Math Matters

Applying Math to the Real World

Richard N. Aufmann | Joanne S. Lockwood |
Richard D. Nation | Daniel K. Clegg

Australia • Brazil • Mexico • Singapore • United Kingdom • United States

Math Matters: Applying Math to the Real World

Mathematical Excursions, Fourth Edition
Richard N. Aufmann, Joanne S. Lockwood, Richard D. Nation, Daniel K. Clegg

For product information and technology assistance, contact us at **Cengage Learning Customer & Sales Support, 1-800-354-9706.**

For permission to use material from this text or product, submit all requests online at **www.cengage.com/permissions.**
Further permissions questions can be emailed to **permissionrequest@cengage.com.**

This book contains select works from existing Cengage learning resources and was produced by Cengage learning Custom Solutions for collegiate use. As such, those adopting and/or contributing to this work are responsible for editorial content accuracy, continuity and completeness.

ISBN: 978-1-337-70270-6

Cengage Learning
20 Channel Street
Boston, MA 02210
USA

Cengage Learning is a leading provider of customized learning solutions with employees residing in nearly 40 different countries and sales in more than 125 countries around the world. Find your local representative at: **www.cengage.com.**

Cengage Learning products are represented in Canada by Nelson Education, Ltd.

For your course and learning solutions, visit **www.cengage.com.**

Purchase any of our products at your local college store or at our preferred online store **www.cengagebrain.com.**

Visit our custom book building website at **www.compose.cengage.com.**

Printed at CLDPC, USA, 07-18

Contents

1 Measurement and Geometry 1

2 Applications of Equations 103

Andy Dean Photography/Shutterstock.com

3 The Mathematics of Finance 163

Eric Fahrner/Shutterstock.com

4 Statistics 231

Introduction to Math Matters: Applying Math to the Real World.

Math Matters - in today's culture, which relies heavily on money calculations, measuring spaces, and using numbers to make persuasive arguments, that is certainly true!

This book is about learning to navigate the math in our everyday lives: the math that makes us better with our personal finances, better at design, and better in business.

Your College Math course is essentially a critical thinking course that focuses on the math you need to know as a working professional. The material in this book has been carefully curated to cover the areas most relevant to your day-to-day life.

As you use this book, make sure you focus on thoroughly understanding the content, not just to do well on tests, but so you can put math to work in your life. After all, math matters!

1

Measurement and Geometry

Much of this chapter concerns geometric figures and their properties. Drawing complex 3D figures by hand can be tedious and time consuming. Fortunately, the advent of 3D computer drawing programs has made the process much easier.

One of the easiest 3D drawing programs to use is Google SketchUp. If you are not familiar with SketchUp, we encourage you to give it a try. A free version is available at http://sketchup.google.com/.

Even if you decide not to produce your own 3D drawings, you can still enjoy looking at some of the drawings that other SketchUp users have produced. For example, the following SketchUp drawing of a country villa incorporates many of the geometric figures presented in this chapter. After you download this drawing[1], you can use rotation and zoom tools to view the villa from any angle and distance. Use the rotation and zoom tools to check out the grand piano on the second floor.

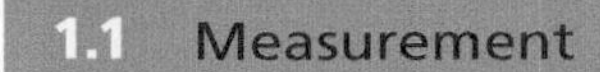

Google SketchUp™/josh86

3D drawing programs have been used to design video games. For instance, art director Robh Ruppel used SketchUp to design the video game *Uncharted 2: Among Thieves*. He discusses some of the details concerning the design of *Uncharted 2* in a YouTube video available at http://www.youtube.com/watch?v=8mkPRmqUlFw.

Sony Corporation of America.

[1] The URL for the above country villa drawing is: http://sketchup.google.com/3dwarehouse/details?mid=79a4f741cbf41e86a1c299db94b0d06b&prevstart=0

SECTION 1.1 Measurement

U.S. Customary Units of Measure

Units of measure are a way to give a magnitude or size to a number. For instance, there is quite a difference between 7 feet and 7 miles. The units *feet* and *miles* are units of measure in the U.S. Customary System. In this section we are going to focus on units of length, weight, and capacity.

Here are some of the U.S. Customary units and their equivalences.

Equivalences Between Units of Length in the U.S. Customary System

12 inches (in.) = 1 foot (ft)
3 ft = 1 yard (yd)
5280 ft = 1 mile (mi)

Equivalences Between Units of Weight in the U.S. Customary System

16 ounces (oz) = 1 pound (lb)
2000 lb = 1 ton

Equivalences Between Units of Capacity in the U.S. Customary System

8 fluid ounces (fl oz) = 1 cup (c)
2 c = 1 pint (pt)
2 pt = 1 quart (qt)
4 qt = 1 gallon (gal)

These equivalences can be used to change from one unit to another unit by using a **conversion rate**. For instance, because 12 in. = 1 ft, we can write two conversion rates,

$$\frac{12\text{ in.}}{1\text{ ft}} \text{ and } \frac{1\text{ ft}}{12\text{ in.}}$$

Dimensional analysis involves using conversion rates to change from one unit of measurement to another.

EXAMPLE 1 Convert Between Units of Length

Convert 18 in. to feet.

Solution

Choose a conversion rate so that the unit in the numerator of the conversion rate is the same as the unit needed in the answer ("feet" for this problem). The unit in the denominator of the conversion rate is the same as the unit in the given measurement ("inches" for this problem). The conversion rate is $\frac{1\text{ ft}}{12\text{ in.}}$.

$$18\text{ in.} = 18\,\cancel{\text{in.}} \times \frac{1\text{ ft}}{12\,\cancel{\text{in.}}}$$

The unit in the numerator is the same as the unit needed in the answer.
The unit in the denominator is the same as the unit in the given measurement.

$$= \frac{18\text{ ft}}{12} = \frac{3}{2}\text{ ft}$$

$$= 1\frac{1}{2}\text{ ft}$$

$$18\text{ in.} = 1\frac{1}{2}\text{ ft}$$

CHECK YOUR PROGRESS 1

Convert 14 ft to yards.

Solution See page S1.

EXAMPLE 2 Convert Between Units of Weight

Convert $3\frac{1}{2}$ tons to pounds.

Solution

Write a conversion rate with pounds in the numerator and tons in the denominator. The conversion rate is $\frac{2000 \text{ lb}}{1 \text{ ton}}$.

$$3\frac{1}{2} \text{ tons} = \frac{7}{2} \cancel{\text{tons}} \times \frac{2000 \text{ lb}}{1 \cancel{\text{ton}}}$$

$$= \frac{14{,}000 \text{ lb}}{2} = 7000 \text{ lb}$$

$$3\frac{1}{2} \text{ tons} = 7000 \text{ lb}$$

CHECK YOUR PROGRESS 2

Convert 3 lb to ounces.

Solution See page S1.

Sometimes one unit cannot be converted directly to another. For instance, consider trying to convert quarts to cups using only the capacity equivalences given earlier. In this case, it is necessary to use more than one conversion factor, as shown next.

Convert 3 qt to cups.

$$3 \text{ qt} = 3 \text{ qt} \times \boxed{\frac{2 \text{ pt}}{1 \text{ qt}}} \times \boxed{\frac{2 \text{ c}}{1 \text{ pt}}}$$

$$= \frac{3 \cancel{\text{qt}}}{1} \times \frac{2 \cancel{\text{pt}}}{1 \cancel{\text{qt}}} \times \frac{2 \text{ c}}{1 \cancel{\text{pt}}}$$

$$= \frac{12 \text{ c}}{1} = 12 \text{ c}$$

$$3 \text{ qt} = 12 \text{ c}$$

- The direct equivalence between quarts and cups was not given earlier in the section. Use two conversion rates. First convert quarts to pints, and then convert pints to cups.

EXAMPLE 3 Convert Between Units of Capacity

Convert 42 c to quarts.

Solution

First convert cups to pints, and then convert pints to quarts.

$$42 \text{ c} = 42 \cancel{\text{c}} \times \frac{1 \cancel{\text{pt}}}{2 \cancel{\text{c}}} \times \frac{1 \text{ qt}}{2 \cancel{\text{pt}}}$$

$$= \frac{42 \text{ qt}}{4} = 10\frac{1}{2} \text{ qt}$$

$$42 \text{ c} = 10\frac{1}{2} \text{ qt}$$

CHECK YOUR PROGRESS 3

Convert 18 pt to gallons.

Solution See page S1.

The Metric System

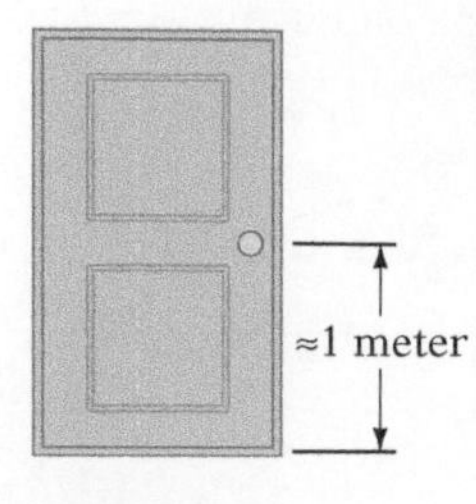

In 1789, an attempt was made to standardize units of measurement internationally in order to simplify trade and commerce between nations. A commission in France developed a system of measurement known as the **metric system**.

The basic unit of length in the metric system is the **meter**. One meter is approximately the distance from a doorknob to the floor. All units of length in the metric system are derived from the meter. Prefixes to the basic unit denote the length of each unit. For example, the prefix "centi-" means one-hundredth, so 1 centimeter is 1 one-hundredth of a meter.

Prefixes and Units of Length in the Metric System

Prefix	Unit
kilo- = 1000	1 kilometer (km) = 1000 meters (m)
hecto- = 100	1 hectometer (hm) = 100 m
deca- = 10	1 decameter (dam) = 10 m
	1 meter (m) = 1 m
deci- = 0.1	1 decimeter (dm) = 0.1 m
centi- = 0.01	1 centimeter (cm) = 0.01 m
milli- = 0.001	1 millimeter (mm) = 0.001 m

Conversion between units of length in the metric system involves moving the decimal point to the right or to the left. Listing the units in order from largest to smallest will indicate how many places to move the decimal point and in which direction.

To convert 4200 cm to meters, write the units in order from largest to smallest.

km hm dam m dm cm mm
2 positions

- Converting centimeters to meters requires moving 2 positions to the left.

4200 cm = 42.00 m
2 places

- Move the decimal point the same number of places and in the same direction.

A metric measurement that involves two units is customarily written in terms of one unit. Convert the smaller unit to the larger unit, and then add.

To convert 8 km 32 m to kilometers, first convert 32 m to kilometers.

km hm dam m dm cm mm

- Converting meters to kilometers requires moving 3 positions to the left.

32 m = 0.032 km

- Move the decimal point the same number of places and in the same direction.

8 km 32 m = 8 km + 0.032 km
= 8.032 km

- Add the result to 8 km.

EXAMPLE 4 **Convert Between Units of Length**

Convert 0.38 m to millimeters.

Solution

0.38 m = 380 mm

CHECK YOUR PROGRESS 4

Convert 3.07 m to centimeters.

Solution See page S1.

Mass and weight are closely related. Weight is a measure of how strongly Earth is pulling on an object. Therefore, an object's weight is less in space than on Earth's surface. However, the amount of material in the object, its **mass**, remains the same. On the surface of Earth, *mass* and *weight* can be used interchangeably.

The gram is the unit of mass in the metric system to which prefixes are added. One gram is about the weight of a paper clip.

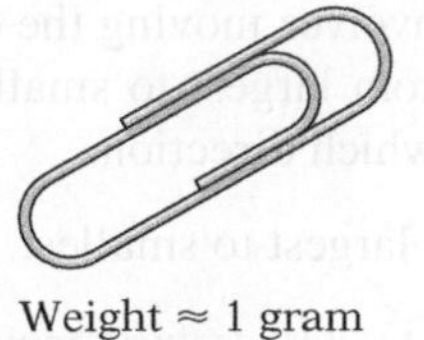

Weight ≈ 1 gram

Units of Mass in the Metric System

1 kilogram (kg) = 1000 grams (g)
1 hectogram (hg) = 100 g
1 decagram (dag) = 10 g
1 gram (g) = 1 g
1 decigram (dg) = 0.1 g
1 centigram (cg) = 0.01 g
1 milligram (mg) = 0.001 g

Conversion between units of mass in the metric system involves moving the decimal point to the right or to the left. Listing the units in order from largest to smallest will indicate how many places to move the decimal point and in which direction.

To convert 324 g to kilograms, write the units in order from largest to smallest.

kg hg dag g dg cg mg
3 positions

- Converting grams to kilograms requires moving 3 positions to the left.

324 g = 0.324 kg
3 places

- Move the decimal point the same number of places and in the same direction.

EXAMPLE 5 Convert Between Units of Mass

Convert 4.23 g to milligrams.

Solution

4.23 g = 4230 mg

CHECK YOUR PROGRESS 5

Convert 42.3 mg to grams.

Solution See page S1.

The basic unit of capacity in the metric system is the liter. One **liter** is defined as the capacity of a box that is 10 cm long on each side.

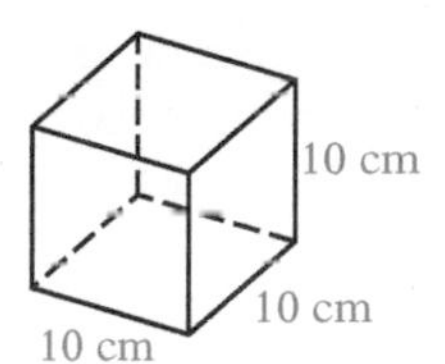

The units of capacity in the metric system have the same prefixes as the units of length.

Units of Capacity in the Metric System

1 kiloliter (kl) = 1000 L
1 hectoliter (hl) = 100 L
1 decaliter (dal) = 10 L
1 liter (L) = 1 L
1 deciliter (dl) = 0.1 L
1 centiliter (cl) = 0.01 L
1 milliliter (ml) = 0.001 L

The milliliter is equal to 1 **cubic centimeter** (cm^3). In medicine, cubic centimeter is often abbreviated cc.

1 cm
1 cm
1 cm
1 ml = 1 cm^3

Conversion between units of capacity in the metric system involves moving the decimal point to the right or to the left. Listing the units in order from largest to smallest will indicate how many places to move the decimal point and in which direction.

To convert 824 ml to liters, first write the units in order from largest to smallest.

kl hl dal L dl cl ml
3 positions

- Converting milliliters to liters requires moving 3 positions to the left.

824 ml = 0.824 L
3 places

- Move the decimal point the same number of places and in the same direction.

EXAMPLE 6 Convert Between Units of Capacity

Convert 4 L 32 ml to liters.

Solution

32 ml = 0.032 L

4 L 32 ml = 4 L + 0.032 L

= 4.032 L

CHECK YOUR PROGRESS 6

Convert 2 kl 167 L to liters.

Solution See page S1.

Convert Between U.S. Customary Units and Metric Units

More than 90% of the world's population uses the metric system of measurement. Therefore, converting U.S. Customary units to metric units is essential in trade and commerce—for example, in importing foreign goods and exporting domestic goods. Approximate equivalences between the two systems follow.

Units of Length	Units of Weight	Units of Capacity
1 in. = 2.54 cm	1 oz ≈ 28.35 g	1 L ≈ 1.06 qt
1 m ≈ 3.28 ft	1 lb ≈ 454 g	1 gal ≈ 3.79 L
1 m ≈ 1.09 yd	1 kg ≈ 2.2 lb	
1 mi ≈ 1.61 km		

These equivalences can be used to form conversion rates to change from one unit of measurement to another. For example, because 1 mi ≈ 1.61 km, the conversion rates $\frac{1 \text{ mi}}{1.61 \text{ km}}$ and $\frac{1.61 \text{ km}}{1 \text{ mi}}$ are both approximately equal to 1.

Convert 55 mi to kilometers.

$$55 \text{ mi} \approx 55 \text{ mi} \times \boxed{\frac{1.61 \text{ km}}{1 \text{ mi}}}$$

- The conversion rate must contain kilometers in the numerator and miles in the denominator.

$$= \frac{55 \not{\text{mi}}}{1} \times \frac{1.61 \text{ km}}{1 \not{\text{mi}}}$$

$$= \frac{88.55 \text{ km}}{1}$$

$$55 \text{ mi} \approx 88.55 \text{ km}$$

EXAMPLE 7 Convert U.S. Customary Units to Metric Units

The price of gasoline is \$3.89/gal. Find the cost per liter. Round to the nearest tenth of a cent.

Solution

$$\frac{\$3.89}{\text{gal}} \approx \frac{\$3.89}{\cancel{\text{gal}}} \times \frac{1\ \cancel{\text{gal}}}{3.79\ \text{L}} = \frac{\$3.89}{3.79\ \text{L}} \approx \frac{\$1.026}{1\ \text{L}}$$

$\$3.89/\text{gal} \approx \$1.026/\text{L}$

CHECK YOUR PROGRESS 7

The price of milk is \$3.69/gal. Find the cost per liter. Round to the nearest cent.

Solution See page S1.

Metric units are used in the United States. Cereal is sold by the gram, 35-mm film is available, and soda is sold by the liter. The same conversion rates used to convert U.S. Customary units to metric units are used to convert metric units to U.S. Customary units.

EXAMPLE 8 Convert Metric Units to U.S. Customary Units

Convert 200 m to feet.

Solution

$$200\ \text{m} \approx 200\ \cancel{\text{m}} \times \frac{3.28\ \text{ft}}{1\ \cancel{\text{m}}} = \frac{656\ \text{ft}}{1}$$

$200\ \text{m} \approx 656\ \text{ft}$

CHECK YOUR PROGRESS 8

Convert 45 cm to inches. Round to the nearest hundredth.

Solution See page S1.

EXAMPLE 9 Convert Metric Units to U.S. Customary Units

Convert 90 km/h to miles per hour. Round to the nearest hundredth.

Solution

$$\frac{90\ \text{km}}{\text{h}} \approx \frac{90\ \text{km}}{\text{h}} \times \frac{1\ \text{mi}}{1.61\ \text{km}} = \frac{90\ \text{mi}}{1.61\ \text{h}} \approx \frac{55.90\ \text{mi}}{1\ \text{h}}$$

$90\ \text{km/h} \approx 55.90\ \text{mi/h}$

CHECK YOUR PROGRESS 9

Express 75 km/h in miles per hour. Round to the nearest hundredth.

Solution See page S1.

EXCURSION

Drawing with a Straightedge and a Compass

The Elements, written by Euclid about 2300 years ago, is arguably the most influential treatise on geometry ever written. One of the most remarkable aspects of this work is that all measurements necessary for the proofs were accomplished using only a straightedge and a compass. Neither of these devices had any units written on it—Euclid used just a straight, blank piece of wood as his straightedge and a compass that could be adjusted but was not demarked by degrees.

Using these two instruments, Euclid showed how to find the midpoint of a line segment, how to construct a 90° angle, and how to draw parallel lines and many other geometric figures. For instance, here is Euclid's method for constructing a 90° angle at a point.

1. Start with a point on a line. The 90° angle will be created at this point.

2. Set the compass to a specific width and, from the point, draw two arcs that intersect the line.

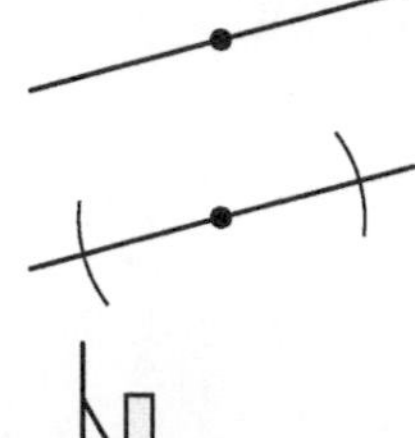

3. Increase the width of the compass by some arbitrary amount. Place the point of the compass at each point where the arcs intersect the line, and draw two intersecting arcs.

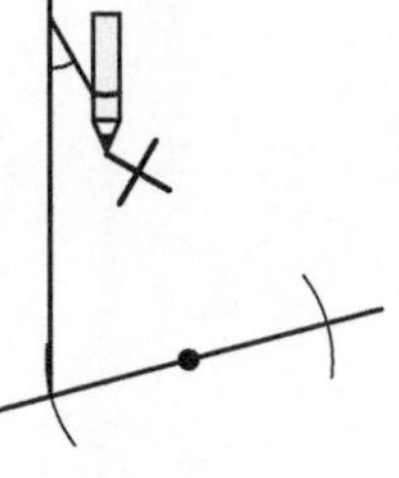

4. Draw a line through the point on the line and the intersection of the two arcs.

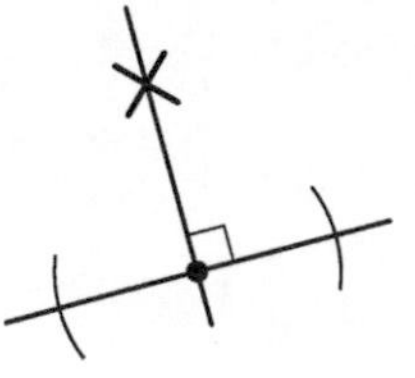

It is possible to bisect any angle using only a compass and a straightedge.

1. Start with an angle. Draw an arc through the angle with the point of the compass at the vertex of the angle.

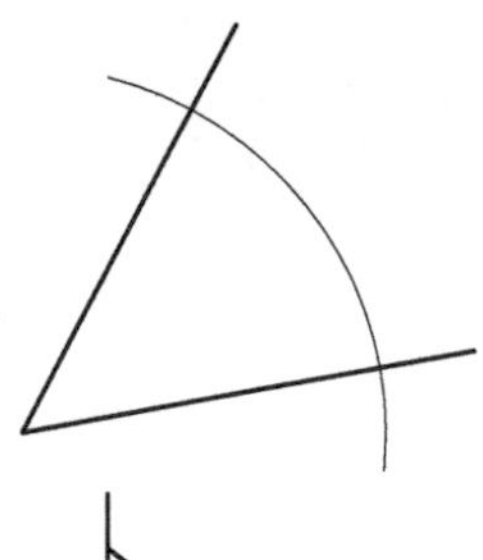

2. Draw two intersecting arcs by placing the compass at the points where the original arc intersects each side of the angle. Then draw a line between the vertex of the angle and the intersection of the two arcs.

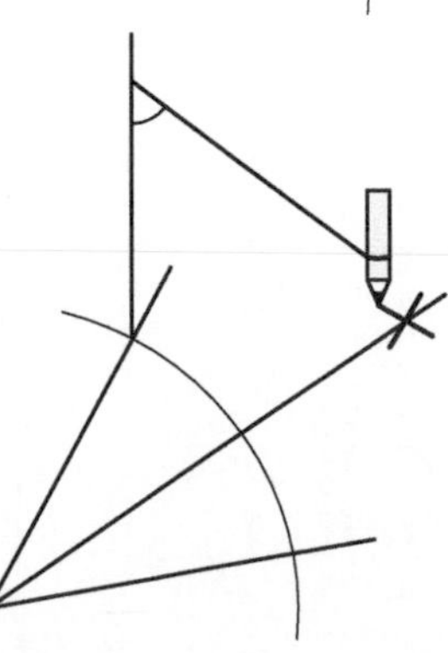

EXCURSION EXERCISES

Complete the following exercises using only a straightedge and a compass. If you get stuck, do some research on how to draw the figure with a straightedge and compass.

1. Draw the yin-and-yang symbol shown at the right. *Hint:* This symbol consists of multiple circles, each with its center on a vertical line.

2. Draw a hexagon with all sides the same length. Here is a suggestion on how to begin. First, draw two circles that are equal in size. Then add lines as shown in the diagram at the far right.

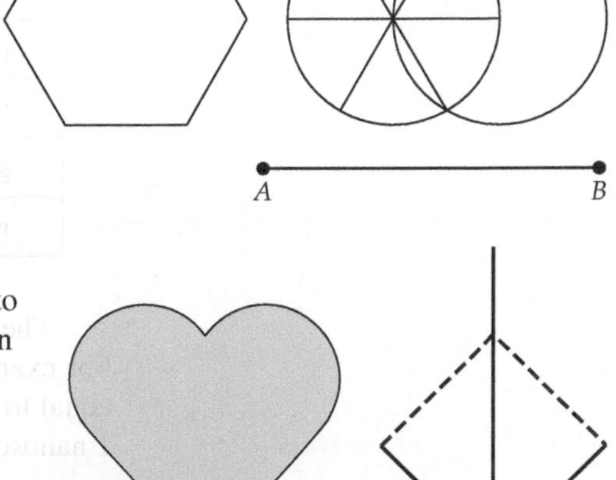

3. Find the midpoint of the line segment *AB*.

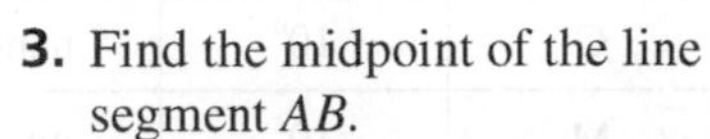

4. Draw the heart-shaped figure shown at the right. Here is a suggestion on how to begin. First, use the construction shown at the far right to draw a right triangle. Then bisect the angle and draw some circles.

EXERCISE SET 1.1

■ For Exercises 1 to 24, convert between the two measurements.

1. 6 ft = ______ in.

2. 7920 ft = ______ mi

3. 5 yd = ______ in.

4. $\frac{1}{2}$ mi = ______ yd

5. 64 oz = ______ lb

6. 9000 lb = ______ tons

7. $1\frac{1}{2}$ lb = ______ oz

8. $\frac{4}{5}$ ton = ______ lb

9. $2\frac{1}{2}$ c = ______ fl oz

10. 10 qt = ______ gal

11. 7 gal = ______ pt

12. $1\frac{1}{2}$ qt = ______ c

13. 62 cm = ______ mm

14. 6804 m = ______ km

15. 3.21 m = ______ cm

16. 260 cm = ______ m

17. 7421 g = ______ kg

18. 43 mg = ______ g

19. 0.45 g = ______ dg

20. 0.0456 g = ______ mg

21. 7.5 ml = ______ L

22. 0.037 L = ______ ml

23. 0.435 L = ______ cm^3

24. 897 L = ______ kl

■ For Exercises 25 to 34, solve. Round to the nearest hundredth if necessary.

25. Find the weight in kilograms of a 145-pound person.

26. Find the number of liters in 14.3 gal of gasoline.

27. Express 30 mi/h in kilometers per hour.

28. Seedless watermelon costs \$0.59/lb. Find the cost per kilogram.

29. Deck stain costs \$32.99/gal. Find the cost per liter.

30. Find the weight, in pounds, of an 86-kilogram person.

31. Find the width, in inches, of 35-mm film.

32. Express 30 m/s in feet per second.

33. A 5-kg ham costs \$10/kg. Find the cost per pound.

34. A 2.5-kg bag of grass seed costs \$10.99. Find the cost per pound.

EXTENSIONS

As our scientific and technical knowledge has increased, so has our need for ever-smaller and ever-larger units of measure. The prefixes used to denote some of these units of measure are listed in the table below.

Prefixes for large units		10^n	Prefixes for small units		10^n
Name	Symbol		Name	Symbol	
yotta	Y	10^{24}	yocto	y	10^{-24}
zetta	Z	10^{21}	zepto	z	10^{-21}
exa	E	10^{18}	atto	a	10^{-18}
peta	P	10^{15}	femto	f	10^{-15}
tera	T	10^{12}	pico	p	10^{-12}
giga	G	10^{9}	nano	n	10^{-9}
mega	M	10^{6}	micro	μ	10^{-6}

These new units of measure are quickly working their way into our everyday lives. For example, it is quite easy to purchase a 1-terabyte hard drive. One terabyte (TB) is equal to 10^{12} bytes. As another example, many computers can do multiple operations in 1 nanosecond (ns). One nanosecond is equal to 10^{-9} s.

■ For Exercises 35 to 40, convert between the two units.

35. 2.3 T = ________ Y

36. 4.51 n = ________ p

37. 0.65 Z = ________ G

38. 9.46 a = ________ μ

39. 4.01 G = ________ E

40. 7.15 y = ________ f

41. The speed of light is approximately 3×10^8 m/s. What is the speed of light in Zm (zettameters) per second?

42. A light year is approximately 6,000,000,000,000,000 mi. Describe a light year using Ym (yottameters).

43. In the 1980s, it became possible to measure optical events in nanoseconds and picoseconds. Express 1 ps as a decimal.

44. A tau lepton, which is an extremely small elementary particle, has a lifetime of 3×10^{-13} s. What is the lifetime of a tau lepton in femtoseconds?

SECTION 1.2 Basic Concepts of Euclidean Geometry

Lines, Rays, Line Segments, and Angles

The word *geometry* comes from the Greek words for "earth" and "measure." Geometry has applications in such disciplines as physics, medicine, and geology. Geometry is also used in applied fields such as mechanical drawing and astronomy. Geometric forms are used in art and design. We will begin our study by introducing two basic geometric concepts: point and line.

A **point** is symbolized by drawing a dot. A **line** is determined by two distinct points and extends indefinitely in both directions, as the arrows on the line at the right indicate. This line contains points A and B and is represented by $\overleftrightarrow{AB}$. A line can also be represented by a single letter, such as ℓ.

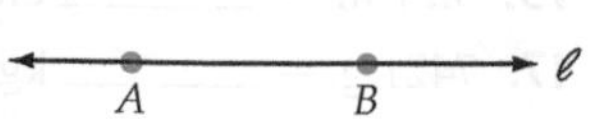

HISTORICAL NOTE

Science Photo Library/ Photo Researchers/Science Source

Geometry is one of the oldest branches of mathematics. Around 350 BC, Euclid (yoo'klĭd) of Alexandria wrote *The Elements,* which contained all of the known concepts of geometry. Euclid's contribution to geometry was to unify various concepts into a single deductive system that was based on a set of postulates.

A **ray** starts at a point and extends indefinitely in *one* direction. The point at which a ray starts is called the **endpoint** of the ray. The ray shown at the right is denoted $\overrightarrow{AB}$. Point A is the endpoint of the ray.

A **line segment** is part of a line and has two endpoints. The line segment shown at the right is denoted by $\overline{AB}$. The distance between the endpoints of $\overline{AB}$ is denoted by AB.

QUESTION Classify each diagram as a line, a ray, or a line segment.

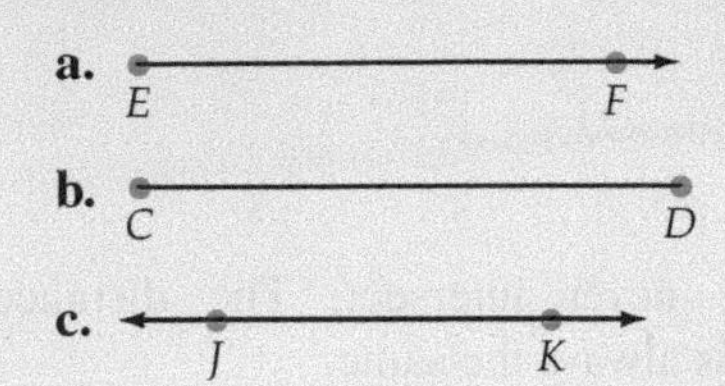

Given $AB = 22$ cm and $BC = 13$ cm in the figure at the right, then AC is the sum of the distances AB and BC.

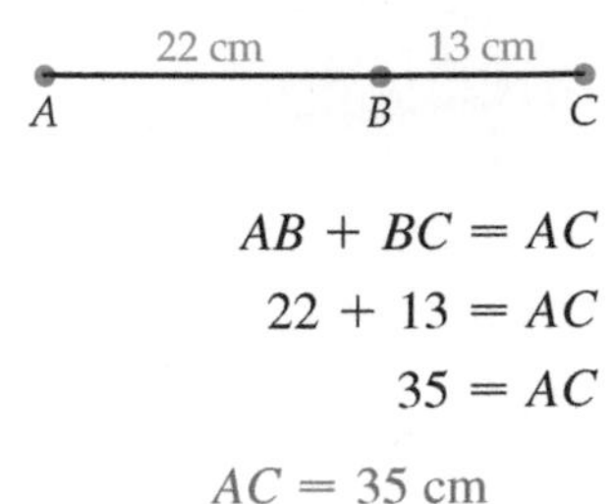

$$AB + BC = AC$$
$$22 + 13 = AC$$
$$35 = AC$$

$AC = 35$ cm

EXAMPLE 1 Use an Equation to Find a Distance on a Line Segment

X, Y, and Z are all on line ℓ. Given $XY = 9$ m and YZ is twice XY, find XZ.

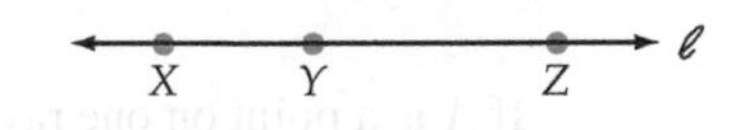

Solution

$XZ = XY + YZ$

$XZ = XY + 2(XY)$ • YZ is twice XY.

$XZ = 9 + 2(9)$ • Replace XY by 9.

$XZ = 9 + 18$ • Solve for XZ.

$XZ = 27$

$XZ = 27$ m

CHECK YOUR PROGRESS 1 A, B, and C are all on line ℓ. Given $BC = 16$ ft and $AB = \frac{1}{4}(BC)$, find AC.

Solution See page S1.

ANSWER **a.** Ray. **b.** Line segment. **c.** Line.

In this section, we are discussing figures that lie in a plane. A **plane** is a flat surface with no thickness and no boundaries. It can be pictured as a desktop or whiteboard that extends forever. Figures that lie in a plane are called **plane figures.**

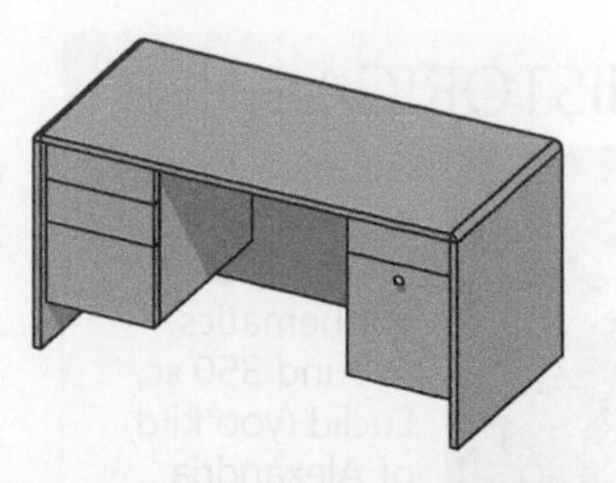

Lines in a plane can be intersecting or parallel. **Intersecting lines** cross at a point in the plane.

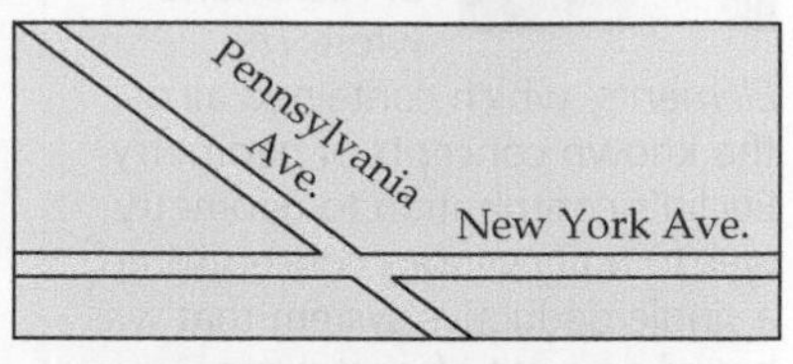

Parallel lines never intersect. The distance between them is always the same.

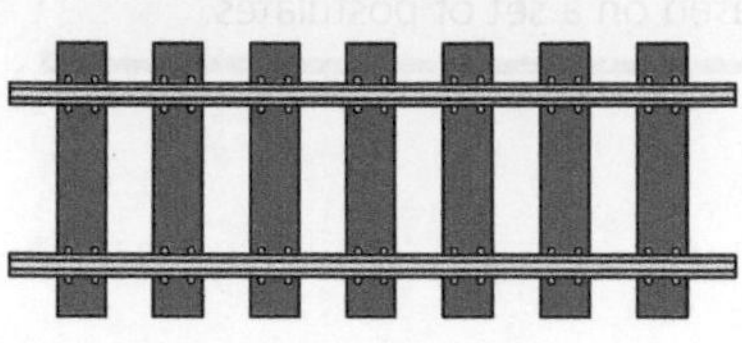

The symbol $\|$ means "is parallel to." In the figure at the right, $j \| k$ and $\overline{AB} \| \overline{CD}$.

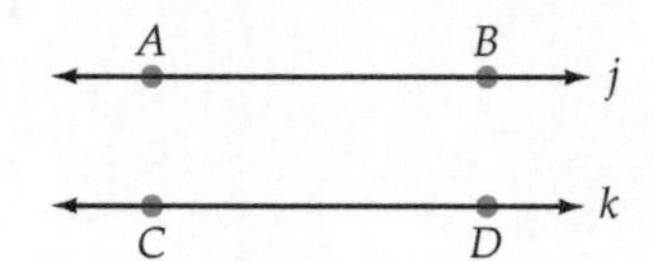

Angles

An **angle** is formed by two rays with the same endpoint. The **vertex** of the angle is the point at which the two rays meet. The rays are called the **sides** of the angle.

Side
Vertex
Side

If A is a point on one ray of an angle, C is a point on the other ray, and B is the vertex, then the angle is called $\angle B$ or $\angle ABC$, where $\angle$ is the symbol for angle. Note that an angle can be named by the vertex, or by giving three points, where the second point listed is the vertex. $\angle ABC$ could also be called $\angle CBA$.

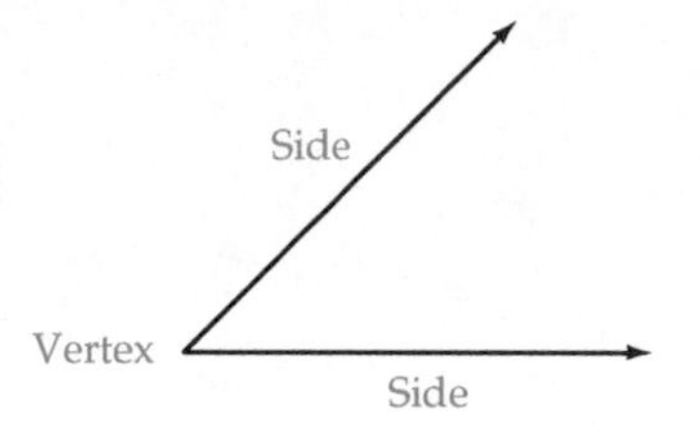

An angle can also be named by a variable written between the rays close to the vertex. In the figure at the right, $\angle x$ and $\angle QRS$ are two different names for the same angle. $\angle y$ and $\angle SRT$ are two different names for the same angle. Note that in this figure, more than two rays meet at R. In this case, the vertex alone cannot be used to name $\angle QRT$.

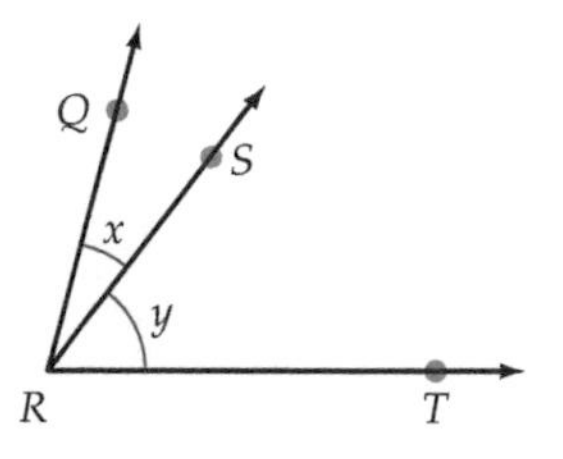

An angle is often measured in **degrees.** The symbol for degrees is a small raised circle, °. The angle formed by rotating a ray through a complete circle has a measure of 360°.

360°

A 90° angle is called a **right angle.** The symbol ⌐ represents a right angle.

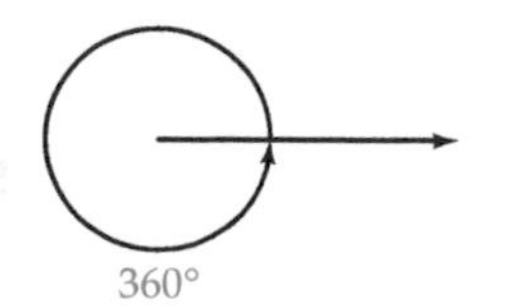

HISTORICAL NOTE

The Babylonians knew that one solar year, or the length of time it takes for the the sun to return to the same position in the cycle of seasons, as seen from Earth, was approximately 365 days. Historians suggest that the reason one complete revolution of a circle is 360° that 360 is the closest number that is divisible by many nbers.

POINT OF INTEREST

Julius Elias/Shutterstock.com

The Leaning Tower of Pisa is the bell tower of the Cathedral in Pisa, Italy. The tower was designed to be vertical, but it started to lean soon after construction began in 1173. By 1990, when restoration work began, the tower was 5.5° off from the vertical. Now, post restoration, the structure leans 3.99°. (*Source:* http://en.wikipedia.org)

Perpendicular lines are intersecting lines that form right angles.

The symbol $\perp$ means "is perpendicular to." In the figure at the right, $p \perp q$ and $\overline{AB} \perp \overline{CD}$.

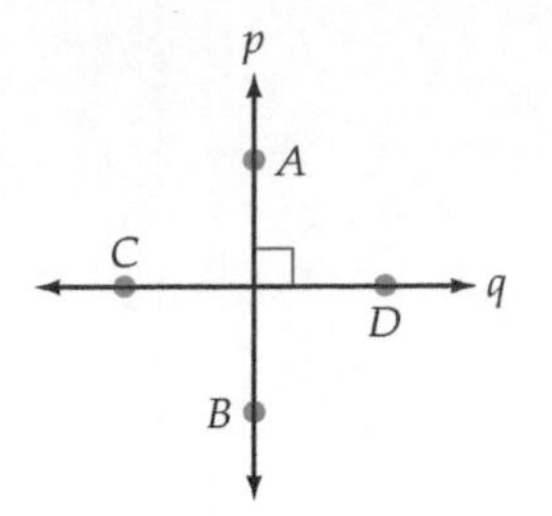

A **straight angle** is an angle whose measure is 180°. $\angle AOB$ is a straight angle.

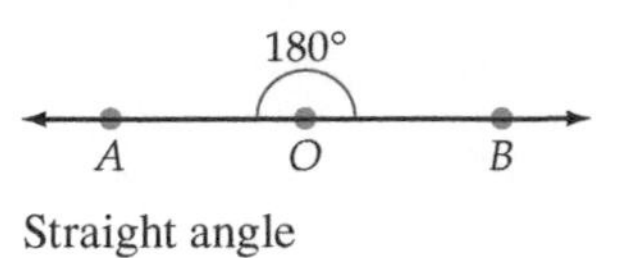

Straight angle

Complementary angles are two angles whose measures have the sum 90°.

$\angle A$ and $\angle B$ at the right are complementary angles.

Supplementary angles are two angles whose measures have the sum 180°.

$\angle C$ and $\angle D$ at the right are supplementary angles.

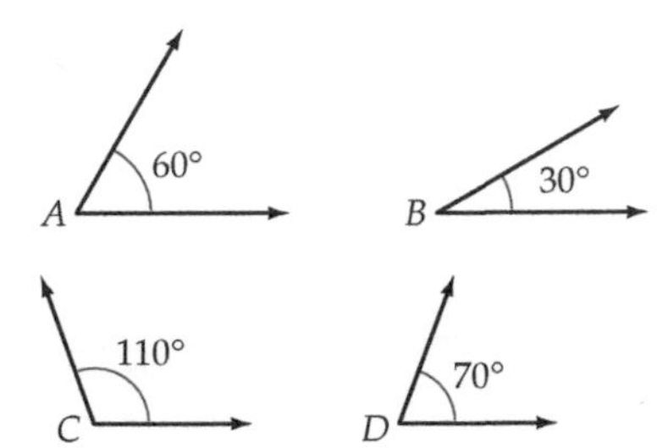

An **acute angle** is an angle whose measure is between 0° and 90°. $\angle D$ above is an acute angle. An **obtuse angle** is an angle whose measure is between 90° and 180°. $\angle C$ above is an obtuse angle.

The measure of $\angle C$ is 110°. This is often written as $m\angle C - 110°$, where m is an abbreviation for "the measure of."

EXAMPLE 2 Find the Measure of the Complement of an Angle

Find the measure of the complement of a 38° angle.

Solution

Complementary angles are two angles the sum of whose measures is 90°. To find the measure of the complement, let x represent the complement of a 38° angle. Write an equation and solve for x.

$$x + 38° = 90°$$
$$x = 52°$$

CHECK YOUR PROGRESS 2 Find the measure of the supplement of a 129° angle.

Solution See page S1.

TAKE NOTE

Co-planar means "in the same plane."

Adjacent angles are two co-planar, nonoverlapping angles that share a common vertex and a common side. In the figure at the right, $\angle DAC$ and $\angle CAB$ are adjacent angles.

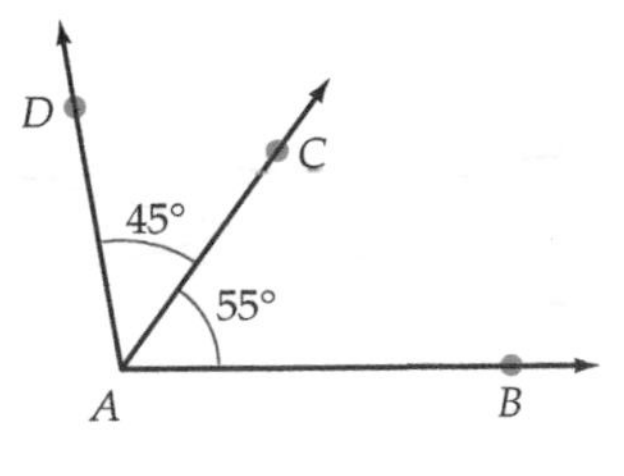

$$m\angle DAC = 45° \text{ and } m\angle CAB = 55°.$$
$$m\angle DAB = m\angle DAC + m\angle CAB$$
$$= 45° + 55° = 100°$$

In the figure at the right, $m\angle EDG = 80°$. The measure of $\angle FDG$ is three times the measure of $\angle EDF$. Find the measure of $\angle EDF$.

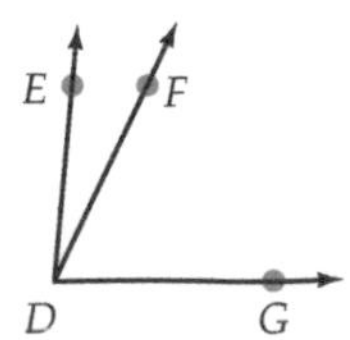

Let $x =$ the measure of $\angle EDF$.
Then $3x =$ the measure of $\angle FDG$.
Write an equation and solve for x.

$$m\angle EDF + m\angle FDG = m\angle EDG$$
$$x + 3x = 80°$$
$$4x = 80°$$
$$x = 20°$$

$$m\angle EDF = 20°$$

EXAMPLE 3 **Find the Measure of an Adjacent Angle**

Given that $m\angle ABC$ is 84°, find the measure of $\angle x$.

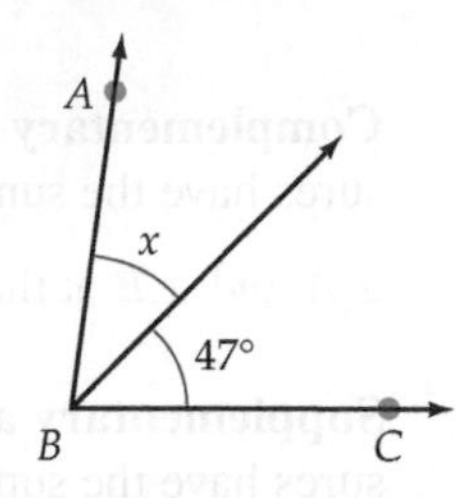

Solution

To find the measure of $\angle x$, write an equation using the fact that the sum of the measures of $\angle x$ and 47° is 84°. Solve for $m\angle x$.

$$m\angle x + 47° = 84°$$

$$m\angle x = 37°$$

CHECK YOUR PROGRESS 3 Given that the $m\angle DEF$ is 118°, find the measure of $\angle a$.

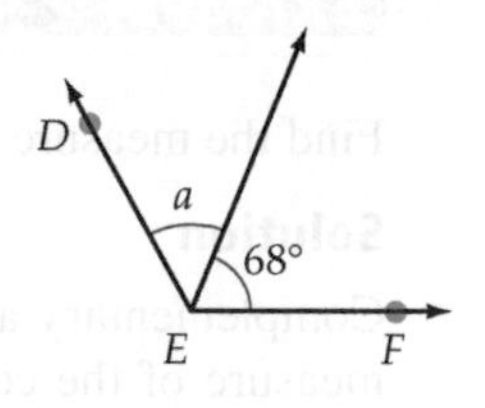

Solution See page S1.

Angles Formed by Intersecting Lines

Four angles are formed by the intersection of two lines. If the two lines are not perpendicular, then two of the angles formed are acute angles and two of the angles formed are obtuse angles. The two acute angles are always opposite each other, and the two obtuse angles are always opposite each other.

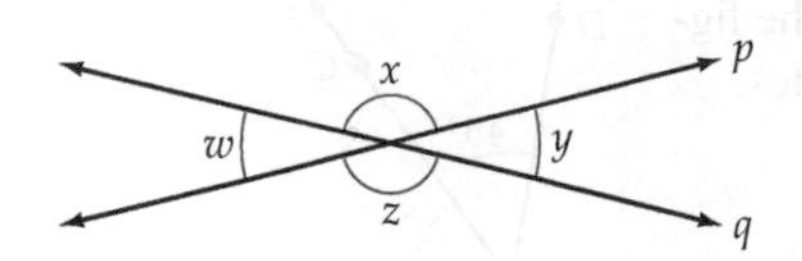

The nonadjacent angles formed by two intersecting lines are called **vertical angles.** $\angle w$ and $\angle y$ are vertical angles. $\angle x$ and $\angle z$ are vertical angles.

Vertical angles have the same measure.

$m\angle w = m\angle y$ $\qquad$ $m\angle x = m\angle z$

In the figure at the left, $\angle x$ and $\angle y$ are adjacent angles, as are $\angle y$ and $\angle z$, $\angle z$ and $\angle w$, and $\angle w$ and $\angle x$.

Adjacent angles formed by intersecting lines are supplementary angles.

$m\angle x + m\angle y = 180°$ $\qquad$ $m\angle z + m\angle w = 180°$

$m\angle y + m\angle z = 180°$ $\qquad$ $m\angle w + m\angle x = 180°$

EXAMPLE 4 Solve a Problem Involving Intersecting Lines

In the diagram at the right, $m\angle b = 115°$. Find the measures of angles a, c, and d.

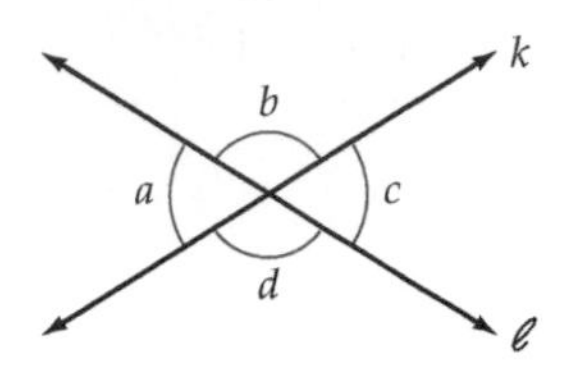

Solution

$m\angle a + m\angle b = 180°$ • $\angle a$ is supplementary to $\angle b$ because $\angle a$ and $\angle b$ are adjacent angles of intersecting lines.

$m\angle a + 115° = 180°$ • Replace $m\angle b$ with 115°.

$m\angle a = 65°$ • Subtract 115° from each side of the equation.

$m\angle c = 65°$ • $m\angle c = m\angle a$ because $\angle c$ and $\angle a$ are vertical angles.

$m\angle d = 115°$ • $m\angle d = m\angle b$ because $\angle d$ and $\angle b$ are vertical angles.

$m\angle a = 65°$, $m\angle c = 65°$, and $m\angle d = 115°$.

CHECK YOUR PROGRESS 4

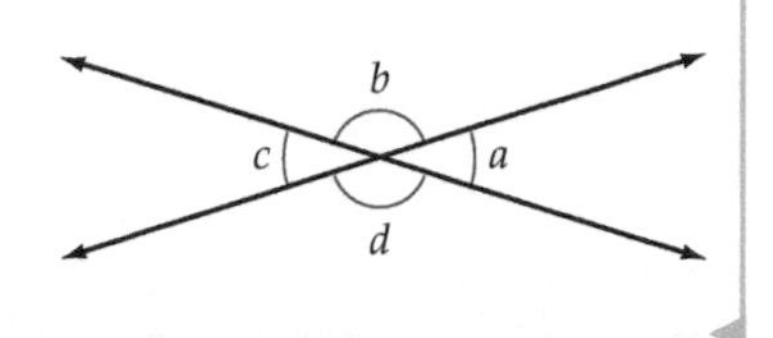

In the diagram at the right, $m\angle a = 35°$. Find the measures of angles b, c, and d.

Solution See page S1.

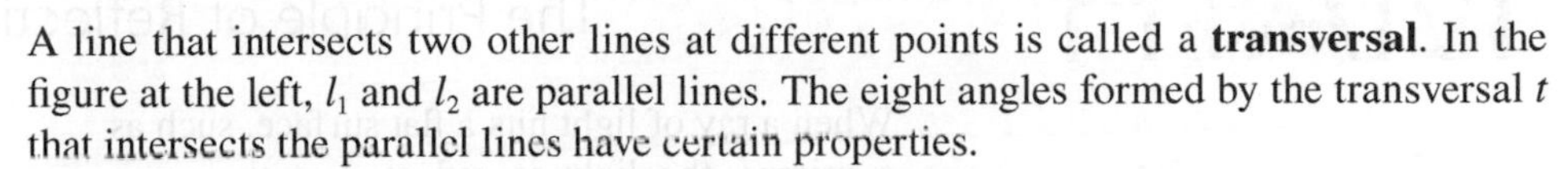

A line that intersects two other lines at different points is called a **transversal**. In the figure at the left, l_1 and l_2 are parallel lines. The eight angles formed by the transversal t that intersects the parallel lines have certain properties.

$\angle c$ and $\angle w$ are **alternate interior angles**; $\angle d$ and $\angle x$ are also alternate interior angles.

Alternate interior angles are equal.

$m\angle c = m\angle w$ $\qquad$ $m\angle d = m\angle x$

$\angle a$ and $\angle y$ are **alternate exterior angles**; $\angle b$ and $\angle z$ are also alternate exterior angles.

Alternate exterior angles are equal.

$m\angle a = m\angle y$ $\qquad$ $m\angle b = m\angle z$

$\angle a$ and $\angle w$, $\angle d$ and $\angle z$, $\angle b$ and $\angle x$, and $\angle c$ and $\angle y$ are **corresponding angles**.

Corresponding angles are equal.

$m\angle a = m\angle w$ $\qquad$ $m\angle b = m\angle x$

$m\angle d = m\angle z$ $\qquad$ $m\angle c = m\angle y$

QUESTION Which angles in the figure at the left above have the same measure as angle a? Which angles have the same measure as angle b?

POINT OF INTEREST

Many cities in the New World, unlike those in Europe, were designed using rectangular street grids. Washington, D.C. was designed this way, except that diagonal avenues were added, primarily for the purpose of enabling troop movement in the event the city required defense. As an added precaution, monuments were constructed at major intersections so that attackers would not have a straight shot down a boulevard.

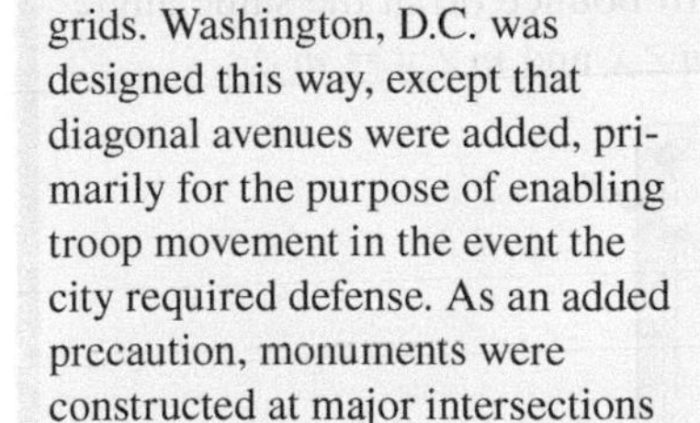

EXAMPLE 5 Solve a Problem Involving Parallel Lines Cut by a Transversal

In the diagram at the right, $\ell_1 \| \ell_2$ and $m\angle f = 58°$. Find the measures of $\angle a$, $\angle c$, and $\angle d$.

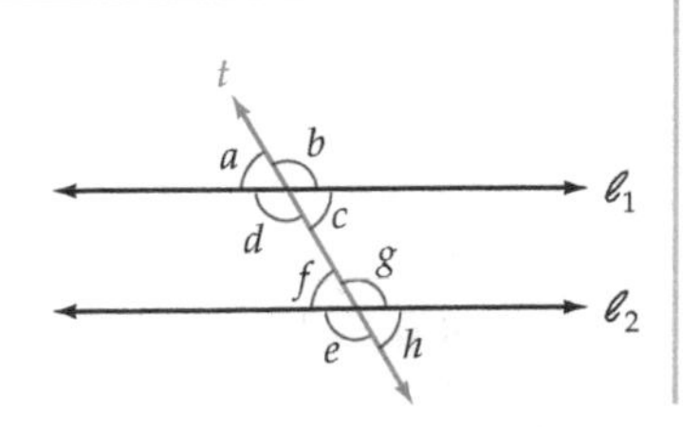

ANSWER Angles c, w, and y have the same measure as angle a. Angles d, x, and z have the same measure as angle b.

Solution

$m\angle a = m\angle f = 58°$ • $\angle a$ and $\angle f$ are corresponding angles.

$m\angle c = m\angle f = 58°$ • $\angle c$ and $\angle f$ are alternate interior angles.

$m\angle d + m\angle a = 180°$ • $\angle d$ is supplementary to $\angle a$.

$m\angle d + 58° = 180°$ • Replace $m\angle a$ with 58°.

$m\angle d = 122°$ • Subtract 58° from each side of the equation.

$m\angle a = 58°, m\angle c = 58°$, and $m\angle d = 122°$.

CHECK YOUR PROGRESS 5

In the diagram at the right, $\ell_1 \parallel \ell_2$ and $m\angle g = 124°$. Find the measures of $\angle b$, $\angle c$, and $\angle d$.

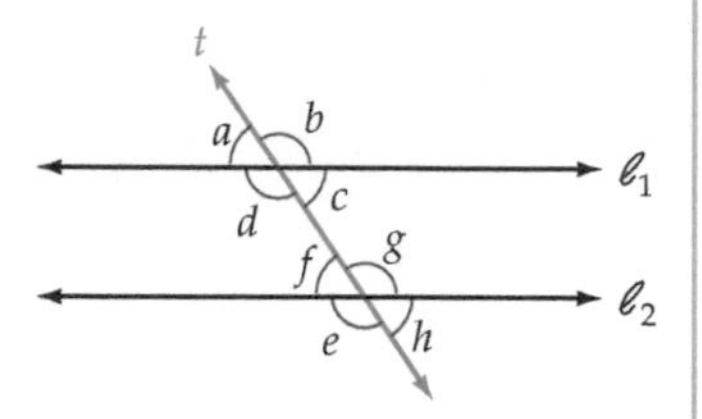

Solution See page S1.

MATH MATTERS The Principle of Reflection

When a ray of light hits a flat surface, such as a mirror, the light is reflected at the same angle at which it hit the surface. For example, in the diagram at the left, $m\angle x = m\angle y$.

This principle of reflection is in operation in a simple periscope. In a periscope, light is reflected twice, with the result that light rays entering the periscope are parallel to the light rays at eye level.

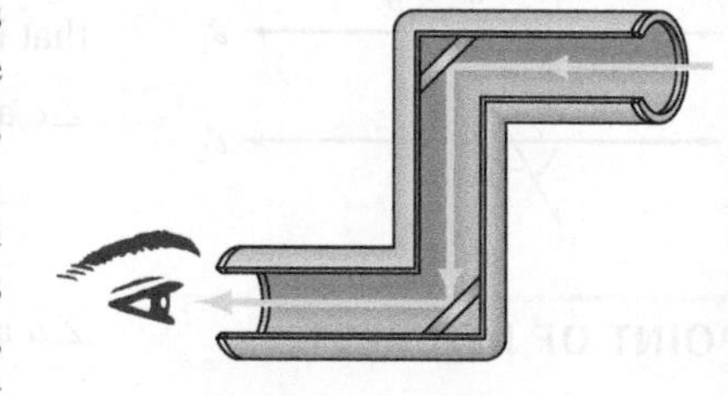

The same principle is in operation on a billiard table. Assuming that it has no "side spin," a ball bouncing off the side of the table will bounce off at the same angle at which it hit the side. In the figure below, $m\angle w = m\angle x$ and $m\angle y = m\angle z$.

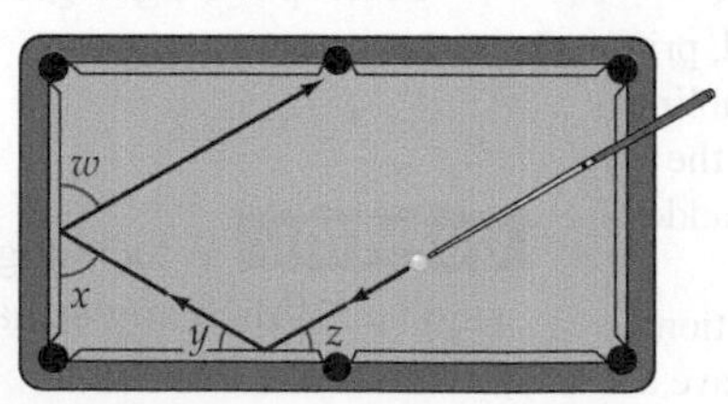

In the miniature golf shot illustrated below, $m\angle w = m\angle x$ and $m\angle y = m\angle z$.

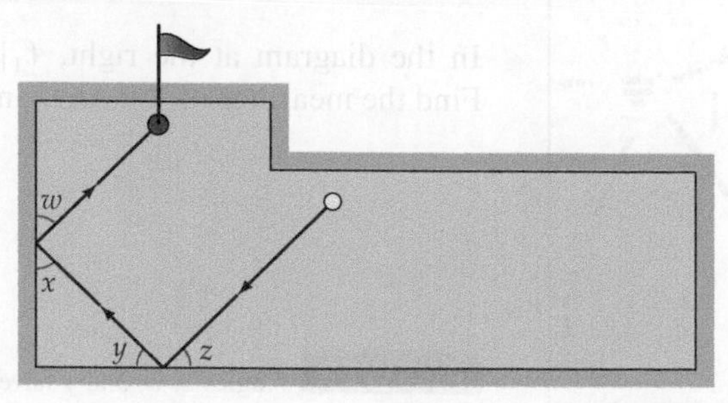

Angles of a Triangle

The figure at the right shows three intersecting lines. The plane figure formed by the line segments AB, BC, and AC is called a **triangle**.

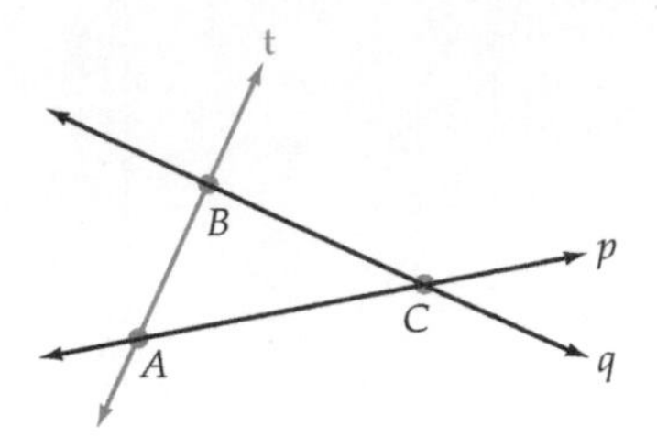

The angles within the region enclosed by the triangle are called **interior angles**. In the figure at the right, angles a, b, and c are interior angles. The sum of the measures of the interior angles of a triangle is 180°.

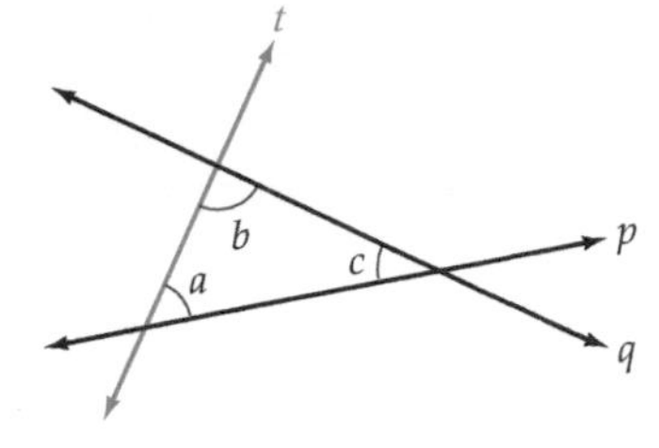

$$m\angle a + m\angle b + m\angle c = 180^\circ$$

The Sum of the Measures of the Interior Angles of a Triangle

The sum of the measures of the interior angles of a triangle is 180°.

QUESTION Can the measures of the three interior angles of a triangle be 87°, 51°, and 43°?

An **exterior angle of a triangle** is an angle that is adjacent to an interior angle of the triangle and is supplemental to the interior angle. In the figure at the right, angles m and n are exterior angles for angle a. The sum of the measure of an interior angle and one of its exterior angles is 180°.

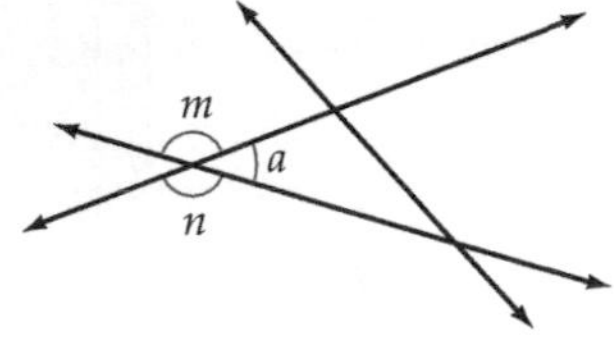

$$m\angle a + m\angle m = 180^\circ$$
$$m\angle a + m\angle n = 180^\circ$$

EXAMPLE 6 Find the Measure of the Third Angle of a Triangle

Two angles of a triangle measure 43° and 86°. Find the measure of the third angle.

Solution

Use the fact that the sum of the measures of the interior angles of a triangle is 180°. Write an equation using x to represent the measure of the third angle. Solve the equation for x.

$$x + 43^\circ + 86^\circ = 180^\circ$$
$$x + 129^\circ = 180^\circ \quad \text{• Add } 43^\circ + 86^\circ.$$
$$x = 51^\circ \quad \text{• Subtract } 129^\circ \text{ from each side of the equation.}$$

The measure of the third angle is 51°.

CHECK YOUR PROGRESS 6 One angle in a triangle is a right angle, and one angle measures 27°. Find the measure of the third angle.

Solution See page S1.

TAKE NOTE

In this text, when we refer to the angles of a triangle, we mean the interior angles of the triangle unless specifically stated otherwise.

ANSWER No, because 87° + 51° + 43° = 181°, and the sum of the measures of the three interior angles of a triangle must be 180°.

EXAMPLE 7 **Solve a Problem Involving the Angles of a Triangle**

In the diagram at the right, $m\angle c = 40°$ and $m\angle e = 60°$. Find the measure of $\angle d$.

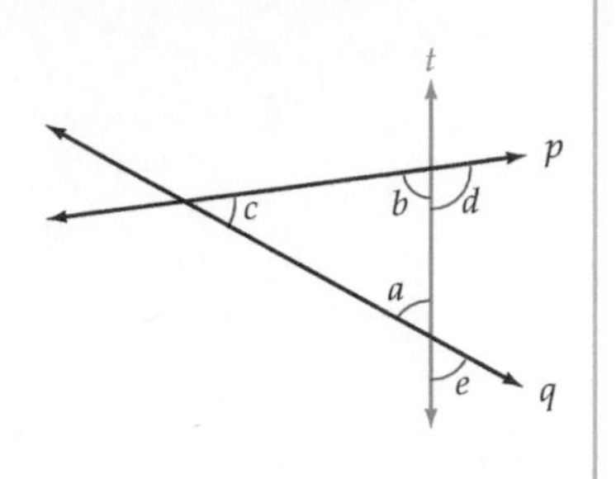

Solution

$m\angle a = m\angle e = 60°$ • $\angle a$ and $\angle e$ are vertical angles.

$m\angle c + m\angle a + m\angle b = 180°$ • The sum of the interior angles is 180°.

$40° + 60° + m\angle b = 180°$ • Replace $m\angle c$ with 40° and $m\angle a$ with 60°.

$100° + m\angle b = 180°$ • Add 40° + 60°.

$m\angle b = 80°$ • Subtract 100° from each side of the equation.

$m\angle b + m\angle d = 180°$ • $\angle b$ and $\angle d$ are supplementary angles.

$80° + m\angle d = 180°$ • Replace $m\angle b$ with 80°.

$m\angle d = 100°$ • Subtract 80° from each side of the equation.

$m\angle d = 100°$

CHECK YOUR PROGRESS 7

In the diagram at the right, $m\angle c = 35°$ and $m\angle d = 105°$. Find the measure of $\angle e$.

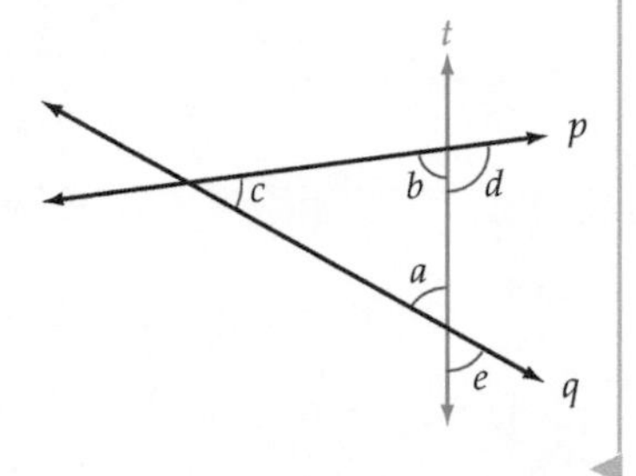

Solution See page S2.

Preparing a Circle Graph

A circle graph, sometimes called a pie chart, is a circular chart divided into sectors. The ratio of the angle measure of each sector to 360 (the number of degrees in a circle) is proportional to the ratio of the number of data values represented by the sector to the total number of data values.

The circle graph at the right represents the preferences of 200 people who were asked about the temperature range they considered most comfortable for walking. The data are given in the table below.

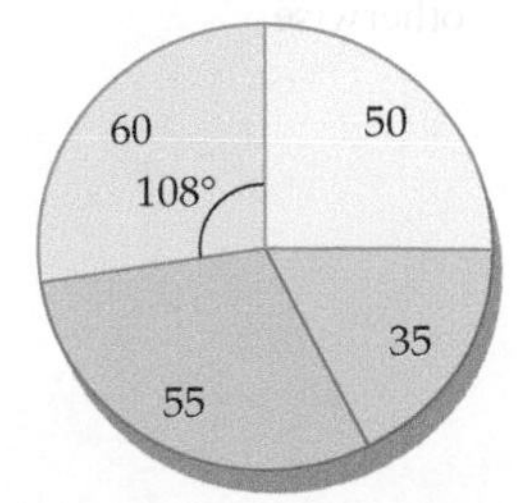

Temperature, °F	Number of people
60–64	50
65–69	55
70–74	60
75–79	35

The angle measure of the sector that represents people who chose a temperature between 70°F and 74°F is 108°. Note that $\frac{108}{360} = \frac{60}{200}$. That is, the ratio of the size of the angle, 108, to the total number of degrees in a circle, 360, is proportional to the magnitude of the data in that sector, 60, to the sum of all the data in the circle graph, 200.

Spreadsheet programs such as Excel and Numbers have built-in functions that will create a circle graph. Use such a program to prepare a circle graph for each of the exercises below.

EXCURSION EXERCISES

Prepare a circle graph for the data provided in each exercise.

1. A survey asked adults to name their favorite pizza topping. The results are shown in the table below.

Pepperoni	43%
Sausage	19%
Mushrooms	14%
Vegetables	13%
Other	7%
Onions	4%

2. A survey of children between 10 and 14 years old was conducted to determine the average amount of time they spent consuming media each day. The results are shown in the table below.

Watching TV	63 minutes
Listening to music	105 minutes
Nonschool computer use	42 minutes
Text messaging	84 minutes
Playing video games	76 minutes
Talking on cell phones	50 minutes

EXERCISE SET 1.2

1. Provide three names for the angle below.

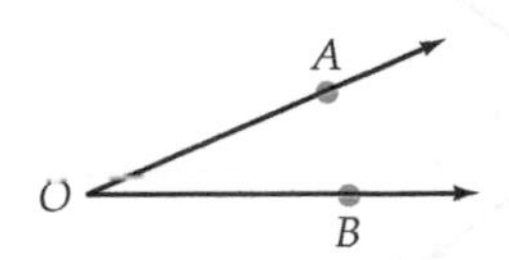

2. State the number of degrees in a full circle, a straight angle, and a right angle.

3. Find the complement of a 62° angle.

4. Find the complement of a 31° angle.

5. Find the supplement of a 162° angle.

6. Find the supplement of a 72° angle.

■ For Exercises 7 to 10, determine whether the described angle is an acute angle, is a right angle, is an obtuse angle, or does not exist.

7. The complement of an acute angle

8. The supplement of a right angle

9. The supplement of an acute angle

10. The supplement of an obtuse angle

11. Given $AB = 12$ cm, $CD = 9$ cm, and $AD = 35$ cm, find the length of $\overline{BC}$.

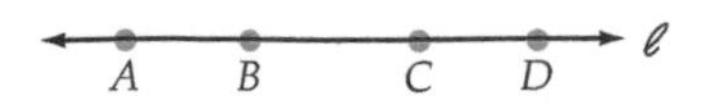

12. Given $AB = 21$ mm, $BC = 14$ mm, and $AD = 54$ mm, find the length of $\overline{CD}$.

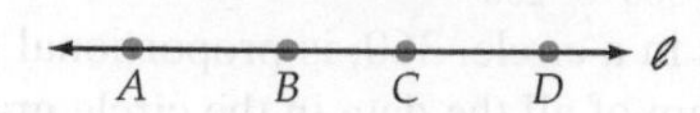

13. Given $QR = 7$ ft and RS is three times the length of $\overline{QR}$, find the length of $\overline{QS}$.

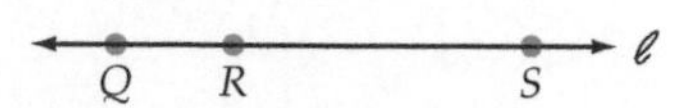

14. Given $QR = 15$ in. and RS is twice the length of $\overline{QR}$, find the length of $\overline{QS}$.

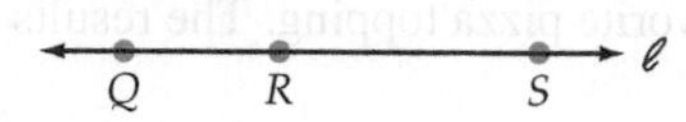

15. Given $m\angle LOM = 53°$ and $m\angle LON = 139°$, find the measure of $\angle MON$.

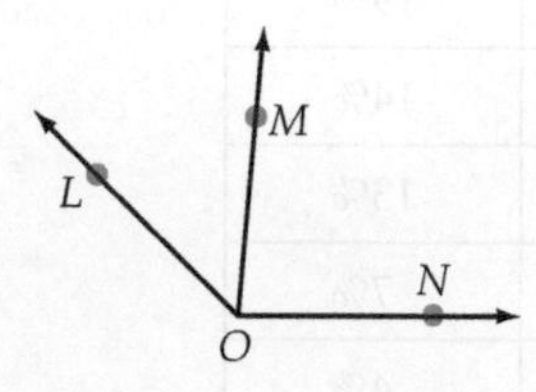

16. Given $m\angle MON = 38°$ and $m\angle LON = 85°$, find the measure of $\angle LOM$.

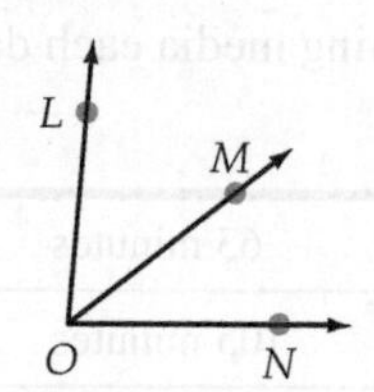

■ In Exercises 17 and 18, find the measure of $\angle x$.

17.

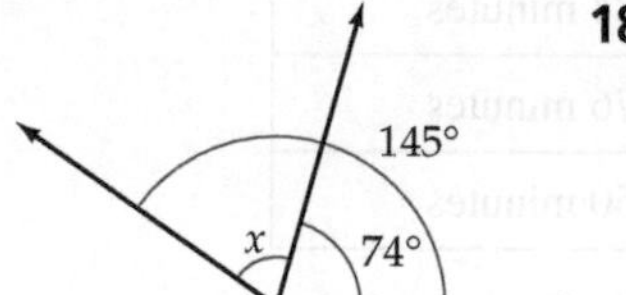

18.

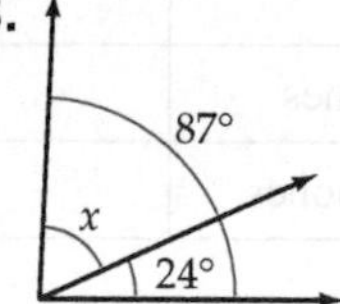

■ In Exercises 19 and 20, given that $\angle LON$ is a right angle, find the measure of $\angle x$.

19.

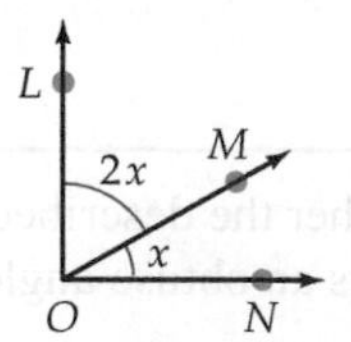

20.

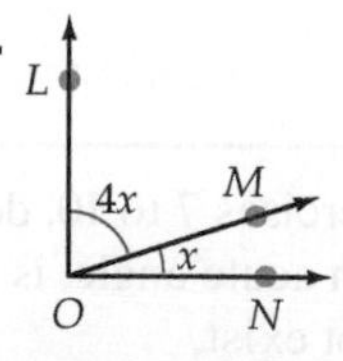

■ In Exercises 21 to 24, find the measure of $\angle a$.

21.

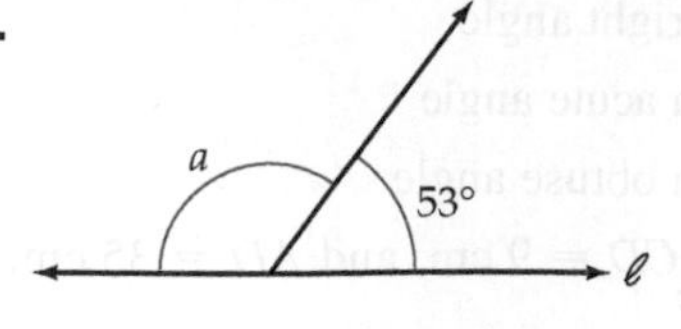

22.

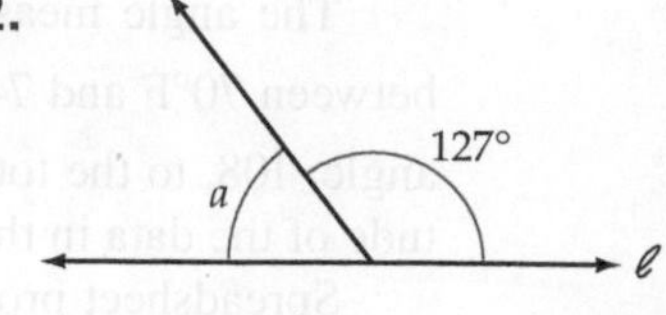

23.

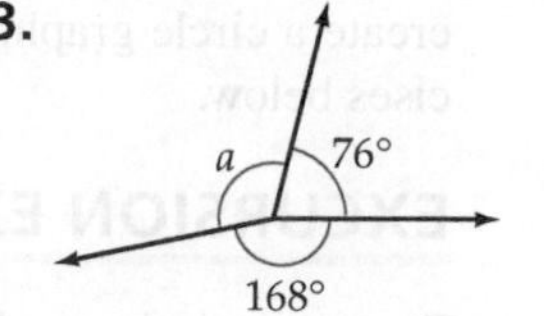

24.

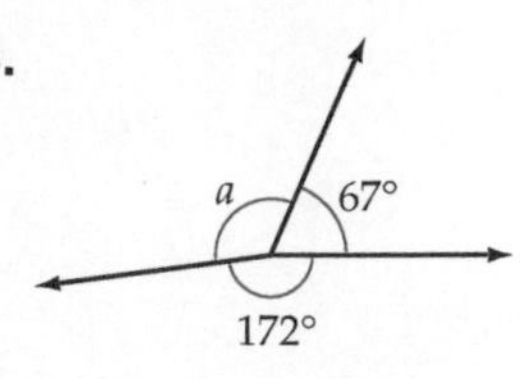

■ In Exercises 25 to 28, find the value of x.

25.

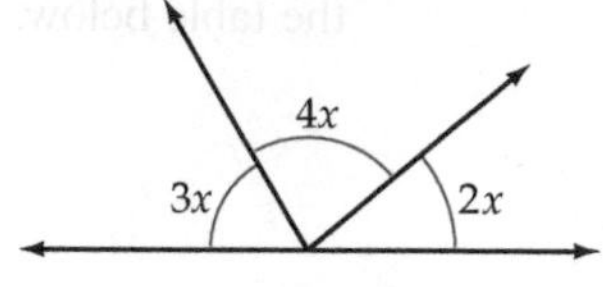

26.

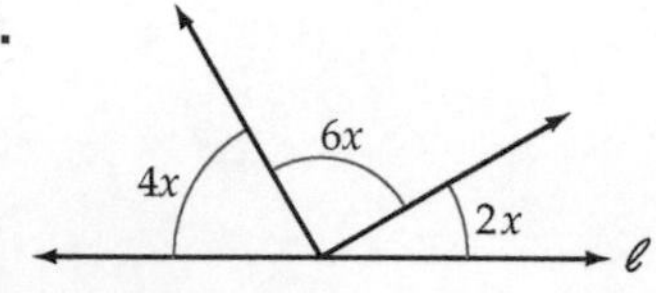

27.

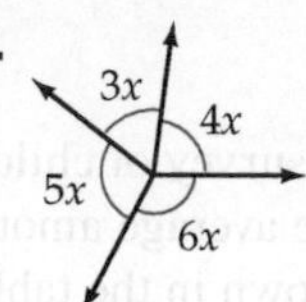

28.

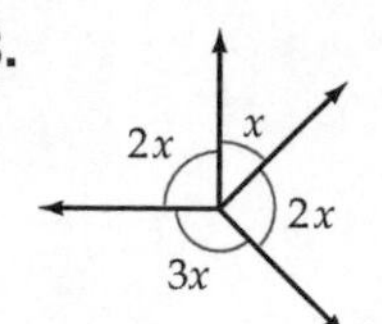

29. Given $m\angle a = 51°$, find the measure of $\angle b$.

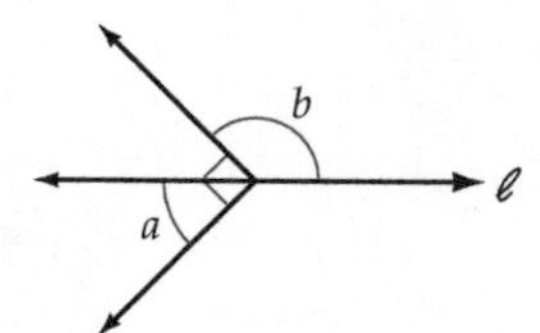

30. Given $m\angle a = 38°$, find the measure of $\angle b$.

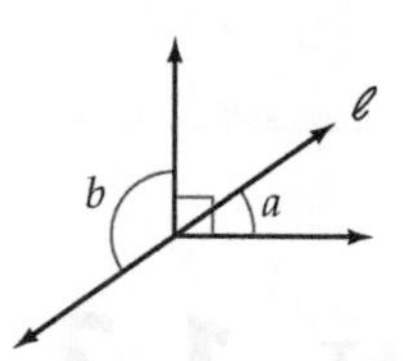

■ In Exercises 31 and 32, find the measure of $\angle x$.

31.

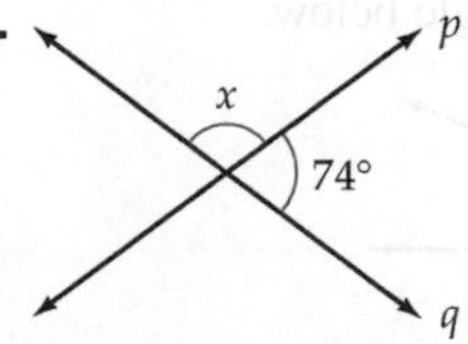

32.

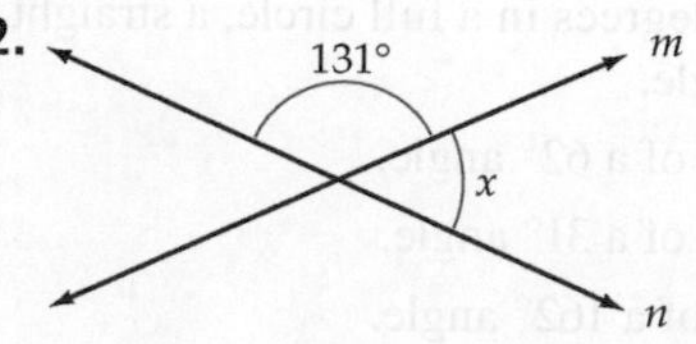

■ In Exercises 33 and 34, find the value of x.

33.

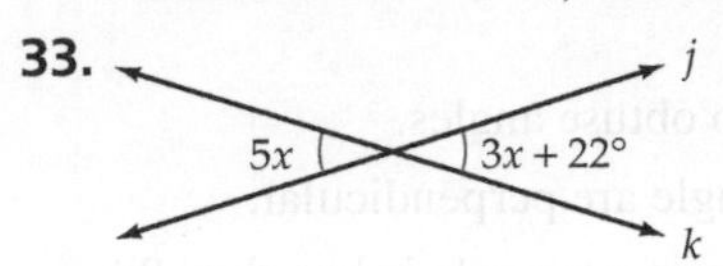

34.

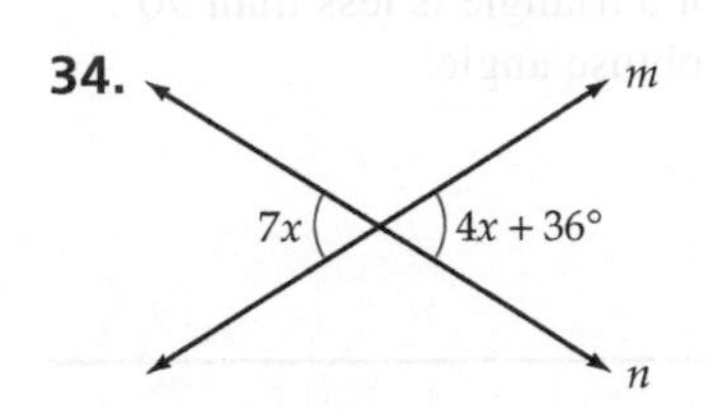

■ In Exercises 35 to 38, given that $\ell_1 \parallel \ell_2$, find the measures of angles a and b.

35.

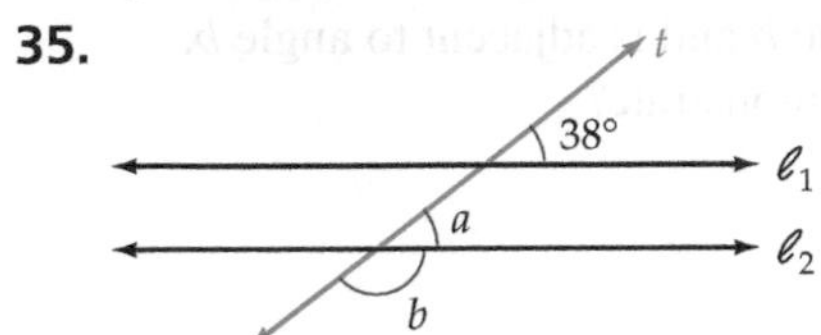

36.

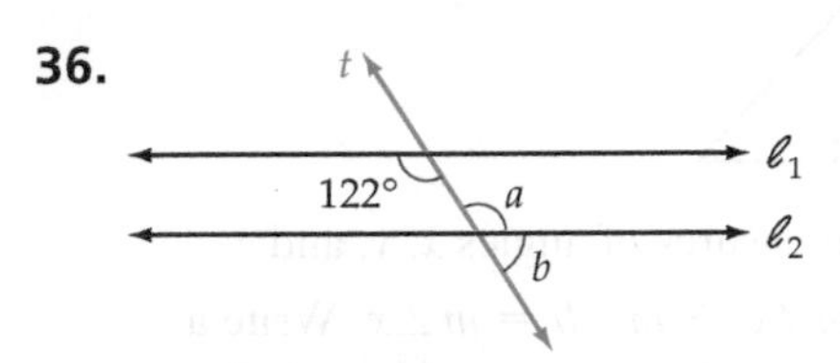

37.

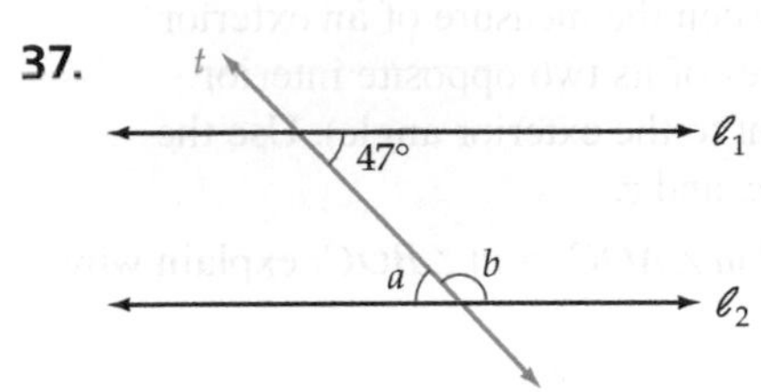

38.

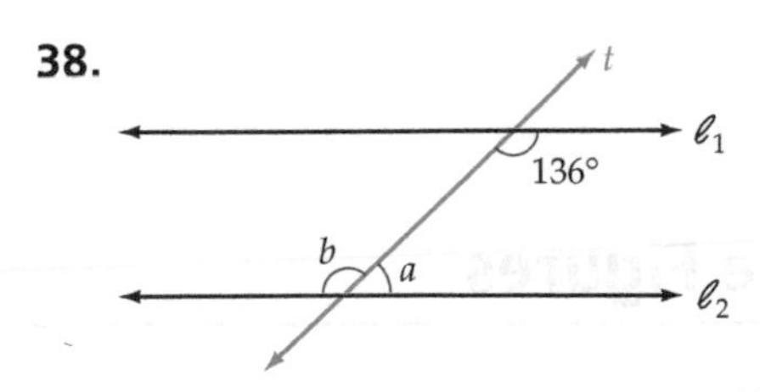

■ In Exercises 39 to 42, given that $\ell_1 \parallel \ell_2$, find x.

39.

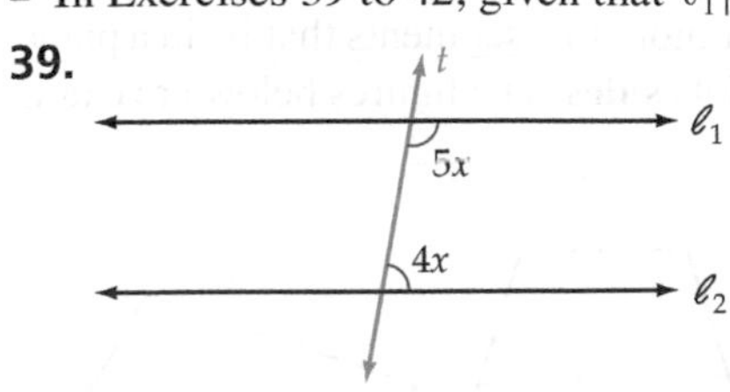

40.

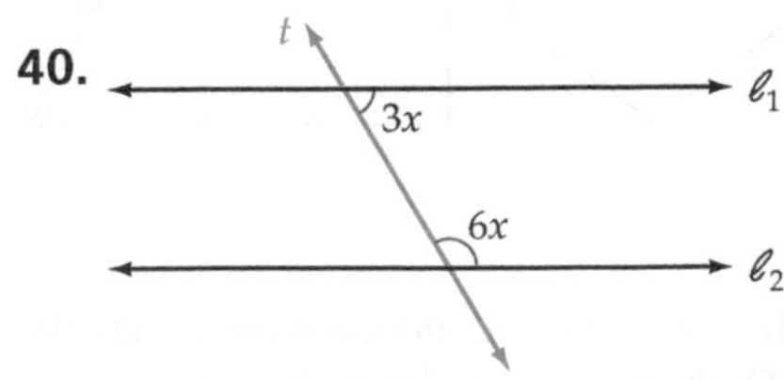

41.

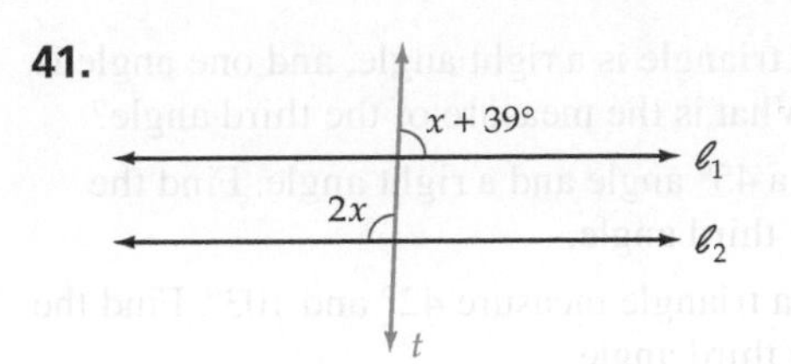

42.

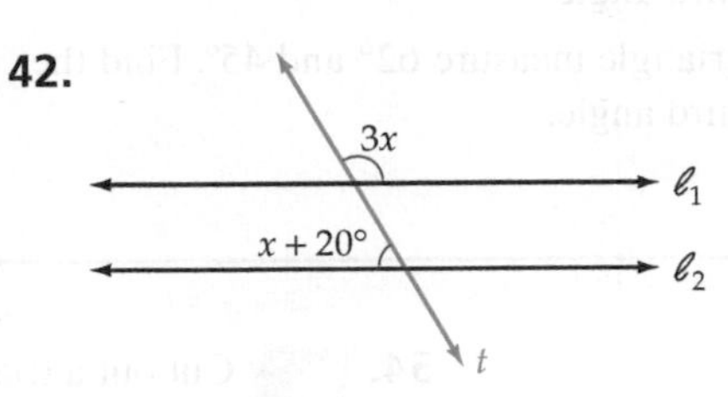

43. Given that $m\angle a = 95°$ and $m\angle b = 70°$, find the measures of angles x and y.

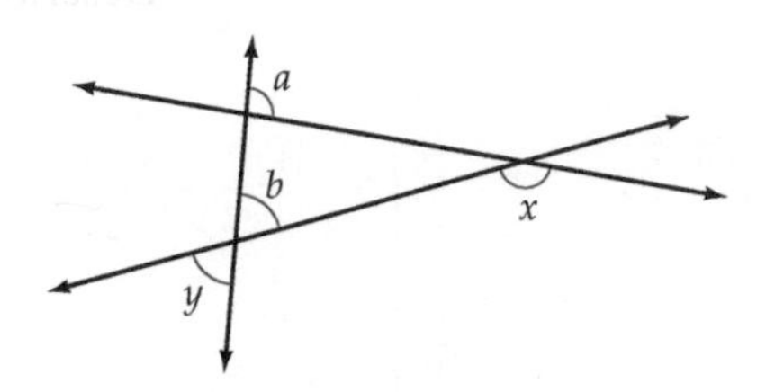

44. Given that $m\angle a = 35°$ and $m\angle b = 55°$, find the measures of angles x and y.

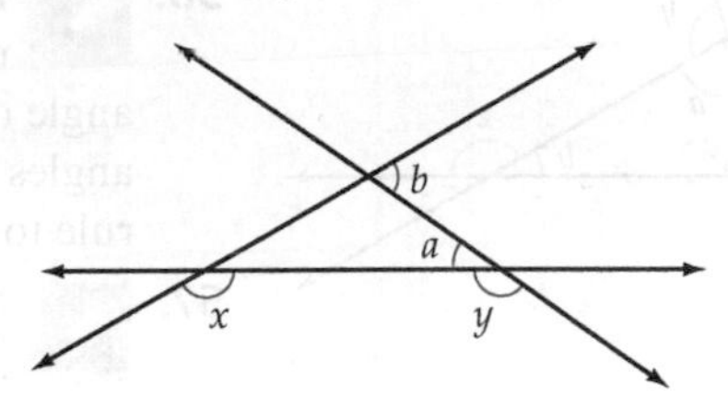

45. Given that $m\angle y = 45°$, find the measures of angles a and b.

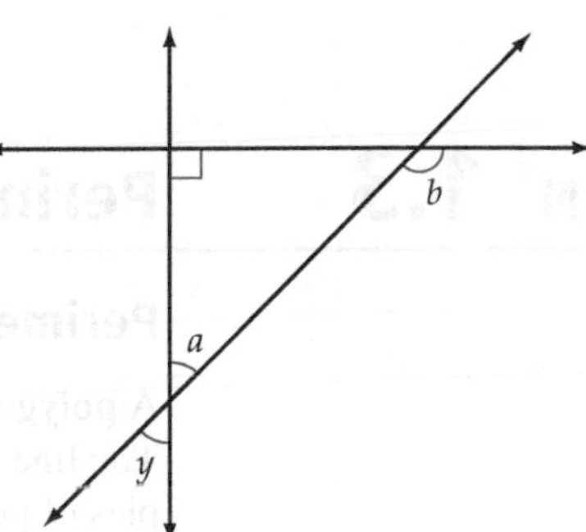

46. Given that $m\angle y = 130°$, find the measures of angles a and b.

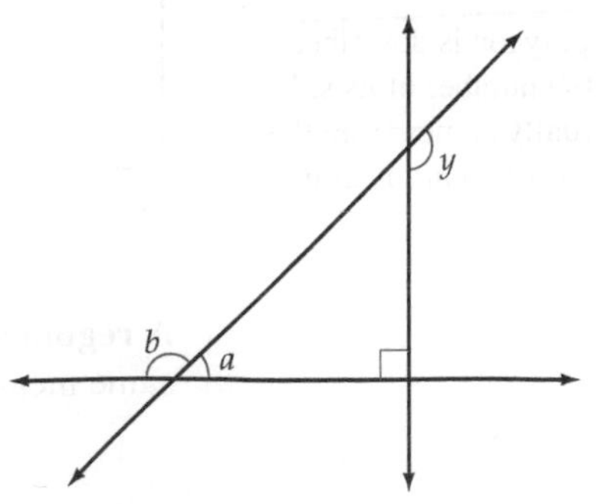

47. One angle in a triangle is a right angle, and one angle is equal to 30°. What is the measure of the third angle?

48. A triangle has a 45° angle and a right angle. Find the measure of the third angle.

49. Two angles of a triangle measure 42° and 103°. Find the measure of the third angle.

50. Two angles of a triangle measure 62° and 45°. Find the measure of the third angle.

■ For Exercises 51 to 53, determine whether the statement is true or false.

51. A triangle can have two obtuse angles.

52. The legs of a right triangle are perpendicular.

53. If the sum of two angles of a triangle is less than 90°, then the third angle is an obtuse angle.

EXTENSIONS

54. Cut out a triangle and then tear off two of the angles, as shown below. Position angle a so that it is to the left of angle b and is adjacent to angle b. Now position angle c so that it is to the right of angle b and is adjacent to angle b. Describe what you observe. What does this demonstrate?

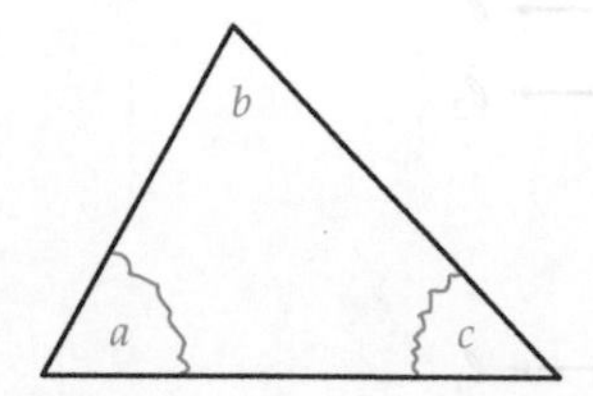

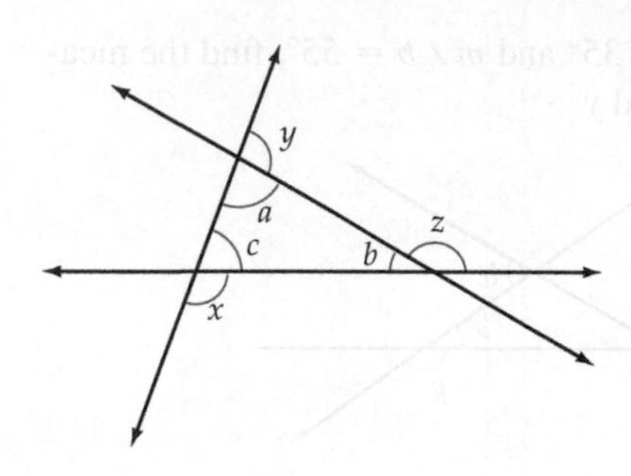

55. For the figure at the left, find the sum of the measures of angles x, y, and z.

56. For the figure at the left, explain why $m\angle a + m\angle b = m\angle x$. Write a rule that describes the relationship between the measure of an exterior angle of a triangle and the sum of the measures of its two opposite interior angles (the interior angles that are nonadjacent to the exterior angle). Use the rule to write an equation involving angles a, c, and z.

57. If $\overline{AB}$ and $\overline{CD}$ intersect at point O, and $m\angle AOC = m\angle BOC$, explain why $\overline{AB} \perp \overline{CD}$.

SECTION 1.3 Perimeter and Area of Plane Figures

Perimeter of Plane Geometric Figures

A **polygon** is a closed figure determined by three or more line segments that lie in a plane. The line segments that form the polygon are called its **sides**. The figures below are examples of polygons.

POINT OF INTEREST

Although a polygon is described in terms of the number of its sides, the word actually comes from the Latin word *polygonum*, meaning "many *angles*."

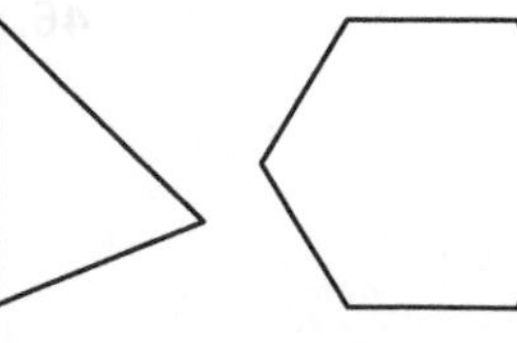
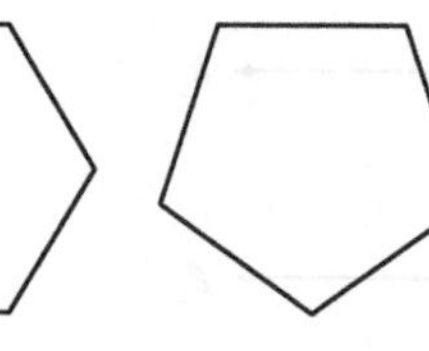
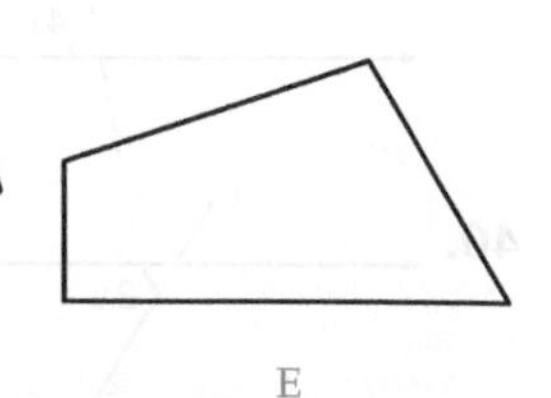

A B C D E

A **regular polygon** is one in which each side has the same length and each angle has the same measure. The polygons in Figures A, C, and D above are regular polygons.

AP Images

The Pentagon in Arlington, Virginia

The name of a polygon is based on the number of its sides. The table below lists the names of polygons that have from 3 to 10 sides.

Number of sides	Name of polygon
3	Triangle
4	Quadrilateral
5	Pentagon
6	Hexagon
7	Heptagon
8	Octagon
9	Nonagon
10	Decagon

Triangles and quadrilaterals are two of the most common types of polygons. Triangles are distinguished by the number of equal sides and also by the measures of their angles.

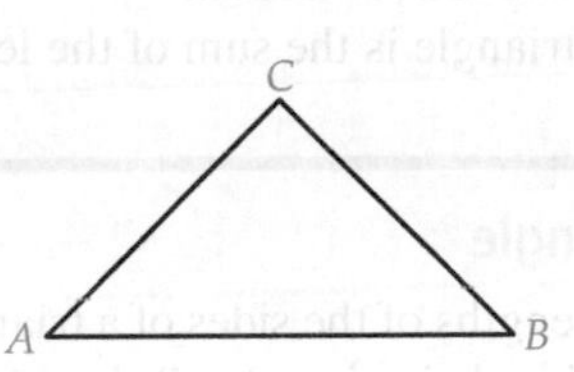

An **isosceles triangle** has exactly two sides of equal length. The angles opposite the equal sides are of equal measure.

$AC = BC$

$m\angle A = m\angle B$

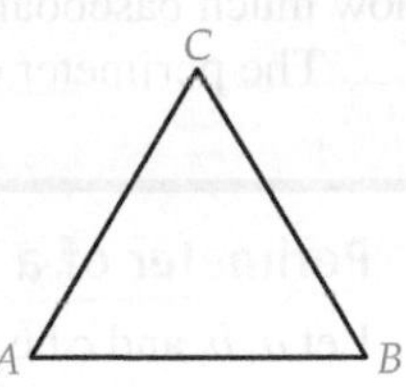

The three sides of an **equilateral triangle** are of equal length. The three angles are of equal measure.

$AB = BC = AC$

$m\angle A = m\angle B$
$= m\angle C$

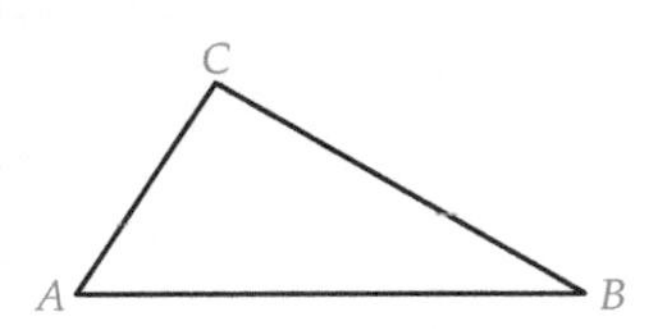

A **scalene triangle** has no two sides of equal length. No two angles are of equal measure.

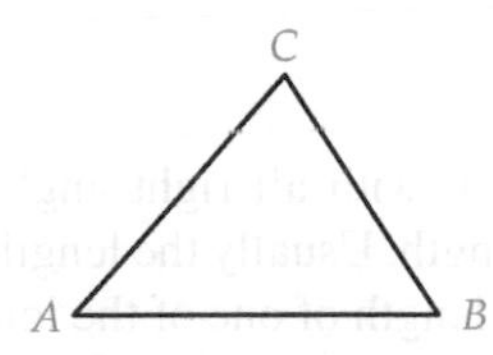

An **acute triangle** has three acute angles.

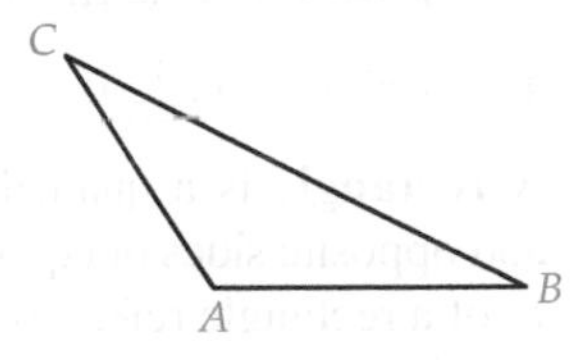

An **obtuse triangle** has one obtuse angle.

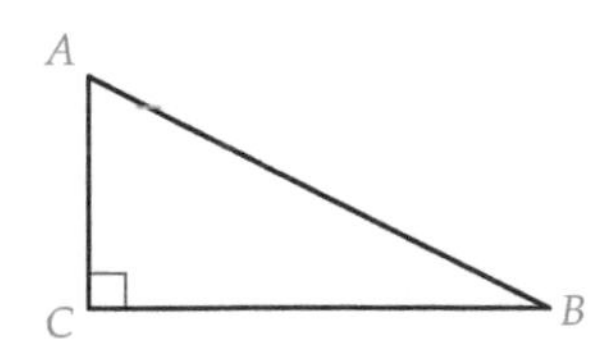

A **right triangle** has a right angle.

A **quadrilateral** is a four-sided polygon. Quadrilaterals are also distinguished by their sides and angles, as shown in Figure 1.1 on the next page. Note that a rectangle, a square, and a rhombus are different forms of a parallelogram.

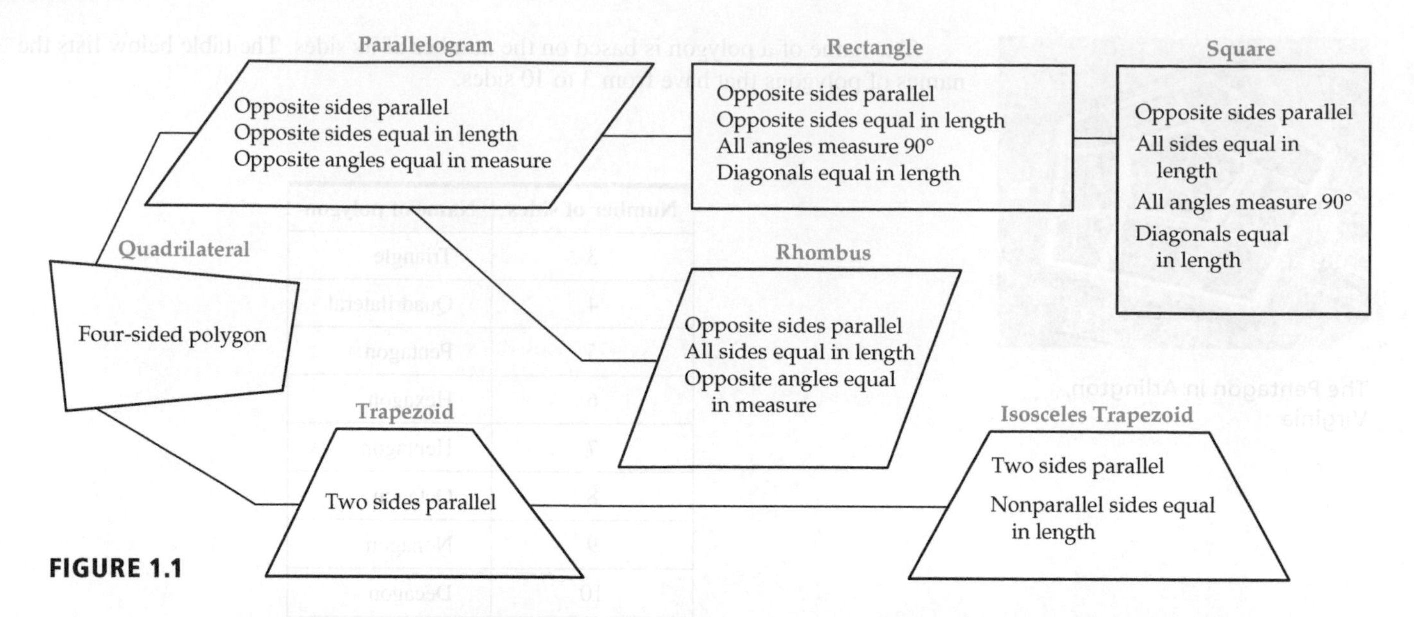

FIGURE 1.1

QUESTION **a.** What distinguishes a rectangle from other parallelograms?
b. What distinguishes a square from other rectangles?

The **perimeter** of a plane geometric figure is a measure of the distance around the figure. Perimeter is used, for example, when buying fencing for a garden or determining how much baseboard is needed for a room.

The perimeter of a triangle is the sum of the lengths of the three sides.

Perimeter of a Triangle

Let a, b, and c be the lengths of the sides of a triangle. The perimeter, P, of the triangle is given by $P = a + b + c$.

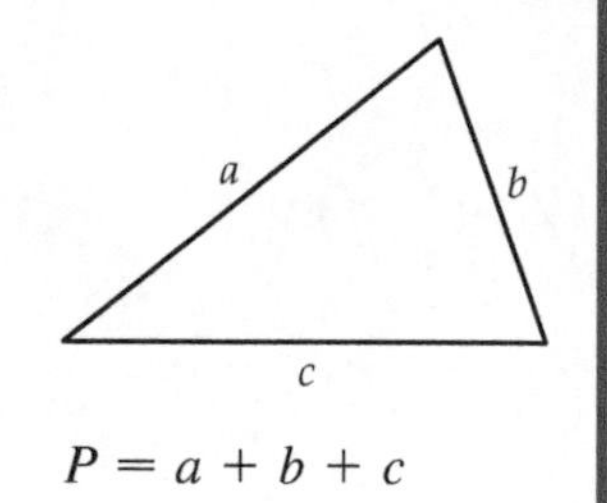

$P = a + b + c$

To find the perimeter of the triangle shown at the right, add the lengths of the three sides.

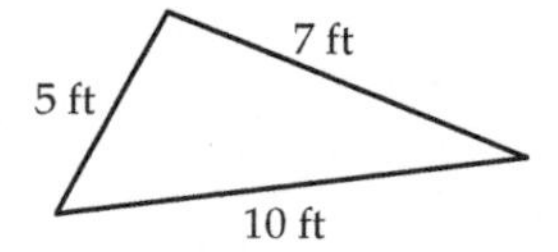

$P = 5 + 7 + 10 = 22$

The perimeter is 22 ft.

A **rectangle** is a quadrilateral with all right angles and opposite sides of equal length. Usually the length, L, of a rectangle refers to the length of one of the longer sides of the rectangle and the width, W, refers to the length of one of the shorter sides. The perimeter can then be represented as $P = L + W + L + W$.

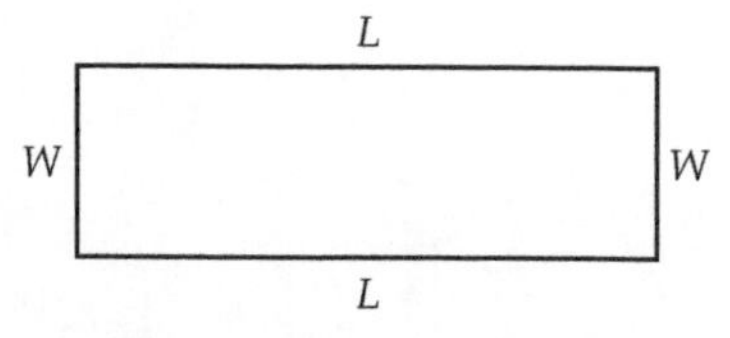

The formula for the perimeter of a rectangle is derived by combining like terms.

$P = L + W + L + W$
$P = 2L + 2W$

ANSWER **a.** In a rectangle, all angles measure 90°. **b.** In a square, all sides are equal in length.

Perimeter of a Rectangle

Let L represent the length and W the width of a rectangle. The perimeter, P, of the rectangle is given by $P = 2L + 2W$.

A **square** is a rectangle in which each side has the same length. Letting s represent the length of each side of a square, the perimeter of the square can be represented by $P = s + s + s + s$.

The formula for the perimeter of a square is derived by combining like terms.

$$P = s + s + s + s$$
$$P = 4s$$

Perimeter of a Square

Let s represent the length of a side of a square. The perimeter, P, of the square is given by $P = 4s$.

Figure $ABCD$ is a parallelogram. $\overline{BC}$ is the **base** of the parallelogram. Opposite sides of a parallelogram are equal in length, so $\overline{AD}$ is the same length as $\overline{BC}$, and $\overline{AB}$ is the same length as $\overline{CD}$.

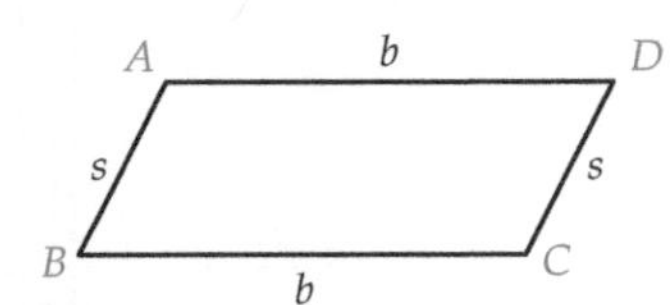

Let b represent the length of the base and s the length of an adjacent side. Then the perimeter of a parallelogram can be represented as $P = b + s + b + s$.

$$P = b + s + b + s$$

The formula for the perimeter of a parallelogram is derived by combining like terms.

$$P = 2b + 2s$$

HISTORICAL NOTE

The Granger Collection, NY

Benjamin Banneker (băn'ĭ-kər) (1731–1806), a noted American scholar who was largely self-taught, was both a surveyor and an astronomer. As a surveyor, he was a member of the commission that defined the boundary lines and laid out the streets of the District of Columbia. (See the Point of Interest on page 15.)

Perimeter of a Parallelogram

Let b represent the length of the base of a parallelogram and s the length of a side adjacent to the base. The perimeter, P, of the parallelogram is given by $P = 2b + 2s$.

EXAMPLE 1 Find the Perimeter of a Rectangle

You want to trim a rectangular frame with a metal strip. The frame measures 30 in. by 20 in. Find the length of metal strip you will need to trim the frame.

Solution

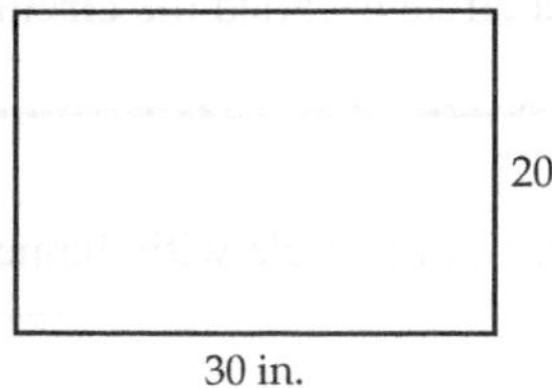

• Draw a diagram.

$P = 2L + 2W$ • Use the formula for the perimeter of a rectangle.

$P = 2(30) + 2(20)$ • The length is 30 in. Substitute 30 for L. The width is 20 in. Substitute 20 for W.

$P = 60 + 40$

$P = 100$

You will need 100 in. of the metal strip.

CHECK YOUR PROGRESS 1 Find the length of decorative molding needed to edge the top of the walls in a rectangular room that is 12 ft long and 8 ft wide.

Solution See page S2.

EXAMPLE 2 **Find the Perimeter of a Square**

Find the length of fencing needed to surround a square corral that measures 60 ft on each side.

Solution

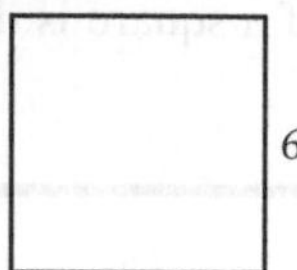

• Draw a diagram.

$P = 4s$ • Use the formula for the perimeter of a square.

$P = 4(60)$ • The length of a side is 60 ft. Substitute 60 for s.

$P = 240$

240 ft of fencing are needed.

CHECK YOUR PROGRESS 2 A homeowner plans to fence in the area around the swimming pool in the backyard. The area to be fenced in is a square measuring 24 ft on each side. How many feet of fencing should the homeowner purchase?

Solution See page S2.

POINT OF INTEREST

A **glazier** is a person who cuts, fits, and installs glass, generally in doors and windows. Of particular challenge to a glazier are intricate stained glass window designs.

Luca Moi/Shutterstock.com

A **circle** is a plane figure in which all points are the same distance from point O, called the **center** of the circle.

A **diameter** of a circle is a line segment with endpoints on the circle and passing through the center. $\overline{AB}$ is a diameter of the circle at the right. The variable d is used to designate the length of a diameter of a circle.

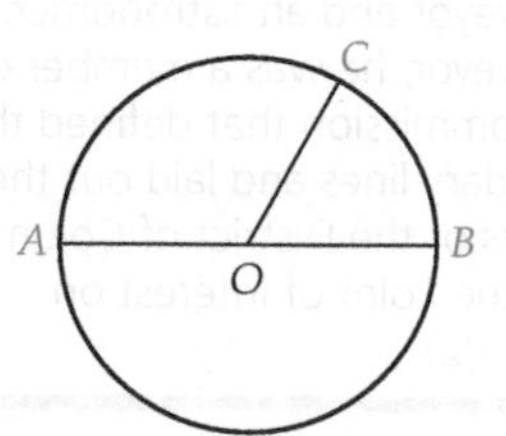

A **radius** of a circle is a line segment from the center of the circle to a point on the circle. $\overline{OC}$ is a radius of the circle at the right above. The variable r is used to designate the length of a radius of a circle.

The length of the diameter is twice the length of the radius.

$$d = 2r \text{ or } r = \frac{1}{2}d$$

The distance around a circle is called the **circumference**.

POINT OF INTEREST

Archimedes (ar-kə-mē′dēz) (c. 287–212 BC) is the person who calculated that $\pi \approx 3\frac{1}{7}$. He actually showed that $3\frac{10}{71} < \pi < 3\frac{1}{7}$. The approximation $3\frac{10}{71}$ is a more accurate approximation of π than $3\frac{1}{7}$, but it is more difficult to use without a calculator.

Circumference of a Circle

The circumference, C, of a circle with diameter d and radius r is given by $C = \pi d$ or $C = 2\pi r$.

The formula for circumference uses the number π (pi), which is an irrational number.

The value of π can be approximated by a fraction or by a decimal.

$$\pi \approx 3\frac{1}{7} = \frac{22}{7} \text{ or } \pi \approx 3.14$$

The π key on a scientific calculator gives a closer approximation of π than 3.14. A scientific calculator is used in this section to find approximate values in calculations involving π.

CALCULATOR NOTE 

To approximate 16π on your calculator, enter

16 [×] [π] [=]

EXAMPLE 3 **Find the Circumference of a Circle**

Find the circumference of a circle with a radius of 15 cm. Round to the nearest hundredth of a centimeter.

Solution

$C = 2\pi r$ • The radius is given. Use the circumference formula that involves the radius.

$C = 2\pi(15)$ • Replace r with 15.

$C = 30\pi$ • Multiply 2 times 15.

$C \approx 94.25$ • An approximation is asked for. Use the π key on a calculator.

The circumference of the circle is approximately 94.25 cm.

CHECK YOUR PROGRESS 3 Find the circumference of a circle with a diameter of 9 km. Give the exact measure.

Solution See page S2.

EXAMPLE 4 **Application of Finding the Circumference of a Circle**

A bicycle tire has a diameter of 24 in. How many feet does the bicycle travel when the wheel makes 8 revolutions? Round to the nearest hundredth of a foot.

Solution

24 in. = 2 ft • The diameter is given in inches, but the answer must be expressed in feet. Convert the diameter (24 in.) to feet. There are 12 in. in 1 ft. Divide 24 by 12.

$C = \pi d$ • The diameter is given. Use the circumference formula that involves the diameter.

$C = \pi(2)$ • Replace d with 2.

$C = 2\pi$ • This is the distance traveled in 1 revolution.

$8C = 8(2\pi) = 16\pi \approx 50.27$ • Find the distance traveled in 8 revolutions.

The bicycle will travel about 50.27 ft when the wheel makes 8 revolutions.

CHECK YOUR PROGRESS 4 A tricycle tire has a diameter of 12 in. How many feet does the tricycle travel when the wheel makes 12 revolutions? Round to the nearest hundredth of a foot.

Solution See page S2.

Area of Plane Geometric Figures

Area is the amount of surface in a region. Area can be used to describe, for example, the size of a rug, a parking lot, a farm, or a national park. Area is measured in square units.

A square that measures 1 in. on each side has an area of 1 square inch, written 1 in^2.

A square that measures 1 cm on each side has an area of 1 square centimeter, written 1 cm^2.

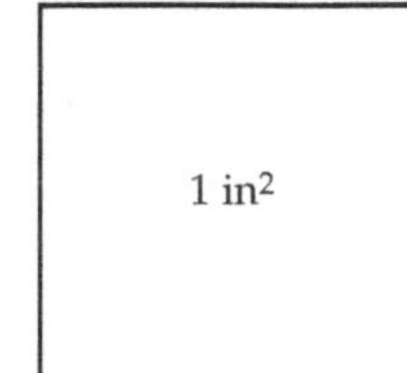

Larger areas are often measured in square feet (ft^2), square meters (m^2), square miles (mi^2), acres (43,560 ft^2), or any other square unit.

QUESTION **a.** What is the area of a square that measures 1 yd on each side?
b. What is the area of a square that measures 1 km on each side?

Area of a Rectangle

Let L represent the length and W the width of a rectangle. The area, A, of the rectangle is given by $A = LW$.

QUESTION How many squares, each 1 in. on a side, are needed to cover a rectangle that has an area of 18 in^2?

EXAMPLE 5 Find the Area of a Rectangle

How many square feet of sod are needed to cover a football field? A football field measures 360 ft by 160 ft.

Solution

160 ft, 360 ft • Draw a diagram.

$A = LW$ • Use the formula for the area of a rectangle.

$A = 360(160)$ • The length is 360 ft. Substitute 360 for L. The width is 160 ft. Substitute 160 for W. Remember that LW means "L times W."

$A = 57{,}600$

57,600 ft^2 of sod is needed. • Area is measured in square units.

CHECK YOUR PROGRESS 5 Find the amount of fabric needed to make a rectangular flag that measures 308 cm by 192 cm.

Solution See page S2.

TAKE NOTE

Recall that the rules of exponents state that when multiplying variables with like bases, we add the exponents.

A square is a rectangle in which all sides are the same length. Therefore, both the length and the width of a square can be represented by s, and $A = LW = s \cdot s = s^2$.

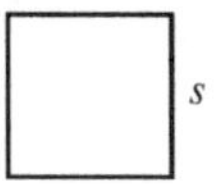

$A = s \cdot s$
$A = s^2$

Area of a Square

Let s represent the length of a side of a square. The area, A, of the square is given by $A = s^2$.

ANSWER **a.** The area is 1 square yard, written 1 yd^2. **b.** The area is 1 square kilometer, written 1 km^2.

ANSWER 18 squares, each 1 in. on a side, are needed to cover the rectangle.

EXAMPLE 6 Find the Area of a Square

A homeowner wants to carpet the family room. The floor is square and measures 6 m on each side. How much carpet should be purchased?

Solution

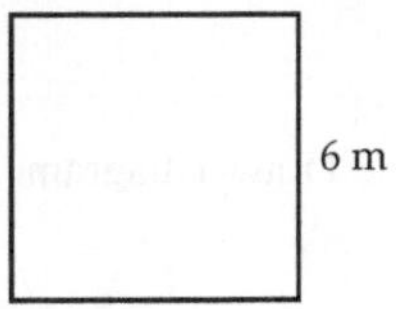

• Draw a diagram.

$A = s^2$ • Use the formula for the area of a square.

$A = 6^2$ • The length of a side is 6 m. Substitute 6 for *s*.

$A = 36$

36 m^2 of carpet should be purchased. • Area is measured in square units.

CHECK YOUR PROGRESS 6 Find the area of the floor of a two-car garage that is in the shape of a square that measures 24 ft on a side.

Solution See page S2.

Figure *ABCD* is a parallelogram. $\overline{BC}$ is the **base** of the parallelogram. $\overline{AE}$, perpendicular to the base, is the **height** of the parallelogram.

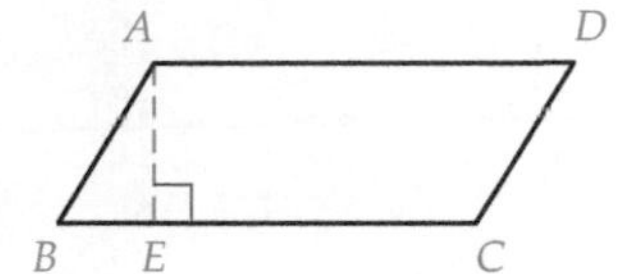

Any side of a parallelogram can be designated as the base. The corresponding height is found by drawing a line segment perpendicular to the base from the opposite side. In the figure at the right, $\overline{CD}$ is the base and $\overline{AE}$ is the height.

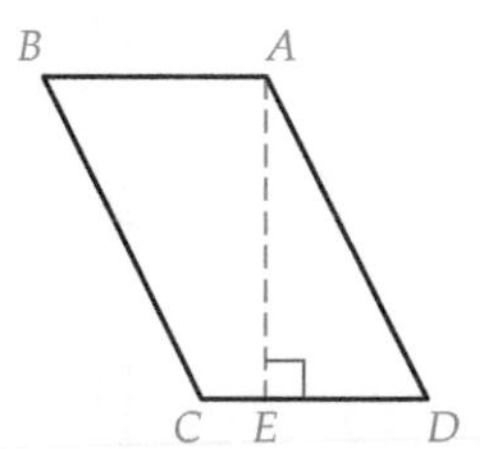

A rectangle can be formed from a parallelogram by cutting a right triangle from one end of the parallelogram and attaching it to the other end. The area of the resulting rectangle will equal the area of the original parallelogram.

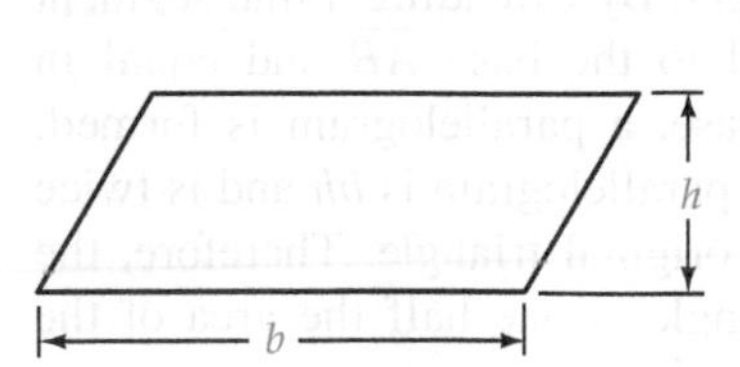

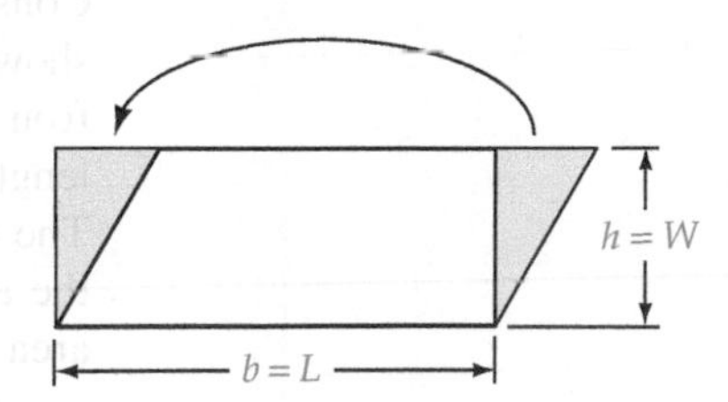

Area of a Parallelogram

Let b represent the length of the base and h the height of a parallelogram. The area, A, of the parallelogram is given by $A = bh$.

EXAMPLE 7 Find the Area of a Parallelogram

A solar panel is in the shape of a parallelogram that has a base of 2 ft and a height of 3 ft. Find the area of the solar panel.

Solution

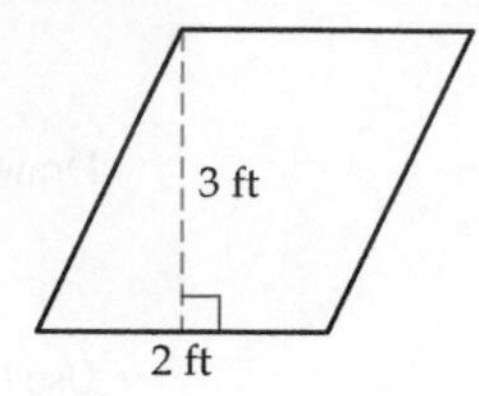

• Draw a diagram.

$A = bh$ • Use the formula for the area of a parallelogram.

$A = 2(3)$ • The base is 2 ft. Substitute 2 for b. The height is 3 ft. Substitute 3 for h. Remember that bh means "b times h."

$A = 6$

The area is 6 ft^2. • Area is measured in square units.

CHECK YOUR PROGRESS 7 A fieldstone patio is in the shape of a parallelogram that has a base measuring 14 m and a height measuring 8 m. What is the area of the patio?

Solution See page S2.

Figure ABC is a triangle. $\overline{AB}$ is the **base** of the triangle. $\overline{CD}$, perpendicular to the base, is the **height** of the triangle.

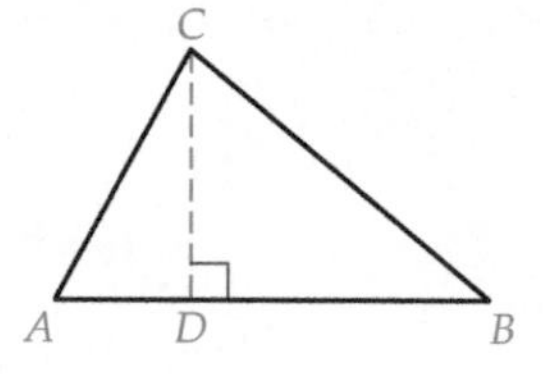

Any side of a triangle can be designated as the base. The corresponding height is found by drawing a line segment perpendicular to the base from the vertex opposite the base.

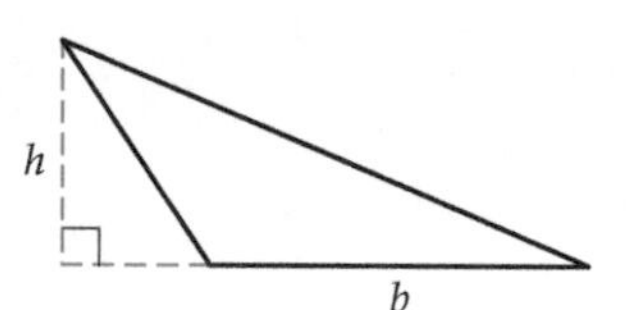

Consider triangle ABC with base b and height h, shown at the right. By extending a line segment from C parallel to the base $\overline{AB}$ and equal in length to the base, a parallelogram is formed. The area of the parallelogram is bh and is twice the area of the original triangle. Therefore, the area of the triangle is one half the area of the parallelogram, or $\frac{1}{2}bh$.

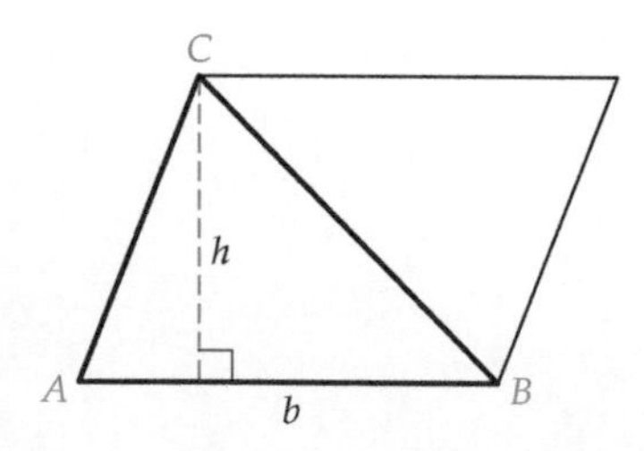

Area of a Triangle

Let b represent the length of the base and h the height of a triangle. The area, A, of the triangle is given by $A = \frac{1}{2}bh$.

EXAMPLE 8 **Find the Area of a Triangle**

A riveter uses metal plates that are in the shape of a triangle with a base of 12 cm and a height of 6 cm. Find the area of one metal plate.

Solution

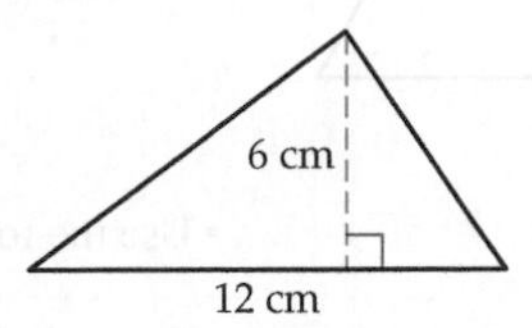

• Draw a diagram.

$A = \frac{1}{2}bh$ • Use the formula for the area of a triangle.

$A = \frac{1}{2}(12)(6)$ • The base is 12 cm. Substitute 12 for b. The height is 6 cm. Substitute 6 for h. Remember that bh means "b times h."

$A = 6(6)$

$A = 36$

The area is 36 cm^2. • Area is measured in square units.

CHECK YOUR PROGRESS 8 Find the amount of felt needed to make a banner that is in the shape of a triangle with a base of 18 in. and a height of 9 in.

Solution See page S2.

TAKE NOTE

The bases of a trapezoid are the parallel sides of the figure.

Figure $ABCD$ is a trapezoid. $\overline{AB}$, with length b_1, is one **base** of the trapezoid and $\overline{CD}$, with length b_2, is the other base. $\overline{AE}$, perpendicular to the two bases, is the **height**.

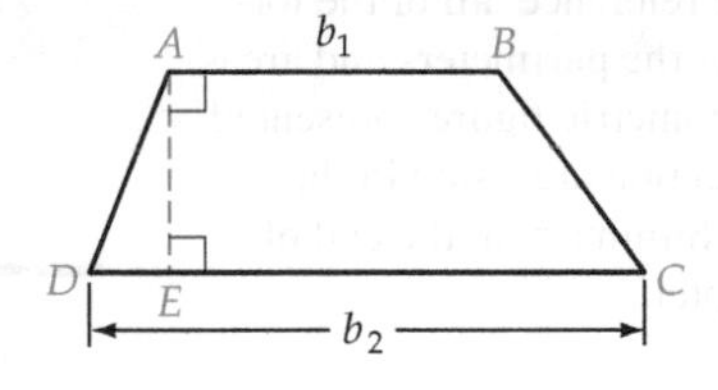

In the trapezoid at the right, the line segment $\overline{BD}$ divides the trapezoid into two triangles, ABD and BCD. In triangle ABD, b_1 is the base and h is the height. In triangle BCD, b_2 is the base and h is the height. The area of the trapezoid is the sum of the areas of the two triangles.

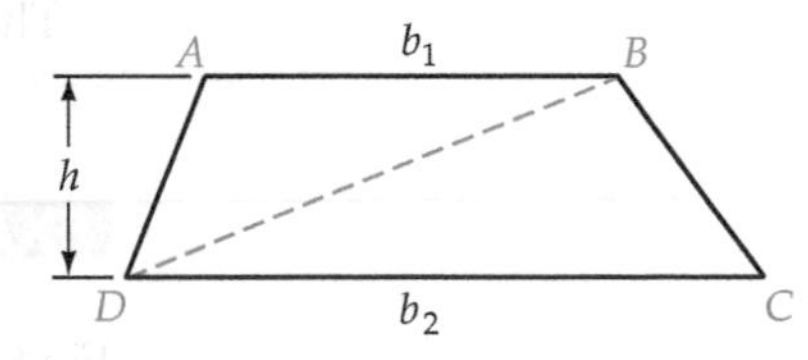

Area of trapezoid $ABCD$ = Area of triangle ABD + area of triangle BCD

$$= \frac{1}{2}b_1h + \frac{1}{2}b_2h = \frac{1}{2}h(b_1 + b_2)$$

Area of a Trapezoid

Let b_1 and b_2 represent the lengths of the bases and h the height of a trapezoid. The area, A, of the trapezoid is given by $A = \frac{1}{2}h(b_1 + b_2)$.

EXAMPLE 9 **Find the Area of a Trapezoid**

A boat dock is built in the shape of a trapezoid with bases measuring 14 ft and 6 ft and a height of 7 ft. Find the area of the dock.

Solution

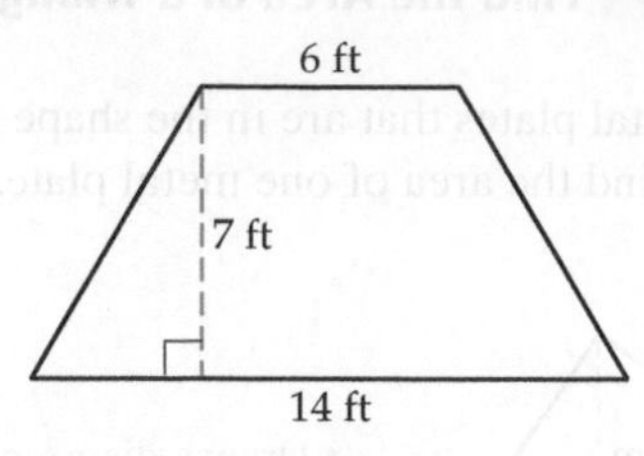

• Draw a diagram.

$A = \frac{1}{2}h(b_1 + b_2)$ • Use the formula for the area of a trapezoid.

$A = \frac{1}{2} \cdot 7(14 + 6)$ • The height is 7 ft. Substitute 7 for h. The bases measure 14 ft and 6 ft. Substitute 14 and 6 for b_1 and b_2.

$A = \frac{1}{2} \cdot 7(20)$

$A = 70$

The area is 70 ft^2. • Area is measured in square units.

CHECK YOUR PROGRESS 9 Find the area of a patio that has the shape of a trapezoid with a height of 9 ft and bases measuring 12 ft and 20 ft.

Solution See page S2.

TAKE NOTE

For your reference, all of the formulas for the perimeters and areas of the geometric figures presented in this section are listed in the Chapter Summary at the end of this chapter.

The area of a circle is the product of π and the square of the radius.

$A = \pi r^2$

The Area of a Circle

The area, A, of a circle with radius of length r is given by $A = \pi r^2$.

EXAMPLE 10 Find the Area of a Circle

Find the area of a circle with a diameter of 10 m. Round to the nearest hundredth of a square meter.

CALCULATOR NOTE

To evaluate the expression $\pi (5)^2$ on your calculator, enter

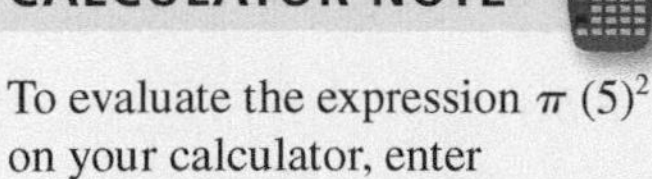

or

Solution

$r = \frac{1}{2}d = \frac{1}{2}(10) = 5$ • Find the radius of the circle.

$A = \pi r^2$ • Use the formula for the area of a circle.

$A = \pi(5)^2$ • Replace r with 5.

$A = \pi(25)$ • Square 5.

$A \approx 78.54$ • An approximation is asked for. Use the π key on a calculator.

The area of the circle is approximately 78.54 m^2.

CHECK YOUR PROGRESS 10 Find the area of a circle with a diameter of 12 km. Give the exact measure.

Solution See page S2.

EXAMPLE 11 **Application of Finding the Area of a Circle**

How large a cover is needed for a circular hot tub that is 8 ft in diameter? Round to the nearest tenth of a square foot.

Solution

$r = \frac{1}{2}d = \frac{1}{2}(8) = 4$ • Find the radius of a circle with a diameter of 8 ft.

$A = \pi r^2$ • Use the formula for the area of a circle.

$A = \pi(4)^2$ • Replace r with 4.

$A = \pi(16)$ • Square 4.

$A \approx 50.3$ • Use the π key on a calculator.

The cover for the hot tub must be 50.3 ft².

CHECK YOUR PROGRESS 11 How much material is needed to make a circular tablecloth that is to have a diameter of 4 ft? Round to the nearest hundredth of a square foot.

Solution See page S2.

MATH MATTERS Möbius Bands

Cut out a long, narrow rectangular strip of paper.

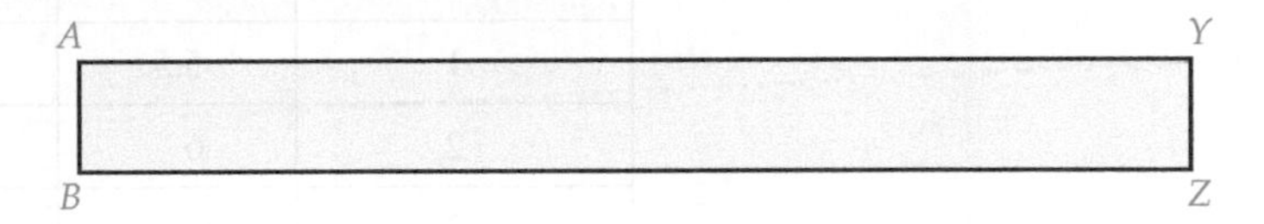

Give the strip of paper a half-twist.

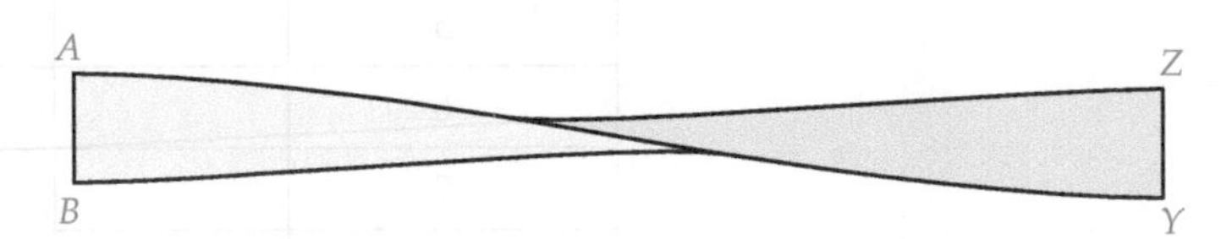

Put the ends together so that A meets Z and B meets Y. Tape the ends together. The result is a *Möbius band.* A Möbius band is also called a Möbius strip.

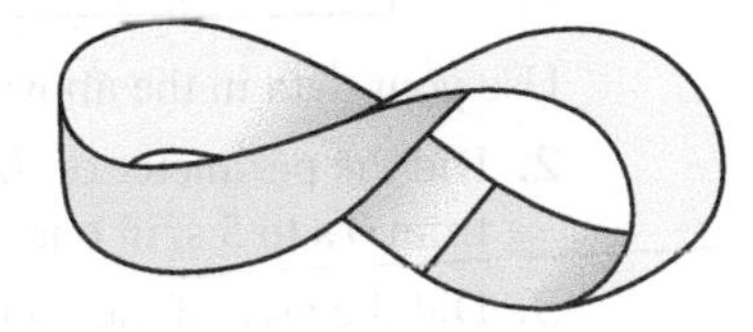

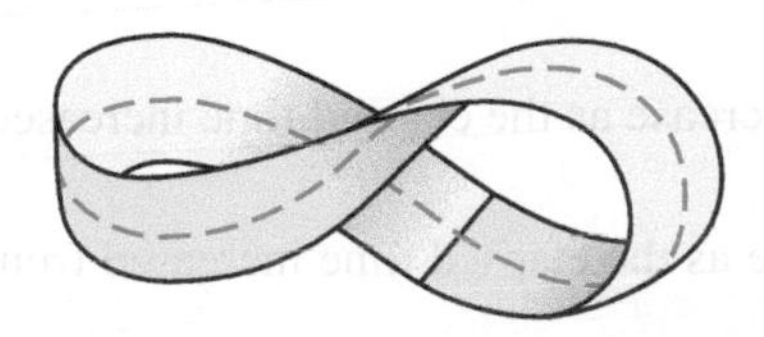

Make a Möbius band that is $1\frac{1}{2}$ in. wide. Use a pair of scissors to cut the Möbius band lengthwise down the middle, staying $\frac{3}{4}$ in. from each edge. Describe the result.

Make a Möbius band from plain white paper and then shade one side. Describe what remains unshaded on the Möbius band, and state the number of sides a Möbius band has.

EXCURSION

Perimeter and Area of a Rectangle with Changing Dimensions

A graphic artist has drawn a 5-inch by 4-inch rectangle on a computer screen. The artist is scaling the size of the rectangle in such a way that every second the upper right corner of the rectangle moves to the right 0.5 in. and downward 0.2 in.

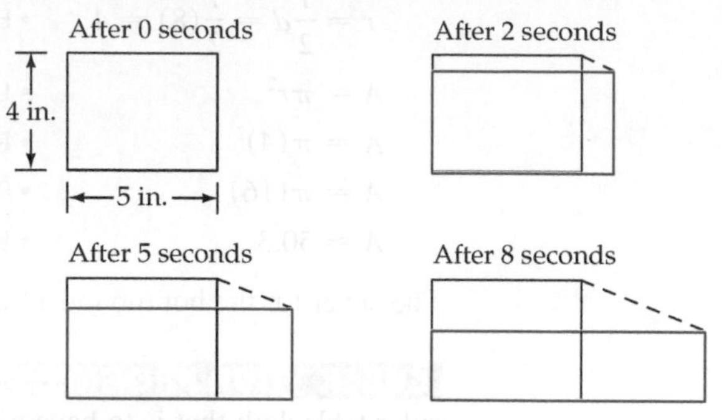

Thus after 1 s, the length of the rectangle is 5.5 in. and the width is 3.8 in. After 2 s, the length is 6 in. and the width is 3.6 in.

EXCURSION EXERCISES

1. Complete the table below by calculating the length, width, perimeter, and area of the rectangle after the given number of seconds have elapsed.

Number of seconds elapsed	Length (in inches)	Width (in inches)	Perimeter (in inches)	Area (in square inches)
0	5	4		
1	5.5	3.8		
2	6	3.6		
3				
4				
5				
6				
7				
8				
9				
10				

Use your data in the above table to answer Exercises 2 to 6.

2. Did the perimeter of the rectangle increase or decrease as the elapsed time increased from 0 s to 5 s, in one-second increments?

3. Did the area of the rectangle increase or decrease as the elapsed time increased from 0 s to 5 s, in one-second increments?

4. Did the perimeter of the rectangle increase or decrease as the elapsed time increased from 5 s to 10 s, in one-second increments?

5. Did the area of the rectangle increase or decrease as the elapsed time increased from 5 s to 10 s, in one-second increments?

6. If the perimeter of a rectangle is increasing, does this mean that the area of the rectangle is also increasing?

EXERCISE SET 1.3

1. What is wrong with each statement?

a. The perimeter is 40 m^2.

b. The area is 120 ft.

■ In Exercises 2 to 8, find **(a)** the perimeter and **(b)** the area of the figure.

2.

7 in.

11 in.

3.

10 m

5 m

4.

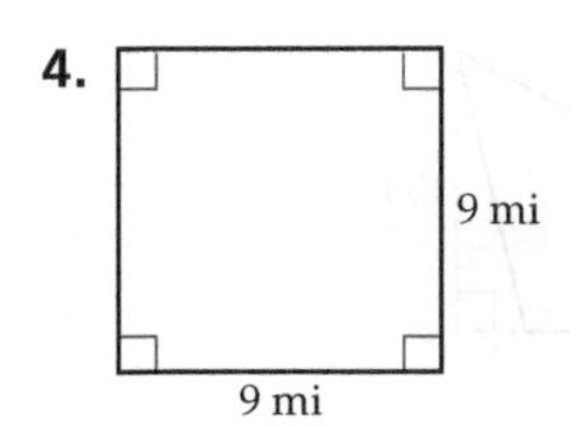

5.

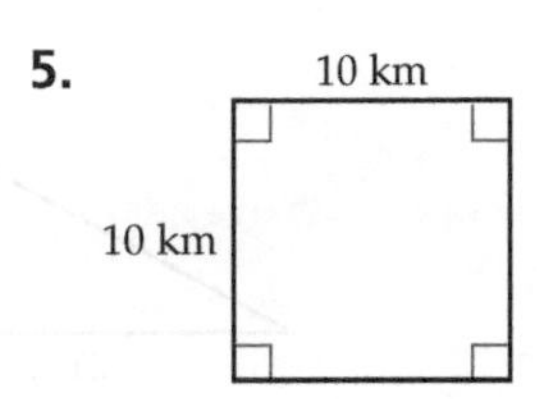

6.

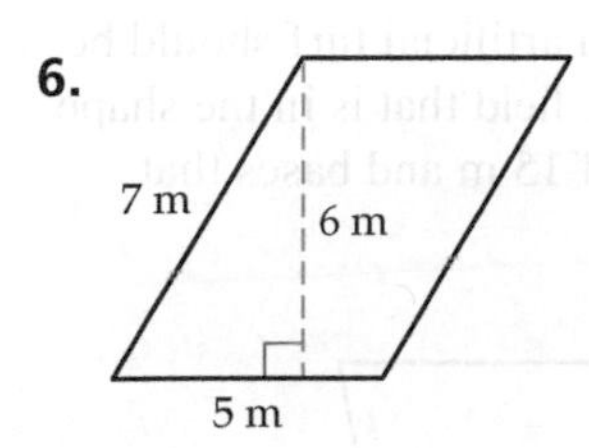

7.

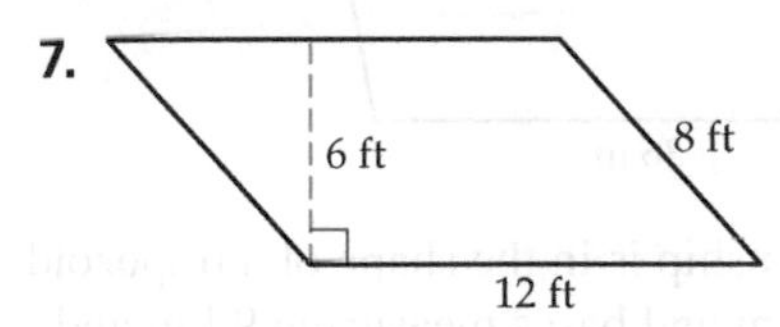

8.

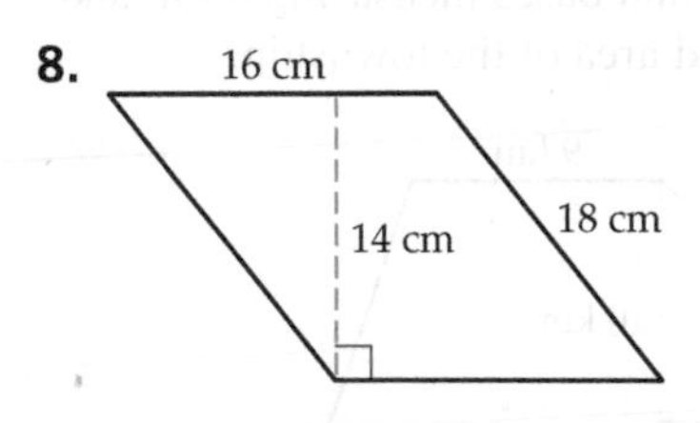

■ In Exercises 9 to 14, find **(a)** the circumference and **(b)** the area of the figure. State an exact answer and a decimal approximation rounded to the nearest hundredth.

9.

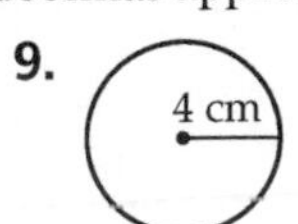

10.

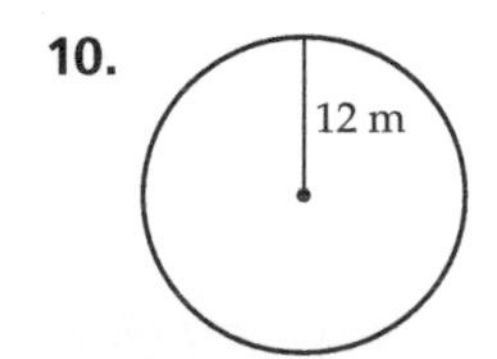

11.

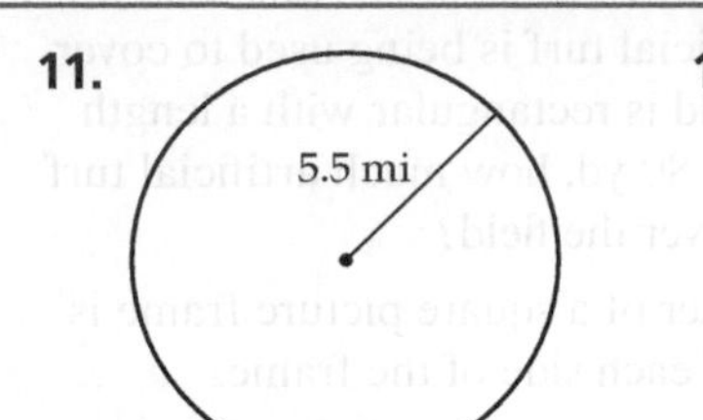

12.

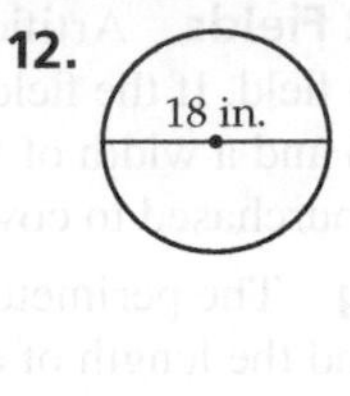

13.

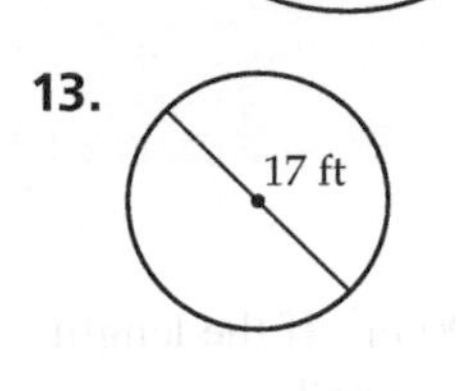

14.

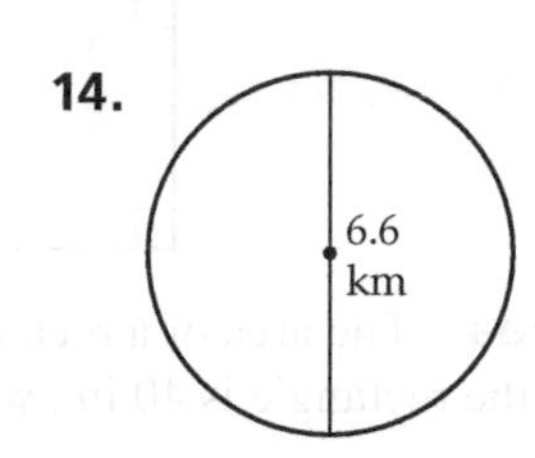

15. Perimeter Find the perimeter of a regular pentagon that measures 4 in. on each side.

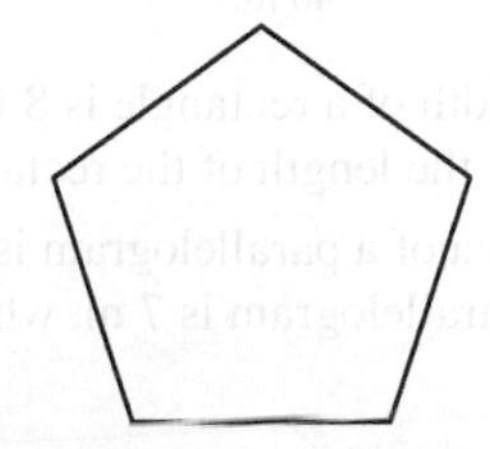

16. Interior Decorating Wall-to-wall carpeting is installed in a room that is 15 ft long and 10 ft wide. The edges of the carpet are held down by tack strips. How many feet of tack-strip material are needed?

17. Cross-Country A cross-country course is in the shape of a parallelogram with a base of length 3 mi and a side of length 2 mi. What is the total length of the cross-country course?

18. Parks and Recreation A rectangular playground has a length of 160 ft and a width of 120 ft. Find the length of hedge that surrounds the playground.

19. Sewing Bias binding is to be sewn around the edge of a rectangular tablecloth measuring 68 in. by 42 in. If the bias binding comes in packages containing 15 ft of binding, how many packages of bias binding are needed for the tablecloth?

20. Race Tracks The first circular dog race track opened in 1919 in Emeryville, California. The radius of the circular track was 157.64 ft. Find the circumference of the track. Use 3.14 for π. Round to the nearest foot.

21. The length of a side of a square is equal to the diameter of a circle. Which is greater, the perimeter of the square or the circumference of the circle?

22. The length of a rectangle is equal to the diameter of a circle, and the width of the rectangle is equal to the radius of the same circle. Which is greater, the perimeter of the rectangle or the circumference of the circle?

23. Construction What is the area of a square patio that measures 12 m on each side?

24. Athletic Fields Artificial turf is being used to cover a playing field. If the field is rectangular with a length of 110 yd and a width of 80 yd, how much artificial turf must be purchased to cover the field?

25. Framing The perimeter of a square picture frame is 36 in. Find the length of each side of the frame.

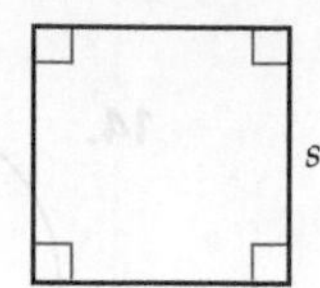

26. Area The area of a rectangle is 400 in^2. If the length of the rectangle is 40 in., what is the width?

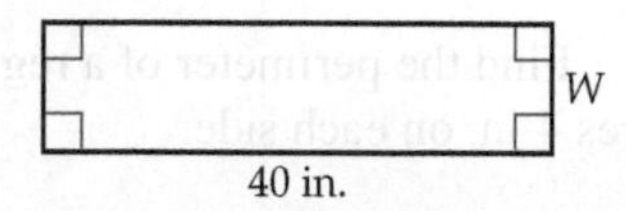

27. Area The width of a rectangle is 8 ft. If the area is 312 ft^2, what is the length of the rectangle?

28. Area The area of a parallelogram is 56 m^2. If the height of the parallelogram is 7 m, what is the length of the base?

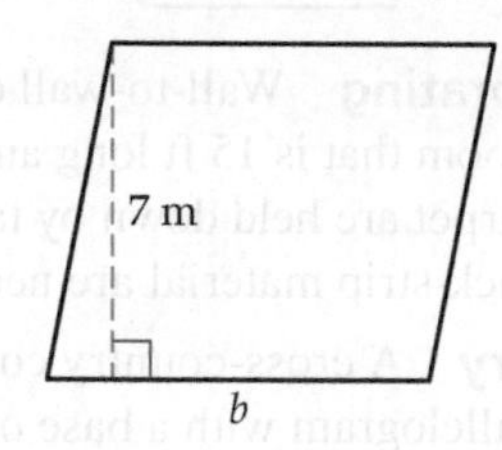

29. Storage Units You want to rent a storage unit. You estimate that you will need 175 ft^2 of floor space. You see the ad below on the Internet. You want to rent the smallest possible unit that will hold everything you want to store. Which of the six units pictured in the ad should you select?

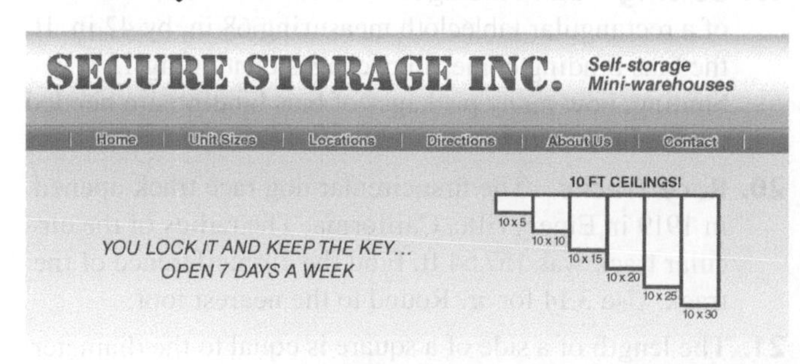

30. Sailing A sail is in the shape of a triangle with a base of 12 m and a height of 16 m. How much canvas was needed to make the body of the sail?

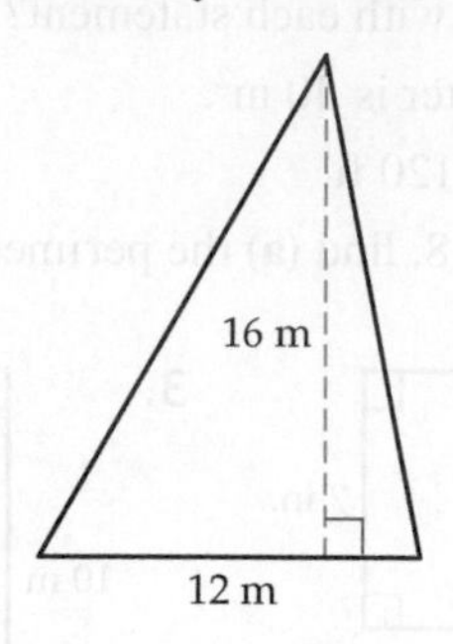

31. Gardens A vegetable garden is in the shape of a triangle with a base of 21 ft and a height of 13 ft. Find the area of the vegetable garden.

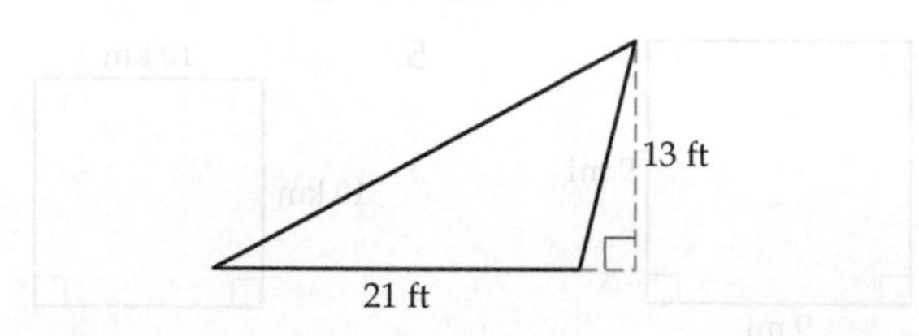

32. Athletic Fields How much artificial turf should be purchased to cover an athletic field that is in the shape of a trapezoid with a height of 15 m and bases that measure 45 m and 36 m?

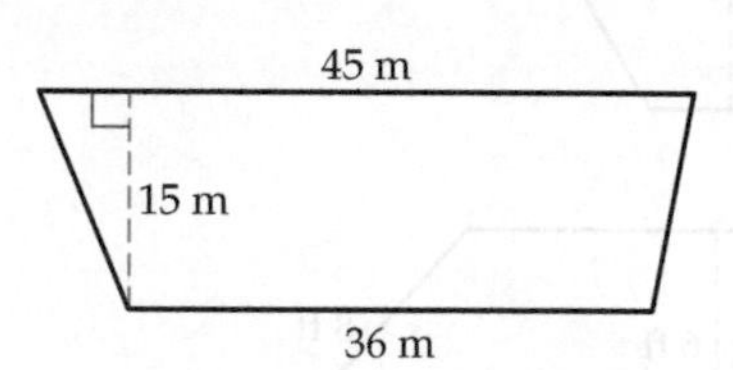

33. Land Area A township is in the shape of a trapezoid with a height of 10 km and bases measuring 9 km and 23 km. What is the land area of the township?

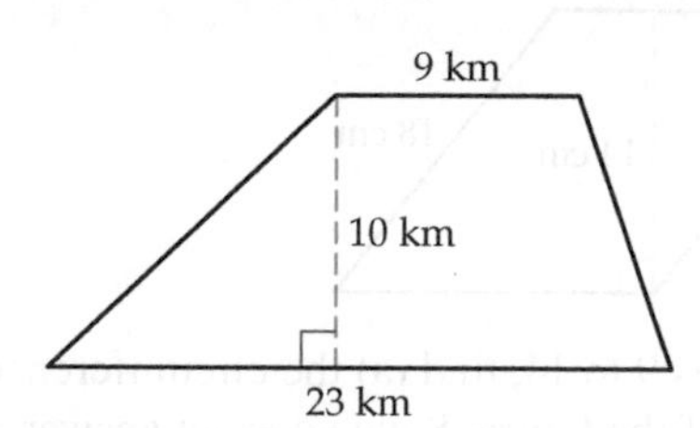

34. Parks and Recreation A city plans to plant grass seed in a public playground that has the shape of a triangle with a height of 24 m and a base of 20 m. Each bag of grass seed will seed 120 m^2. How many bags of seed should be purchased?

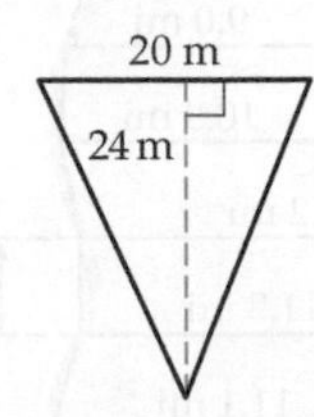

35. Home Maintenance You plan to stain the wooden deck at the back of your house. The deck is in the shape of a trapezoid with bases that measure 10 ft and 12 ft and a height of 10 ft. A quart of stain will cover 55 ft^2. How many quarts of stain should you purchase?

36. Interior Decorating A fabric wall hanging is in the shape of a triangle that has a base of 4 ft and a height of 3 ft. An additional 1 ft^2 of fabric is needed for hemming the material. How much fabric should be purchased to make the wall hanging?

37. Interior Decorating You are wallpapering two walls of a den, one measuring 10 ft by 8 ft and the other measuring 12 ft by 8 ft. The wallpaper costs $96 per roll, and each roll will cover 40 ft^2. What is the cost to wallpaper the two walls?

38. Gardens An urban renewal project involves reseeding a garden that is in the shape of a square, 80 ft on each side. Each bag of grass seed costs $12 and will seed 1500 ft^2. How much money should be budgeted for buying grass seed for the garden?

39. Carpeting You want to install wall-to-wall carpeting in the family room. The floor plan is shown below. If the cost of the carpet you would like to purchase is $38 per square yard, what is the cost of carpeting your family room? Assume that there is no waste. *Hint:* 9 ft^2 = 1 yd^2.

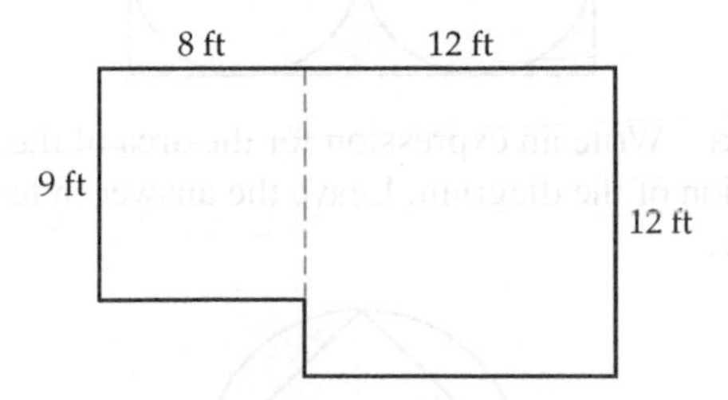

40. Interior Decorating You want to paint the rectangular walls of your bedroom. Two walls measure 16 ft by 8 ft, and the other two walls measure 12 ft by 8 ft. The paint you wish to purchase costs $28 per gallon, and each gallon will cover 400 ft^2 of wall. Find the minimum amount you will need to spend on paint.

41. Landscaping A walkway 2 m wide surrounds a rectangular plot of grass. The plot is 25 m long and 15 m wide. What is the area of the walkway?

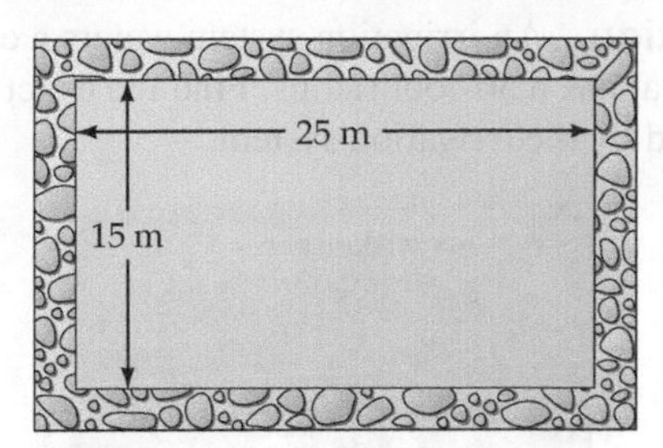

42. Draperies The material used to make pleated draperies for a window must be twice as wide as the width of the window. Draperies are being made for four windows, each 3 ft wide and 4 ft high. Because the drapes will fall slightly below the window sill and extra fabric is needed for hemming the drapes, 1 ft must be added to the height of the window. How much material must be purchased to make the drapes?

43. Carpentry Find the length of molding needed to put around a circular table that is 4.2 ft in diameter. Round to the nearest hundredth of a foot.

44. Sewing How much binding is needed to bind the edge of a circular rug that is 3 m in diameter? Round to the nearest hundredth of a meter.

45. Pulleys A pulley system is diagrammed below. If pulley B has a diameter of 16 in. and is rotating at 240 revolutions per minute, how far does a given point on the belt travel each minute that the pulley system is in operation? Assume the belt does not slip as the pulley rotates. Round to the nearest inch.

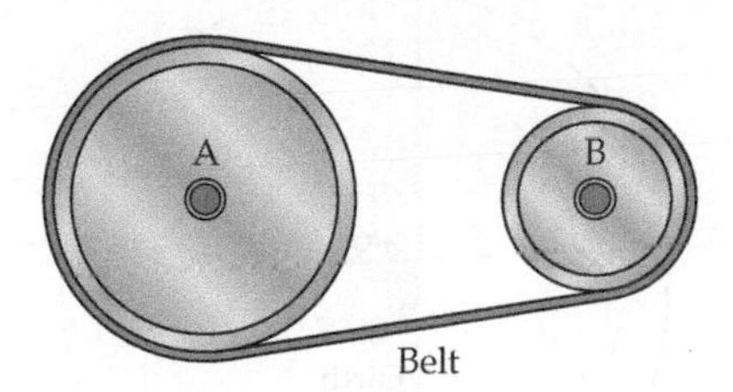

46. Bicycles A bicycle tire has a diameter of 18 in. How many feet does the bicycle travel when the wheel makes 20 revolutions? Round to the nearest hundredth of a foot.

47. Tricycles The front wheel of a tricycle has a diameter of 16 in. How many feet does the tricycle travel when the wheel makes 15 revolutions? Round to the nearest hundredth of a foot.

48. Telescopes The circular lens located on an astronomical telescope has a diameter of 24 in. Find the exact area of the lens.

49. Irrigation An irrigation system waters a circular field that has a 50-foot radius. Find the exact area watered by the irrigation system.

David Frazier/Spirit/Corbis

50. Pizza How much greater is the area of a pizza that has a radius of 10 in. than the area of a pizza that has a radius of 8 in.? Round to the nearest hundredth of a square inch.

51. Pizza A restaurant serves a small pizza that has a radius of 6 in. The restaurant's large pizza has a radius that is twice the radius of the small pizza. How much larger is the area of the large pizza? Round to the nearest hundredth of a square inch. Is the area of the large pizza more or less than twice the area of the small pizza?

52. Satellites A geostationary satellite (GEO) orbits Earth over the Equator. The orbit is circular and at a distance of 36,000 km above Earth. An orbit at this altitude allows the satellite to maintain a fixed position in relation to Earth. What is the distance traveled by a GEO satellite in one orbit around Earth? The radius of Earth is 6380 km. Round to the nearest kilometer.

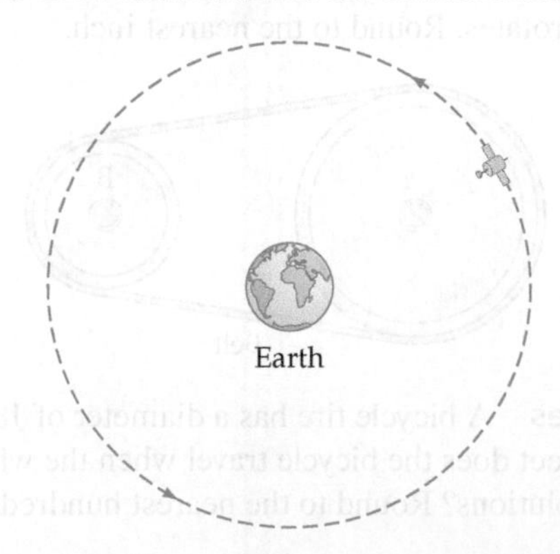

53. Lake Tahoe One way to measure the area of an irregular figure, such as a lake, is to divide the area into trapezoids that have the same height. Then measure the length of each base, calculate the area of each trapezoid, and add the areas. The following figure gives approximate dimensions for Lake Tahoe, which straddles the California and Nevada borders. Approximate the area of Lake Tahoe using the given trapezoids. Round to the nearest tenth of a square mile.

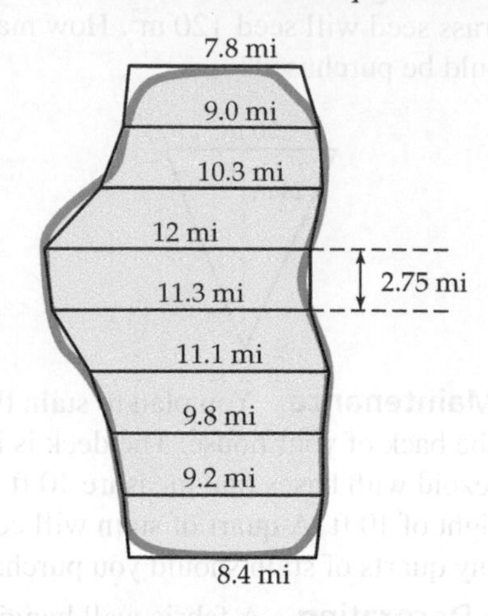

54. Ball Fields How much farther is it around the bases of a baseball diamond than around the bases of a softball diamond? *Hint:* Baseball and softball diamonds are squares.

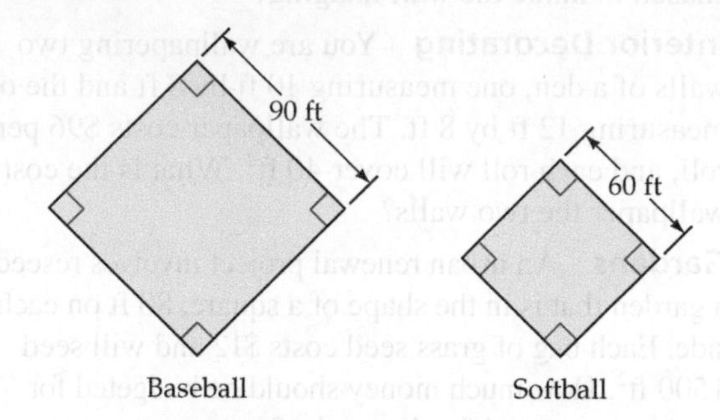

55. Area Write an expression for the area of the shaded portion of the diagram. Leave the answer in terms of π and r.

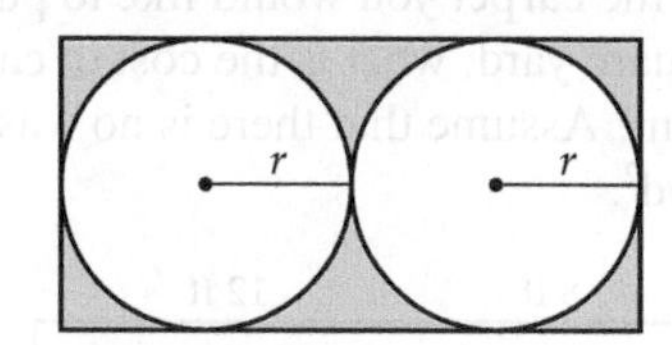

56. Area Write an expression for the area of the shaded portion of the diagram. Leave the answer in terms of π and r.

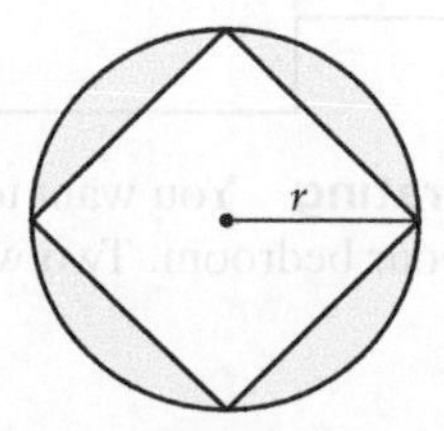

57. Area If both the length and width of a rectangle are doubled, how many times as large is the area of the resulting rectangle compared to the area of the original rectangle?

EXTENSIONS

58. A circle with radius r and circumference C is sliced into 16 identical sectors which are then arranged as shown below.

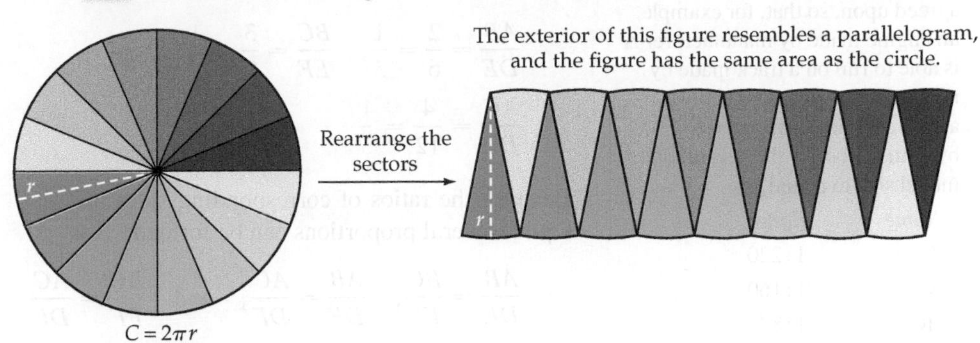

The exterior of the figure shown by the rearranged sectors resembles a parallelogram.

a. What dimension of the circle approximates the height of the parallelogram?

b. What dimension of the circle approximates the base of the parallelogram?

c. Explain how the formula for the area of a circle can be derived by using this slicing approach.

59. Heron's (or Hero's) formula is sometimes used to calculate the area of a triangle.

Heron's Formula

The area of a triangle with sides of lengths a, b, and c is given by

$$A = \sqrt{s(s-a)(s-b)(s-c)}$$

where s is the semiperimeter of the triangle:

$$s = \frac{a+b+c}{2}$$

a. Use Heron's formula to find the area of a triangle with sides that measure 4.4 in., 5.7 in., and 6.2 in. Round to the nearest tenth of a square inch.

b. Use Heron's formula to find the area of an equilateral triangle with sides that measure 8.3 cm. Round to the nearest tenth of a square centimeter.

c. Find the lengths of the sides of a triangle that has a perimeter of 12 in., given that the length of each side, in inches, is a counting number and the area of the triangle, in square inches, is also a counting number. *Hint:* All three sides are different lengths.

SECTION 1.4 Properties of Triangles

Similar Triangles

Similar objects have the same shape but not necessarily the same size. A tennis ball is similar to a basketball. A model ship is similar to an actual ship.

Similar objects have corresponding parts; for example, the rudder on the model ship corresponds to the rudder on the actual ship. The relationship between the sizes of the corresponding parts can be written as a ratio. All corresponding parts of two similar figures share the same ratio. If the rudder on the model ship is $\frac{1}{100}$ the size of the rudder on the actual ship, then the model mast is $\frac{1}{100}$ of the size of the actual mast, the width of the model is $\frac{1}{100}$ the width of the actual ship, and so on.

POINT OF INTEREST

Model trains are similar to actual trains. They come in a variety of sizes that manufacturers have agreed upon, so that, for example, an engine made by manufacturer A is able to run on a track made by manufacturer B. Listed below are three model railroad sizes by name, along with the ratio of model size to actual size.

Name	*Ratio*
Z	1:220
N	1:160
HO	1:87

Z Scale

N Scale

HO Scale

HO's ratio of 1:87 means that in every dimension, an HO scale model railroad car is $\frac{1}{87}$ the size of the real railroad car.

The two triangles ABC and DEF shown at the right are similar. Side $\overline{AB}$ corresponds to side $\overline{DE}$, side $\overline{BC}$ corresponds to side $\overline{EF}$, and side $\overline{AC}$ corresponds to side $\overline{DF}$. The ratios of the lengths of corresponding sides are equal.

$$\frac{AB}{DE} = \frac{2}{6} = \frac{1}{3}, \quad \frac{BC}{EF} = \frac{3}{9} = \frac{1}{3}, \quad \text{and}$$

$$\frac{AC}{DF} = \frac{4}{12} = \frac{1}{3}$$

Because the ratios of corresponding sides are equal, several proportions can be formed.

$$\frac{AB}{DE} = \frac{BC}{EF}, \quad \frac{AB}{DE} = \frac{AC}{DF}, \quad \text{and} \quad \frac{BC}{EF} = \frac{AC}{DF}$$

The measures of corresponding angles in similar triangles are equal. Therefore,

$$m\angle A = m\angle D, \quad m\angle B = m\angle E, \quad \text{and}$$
$$m\angle C = m\angle F$$

Triangles ABC and DEF at the right are similar triangles. AH and DK are the heights of the triangles. The ratio of the heights of similar triangles equals the ratio of the lengths of corresponding sides.

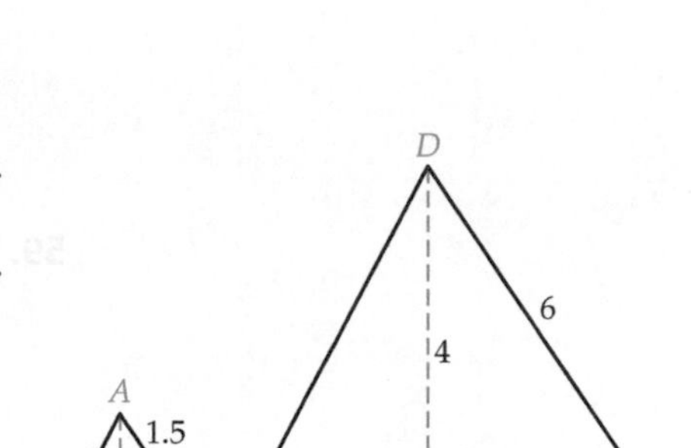

Ratio of corresponding sides $= \frac{1.5}{6} = \frac{1}{4}$

Ratio of heights $= \frac{1}{4}$

Properties of Similar Triangles

For similar triangles, the ratios of corresponding sides are equal. The ratio of corresponding heights is equal to the ratio of corresponding sides. The measures of corresponding angles are equal.

The two triangles at the right are similar triangles. Find the length of side $\overline{EF}$. Round to the nearest tenth of a meter.

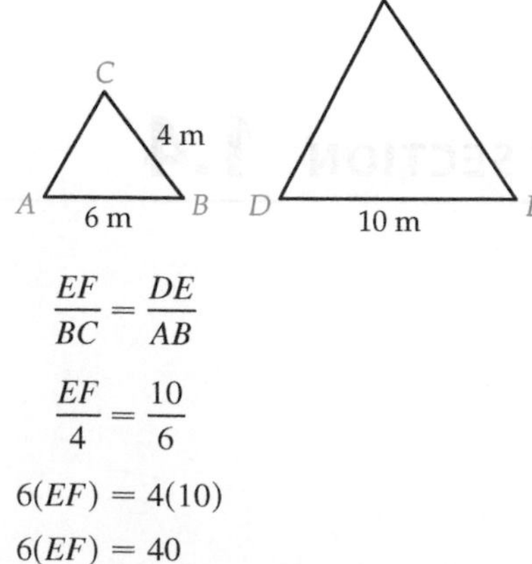

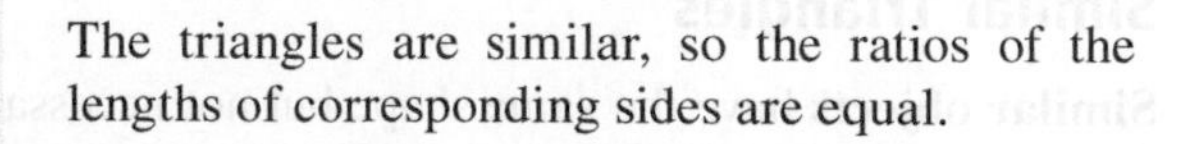

The triangles are similar, so the ratios of the lengths of corresponding sides are equal.

$$\frac{EF}{BC} = \frac{DE}{AB}$$

$$\frac{EF}{4} = \frac{10}{6}$$

$$6(EF) = 4(10)$$

$$6(EF) = 40$$

$$EF \approx 6.7$$

The length of side EF is approximately 6.7 m.

TAKE NOTE

The notation $\triangle ABC \sim \triangle DEF$ is used to indicate that triangle ABC is similar to triangle DEF.

QUESTION What are two other proportions that can be written for the similar triangles shown in the preceding example?

EXAMPLE 1 Use Similar Triangles to Find the Unknown Height of a Triangle

Triangles ABC and DEF are similar. Find FG, the height of triangle DEF.

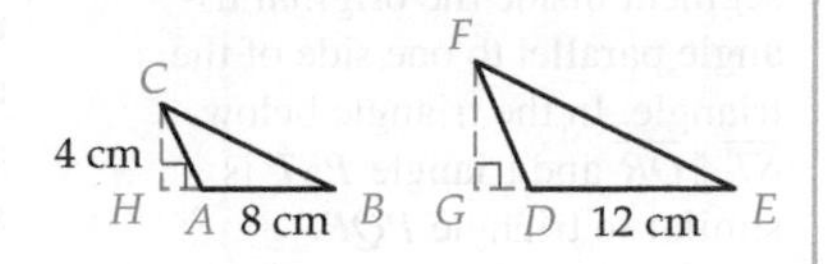

Solution

$\frac{AB}{DE} = \frac{CH}{FG}$ • For similar triangles, the ratio of corresponding sides equals the ratio of corresponding heights.

$\frac{8}{12} = \frac{4}{FG}$ • Replace AB, DE, and CH with their values.

$8(FG) = 12(4)$ • The cross products are equal.

$8(FG) = 48$

$FG = 6$ • Divide both sides of the equation by 8.

The height FG of triangle DEF is 6 cm.

CHECK YOUR PROGRESS 1

Triangles ABC and DEF are similar. Find FG, the height of triangle DEF.

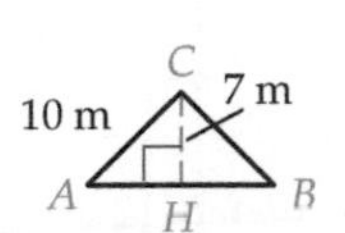

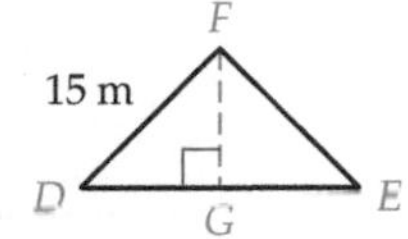

Solution See page S2.

Triangles ABC and DEF are similar triangles. Find the area of triangle ABC.

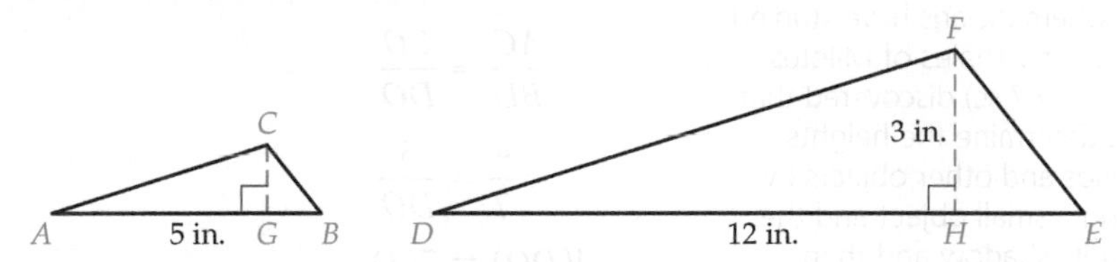

Solve a proportion to find the height of triangle ABC.

$$\frac{AB}{DE} = \frac{CG}{FH}$$
$$\frac{5}{12} = \frac{CG}{3}$$
$$12(CG) = 5(3)$$
$$12(CG) = 15$$
$$CG = 1.25$$

Use the formula for the area of a triangle. $A = \frac{1}{2}bh$

The base is 5 in. The height is 1.25 in. $A = \frac{1}{2}(5)(1.25)$

The area of triangle ABC is 3.125 in^2. $A = 3.125$

ANSWER In addition to $\frac{EF}{BC} = \frac{DE}{AB}$, we can write the proportions $\frac{DE}{AB} = \frac{DF}{AC}$ and $\frac{EF}{BC} = \frac{DF}{AC}$. These three proportions can also be written using the reciprocal of each fraction: $\frac{BC}{EF} = \frac{AB}{DE}$, $\frac{AB}{DE} = \frac{AC}{DF}$, and $\frac{BC}{EF} = \frac{AC}{DF}$. Also, the right and left sides of each proportion can be interchanged.

If the three angles of one triangle are equal in measure to the three angles of another triangle, then the triangles are similar.

TAKE NOTE

You can always create similar triangles by drawing a line segment inside the original triangle parallel to one side of the triangle. In the triangle below, $\overline{ST} \parallel \overline{QR}$ and triangle PST is similar to triangle PQR.

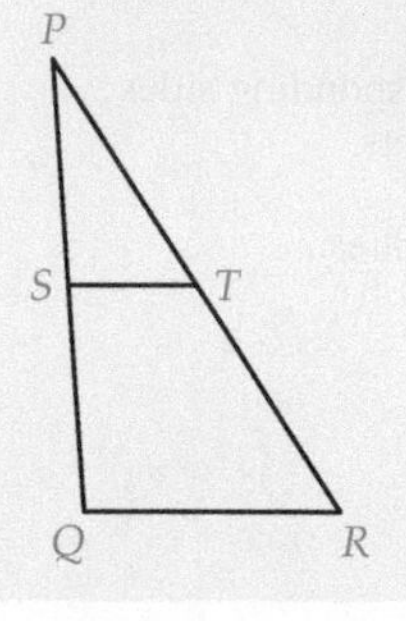

In triangle ABC at the right, line segment $\overline{DE}$ is drawn parallel to the base $\overline{AB}$. Because the measures of corresponding angles are equal, $m\angle x = m\angle r$ and $m\angle y = m\angle n$. We know that $m\angle C = m\angle C$. Thus the measures of the three angles of triangle ABC are equal, respectively, to the measures of the three angles of triangle DEC. Therefore, triangles ABC and DEC are similar triangles.

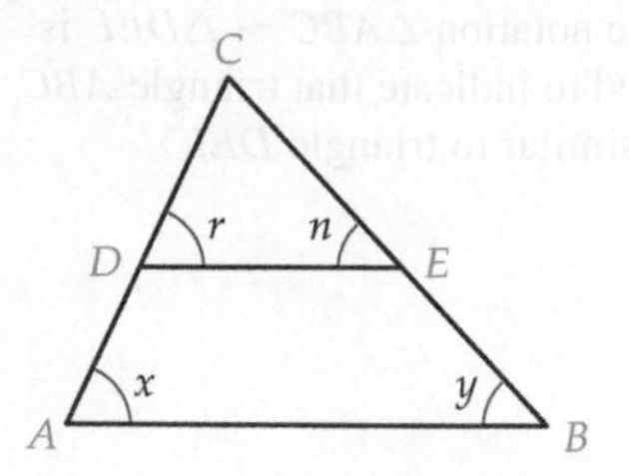

The sum of the measures of the three angles of a triangle is 180°. If two angles of one triangle are equal in measure to two angles of another triangle, then the third angles must be equal. Thus we can say that if two angles of one triangle are equal in measure to two angles of another triangle, then the two triangles are similar.

In the figure at the right, $\overline{AB}$ intersects $\overline{CD}$ at point O. Angles C and D are right angles. Find the length of $\overline{DO}$.

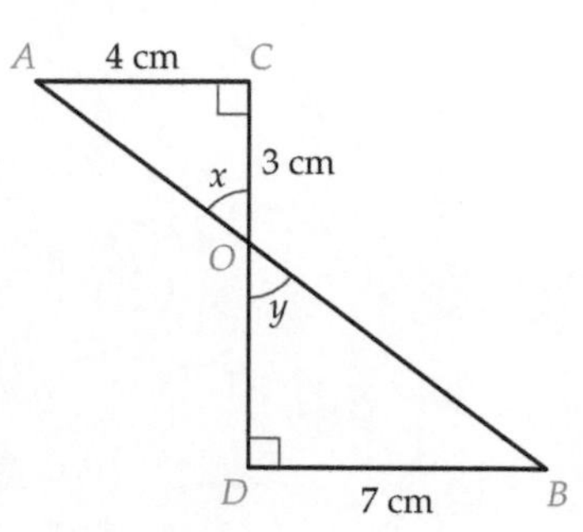

First determine whether triangles AOC and BOD are similar.

$m\angle C = m\angle D$ because they are both right angles.

$m\angle x = m\angle y$ because vertical angles have the same measure.

Because two angles of triangle AOC are equal in measure to two angles of triangle BOD, triangles AOC and BOD are similar.

Use a proportion to find the length of the unknown side.

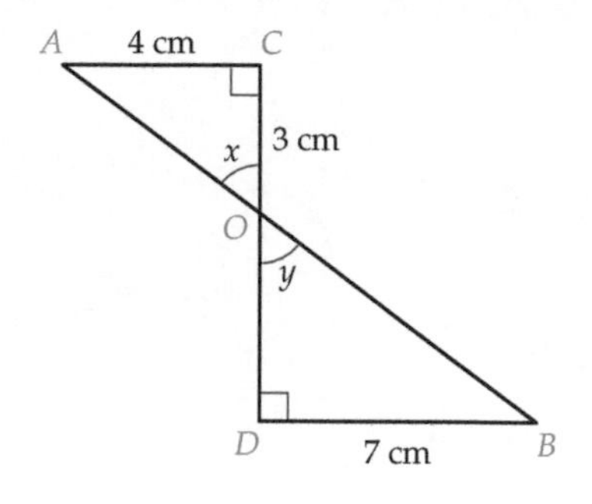

$$\frac{AC}{BD} = \frac{CO}{DO}$$

$$\frac{4}{7} = \frac{3}{DO}$$

$$4(DO) = 7(3)$$

$$4(DO) = 21$$

$$DO = 5.25$$

The length of $\overline{DO}$ is 5.25 cm.

HISTORICAL NOTE

Many mathematicians have studied similar objects. Thales of Miletus (ca. 624 BC–547 BC) discovered that he could determine the heights of pyramids and other objects by measuring a small object and the length of its shadow and then making use of similar triangles.

Fibonacci (1170–1250) also studied similar objects. The second section of Fibonacci's text *Liber abaci* contains practical information for merchants and surveyors. There is a chapter devoted to using similar triangles to determine the heights of tall objects.

EXAMPLE 2 Solve a Problem Involving Similar Triangles

In the figure at the right, $\angle B$ and $\angle D$ are right angles, $AB = 12$ m, $DC = 4$ m, and $AC = 18$ m. Find the length of $\overline{CO}$.

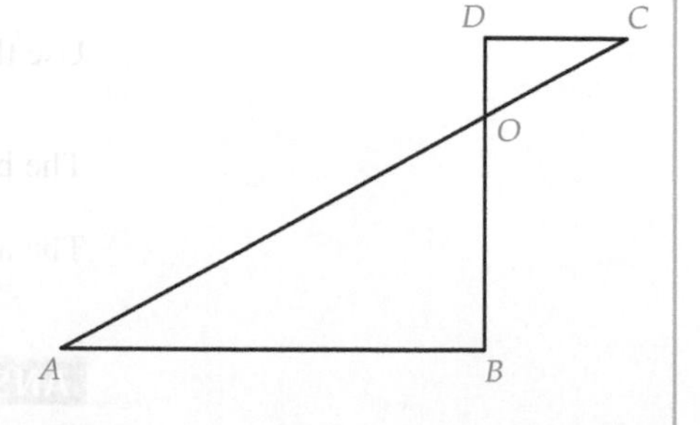

Solution

$\angle B$ and $\angle D$ are right angles. Therefore, $\angle B = \angle D$. $\angle AOB$ and $\angle COD$ are vertical angles. Therefore, $\angle AOB = \angle COD$.

Because two angles of triangle *AOB* are equal in measure to two angles of triangle *COD*, triangles *AOB* and *COD* are similar triangles.

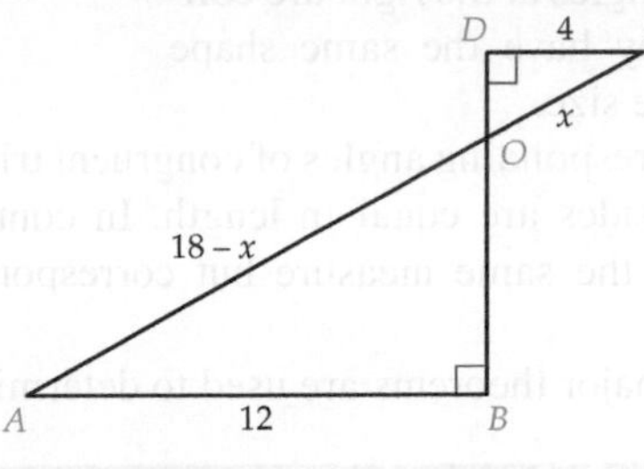

• Label the diagram using the given information. Let x represent CO. $AC = AO + CO$. Because $AC = 18$, $AO = 18 - x$.

$$\frac{DC}{BA} = \frac{CO}{AO}$$

• Triangles *AOB* and *COD* are similar triangles. The ratios of corresponding sides are equal.

$$\frac{4}{12} = \frac{x}{18 - x}$$

$$12x = 4(18 - x)$$

$$12x = 72 - 4x$$

• Use the distributive property.

$$16x = 72$$

$$x = 4.5$$

The length of $\overline{CO}$ is 4.5 m.

CHECK YOUR PROGRESS 2

In the figure at the right, $\angle A$ and $\angle D$ are right angles, $AB = 10$ cm, $CD = 4$ cm, and $DO = 3$ cm. Find the area of triangle *AOB*.

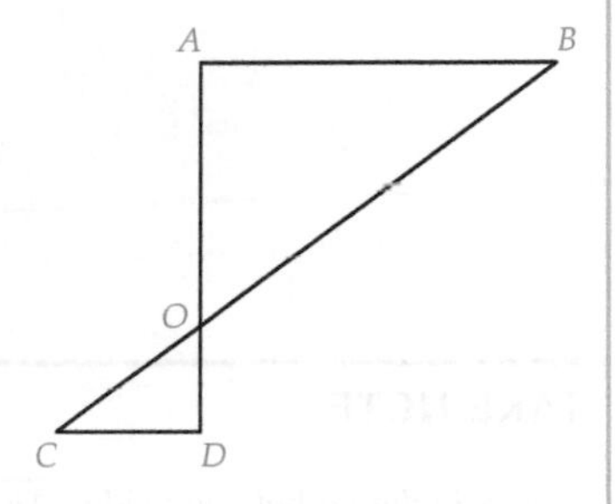

Solution See pages S3.

MATH MATTERS Similar Polygons

For similar triangles, the measures of corresponding angles are equal and the ratios of the lengths of corresponding sides are equal. The same is true for similar polygons.

Quadrilaterals *ABCD* and *LMNO* are similar.

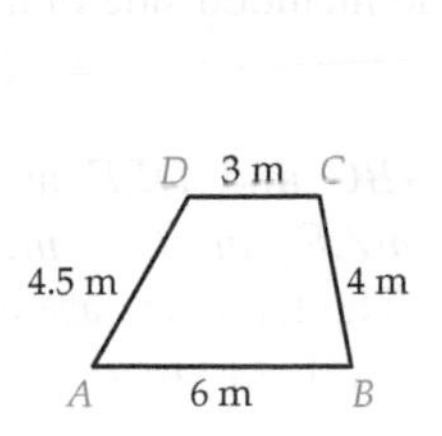

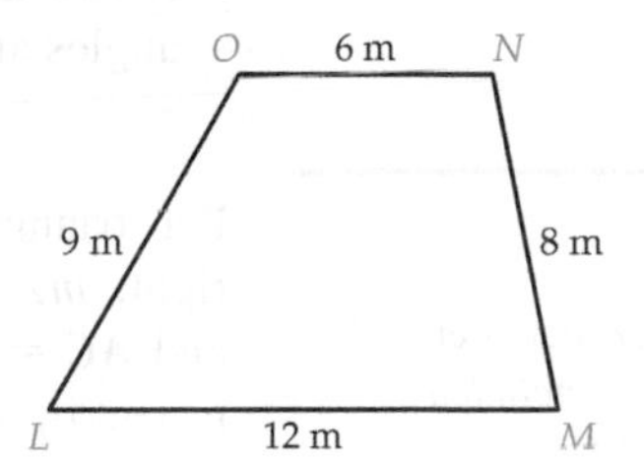

The ratio of the lengths of corresponding sides is: $\frac{AB}{LM} = \frac{6}{12} = \frac{1}{2}$

The ratio of the perimeter of *ABCD* to the perimeter of *LMNO* is:

$$\frac{\text{perimeter of } ABCD}{\text{perimeter of } LMNO} = \frac{17.5}{35} = \frac{1}{2}$$

Note that this ratio is the same as the ratio of corresponding sides. This is true for all similar polygons: If two polygons are similar, the ratio of their perimeters is equal to the ratio of the lengths of any pair of corresponding sides.

Congruent Triangles

> **TAKE NOTE**
>
> The notation $\triangle ABC \cong \triangle DEF$ is used to indicate that triangle ABC is congruent to triangle DEF.

The two triangles at the right are **congruent**. They have the same shape and the same size.

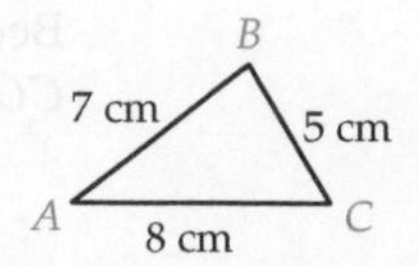

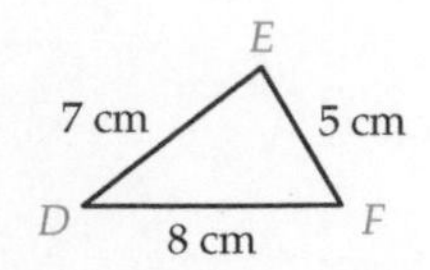

The corresponding angles of congruent triangles have the same measure and the corresponding sides are equal in length. In contrast, for similar triangles, corresponding angles have the same measure but corresponding sides are not necessarily the same length.

Three major theorems are used to determine whether two triangles are congruent.

> **Side-Side-Side Theorem (SSS)**
>
> If the three sides of one triangle are equal in measure to the corresponding three sides of a second triangle, the two triangles are congruent.

In the triangles at the right, $AC = DE$, $AB = EF$, and $BC = DF$. The corresponding sides of triangles ABC and DEF are equal in measure. The triangles are congruent by the SSS theorem.

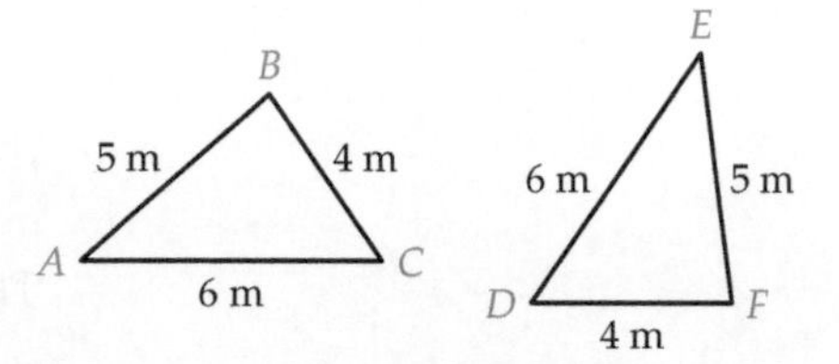

> **Side-Angle-Side Theorem (SAS)**
>
> If two sides and the included angle of one triangle are equal in measure to two sides and the included angle of a second triangle, the two triangles are congruent.

> **TAKE NOTE**
>
> $\angle A$ is *included* between sides $\overline{AB}$ and $\overline{AC}$. $\angle E$ is *included* between sides $\overline{DE}$ and $\overline{EF}$.

In the two triangles at the right, $AB = EF$, $AC = DE$, and $m\angle BAC = m\angle DEF$. The triangles are congruent by the SAS theorem.

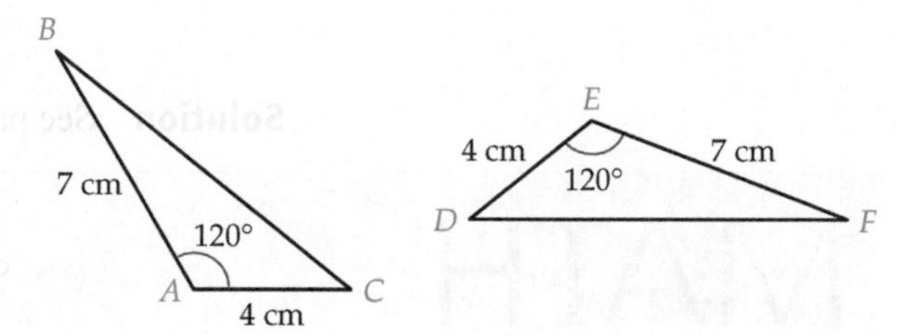

> **Angle-Side-Angle Theorem (ASA)**
>
> If two angles and the included side of one triangle are equal in measure to two angles and the included side of a second triangle, the two triangles are congruent.

> **TAKE NOTE**
>
> Side $\overline{AC}$ is *included* between $\angle A$ and $\angle C$. Side $\overline{EF}$ is *included* between $\angle E$ and $\angle F$.

For triangles ABC and DEF at the right, $m\angle A = m\angle F$, $m\angle C = m\angle E$, and $AC = EF$. The triangles are congruent by the ASA theorem.

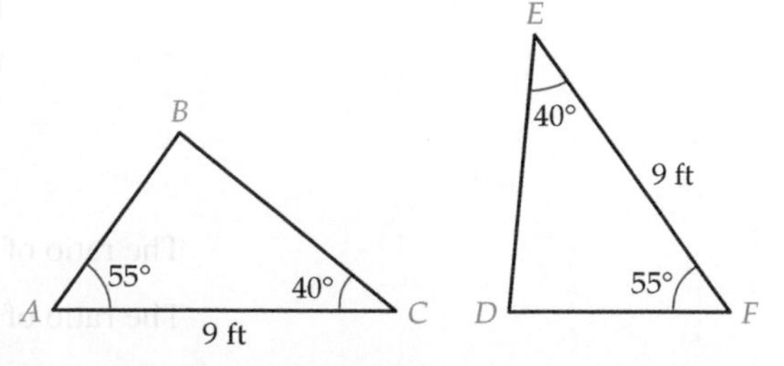

Given triangles PQR and MNO, do the conditions $m\angle P = m\angle O$, $m\angle Q = m\angle M$, and $PQ = MO$ guarantee that triangle PQR is congruent to triangle MNO?

Draw a sketch of the two triangles and determine whether one of the theorems for congruence is satisfied.

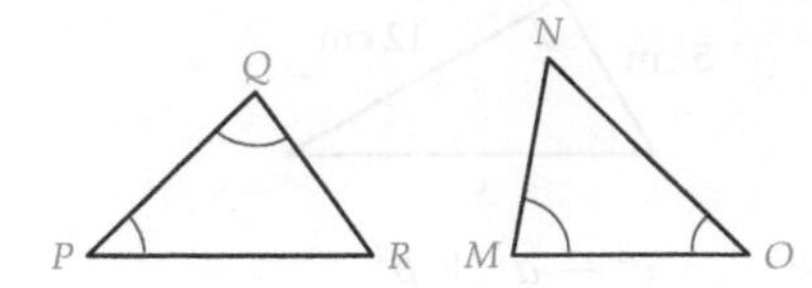

See the figures at the left. Because two angles and the included side of one triangle are equal in measure to two angles and the included side of the second triangle, the triangles are congruent by the ASA theorem.

EXAMPLE 3 **Determine Whether Two Triangles Are Congruent**

In the figure at the right, is triangle *ABC* congruent to triangle *DEF*?

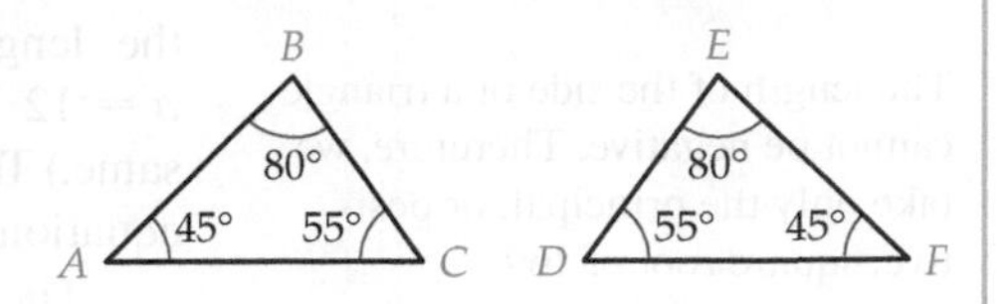

Solution

To determine whether the triangles are congruent, determine whether one of the theorems for congruence is satisfied.

The triangles do not satisfy the SSS theorem, the SAS theorem, or the ASA theorem. The triangles are not necessarily congruent.

CHECK YOUR PROGRESS 3

In the figure at the right, is triangle *PQR* congruent to triangle *MNO*?

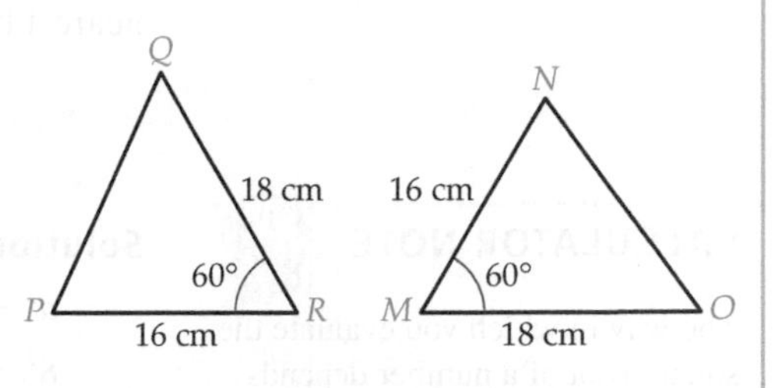

Solution See page S3.

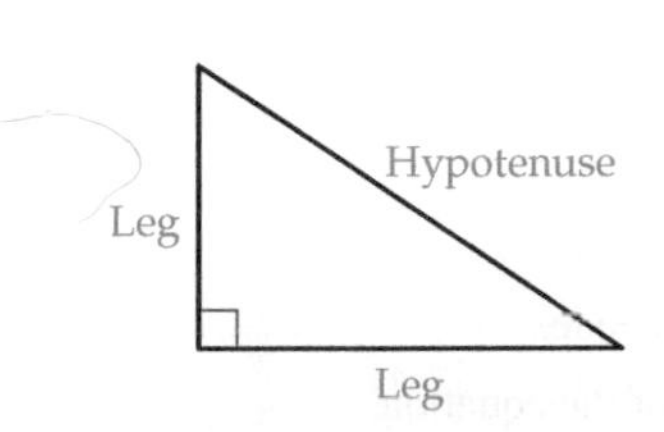

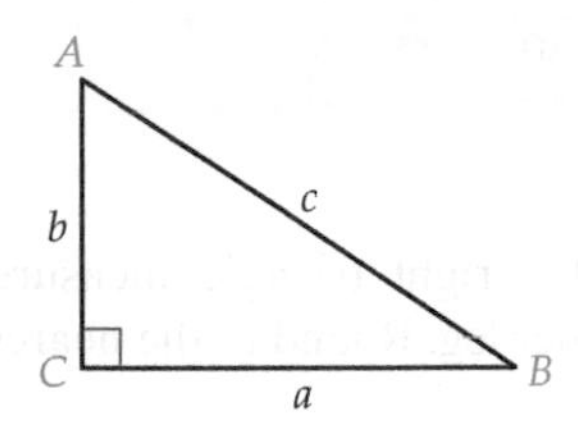

The Pythagorean Theorem

Recall that a right triangle contains one right angle. The side opposite the right angle is called the **hypotenuse**. The other two sides are called **legs**.

The angles in a right triangle are usually labeled with the capital letters *A*, *B*, and *C*, with *C* reserved for the right angle. The side opposite angle *A* is side *a*, the side opposite angle *B* is side *b*, and *c* is the hypotenuse.

The figure at the right is a right triangle with legs measuring 3 units and 4 units and a hypotenuse measuring 5 units. Each side of the triangle is also the side of a square. The number of square units in the area of the largest square is equal to the sum of the numbers of square units in the areas of the smaller squares.

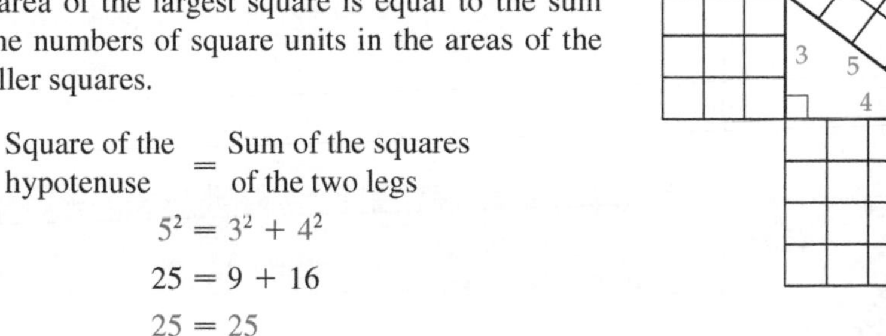

Square of the hypotenuse = Sum of the squares of the two legs

$$5^2 = 3^2 + 4^2$$
$$25 = 9 + 16$$
$$25 = 25$$

The Greek mathematician Pythagoras is generally credited with the discovery that the square of the hypotenuse of a right triangle is equal to the sum of the squares of the two legs. This is called the **Pythagorean theorem**.

The Pythagorean Theorem

If a and b are the lengths of the legs of a right triangle and c is the length of the hypotenuse, then $c^2 = a^2 + b^2$.

POINT OF INTEREST

The first known proof of the Pythagorean theorem is in a Chinese textbook that dates from 150 BC. The book is called *Nine Chapters on the Mathematical Art.* The diagram below is from that book and was used in the proof of the theorem.

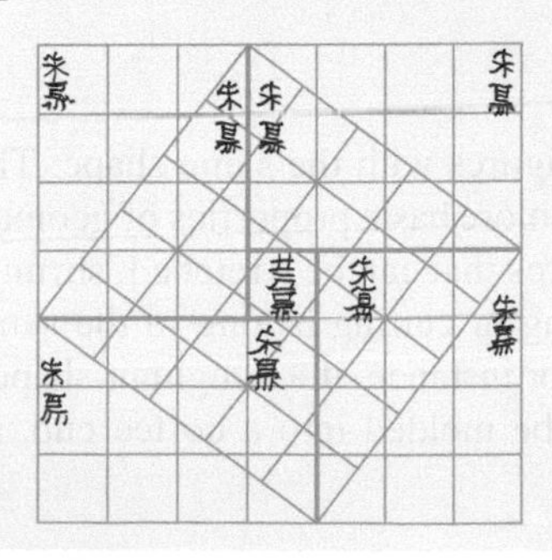

If the lengths of two sides of a right triangle are known, the Pythagorean theorem can be used to find the length of the third side.

Consider a right triangle with legs that measure 5 cm and 12 cm. Use the Pythagorean theorem, with $a = 5$ and $b = 12$, to find the length of the hypotenuse. (If you let $a = 12$ and $b = 5$, the result will be the same.) Take the square root of each side of the equation.

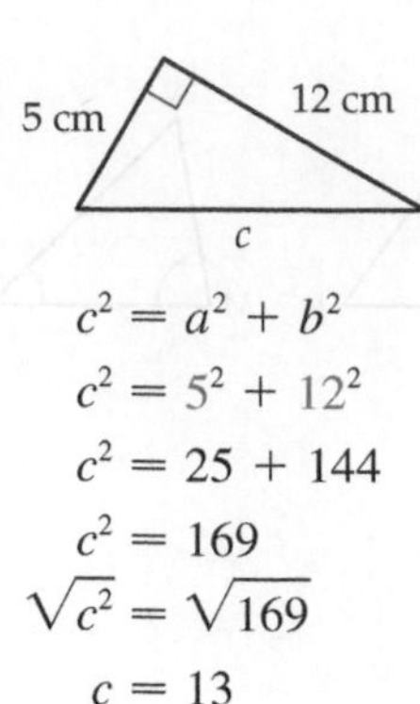

$$c^2 = a^2 + b^2$$
$$c^2 = 5^2 + 12^2$$
$$c^2 = 25 + 144$$
$$c^2 = 169$$
$$\sqrt{c^2} = \sqrt{169}$$
$$c = 13$$

The length of the hypotenuse is 13 cm.

TAKE NOTE

The length of the side of a triangle cannot be negative. Therefore, we take only the principal, or positive, square root of 169.

EXAMPLE 4 Determine the Length of the Unknown Side of a Right Triangle

The length of one leg of a right triangle is 8 in. The length of the hypotenuse is 12 in. Find the length of the other leg. Round to the nearest hundredth of an inch.

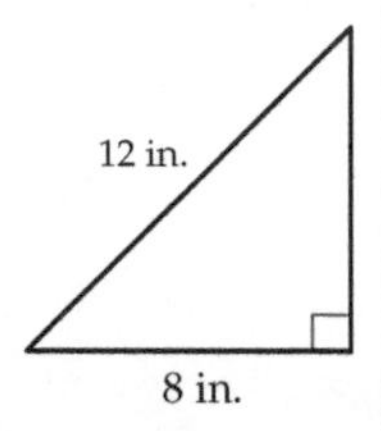

Solution

$a^2 + b^2 = c^2$ • Use the Pythagorean theorem.

$8^2 + b^2 = 12^2$ • $a = 8$, $c = 12$

$64 + b^2 = 144$

$b^2 = 80$ • Solve for b^2. Subtract 64 from each side.

$\sqrt{b^2} = \sqrt{80}$ • Take the square root of each side of the equation.

$b \approx 8.94$ • Use a calculator to approximate $\sqrt{80}$.

The length of the other leg is approximately 8.94 in.

CALCULATOR NOTE

The way in which you evaluate the square root of a number depends on the type of calculator you have. Here are two possible keystrokes to find $\sqrt{80}$:

80 [√] [=]

or

[√] 80 [ENTER]

The first method is used on many scientific calculators. The second method is used on many graphing calculators.

CHECK YOUR PROGRESS 4 The hypotenuse of a right triangle measures 6 m, and one leg measures 2 m. Find the measure of the other leg. Round to the nearest hundredth of a meter.

Solution See page S3.

EXCURSION

Topology: A Brief Introduction

In this section, we discussed similar figures—that is, figures with the same shape. The branch of geometry called **topology** is the study of even more basic properties of geometric figures than their sizes and shapes. In topology, figures that can be stretched, shrunk, molded, or bent into the same shape without puncturing or cutting belong to the same family. They are said to be **topologically equivalent**. For instance, if a doughnut-shaped figure were made out of modeling clay, then it could be molded into a coffee cup, as shown on the next page.

A transformation of a doughnut into a coffee cup

In topology, figures are classified according to their **genus**, where the genus is given by the number of holes in the figure. An inlet in a figure is considered to be a hole if water poured into it passes through the figure. For example, a coffee cup has a hole that is created by its handle; however, the inlet at the top of a coffee cup is not considered to be a hole, because water that is poured into this inlet does not pass through the coffee cup.

Several common geometric figures with genuses 0, 1, 2, and 3 are illustrated below. Figures with the same genus are topogically equivalent.

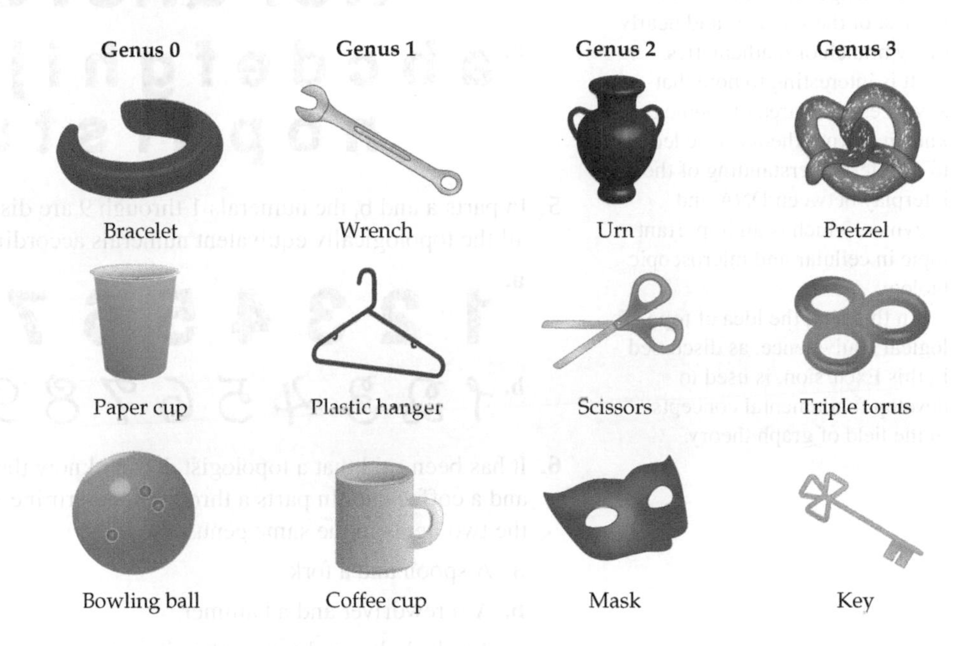

EXCURSION EXERCISES

1. Name the genus of each figure.

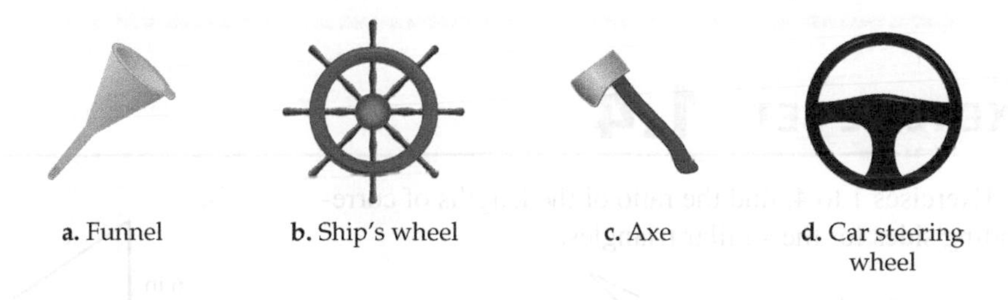

2. Which one of the following figures is not topologically equivalent to the others?

3. Which one of the following figures is not topologically equivalent to the others?

Comb Spatula Block Oar

POINT OF INTEREST

Since its early beginnings in 1736, the subject matter known as topology has expanded from a few novel ideas into a vast body of knowledge with applications in most of the sciences and nearly every branch of mathematics.

It is interesting to note that advances in an area of topology known as knot theory have led to a better understanding of the interplay between DNA and enzymes, which is an important topic in cellular and microscopic biology.

In this text, the idea of topological equivalence, as discussed in this Excursion, is used to develop fundamental concepts in the field of graph theory.

4. In parts a and b, the letters of the alphabet are displayed using a particular font. List all the topogically equivalent letters according to their genus of 0, 1, or 2.

a. ABCDEFGHIJKLM
NOPQRSTUVWXYZ

b. a b c d e f g h i j k l m
n o p q r s t u v w x y z

5. In parts a and b, the numerals 1 through 9 are displayed using a particular font. List all the topologically equivalent numerals according to their genus of 0, 1, or 2.

a. 1 2 3 4 5 6 7 8 9

b. 1 2 3 4 5 6 7 8 9

6. It has been said that a topologist doesn't know the difference between a doughnut and a coffee cup. In parts a through f, determine whether a topologist would classify the two items in the same genus.

a. A spoon and a fork

b. A screwdriver and a hammer

c. A salt shaker and a sugar bowl

d. A bolt and its nut

e. A slice of American cheese and a slice of Swiss cheese

f. A mixing bowl and a strainer

EXERCISE SET 1.4

■ In Exercises 1 to 4, find the ratio of the lengths of corresponding sides for the similar triangles.

1.

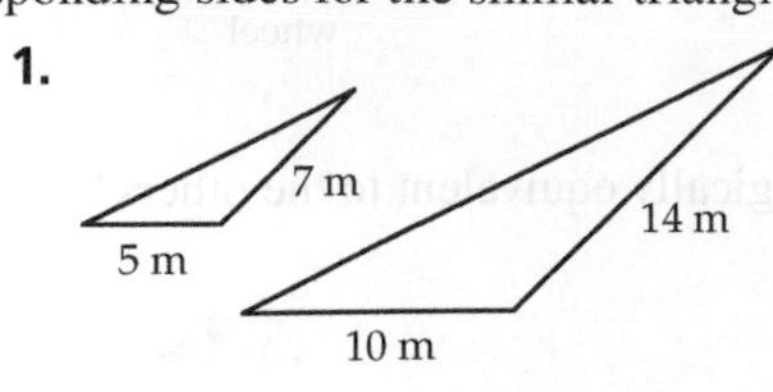

2.

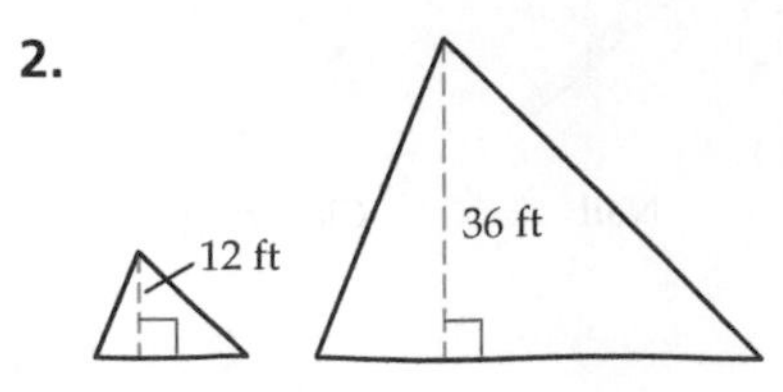

3.

6 in. 9 in. 8 in. 12 in.

4.

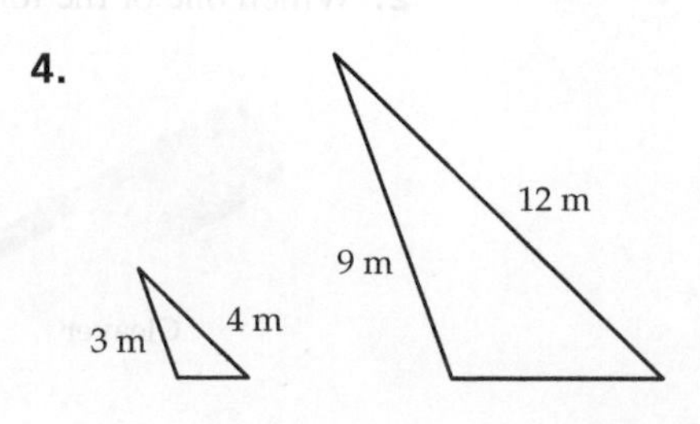

■ In Exercises 5 to 14, triangles ABC and DEF are similar triangles. Use this fact to solve each exercise. Round to the nearest tenth.

5. Find side DE.

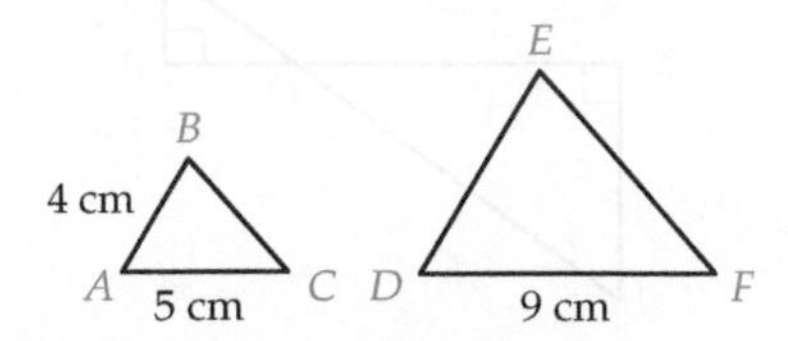

6. Find side DE.

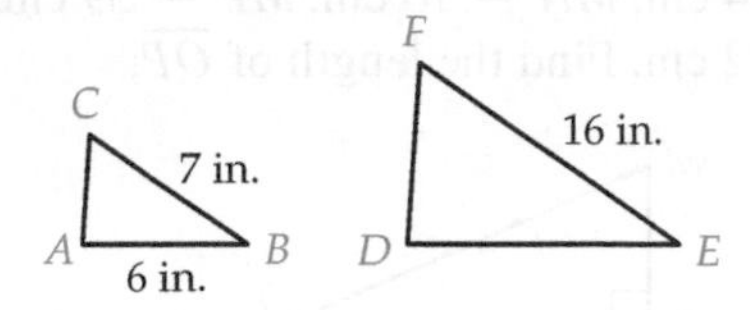

7. Find the height of triangle DEF.

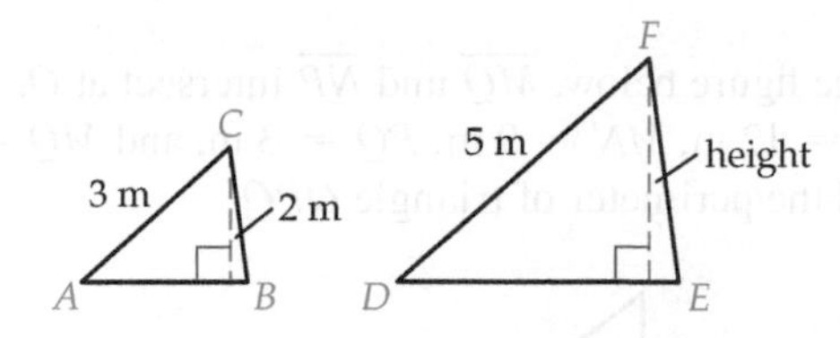

8. Find the height of triangle ABC.

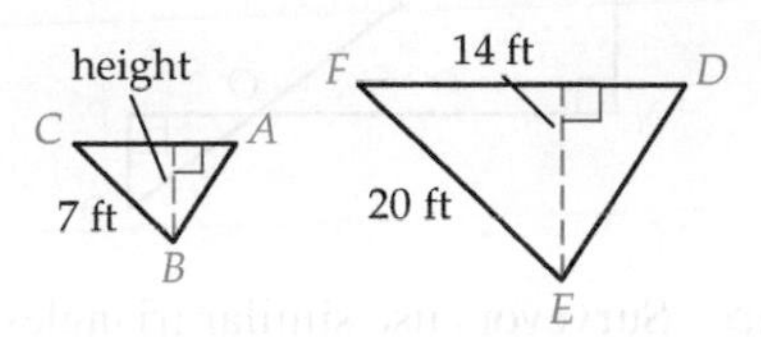

9. Find the perimeter of triangle ABC.

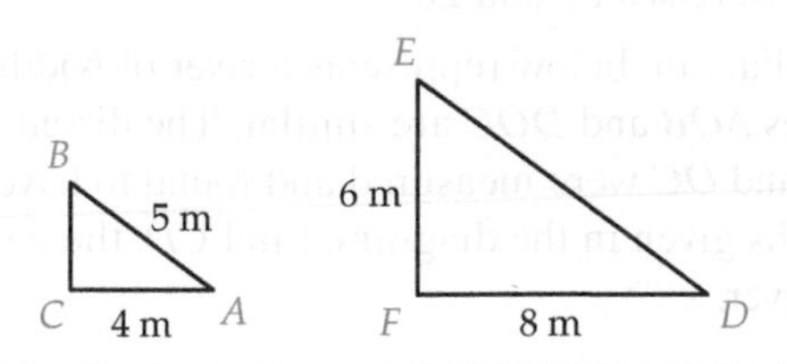

10. Find the perimeter of triangle DEF.

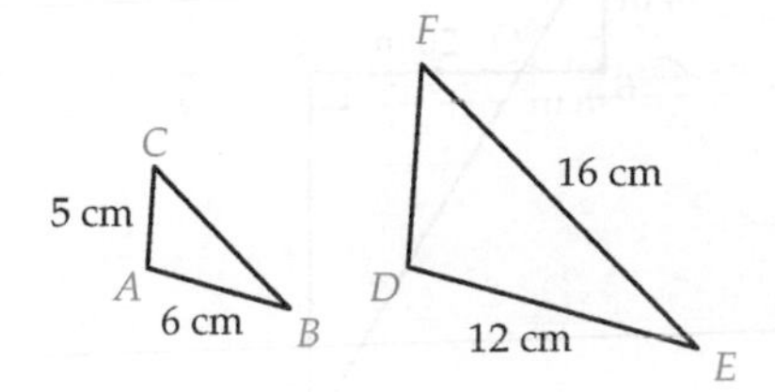

11. Find the perimeter of triangle ABC.

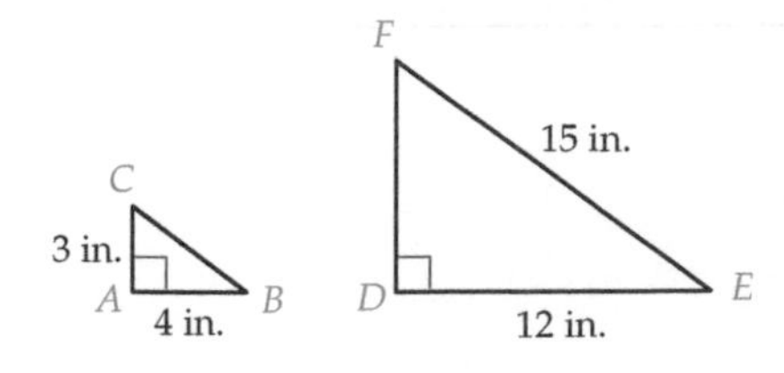

12. Find the area of triangle DEF.

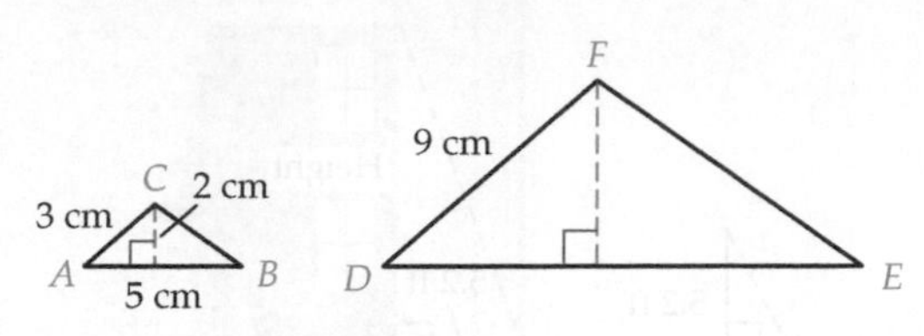

13. Find the area of triangle ABC.

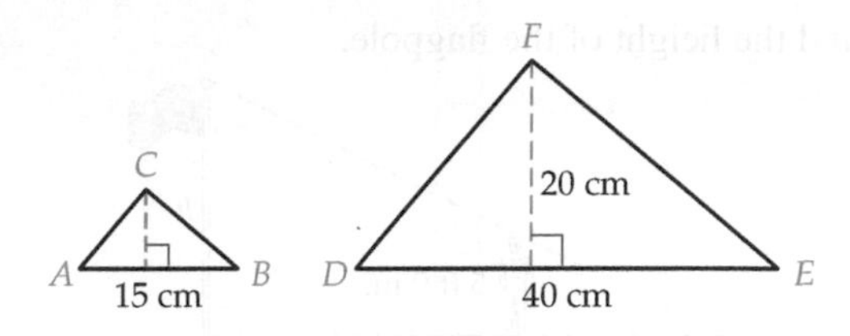

14. Find the area of triangle DEF.

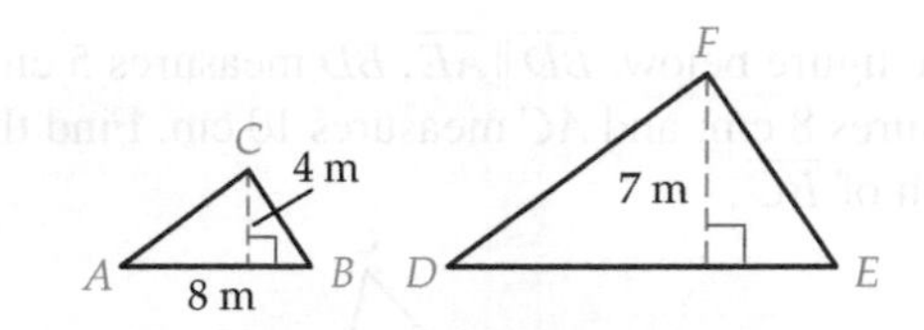

■ In Exercises 15 to 19, the given triangles are similar triangles. Use this fact to solve each exercise.

15. Find the height of the flagpole.

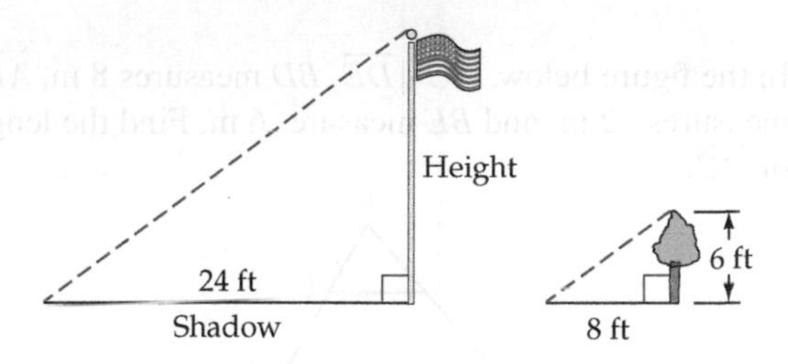

16. Find the height of the flagpole.

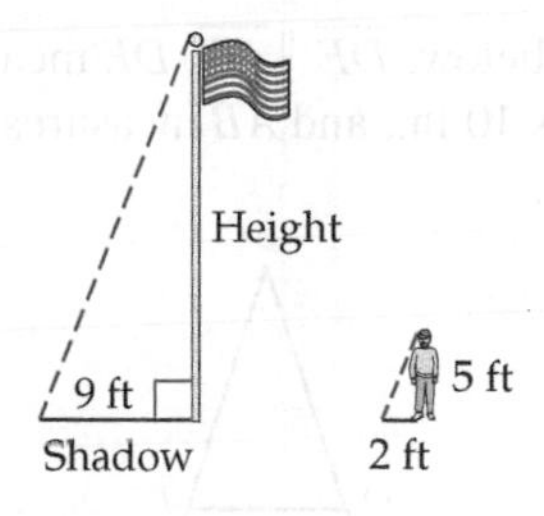

17. Find the height of the building.

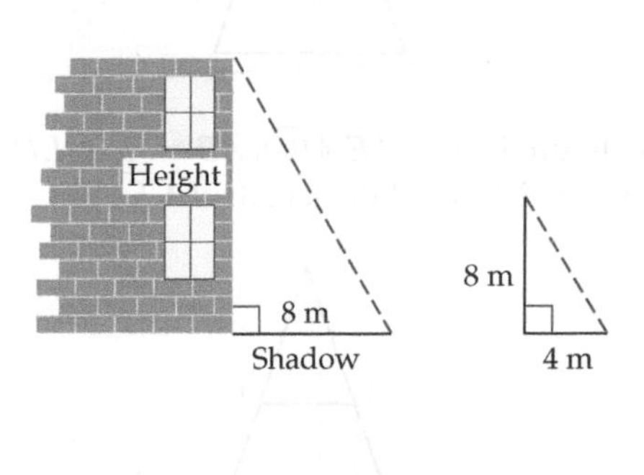

18. Find the height of the building.

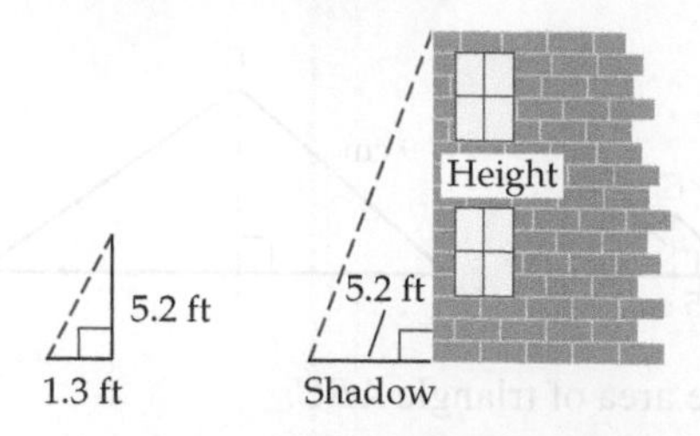

19. Find the height of the flagpole.

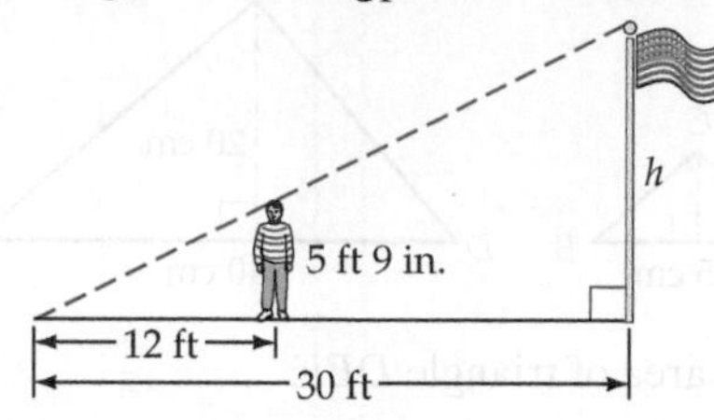

20. In the figure below, $\overline{BD} \parallel \overline{AE}$, BD measures 5 cm, AE measures 8 cm, and AC measures 10 cm. Find the length of $\overline{BC}$.

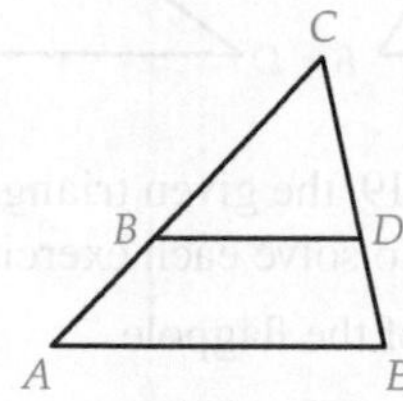

21. In the figure below, $\overline{AC} \parallel \overline{DE}$, BD measures 8 m, AD measures 12 m, and BE measures 6 m. Find the length of $\overline{BC}$.

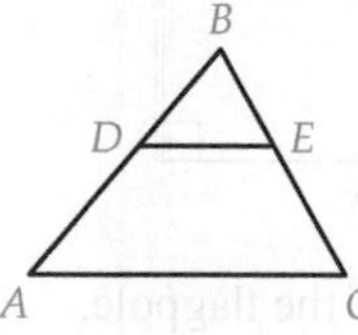

22. In the figure below, $\overline{DE} \parallel \overline{AC}$, DE measures 6 in., AC measures 10 in., and AB measures 15 in. Find the length of $\overline{DA}$.

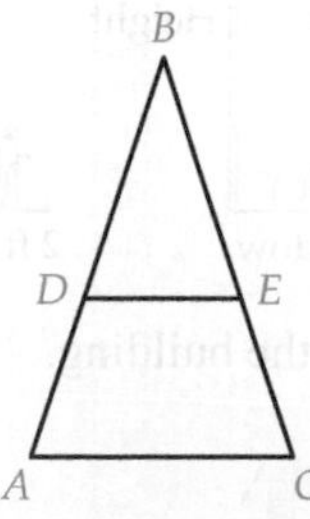

23. In the figure below, $\overline{AE} \parallel \overline{BD}$, $AB = 3$ ft, $ED = 4$ ft, and $BC = 3$ ft. Find the length of $\overline{CE}$.

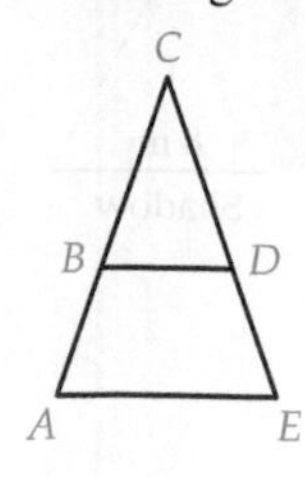

24. In the figure below, $\overline{MP}$ and $\overline{NQ}$ intersect at O, $NO = 25$ ft, $MO = 20$ ft, and $PO = 8$ ft. Find the length of $\overline{QO}$.

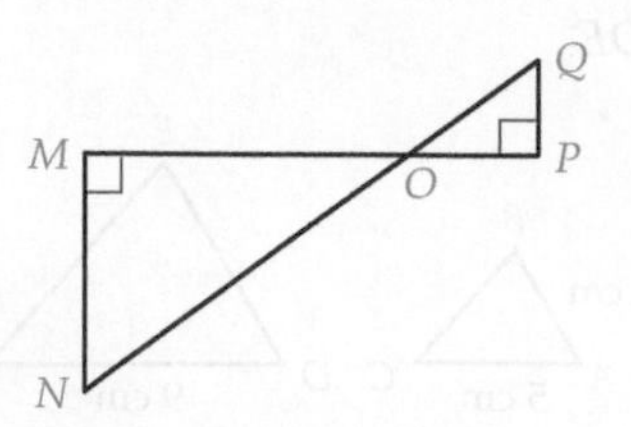

25. In the figure below, $\overline{MP}$ and $\overline{NQ}$ intersect at O, $NO = 24$ cm, $MN = 10$ cm, $MP = 39$ cm, and $QO = 12$ cm. Find the length of $\overline{OP}$.

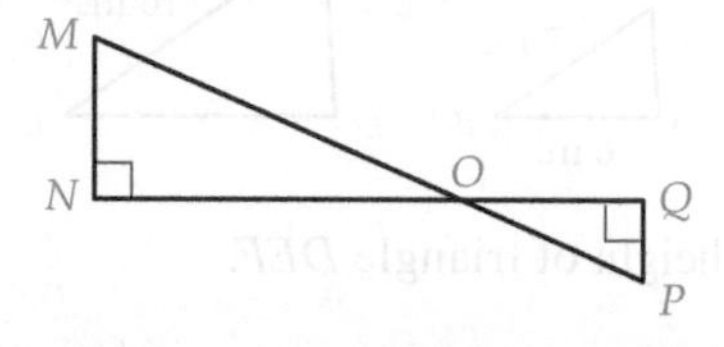

26. In the figure below, $\overline{MQ}$ and $\overline{NP}$ intersect at O, $NO = 12$ m, $MN = 9$ m, $PQ = 3$ m, and $MQ = 20$ m. Find the perimeter of triangle OPQ.

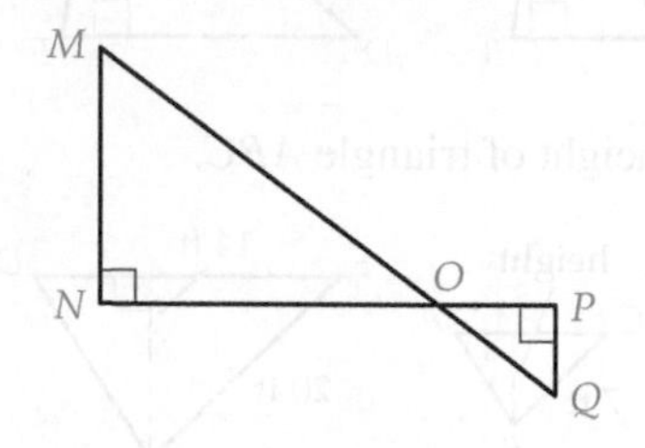

■ **Surveying** Surveyors use similar triangles to measure distances that cannot be measured directly. This is illustrated in Exercises 27 and 28.

27. The diagram below represents a river of width CD. Triangles AOB and DOC are similar. The distances AB, BO, and OC were measured and found to have the lengths given in the diagram. Find CD, the width of the river.

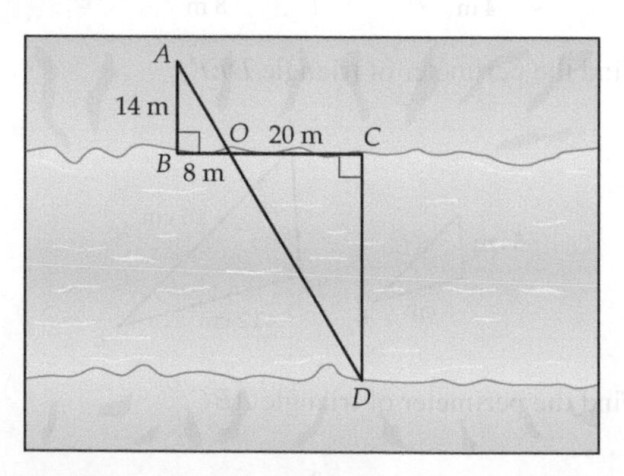

28. The diagram below shows how surveyors laid out similar triangles along the Winnepaugo River. Find the width, d, of the river.

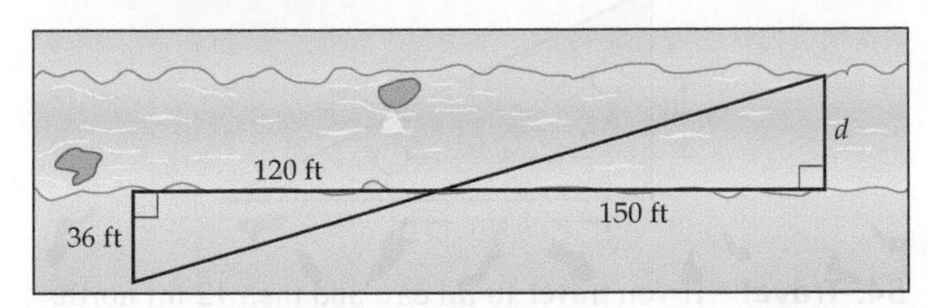

■ In Exercises 29 to 36, determine whether the two triangles are congruent. If they are congruent, state by what theorem (SSS, SAS, or ASA) they are congruent.

29.

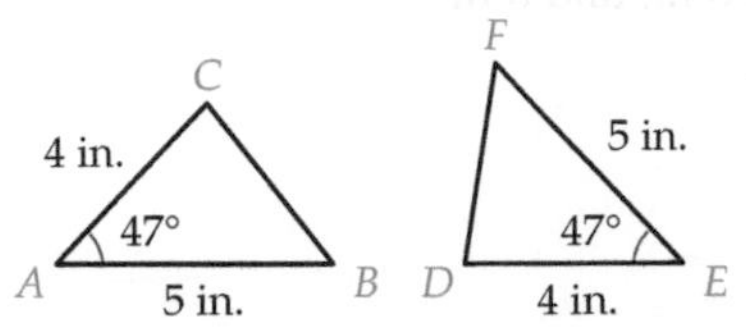

30.

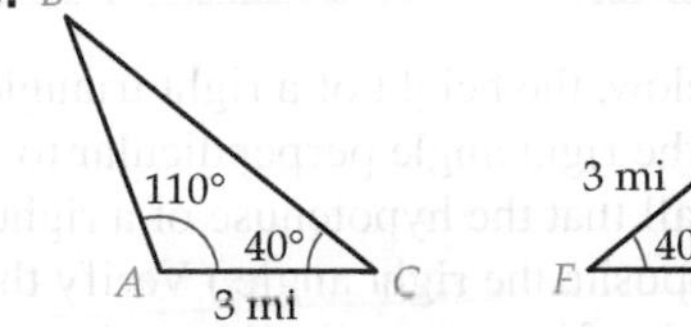

31.

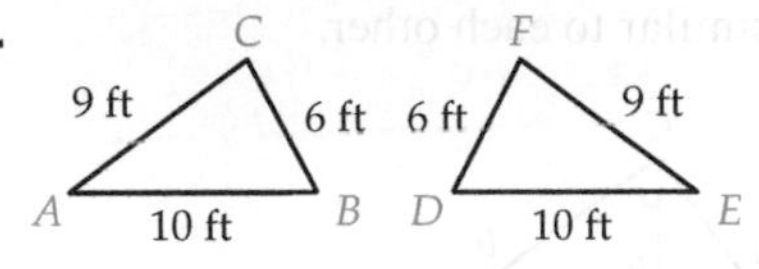

32.

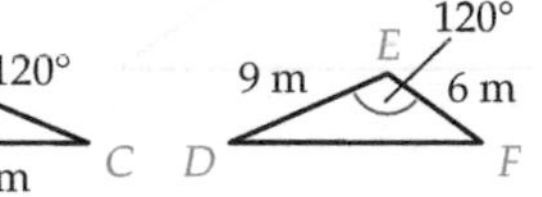

33.

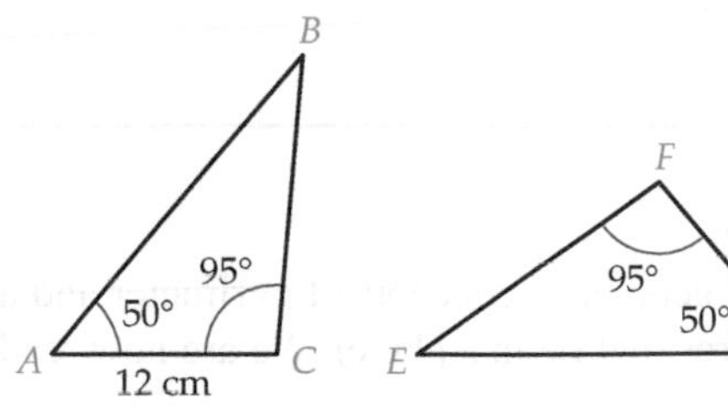

34.

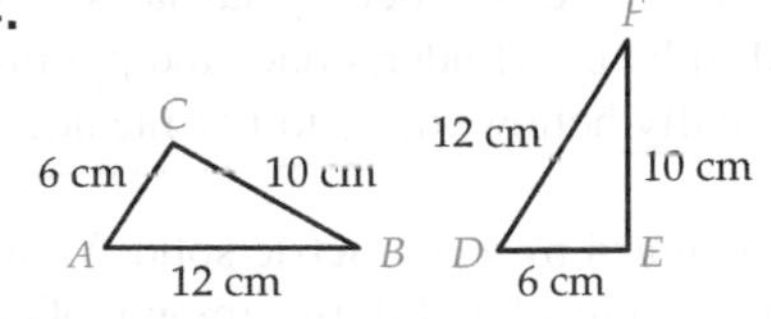

35.

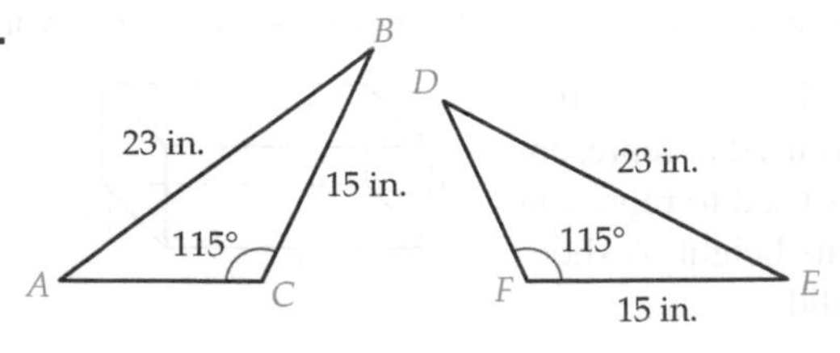

36. B, 10 cm, 45°, A, 14 cm, C; D, 10 cm, 45°, F, 14 cm, E

37. Given triangle ABC and triangle DEF, do the conditions $m\angle C = m\angle E$, $AC = EF$, and $BC = DE$ guarantee that triangle ABC is congruent to triangle DEF? If they are congruent, by what theorem are they congruent?

38. Given triangle PQR and triangle MNO, do the conditions $PR = NO$, $PQ = MO$, and $QR = MN$ guarantee that triangle PQR is congruent to triangle MNO? If they are congruent, by what theorem are they congruent?

39. Given triangle LMN and triangle QRS, do the conditions $m\angle M = m\angle S$, $m\angle N = m\angle Q$, and $m\angle L = m\angle R$ guarantee that triangle LMN is congruent to triangle QRS? If they are congruent, by what theorem are they congruent?

40. Given triangle DEF and triangle JKL, do the conditions $m\angle D = m\angle K$, $m\angle E = m\angle L$, and $DE = KL$ guarantee that triangle DEF is congruent to triangle JKL? If they are congruent, by what theorem are they congruent?

41. Given triangle ABC and triangle PQR, do the conditions $m\angle B = m\angle P$, $BC = PQ$, and $AC = QR$ guarantee that triangle ABC is congruent to triangle PQR? If they are congruent, by what theorem are they congruent?

42. True or false? If the ratio of the corresponding sides of two similar triangles is 1 to 1, then the two triangles are congruent.

■ In Exercises 43 to 51, find the length of the unknown side of the triangle. Round to the nearest tenth.

43.

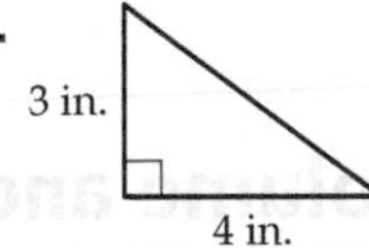

44.

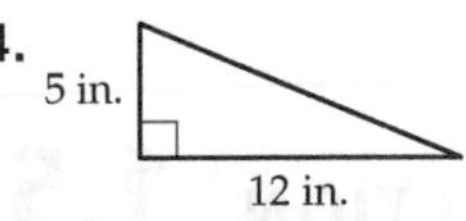

45.

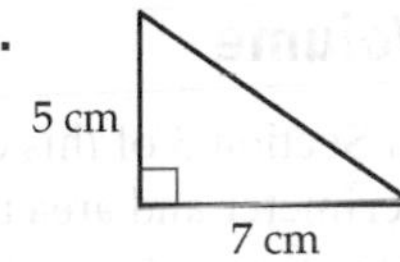

46.

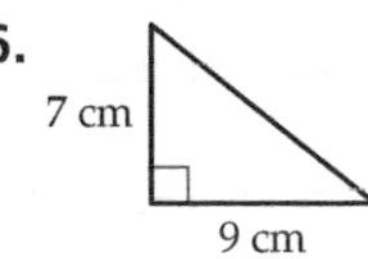

47.

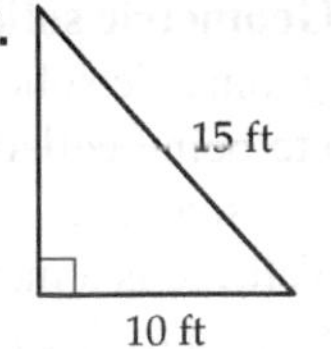

48.

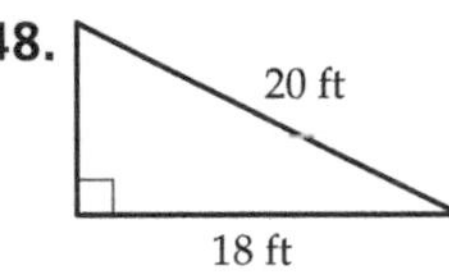

49.

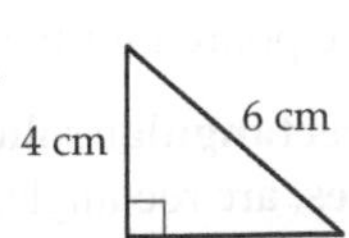

50.

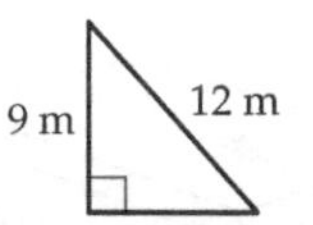

51.

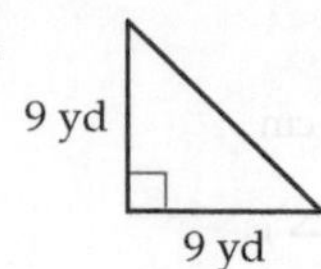

■ In Exercises 52 to 56, use the given information to solve each exercise. Round to the nearest tenth.

52. Home Maintenance A ladder 8 m long is leaning against a building. How high on the building will the ladder reach when the bottom of the ladder is 3 m from the building?

53. Mechanics Find the distance between the centers of the holes in the metal plate.

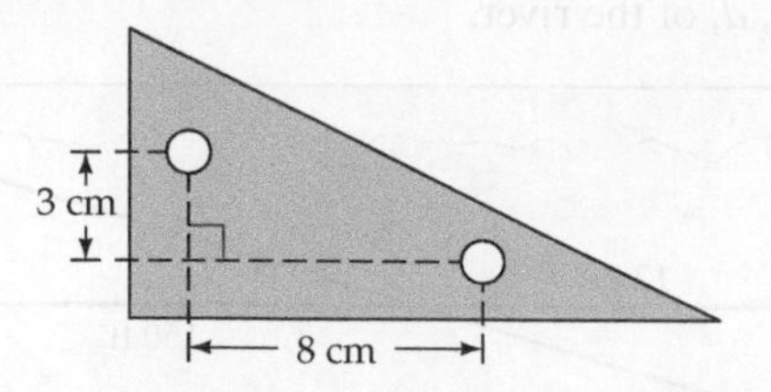

54. Travel If you travel 18 mi east and then 12 mi north, how far are you from your starting point?

55. Perimeter Find the perimeter of a right triangle with legs that measure 5 cm and 9 cm.

56. Perimeter Find the perimeter of a right triangle with legs that measure 6 in. and 8 in.

EXTENSIONS

57. Determine whether the statement is always true, sometimes true, or never true.

a. If two angles of one triangle are equal to two angles of a second triangle, then the triangles are similar triangles.

b. Two isosceles triangles are similar triangles.

c. Two equilateral triangles are similar triangles.

d. If an acute angle of a right triangle is equal to an acute angle of another right triangle, then the triangles are similar triangles.

58. In the figure below, the height of a right triangle is drawn from the right angle perpendicular to the hypotenuse. (Recall that the hypotenuse of a right triangle is the side opposite the right angle.) Verify that the two smaller triangles formed are similar to the original triangle and similar to each other.

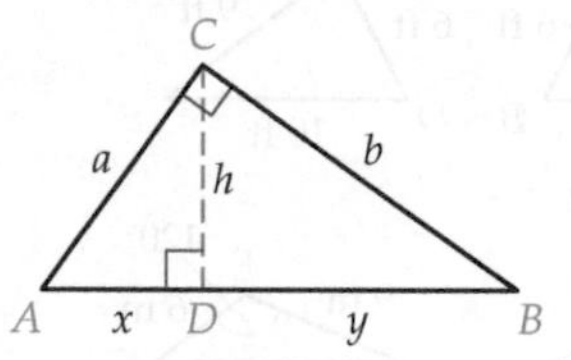

SECTION 1.5 Volume and Surface Area

Volume

In Section 3 of this chapter, we developed the geometric concepts of perimeter and area. Perimeter and area refer to plane figures (figures that lie in a plane). We are now ready to introduce *volume* of geometric solids.

Geometric solids are three-dimensional shapes that are bounded by surfaces. Common geometric solids include the rectangular solid, sphere, cylinder, cone, and pyramid. Despite being called "solids," these figures are actually hollow; they do not include the points inside their surfaces.

Volume is a measure of the amount of space occupied by a geometric solid. Volume can be used to describe, for example, the amount of trash in a landfill, the amount of concrete poured for the foundation of a house, or the amount of water in a town's reservoir.

A **rectangular solid** is one in which all six sides, called **faces**, are rectangles. The variable L is used to represent the length of a rectangular solid, W is used to represent its width, and H is used to represent its height. A shoebox is an example of a rectangular solid.

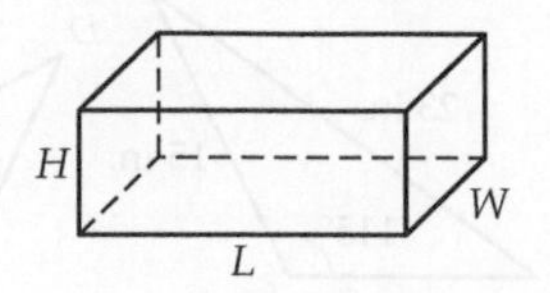

A **cube** is a special type of rectangular solid. Each of the six faces of a cube is a square. The variable s is used to represent the length of one side of a cube. A baby's block is an example of a cube.

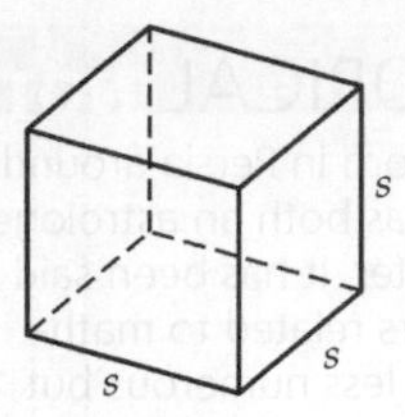

A cube that is 1 ft on each side has a volume of 1 cubic foot, which is written 1 ft^3. A cube that measures 1 cm on each side has a volume of 1 cubic centimeter, written 1 cm^3.

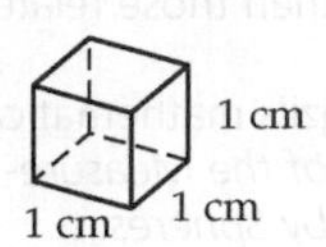

The volume of a solid is the number of cubes, each of volume 1 cubic unit, that are necessary to exactly fill the solid. The volume of the rectangular solid at the right is 24 cm^3 because it will hold exactly 24 cubes, each 1 cm on a side. Note that the volume can be found by multiplying the length times the width times the height.

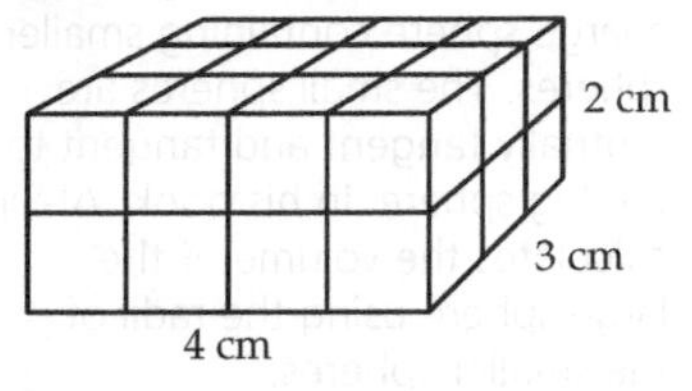

$4 \cdot 3 \cdot 2 = 24$

The volume of the solid is 24 cm^3.

Volume of a Rectangular Solid

The volume, V, of a rectangular solid with length L, width W, and height H is given by $V = LWH$.

Volume of a Cube

The volume, V, of a cube with side of length s is given by $V = s^3$.

QUESTION Which of the following are rectangular solids: juice box, baseball, can of soup, compact disc, or jewel box (plastic container) that a compact disc is packaged in?

A **sphere** is a solid in which all points are the same distance from a point O, called the **center** of the sphere. A **diameter** of a sphere is a line segment with endpoints on the sphere and passing through the center. A **radius** is a line segment from the center to a point on the sphere. $\overline{AB}$ is a diameter and $\overline{OC}$ is a radius of the sphere shown at the right. A basketball is an example of a sphere.

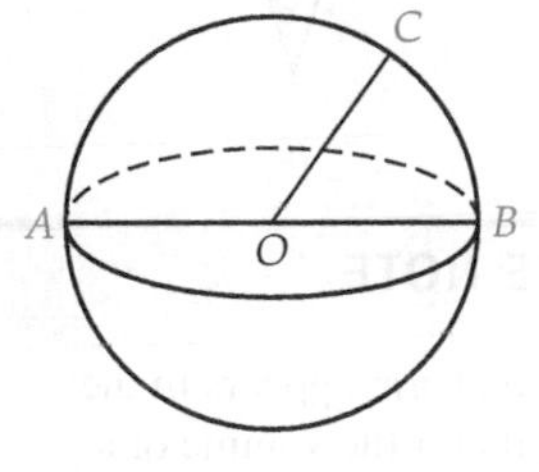

If we let d represent the length of a diameter and r represent the length of a radius, then $d = 2r$ or $r = \frac{1}{2}d$.

$$d = 2r \quad \text{or} \quad r = \frac{1}{2}d$$

Volume of a Sphere

The volume, V, of a sphere with radius of length r is given by $V = \frac{4}{3}\pi r^3$.

ANSWER A juice box and a jewel box are rectangular solids.

HISTORICAL NOTE

Al-Sijzi was born in Persia around AD 945. He was both an astrologer and a geometer. It has been said that his papers related to mathematics were less numerous but more significant than those related to astrology.

One of Al-Sijzi's mathematical works was *Book of the Measurement of Spheres by Spheres.* It contains 12 theorems regarding a large sphere containing smaller spheres. The small spheres are mutually tangent and tangent to the big sphere. In his book, Al-Sijzi calculates the volume of the large sphere using the radii of the smaller spheres.

CALCULATOR NOTE

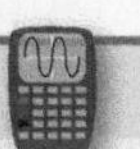

To approximate 36π on a scientific calculator, enter

36 [×] [π] [=]

TAKE NOTE

Note that πr^2 appears in the formula for the volume of a right circular cylinder and in the formula for the volume of a right circular cone. This is because, in each case, the base of the figure is a circle.

Find the volume of a rubber ball that has a diameter of 6 in.

First find the length of a radius of the sphere. $r = \frac{1}{2}d = \frac{1}{2}(6) = 3$

Use the formula for the volume of a sphere. $V = \frac{4}{3}\pi r^3$

Replace r with 3. $V = \frac{4}{3}\pi(3)^3$

$V = \frac{4}{3}\pi(27)$

$V = 36\pi$

The exact volume of the rubber ball is 36π in^3.

An approximate measure can be found by using the π key on a calculator. $V \approx 113.10$

The volume of the rubber ball is approximately 113.10 in^3.

The most common cylinder, called a **right circular cylinder**, is one in which the bases are circles and are perpendicular to the height of the cylinder. The variable r is used to represent the length of the radius of a base of a cylinder, and h represents the height of the cylinder. In this text, only right circular cylinders are discussed.

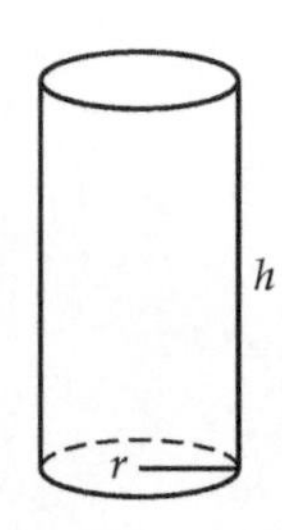

Volume of a Right Circular Cylinder

The volume, V, of a right circular cylinder is given by $V = \pi r^2 h$, where r is the radius of the base and h is the height of the cylinder.

A **right circular cone** is obtained when one base of a right circular cylinder is shrunk to a point, called the **vertex**, V. The variable r is used to represent the radius of the base of the cone, and h represents the height of the cone. The variable l is used to represent the **slant height**, which is the distance from a point on the circumference of the base to the vertex. In this text, only right circular cones are discussed. An ice cream cone is an example of a right circular cone.

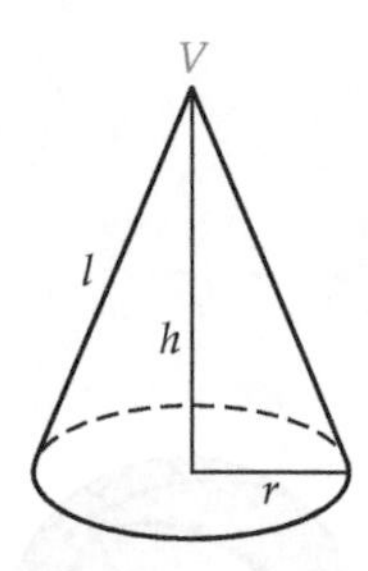

Volume of a Right Circular Cone

The volume, V, of a right circular cone is given by $V = \frac{1}{3}\pi r^2 h$, where r is the length of a radius of the circular base and h is the height of the cone.

The base of a **regular pyramid** is a regular polygon, and the sides are isosceles triangles (two sides of the triangle are the same length). The height, h, is the distance from the vertex, V, to the base and is perpendicular to the base. The variable l is used to represent the **slant height**, which is the height of one of the isosceles triangles on the face of the pyramid. The regular square pyramid at the right has a square base. This is the only type of pyramid discussed in this text. Many Egyptian pyramids are regular square pyramids.

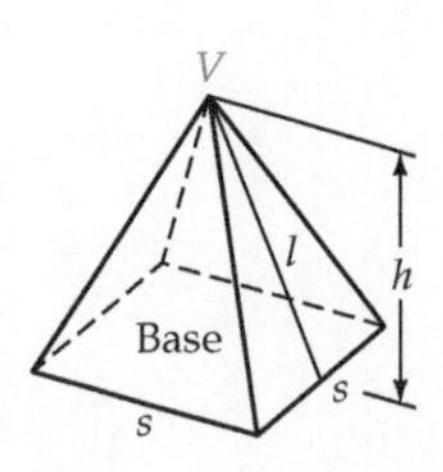

Dudarev Mikhail/Shutterstock.com

Pyramid at Giza

Volume of a Regular Square Pyramid

The volume, V, of a regular square pyramid is given by $V = \frac{1}{3}s^2h$, where s is the length of a side of the base and h is the height of the pyramid.

QUESTION Which of the following units could be used to measure the volume of a regular square pyramid?

a. ft^3 **b.** m^3 **c.** yd^2 **d.** cm^3 **e.** mi

EXAMPLE 1 Find the Volume of a Geometric Solid

Find the volume of a cube that measures 1.5 m on a side.

Solution

$V = s^3$ • Use the formula for the volume of a cube.

$V = 1.5^3$ • Replace s with 1.5.

$V = 3.375$

The volume of the cube is $3.375\ \text{m}^3$.

CHECK YOUR PROGRESS 1 The length of a rectangular solid is 5 m, the width is 3.2 m, and the height is 4 m. Find the volume of the solid.

Solution See page S3.

EXAMPLE 2 Find the Volume of a Geometric Solid

The radius of the base of a cone is 8 cm. The height of the cone is 12 cm. Find the volume of the cone. Round to the nearest hundredth of a cubic centimeter.

Solution

$V = \frac{1}{3}\pi r^2 h$ • Use the formula for the volume of a cone.

$V = \frac{1}{3}\pi(8)^2(12)$ • Replace r with 8 and h with 12.

$V = \frac{1}{3}\pi(64)(12)$

$V = 256\pi$ • Exact volume

$V \approx 804.25$ • Use the π key on a calculator.

The volume of the cone is approximately $804.25\ \text{cm}^3$.

CHECK YOUR PROGRESS 2 The length of a side of the base of a regular square pyramid is 15 m and the height of the pyramid is 25 m. Find the volume of the pyramid.

Solution See page S3.

POINT OF INTEREST

A few years ago, astronomers identified a trio of supergiant stars, which were subsequently named KW Sagitarii, V354 Cephei, and KY Cygni. All three have diameters of more than 1 billion miles, or 1500 times the diameter of our sun. If one of these stars were placed in the same location as our sun, it would not only engulf Earth, but its outer boundary would extend to a point between the orbits of Jupiter and Saturn.

ANSWER Volume is measured in cubic units. Therefore, the volume of a regular square pyramid could be measured in ft^3, m^3, or cm^3, but not in yd^2 or mi.

EXAMPLE 3 **Find the Volume of a Geometric Solid**

An oil storage tank in the shape of a cylinder is 4 m high and has a diameter of 6 m. The oil tank is two-thirds full. Find the number of cubic meters of oil in the tank. Round to the nearest hundredth of a cubic meter.

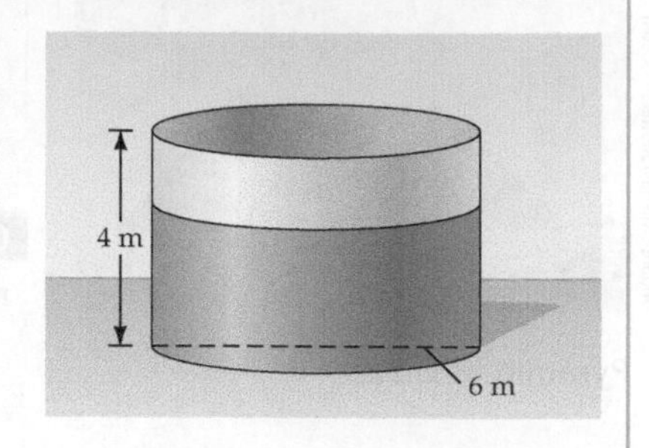

Solution

$r = \frac{1}{2}d = \frac{1}{2}(6) = 3$ • Find the radius of the base.

$V = \pi r^2 h$ • Use the formula for the volume of a cylinder.

$V = \pi(3)^2(4)$ • Replace r with 3 and h with 4.

$V = \pi(9)(4)$

$V = 36\pi$

$\frac{2}{3}(36\pi) = 24\pi$ • Multiply the volume by $\frac{2}{3}$.

≈ 75.40 • Use the π key on a calculator.

There are approximately 75.40 m^3 of oil in the storage tank.

CHECK YOUR PROGRESS 3

A silo in the shape of a cylinder is 16 ft in diameter and has a height of 30 ft. The silo is three-fourths full. Find the volume of the portion of the silo that is not being used for storage. Round to the nearest hundredth of a cubic foot.

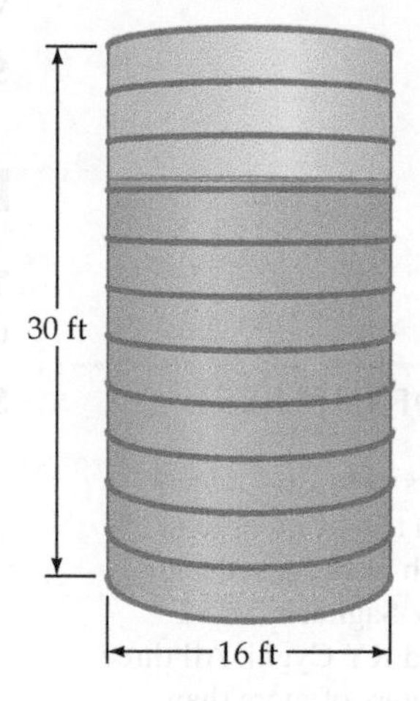

Solution See page S3.

Surface Area

The **surface area** of a solid is the total area on the surface of the solid. Suppose you want to cover a geometric solid with wallpaper. The amount of wallpaper needed is equal to the surface area of the figure.

When a rectangular solid is cut open and flattened out, each face is a rectangle. The surface area, S, of the rectangular solid is the sum of the areas of the six rectangles:

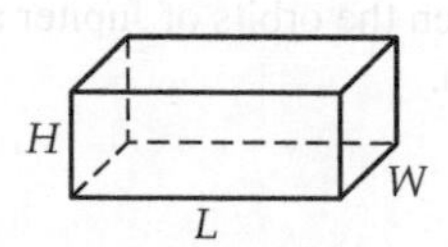

$$S = LW + LH + WH + LW + WH + LH$$

which simplifies to

$$S = 2LW + 2LH + 2WH$$

	LW	
	LH	
WH	LW	WH
	LH	

If the rectangular solid is a cube, then all three sides L, W, and H are equal. Therefore, each side can be represented by s. The surface area of a cube is

$$S = 2LW + 2LH + 2WH$$
$$S = 2 \cdot s \cdot s + 2 \cdot s \cdot s + 2 \cdot s \cdot s = 2s^2 + 2s^2 + 2s^2$$
$$S = 6s^2$$

> **HISTORICAL NOTE**
>
> **Pappus** (păp'ŭs) of Alexandria (ca. 290–350) was born in Egypt. We know the time period in which he lived because he wrote about his observation of the eclipse of the sun that took place in Alexandria on October 18, 320.
>
> Pappus has been called the last of the great Greek geometers. His major work in geometry is *Synagoge*, or the *Mathematical Collection*. It consists of eight books. In Book V, Pappus proves that the sphere has a greater volume than any regular geometric solid with equal surface area. He also proves that if two regular solids have equal surface areas, the solid with the greater number of faces has the greater volume.

When a cylinder is cut open and flattened out, the top and bottom of the cylinder are circles. The side of the cylinder flattens out to a rectangle. The length of the rectangle is the circumference of the base, which is $2\pi r$; the width is h, the height of the cylinder. Therefore, the area of the rectangle is $2\pi rh$. The surface area, S, of the cylinder is

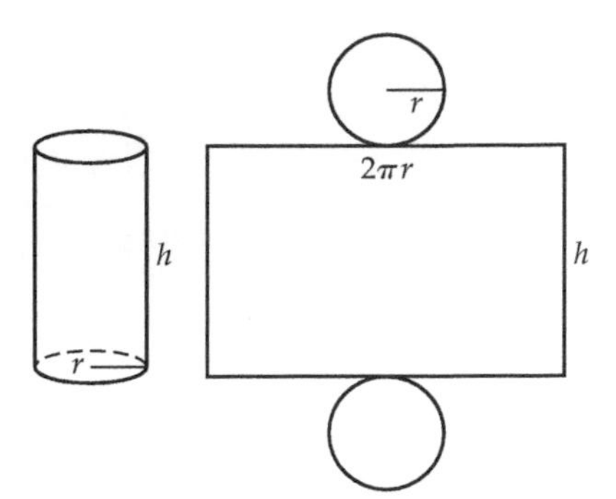

$$S = \pi r^2 + 2\pi rh + \pi r^2$$

which simplifies to

$$S = 2\pi r^2 + 2\pi rh$$

The surface area of a regular square pyramid is the area of the base plus the area of the four isosceles triangles. The length of a side of the square base is s; therefore, the area of the base is s^2. The slant height, l, is the height of each triangle, and s is the length of the base of each triangle. The surface area, S, of a regular square pyramid is

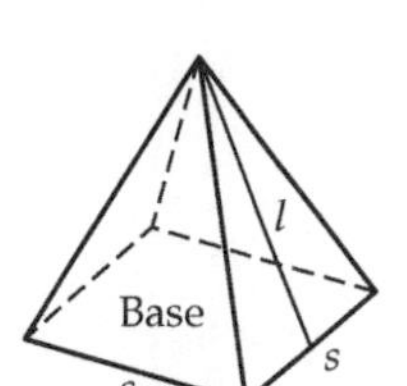

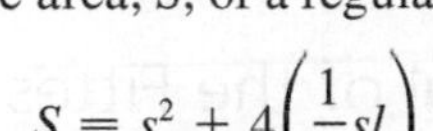

$$S = s^2 + 4\left(\frac{1}{2}sl\right)$$

which simplifies to

$$S = s^2 + 2sl$$

Formulas for the surface areas of geometric solids are given below.

Surface Areas of Geometric Solids

The surface area, S, of a **rectangular solid** with length L, width W, and height H is given by $S = 2LW + 2LH + 2WH$.

The surface area, S, of a **cube** with sides of length s is given by $S = 6s^2$.

The surface area, S, of a **sphere** with radius r is given by $S = 4\pi r^2$.

The surface area, S, of a **right circular cylinder** is given by $S = 2\pi r^2 + 2\pi rh$, where r is the radius of the base and h is the height.

The surface area, S, of a **right circular cone** is given by $S = \pi r^2 + \pi rl$, where r is the radius of the circular base and l is the slant height.

The surface area, S, of a **regular square pyramid** is given by $S = s^2 + 2sl$, where s is the length of a side of the base and l is the slant height.

QUESTION Which of the following units could be used to measure the surface area of a rectangular solid?

a. in^2 **b.** m^3 **c.** cm^2 **d.** ft^3 **e.** yd

ANSWER Surface area is measured in square units. Therefore, the surface area of a rectangular solid could be measured in in^2 or cm^2, but not in m^3, ft^3, or yd.

EXAMPLE 4 **Find the Surface Area of a Geometric Solid**

The diameter of the base of a cone is 5 m and the slant height is 4 m. Find the surface area of the cone. Round to the nearest hundredth of a square meter.

Solution

$r = \frac{1}{2}d = \frac{1}{2}(5) = 2.5$ • Find the radius of the cone.

$S = \pi r^2 + \pi rl$ • Use the formula for the surface area of a cone.

$S = \pi(2.5)^2 + \pi(2.5)(4)$ • Replace r with 2.5 and l with 4.

$S = \pi(6.25) + \pi(2.5)(4)$

$S = 6.25\pi + 10\pi$

$S = 16.25\pi$

$S \approx 51.05$

The surface area of the cone is approximately 51.05 m^2.

CHECK YOUR PROGRESS 4 The diameter of the base of a cylinder is 6 ft and the height is 8 ft. Find the surface area of the cylinder. Round to the nearest hundredth of a square foot.

Solution See page S3.

MATH MATTERS Survival of the Fittest

hallam creations/Shutterstock.com

The ratio of an animal's surface area to the volume of its body is a crucial factor in its survival. The more square units of skin for every cubic unit of volume, the more rapidly the animal loses body heat. Therefore, animals living in a warm climate benefit from a higher ratio of surface area to volume, whereas those living in a cool climate benefit from a lower ratio.

EXCURSION

Water Displacement

A recipe for peanut butter cookies calls for 1 cup of peanut butter. Peanut butter is difficult to measure. If you have ever used a measuring cup to measure peanut butter, you know that there tend to be pockets of air at the bottom of the cup. And trying to scrape all of the peanut butter out of the cup and into the mixing bowl is a challenge.

A more convenient method of measuring 1 cup of peanut butter is to fill a 2-cup measuring cup with 1 cup of water. Then add peanut butter to the water until the water reaches the 2-cup mark. (Make sure all the peanut butter is below the top of the water.) Drain off the water, and the one cup of peanut butter drops easily into the mixing bowl.

POINT OF INTEREST

King Hiero of Syracuse commissioned a new crown from his goldsmith. When the crown was completed, Hiero suspected that the goldsmith had stolen some of the gold and replaced it with lead. Hiero asked Archimedes to determine, without defacing the surface of the crown, whether the crown was pure gold.

Archimedes knew that the first problem he had to solve was how to determine the volume of the crown. Legend has it that one day he was getting into a bathtub that was completely full of water, and the water splashed over the side. He surmised that the volume of water that poured over the side was equal to the volume of his submerged body. Supposedly, he was so excited that he jumped from the tub and went running through the streets yelling "Eureka! Eureka!," meaning "I found it! I found it!"—referring to the solution of the problem of determining the volume of the crown.

This method of measuring peanut butter works because when an object sinks below the surface of the water, the object displaces an amount of water that is equal to the volume of the object.

A sphere with a diameter of 4 in. is placed in a rectangular tank of water that is 6 in. long and 5 in. wide. How much does the water level rise? Round to the nearest hundredth of an inch.

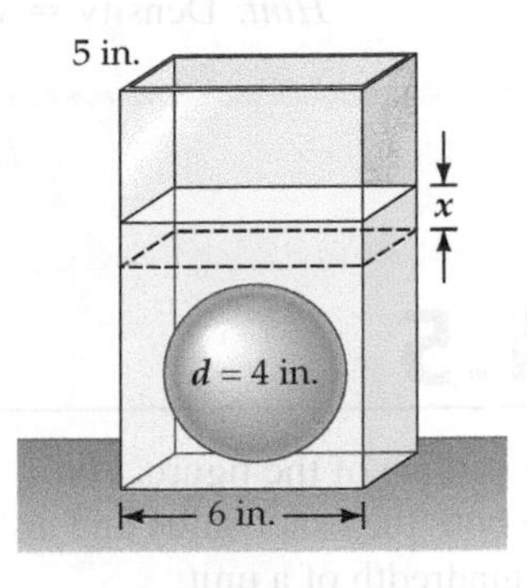

$V = \frac{4}{3}\pi r^3$ • Use the formula for the volume of a sphere.

$V = \frac{4}{3}\pi(2^3) = \frac{32}{3}\pi$ • $r = \frac{1}{2}d = \frac{1}{2}(4) = 2$

Let x represent the amount of the rise in water level. The volume of the sphere will equal the volume of the water displaced. As shown above, this volume is the volume of a rectangular solid with width 5 in., length 6 in., and height x in.

$V = LWH$ • Use the formula for the volume of a rectangular solid.

$\frac{32}{3}\pi = (6)(5)x$ • Substitute $\frac{32}{3}\pi$ for V, 6 for L, 5 for W, and x for H.

$\frac{32}{90}\pi = x$ • The exact height that the water will rise is $\frac{32}{90}\pi$.

$1.12 \approx x$ • Use a calculator to find an approximation.

The water will rise approximately 1.12 in.

EXCURSION EXERCISES

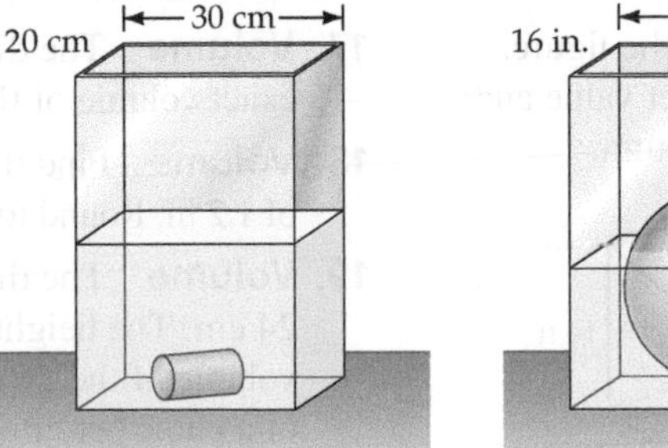

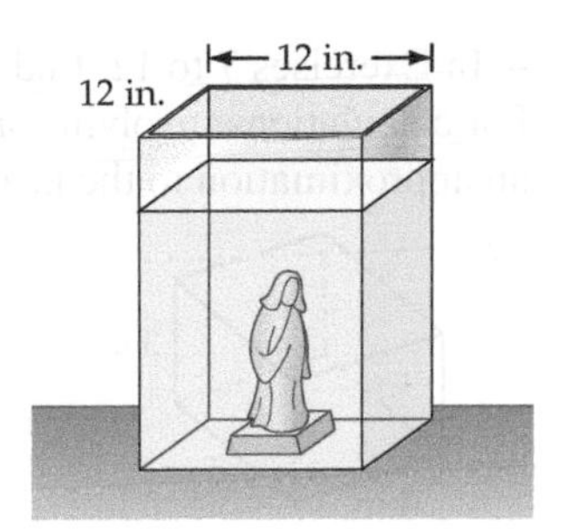

FIGURE 1 FIGURE 2 FIGURE 3

1. A cylinder with a 2-cm radius and a height of 10 cm is submerged in a tank of water that is 20 cm wide and 30 cm long (see Figure 1). How much does the water level rise? Round to the nearest hundredth of a centimeter.

2. A sphere with a radius of 6 in. is placed in a rectangular tank of water that is 16 in. wide and 20 in. long (see Figure 2). The sphere displaces water until two-thirds of

the sphere, with respect to its volume, is submerged. How much does the water level rise? Round to the nearest hundredth of an inch.

3. A chemist wants to know the density of a statue that weighs 15 lb. The statue is placed in a rectangular tank of water that is 12 in. long and 12 in. wide (see Figure 3 on page 59). The water level rises 0.42 in. Find the density of the statue. Round to the nearest hundredth of a pound per cubic inch.
Hint: Density = weight ÷ volume.

EXERCISE SET 1.5

■ In Exercises 1 to 6, find the volume of the figure. For calculations involving π, give both the exact value and an approximation to the nearest hundredth of a unit.

1.

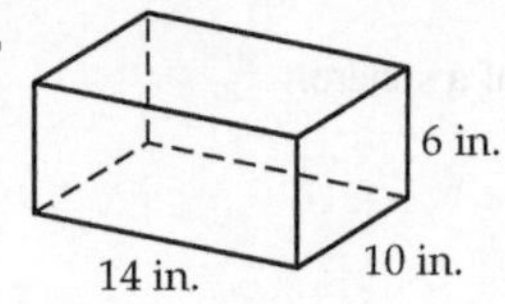

2.

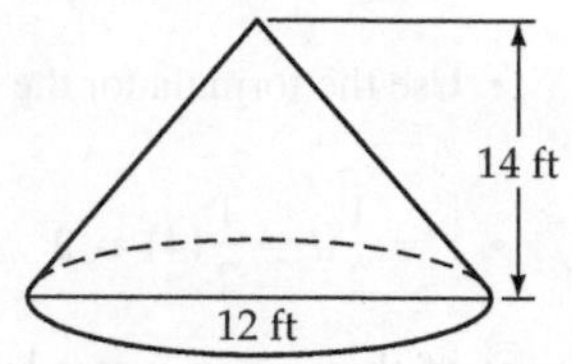

3.

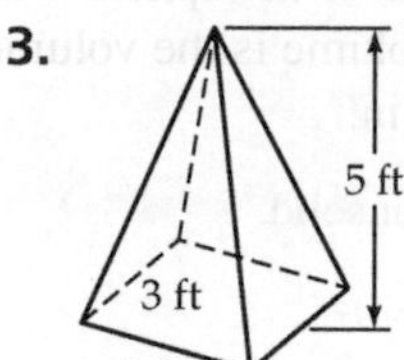

4.

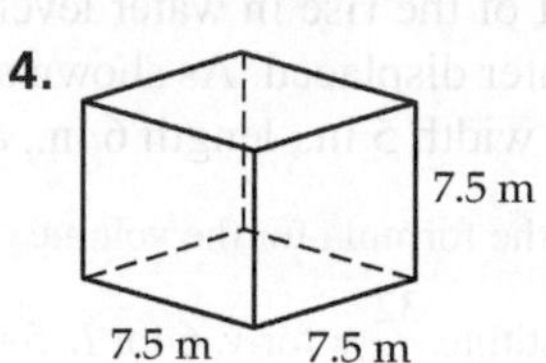

5.

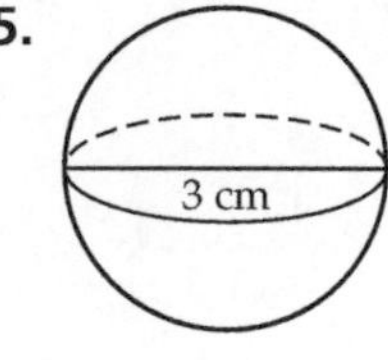

6.

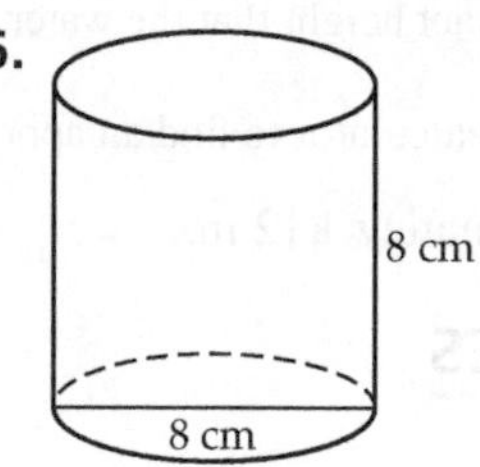

■ In Exercises 7 to 12, find the surface area of the figure. For calculations involving π, give both the exact value and an approximation to the nearest hundredth of a unit.

7.

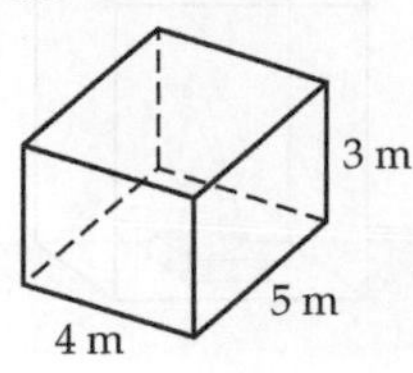

8.

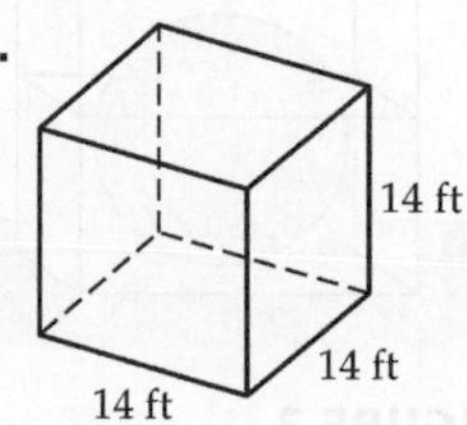

9.

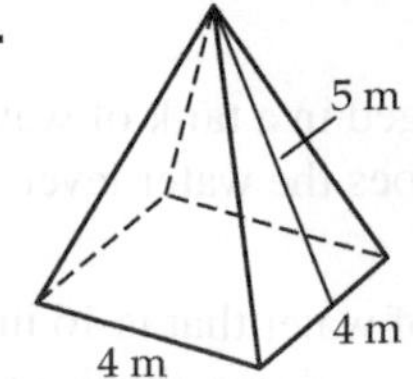

10.

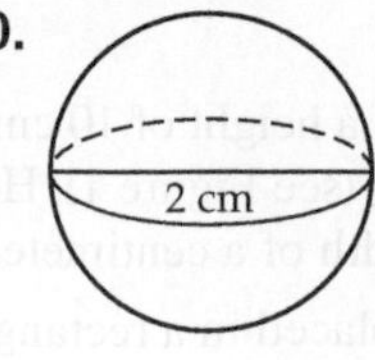

11.

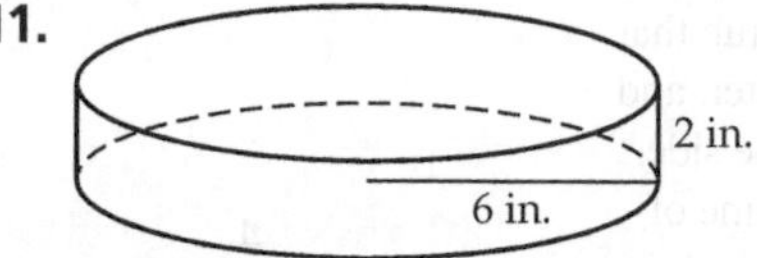

12.

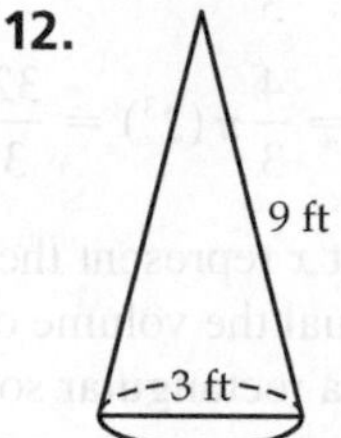

■ In Exercises 13 to 45, solve.

13. **Volume** A rectangular solid has a length of 6.8 m, a width of 2.5 m, and a height of 2 m. Find the volume of the solid.

14. **Volume** Find the volume of a rectangular solid that has a length of 4.5 ft, a width of 3 ft, and a height of 1.5 ft.

15. **Volume** Find the volume of a cube whose side measures 2.5 in.

16. **Volume** The length of a side of a cube is 7 cm. Find the volume of the cube.

17. **Volume** The diameter of a sphere is 6 ft. Find the exact volume of the sphere.

18. **Volume** Find the volume of a sphere that has a radius of 1.2 m. Round to the nearest hundredth of a cubic meter.

19. **Volume** The diameter of the base of a cylinder is 24 cm. The height of the cylinder is 18 cm. Find the volume of the cylinder. Round to the nearest hundredth of a cubic centimeter.

20. **Volume** The height of a cylinder is 7.2 m. The radius of the base is 4 m. Find the exact volume of the cylinder.

21. **Volume** The radius of the base of a cone is 5 in. The height of the cone is 9 in. Find the exact volume of the cone.

22. **Volume** The height of a cone is 15 cm. The diameter of the cone is 10 cm. Find the volume of the cone. Round to the nearest hundredth of a cubic centimeter.

23. Volume The length of a side of the base of a regular square pyramid is 6 in. and the height of the pyramid is 10 in. Find the volume of the pyramid.

24. Volume The height of a regular square pyramid is 8 m and the length of a side of the base is 9 m. What is the volume of the pyramid?

25. The length of a side of a cube is equal to the radius of a sphere. Which solid has the greater volume?

26. A sphere and a cylinder have the same radius. The height of the cylinder is equal to the radius of its base. Which solid has the greater volume?

27. The Statue of Liberty The index finger of the Statue of Liberty is 8 ft long. The circumference at the second joint is 3.5 ft. Use the formula for the volume of a cylinder to approximate the volume of the index finger on the Statue of Liberty. Round to the nearest hundredth of a cubic foot.

28. Fish Hatchery A rectangular tank at a fish hatchery is 9 m long, 3 m wide, and 1.5 m deep. Find the volume of the water in the tank when the tank is full.

Sukpaiboonwat/Shutterstock.com

29. The Panama Canal When the lock is full, the water in the Pedro Miguel Lock near the Pacific Ocean side of the Panama Canal fills a rectangular solid of dimensions 1000 ft long, 110 ft wide, and 43 ft deep. There are 7.48 gal of water in each cubic foot. How many gallons of water are in the lock?

Chris Jenner/Shutterstock.com

Panama Canal

30. Surface Area The width of a rectangular solid is 32 cm, the length is 60 cm, and the height is 14 cm. What is the surface area of the solid?

31. Surface Area The side of a cube measures 3.4 m. Find the surface area of the cube.

32. Surface Area Find the surface area of a cube with a side measuring 1.5 in.

33. Surface Area Find the exact surface area of a sphere with a diameter of 15 cm.

34. Surface Area The radius of a sphere is 2 in. Find the surface area of the sphere. Round to the nearest hundredth of a square inch.

35. Surface Area The radius of the base of a cylinder is 4 in. The height of the cylinder is 12 in. Find the surface area of the cylinder. Round to the nearest hundredth of a square inch.

36. Surface Area The diameter of the base of a cylinder is 1.8 m. The height of the cylinder is 0.7 m. Find the exact surface area of the cylinder.

37. Surface Area The slant height of a cone is 2.5 ft. The radius of the base is 1.5 ft. Find the exact surface area of the cone. The formula for the surface area of a cone is given on page 57.

38. Surface Area The diameter of the base of a cone is 21 in. The slant height is 16 in. What is the surface area of the cone? The formula for the surface area of a cone is given on page 57. Round to the nearest hundredth of a square inch.

39. Surface Area The length of a side of the base of a regular square pyramid is 9 in., and the pyramid's slant height is 12 in. Find the surface area of the pyramid.

40. Surface Area The slant height of a regular square pyramid is 18 m, and the length of a side of the base is 16 m. What is the surface area of the pyramid?

41. Appliances The volume of a freezer that is a rectangular solid with a length of 7 ft and a height of 3 ft is 52.5 ft^3. Find the width of the freezer.

42. Aquariums The length of a rectangular solid aquarium is 18 in. and the width is 12 in. If the volume of the aquarium is 1836 in^3, what is the height of the aquarium?

43. Paint A can of paint will cover 300 ft^2 of surface. How many cans of paint should be purchased to paint a cylinder that has a height of 30 ft and a radius of 12 ft?

44. Ballooning A hot air balloon is in the shape of a sphere. Approximately how much fabric was used to construct the balloon if its diameter is 32 ft? Round to the nearest square foot.

45. Surface Area The length of a side of the base of a regular square pyramid is 5 cm and the slant height of the pyramid is 8 cm. How much larger is the surface area of this pyramid than the surface area of a cone with a diameter of 5 cm and a slant height of 8 cm? Round to the nearest hundredth of a square centimeter.

■ In Exercises 46 to 51, find the volume of the figure. Round to the nearest hundredth of a unit.

46.

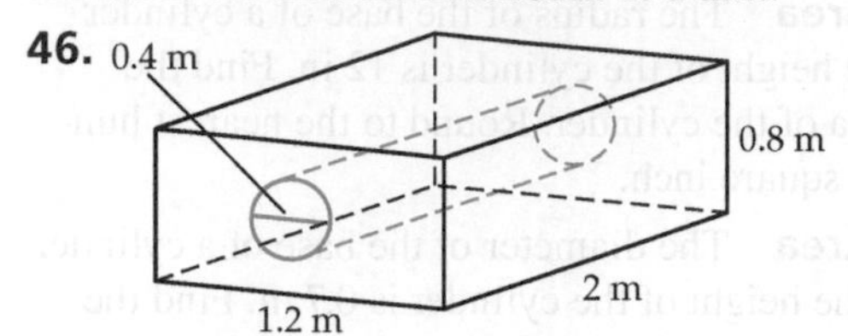

47.

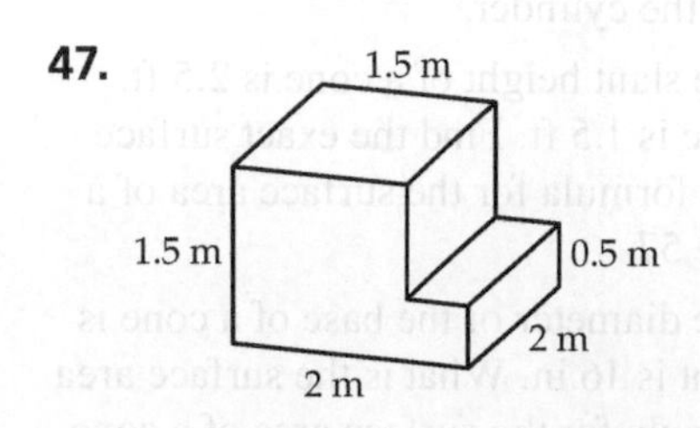

48.

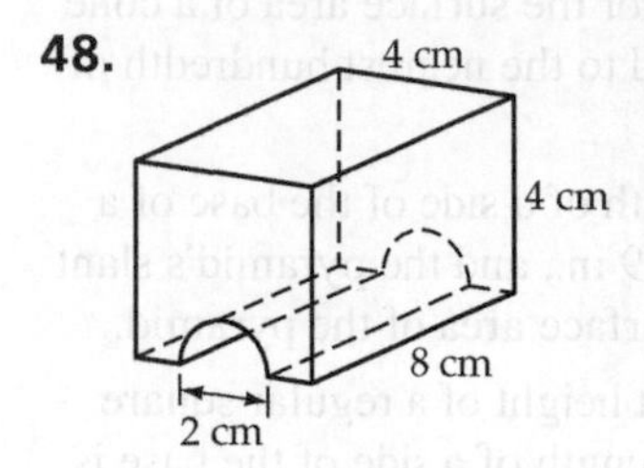

49.

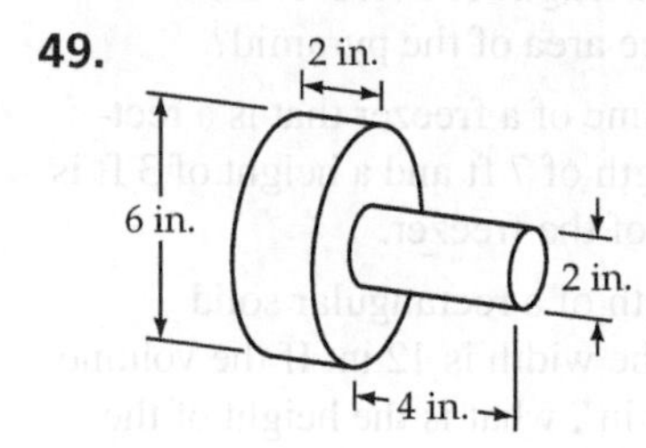

50.

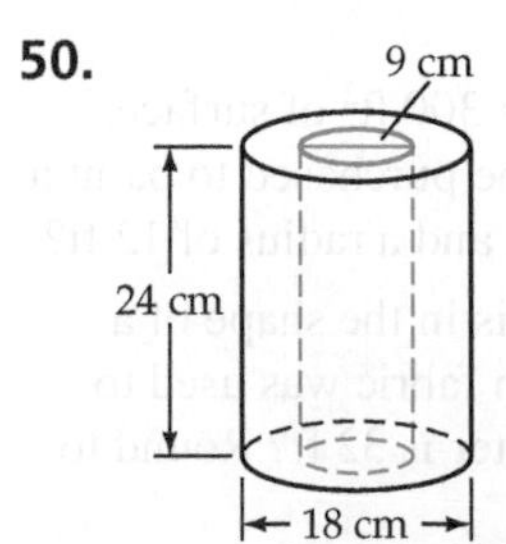

51.

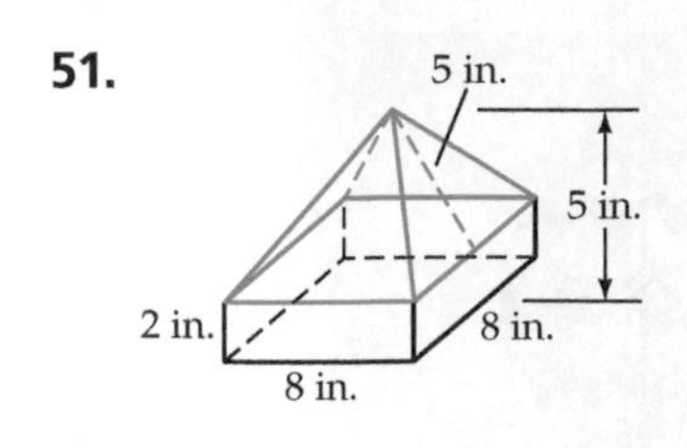

■ In Exercises 52 to 55, find the surface area of the figure. Round to the nearest hundredth of a unit.

52.

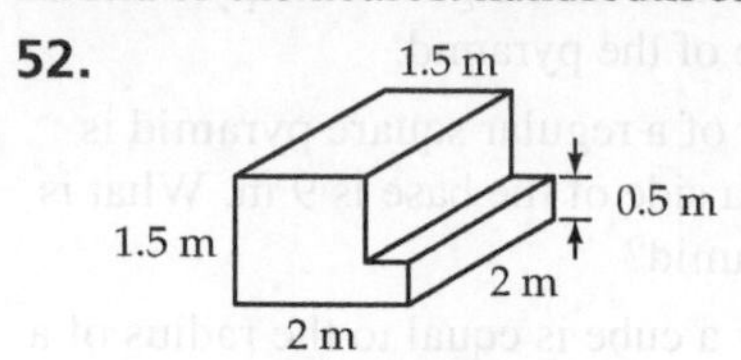

53.

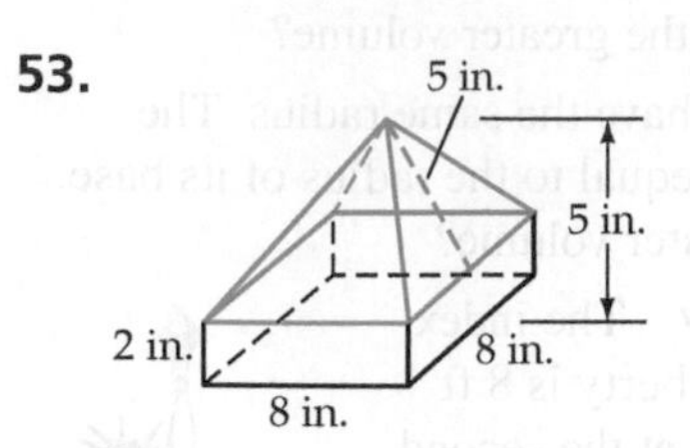

54.

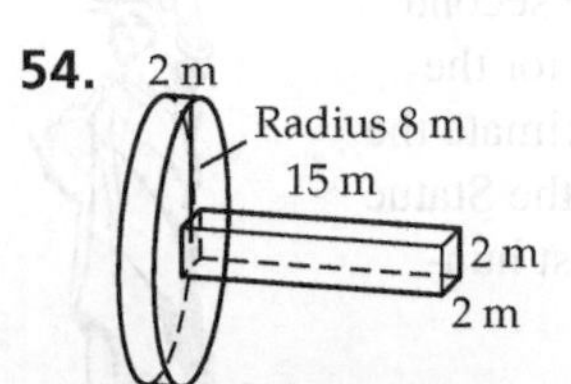

55.

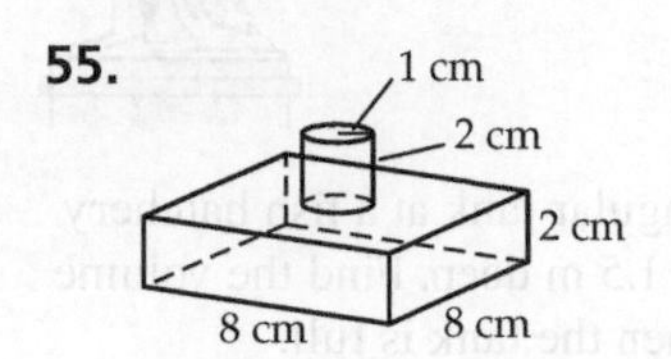

56. Oil Tanks A truck is carrying an oil tank. The tank consists of a circular cylinder with a hemisphere on each end, as shown. If the tank is half full, how many cubic feet of oil is the truck carrying? Round to the nearest hundredth of a cubic foot.

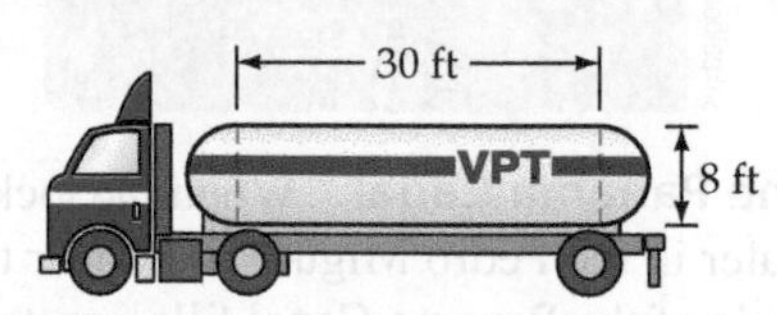

57. Swimming Pools How many liters of water are needed to fill the swimming pool shown below? (1 m^3 contains 1000 L.)

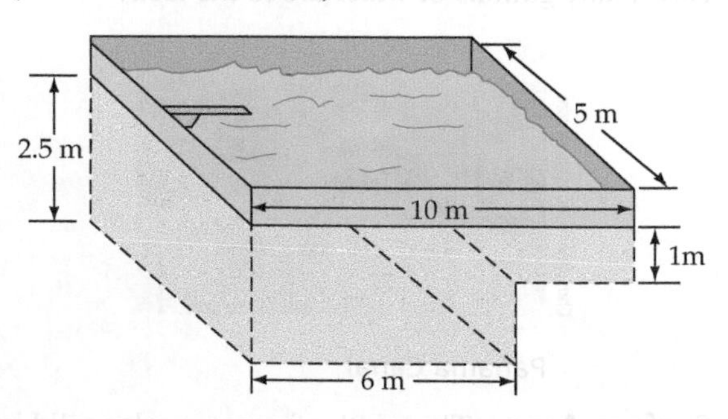

58. Metallurgy A piece of sheet metal is cut and formed into the shape shown below. Given that there are 0.24 g in 1 cm^2 of the metal, find the total number of grams of metal used. Round to the nearest hundredth of a gram.

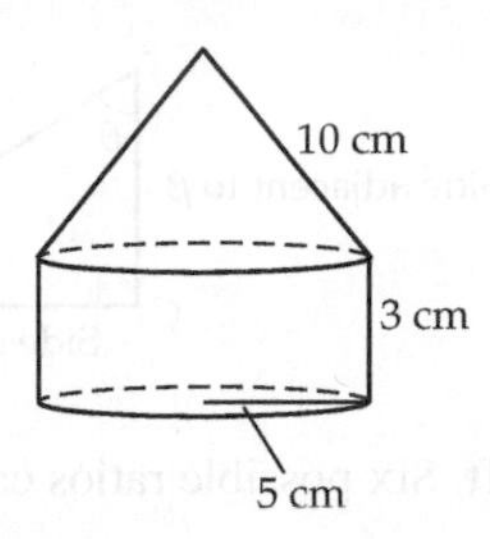

59. Gold A solid sphere of gold alloy with a radius of 0.5 cm has a value of $180. Find the value of a solid sphere of the same alloy with a radius of 1.5 cm.

60. Swimming Pools A swimming pool is built in the shape of a rectangular solid. It holds 32,000 gal of water. If the length, width, and height of the pool are each doubled, how many gallons of water will be needed to fill the pool?

EXTENSIONS

61. a. Draw a two-dimensional figure that can be cut out and made into a right circular cone.

b. Draw a two-dimensional figure that can be cut out and made into a regular square pyramid.

62. A sphere fits inside a cylinder as shown in the figure below. The height of the cylinder equals the diameter of the sphere. Show that the surface area of the sphere equals the surface area of the side of the cylinder.

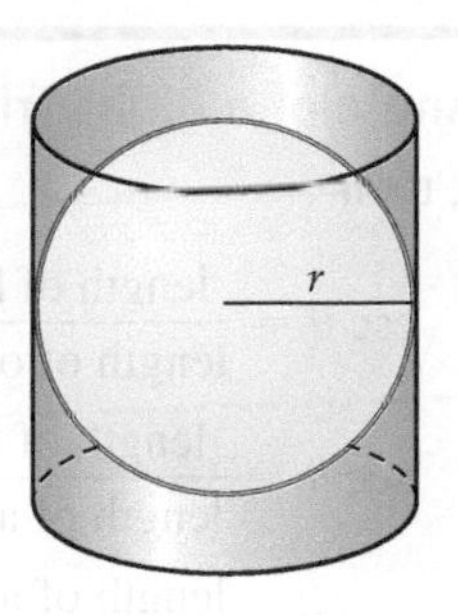

63. Determine whether the statement is always true, sometimes true, or never true.

a. The slant height of a regular square pyramid is longer than the height.

b. The slant height of a cone is shorter than the height.

c. The four triangular faces of a regular square pyramid are equilateral triangles.

64. a. What is the effect on the surface area of a rectangular solid of doubling the width and height?

b. What is the effect on the volume of a rectangular solid of doubling the length and width?

c. What is the effect on the volume of a cube of doubling the length of each side of the cube?

d. What is the effect on the surface area of a cylinder of doubling the radius and height?

65. Explain how you could cut through a cube so that the face of the resulting solid is

a. a square.

b. an equilateral triangle.

c. a trapezoid.

d. a hexagon.

SECTION 1.6 Right Triangle Trigonometry

Trigonometric Ratios of an Acute Angle

Consider the problem of engineers trying to determine the distance across a ravine in order to design a bridge. Look at the diagram at the left. It is fairly easy to measure the length of the side of the triangle that is on the land (100 ft), but the lengths of sides a and c cannot be measured easily because of the ravine.

The study of *trigonometry*, a term that comes from two Greek words meaning "triangle measurement," began about 2000 years ago, partially as a means of solving surveying problems such as the one described above. In this section, we will examine *right triangle* trigonometry—that is, trigonometry that applies only to right triangles.

When working with right triangles, it is convenient to refer to the side *opposite* an angle and the side *adjacent to* (next to) an angle. The hypotenuse of a right triangle is not adjacent to or opposite either of the acute angles of the triangle.

TAKE NOTE

In trigonometry, it is common practice to use Greek letters for the angles of a triangle. Here are some frequently used letters: α (alpha), β (beta), and θ (theta). The word *alphabet* is derived from the first two letters of the Greek alphabet, α and β.

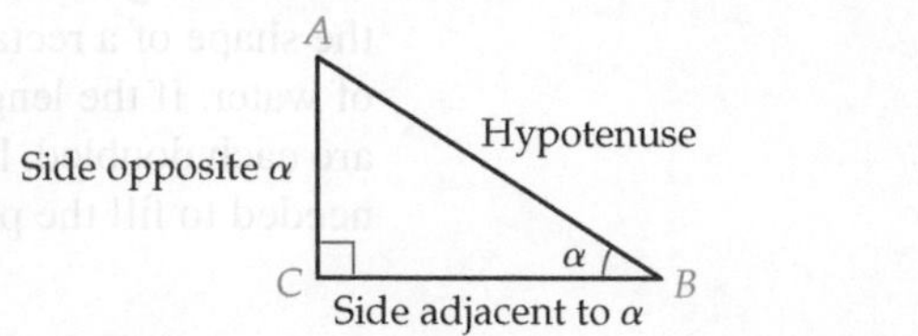

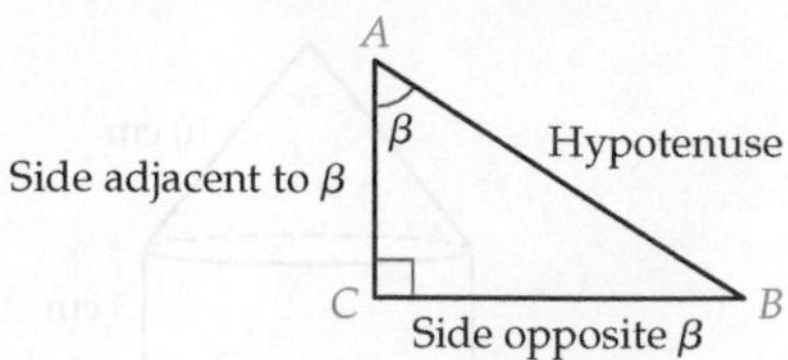

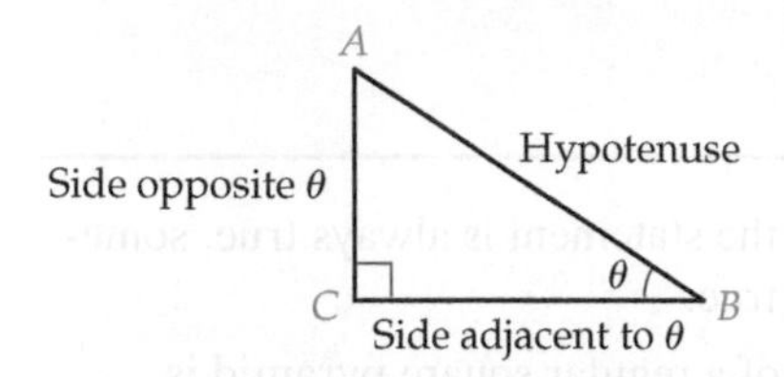

Consider the right triangle shown at the left. Six possible ratios can be formed using the lengths of the sides of the triangle.

$$\frac{\text{length of opposite side}}{\text{length of hypotenuse}} \qquad \frac{\text{length of hypotenuse}}{\text{length of opposite side}}$$

$$\frac{\text{length of adjacent side}}{\text{length of hypotenuse}} \qquad \frac{\text{length of hypotenuse}}{\text{length of adjacent side}}$$

$$\frac{\text{length of opposite side}}{\text{length of adjacent side}} \qquad \frac{\text{length of adjacent side}}{\text{length of opposite side}}$$

These ratios are called the **sine** (sin), **cosine** (cos), **tangent** (tan), **cosecant** (csc), **secant** (sec), and **cotangent** (cot) of the right triangle.

The Trigonometric Ratios of an Acute Angle of a Right Triangle

If θ is an acute angle of a right triangle ABC, then

$$\sin\theta = \frac{\text{length of opposite side}}{\text{length of hypotenuse}} \qquad \csc\theta = \frac{\text{length of hypotenuse}}{\text{length of opposite side}}$$

$$\cos\theta = \frac{\text{length of adjacent side}}{\text{length of hypotenuse}} \qquad \sec\theta = \frac{\text{length of hypotenuse}}{\text{length of adjacent side}}$$

$$\tan\theta = \frac{\text{length of opposite side}}{\text{length of adjacent side}} \qquad \cot\theta = \frac{\text{length of adjacent side}}{\text{length of opposite side}}$$

As a convenience, we will write opp, adj, and hyp as abbreviations for *the length of the* opposite side, adjacent side, and hypotenuse, respectively. Using this convention, the definitions of the trigonometric ratios are written as follows:

$$\sin\theta = \frac{\text{opp}}{\text{hyp}} \qquad \csc\theta = \frac{\text{hyp}}{\text{opp}}$$

$$\cos\theta = \frac{\text{adj}}{\text{hyp}} \qquad \sec\theta = \frac{\text{hyp}}{\text{adj}}$$

$$\tan\theta = \frac{\text{opp}}{\text{adj}} \qquad \cot\theta = \frac{\text{adj}}{\text{opp}}$$

For the remainder of this section, we will focus on the sine, cosine, and tangent ratios.

When working with trigonometric ratios, be sure to draw a diagram and label the adjacent and opposite sides of an angle. For instance, in the definition above, if we had placed θ at angle A, then the triangle would have been labeled as shown at the left. The definitions of the ratios remain the same.

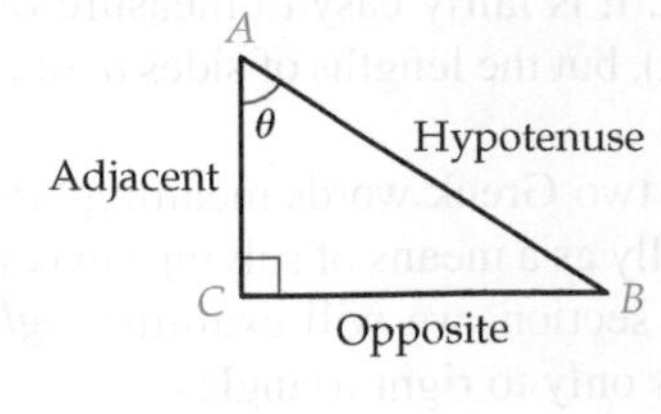

$$\sin\theta = \frac{\text{opp}}{\text{hyp}} \qquad \cos\theta = \frac{\text{adj}}{\text{hyp}} \qquad \tan\theta = \frac{\text{opp}}{\text{adj}}$$

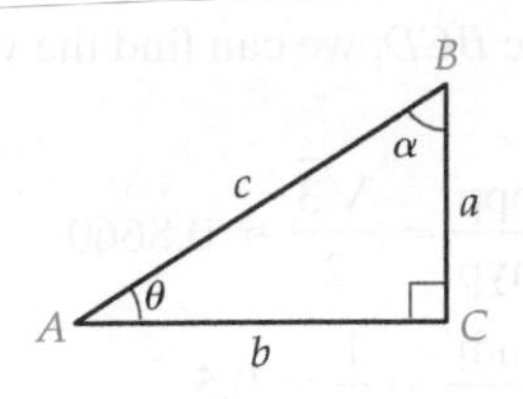

QUESTION For the right triangle shown at the left, indicate which side is

a. adjacent to $\angle A$ **b.** opposite θ **c.** adjacent to α **d.** opposite $\angle B$

EXAMPLE 1 Find the Values of Trigonometric Ratios

For the right triangle at the right, find the values of $\sin\theta$, $\cos\theta$, and $\tan\theta$.

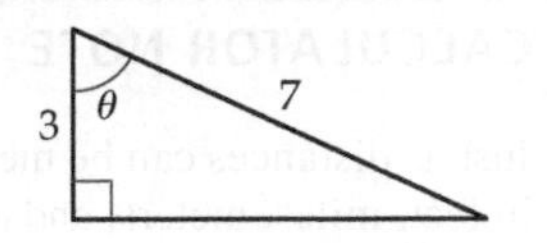

Solution

Use the Pythagorean theorem to find the length of the side opposite θ.

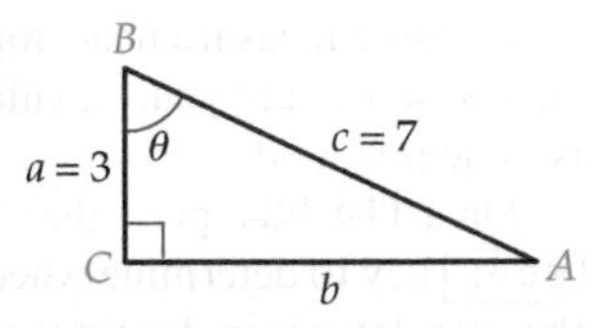

$$\begin{aligned} a^2 + b^2 &= c^2 && \bullet \text{ See the figure at the right.} \\ 3^2 + b^2 &= 7^2 && \bullet\ a = 3,\ c = 7 \\ 9 + b^2 &= 49 \\ b^2 &= 40 \\ b &= \sqrt{40} = 2\sqrt{10} \end{aligned}$$

Using the definitions of the trigonometric ratios, we have

$$\sin\theta = \frac{\text{opp}}{\text{hyp}} = \frac{2\sqrt{10}}{7} \qquad \cos\theta = \frac{\text{adj}}{\text{hyp}} = \frac{3}{7} \qquad \tan\theta = \frac{\text{opp}}{\text{adj}} = \frac{2\sqrt{10}}{3}$$

CHECK YOUR PROGRESS 1

For the right triangle at the right, find the values of $\sin\theta$, $\cos\theta$, and $\tan\theta$.

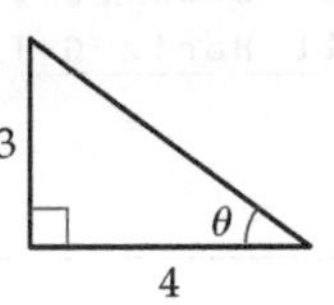

Solution See page S3.

In Example 1, we gave the exact answers. In many cases, approximate values of trigonometric ratios are given. The answers to Example 1, rounded to the nearest ten-thousandth, are

$$\sin\theta = \frac{2\sqrt{10}}{7} \approx 0.9035 \qquad \cos\theta = \frac{3}{7} \approx 0.4286 \qquad \tan\theta = \frac{2\sqrt{10}}{3} \approx 2.1082$$

We will sometimes want to know the value of a trigonometric ratio for a given angle. Triangle ABC at the left is an equilateral triangle with sides of length 2 units and angle bisector $\overline{BD}$. Because $\overline{BD}$ bisects $\angle ABC$, the measures of $\angle ABD$ and $\angle DBC$ are both 30°. The angle bisector $\overline{BD}$ also bisects $\overline{AC}$. Therefore, $AD = 1$ and $DC = 1$. Using the Pythagorean theorem, we can find the measure of BD.

$$\begin{aligned} (DC)^2 + (BD)^2 &= (BC)^2 \\ 1^2 + (BD)^2 &= 2^2 && \bullet\ DC = 1,\ BC = 2 \\ 1 + (BD)^2 &= 4 && \bullet \text{ Solve for } BD. \\ (BD)^2 &= 3 \\ BD &= \sqrt{3} \end{aligned}$$

ANSWER **a.** b **b.** a **c.** a **d.** b

Using the definitions of the trigonometric ratios and triangle BCD, we can find the values of the sine, cosine, and tangent of 30° and 60°.

$$\sin 30° = \frac{\text{opp}}{\text{hyp}} = \frac{1}{2} = 0.5 \qquad \sin 60° = \frac{\text{opp}}{\text{hyp}} = \frac{\sqrt{3}}{2} \approx 0.8660$$

$$\cos 30° = \frac{\text{adj}}{\text{hyp}} = \frac{\sqrt{3}}{2} \approx 0.8660 \qquad \cos 60° = \frac{\text{adj}}{\text{hyp}} = \frac{1}{2} = 0.5$$

$$\tan 30° = \frac{\text{opp}}{\text{adj}} = \frac{1}{\sqrt{3}} \approx 0.5774 \qquad \tan 60° = \frac{\text{opp}}{\text{adj}} = \sqrt{3} \approx 1.7320$$

CALCULATOR NOTE

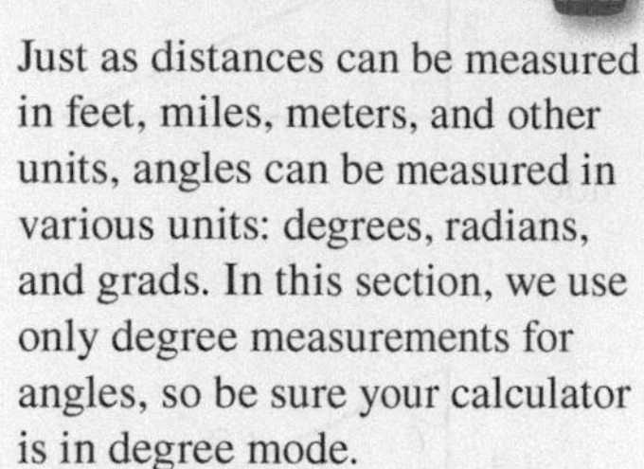

Just as distances can be measured in feet, miles, meters, and other units, angles can be measured in various units: degrees, radians, and grads. In this section, we use only degree measurements for angles, so be sure your calculator is in degree mode.

On a TI-83/84, press the MODE key to determine whether the calculator is in degree mode.

```
Normal Sci Eng
Float 0123456789
Radian Degree
Func Par Pol Seq
Connected Dot
Sequential Simul
Real a+bi re^θi
Full Horiz G-T
```

The properties of an equilateral triangle enabled us to calculate the values of the trigonometric ratios for 30° and 60°. Calculating values of the trigonometric ratios for most other angles, however, would be quite difficult. Fortunately, many calculators have been programmed to allow us to estimate these values.

To find tan 30° on a TI-83/84 calculator, first confirm that your calculator is in "degree mode." Press the TAN key and type in 30). Then press ENTER.

$\tan 30° \approx 0.5774$

On a scientific calculator, type in 30, and then press the TAN key.

Use a calculator to find sin 43.8° and tan 37.1° to the nearest ten-thousandth.

$\sin 43.8° \approx 0.6921$

$\tan 37.1° \approx 0.7563$

The engineers mentioned at the beginning of this section could use trigonometry to determine the distance across the ravine. Suppose the engineers measure angle A as 33.8°. Now they would ask, "Which trigonometric ratio, sine, cosine, or tangent, involves the side opposite angle A and the side adjacent to angle A?" Knowing that the tangent ratio is the required ratio, the engineers could write and solve the equation

$$\tan 33.8° = \frac{a}{100}$$

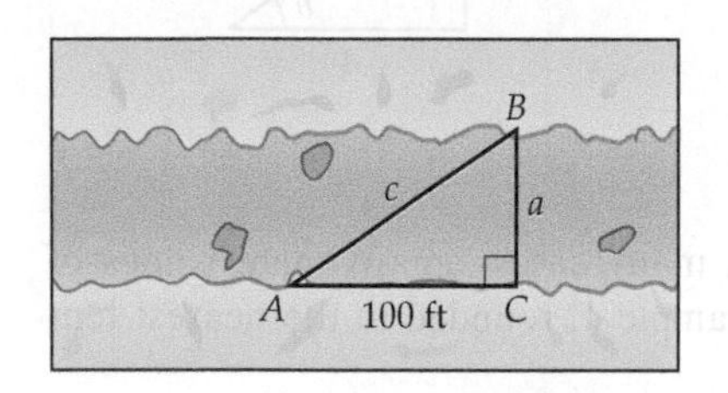

$\tan 33.8° = \frac{a}{100}$

$100(\tan 33.8°) = a$ • Multiply each side of the equation by 100.

$66.9 \approx a$ • Use a calculator to find tan 33.8°. Multiply the result in the display by 100.

The distance across the ravine is approximately 66.9 feet.

EXAMPLE 2 Find the Length of a Side of a Triangle

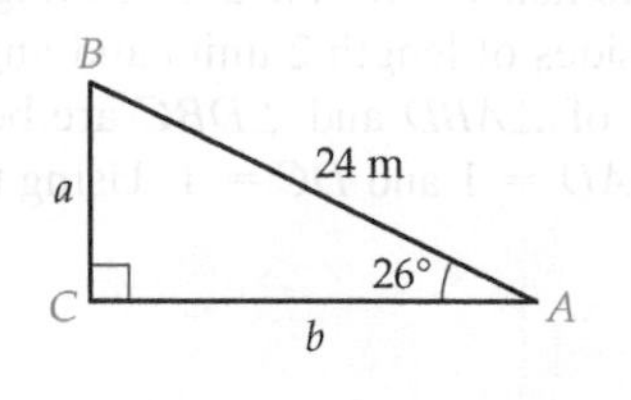

For the right triangle shown at the left, find the length of side a. Round to the nearest tenth of a meter.

Solution

We are given the measure of $\angle A$ and the hypotenuse. We want to find the length of side a. Side a is opposite $\angle A$. The sine function involves the side opposite an angle and the hypotenuse.

$\sin A = \frac{\text{opp}}{\text{hyp}}$

$\sin 26° = \frac{a}{24}$ • $A = 26°$, hypotenuse $= 24$ m

$24(\sin 26°) = a$ • Multiply each side by 24.

$10.5 \approx a$ • Use a calculator to find sin 26°. Multiply the result in the display by 24.

The length of side a is approximately 10.5 m.

CHECK YOUR PROGRESS 2

For the right triangle shown at the right, find the length of side a. Round to the nearest tenth of a foot.

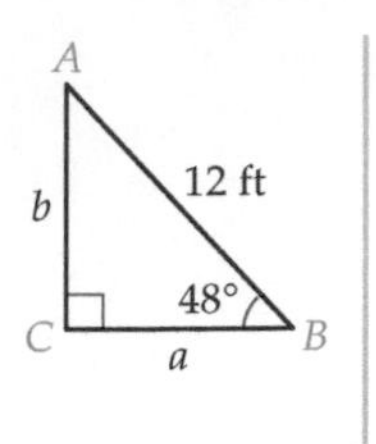

Solution See page S3.

Inverse Sine, Inverse Cosine, and Inverse Tangent

Suppose it is necessary to find the measure of $\angle A$ in the figure at the left. Because the length of the side adjacent to $\angle A$ is known and the length of the hypotenuse is known, we can write

$$\cos A = \frac{\text{adj}}{\text{hyp}}$$

$$\cos A = \frac{25}{27}$$

The solution of this equation is the angle whose cosine is $\frac{25}{27}$. This angle can be found by using the $\cos^{-1}$ key on a calculator. The expression $\cos^{-1}$ is read "the inverse cosine of."

$$\cos^{-1}\left(\frac{25}{27}\right) \approx 22.19160657$$

To the nearest tenth of a degree, the measure of $\angle A$ is 22.2°.

TAKE NOTE

The expression $\sin^{-1}(x)$ is sometimes written $\arcsin(x)$. The two expressions are equivalent. The expressions $\cos^{-1}(x)$ and $\arccos(x)$ are equivalent, as are $\tan^{-1}(x)$ and $\arctan(x)$.

Inverse Sine, Inverse Cosine, and Inverse Tangent

$\sin^{-1}(x)$ is defined as the angle whose sine is x, $0 < x < 1$.
$\cos^{-1}(x)$ is defined as the angle whose cosine is x, $0 < x < 1$.
$\tan^{-1}(x)$ is defined as the angle whose tangent is x, $x > 0$.

CALCULATOR NOTE

To find an inverse on a calculator, usually the INV or 2ND key is pressed prior to pushing the SIN, COS, or TAN key. Some calculators have $\sin^{-1}$, $\cos^{-1}$, and $\tan^{-1}$ keys. Consult the instruction manual for your calculator.

EXAMPLE 3 Evaluate an Inverse Sine Expression

Use a calculator to find $\sin^{-1}(0.9171)$. Round to the nearest tenth of a degree.

Solution

$\sin^{-1}(0.9171) \approx 66.5°$ • The calculator must be in degree mode. Press the keys for inverse sine followed by .9171). Press ENTER.

CHECK YOUR PROGRESS 3 Use a calculator to find $\tan^{-1}(0.3165)$. Round to the nearest tenth of a degree.

Solution See page S3.

TAKE NOTE

If

$\sin\theta = 0.7239$,

then

$\theta = \sin^{-1}(0.7239)$.

EXAMPLE 4 Find the Measure of an Angle Using Inverse Sine

Given $\sin\theta = 0.7239$, find θ. Use a calculator. Round to the nearest tenth of a degree.

Solution

This is equivalent to finding $\sin^{-1}(0.7239)$. The calculator must be in degree mode.

$$\sin^{-1}(0.7239) \approx 46.4°$$
$$\theta \approx 46.4°$$

CHECK YOUR PROGRESS 4 Given $\tan\theta = 0.5681$, find θ. Use a calculator. Round to the nearest tenth of a degree.

Solution See page S3.

EXAMPLE 5 Find the Measure of an Angle in a Right Triangle

For the right triangle shown at the left, find the measure of $\angle B$. Round to the nearest tenth of a degree.

Solution

We want to find the measure of $\angle B$, and we are given the lengths of the sides opposite $\angle B$ and adjacent to $\angle B$. The tangent ratio involves the side opposite an angle and the side adjacent to that angle.

$$\tan B = \frac{\text{opp}}{\text{adj}}$$

$$\tan B = \frac{24}{16}$$

$$B = \tan^{-1}\left(\frac{24}{16}\right)$$

$$B \approx 56.3^\circ$$ • Use the $\tan^{-1}$ key on a calculator.

The measure of $\angle B$ is approximately 56.3°.

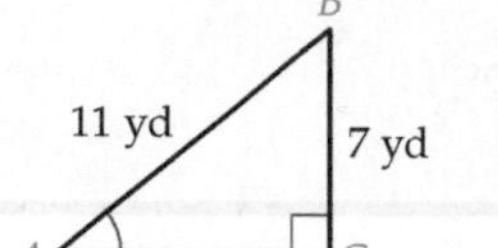

CHECK YOUR PROGRESS 5 For the right triangle shown at the left, find the measure of $\angle A$. Round to the nearest tenth of a degree.

Solution See page S4.

Angles of Elevation and Depression

One application of trigonometry, called **line-of-sight problems**, concerns an observer looking at an object.

Angles of elevation and depression are measured with respect to a horizontal line. If the object being sighted is above the observer, the acute angle formed by the line of sight and the horizontal line is an **angle of elevation**. If the object being sighted is below the observer, the acute angle formed by the line of sight and the horizontal line is an **angle of depression**.

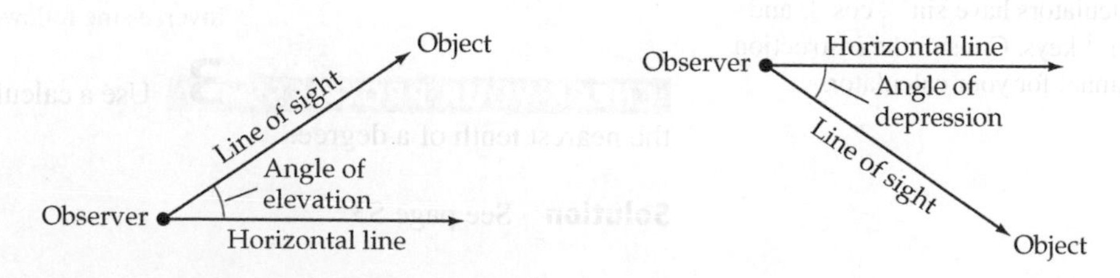

EXAMPLE 6 Solve an Angle of Elevation Problem

The angle of elevation from a point 62 ft away from the base of a flagpole to the top of the flagpole is 34°. Find the height of the flagpole. Round to the nearest tenth of a foot.

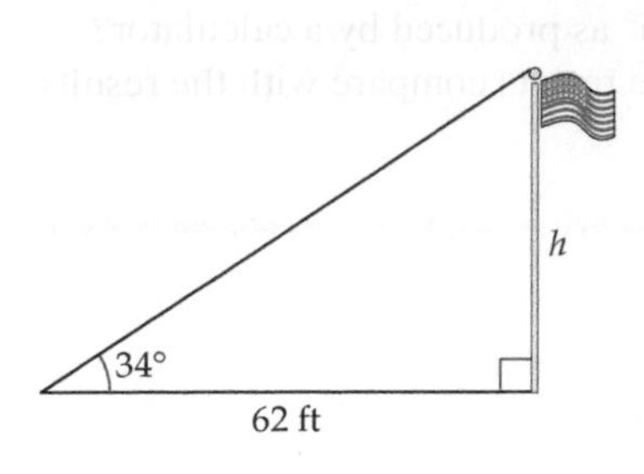

Solution

Draw a diagram. To find the height, h, write a trigonometric ratio that relates the given information and the unknown side of the triangle.

$$\tan 34° = \frac{h}{62}$$

$$62(\tan 34°) = h \quad \text{• Solve for } h.$$

$$41.8 \approx h \quad \text{• Use a calculator to find } \tan 34°. \text{ Multiply the result in the display by 62.}$$

The height of the flagpole is approximately 41.8 ft.

CHECK YOUR PROGRESS 6 The angle of depression from the top of a lighthouse that is 20 m high to a boat on the water is 25°. How far is the boat from the base of the lighthouse? Round to the nearest tenth of a meter.

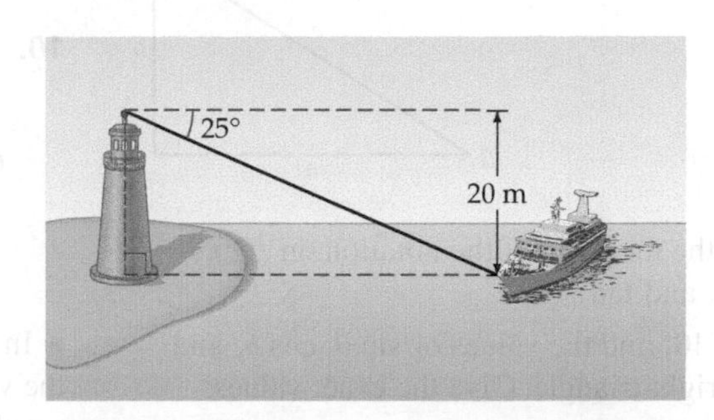

Solution See page S4.

EXCURSION

Approximating the Value of a Trigonometric Ratio

The value of a trigonometric ratio can be approximated by drawing a triangle with a given angle. To illustrate, we will choose an angle of 35°.

To find the tangent of 35° using the definitions given in this section, we can carefully construct a right triangle containing an angle of 35°. Because any two right triangles containing an angle of 35° are similar, *the value of tan 35° is the same no matter what triangle we draw.*

EXCURSION EXERCISES

1. Draw a horizontal line segment 10 cm long with left endpoint A and right endpoint C. See the diagram at the left.
2. Using a protractor, construct at A a 35° angle.
3. Draw at C a vertical line that intersects the terminal side of angle A at B. Your drawing should be similar to the one at the left.
4. Measure line segment BC to the nearest tenth of a centimeter.
5. Use your measurements to determine the approximate value of tan 35°.
6. Using your value for BC and the Pythagorean theorem, estimate AB. Round to the nearest centimeter.

7. Estimate sin 35° and cos 35°.

8. What are the values of sin 35°, cos 35°, and tan 35° as produced by a calculator? Round to the nearest ten-thousandth. How do these results compare with the results you obtained in Exercises 5 and 7?

EXERCISE SET 1.6

1. Use the right triangle below and sides a, b, and c to do the following:

a. Find sin A.

b. Find sin B.

c. Find cos A.

d. Find cos B.

e. Find tan A.

f. Find tan B.

A c b B a C

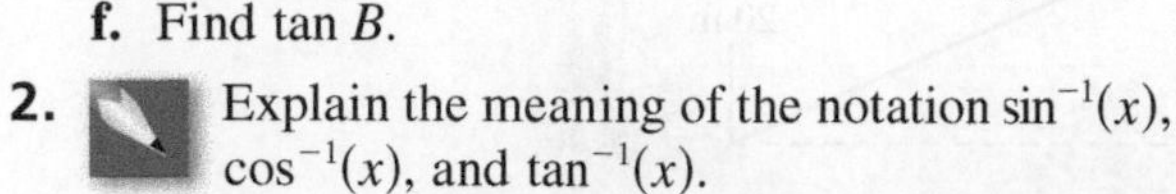

2. Explain the meaning of the notation $\sin^{-1}(x)$, $\cos^{-1}(x)$, and $\tan^{-1}(x)$.

■ In Exercises 3 to 10, find the values of sin θ, cos θ, and tan θ for the given right triangle. Give the exact values.

3.

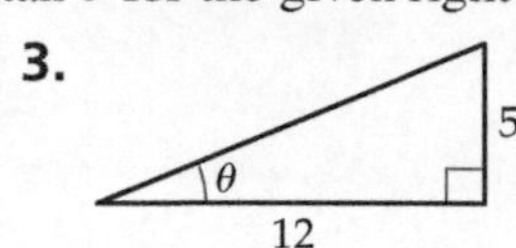

4.

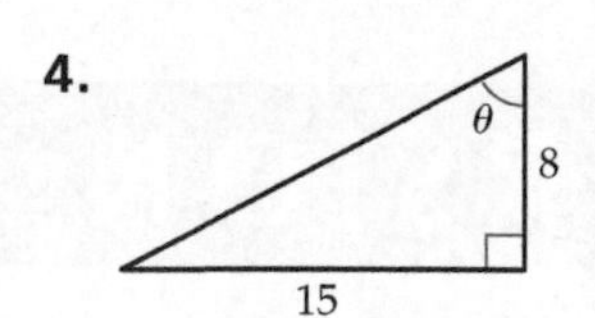

5.

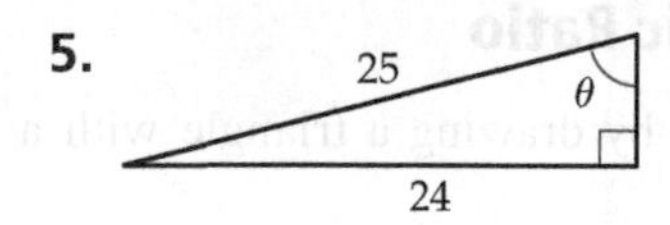

6.

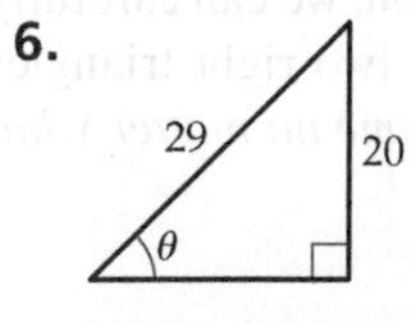

7.

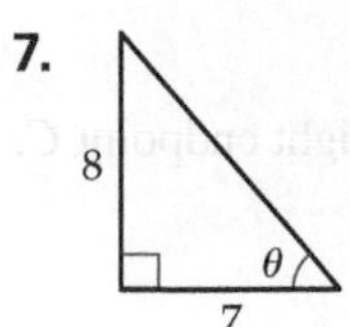

8.

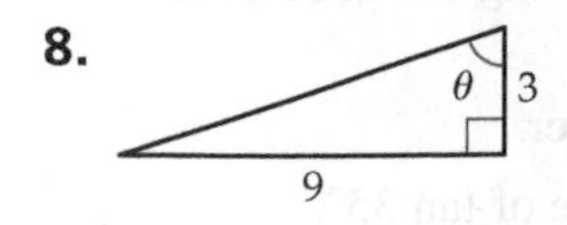

9.

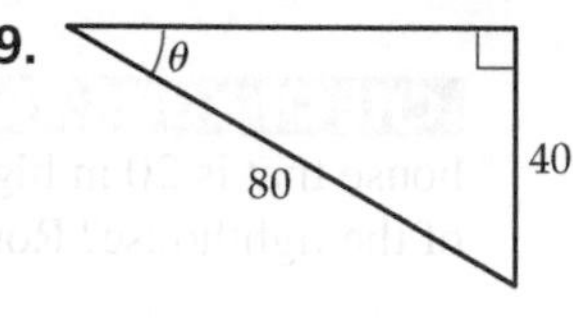

10.

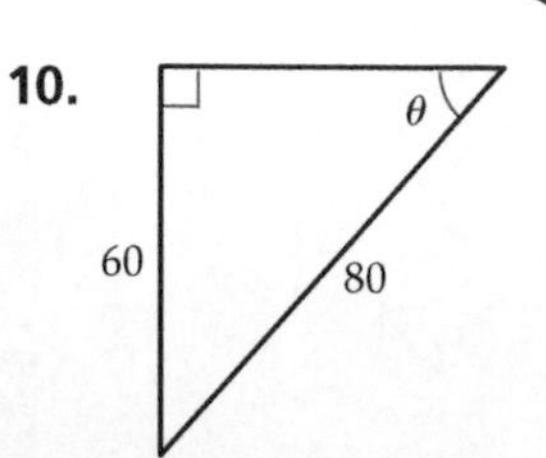

■ In Exercises 11 to 26, use a calculator to estimate the value of each of the following. Round to the nearest ten-thousandth.

11. cos 47° **12.** sin 62° **13.** tan 55°

14. cos 11° **15.** sin 85.6° **16.** cos 21.9°

17. tan 63.4° **18.** sin 7.8° **19.** tan 41.6°

20. cos 73° **21.** sin 57.7° **22.** tan 39.2°

23. sin 58.3° **24.** tan 35.1° **25.** cos 46.9°

26. sin 50°

■ In Exercises 27 to 42, use a calculator. Round to the nearest tenth of a degree.

27. Given $\sin\theta = 0.6239$, find θ.

28. Given $\cos\beta = 0.9516$, find β.

29. Find $\cos^{-1}(0.7536)$.

30. Find $\sin^{-1}(0.4478)$.

31. Given $\tan\alpha = 0.3899$, find α.

32. Given $\sin\beta = 0.7349$, find β.

33. Find $\tan^{-1}(0.7815)$.

34. Find $\cos^{-1}(0.6032)$.

35. Given $\cos\theta = 0.3007$, find θ.

36. Given $\tan\alpha = 1.588$, find α.

37. Find $\sin^{-1}(0.0105)$.

38. Find $\tan^{-1}(0.2438)$.

39. Given $\sin\beta = 0.9143$, find β.

40. Given $\cos\theta = 0.4756$, find θ.

41. Find $\cos^{-1}(0.8704)$.

42. Find $\sin^{-1}(0.2198)$.

■ For Exercises 43 to 56, draw a picture and label it. Then set up an equation and solve it. Show all your work. Round the measure of each angle to the nearest tenth of a degree. Round the length of a side to the nearest tenth of a unit. Assume the ground is level unless indicated otherwise.

43. Ballooning A balloon, tethered by a cable 997 ft long, was blown by a wind so that the cable made an angle of 57.6° with the ground. Find the height of the balloon off the ground.

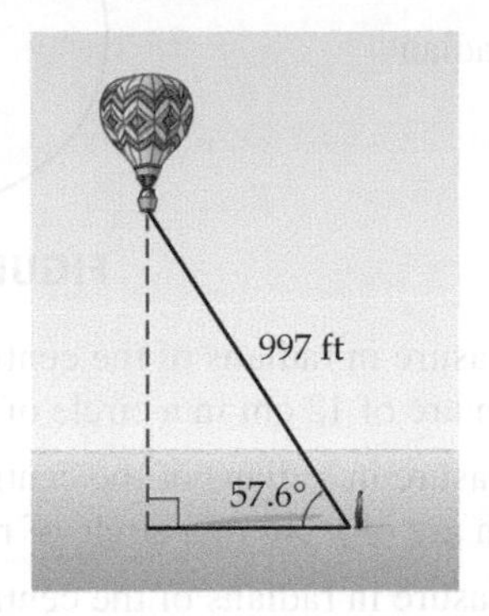

44. Roadways A road is inclined at an angle of 9.8° with the horizontal. Find the distance that one must drive on this road in order to be elevated 14.8 ft above the horizontal.

45. Home Maintenance A ladder 30.8 ft long leans against a building. If the foot of the ladder is 7.25 ft from the base of the building, find the angle the top of the ladder makes with the building.

46. Aviation A plane takes off from a field and rises at an angle of 11.4° with the horizontal. Find the height of the plane after it has traveled a distance of 1250 ft.

47. Guy Wires A guy wire whose grounded end is 16 ft from the telephone pole it supports makes an angle of 56.7° with the ground. How long is the wire?

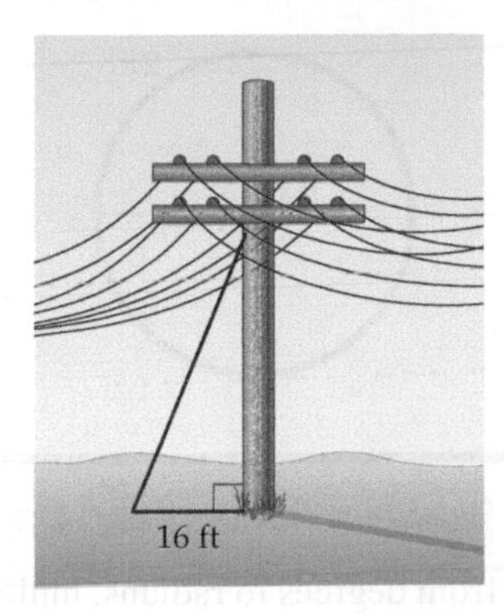

48. Angle of Depression A lighthouse built at sea level is 169 ft tall. From its top, the angle of depression to a boat below measures 25.1°. Find the distance from the boat to the foot of the lighthouse.

49. Angle of Elevation At a point 39.3 ft from the base of a tree, the angle of elevation of its top measures 53.4°. Find the height of the tree.

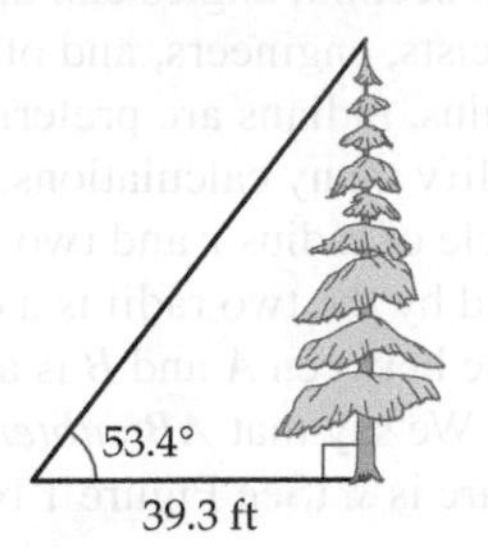

50. Angle of Depression An artillery spotter in a plane that is at an altitude of 978 ft measures the angle of depression of an enemy tank as 28.5°. How far is the enemy tank from the point on the ground directly below the spotter?

51. Home Maintenance A 15-foot ladder leans against a house. The ladder makes an angle of 65° with the ground. How far up the side of the house does the ladder reach?

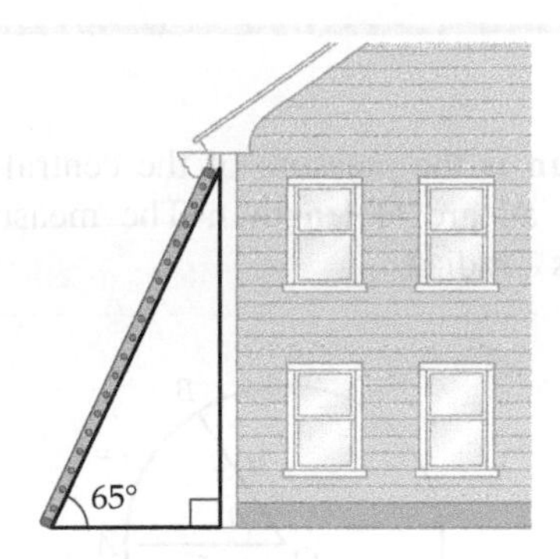

52. Angle of Elevation Find the angle of elevation of the sun when a tree 40.5 ft high casts a shadow 28.3 ft long.

53. Guy Wires A television transmitter tower is 600 ft high. If the angle between the guy wire (attached at the top) and the tower is 55.4°, how long is the guy wire?

54. Ramps A ramp used to load a racing car onto a flatbed carrier is 5.25 m long, and its upper end is 1.74 m above the lower end. Find the angle between the ramp and the road.

55. Angle of Elevation The angle of elevation of the sun is 51.3° at a time when a tree casts a shadow 23.7 yd long. Find the height of the tree.

56. Angle of Depression From the top of a building 312 ft tall, the angle of depression to a flower bed on the ground below is 12.0°. What is the distance between the base of the building and the flower bed?

EXTENSIONS

As we noted in this section, angles can also be measured in *radians*. For physicists, engineers, and other applied scientists who use calculus, radians are preferred over degrees because they simplify many calculations. To define a radian, first consider a circle of radius r and two radii $\overline{OA}$ and $\overline{OB}$. The angle θ formed by the two radii is a **central angle**. The portion of the circle between A and B is an **arc** of the circle and is written $\widehat{AB}$. We say that $\widehat{AB}$ *subtends* the angle θ. The length of the arc is s. (See Figure 1 below.)

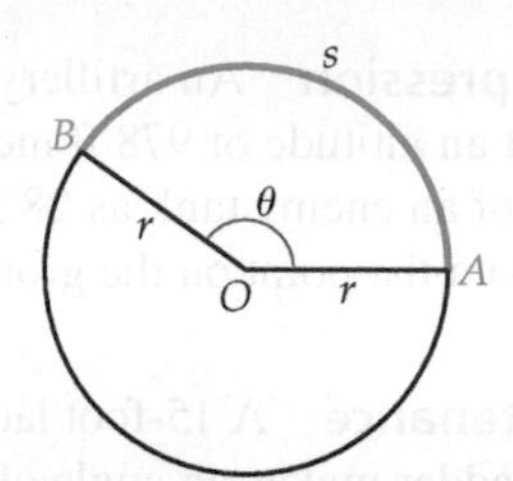

FIGURE 1

Radian

One **radian** is the measure of the central angle subtended by an arc of length r. The measure of θ in Figure 2 is 1 radian.

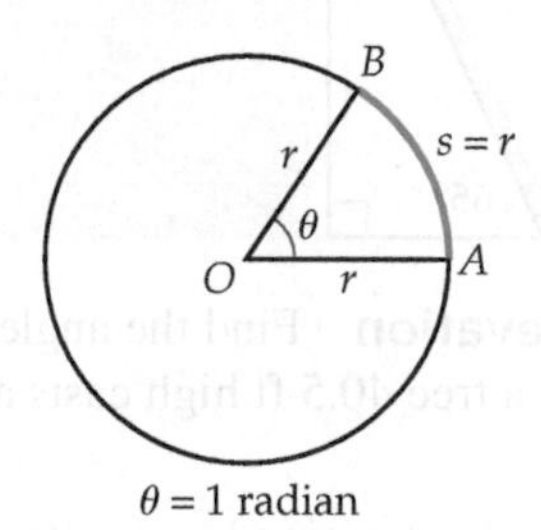

FIGURE 2

To find the radian measure of an angle subtended by an arc of length s, use the following formula.

Radian Measure

Given an arc of length s on a circle of radius r, the measure of the central angle subtended by the arc is

$\theta = \dfrac{s}{r}$ radians.

For example, to find the measure in radians of the central angle subtended by an arc of 9 in. in a circle of radius 12 in., divide the length of the arc ($s = 9$ in.) by the length of the radius ($r = 12$ in.). See Figure 3.

$$\theta = \frac{9 \text{ in.}}{12 \text{ in.}} \text{ radian}$$

$$= \frac{3}{4} \text{ radian}$$

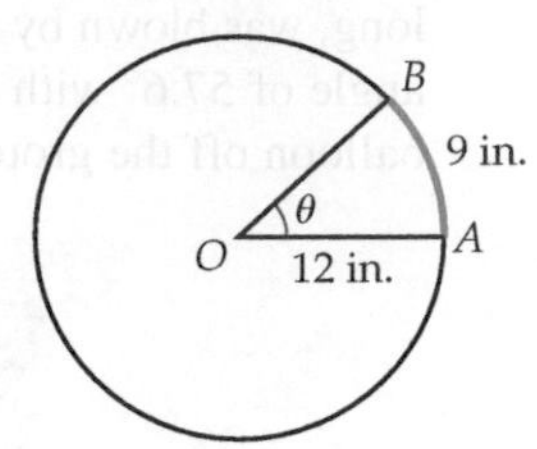

FIGURE 3

57. Find the measure in radians of the central angle subtended by an arc of 12 cm in a circle of radius 3 cm.

58. Find the measure in radians of the central angle subtended by an arc of 4 cm in a circle of radius 8 cm.

59. Find the measure in radians of the central angle subtended by an arc of 6 in. in a circle of radius 9 in.

60. Find the measure in radians of the central angle subtended by an arc of 12 ft in a circle of radius 10 ft.

Recall that the circumference of a circle is given by $C = 2\pi r$. Therefore, the radian measure of the central angle subtended by the circumference is $\theta = \dfrac{2\pi r}{r} = 2\pi$.

In degree measure, the central angle has a measure of 360°. Thus we have 2π radians = 360°. Dividing each side of the equation by 2 gives π radians = 180°. From the last equation, we can establish the conversion factors $\dfrac{\pi \text{ radians}}{180°}$ and $\dfrac{180°}{\pi \text{ radians}}$. These conversion factors are used to convert between radians and degrees.

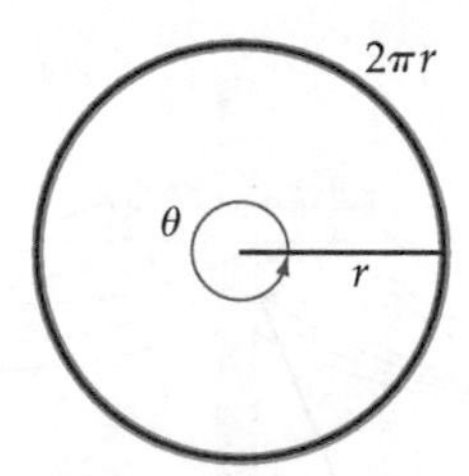

Conversion Between Radians and Degrees

- To convert from degrees to radians, multiply by $\dfrac{\pi \text{ radians}}{180°}$.
- To convert from radians to degrees, multiply by $\dfrac{180°}{\pi \text{ radians}}$.

For instance, to convert 30° to radians, multiply 30° by $\frac{\pi \text{ radians}}{180°}$.

$$30° = 30°\left(\frac{\pi \text{ radians}}{180°}\right)$$
$$= \frac{\pi}{6} \text{ radian} \quad \text{• Exact answer}$$
$$\approx 0.5236 \text{ radian} \quad \text{• Approximate answer}$$

To convert 2 radians to degrees, multiply 2 by $\frac{180°}{\pi \text{ radians}}$.

$$2 \text{ radians} = 2\left(\frac{180°}{\pi \text{ radians}}\right)$$
$$= \left(\frac{360}{\pi}\right)° \quad \text{• Exact answer}$$
$$\approx 114.5916° \quad \text{• Approximate answer}$$

61. What is the measure in degrees of 1 radian?

62. Is the measure of 1 radian larger or smaller than the measure of 1°?

■ In Exercises 63 to 68, convert degree measure to radian measure. Find an exact answer and an answer rounded to the nearest ten-thousandth.

63. 45° **64.** 180° **65.** 315°

66. 90° **67.** 210° **68.** 18°

■ In Exercises 69 to 74, convert radian measure to degree measure. For Exercises 72 to 74, find an exact answer and an answer rounded to the nearest ten-thousandth.

69. $\frac{\pi}{3}$ radians **70.** $\frac{11\pi}{6}$ radians

71. $\frac{4\pi}{3}$ radians **72.** 1.2 radians

73. 3 radians **74.** 2.4 radians

SECTION 1.7 Non-Euclidean Geometry

Euclidean Geometry vs. Non-Euclidean Geometry

Some of the most popular games are based on a handful of rules that are easy to learn but still allow the game to develop into complex situations. The ancient Greek mathematician Euclid wanted to establish a geometry that was based on the *fewest* possible number of rules. He called these rules **postulates**. Euclid based his geometry on the following five postulates.

TAKE NOTE

In addition to postulates, Euclid's geometry, referred to as *Euclidean geometry*, involves definitions and some *undefined terms*. For instance, the term *point* is an undefined term in Euclidean geometry because any definition of the term *point* would require additional undefined terms. In a similar way, the term *line* is also an undefined term in Euclidean geometry.

Euclid's Postulates

P1: A line segment can be drawn from any point to any other point.

P2: A line segment can be extended continuously in a straight line.

P3: A circle can be drawn with any center and any radius.

P4: All right angles have the same measure.

P5: ***The Parallel Postulate*** Through a given point not on a given line, exactly one line can be drawn parallel to the given line.

For many centuries, the truth of these postulates was felt to be self-evident. However, a few mathematicians suspected that the fifth postulate, known as the parallel postulate, could be deduced from the other postulates. Over the years, many mathematicians tried to prove the parallel postulate, but none were successful.

Carl Friedrich Gauss (gaus') (1777–1855) was one such mathematician. After many failed attempts to establish the parallel postulate as a theorem, Gauss came to the conclusion that the parallel postulate was an independent postulate. However, he noted that by changing this one postulate, he could create a whole new type of geometry! This is analogous to changing one of the rules of a game to create a new game.

Gauss's Alternative to the Parallel Postulate

Through a given point not on a given line, there are *at least two* lines parallel to the given line.

HISTORICAL NOTE

Nikolai Lobachevsky (lō′bə-chĕf′skē) (1793–1856) was a noted Russian mathematician. Lobachevsky's concept of a non-Euclidean geometry was so revolutionary that he is called the Copernicus of geometry.

The Granger Collection, NY

Another pioneer in **non-Euclidean geometry** (any geometry that does not include Euclid's parallel postulate) was the Russian mathematician Nikolai Lobachevsky. In a series of monthly articles that appeared in the academic journal of the University of Kazan in 1829, Lobachevsky provided a detailed investigation into the problem of the parallel postulate. He proposed that a consistent new geometry could be developed by replacing the parallel postulate with the alternative postulate, which assumes that *more than one* parallel line can be drawn through a point not on a given line. This new geometry, developed independently by both Gauss and Lobachevsky, is often called *hyperbolic geometry*.

The year 1826, in which Lobachevsky first lectured about a new non-Euclidean geometry, also marks the birth of the mathematician Bernhard Riemann. Although Riemann died of tuberculosis at age 39, he made major contributions in several areas of mathematics and physics. Riemann was the first person to consider a geometry in which the parallel postulate was replaced with the following postulate.

HISTORICAL NOTE

Bernhard Riemann (rē′mən) (1826–1866). "Riemann's achievement has taught mathematicians to disbelieve in *any* geometry, or any space, as a necessary mode of human perception."[2]

The Granger Collection, NY

Riemann's Alternative to the Parallel Postulate

Through a given point not on a given line, there exist *no* lines parallel to the given line.

Unlike the geometry developed by Lobachevsky, which was not based on a physical model, the non-Euclidean geometry of Riemann was closely associated with a sphere and the remarkable idea that because a line is an undefined term, a line on the surface of a sphere can be different from a line on a plane. It seems reasonable to suspect that "spherical lines" should retain some of the properties of lines on a plane. For example, on a plane, the shortest distance between two points is measured along the line that connects the points. The line that connects the points is an example of what is called a *geodesic*.

Geodesic

A **geodesic** is a curve C on a surface S such that for any two points on C, the portion of C between these points is the shortest path on S that joins these points.

On a sphere, the geodesic between two points is a *great circle* that connects the points.

Great Circle

A **great circle** of a sphere is a circle on the surface of the sphere whose center is at the center of the sphere. Any two points on a great circle divide the circle into two arcs. The shorter arc is the **minor arc**, and the longer arc is the **major arc**.

[2] Bell, E. T. *Men of Mathematics*. New York: Touchstone Books, Simon and Schuster, 1986.

In *Riemannian geometry*, which is also called *spherical geometry* or *elliptical geometry*, great circles, which are the geodesics of a sphere, are thought of as lines. Figure 1.2 shows a sphere and two of its great circles. Because all great circles of a sphere intersect, a sphere provides us with a model of a geometry in which there are no parallel lines.

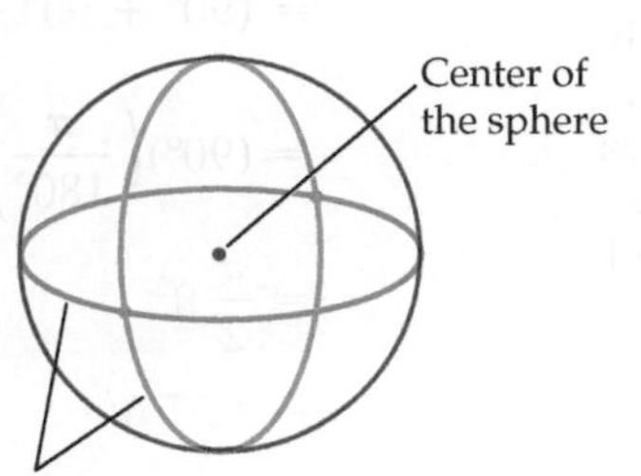

FIGURE 1.2 A sphere and its great circles serve as a physical model for Riemannian geometry.

TAKE NOTE

Riemannian geometry has many applications. For instance, because Earth is nearly spherical, navigation over long distances is facilitated by the use of Riemannian geometry as opposed to Euclidean geometry.

In Riemannian geometry, a triangle may have as many as three right angles. Figure 1.3 illustrates a spherical triangle with one right angle, a spherical triangle with two right angles, and a spherical triangle with three right angles.

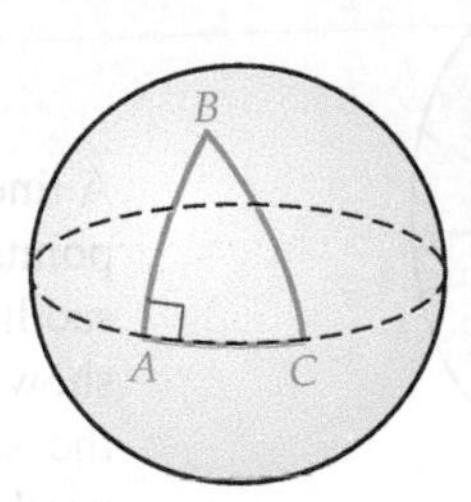

a. A spherical triangle with one right angle

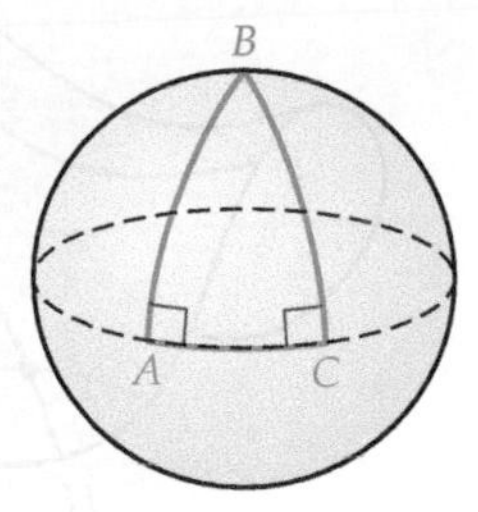

b. A spherical triangle with two right angles

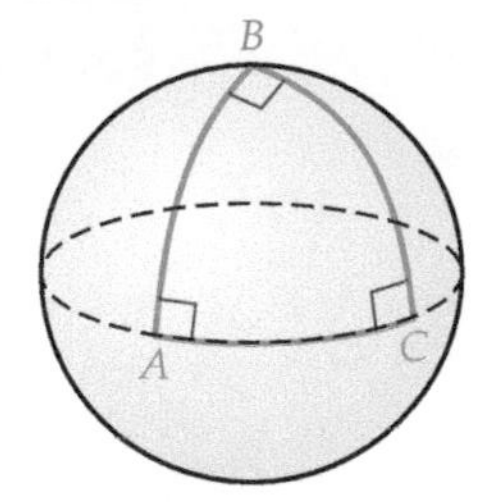

c. A spherical triangle with three right angles

FIGURE 1.3

The Spherical Triangle Area Formula

The area S of the spherical triangle ABC on a sphere with radius r is given by

$$S = (m\angle A + m\angle B + m\angle C - 180°)\left(\frac{\pi}{180°}\right)r^2$$

where each angle is measured in degrees.

EXAMPLE 1 Find the Area of a Spherical Triangle

Find the area of a spherical triangle with three right angles on a sphere with a radius of 1 ft. Find both the exact area and the approximate area rounded to the nearest hundredth of a square foot.

TAKE NOTE

To check the result in Example 1, use the fact that the given triangle covers $\frac{1}{8}$ of the surface of the sphere. See Figure 1.3c. The total surface area of a sphere is $4\pi r^2$. In Example 1, $r = 1$ ft, so the sphere has a surface area of 4π ft². Thus the area of the spherical triangle in Example 1 should be

$$\left(\frac{1}{8}\right)(4\pi) = \frac{\pi}{2}\text{ ft}^2$$

Solution

Apply the spherical triangle area formula.

$$S = (m\angle A + m\angle B + m\angle C - 180°)\left(\frac{\pi}{180°}\right)r^2$$
$$= (90° + 90° + 90° - 180°)\left(\frac{\pi}{180°}\right)(1)^2$$
$$= (90°)\left(\frac{\pi}{180°}\right)$$
$$= \frac{\pi}{2}\text{ ft}^2 \quad \text{• Exact area}$$
$$\approx 1.57\text{ ft}^2 \quad \text{• Approximate area}$$

CHECK YOUR PROGRESS 1 Find the area of the spherical triangle whose angles measure 200°, 90°, and 90° on a sphere with a radius of 6 in. Find both the exact area and the approximate area rounded to the nearest hundredth of a square inch.

Solution See page S4.

Mathematicians have not been able to create a three-dimensional model that *perfectly* illustrates all aspects of hyperbolic geometry. However, an infinite saddle surface can be used to visualize some of the basic aspects of hyperbolic geometry. Figure 1.4 shows a portion of an infinite saddle surface.

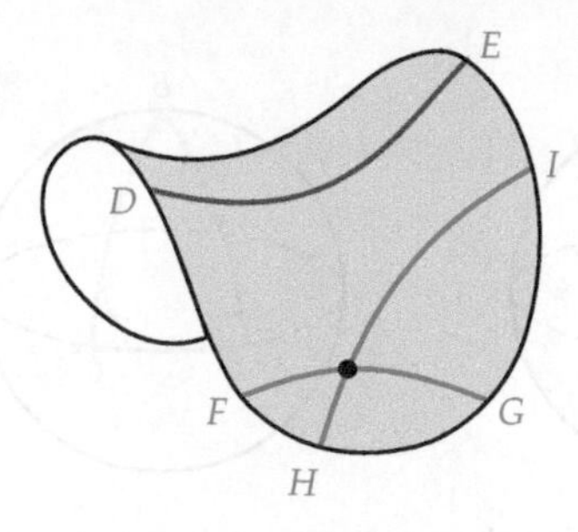

FIGURE 1.4 Portion of an infinite saddle surface

A line (geodesic) can be drawn through any two points on the saddle surface. Most lines on the saddle surface have a concave curvature, as shown by $\overleftrightarrow{DE}$, $\overleftrightarrow{FG}$, and $\overleftrightarrow{HI}$. Keep in mind that the saddle surface is an infinite surface. Figure 1.4 shows only a portion of the surface.

Parallel lines on an infinite saddle surface are defined as two lines that do not intersect. In Figure 1.4, $\overleftrightarrow{FG}$ and $\overleftrightarrow{HI}$ are *not* parallel because they intersect at a point. The lines $\overleftrightarrow{DE}$ and $\overleftrightarrow{FG}$ are parallel because they do not intersect. The lines $\overleftrightarrow{DE}$ and $\overleftrightarrow{HI}$ are also parallel lines. Figure 1.4 provides a geometric model of a hyperbolic geometry because for a given line, *more than one* parallel line exists through a point not on the given line.

Figure 1.5 shows a triangle drawn on a saddle surface. The triangle is referred to as a *hyperbolic triangle.* Due to the curvature of the sides of the hyperbolic triangle, the sum of the measures of the angles of the triangle is less than 180°. This is true for all hyperbolic triangles.

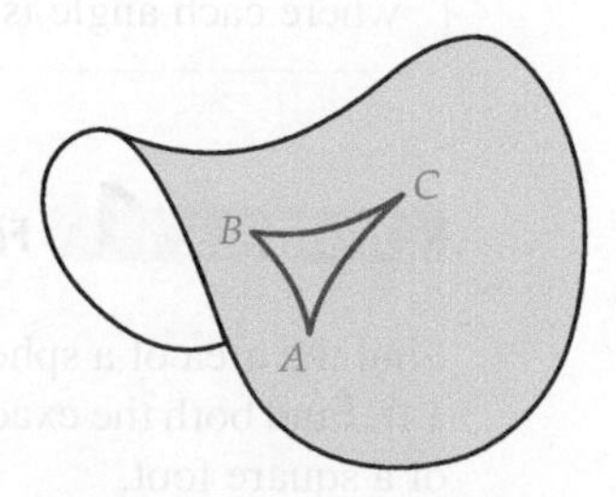

FIGURE 1.5 Hyperbolic triangle

The following chart summarizes some of the properties of plane, hyperbolic, and spherical geometries.

<table>
<tr><th>Euclidean Geometry</th><th colspan="2">Non-Euclidean Geometries</th></tr>
<tr><td>Euclidean or Plane Geometry (ca. 300 BC):
Through a given point not on a given line, exactly one line can be drawn parallel to the given line.
Geometry on a plane</td><td>Lobachevskian or Hyperbolic Geometry (1826):
Through a given point not on a given line, there are at least two lines parallel to the given line.
Geometry on an infinite saddle surface</td><td>Riemannian or Spherical Geometry (1855):
Through a given point not on a given line, there exist no lines parallel to the given line.
Geometry on a sphere</td></tr>
<tr><td>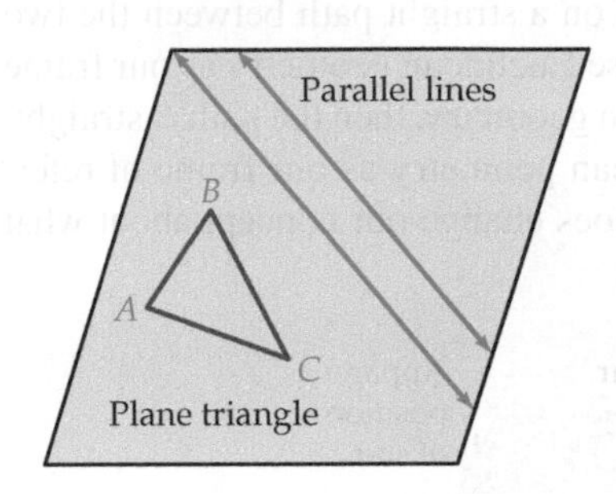</td><td>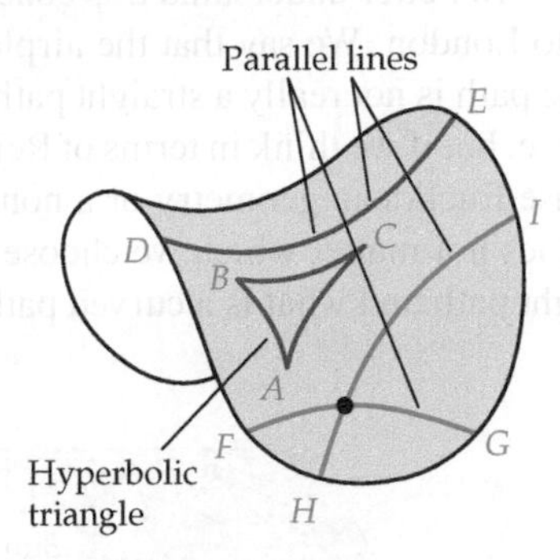</td><td>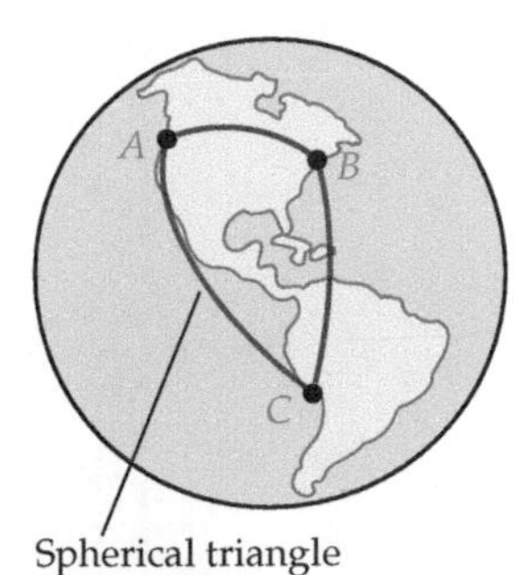</td></tr>
<tr><td>For any triangle ABC,
$m\angle A + m\angle B + m\angle C = 180°$
A triangle can have at most one right angle.
The shortest path between two points is the line segment that connects the points.</td><td>For any triangle ABC,
$m\angle A + m\angle B + m\angle C < 180°$
A triangle can have at most one right angle.
The curves shown in the above figure illustrate some of the geodesics of an infinite saddle surface.</td><td>For any triangle ABC,
$180° < m\angle A + m\angle B + m\angle C < 540°$
A triangle can have one, two, or three right angles.
The shortest path between two points is the minor arc of a great circle that passes through the points.</td></tr>
</table>

EXAMPLE 2 Euclidean and Non-Euclidean Geometries

Determine the type of geometry (Euclidean, Riemannian, or Lobachevskian) in which two lines can intersect at a point and both of the lines can be parallel to a third line that does not pass through the intersection point.

Solution

Euclid's parallel postulate states that through a given point not on a given line, exactly one line can be drawn parallel to the given line.

Riemann's alternative to the parallel postulate states that through a given point not on a given line, there exist no lines parallel to the given line.

Gauss's alternative to the parallel postulate, which is assumed in Lobachevskian geometry, states that through a given point not on a given line, there are at least two lines parallel to the given line.

Thus, if we consider only Euclidean, Riemannian, and Lobachevskian geometries, then the condition that "two lines can intersect at a point and both of the lines can be parallel to a third line that does not pass through the intersection point" can be true only in Lobachevskian geometry.

CHECK YOUR PROGRESS 2 Determine the type of geometry in which there are no lines parallel to a given line.

Solution See page S4.

MATH MATTERS Curved Space

In 1915, Albert Einstein proposed a revolutionary theory that is now called the *general theory of relativity*. One of the major ideas of this theory is that space is curved, or "warped," by the mass of stars and planets. The greatest curvature occurs around those stars with the largest mass. Light rays in space do not travel in a straight path, but rather follow the geodesics of this curved space. Recall that the shortest path that joins two points on a given surface is on a geodesic of the surface.

It is interesting to consider the paths of light rays in space from a different perspective, in which the light rays travel along straight paths in a space that is non-Euclidean. To better understand this concept, consider an airplane that flies from Los Angeles to London. We say that the airplane flies on a straight path between the two cities. The path is not really a straight path if we use Euclidean geometry as our frame of reference, but if we think in terms of Reimannian geometry, then the path *is* straight. We can use Euclidean geometry or a non-Euclidean geometry as our frame of reference. It does not matter which we choose, but it does change our concept about what is a straight path and what is a curved path.

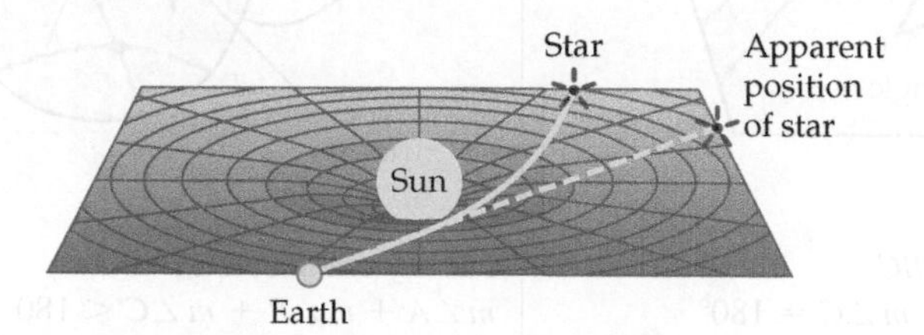

Light rays from a star follow the geodesics of space. Any light rays that pass near the sun are slightly bent. This causes some stars to appear to an observer on Earth to be in different positions than their actual positions.

City Geometry: A Contemporary Geometry

Consider the geometric model of a city shown in Figure 1.6. In this city, all of the streets run either straight north and south or straight east and west. The distance between adjacent north–south streets is 1 block, and the distance between adjacent east–west streets is 1 block. In a city it is generally not possible to travel from P to Q along a straight path. Instead, one must travel between P and Q by traveling along the streets. As you travel from P to Q, we assume that you always travel in a direction that gets you closer to point Q. Two such paths are shown by the red and the green dashed line segments in Figure 1.6.

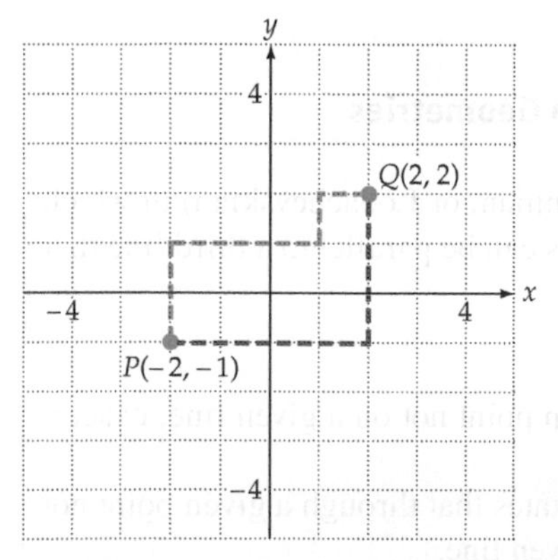

FIGURE 1.6 Two city paths from P to Q

We will use the notation $d_C(P, Q)$ to represent the *city distance* between the points P and Q. For P and Q as shown in Figure 1.6, $d_C(P, Q) = 7$ blocks. This distance can be determined by counting the number of blocks needed to travel along the streets from P to Q or by using the following formula.

POINT OF INTEREST

The city distance formula is also called the *Manhattan metric*. It first appeared in an article published by the mathematician Hermann Minkowski (1864–1909).

The City Distance Formula

If $P(x_1, y_1)$ and $Q(x_2, y_2)$ are two points in a city, then the **city distance** between P and Q is given by

$$d_C(P, Q) = |x_2 - x_1| + |y_2 - y_1|$$

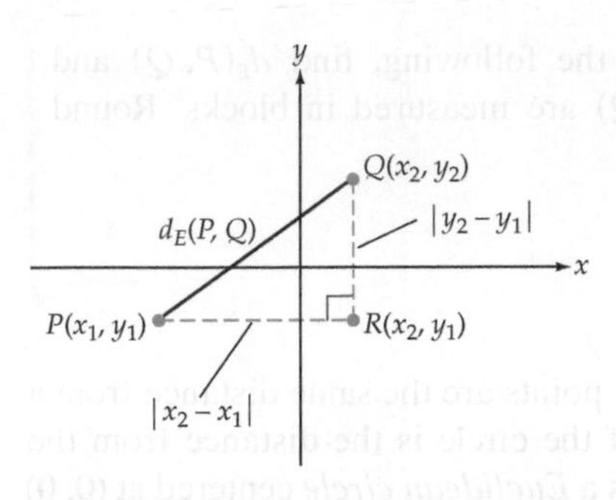

FIGURE 1.7

In Euclidean geometry, the distance between the points P and Q is defined as the length of $\overline{PQ}$. To determine a *Euclidean distance formula* for the distance between $P(x_1, y_1)$ and $Q(x_2, y_2)$, we first locate the point $R(x_2, y_1)$. See Figure 1.7.

Note that R has the same x-coordinate as Q and that R has the same y-coordinate as P. The horizontal distance between P and R is $|x_2 - x_1|$, and the vertical distance between R and Q is $|y_2 - y_1|$. Apply the Pythagorean theorem to the right triangle PRQ to produce

$$[d_E(P, Q)]^2 = |x_2 - x_1|^2 + |y_2 - y_1|^2$$

Because the square of a number cannot be negative, the absolute value signs are not necessary.

$$[d_E(P, Q)]^2 = (x_2 - x_1)^2 + (y_2 - y_1)^2$$

Take the square root of each side of the equation to produce

$$d_E(P, Q) = \sqrt{(x_2 - x_1)^2 + (y_2 - y_1)^2}$$

The Euclidean Distance Formula

If $P(x_1, y_1)$ and $Q(x_2, y_2)$ are two points in a plane, then the **Euclidean distance** between P and Q is given by

$$d_E(P, Q) = \sqrt{(x_2 - x_1)^2 + (y_2 - y_1)^2}$$

EXAMPLE 3 Find the Euclidean Distance and the City Distance Between Two Points

For each of the following, find $d_E(P, Q)$ and $d_C(P, Q)$. Assume that both $d_E(P, Q)$ and $d_C(P, Q)$ are measured in blocks. Round approximate results to the nearest tenth of a block.

a. $P(-4, -3), Q(2, -1)$ **b.** $P(2, -3), Q(-5, 4)$

Solution

a.
$$\begin{aligned} d_E(P, Q) &= \sqrt{(x_2 - x_1)^2 + (y_2 - y_1)^2} \\ &= \sqrt{[2 - (-4)]^2 + [(-1) - (-3)]^2} \\ &= \sqrt{6^2 + 2^2} \\ &= \sqrt{40} \approx 6.3 \text{ blocks} \end{aligned}$$

$$\begin{aligned} d_C(P, Q) &= |x_2 - x_1| + |y_2 - y_1| \\ &= |2 - (-4)| + |(-1) - (-3)| \\ &= |6| + |2| \\ &= 6 + 2 \\ &= 8 \text{ blocks} \end{aligned}$$

b.
$$\begin{aligned} d_E(P, Q) &= \sqrt{(x_2 - x_1)^2 + (y_2 - y_1)^2} \\ &= \sqrt{[(-5) - 2]^2 + [4 - (-3)]^2} \\ &= \sqrt{(-7)^2 + 7^2} \\ &= \sqrt{98} \approx 9.9 \text{ blocks} \end{aligned}$$

$$\begin{aligned} d_C(P, Q) &= |x_2 - x_1| + |y_2 - y_1| \\ &= |(-5) - 2| + |4 - (-3)| \\ &= |-7| + |7| \\ &= 7 + 7 \\ &= 14 \text{ blocks} \end{aligned}$$

TAKE NOTE

In Example 3 we have calculated the city distances by using the city distance formula. These distances can also be determined by counting the number of blocks needed to travel along the streets from P to Q on a rectangular coordinate grid.

CHECK YOUR PROGRESS 3 For each of the following, find $d_E(P, Q)$ and $d_C(P, Q)$. Assume that both $d_E(P, Q)$ and $d_C(P, Q)$ are measured in blocks. Round approximate results to the nearest tenth of a block.

a. $P(-1, 4), Q(3, 2)$ **b.** $P(3, -4), Q(-1, 5)$

Solution See page S4.

Recall that a circle is a plane figure in which all points are the same distance from a given center point and the length of the radius r of the circle is the distance from the center point to a point on the circle. Figure 1.8 shows a *Euclidean circle* centered at (0, 0) with a radius of 3 blocks. Figure 1.9 shows all the points in a city that are 3 blocks from the center point (0, 0). These points form a *city circle* with a radius of 3 blocks.

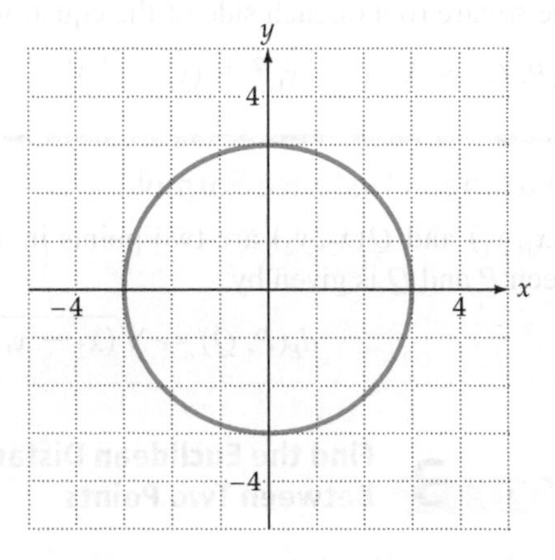

FIGURE 1.8 A Euclidean circle with center (0, 0) and a radius of 3 blocks

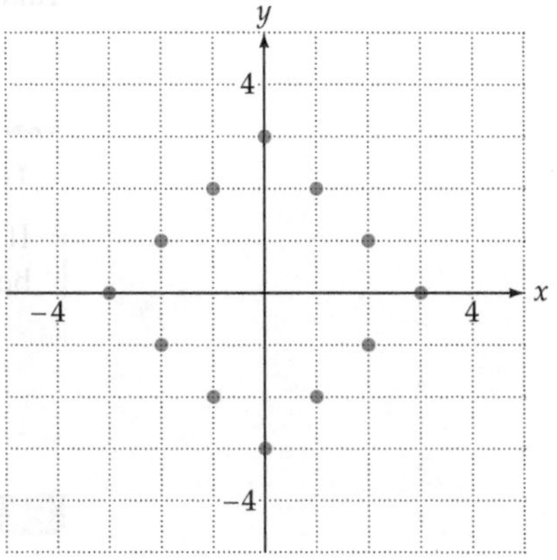

FIGURE 1.9 A city circle with center (0, 0) and a radius of 3 blocks

It is interesting to observe that the *city circle* shown in Figure 1.9 consists of just 12 points and that these points all lie on a square with vertices (3, 0), (0, 3), (−3, 0), and (0, −3).

EXCURSION

Finding Geodesics

Form groups of three or four students. Each group needs a roll of narrow tape or a ribbon and the two geometrical models shown at the right. The purpose of this Excursion is to use the tape (ribbon) to determine the geodesics of a surface.

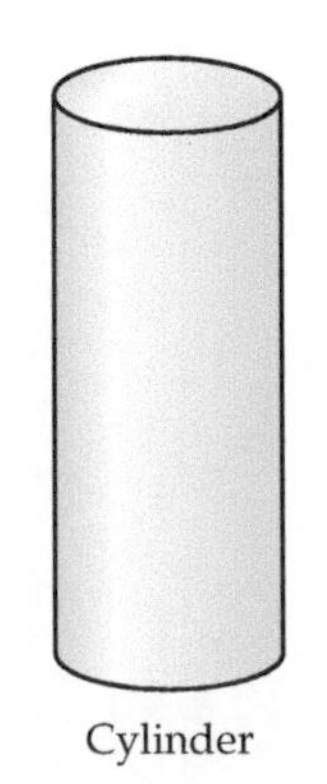

Cylinder

Paper cup

The following three theorems can be used to determine the geodesics of a surface.

Geodesic Theorems

Theorem 1 If a surface is smooth with no edges or holes, then the shortest path between any two points is on a geodesic of the surface.

Theorem 2 ***The Tape Test*** If a piece of tape is placed so that it lies flat on a smooth surface, then the center line of the tape is on a geodesic of the surface.

Theorem 3 ***Inverse of the Tape Test*** If a piece of tape does not lie flat on a smooth surface, then the center line of the tape is not on a geodesic of the surface.

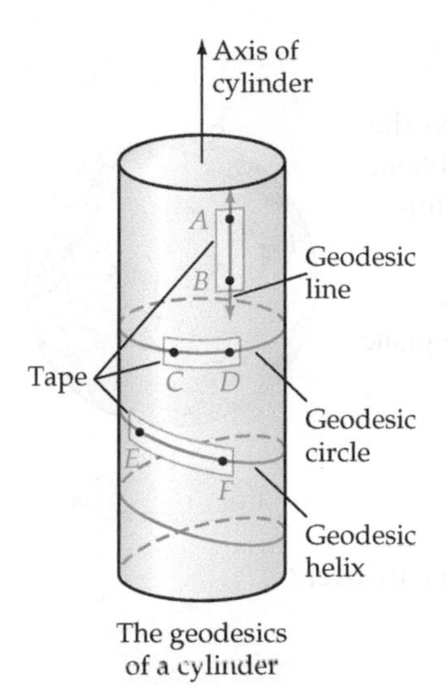

The geodesics of a cylinder

FIGURE 1.10

What are the geodesics of a cylinder? If two points A and B are as shown in Figure 1.10, then the vertical line segment between A and B is the shortest path between the points. A piece of tape can be placed so that it covers point A and point B and lies flat on the cylinder. Thus, by Theorem 2, line segment $\overline{AB}$ is on a geodesic of the cylinder.

If two points C and D are as shown in Figure 1.10, then the minor arc of a circle is the shortest path between the points. Once again we see that a piece of tape can be placed so that it covers points C and D and lies flat on the cylinder. Theorem 2 indicates that the arc $\overset{\frown}{CD}$ is on a geodesic of the cylinder.

To find a geodesic that passes through the two points E and F, start your tape at E and proceed slightly downward and to the right, toward point F. If your tape lies flat against the cylinder, you have found the geodesic for the two points. If your tape does not lie flat against the surface, then your path is not a geodesic and you need to experiment further. Eventually you will find the *circular helix* curve, shown in Figure 1.10, that allows the tape to lie flat on the cylinder.[3]

Additional experiments with the tape and the cylinder should convince you that a geodesic of a cylinder is one of the following: (a) a line parallel to the axis of the cylinder, (b) a circle with its center on the axis of the cylinder and its diameter perpendicular to the axis, or (c) a circular helix curve that has a constant slope and a center on the axis of the cylinder.

EXCURSION EXERCISES

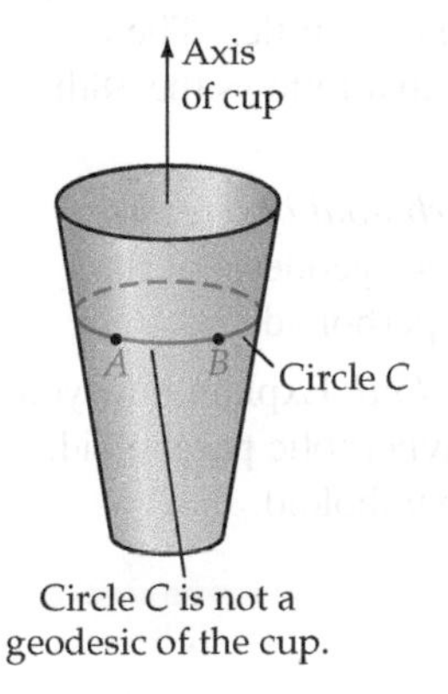

Circle C is not a geodesic of the cup.

FIGURE 1.11

1. **a.** Place two points A and B on a paper cup so that A and B are both at the same height, as in Figure 1.11. We know circle C that passes through A and B is *not* a geodesic of the cup because a piece of tape will not lie flat when placed directly on top of circle C. Experiment with a piece of tape to determine the *actual* geodesic that passes through A and B. Make a drawing that shows this geodesic and illustrate how it differs from circle C.

   b. Use a cup similar to the one in Figure 1.11 and a piece of tape to determine two other types of geodesics of the cup. Make a drawing that shows each of these two additional types of geodesics.

2. The only geodesics of a sphere are great circles. Write a sentence that explains how you can use a piece of tape to show that circle D in Figure 1.12 is not a geodesic of the sphere.

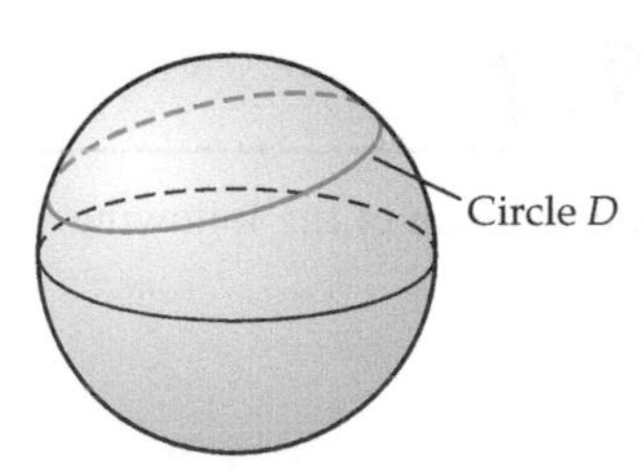

FIGURE 1.12

[3] The thread of a bolt is an example of a circular helix.

3.  Write a sentence that explains how you know that circle E in Figure 1.13 is not a geodesic of the figure.

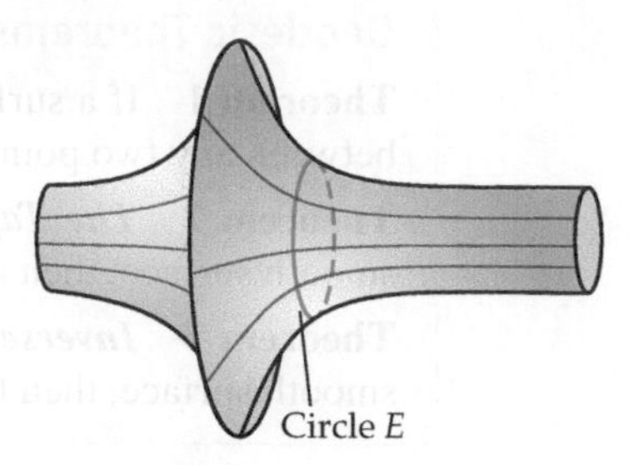

FIGURE 1.13

Excursion Exercises 4 to 6 require a world globe that shows the locations of major cities. We suggest that you use a thin ribbon, instead of tape, to determine the great circle routes in the following exercises, because tape may damage the globe.

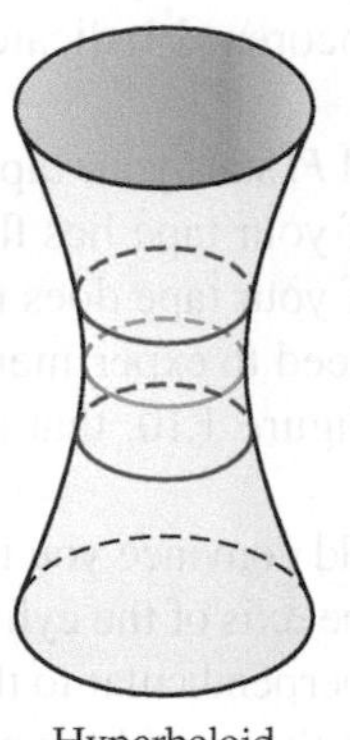

Hyperboloid of one sheet

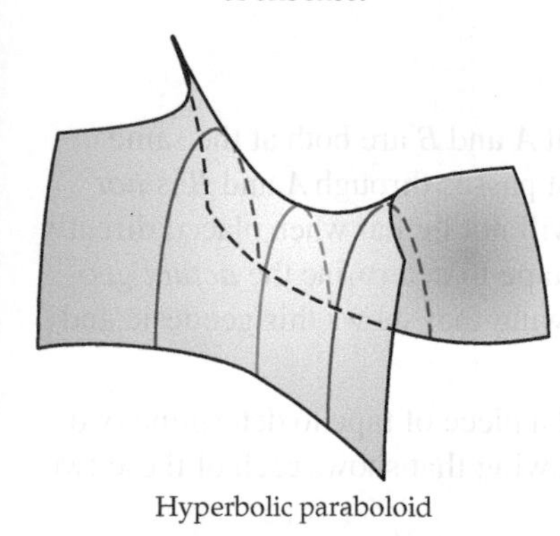

Hyperbolic paraboloid

4. A pilot flies a great circle route from Miami, Florida, to Hong Kong. Which one of the following states will the plane fly over?
   a. California b. Oregon
   c. Washington d. Alaska

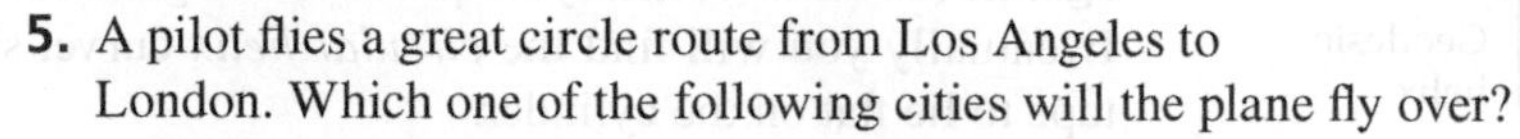

5. A pilot flies a great circle route from Los Angeles to London. Which one of the following cities will the plane fly over?
   a. New York b. Chicago
   c. Godthaab, Greenland d. Vancouver, Canada

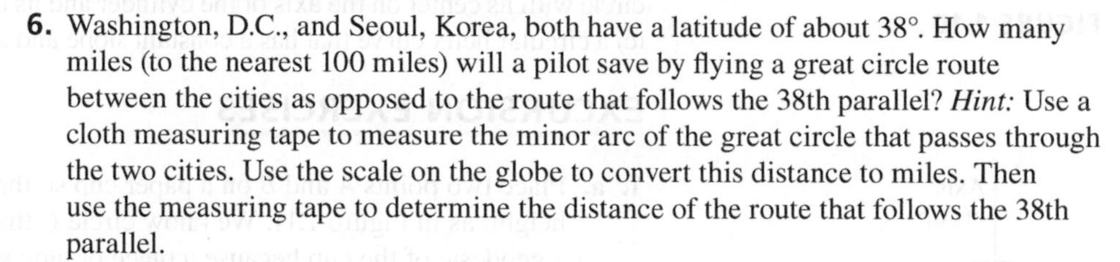

6. Washington, D.C., and Seoul, Korea, both have a latitude of about 38°. How many miles (to the nearest 100 miles) will a pilot save by flying a great circle route between the cities as opposed to the route that follows the 38th parallel? *Hint:* Use a cloth measuring tape to measure the minor arc of the great circle that passes through the two cities. Use the scale on the globe to convert this distance to miles. Then use the measuring tape to determine the distance of the route that follows the 38th parallel.

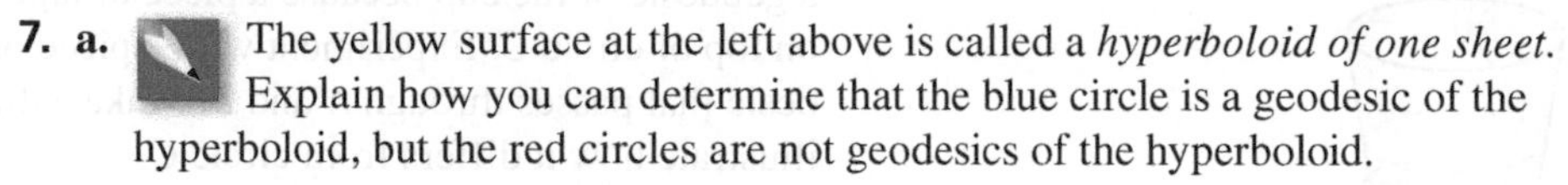

7. a. The yellow surface at the left above is called a *hyperboloid of one sheet.* Explain how you can determine that the blue circle is a geodesic of the hyperboloid, but the red circles are not geodesics of the hyperboloid.
   b. The saddle surface at the left is called a *hyperbolic paraboloid.* Explain how you can determine that the blue parabola is a geodesic of the hyperbolic paraboloid, but the red parabolas are not geodesics of the hyperbolic paraboloid.

EXERCISE SET 1.7

1. State the parallel postulate for each of the following.
   a. Euclidean geometry
   b. Lobachevskian geometry
   c. Riemannian geometry
2. Name the mathematician who is called the Copernicus of geometry.
3. Name the mathematician who was the first to consider a geometry in which Euclid's parallel postulate was replaced with "Through a given point not on a given line, there are *at least two* lines parallel to the given line."
4. What is the maximum number of right angles a triangle can have in
   a. Euclidean geometry?
   b. Lobachevskian geometry?
   c. Riemannian geometry?

5. What name did Lobachevsky give to the geometry that he created?

6. Explain why great circles in Riemannian geometry are thought of as lines.

7. What is a geodesic?

8. In which geometry can two distinct lines be parallel to a third line but not parallel to each other?

9. What model was used in this text to illustrate hyperbolic geometry?

10. In which geometry do all perpendiculars to a given line intersect each other?

11. Find the exact area of a spherical triangle with angles of 150°, 120°, and 90° on a sphere with a radius of 1.

12. Find the area of a spherical triangle with three right angles on a sphere with a radius of 1980 mi. Round to the nearest ten thousand square miles.

■ **City Geometry** In Exercises 13 to 20, find the Euclidean distance between the points and the city distance between the points. Assume that both $d_E(P, Q)$ and $d_C(P, Q)$ are measured in blocks. Round approximate results to the nearest tenth of a block.

13. $P(-3, 1), Q(4, 1)$
14. $P(-2, 4), Q(3, -1)$
15. $P(2, -3), Q(-3, 5)$
16. $P(-2, 0), Q(3, 7)$
17. $P(-1, 4), Q(5, -2)$
18. $P(-5, 2), Q(3, -4)$
19. $P(2, 0), Q(3, -6)$
20. $P(2, -2), Q(5, -2)$

A Distance Conversion Formula The following formula can be used to convert the Euclidean distance between the points P and Q to the city distance between P and Q. In this formula, the variable m represents the slope of the line segment $\overline{PQ}$.

$$d_C(P, Q) = \frac{1 + |m|}{\sqrt{1 + m^2}} d_E(P, Q)$$

■ In Exercises 21 to 26, use the preceding formula to find the city distance between P and Q.

21. $d_E(P, Q) = 5$ blocks, slope of $\overline{PQ} = \frac{3}{4}$

22. $d_E(P, Q) = \sqrt{29}$ blocks, slope of $\overline{PQ} = \frac{2}{5}$

23. $d_E(P, Q) = \sqrt{13}$ blocks, slope of $\overline{PQ} = -\frac{2}{3}$

24. $d_E(P, Q) = 2\sqrt{10}$ blocks, slope of $\overline{PQ} = -3$

25. $d_E(P, Q) = \sqrt{17}$ blocks, slope of $\overline{PQ} = \frac{1}{4}$

26. $d_E(P, Q) = 4\sqrt{2}$ blocks, slope of $\overline{PQ} = -1$

27. Explain why there is no formula that can be used to convert $d_C(P, Q)$ to $d_E(P, Q)$. Assume that no additional information is given other than the value of $d_C(P, Q)$.

28. a. If $d_E(P, Q) = d_E(R, S)$, must $d_C(P, Q) = d_C(R, S)$? Explain.
    b. If $d_C(P, Q) = d_C(R, S)$, must $d_E(P, Q) = d_E(R, S)$? Explain.

29. Plot the points in the city circle with center $(-2, -1)$ and radius $r = 2$ blocks.

30. Plot the points in the city circle with center $(1, -1)$ and radius $r = 3$ blocks.

31. Plot the points in the city circle with center (0, 0) and radius $r = 2.5$ blocks.

32. Plot the points in the city circle with center (0, 0) and radius $r = 3.5$ blocks.

33. How many points are on the city circle with center (0, 0) and radius $r = n$ blocks, where n is a natural number?

34. Which of the following city circles has the most points, a city circle with center (0, 0) and radius 4.5 blocks or a city circle with center (0, 0) and radius 5 blocks?

EXTENSIONS

Apartment Hunting in a City Use the following information to answer each of the questions in Exercises 35 and 36.

Amy and her husband Ryan are looking for an apartment located adjacent to a city street. Amy works at $P(-3, -1)$ and Ryan works at $Q(2, 3)$. Both Amy and Ryan plan to walk from their apartment to work along routes that follow the north–south and the east–west streets.

35. a. Plot the points where Amy and Ryan should look for an apartment if they wish the sum of the city distances they need to walk to work to be a minimum.
    b. Plot the points where Amy and Ryan should look for an apartment if they wish the sum of the city distances they need to walk to work to be a minimum and they both will walk the same distance. *Hint:* Find the intersection of the city circle with center P and radius of 4.5 blocks, and the city circle with center Q and radius of 4.5 blocks.

36. a. Plot the points where Amy and Ryan should look for an apartment if they wish the sum of the city distances they need to walk to work to be less than or equal to 10 blocks.
    b. Plot the points where Amy and Ryan should look for an apartment if they wish the sum of the city distances they need to walk to work to be less than or equal to 10 blocks and they both will walk the same distance. *Hint:* Find the intersection of the city circle with center P and radius of 5.5 blocks, and the city circle with center Q and radius of 5.5 blocks.

37. A Finite Geometry Consider a finite geometry with exactly five points: A, B, C, D, and E. In this geometry a line is any two of the five points. For example, the two points A and B together form the line denoted by AB. Parallel lines are defined as two lines that do not share a common point.

a. How many lines are in this geometry?

b. How many of the lines are parallel to line AB?

38. A Finite Geometry Consider a finite geometry with exactly six points: A, B, C, D, E, and F. In this geometry a line is any two of the six points. Parallel lines are defined as two lines that do not share a common point.

a. How many lines are in this geometry?

b. How many of the lines are parallel to line AB?

SECTION 1.8 Fractals

Fractals—Endlessly Repeated Geometric Figures

Have you ever used a computer program to enlarge a portion of a photograph? Sometimes the result is a satisfactory enlargement; however, if the photograph is enlarged too much, the image becomes blurred. For example, the photograph in Figure 1.14 below is shown at its original size. The image in Figure 1.15 is an enlarged portion of Figure 1.14, and the image in Figure 1.16 is an enlarged portion of Figure 1.15. If we continue to make enlargements of enlargements, we will produce extremely blurred images that provide little information about the original photograph.

A computer monitor displays an image using small dots called *pixels*. If a computer image is enlarged using a software program, the program must determine the color of each pixel in the enlargement. If the image file for the photograph cannot supply the needed color information for each pixel, the color of some pixels is calculated by *averaging* the numerical color values of neighboring pixels for which the image file has the color information.

Shipfactory/Shutterstock.com

FIGURE 1.14

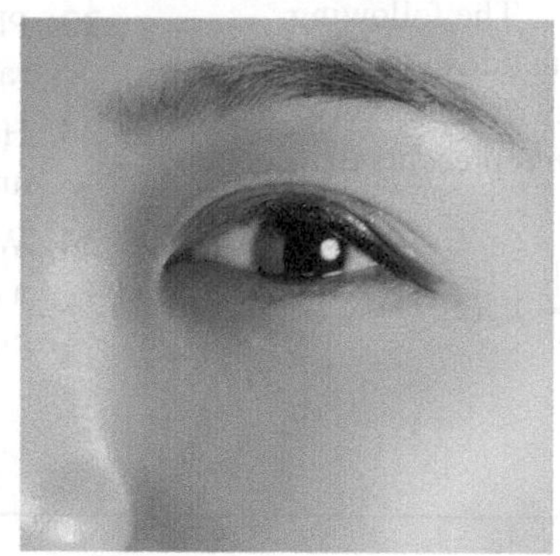
Shipfactory/Shutterstock.com

FIGURE 1.15

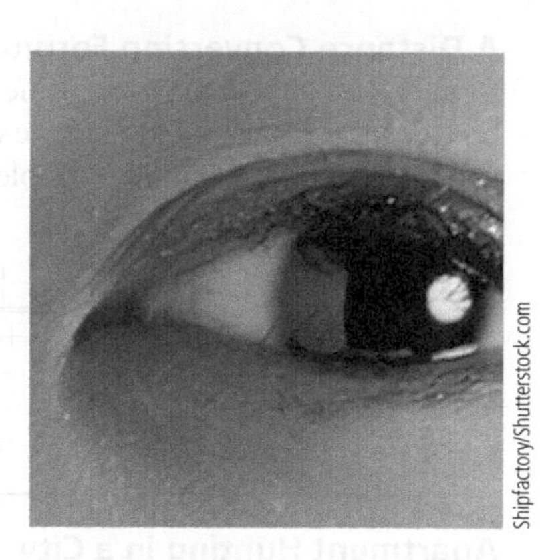
Shipfactory/Shutterstock.com

FIGURE 1.16

In the 1970s, the mathematician Benoit Mandelbrot discovered some remarkable methods that enable us to create geometric figures with a special property: if any portion of the figure is enlarged repeatedly, then additional details (not fewer details, as with the enlargement of a photograph) of the figure are displayed. Mandelbrot called these endlessly repeated geometric figures *fractals*. The fractals that we will study in this lesson can be defined as follows. A **fractal** is a geometric figure in which a self-similar motif repeats itself on an ever-diminishing scale.

Fractals are generally constructed by using **iterative processes** in which the fractal is more closely approximated as a repeated cycle of procedures is performed. For example, a fractal known as the *Koch curve* is constructed as follows.

Construction of the Koch Curve

Step 0: Start with a line segment. This initial segment is shown as stage 0 in Figure 1.17. Stage 0 of a fractal is called the **initiator** of the fractal.

Step 1: On the middle third of the line segment, draw an equilateral triangle and remove its base. The resulting curve is stage 1 in Figure 1.17. Stage 1 of a fractal is called the **generator** of the fractal.

Step 2: Replace each initiator shape (line segment, in this example) with a *scaled version* of the generator to produce the next stage of the Koch curve. The width of the scaled version of the generator is the same as the width of the line segment it replaces. Continue to repeat this step ad infinitum to create additional stages of the Koch curve.

Three applications of step 2 produce stage 2, stage 3, and stage 4 of the Koch curve, as shown in Figure 1.17.

TAKE NOTE

The line segments at any stage of the Koch curve are $\frac{1}{3}$ the length of the line segments at the previous stage. To create the next stage of the Koch curve (after stage 1), replace each line segment with a scaled version of the generator.

At any stage after stage 2, the scaled version of the generator is $\frac{1}{3}$ the size of the preceding scaled generator.

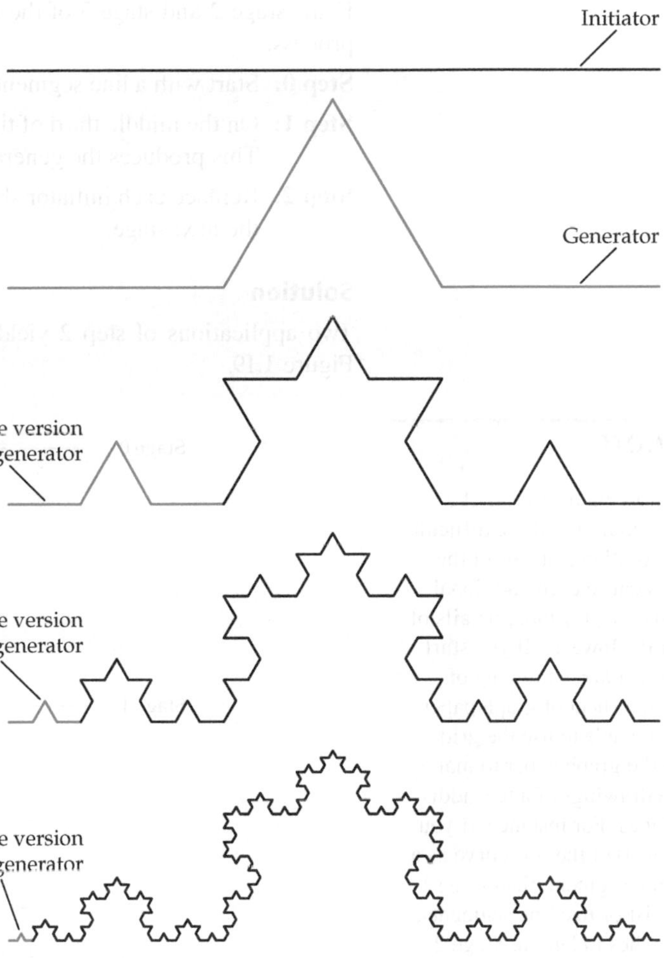

Initiator
Stage 0
Generator
Stage 1
1/3 scale version of the generator
Stage 2
1/9 scale version of the generator
Stage 3
1/27 scale version of the generator
Stage 4

FIGURE 1.17 The first five stages of the Koch curve

HISTORICAL NOTE

The Koch curve was created by the mathematician Niels Fabian Helge von Koch (kôkh) (1870–1924). Von Koch attended Stockholm University and in 1911 became a professor of mathematics at Stockholm University. In addition to his early pioneering work with fractals, he wrote several papers on number theory.

None of the curves shown in Figure 1.17 is the Koch curve. The Koch curve is the curve that would be produced if step 2 in the above construction process were repeated ad infinitum. No one has ever seen the Koch curve, but we know that it is a very jagged curve in which the self-similar motif shown in Figure 1.17 repeats itself on an ever-diminishing scale.

POINT OF INTEREST

It can be shown that the Koch snowflake has a finite area but an infinite perimeter. Thus it has the remarkable property that you could paint the surface of the snowflake, but you could never get enough paint to paint its boundary.

The curves shown in Figure 1.18 are the first five stages of the *Koch snowflake*.

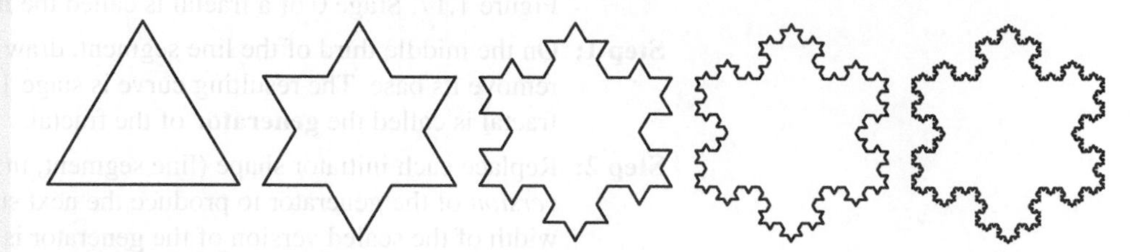

FIGURE 1.18 The first five stages of the Koch snowflake

EXAMPLE 1 Draw Stages of a Fractal

Draw stage 2 and stage 3 of the *box curve*, which is defined by the following iterative process.

Step 0: Start with a line segment as the initiator. See stage 0 in Figure 1.19.

Step 1: On the middle third of the line segment, draw a square and remove its base. This produces the generator of the box curve. See stage 1 in Figure 1.19.

Step 2: Replace each initiator shape with a scaled version of the generator to produce the next stage.

Solution

Two applications of step 2 yield stage 2 and stage 3 of the box curve, as shown in Figure 1.19.

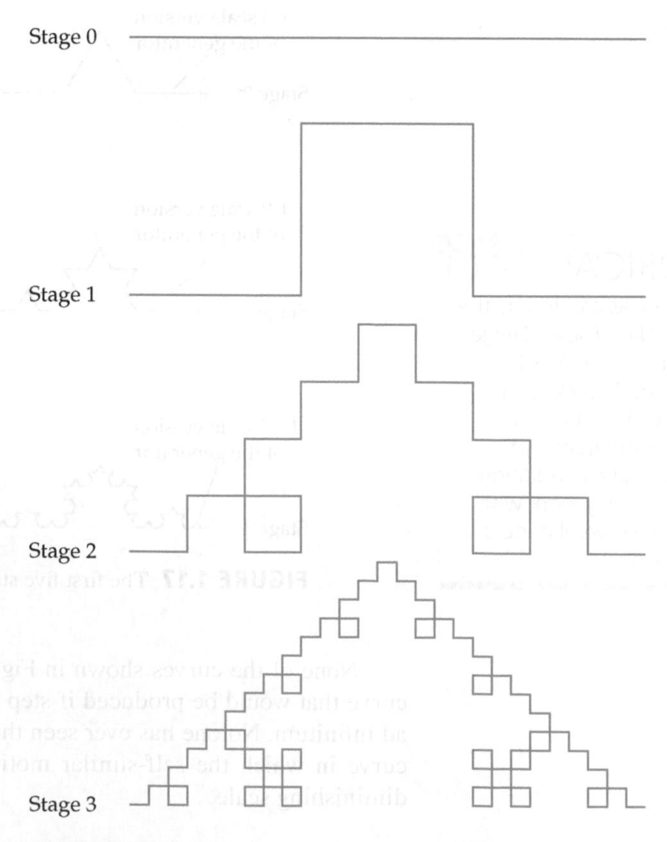

FIGURE 1.19 The first four stages of the box curve

TAKE NOTE

If your drawing of stage 0 of a fractal is small, it will be difficult to draw additional stages of the fractal, because each additional stage must display more details of the fractal. However, if you start by making a *large* drawing of stage 0 on a sheet of graph paper, you will be able to use the grid lines on the graph paper to make accurate drawings of a few additional stages. For instance, if you draw stage 0 of the box curve as a 9-inch line segment, then stage 1 will consist of five line segments, each 3 inches in length. Stage 2 will consist of 25 line segments, each 1 inch in length. The 125 line segments of stage 3 will each be $\frac{1}{3}$ of an inch in length.

Instead of erasing and drawing each new stage of the fractal on top of the previous stage, it is advantageous to draw each new stage directly below the previous stage, as shown in Figure 1.19.

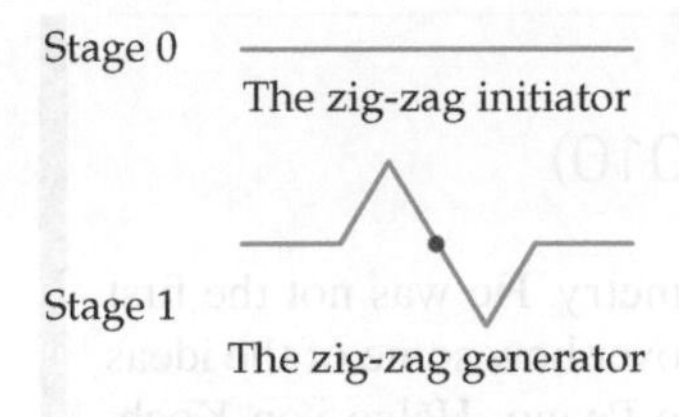

FIGURE 1.20 The initiator and generator of the zig-zag curve

CHECK YOUR PROGRESS 1 Draw stage 2 of the *zig-zag curve*, which is defined by the following iterative process.

Step 0: Start with a line segment. See stage 0 of Figure 1.20.

Step 1: Remove the middle half of the line segment and draw a zig-zag, as shown in stage 1 of Figure 1.20. Each of the six line segments in the generator is a $\frac{1}{4}$-scale replica of the initiator.

Step 2: Replace each initiator shape with the scaled version of the generator to produce the next stage. Repeat this step to produce additional stages.

Solution See page S4.

In each of the previous fractals, the initiator was a line segment. In Example 2, we use a triangle and its interior as the initiator.

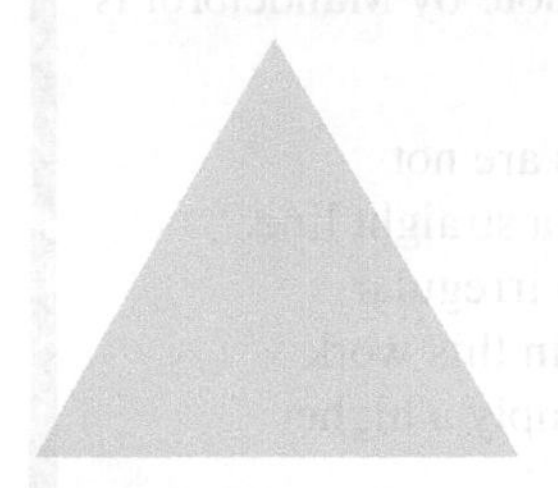
Stage 0 (the initiator)

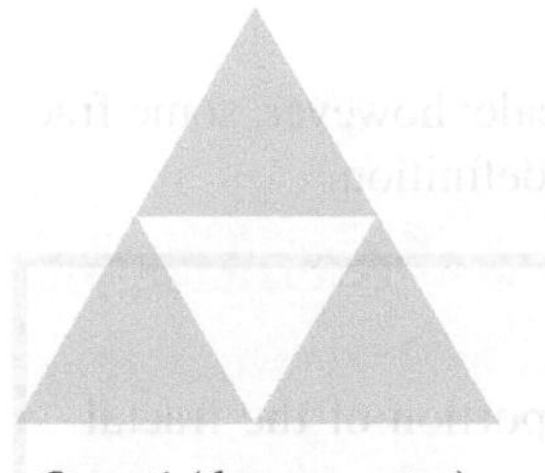
Stage 1 (the generator)

FIGURE 1.21 The initiator and generator of the Sierpinski gasket

EXAMPLE 2 Draw Stages of a Fractal

Draw stage 2 and stage 3 of the *Sierpinski gasket* (also known as the *Sierpinski triangle*), which is defined by the following iterative process.

Step 0: Start with an equilateral triangle and its interior. This is stage 0 of the Sierpinski gasket. See Figure 1.21.

Step 1: Form a new triangle by connecting the midpoints of the sides of the triangle. Remove this center triangle. The result is the three green triangles shown in stage 1 in Figure 1.21.

Step 2: Replace each initiator (green triangle) with a scaled version of the generator.

Solution

Two applications of step 2 of the above process produce stage 2 and stage 3 of the Sierpinski gasket, as shown in Figure 1.22.

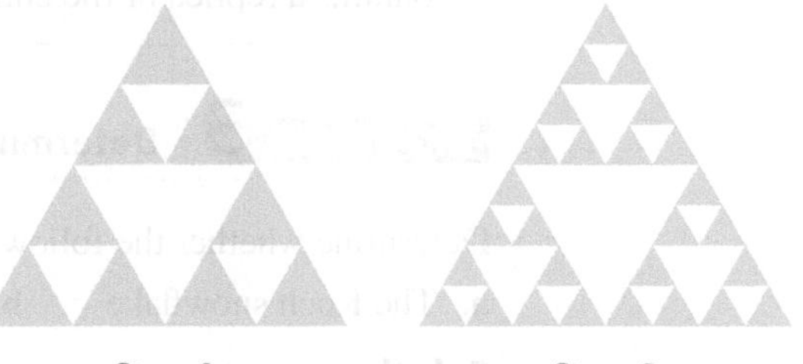

FIGURE 1.22 Stages 2 and 3 of the Sierpinski gasket

CHECK YOUR PROGRESS 2 Draw stage 2 of the *Sierpinski carpet*, which is defined by the following process.

Step 0: Start with a square and its interior. See stage 0 in Figure 1.23.

Step 1: Subdivide the square into nine smaller congruent squares and remove the center square. This yields stage 1 (the generator) shown in Figure 1.23.

Step 2: Replace each initiator (tan square) with a scaled version of the generator. Repeat this step to create additional stages of the Sierpinski carpet.

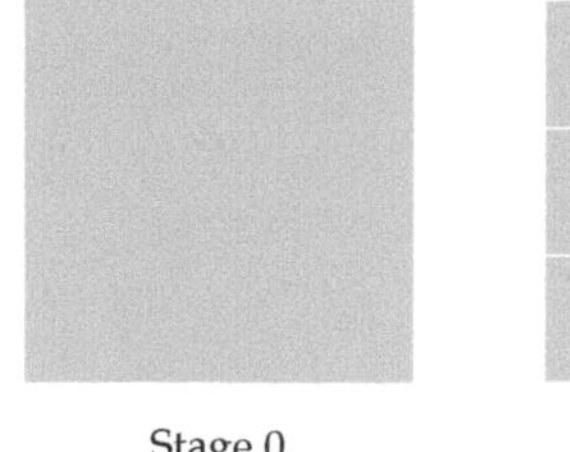
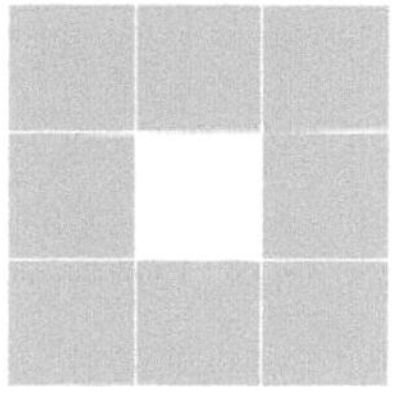

FIGURE 1.23 The initiator and generator of the Sierpinski carpet

Solution See page S4.

MATH MATTERS Benoit Mandelbrot (1924–2010)

POINT OF INTEREST

Hank Morgan/Science Photo Library/Photo Researchers/Science Source

Fractal geometry is not just a chapter of mathematics, but one that helps Everyman to see the same old world differently.—Benoit Mandelbrot, IBM Research (*Source:* http://php.iupui.edu/~wijackso/fractal3.htm)

Benoit Mandelbrot is often called the father of fractal geometry. He was not the first person to create a fractal, but he was the first person to discover how some of the ideas of earlier mathematicians such as Georg Cantor, Giuseppe Peano, Helge von Koch, Waclaw Sierpinski, and Gaston Julia could be united to form a new type of geometry. Mandelbrot also recognized that many fractals share characteristics with shapes and curves found in nature. For instance, the leaves of a fern, when compared with the whole fern, are almost identical in shape, only smaller. This self-similarity characteristic is evident (to some degree) in all fractals. The following quote by Mandelbrot is from his 1983 book, *The Fractal Geometry of Nature.*[4]

> Clouds are not spheres, mountains are not cones, coastlines are not circles, and bark is not smooth, nor does lightning travel in a straight line. More generally, I claim that many patterns of Nature are so irregular and fragmented, that, compared with Euclid—a term used in this work to denote all of standard geometry—Nature exhibits not simply a higher degree but an altogether different level of complexity.

Strictly Self-Similar Fractals

All fractals show a self-similar motif on an ever-diminishing scale; however, some fractals are *strictly self-similar* fractals, according to the following definition.

Strictly Self-Similar Fractal

A fractal is said to be **strictly self-similar** if any arbitrary portion of the fractal contains a replica of the entire fractal.

EXAMPLE 3 Determine Whether a Fractal Is Strictly Self-Similar

Determine whether the following fractals are strictly self-similar.

a. The Koch snowflake **b.** The Koch curve

Solution

a. The Koch snowflake is a closed figure. Any portion of the Koch snowflake (like the portion circled in Figure 1.24) is not a closed figure. Thus the Koch snowflake is *not* a strictly self-similar fractal.

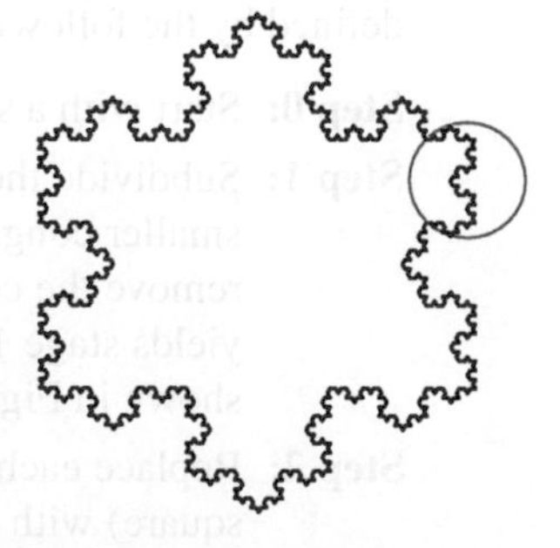

FIGURE 1.24 The portion of the Koch snowflake shown in the circle is not a replica of the entire snowflake.

[4] Mandelbrot, Benoit B. *The Fractal Geometry of Nature.* New York: W. H. Freeman and Company, 1983, p. 1.

b. Because any portion of the Koch curve replicates the entire fractal, the Koch curve is a strictly self-similar fractal. See Figure 1.25.

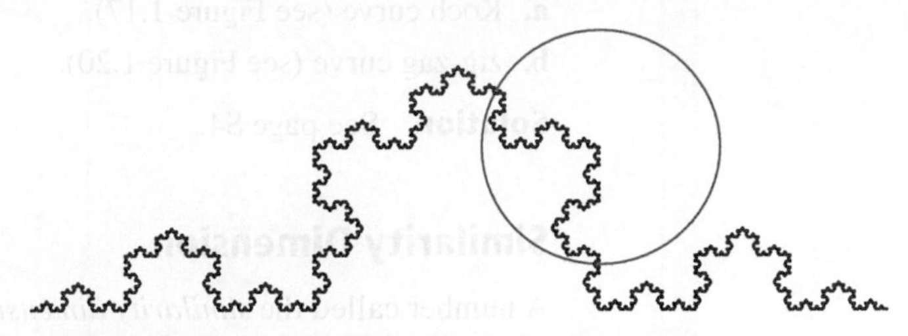

FIGURE 1.25 Any portion of the Koch curve is a replica of the entire Koch curve.

CHECK YOUR PROGRESS 3 Determine whether the following fractals are strictly self-similar.

a. The box curve (see Example 1) **b.** The Sierpinski gasket (see Example 2)

Solution See page S4.

Replacement Ratio and Scaling Ratio

Mathematicians like to assign numbers to fractals so that they can objectively compare fractals. Two numbers that are associated with many fractals are the *replacement ratio* and the *scaling ratio.*

Replacement Ratio and Scaling Ratio of a Fractal

- If the generator of a fractal consists of N replicas of the initiator, then the **replacement ratio** of the fractal is N.
- If the initiator of a fractal has linear dimensions that are r times the corresponding linear dimensions of its replicas in the generator, then the **scaling ratio** of the fractal is r.

EXAMPLE 4 **Find the Replacement Ratio and the Scaling Ratio of a Fractal**

Find the replacement ratio and the scaling ratio of the

a. box curve. **b.** Sierpinski gasket.

Solution

a. Figure 1.19 on page 86 shows that the generator of the box curve consists of five line segments and that the initiator consists of only one line segment. Thus the replacement ratio of the box curve is 5:1, or 5.

The initiator of the box curve is a line segment that is 3 times as long as the replica line segments in the generator. Thus the scaling ratio of the box curve is 3:1, or 3.

b. Figure 1.21 on page 87 shows that the generator of the Sierpinski gasket consists of three triangles and that the initiator consists of only one triangle. Thus the replacement ratio of the Sierpinski gasket is 3:1, or 3.

The initiator triangle of the Sierpinski gasket has a width that is 2 times the width of the replica triangles in the generator. Thus the scaling ratio of the Sierpinski gasket is 2:1, or 2.

CHECK YOUR PROGRESS 4 Find the replacement ratio and the scaling ratio of the

a. Koch curve (see Figure 1.17).

b. zig-zag curve (see Figure 1.20).

Solution See page S4.

Similarity Dimension

A number called the *similarity dimension* is used to quantify how densely a strictly self-similar fractal fills a region.

Similarity Dimension

The **similarity dimension** D of a strictly self-similar fractal is given by

$$D = \frac{\log N}{\log r}$$

where N is the replacement ratio of the fractal and r is the scaling ratio.

EXAMPLE 5 **Find the Similarity Dimension of a Fractal**

Find the similarity dimension, to the nearest thousandth, of the

a. Koch curve.

b. Sierpinski gasket.

Solution

a. Because the Koch curve is a strictly self-similar fractal, we can find its similarity dimension. Figure 1.17 on page 85 shows that stage 1 of the Koch curve consists of four line segments and stage 0 consists of only one line segment. Hence the replacement ratio is 4:1, or 4. The line segment in stage 0 is 3 times as long as each of the replica line segments in stage 1, so the scaling ratio is 3. Thus the Koch curve has a similarity dimension of

$$D = \frac{\log 4}{\log 3} \approx 1.262$$

b. In Example 4, we found that the Sierpinski gasket has a replacement ratio of 3 and a scaling ratio of 2. Thus the Sierpinski gasket has a similarity dimension of

$$D = \frac{\log 3}{\log 2} \approx 1.585$$

TAKE NOTE

Because the Koch snowflake is not a strictly self-similar fractal, we cannot compute its similarity dimension.

CHECK YOUR PROGRESS 5 Compute the similarity dimension, to the nearest thousandth, of the

a. box curve (see Example 1). **b.** Sierpinski carpet (see Check Your Progress 2).

Solution See page S5.

The results of Example 5 show that the Sierpinski gasket has a larger similarity dimension than the Koch curve. This means that the Sierpinski gasket fills a flat two-dimensional surface more densely than does the Koch curve.

Computers are used to generate fractals such as those shown in Figure 1.26. These fractals were *not* rendered by using an initiator and a generator, but they were rendered using iterative procedures.

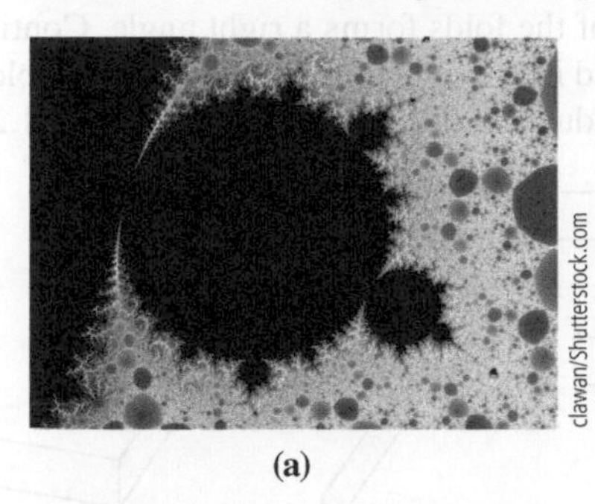

(a)

(b)

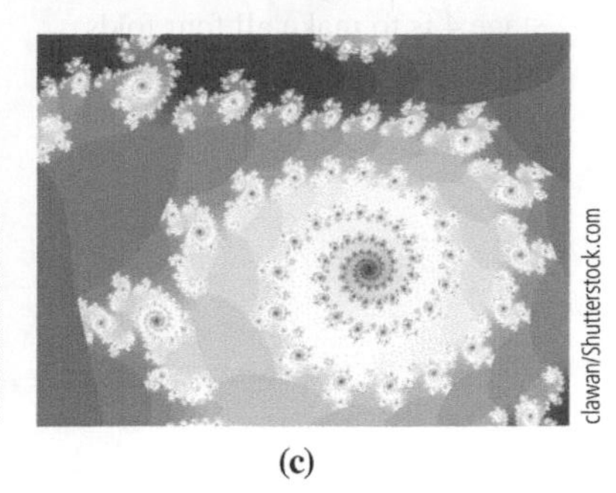

(c)

FIGURE 1.26 Computer-generated fractals

Fractals have other applications in addition to being used to produce intriguing images. For example, computer scientists have recently developed fractal image compression programs based on self-transformations of an image. An image compression program is a computer program that converts an image file to a smaller file that requires less computer memory. In some situations, these fractal compression programs outperform standardized image compression programs such as JPEG (*jay-peg*), which was developed by the Joint Photographic Experts Group.

Some cellular telephones have been manufactured with internal antennas that are fractal in design. Figure 1.27 shows a cellular telephone with an internal antenna in the shape of a stage of the Sierpinski carpet fractal. The antenna in Figure 1.28 is in the shape of a stage of the Koch curve.

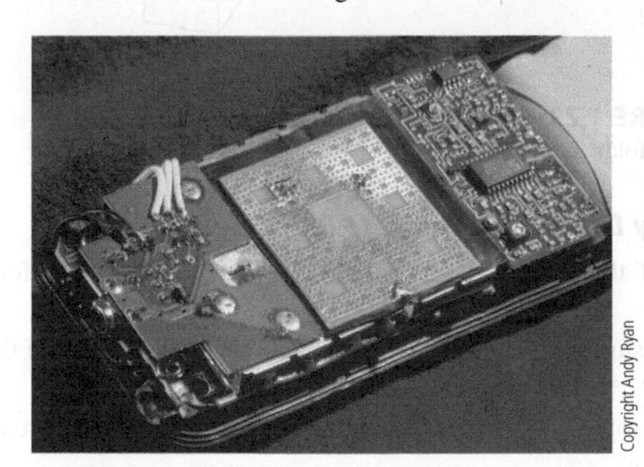

FIGURE 1.27 A Sierpinski carpet fractal antenna hidden inside a cellular telephone

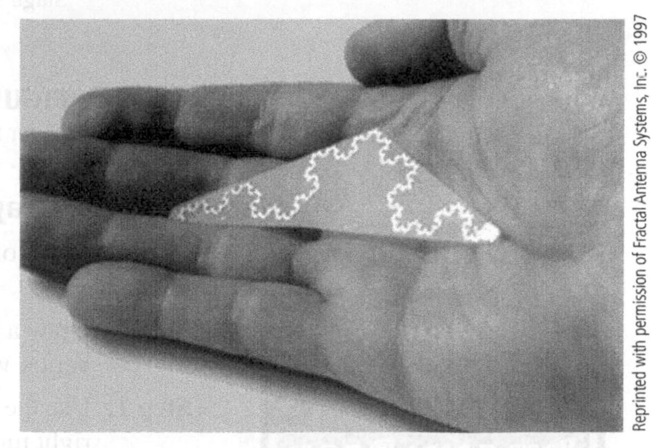

FIGURE 1.28 A Koch curve antenna designed for use in wireless communication devices

EXCURSION

The Heighway Dragon Fractal

In this Excursion, we illustrate two methods of constructing the stages of a fractal known as the *Heighway dragon.*

The Heighway Dragon via Paper Folding

The first few stages of the Heighway dragon fractal can be constructed by the repeated folding of a strip of paper. In the following discussion, we use a 1-inch-wide strip of paper

TAKE NOTE

The easiest way to construct stage 4 is to make all four folds before you open the paper. All folds must be made in the same direction.

that is 14 in. in length as stage 0. To create stage 1 of the dragon fractal, just fold the strip in half and open it so that the fold forms a right angle (see Figure 1.29). To create stage 2, fold the original strip twice. The second fold should be in the same direction as the first fold. Open the paper so that each of the folds forms a right angle. Continue the iterative process of making an additional fold in the same direction as the first fold and then forming a right angle at each fold to produce additional stages. See Figure 1.29.

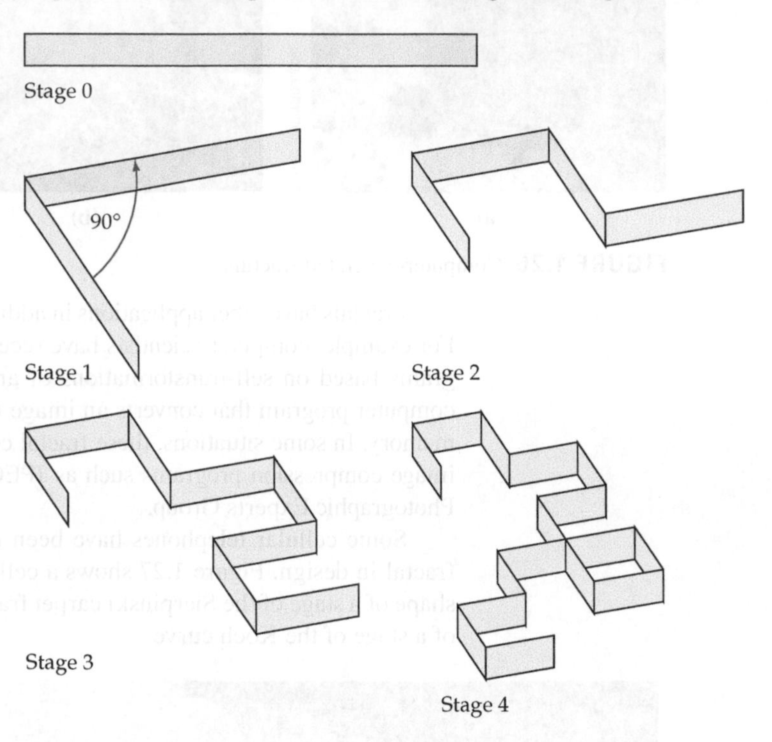

FIGURE 1.29 The first five stages of the Heighway dragon via paper folding

The Heighway Dragon via the Left-Right Rule

The nth stage of the Heighway dragon can also be created by the following drawing procedure.

Step 0: Draw a small vertical line segment. Label the bottom point of this segment as vertex $v = 0$ and label the top as vertex $v = 1$.

Step 1: Use the following left-right rule to determine whether to make a left turn or a right turn.

The Left-Right Rule

At vertex v, where v is an *odd* number, go

- **right** if the remainder of v divided by 4 is 1.
- **left** if the remainder of v divided by 4 is 3.

At vertex 2, go to the right. At vertex v, where v is an *even* number greater than 2, go in the same direction in which you went at vertex $\frac{v}{2}$.

Draw another line segment of the same length as the original segment. Label the endpoint of this segment with a number that is 1 larger than the number used for the preceding vertex.

Step 2: Continue to repeat step 1 until you reach the last vertex. The last vertex of an n-stage Heighway dragon is the vertex numbered 2^n.

POINT OF INTEREST

The Heighway dragon is sometimes called the "Jurassic Park fractal" because it was used in the book *Jurassic Park* to illustrate some of the surprising results that can be obtained by iterative processes.

EXCURSION EXERCISES

1. Use a strip of paper and the folding procedure explained on page 92 to create models of the first five stages (stage 0 through stage 4) of the Heighway dragon. Explain why it would be difficult to create the 10th stage of the Heighway dragon using the paper-folding procedure.
2. Use the left-right rule to draw stage 2 of the Heighway dragon.
3. Use the left-right rule to determine the direction in which to turn at vertex 7 of the Heighway dragon.
4. Use the left-right rule to determine the direction in which to turn at vertex 50 of the Heighway dragon.
5. Use the left-right rule to determine the direction in which to turn at vertex 64 of the Heighway dragon.

EXERCISE SET 1.8

■ In Exercises 1 and 2, use an iterative process to draw stage 2 and stage 3 of the fractal with the given initiator (stage 0) and the given generator (stage 1).

1. The Cantor point set

Stage 0

Stage 1

2. Lévy's curve

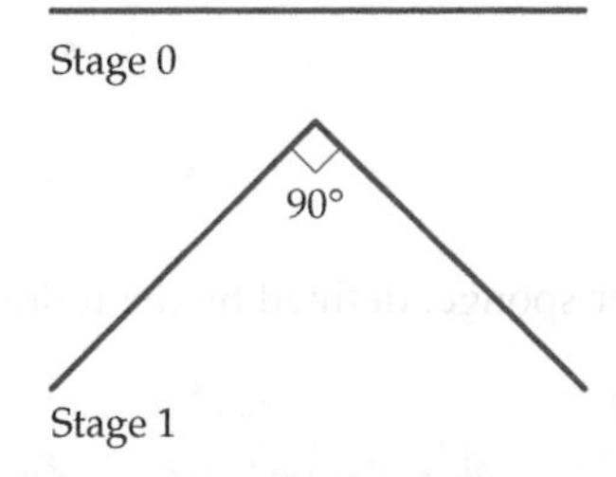

■ In Exercises 3 to 8, use an iterative process to draw stage 2 of the fractal with the given initiator (stage 0) and the given generator (stage 1).

3. The Sierpinski carpet, variation 1

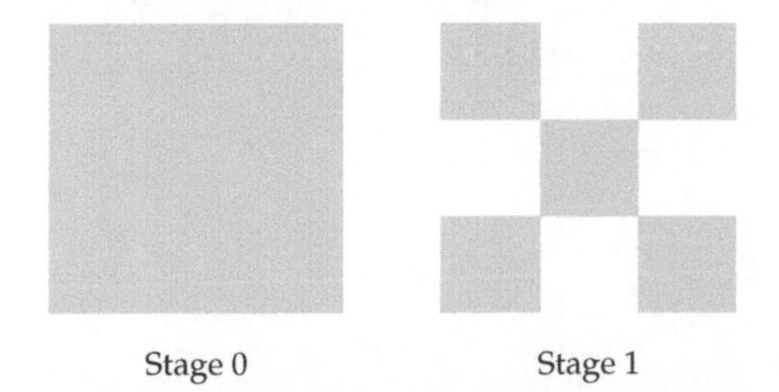

4. The Sierpinski carpet, variation 2

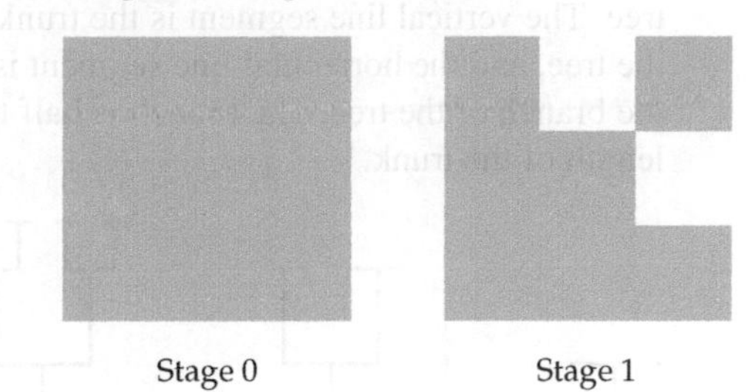

5. The river tree of Peano Cearo

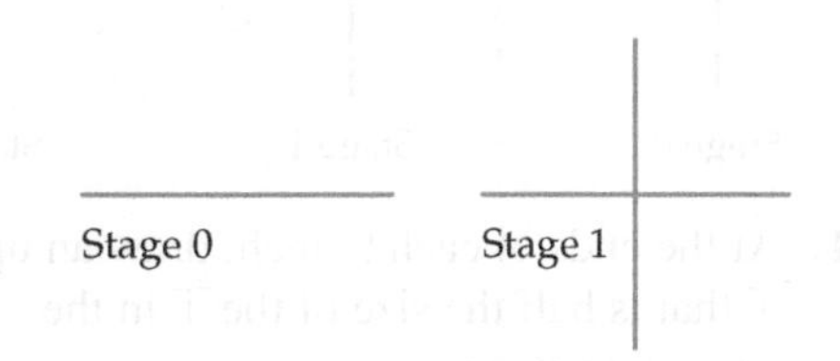

6. Minkowski's fractal

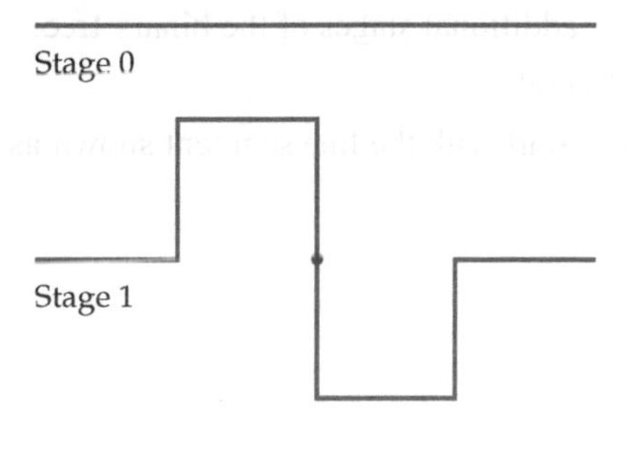

7. The square fractal

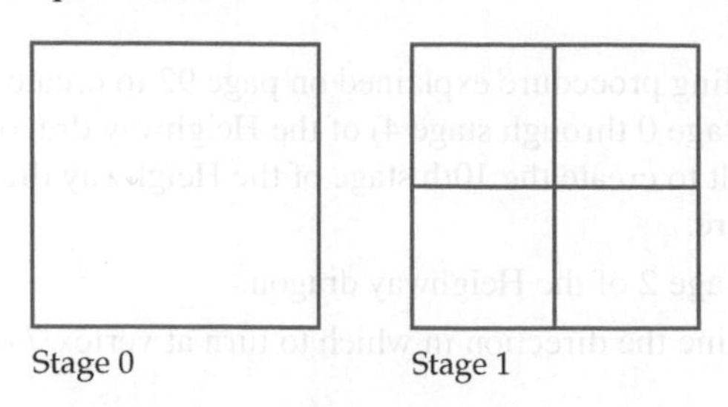

8. The cube fractal

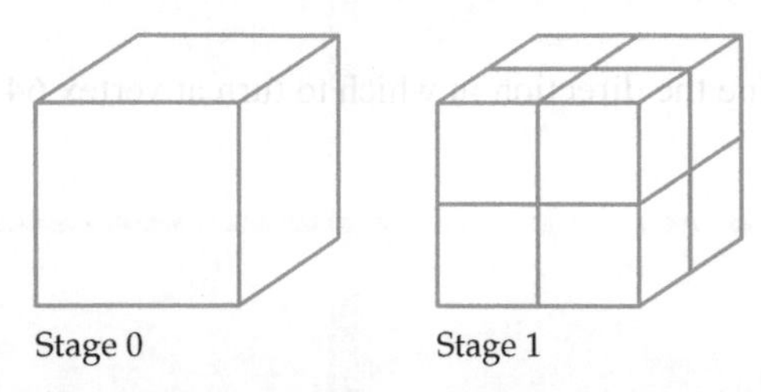

■ In Exercises 9 and 10, draw stage 3 and stage 4 of the fractal defined by the given iterative process.

9. The binary tree

Step 0: Start with a "T." This is stage 0 of the binary tree. The vertical line segment is the trunk of the tree, and the horizontal line segment is the branch of the tree. The branch is half the length of the trunk.

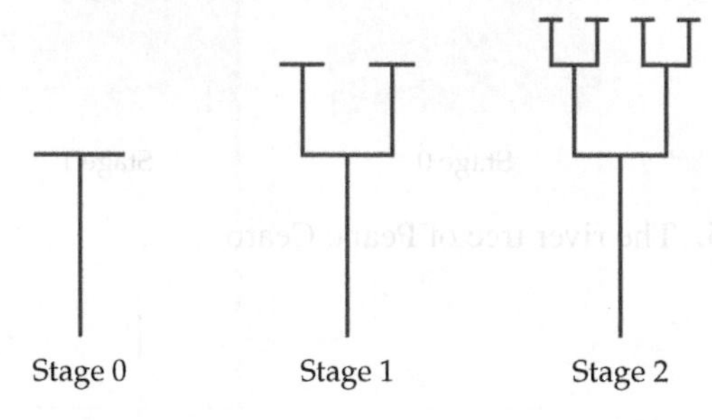

Step 1: At the ends of each branch, draw an upright T that is half the size of the T in the preceding stage.

Step 2: Continue to repeat step 1 to generate additional stages of the binary tree.

10. The I-fractal

Step 0: Start with the line segment shown as stage 0 below.

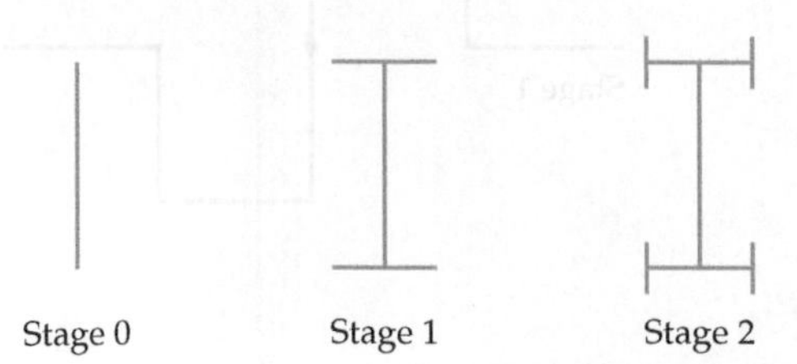

Step 1: At each end of the line segment, draw a crossbar that is half the length of the line segment it contacts. (This produces stage 1 of the I-fractal.)

Step 2: Use each crossbar from the preceding step as the connecting segment of a new "I." Attach new crossbars that are half the length of the connecting segment.

Step 3: Continue to repeat step 2 to generate additional stages of the I-fractal.

■ In Exercises 11 to 20, compute, if possible, the similarity dimension of the fractal. Round to the nearest thousandth.

11. The Cantor point set (see Exercise 1)

12. Lévy's curve (see Exercise 2)

13. The Sierpinski carpet, variation 1 (see Exercise 3)

14. The Sierpinski carpet, variation 2 (see Exercise 4)

15. The river tree of Peano Cearo (see Exercise 5)

16. Minkowski's fractal (see Exercise 6)

17. The square fractal (see Exercise 7)

18. The cube fractal (see Exercise 8)

19. The quadric Koch curve, defined by the following stages

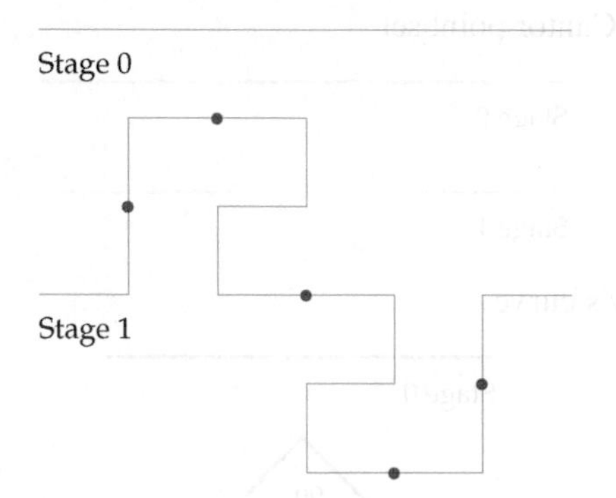

20. The Menger sponge, defined by the following stages

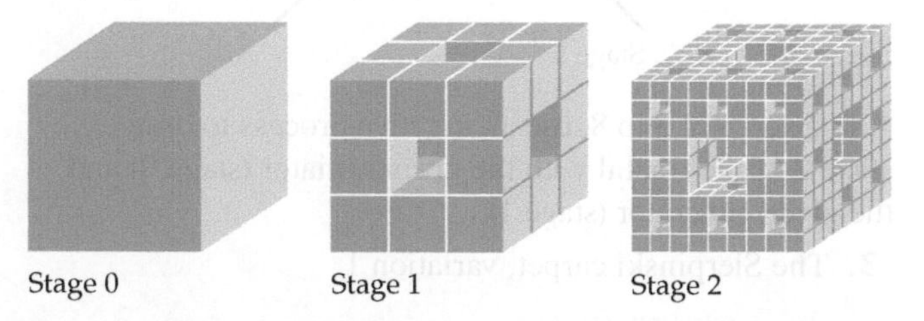

EXTENSIONS

21. Compare Similarity Dimensions

a. Rank, from largest to smallest, the similarity dimensions of the Sierpinski carpet; the Sierpinski carpet, variation 1 (see Exercise 3); and the Sierpinski carpet, variation 2 (see Exercise 4).

b. Which of the three fractals is the most dense?

22. The Peano Curve The *Peano curve* is defined by the following stages.

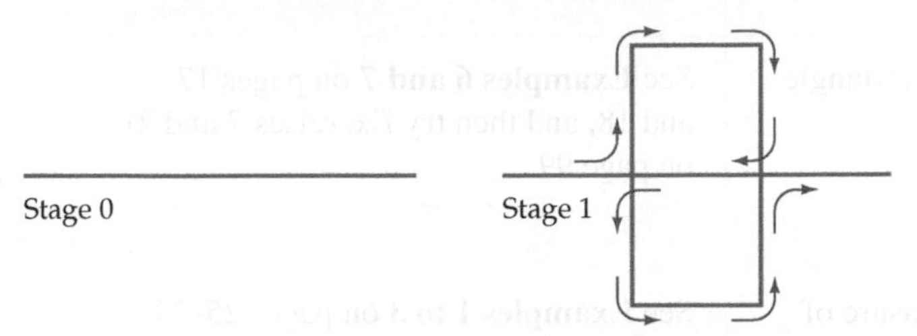

The arrows show the route used to trace the generator.

a. What is the similarity dimension of the Peano curve?

b. Explain why the Peano curve is referred to as a plane-filling curve.

23. Explain why the similarity dimension formula cannot be used to find the similarity dimension of the binary tree defined in Exercise 9.

24. Stage 0 and stage 1 of Lévy's curve (see Exercise 2) and the Heighway dragon (see page 92) are identical, but the fractals start to differ at stage 2. Make two drawings that illustrate how they differ at stage 2.

CHAPTER 1 SUMMARY

The following table summarizes essential concepts in this chapter. The references given in the right-hand column list Examples and Exercises that can be used to test your understanding of a concept.

1.1 Measurement	
U.S. Customary Units of Measure ■ Measures of length: inches, feet, yards, miles ■ Measures of weight: ounces, pounds, tons ■ Measures of capacity: fluid ounces, cups, pints, quarts, gallons	See **Examples 1 to 3** on pages 2 and 3. Then try Exercises 1 and 2 on page 99.
The Metric System The metric system uses a prefix of a base unit to denote the magnitude of a measurement. ■ Base unit of length: meter ■ Base unit of mass: gram ■ Base unit of capacity: liter Some of the prefixes used in the metric system are kilo (1000), hecto (100), deca (10), deci (0.1), centi (0.01), and milli (0.001).	See **Examples 4, 5, and 6** on pages 4–6. Then try Exercises 3, 4, and 5 on page 99.
Convert Between U.S. Customary Units and Metric Units	See **Example 7** on page 7. Then try Exercise 6 on page 99.

continued

1.2 Basic Concepts of Euclidean Geometry	
Vertical Angles The nonadjacent angles formed by two intersecting lines are called vertical angles. Vertical angles have the same measure.	See **Example 4** on page 15, and then try Exercise 14 on page 99.
Lines and Angles A line that intersects two other lines at different points is a transversal. If the lines cut by a transversal are parallel lines, several angles of equal measure are formed. ■ Pairs of alternate interior angles have the same measure. ■ Pairs of alternate exterior angles have the same measure. ■ Pairs of corresponding angles have the same measure.	See **Example 5** on page 15, and then try Exercise 18 on page 99.
Triangles The sum of the measures of the interior angles of a triangle is 180°.	See **Examples 6 and 7** on pages 17 and 18, and then try Exercises 7 and 21 on page 99.
1.3 Perimeter and Area of Plane Figures	
Perimeter The perimeter of a plane geometric figure is a measure of the distance around the figure. Triangle: $P = a + b + c$ Rectangle: $P = 2L + 2W$ Square: $P = 4s$ Parallelogram: $P = 2b + 2s$ Circle: $C = \pi d$ or $C = 2\pi r$	See **Examples 1 to 3** on pages 25–27, and then try Exercises 17, 24, and 26 on pages 99 and 100.
Area Area is the amount of surface in a region. Area is measured in square units. Triangle: $A = \frac{1}{2}bh$ Rectangle: $A = LW$ Square: $A = s^2$ Parallelogram: $A = bh$ Trapezoid: $A = \frac{1}{2}h(b_1 + b_2)$ Circle: $A = \pi r^2$	See **Examples 5 to 10** on pages 28–32, and then try Exercises 15, 22, 27, and 28 on pages 99 and 100.
1.4 Properties of Triangles	
Similar Triangles The ratios of corresponding sides are equal. The ratio of corresponding heights is equal to the ratio of corresponding sides. The measures of corresponding angles are equal.	See **Examples 1 and 2** on pages 41–43, and then try Exercise 8 on page 99.
Congruent Triangles **Side-Side-Side Theorem (SSS)** If the three sides of one triangle are equal in measure to the three sides of a second triangle, the two triangles are congruent. **Side-Angle-Side Theorem (SAS)** If two sides and the included angle of one triangle are equal in measure to two sides and the included angle of a second triangle, the two triangles are congruent. **Angle-Side-Angle Theorem (ASA)** If two angles and the included side of one triangle are equal in measure to two angles and the included side of a second triangle, the two triangles are congruent.	See **Example 3** on page 45, and then try Exercise 29 on page 100.

continued

The Pythagorean Theorem If a and b are the lengths of the legs of a right triangle and c is the length of the hypotenuse, then $c^2 = a^2 + b^2$.	See **Example 4** on page 46, and then try Exercise 30 on page 100.
1.5 Volume and Surface Area	
Volume Volume is a measure of the amount of space occupied by a geometric solid. Volume is measured in cubic units. Rectangular solid: $V = LWH$ Cube: $V = s^3$ Sphere: $V = \frac{4}{3}\pi r^3$ Right circular cylinder: $V = \pi r^2 h$ Right circular cone: $V = \frac{1}{3}\pi r^2 h$ Regular square pyramid: $V = \frac{1}{3}s^2 h$	See **Examples 1, 2, and 3** on pages 55 and 56, and then try Exercises 9, 16, 20, and 23 on page 99.
Surface Area The surface area of a solid is the total area on the surface of the solid. Rectangular solid: $S = 2LW + 2LH + 2WH$ Cube: $S = 6s^2$ Sphere: $S = 4\pi r^2$ Right circular cylinder: $S = 2\pi r^2 + 2\pi rh$ Right circular cone: $S = \pi r^2 + \pi rl$ Regular square pyramid: $S = s^2 + 2sl$	See **Example 4** on page 58, and then try Exercises 11, 12, and 25 on page 99.
1.6 Right Triangle Trigonometry	
The Trigonometric Ratios of an Acute Angle of a Right Triangle If θ is an acute angle of a right triangle ABC, then $\sin\theta = \frac{\text{length of opposite side}}{\text{length of hypotenuse}}$ $\cos\theta = \frac{\text{length of adjacent side}}{\text{length of hypotenuse}}$ $\tan\theta = \frac{\text{length of opposite side}}{\text{length of adjacent side}}$ $\csc\theta = \frac{\text{length of hypotenuse}}{\text{length of opposite side}}$ $\sec\theta = \frac{\text{length of hypotenuse}}{\text{length of adjacent side}}$ $\cot\theta = \frac{\text{length of adjacent side}}{\text{length of opposite side}}$	See **Examples 1 and 2** on pages 65 and 66, and then try Exercises 31 and 32 on page 100.
Inverse Sine, Inverse Cosine, and Inverse Tangent $\sin^{-1}(x)$ is defined as the angle whose sine is x, $0 < x < 1$. $\cos^{-1}(x)$ is defined as the angle whose cosine is x, $0 < x < 1$. $\tan^{-1}(x)$ is defined as the angle whose tangent is x, $x > 0$.	See **Examples 3, 4, and 5** on pages 67 and 68, and then try Exercises 33 and 36 on page 100.

continued

Applications of Trigonometry Trigonometry is often used to solve applications that involve right triangles.	See **Example 6** on pages 68 and 69, and then try Exercises 37 and 38 on page 100.
1.7 Non-Euclidean Geometry	
Parallel Postulates **Euclidean Parallel Postulate** (*Euclidean or Plane Geometry*) Through a given point not on a given line, exactly one line can be drawn parallel to the given line. **Gauss's Alternate to the Parallel Postulate** (*Lobachevskian or Hyperbolic Geometry*) Through a given point not on a given line, there are at least two lines parallel to the given line. **Riemann's Alternative to the Parallel Postulate** (*Riemannian or Spherical Geometry*) Through a given point not on a given line, there exist no lines parallel to the given line.	See **Example 2** on page 77, and then try Exercises 42 and 43 on page 100.
The Spherical Triangle Area Formula The area S of the spherical triangle ABC on a sphere with radius r is $S = (m\angle A + m\angle B + m\angle C - 180°)\left(\frac{\pi}{180°}\right)r^2$	See **Example 1** on pages 75 and 76, and then try Exercises 44 and 45 on page 100.
The Euclidean Distance Formula and the City Distance Formula ■ The Euclidean distance between $P(x_1, y_1)$ and $Q(x_2, y_2)$ is $d_E(P, Q) = \sqrt{(x_2 - x_1)^2 + (y_2 - y_1)^2}$ ■ The city distance between $P(x_1, y_1)$ and $Q(x_2, y_2)$ is $d_C(P, Q) = \lvert x_2 - x_1 \rvert + \lvert y_2 - y_1 \rvert$	See **Example 3** on page 79, and then try Exercises 46 and 49 on page 100.
1.8 Fractals	
Strictly Self-Similar Fractal A fractal is a strictly self-similar fractal if any arbitrary portion of the fractal contains a replica of the entire fractal.	See **Example 3** on page 88, and then try Exercise 51 on page 100.
Replacement Ratio and Scaling Ratio of a Fractal ■ If the generator of a fractal consists of N replicas of the initiator, then the replacement ratio of the fractal is N. ■ If the initiator of a fractal has linear dimensions that are r times the corresponding linear dimensions of its replicas in the generator, then the scaling ratio of the fractal is r.	See **Example 4** on page 89, and then try Exercise 53 on page 100.
Similarity Dimension of a Fractal The similarity dimension D of a strictly self-similar fractal is $D = \frac{\log N}{\log r}$ where N is the replacement ratio of the fractal and r is the scaling ratio.	See **Example 5** on page 90, and then try Exercise 54 on page 100.

CHAPTER 1 REVIEW EXERCISES

■ For Exercises 1 to 5, convert one measurement to another.

1. 27 in. = ________ ft

2. 15 cups = ________ pints

3. 37 mm = ________ cm

4. 0.678 g = ________ mg

5. 1273 ml = ________ L

6. The price of a beverage is $3.56 per liter. What is the price of this beverage in dollars per quart? Round to the nearest cent.

7. Given that $m\angle a = 74°$ and $m\angle b = 52°$, find the measures of angles x and y.

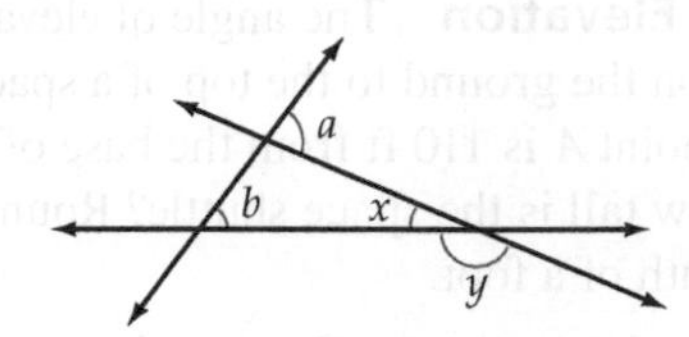

8. Triangles ABC and DEF are similar. Find the perimeter of triangle ABC.

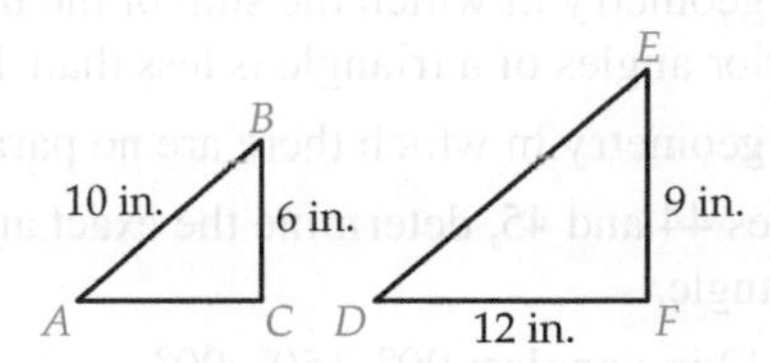

9. Find the volume of the geometric solid.

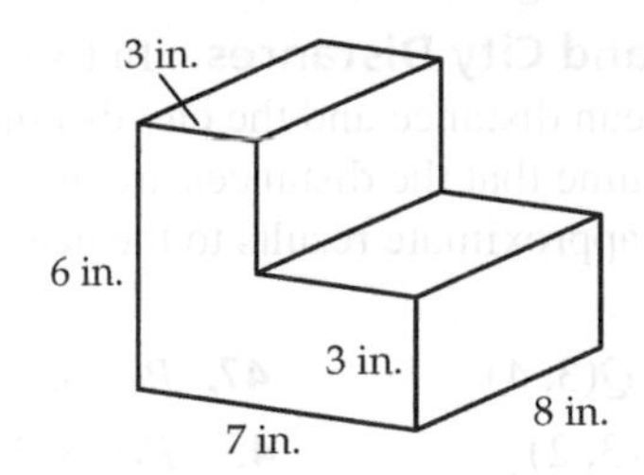

10. Find the measure of $\angle x$.

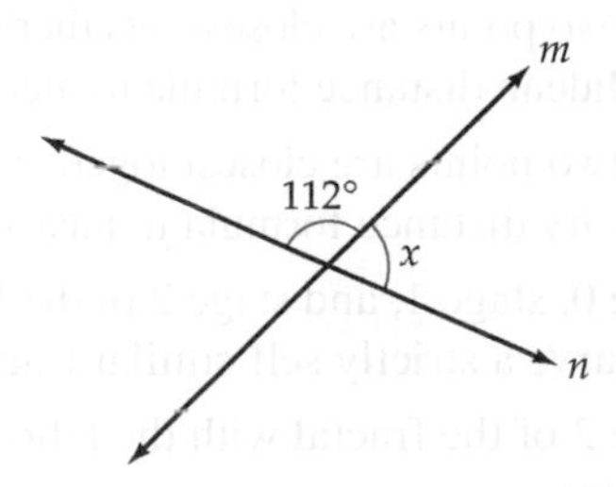

11. Find the surface area of the rectangular solid.

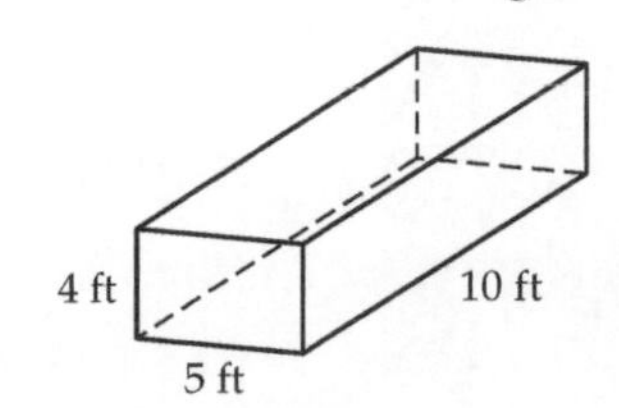

12. The length of a diameter of the base of a cylinder is 4 m, and the height of the cylinder is 8 m. Find the surface area of the cylinder. Give the exact value.

13. Given that $BC = 11$ cm and that AB is three times the length of BC, find the length of AC.

14. Given that $m\angle x = 150°$, find the measures of $\angle w$ and $\angle y$.

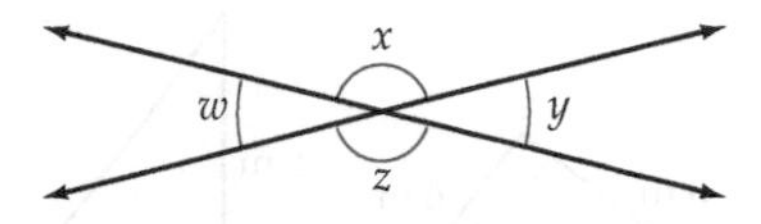

15. Find the area of a parallelogram that has a base of 6 in. and a height of 4.5 in.

16. Find the volume of the square pyramid.

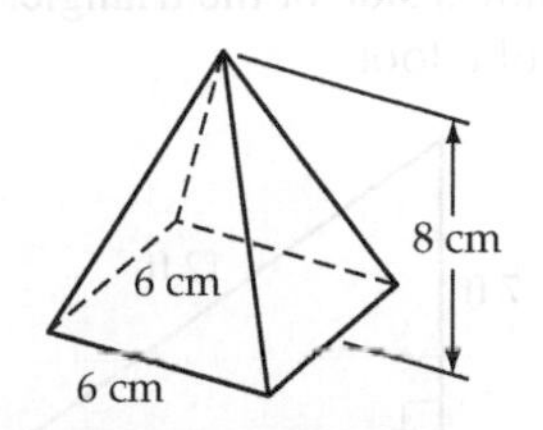

17. Find the circumference of a circle that has a diameter of 4.5 m. Round to the nearest tenth of a meter.

18. Given that $\ell_1 \parallel \ell_2$, find the measures of angles a and b.

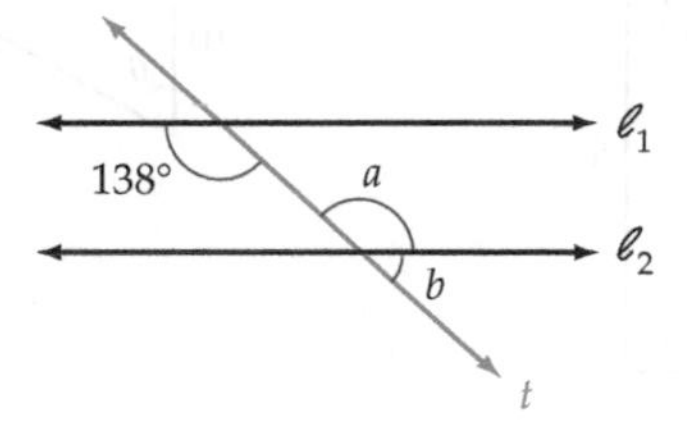

19. Find the supplement of a 32° angle.

20. Find the volume of a rectangular solid with a length of 6.5 ft, a width of 2 ft, and a height of 3 ft.

21. Two angles of a triangle measure 37° and 48°. Find the measure of the third angle.

22. The height of a triangle is 7 cm. The area of the triangle is 28 cm^2. Find the length of the base of the triangle.

23. Find the volume of a sphere that has a diameter of 12 mm. Give the exact value.

24. Framing The perimeter of a square picture frame is 86 cm. Find the length of each side of the frame.

25. Paint A can of paint will cover 200 ft^2 of surface. How many cans of paint should be purchased to paint a cylinder that has a height of 15 ft and a radius of 6 ft?

26. Parks and Recreation The length of a rectangular park is 56 yd. The width is 48 yd. How many yards of fencing are needed to surround the park?

27. Patios What is the area of a square patio that measures 9.5 m on each side?

28. Landscaping A walkway 2 m wide surrounds a rectangular plot of grass. The plot is 40 m long and 25 m wide. What is the area of the walkway?

29. Determine whether the two triangles are congruent. If they are congruent, state by what theorem they are congruent.

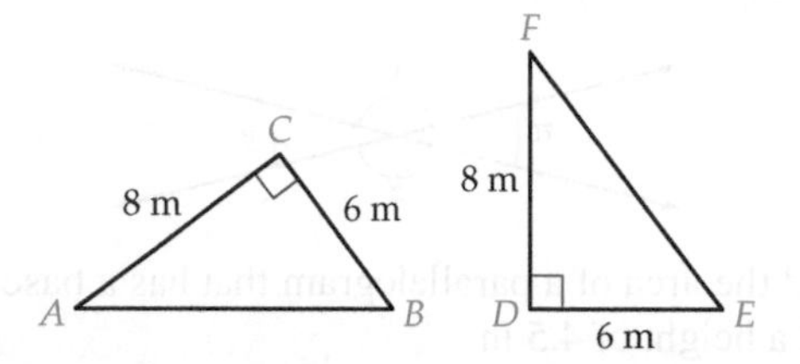

30. Find the unknown side of the triangle. Round to the nearest tenth of a foot.

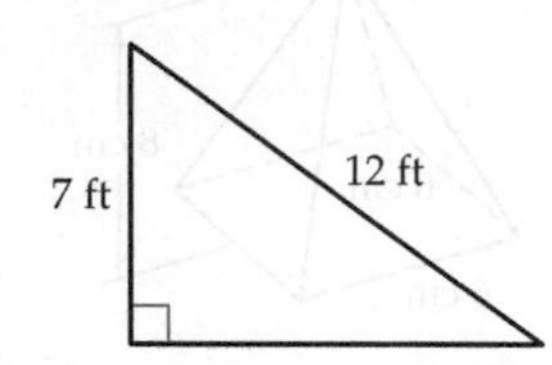

■ In Exercises 31 and 32, find the values of $\sin \theta$, $\cos \theta$, and $\tan \theta$ for the given right triangle.

31. (right triangle: θ, 8, 5)

32. (right triangle: 10, θ, 20)

■ In Exercises 33 to 36, use a calculator. Round to the nearest tenth of a degree.

33. Find $\cos^{-1}(0.9013)$.

34. Find $\sin^{-1}(0.4871)$.

35. Given $\tan \beta = 1.364$, find β.

36. Given $\sin \theta = 0.0325$, find θ.

37. Surveying Find the distance across the marsh in the following figure. Round to the nearest tenth of a foot.

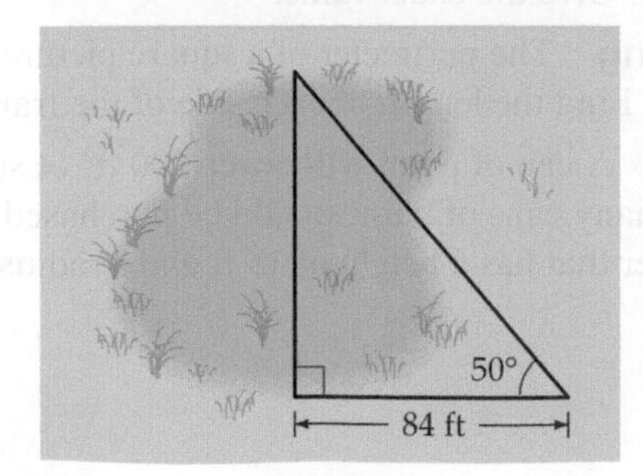

38. Angle of Depression The distance from a plane to a radar station is 200 mi, and the angle of depression is 40°. Find the number of ground miles from a point directly under the plane to the radar station. Round to the nearest tenth of a mile.

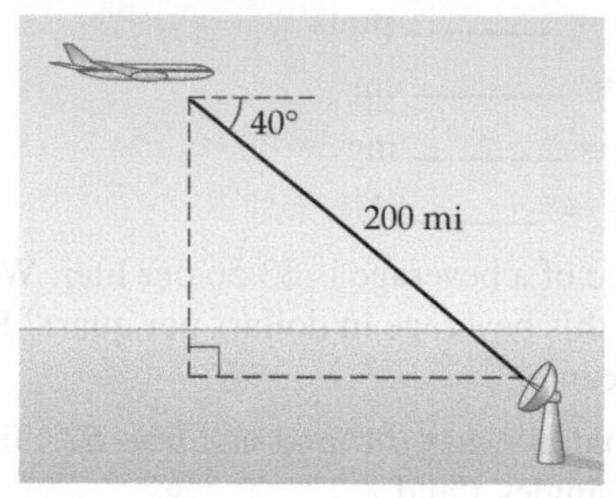

39. Angle of Elevation The angle of elevation from a point A on the ground to the top of a space shuttle is 27°. If point A is 110 ft from the base of the space shuttle, how tall is the space shuttle? Round to the nearest tenth of a foot.

40. What is another name for Riemannian geometry?

41. What is another name for Lobachevskian geometry?

42. Name a geometry in which the sum of the measures of the interior angles of a triangle is less than 180°.

43. Name a geometry in which there are no parallel lines.

■ In Exercises 44 and 45, determine the exact area of the spherical triangle.

44. Radius: 12 in.; angles: 90°, 150°, 90°

45. Radius: 5 ft; angles: 90°, 60°, 90°

■ **Euclidean and City Distances** In Exercises 46 to 49, find the Euclidean distance and the city distance between the points. Assume that the distances are measured in blocks. Round approximate results to the nearest tenth of a block.

46. $P(-1, 1)$, $Q(3, 4)$

47. $P(-5, -2)$, $Q(2, 6)$

48. $P(2, 8)$, $Q(3, 2)$

49. $P(-3, 3)$, $Q(5, -2)$

50. Consider the points $P(1, 1)$, $Q(4, 5)$, and $R(-4, 2)$.

a. Which two points are closest together if you only use the Euclidean distance formula to measure distance?

b. Which two points are closest together if you only use the city distance formula to measure distance?

51. Draw stage 0, stage 1, and stage 2 of the Koch curve. Is the Koch curve a strictly self-similar fractal?

52. Draw stage 2 of the fractal with the following initiator and generator.

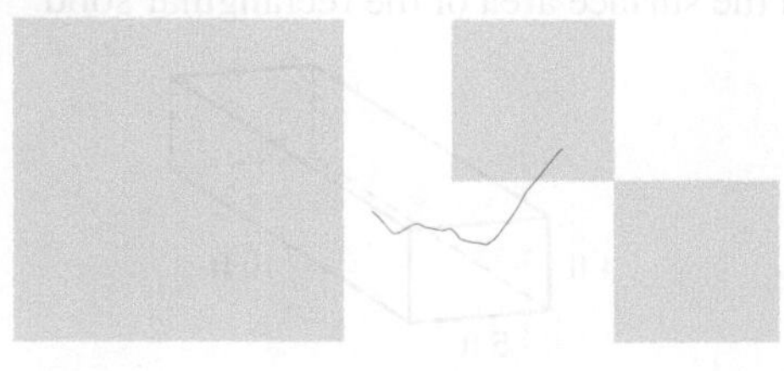

Stage 0 Initiator   Stage 1 Generator

53. For the fractal defined in Exercise 52, determine the

a. relacement ratio.

b. scaling ratio.

c. similarity dimension.

54. Compute the similarity dimension of a strictly self-similar fractal with a replacement ratio of 5 and a scaling ratio of 4. Round to the nearest thousandth.

CHAPTER 1 TEST

1. Find the volume of a cylinder with a height of 6 m and a radius of 3 m. Round to the nearest tenth of a cubic meter.

2. Find the perimeter of a rectangle that has a length of 2 m and a width of 1.4 m.

3. Find the complement of a 32° angle.

4. Find the area of a circle that has a diameter of 2 m. Round to the nearest tenth of a square meter.

5. In the figure below, lines ℓ_1 and ℓ_2 are parallel. Angle x measures 30°. Find the measure of angle y.

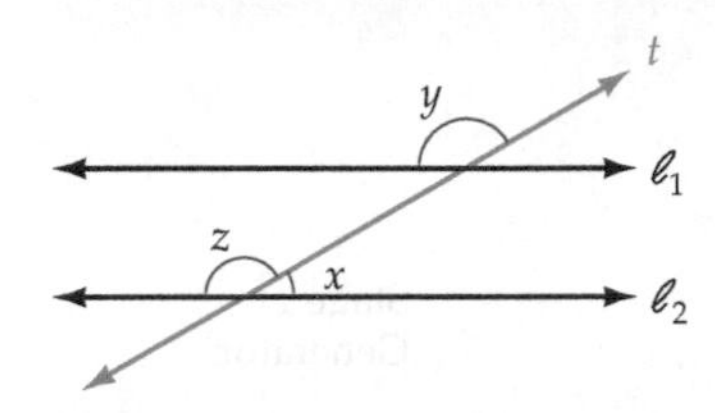

6. In the figure below, lines ℓ_1 and ℓ_2 are parallel. Angle x measures 45°. Find the measures of angles a and b.

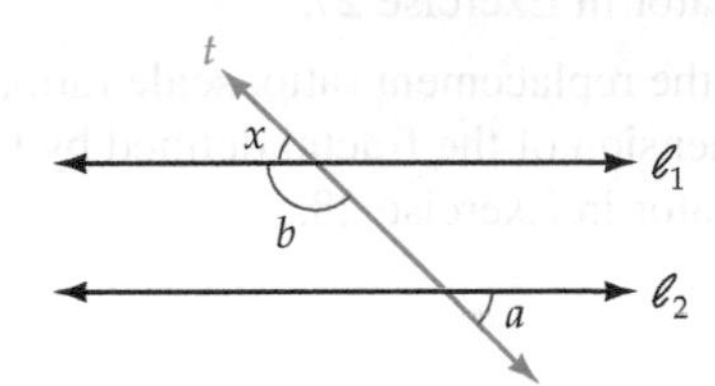

7. Convert: 1.2 m = ______ cm.

8. Find the volume of the figure. Give the exact value.

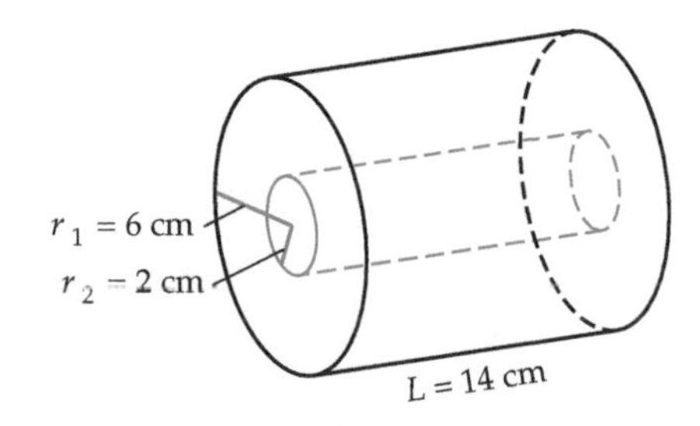

9. Triangles ABC and DEF are similar. Find side BC.

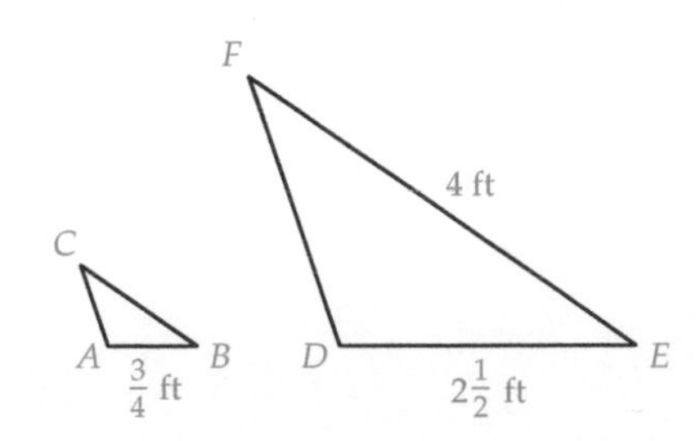

10. A right triangle has a 40° angle. Find the measures of the other two angles.

11. Find the measure of $\angle x$.

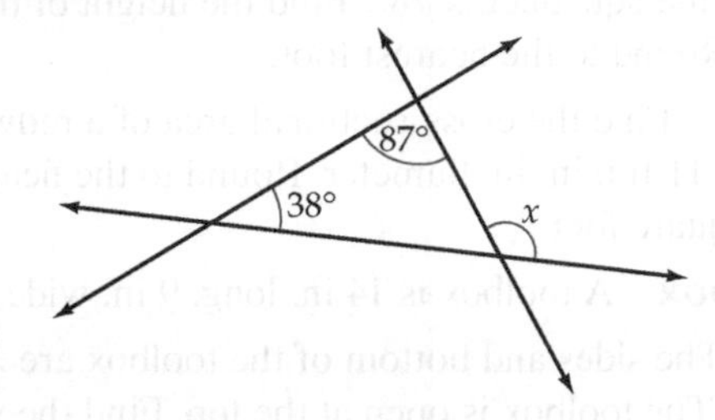

12. Find the area of the parallelogram shown below.

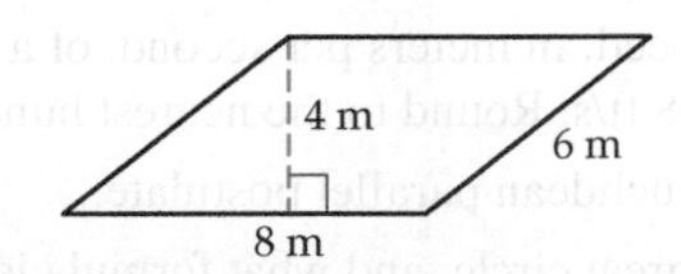

13. Surveying Find the width of the canal shown in the figure below.

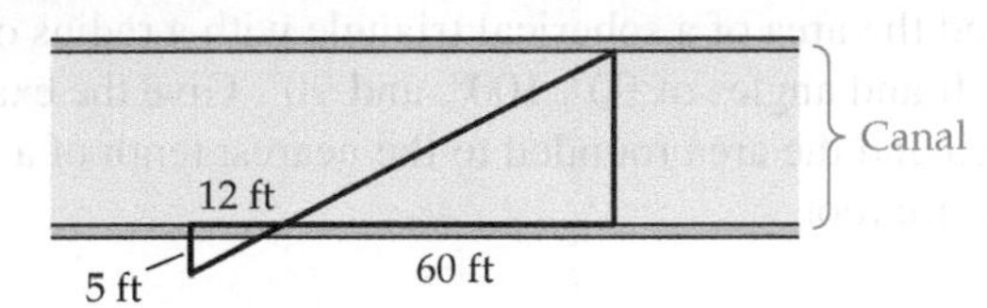

14. Pizza How much more area is in a pizza with radius 10 in. than in a pizza with radius 8 in.? Round to the nearest tenth of a square inch.

15. Determine whether the two triangles are congruent. If they are congruent, state by what theorem they are congruent.

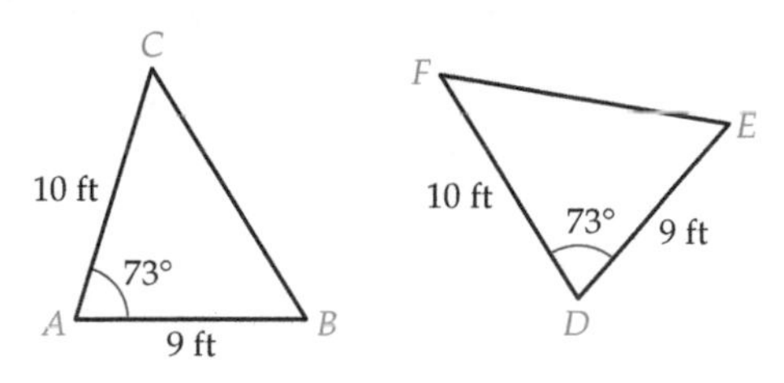

16. For the right triangle shown below, determine the length of side $\overline{BC}$. Round to the nearest tenth of a centimeter.

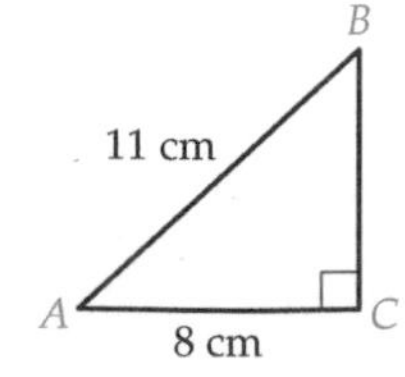

17. Find the values of $\sin \theta$, $\cos \theta$, and $\tan \theta$ for the given right triangle.

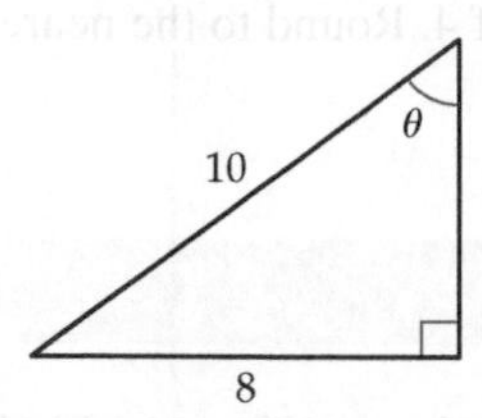

18. Angle of Elevation From a point 27 ft from the base of a Roman aqueduct, the angle of elevation to the top of the aqueduct is 78°. Find the height of the aqueduct. Round to the nearest foot.

19. Trees Find the cross-sectional area of a redwood tree that is 11 ft 6 in. in diameter. Round to the nearest tenth of a square foot.

20. Toolbox A toolbox is 14 in. long, 9 in. wide, and 8 in. high. The sides and bottom of the toolbox are $\frac{1}{2}$ in. thick. The toolbox is open at the top. Find the volume of the interior of the toolbox in cubic inches.

21. Find the speed, in meters per second, of a car that is traveling 88 ft/s. Round to the nearest hundredth.

22. State the Euclidean parallel postulate.

23. What is a great circle, and what formula is used to calculate the area of a spherical triangle formed by three arcs of three great circles?

24. Find the area of a spherical triangle with a radius of 12 ft and angles of 90°, 100°, and 90°. Give the exact area and the area rounded to the nearest tenth of a square foot.

25. City Geometry Find the Euclidean distance and the city distance between the points $P(-4, 2)$ and $Q(5, 1)$. Assume that the distances are measured in blocks. Round approximate results to the nearest tenth of a block.

26. City Geometry How many points are on the city circle with center (0, 0) and radius $r = 4$ blocks?

■ In Exercises 27 and 28, draw stage 2 of the fractal with the given initiator and generator.

27.

28.

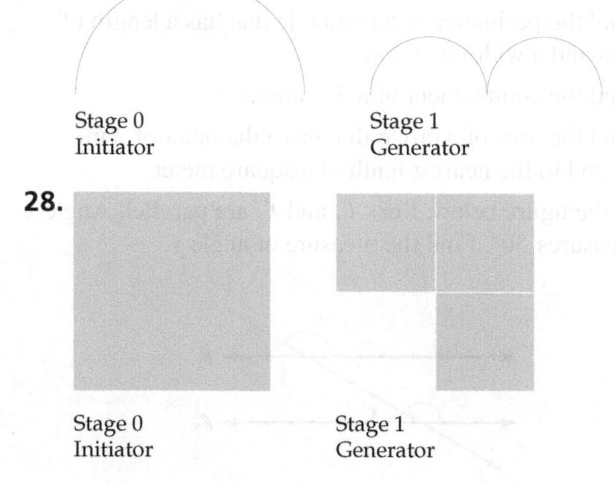

29. Compute the replacement ratio, scale ratio, and similarity dimension of the fractal defined by the initiator and generator in Exercise 27.

30. Compute the replacement ratio, scale ratio, and similarity dimension of the fractal defined by the initiator and generator in Exercise 28.

2

Applications of Equations

In your study of mathematics, you have probably noticed that the problems became less concrete and more abstract. Problems that are concrete provide information pertaining to a specific instance. Abstract problems are theoretical; they are stated without reference to a specific instance. Here's an example of a concrete problem:

If one candy bar costs 75 cents, how many candy bars can be purchased with 3 dollars?

To solve this problem, you need to calculate the number of cents in 3 dollars (multiply 3 by 100), and divide the result by the cost per candy bar (75 cents).

$$\frac{100 \cdot 3}{75} = \frac{300}{75} = 4$$

If one candy bar costs 75 cents, 4 candy bars can be purchased with 3 dollars.

Here is a related abstract problem:

If one candy bar costs c cents, how many candy bars can be purchased with d dollars?

Use the same procedure to solve the related abstract problem. Calculate the number of cents in d dollars (multiply d by 100), and divide the result by the cost per candy bar (c cents).

$$\frac{100 \cdot d}{c} = \frac{100d}{c}$$

If one candy bar costs c cents, $\frac{100d}{c}$ candy bars can be purchased with d dollars.

It is the variables in the problem above that makes it abstract. At the heart of the study of algebra is the use of variables. Variables enable us to generalize situations and state relationships among quantities. These relationships are often stated in the form of equations. In this chapter, we will be using equations to solve applications.

SECTION 2.1 First-Degree Equations and Formulas

Solving First-Degree Equations

Suppose that the fuel economy, in miles per gallon, of a particular car traveling at a speed of v miles per hour can be calculated using the variable expression $-0.02v^2 + 1.6v + 3$, where $10 \le v \le 75$. For example, if the speed of a car is 30 miles per hour, we can calculate the fuel economy by substituting 30 for v in the variable expression and then using the order of operations agreement to evaluate the resulting numerical expression.

$$\begin{aligned} &-0.02v^2 + 1.6v + 3 \\ &-0.02(30)^2 + 1.6(30) + 3 = -0.02(900) + 1.6(30) + 3 \\ &\qquad = -18 + 48 + 3 \\ &\qquad = 33 \end{aligned}$$

The fuel economy is 33 miles per gallon.

The **terms** of a variable expression are the addends of the expression. The expression $-0.02v^2 + 1.6v + 3$ has three terms. The terms $-0.02v^2$ and $1.6v$ are **variable terms** because each contains a variable. The term 3 is a **constant term**; it does not contain a variable.

Each variable term is composed of a **numerical coefficient** and a **variable part** (the variable or variables and their exponents). For the variable term $-0.02v^2$, -0.02 is the coefficient and v^2 is the variable part.

Like terms of a variable expression are terms with the same variable part. Constant terms are also like terms. Examples of like terms are

$4x$ and $7x$

$9y$ and y

$5x^2y$ and $6x^2y$

8 and -3

An **equation** expresses the equality of two mathematical expressions. Each of the following is an equation.

$8 + 5 = 13$

$4y - 6 = 10$

$x^2 - 2x + 1 = 0$

$b = 7$

Each of the equations below is a **first-degree equation in one variable**. *First degree* means that the variable has an exponent of 1.

$x + 11 = 14$

$3z + 5 = 8z$

$2(6y - 1) = 34$

A **solution** of an equation is a number that, when substituted for the variable, results in a true equation.

3 is a solution of the equation $x + 4 = 7$ because $3 + 4 = 7$.

9 is not a solution of the equation $x + 4 = 7$ because $9 + 4 \neq 7$.

To **solve an equation** means to find all solutions of the equation. The following properties of equations are often used to solve equations.

TAKE NOTE

Recall that the order of operations agreement states that when simplifying a numerical expression you should perform the operations in the following order:

1. Perform operations inside parentheses.
2. Simplify exponential expressions.
3. Do multiplication and division from left to right.
4. Do addition and subtraction from left to right.

POINT OF INTEREST

Albert Einstein Archive, Jerusalem, Ferdinand Schmutzer.

One of the most famous equations is $E = mc^2$. This equation, stated by Albert Einstein (īn′stīn), shows that there is a relationship between mass m and energy E. In this equation, c is the speed of light.

TAKE NOTE

It is important to note the difference between an expression and an equation. An equation contains an equals sign; an expression doesn't.

HISTORICAL NOTE

Finding solutions of equations has been a principal aim of mathematics for thousands of years. However, the equals sign did not occur in any text until 1557, when Robert Recorde (ca. 1510–1558) used the symbol in *The Whetstone of Witte.*

QUESTION Which of the following are first-degree equations in one variable?

a. $5y + 4 = 9 - 3(2y + 1)$ **b.** $\sqrt{x} + 9 = 16$ **c.** $p = -14$
d. $2x - 5 = x^2 - 9$ **e.** $3y + 7 = 4z - 10$

Properties of Equations

Addition Property
The same number can be added to each side of an equation without changing the solution of the equation.

If $a = b$, then $a + c = b + c$.

Subtraction Property
The same number can be subtracted from each side of an equation without changing the solution of the equation.

If $a = b$, then $a - c = b - c$.

Multiplication Property
Each side of an equation can be multiplied by the same *nonzero* number without changing the solution of the equation.

If $a = b$ and $c \neq 0$, then $ac = bc$.

Division Property
Each side of an equation can be divided by the same *nonzero* number without changing the solution of the equation.

If $a = b$ and $c \neq 0$, then $\frac{a}{c} = \frac{b}{c}$.

TAKE NOTE

In the multiplication property, it is necessary to state $c \neq 0$ so that the solutions of the equation are not changed.

For example, if $\frac{1}{2}x = 4$, then $x = 8$. But if we multiply each side of the equation by 0, we have

$$0 \cdot \frac{1}{2}x = 0 \cdot 4$$
$$0 = 0$$

The solution $x = 8$ is lost.

In solving a first-degree equation in one variable, the goal is to rewrite the equation with the variable alone on one side of the equation and a constant term on the other side of the equation. The constant term is the solution of the equation.

For example, to solve the equation $t + 9 = -4$, use the subtraction property to subtract the constant term (9) from each side of the equation.

$$t + 9 = -4$$
$$t + 9 - 9 = -4 - 9$$
$$t = -13$$

Now the variable (t) is alone on one side of the equation and a constant term (-13) is on the other side. The solution is -13.

TAKE NOTE

You should always check the solution of an equation. The check for the example at the right is shown below.

$$\begin{array}{c|c} t + 9 & -4 \\ \hline -13 + 9 & -4 \\ -4 & -4 \end{array}$$

$-4 = -4$

This is a true equation. The solution -13 checks.

ANSWER The equations in ***a*** and ***c*** are first-degree equations in one variable. The equation in ***b*** is not a first-degree equation in one variable because it contains the square root of a variable. The equation in ***d*** contains a variable with an exponent other than 1. The equation in ***e*** contains two variables.

To solve the equation $-5q = 120$, use the division property. Divide each side of the equation by the coefficient -5.

$$-5q = 120$$
$$\frac{-5q}{-5} = \frac{120}{-5}$$
$$q = -24$$

Now the variable (q) is alone on one side of the equation and a constant (-24) is on the other side. The solution is -24.

TAKE NOTE

An equation has some properties that are similar to those of a balance scale. For instance, if a balance scale is in balance and equal weights are added to each side of the scale, then the balance scale remains in balance. If an equation is true, then adding the same number to each side of the equation produces another true equation.

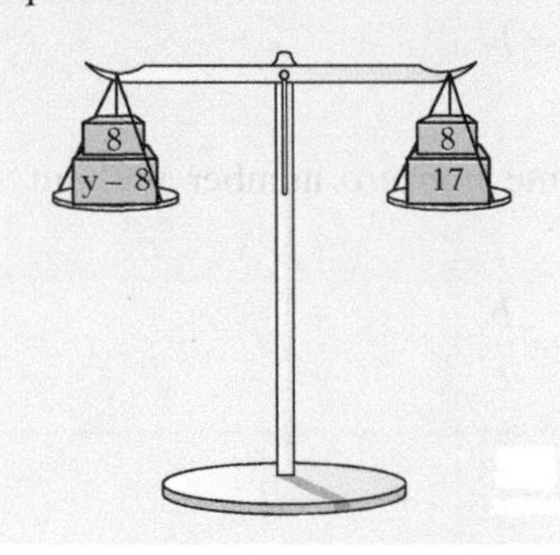

EXAMPLE 1 Solve a First-Degree Equation Using One of the Properties of Equations

Solve.

a. $y - 8 = 17$ **b.** $4x = -2$ **c.** $-5 = 9 + b$ **d.** $-a = -36$

Solution

a. Because 8 is subtracted from y, use the addition property to add 8 to each side of the equation.

$$y - 8 = 17$$
$$y - 8 + 8 = 17 + 8$$
$$y = 25$$

• A check will show that 25 is a solution.

The solution is 25.

b. Because x is multiplied by 4, use the division property to divide each side of the equation by 4.

$$4x = -2$$
$$\frac{4x}{4} = \frac{-2}{4}$$
$$x = -\frac{1}{2}$$

• A check will show that $-\frac{1}{2}$ is a solution.

The solution is $-\frac{1}{2}$.

c. Because 9 is added to b, use the subtraction property to subtract 9 from each side of the equation.

$$-5 = 9 + b$$
$$-5 - 9 = 9 - 9 + b$$
$$-14 = b$$

The solution is -14.

TAKE NOTE

When the coefficient of a variable is 1 or negative 1, the 1 is usually not written; $1a$ is written as a, and $-1a$ is written as $-a$.

d. The coefficient of the variable is -1. Use the multiplication property to multiply each side of the equation by -1. (Alternatively, we can divide both sides by -1.)

$$-a = -36$$
$$-1(-1a) = -1(-36)$$
$$a = 36$$

The solution is 36.

CHECK YOUR PROGRESS 1 Solve.

a. $c - 6 = -13$ **b.** $4 = -8z$ **c.** $22 + m = -9$ **d.** $5x = 0$

Solution See page S5.

When solving more complicated first-degree equations in one variable, use the following sequence of steps.

Steps for Solving a First-Degree Equation in One Variable

1. If the equation contains fractions, multiply each side of the equation by the least common multiple (LCM) of the denominators to clear the equation of fractions.
2. Use the distributive property to remove parentheses.
3. Combine any like terms on the left side of the equation and any like terms on the right side of the equation.
4. Use the addition or subtraction property to rewrite the equation with only one variable term and only one constant term.
5. Use the multiplication or division property to rewrite the equation with the variable alone on one side of the equation and a constant term on the other side of the equation.

If one of the above steps is not needed to solve a given equation, proceed to the next step. Remember that the goal is to rewrite the equation with the variable alone on one side of the equation and a constant term on the other side of the equation.

EXAMPLE 2 Solve a First-Degree Equation Using the Properties of Equations

Solve.

a. $5x + 9 = 23 - 2x$ **b.** $8x - 3(4x - 5) = -2x + 6$

c. $\frac{3x}{4} - 6 = \frac{x}{3} - 1$

Solution

a. There are no fractions (Step 1) or parentheses (Step 2). There are no like terms on either side of the equation (Step 3). Use the addition property to rewrite the equation with only one variable term (Step 4). Add $2x$ to each side of the equation.

$$5x + 9 = 23 - 2x$$
$$5x + 2x + 9 = 23 - 2x + 2x$$
$$7x + 9 = 23$$

Use the subtraction property to rewrite the equation with only one constant term (Step 4). Subtract 9 from each side of the equation.

$$7x + 9 - 9 = 23 - 9$$
$$7x = 14$$

Use the division property to rewrite the equation with the x alone on one side of the equation (Step 5). Divide each side of the equation by 7.

$$\frac{7x}{7} = \frac{14}{7}$$
$$x = 2$$

The solution is 2.

b. There are no fractions (Step 1). Use the distributive property to remove parentheses (Step 2).

$$8x - 3(4x - 5) = -2x + 6$$
$$8x - 12x + 15 = -2x + 6$$

HISTORICAL NOTE

The letter x is used universally as the standard letter for a single unknown, which is why x-rays were so named. The scientists who discovered them did not know what they were, and so labeled them the "unknown rays," or x-rays.

Combine like terms on the left side of the equation (Step 3). Then rewrite the equation with the variable alone on one side and a constant on the other.

$$-4x + 15 = -2x + 6 \quad \bullet \text{ Combine like terms.}$$
$$-4x + 2x + 15 = -2x + 2x + 6 \quad \bullet \text{ The addition property}$$
$$-2x + 15 = 6$$
$$-2x + 15 - 15 = 6 - 15 \quad \bullet \text{ The subtraction property}$$
$$-2x = -9$$
$$\frac{-2x}{-2} = \frac{-9}{-2} \quad \bullet \text{ The division property}$$
$$x = \frac{9}{2}$$

The solution is $\frac{9}{2}$.

TAKE NOTE

Recall that the least common multiple (LCM) of two numbers is the smallest number that both numbers divide into evenly. For the example at the right, the LCM of the denominators 4 and 3 is 12.

c. The equation contains fractions (Step 1); multiply each side of the equation by the LCM of the denominators, 12. Then rewrite the equation with the variable alone on one side and a constant on the other.

$$\frac{3x}{4} - 6 = \frac{x}{3} - 1$$
$$12\left(\frac{3x}{4} - 6\right) = 12\left(\frac{x}{3} - 1\right) \quad \bullet \text{ The multiplication property}$$
$$12 \cdot \frac{3x}{4} - 12 \cdot 6 = 12 \cdot \frac{x}{3} - 12 \cdot 1 \quad \bullet \text{ The distributive property}$$
$$9x - 72 = 4x - 12$$
$$9x - 4x - 72 = 4x - 4x - 12 \quad \bullet \text{ The subtraction property}$$
$$5x - 72 = -12$$
$$5x - 72 + 72 = -12 + 72 \quad \bullet \text{ The addition property}$$
$$5x = 60$$
$$\frac{5x}{5} = \frac{60}{5} \quad \bullet \text{ The division property}$$
$$x = 12$$

The solution is 12.

CHECK YOUR PROGRESS 2 Solve.

a. $4x + 3 = 7x + 9$ **b.** $7 - (5x - 8) = 4x + 3$ **c.** $\frac{3x - 1}{4} + \frac{1}{3} = \frac{7}{3}$

Solution See page S5.

MATH MATTERS The Hubble Space Telescope

The Hubble Space Telescope was launched into orbit on April 24, 1990. Shortly thereafter, the telescope missed the stars it was targeted to photograph because it was pointing in the wrong direction. The direction was off by about one-half of 1 degree as a result of an arithmetic error—an addition instead of a subtraction.

JSC/NASA

Applications

In some applications of equations, we are given an equation that can be used to solve the problem. This is illustrated in Example 3.

EXAMPLE 3 Solve an Application

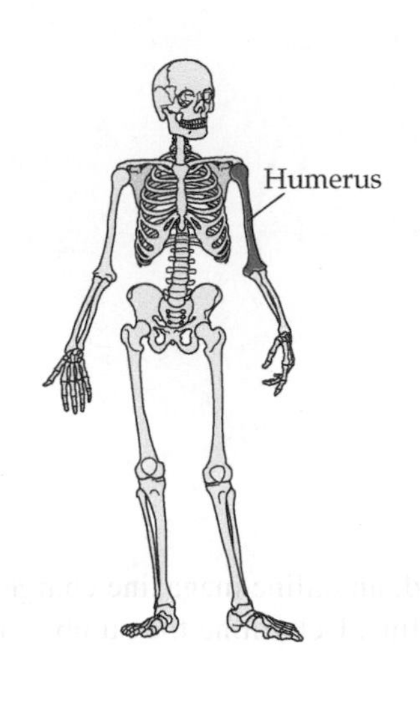

Forensic scientists have determined that the equation $H = 2.9L + 78.1$ can be used to approximate the height H, in centimeters, of an adult on the basis of the length L, in centimeters, of the adult's humerus (the bone extending from the shoulder to the elbow).

a. Use this equation to approximate the height of an adult whose humerus measures 36 cm.

b. According to this equation, what is the length of the humerus of an adult whose height is 168 cm?

Solution

a. Substitute 36 for L in the given equation. Solve the resulting equation for H.

$$H = 2.9L + 78.1$$
$$H = 2.9(36) + 78.1$$
$$H = 104.4 + 78.1$$
$$H = 182.5$$

The adult's height is approximately 182.5 cm.

b. Substitute 168 for H in the given equation. Solve the resulting equation for L.

$$H = 2.9L + 78.1$$
$$168 = 2.9L + 78.1$$
$$168 - 78.1 = 2.9L + 78.1 - 78.1$$
$$89.9 = 2.9L$$
$$\frac{89.9}{2.9} = \frac{2.9L}{2.9}$$
$$31 = L$$

The length of the adult's humerus is approximately 31 cm.

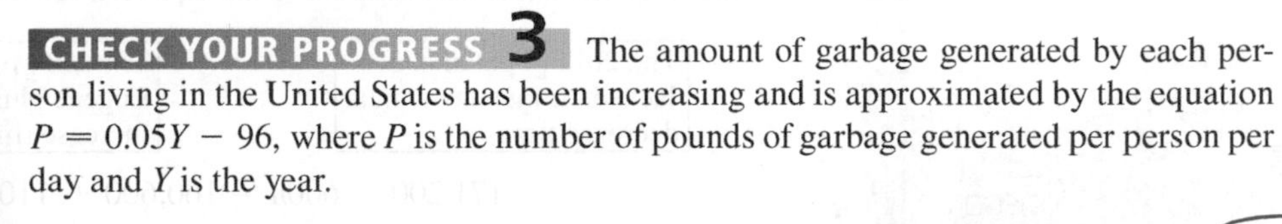

vadim kozlovsky/Shutterstock.com

CHECK YOUR PROGRESS 3 The amount of garbage generated by each person living in the United States has been increasing and is approximated by the equation $P = 0.05Y - 96$, where P is the number of pounds of garbage generated per person per day and Y is the year.

a. Find the amount of garbage generated per person per day in 2015.

b. According to the equation, in what year will 5.5 lb of garbage be generated per person per day?

Solution See page S5.

In many applied problems, we are not given an equation that can be used to solve the problem. Instead, we must use the given information to write an equation whose solution answers the question stated in the problem. This is illustrated in Examples 4 and 5.

EXAMPLE 4 Solve an Application of First-Degree Equations

The cost of electricity in a certain city is \$0.16 for each of the first 300 kWh (kilowatt-hours) and \$0.26 for each kilowatt-hour over 300 kWh. Find the number of kilowatt-hours used by a family that receives a \$103.90 electric bill.

Solution

Let $k =$ the number of kilowatt-hours used by the family. Write an equation and then solve the equation for k.

\$0.16 for each of the first 300 kWh + \$0.26 for each kilowatt-hour over 300	=	\$103.90

$$0.16(300) + 0.26(k - 300) = 103.90$$
$$48 + 0.26k - 78 = 103.90$$
$$0.26k - 30 = 103.90$$
$$0.26k - 30 + 30 = 103.90 + 30$$
$$0.26k = 133.90$$
$$\frac{0.26k}{0.26} = \frac{133.90}{0.26}$$
$$k = 515$$

The family used 515 kWh of electricity.

TAKE NOTE

If the family uses 500 kWh of electricity, they are billed \$0.26/kWh for 200 kWh (500 − 300). If they use 650 kWh, they are billed \$0.26/kWh for 350 kWh (650 − 300). If they use k kWh, $k > 300$, they are billed \$0.26/kWh for $(k - 300)$ kWh.

CHECK YOUR PROGRESS 4 For a classified ad, an online magazine charges \$340 for the first four lines and \$76 for each additional line. Determine the number of lines that can be published in an ad for \$948.

Solution See page S5.

Olinchuk/Shutterstock.com

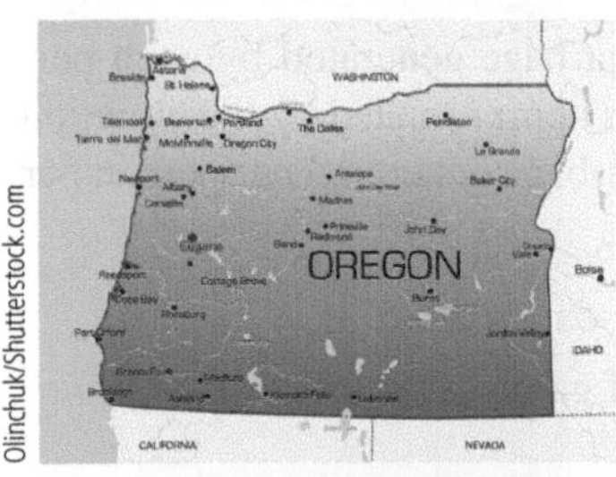

Olinchuk/Shutterstock.com

EXAMPLE 5 Solve an Application of First-Degree Equations

In 2014, the population of Jackson, MS was 171,200, and the population of Eugene, OR was 160,600. In recent years, Jackson's population decreased at an average rate of 600 people per year, while Eugene's increased at an average rate of 1100 people per year. If these rate changes remained stable, in what year would the populations of Jackson and Eugene be the same? Round to the nearest year.

Solution

Let $n =$ the number of years after 2014. Write an equation for when the populations would be the same and then solve the equation for n.

The 2014 population of Jackson minus the annual decrease times n	=	The 2014 population of Eugene plus the annual increase times n

$$171{,}200 - 600n = 160{,}600 + 1100n$$
$$171{,}200 - 600n + 600n = 160{,}600 + 1100n + 600n$$
$$171{,}200 = 160{,}600 + 1700n$$
$$171{,}200 - 160{,}600 = 160{,}600 - 160{,}600 + 1700n$$
$$10{,}600 = 1700n$$
$$\frac{10{,}600}{1700} = \frac{1700n}{1700}$$
$$6 \approx n$$

The variable n is the number of years after 2014. Add 6 to the year 2014.

$$2014 + 6 = 2020$$

To the nearest year, the populations would be the same in 2020.

POINT OF INTEREST

Is the population of your state increasing or decreasing? You can find out by checking a reference such as census.gov, which was the source for the data in Example 5 and Check Your Progress 5.

CHECK YOUR PROGRESS 5 In 2014, the population of Cleveland, OH, was 389,500, and the population of Tampa, FL, was 358,700. In recent years, Cleveland's population decreased at an average rate of 1600 people per year, while Tampa's increased at an average rate of 5700 people per year. If these rate changes remained stable, in what year would the populations of Cleveland and Tampa be the same? Round to the nearest year.

Solution See page S5.

Literal Equations

A **literal equation** is an equation that contains more than one variable. Examples of literal equations are:

$$2x + 3y = 6$$
$$4a - 2b + c = 0$$

A **formula** is a literal equation that states a relationship between two or more quantities in an application problem. Examples of formulas are shown below. These formulas are taken from physics, mathematics, and business.

$$\frac{1}{R_1} + \frac{1}{R_2} = \frac{1}{R}$$
$$s = a + (n - 1)d$$
$$A = P + Prt$$

QUESTION Which of the following are literal equations?

a. $5a - 3b = 7$ **b.** $a^2 + b^2 = c^2$

c. $a_1 + (n - 1)d$ **d.** $3x - 7 = 5 + 4x$

The addition, subtraction, multiplication, and division properties of equations can be used to solve some literal equations for one of the variables. In solving a literal equation for one of the variables, the goal is to rewrite the equation so that the letter being solved for is alone on one side of the equation and all numbers and other variables are on the other side. This is illustrated in Example 6.

EXAMPLE 6 **Solve a Literal Equation**

a. Solve $A = P(1 + i)$ for i.

b. Solve $I = \dfrac{E}{R + r}$ for R.

Solution

a. The goal is to rewrite the equation so that i is alone on one side of the equation and all other numbers and letters are on the other side. We will begin by using the distributive property on the right side of the equation.

$$A = P(1 + i)$$
$$A = P + Pi$$

ANSWER ***a*** and ***b*** are literal equations. ***c*** is not an equation. ***d*** does not have more than one variable.

Subtract P from each side of the equation.

$$A - P = P - P + Pi$$
$$A - P = Pi$$

Divide each side of the equation by P.

$$\frac{A - P}{P} = \frac{Pi}{P}$$
$$\frac{A - P}{P} = i$$

b. The goal is to rewrite the equation so that R is alone on one side of the equation and all other variables are on the other side of the equation. Because the equation contains a fraction, we will first multiply both sides of the equation by the denominator $R + r$ to clear the equation of fractions.

$$I = \frac{E}{R + r}$$
$$(R + r)I = (R + r)\frac{E}{R + r}$$
$$RI + rI = E$$

Subtract from the left side of the equation the term that does not contain a capital R.

$$RI + rI - rI = E - rI$$
$$RI = E - rI$$

Divide each side of the equation by I.

$$\frac{RI}{I} = \frac{E - rI}{I}$$
$$R = \frac{E - rI}{I}$$

CHECK YOUR PROGRESS 6

a. Solve $s = \frac{A + L}{2}$ for L.

b. Solve $L = a(1 + ct)$ for c.

Solution See page S6.

EXCURSION

Body Mass Index

Body mass index, or **BMI**, expresses the relationship between a person's height and weight. It is a measurement for gauging a person's weight-related level of risk for high blood pressure, heart disease, and diabetes. A BMI value of 25 or less indicates a very low to low risk; a BMI value of 25 to 30 indicates a low to moderate risk; a BMI of 30 or more indicates a moderate to very high risk.

The formula for body mass index is

$$B = \frac{703W}{H^2}$$

where B is the BMI, W is weight in pounds, and H is height in inches.

To determine how much a woman who is 5′4″ should weigh in order to have a BMI of 24, first convert 5′4″ to inches.

$$5'4'' = 5(12)'' + 4'' = 60'' + 4'' = 64''$$

Substitute 24 for B and 64 for H in the body mass index formula. Then solve the resulting equation for W.

$$B = \frac{703W}{H^2}$$

$$24 = \frac{703W}{64^2}$$ • $B = 24$, $H = 64$

$$24 = \frac{703W}{4096}$$

$$4096(24) = 4096\left(\frac{703W}{4096}\right)$$ • Multiply each side of the equation by 4096.

$$98{,}304 = 703W$$

$$\frac{98{,}304}{703} = \frac{703W}{703}$$ • Divide each side of the equation by 703.

$$140 \approx W$$

A woman who is 5′4″ should weigh about 140 lb in order to have a BMI of 24.

EXCURSION EXERCISES

1. Amy is 140 lb and 5′8″ tall. Calculate Amy's BMI. Round to the nearest tenth. Rank Amy as a low, moderate, or high risk for weight-related disease.
2. Roger is 5′11″. How much should he weigh in order to have a BMI of 25? Round to the nearest pound.
3. Bohdan weighs 185 lb and is 5′9″. How many pounds must Bohdan lose in order to reach a BMI of 23? Round to the nearest pound.
4. Felicia weighs 160 lb and is 5′7″. She would like to lower her BMI to 20.
   a. By how many points must Felicia lower her BMI? Round to the nearest tenth.
   b. How many pounds must Felicia lose in order to reach a BMI of 20? Round to the nearest pound.
5. **Finding BMI Using a Nomograph** Most medical professionals use a nomograph (or nomogram) to calculate the BMI of their patients. A nomograph is a diagram that shows the relationships among three or more quantities by means of scales that are arranged such that the value of one variable can be found by drawing a straight line from one scale intersecting the other scales at appropriate values. You can download a BMI nomograph from the Internet. One good source is www.pynomo.org/wiki/images/b/b4/Ex_BMI.png. On the nomograph on the next page, the line connecting a height of 5.9 ft and a weight of 150 lb intersects the BMI scale at 21, indicating that a 5.9-foot, 150-pound person has a BMI of 21.
   a. Use the nomograph to calculate Amy's BMI (see Excursion Exercise 1). Compare the results you obtained by using the nomograph with the value you obtained by using a calculator.
   b. Use the nomograph to calculate how much Roger should weigh in order to have a BMI of 25 (see Excursion Exercise 2). How does the result you obtained

by using the nomograph compare with the value you obtained by using a calculator?

c. Explain the advantages and disadvantages of using a nomograph to calculate BMI.

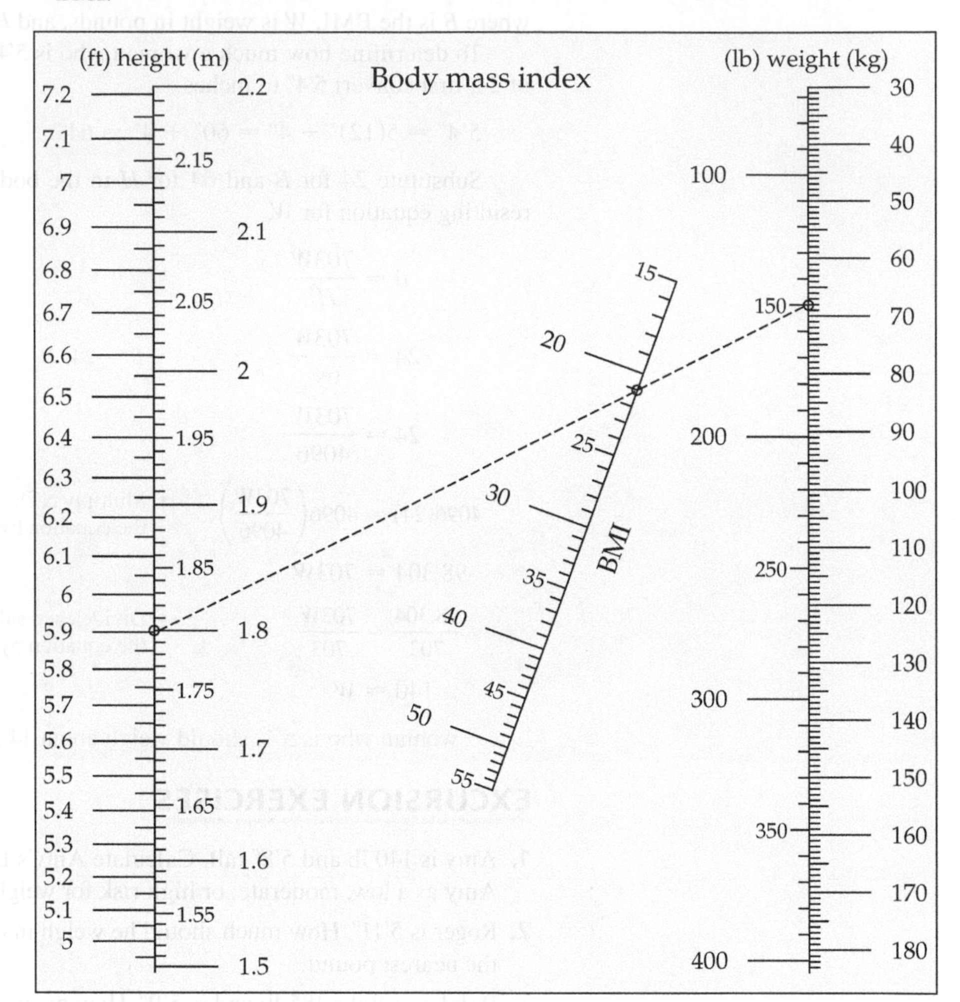

EXERCISE SET 2.1

1. What is the difference between an expression and an equation? Provide an example of each.
2. What is the solution of the equation $x = 8$? Use your answer to explain why the goal in solving an equation is to get the variable alone on one side of the equation.
3. Explain how to check the solution of an equation.

■ In Exercises 4 to 41, solve the equation.

4. $x + 7 = -5$ **5.** $9 + b = 21$

6. $-9 = z - 8$ **7.** $b - 11 = 11$

8. $-3x = 150$ **9.** $-48 = 6z$

10. $-9a = -108$ **11.** $-\frac{3}{4}x = 15$

12. $\frac{5}{2}x = -10$ **13.** $-\frac{x}{4} = -2$

14. $\frac{2x}{5} = -8$ **15.** $4 - 2b = 2 - 4b$

16. $4y - 10 = 6 + 2y$ **17.** $5x - 3 = 9x - 7$

18. $10z + 6 = 4 + 5z$ **19.** $3m + 5 = 2 - 6m$

20. $6a - 1 = 2 + 2a$ **21.** $5x + 7 = 8x + 5$

22. $2 - 6y = 5 - 7y$ **23.** $4b + 15 = 3 - 2b$

24. $2(x + 1) + 5x = 23$ **25.** $9n - 15 = 3(2n - 1)$

26. $7a - (3a - 4) = 12$ **27.** $5(3 - 2y) = 3 - 4y$

28. $9 - 7x = 4(1 - 3x)$

29. $2(3b + 5) - 1 = 10b + 1$

30. $2z - 2 = 5 - (9 - 6z)$

31. $4a + 3 = 7 - (5 - 8a)$

32. $5(6 - 2x) = 2(5 - 3x)$

33. $4(3y + 1) = 2(y - 8)$

34. $2(3b - 5) = 4(6b - 2)$

35. $3(x - 4) = 1 - (2x - 7)$

36. $\frac{2y}{3} - 4 = \frac{y}{6} - 1$

37. $\frac{x}{8} + 2 = \frac{3x}{4} - 3$

38. $\frac{2x - 3}{3} + \frac{1}{2} = \frac{5}{6}$

39. $\frac{2}{3} + \frac{3x + 1}{4} = \frac{5}{3}$

40. $\frac{1}{2}(x + 4) = \frac{1}{3}(3x - 6)$

41. $\frac{3}{4}(x - 8) = \frac{1}{2}(2x + 4)$

■ **Car Payments** The monthly car payment on a 60-month car loan at a 5% rate is calculated by using the formula $P = 0.018417L$, where P is the monthly car payment and L is the loan amount. Use this formula for Exercises 42 and 43.

42. If you can afford a maximum monthly car payment of $300, what is the maximum loan amount you can afford? Round to the nearest cent.

43. If the maximum monthly car payment you can afford is $350, what is the maximum loan amount you can afford? Round to the nearest cent.

■ **Deep-Sea Diving** The pressure on a diver can be calculated using the formula $P = 15 + \frac{1}{2}D$, where P is the pressure in pounds per square inch and D is the depth in feet. Use this formula for Exercises 44 and 45.

44. Find the depth of a diver when the pressure on the diver is 45 lb/in^2.

45. Find the depth of a diver when the pressure on the diver is 55 lb/in^2.

■ **Foot Races** The world-record time for a 1-mile race can be approximated by $t = 16.11 - 0.0062y$, where y is the year of the race, $1950 \leq y \leq 2005$, and t is the time, in minutes, of the race. Use this formula for Exercises 46 and 47.

46. Approximate the year in which the first "4-minute mile" was run. The actual year was 1954.

47. In 1999, the world-record time for a 1-mile race was 3.72 min. For what year does the equation predict this record time?

■ **Black Ice** Black ice is an ice covering on roads that is especially difficult to see and therefore extremely dangerous for motorists. The distance a car traveling at 30 mph will slide after its brakes are applied is related to the outside temperature by the formula $C = \frac{1}{4}D - 45$, where C is the Celsius temperature and D is the distance, in feet, that the car will slide. Use this formula for Exercises 48 and 49.

48. Determine the distance a car will slide on black ice when the outside air temperature is -3°C.

49. How far will a car slide on black ice when the outside air temperature is -11°C?

■ **Crickets** The formula $N = 7C - 30$ approximates N, the number of times per minute a cricket chirps when the air temperature is C degrees Celsius. Use this formula for Exercises 50 and 51.

50. What is the approximate air temperature when a cricket chirps 100 times per minute? Round to the nearest tenth.

51. Determine the approximate air temperature when a cricket chirps 140 times per minute. Round to the nearest tenth.

■ **Bowling** In order to equalize all the bowlers' chances of winning, some players in a bowling league are given a handicap, or a bonus of extra points. Some leagues use the formula $H = 0.8(200 - A)$, where H is the handicap and A is the bowler's average score in past games. Use this formula for Exercises 52 and 53.

52. A bowler has a handicap of 20. What is the bowler's average score?

53. Find the average score of a bowler who has a handicap of 25.

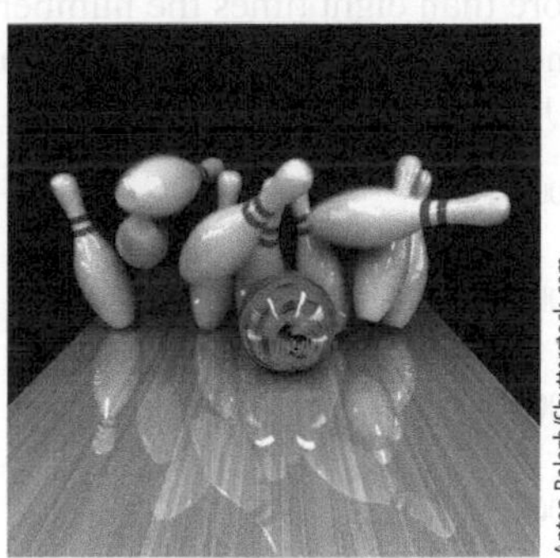

■ In Exercises 54 to 63, write an equation as part of solving the problem.

54. **College Tuition** The graph below shows average tuition and fees at private 4-year colleges for selected years.

a. For the 2003–04 school year, the average tuition and fees at private 4-year colleges were $934 more than four times the average tuition and fees at public 4-year colleges. Find the average tuition and fees at public 4-year colleges for the school year 2003–04.

b. For the 2015–16 school year, the average tuition and fees at private 4-year colleges were $4175 more than three times the average tuition and fees at public 4-year colleges. Determine the average tuition and fees at public 4-year colleges for the 2015–16 school year.

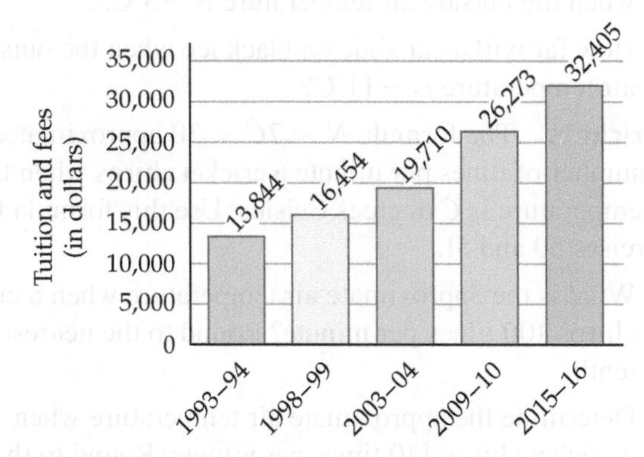

Tuition and Fees at Private 4-Year Colleges
SOURCE: The College Board

55. **Adoption** In a recent year, Americans adopted 17,438 children from foreign countries. In the graph below are the top three countries where the children were born.

a. The number of children adopted from Guatemala was 1052 less than three times the number adopted from Ethiopia. Determine the number of children adopted from Ethiopia that year.

b. The number of children adopted from China was 189 more than eight times the number adopted from Ukraine. Determine the number of children adopted from Ukraine that year.

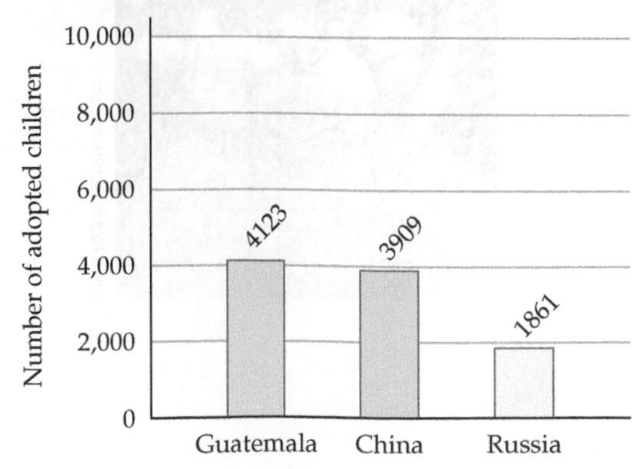

Birth Countries of Adopted American Children
SOURCE: U.S. State Department

56. **Installment Purchases** The purchase price of a large 4K LED TV, including finance charges, was $1425. A down payment of $300 was made, and the remainder was paid in 18 equal monthly installments. Find the monthly payment.

57. **Auto Repair** The cost to replace a water pump in a Corvette was $355. This included $115 for the water pump plus $80/h for labor. How many hours of labor were required to replace the water pump?

58. **Robots** Kiva Systems, Inc., builds robots that companies can use to streamline order fulfillment operations in their warehouses. Salary and other benefits for one human warehouse worker can cost a company about $64,000 a year, an amount that is 103 times the company's yearly maintenance and operation costs for one robot. Find the yearly costs for a robot. Round to the nearest hundred. (*Source: Boston Globe*)

59. **College Staffing** A university employs a total of 600 teaching assistants and research assistants. There are three times as many teaching assistants as research assistants. Find the number of research assistants employed by the university.

60. **Wages** A service station attendant is paid time-and-a-half for working over 40 hours per week. Last week the attendant worked 47 h and earned $631.25. Find the attendant's regular hourly wage.

61. **Investments** An investor deposited $5000 in two accounts. Two times the smaller deposit is $1000 more than the larger deposit. Find the amount deposited in each account.

62. **Shipping** An overnight mail service charges $5.60 for the first 6 oz and $0.85 for each additional ounce or fraction of an ounce. Find the weight, in ounces, of a package that cost $10.70 to deliver.

63. **Telecommunications** A cellular phone company charges $59.95 per month for a service plan that includes 6 GB of data. In addition to the basic monthly rate, the company charges $7.95 for each additional GB of data over 6 GB. A customer on this plan receives a bill for $115.60. How much data did this customer send and receive during the month?

■ In Exercises 64 to 81, solve the formula for the indicated variable.

64. $A = \frac{1}{2}bh$; h (geometry)

65. $P = a + b + c$; b (geometry)

66. $d = rt$; t (physics)

67. $E = IR$; R (physics)

68. $PV = nRT$; R (chemistry)

69. $I = Prt$; r (business)

70. $P = 2L + 2W$; W (geometry)

71. $F = \frac{9}{5}C + 32$; C (temperature conversion)

72. $P = R - C$; C (business)

73. $A = P + Prt$; t (business)

74. $S = V_0t - 16t^2$; V_0 (physics)

75. $T = fm - gm$; f (engineering)

76. $P = \dfrac{R - C}{n}$; R (business)

77. $R = \dfrac{C - S}{t}$; S (business)

78. $V = \dfrac{1}{3}\pi r^2 h$; h (geometry)

79. $A = \dfrac{1}{2}h(b_1 + b_2)$; b_2 (geometry)

80. $a_n = a_1 + (n - 1)d$; d (mathematics)

81. $S = 2\pi r^2 + 2\pi rh$; h (geometry)

■ In Exercises 82 and 83, solve the equation for y.

82. $2x - y = 4$

83. $4x + 3y = 6$

■ In Exercises 84 and 85, solve the equation for x.

84. $ax + by + c = 0$

85. $y - y_1 = m(x - x_1)$

EXTENSIONS

■ In Exercises 86 and 87, solve the equation.

86. $3(4x + 2) = 7 - 4(1 - 3x)$

87. $4(x + 5) = 30 - (10 - 4x)$

88. Use the numbers 5, 10, and 15 to make equations by filling in the boxes: $x + \square = \square - \square$. Each equation must use all three numbers.

a. What is the largest possible solution of these equations?

b. What is the smallest possible solution of these equations?

89. Solve the equation $ax + b = cx + d$ for x. Is your solution valid for all numbers a, b, c, and d? Explain.

■ **Writing Formulas** When we know there is an explicit relationship between two quantities, often we can write a formula to express the relationship.

For example, suppose that a toll of \$3.75 is collected from each vehicle that crosses a particular bridge. Let A be the total amount of money collected, and let c be the number of vehicles that cross the bridge on a given day. Then,

$$A = \$3.75c$$

is a formula that expresses the total amount of money collected from vehicles on any given day.

In Exercises 90 to 93, write a formula for the situation. Include as part of your answer a list of variables that were used, and state what each variable represents.

90. Write a formula to represent the total cost to rent a copier from a company that charges \$325 per month plus \$0.08 per copy made.

91. Suppose you buy a used car with 30,000 mi on it. You expect to drive the car about 750 mi per month. Write a formula to represent the total number of miles the car has been driven after you have owned it for m months.

92. A parking garage charges \$7.50 for the first hour and \$5.25 for each additional hour. Write a formula to represent the parking charge for parking in this garage for h hours. Assume h is a counting number greater than 1.

93. Write a formula to represent the total cost to rent a car from a company that rents cars for \$29.95 per day plus 50¢ for every mile driven over 100 mi. Assume the car will be driven more than 100 mi.

SECTION 2.2 Rate, Ratio, and Proportion

Rates

The word *rate* is used frequently in our everyday lives. It is used in such contexts as unemployment rate, tax rate, interest rate, hourly rate, infant mortality rate, school dropout rate, inflation rate, and postage rate.

A **rate** is a comparison of two quantities and can be written as a fraction. For instance, if a car travels 135 mi on 6 gal of gas, then the miles-to-gallons rate is written

$$\frac{135 \text{ mi}}{6 \text{ gal}}$$

Note that the units (miles and gallons) are written as part of the rate.

> **POINT OF INTEREST**
>
> Unit rates are used in a wide variety of situations. One unit rate you may not be familiar with is used in the airline industry to describe air circulation: cubic feet of air per minute per person. Typical rates are: economy class, 7 ft^3/min/person; first class, 50 ft^3/minute/person; cockpit, 150 ft^3/min/person.

A **unit rate** is a rate in which the number in the denominator is 1. To find a unit rate, divide the number in the numerator of the rate by the number in the denominator of the rate. For the preceding example,

$$135 \div 6 = 22.5$$

The unit rate is $\frac{22.5 \text{ mi}}{1 \text{ gal}}$.

This rate can be written 22.5 mi/gal or 22.5 miles per gallon, where the word *per* has the meaning "for every."

Unit rates make comparisons easier. For example, if you travel 37 mph and I travel 43 mph, we know that I am traveling faster than you are. It is more difficult to compare speeds if we are told that you are traveling $\frac{111 \text{ mi}}{3 \text{ h}}$ and I am traveling $\frac{172 \text{ mi}}{4 \text{ h}}$.

EXAMPLE 1 Calculate a Unit Rate

A dental hygienist earns \$1304 for working a 40-hour week. What is the hygienist's hourly rate of pay?

Solution

The hygienist's rate of pay is $\frac{\$1304}{40 \text{ h}}$.

To find the hourly rate of pay, divide 1304 by 40.

$$1304 \div 40 = 32.6$$

$$\frac{\$1304}{40 \text{ h}} = \frac{\$32.60}{1 \text{ h}} = \$32.60/\text{h}$$

The hygienist's hourly rate of pay is \$32.60/h.

CHECK YOUR PROGRESS 1 You pay \$6.75 for 1.5 lb of hamburger. What is the cost per pound?

Solution See page S6.

EXAMPLE 2 Solve an Application of Unit Rates

A teacher earns a salary of \$53,280 per year. Currently the school year consists of 180 days. If the school year were extended to 220 days, as is proposed in some states, what annual salary should the teacher be paid if the salary is based on the number of days worked per year?

Solution

Find the current salary per day.

$$\frac{\$53{,}280}{180 \text{ days}} = \frac{\$296}{1 \text{ day}} = \$296/\text{day}$$

Multiply the salary per day by the number of days in the proposed school year.

$$\frac{\$296}{1 \text{ day}} \cdot 220 \text{ days} = \$296(220) = \$65{,}120$$

The teacher's annual salary should be \$65,120.

CHECK YOUR PROGRESS 2 In January 2016, the federal minimum wage was \$7.25/h, and the minimum wage in California was \$10.00. How much greater is an employee's pay for working 35 h and earning the California minimum wage rather than the federal minimum wage?

Solution See page S6.

Monkey Business Images/Shutterstock.com

Another application of unit rate is the unit price information that grocery stores are required to provide to customers. The **unit price** of a product is its cost per unit of measure.

Suppose that the price of a 2-pound box of spaghetti is \$2.79. The unit price of the spaghetti is the cost per pound. To find the unit price, write the rate as a unit rate.

The numerator is the price and the denominator is the quantity. Divide the number in the numerator by the number in the denominator.

$$\frac{\$2.79}{2\text{ lb}} = \frac{\$1.395}{1\text{ lb}}$$

The unit price of the spaghetti is \$1.395/lb.

Unit pricing is used by consumers to answer the question "Which is the better buy?" The answer is that the product with the lower unit price is the more economical purchase.

EXAMPLE 3 Determine the More Economical Purchase

Which is the more economical purchase, an 18-ounce jar of peanut butter priced at \$2.69 or a 28-ounce jar of peanut butter priced at \$3.99?

Solution

Find the unit price for each item.

$$\frac{\$2.69}{18\text{ oz}} \approx \frac{\$0.149}{1\text{ oz}} \qquad \frac{\$3.99}{28\text{ oz}} \approx \frac{\$0.143}{1\text{ oz}}$$

Compare the two prices per ounce.

$$\$0.149 > \$0.143$$

The item with the lower unit price is the more economical purchase.
The more economical purchase is the 28-ounce jar priced at \$3.99.

CHECK YOUR PROGRESS 3 Which is the more economical purchase, 32 oz of detergent for \$6.29 or 48 oz of detergent for \$8.29?

Solution See page S6.

POINT OF INTEREST

According to the Centers for Disease Control and Prevention, in a recent year the teen birth rate in the United States declined to 24.2 live births per 1000 females age 15 to 19.

Rates such as crime statistics or data on fatalities are often written as rates per hundred, per thousand, per hundred thousand, or per million. For example, the table below shows bicycle deaths per million people in a recent year in the states with the highest rates. (*Source:* www.nhtsa.dot.gov)

Rates of Bicycle Fatalities (Deaths per Million People)	
Florida	6.8
Arizona	4.7
California	3.7
Oklahoma	3.4
South Carolina	3.1

The rates in this table are easier to read than they would be if they were unit rates. Consider that the bicycle fatalities in South Carolina would be written as 0.0000031 as a unit rate. It is easier to understand that 3.1 out of every million people living in South Carolina die in bicycle accidents.

QUESTION In the table on page 119, what does the rate given for Florida mean?

Ragnarock/Shutterstock.com

Another application of rates is in the area of international trade. Suppose a company in France purchases a shipment of sneakers from an American company. The French company must exchange euros, which is France's currency, for U.S. dollars in order to pay for the order. The number of euros that are equivalent to one U.S. dollar is called the *exchange rate.* The table below shows the exchange rates per U.S. dollar for three foreign countries and the European Union on January 19, 2016. Use this table for Example 4 and Check Your Progress 4.

Exchange Rates per U.S. Dollar	
British pound	0.7058
Canadian dollar	1.4574
Japanese yen	117.44
Euro	0.9156

EXAMPLE 4 **Solve an Application Using Exchange Rates**

a. How many Japanese yen are needed to pay for an order costing \$15,000?

b. Find the number of British pounds that would be exchanged for \$5000.

Solution

a. Multiply the number of yen per \$1 by 15,000.

$$15{,}000(117.44) = 1{,}761{,}600$$

1,761,600 yen are needed to pay for an order costing \$15,000.

b. Multiply the number of pounds per \$1 by 5000.

$$5000(0.7058) = 3529$$

3529 British pounds would be exchanged for \$5000.

CHECK YOUR PROGRESS 4

a. How many Canadian dollars would be needed to pay for an order costing \$20,000?

b. Find the number of euros that would be exchanged for \$25,000.

Solution See page S6.

POINT OF INTEREST

It is believed that billiards was invented in France during the reign of Louis XI (1423–1483). In the United States, the standard billiard table is 4 ft 6 in. by 9 ft. This is a ratio of 1:2. The same ratio holds for carom and snooker tables, which are 5 ft by 10 ft.

Ratios

A **ratio** is the comparison of two quantities that have the same units. A ratio can be written in three different ways:

1. As a fraction $\frac{2}{3}$
2. As two numbers separated by a colon (:) 2:3
3. As two numbers separated by the word *to* 2 to 3

Although units, such as hours, miles, or dollars, are written as part of a rate, units are not written as part of a ratio.

ANSWER Florida's rate of 6.8 means that 6.8 out of every million people living in Florida die in bicycle accidents.

According to the U.S. Bureau of Labor Statistics, there are 123 million married people in the United States, and 82 million of these people are in the labor force. The ratio of the number of married people in the labor force to the total number of married people in the country is calculated below. Note that the ratio is written in simplest form.

$$\frac{82{,}000{,}000}{123{,}000{,}000} = \frac{2}{3} \quad \text{or} \quad 2:3 \quad \text{or} \quad 2 \text{ to } 3$$

The ratio 2 to 3 tells us that 2 out of every 3 married people in the United States are part of the labor force.

Given that 82 million of the 123 million married people in the country work in the labor force, we can calculate the number of married people who do not work in the labor force.

$$123 \text{ million} - 82 \text{ million} = 41 \text{ million}$$

The ratio of the number of married people who are not in the labor force to the number of married people who are is:

$$\frac{41{,}000{,}000}{82{,}000{,}000} = \frac{1}{2} \quad \text{or} \quad 1:2 \quad \text{or} \quad 1 \text{ to } 2$$

The ratio 1 to 2 tells us that for every 1 married person who is not in the labor force, there are 2 married people who are in the labor force.

POINT OF INTEREST

Ratios have applications to many disciplines. Investors talk of price–earnings ratios. Accountants use the current ratio, which is the ratio of current assets to current liabilities. Metallurgists use ratios to make various grades of steel.

EXAMPLE 5 Determine a Ratio in Simplest Form

AVAVA/Shutterstock.com

A survey revealed that, on average, eighth graders watch approximately 21 h of television each week. Find the ratio, as a fraction in simplest form, of the number of hours spent watching television to the total number of hours in a week.

Solution

A ratio is the comparison of two quantities with the same units. In this problem we are given both hours and weeks. We must first convert 1 week to hours.

$$\frac{24 \text{ h}}{1 \text{ day}} \cdot 7 \text{ days} = (24 \text{ h})(7) = 168 \text{ h}$$

Write in simplest form the ratio of the number of hours spent watching television to the number of hours in 1 week.

$$\frac{21 \text{ h}}{1 \text{ wk}} = \frac{21 \text{ h}}{168 \text{ h}} = \frac{21}{168} = \frac{1}{8}$$

The ratio is $\frac{1}{8}$.

CHECK YOUR PROGRESS 5 According to the National Low Income Housing Coalition, a minimum wage worker living in Georgia must work 72 h/wk, 52 wk/yr, to afford the rent on an average one-bedroom apartment and be within the federal standard of not paying more than 30% of income for housing. Find the ratio, as a fraction in simplest form, of the number of hours this worker must spend working per week to the total number of hours in a week.

Solution See page S6.

A **unit ratio** is a ratio in which the number in the denominator is 1. One situation in which a unit ratio is used is student–faculty ratios. The table on page 122 shows the number of full-time men and women undergraduates, as well as the number of full-time faculty, at two universities in the Pacific 10. Use this table for Example 6 and Check Your Progress 6. (*Source:* National Center for Education Statistics, nces.ed.gov)

University	Men	Women	Faculty
Oregon State University	10,018	8459	1471
University of Oregon	8849	9824	1364

EXAMPLE 6 Determine a Unit Ratio

Calculate the student–faculty ratio at Oregon State University. Round to the nearest whole number. Write the ratio using the word *to*.

Solution

Add the number of male undergraduates and the number of female undergraduates to determine the total number of students.

$$10{,}018 + 8459 = 18{,}477$$

Write the ratio of the total number of students to the number of faculty. Divide the numerator and denominator by the denominator. Then round the numerator to the nearest whole number.

$$\frac{18{,}477}{1471} \approx \frac{12.56}{1} \approx \frac{13}{1}$$

The ratio is approximately 13 to 1.

CHECK YOUR PROGRESS 6

Calculate the student–faculty ratio at the University of Oregon. Round to the nearest whole number. Write the ratio using the word *to*.

Solution See page S6.

Proportions

HISTORICAL NOTE

Proportions were studied by the earliest mathematicians. Clay tablets uncovered by archeologists show evidence of the use of proportions in Egyptian and Babylonian cultures dating from 1800 BC.

Now that you have an understanding of rates and ratios, you are ready to work with proportions. A **proportion** is an equation that states the equality of two rates or ratios. The following are examples of proportions.

$$\frac{250 \text{ mi}}{5 \text{ h}} = \frac{50 \text{ mi}}{1 \text{ h}} \qquad \frac{3}{6} = \frac{1}{2}$$

The first example above is the equality of two rates. Note that the units in the numerators (miles) are the same and the units in the denominators (hours) are the same. The second example is the equality of two ratios. Remember that units are not written as part of a ratio.

The definition of a proportion can be stated as follows: If $\frac{a}{b}$ and $\frac{c}{d}$ are equal ratios or rates, then $\frac{a}{b} = \frac{c}{d}$ is a proportion.

Each of the four members in a proportion is called a **term**. Each term is numbered as shown below.

$$\frac{a}{b} = \frac{c}{d}$$

First term: a; Second term: b; Third term: c; Fourth term: d

The second and third terms of the proportion are called the **means** and the first and fourth terms are called the **extremes**.

If we multiply both sides of the proportion by the product of the denominators, we obtain the following result.

$$\frac{a}{b} = \frac{c}{d}$$

$$bd\left(\frac{a}{b}\right) = bd\left(\frac{c}{d}\right)$$

$$ad = bc$$

Note that ad is the product of the extremes and bc is the product of the means. In any proportion, the product of the means equals the product of the extremes. This is sometimes phrased, "the cross products are equal."

In the proportion $\frac{3}{4} = \frac{9}{12}$, the cross products are equal.

$$\frac{3}{4} = \frac{9}{12} \quad 4 \cdot 9 = 36 \leftarrow \text{Product of the means}$$

$$3 \cdot 12 = 36 \leftarrow \text{Product of the extremes}$$

QUESTION For the proportion $\frac{5}{8} = \frac{10}{16}$, **a.** name the first and third terms, **b.** write the product of the means, and **c.** write the product of the extremes.

Sometimes one of the terms in a proportion is unknown. In this case, it is necessary to solve the proportion for the unknown number. The **cross-products method**, which is based on the fact that the product of the means equals the product of the extremes, can be used to solve the proportion. Remember that the cross-products method is just a short cut for multiplying each side of the equation by the least common multiple of the denominators.

Cross-Products Method of Solving a Proportion

If $\frac{a}{b} = \frac{c}{d}$, then $ad = bc$.

EXAMPLE 7 Solve a Proportion

Solve: $\frac{8}{5} = \frac{n}{6}$

Solution

Use the cross-products method of solving a proportion: the product of the means equals the product of the extremes. Then solve the resulting equation for n.

$$\frac{8}{5} = \frac{n}{6}$$

$$8 \cdot 6 = 5 \cdot n$$

$$48 = 5n$$

$$\frac{48}{5} = \frac{5n}{5}$$

$$9.6 = n$$

The solution is 9.6.

TAKE NOTE

Be sure to check the solution.

$$\frac{8}{5} = \frac{9.6}{6}$$

$$8 \cdot 6 = 5 \cdot 9.6$$

$$48 = 48$$

The solution checks.

CHECK YOUR PROGRESS 7 Solve: $\frac{42}{x} = \frac{5}{8}$

Solution See page S6.

ANSWER **a.** The first term is 5. The third term is 10. **b.** The product of the means is 8(10) = 80. **c.** The product of the extremes is 5(16) = 80.

Proportions are useful for solving a wide variety of application problems. Remember that when we use the given information to write a proportion involving two rates, the units in the numerators of the rates need to be the same and the units in the denominators of the rates need to be the same. It is helpful to keep in mind that when we write a proportion, we are stating that two rates or ratios are equal.

EXAMPLE 8 **Solve an Application Using a Proportion**

If you travel 290 mi in your car on 15 gal of gasoline, how far can you travel in your car on 12 gal of gasoline under similar driving conditions?

Solution

Let $x =$ the unknown number of miles.
Write a proportion and then solve the proportion for x.

$$\frac{290 \text{ mi}}{15 \text{ gal}} = \frac{x \text{ mi}}{12 \text{ gal}}$$

• The unit miles is in the numerators. The unit gallons is in the denominators.

$$\frac{290}{15} = \frac{x}{12}$$

$$290 \cdot 12 = 15 \cdot x$$

• Use the cross-products method of solving a proportion.

$$3480 = 15x$$
$$232 = x$$

You can travel 232 mi on 12 gal of gasoline.

TAKE NOTE

We have written a proportion with the unit "miles" in the numerators and the unit "gallons" in the denominators. It would also be correct to have "gallons" in the numerators and "miles" in the denominators.

CHECK YOUR PROGRESS 8 On a map, a distance of 2 cm represents 15 km. What is the distance between two cities that are 7 cm apart on the map?

Solution See page S6.

EXAMPLE 9 **Solve an Application Using a Proportion**

The table below shows three of the universities in the Big Ten Conference and their student–faculty ratios as of 2014. (*Source: U.S. News & World Report*) There are approximately 28,100 full-time undergraduate students at Purdue University. Approximate the number of faculty at Purdue University.

University	Student-faculty ratio
Michigan State University	17 to 1
University of Illinois	18 to 1
Purdue University	13 to 1

Solution

Let $F =$ the number of faculty members.
Write a proportion and then solve the proportion for F.

$$\frac{13 \text{ students}}{1 \text{ faculty}} = \frac{28{,}100 \text{ students}}{F \text{ faculty}}$$

$$13 \cdot F = 1(28{,}100)$$
$$13F = 28{,}100$$
$$\frac{13F}{13} = \frac{28{,}100}{13}$$
$$F \approx 2162$$

There are approximately 2162 faculty members at Purdue University.

TAKE NOTE

Student–faculty ratios are rounded to the nearest whole number, so they are approximations. When we use an approximate ratio in a proportion, the solution will be an approximation.

CHECK YOUR PROGRESS 9 The profits of a firm are shared by its two partners in the ratio 7:5. If the partner receiving the larger amount of this year's profits receives $84,000, what amount does the other partner receive?

Solution See page S6.

EXAMPLE 10 Solve an Application Using a Proportion

The dosage for a certain medication is 2 oz for every 50 lb of body weight. How many ounces of this medication are required for a person who weighs 175 lb?

Solution

Let $n =$ the number of ounces required for a person who weighs 175 lb. Write and solve a proportion. One rate is 2 oz per 50 lb of body weight.

$$\frac{2 \text{ oz}}{50 \text{ lb}} = \frac{n \text{ oz}}{175 \text{ lb}}$$
$$2(175) = 50 \cdot n$$
$$350 = 50n$$
$$\frac{350}{50} = \frac{50n}{50}$$
$$7 = n$$

A 175-pound person requires 7 oz of the medication.

CHECK YOUR PROGRESS 10

In 2013, the number of deaths from fire in the United States was 11.0 deaths per million people. How many people died from fire in the United States in 2013? Use a figure of 318 million for the population of the United States. Round your answer to the nearest thousand. (*Source:* U.S. Fire Administration, www.usfa.dhs.gov)

Solution See page S6.

MATH MATTERS Scale Models for Special Effects

Olivier LeClerc/Gamma Presse

When you see an exploding spacecraft or a sprinting dinosaur in a film, you are experiencing the work of special effects artists. These professionals often create physical scale models of buildings, vehicles, or creatures that appear full size when we witness them in a film. Artists also create three-dimensional computer models, sometimes by using 3D scanners with physical models, to design computer-generated imagery for films. Whether working in the physical or digital realm, the artists use ratios and proportions to determine the correct sizes and dimensions of these models.

EXCURSION

Earned Run Average

One measure of a pitcher's success is earned run average. **Earned run average (ERA)** is the number of earned runs a pitcher gives up for every nine innings pitched. The definition of an earned run is somewhat complicated, but basically an earned run is a run that is scored as a result of hits and base running that involves no errors on the part of the pitcher's team. If the opposing team scores a run on an error (for example, a fly ball that should have been caught in the outfield was fumbled), then that run is not an earned run.

A proportion is used to calculate a pitcher's ERA. Remember that the statistic involves the number of earned runs per *nine innings*. The answer is always rounded to the nearest hundredth. Here is an example.

Earned Run Average Leaders		
Major League Baseball		
Year	Player, club	ERA
2005	Roger Clemens, Houston	1.87
2006	Johan Santana, Minnesota	2.77
2007	Jake Peavy, San Diego	2.54
2008	Johan Santana, New York	2.53
2009	Zack Greinke, Kansas City	2.16
2010	Felix Hernandez, Seattle	2.27
2011	Clayton Kershaw, Los Angeles	2.28
2012	Clayton Kershaw, Los Angeles	2.53
2013	Clayton Kershaw, Los Angeles	1.83
2014	Clayton Kershaw, Los Angeles	1.77
2015	Zack Greinke, Los Angeles	1.66

During the 2015 baseball season, Clayton Kershaw gave up 55 earned runs and pitched 232.2 innings for the Los Angeles Dodgers. To calculate Clayton Kershaw's ERA, let $x =$ the number of earned runs for every nine innings pitched. Write a proportion and then solve it for x.

$$\frac{55 \text{ earned runs}}{232.2 \text{ innings}} = \frac{x}{9 \text{ innings}}$$

$$55 \cdot 9 = 232.2 \cdot x$$

$$495 = 232.2x$$

$$\frac{495}{232.2} = \frac{232.2x}{232.2}$$

$$2.13 \approx x$$

Clayton Kershaw

Clayton Kershaw's ERA for the 2015 season was 2.13.

EXCURSION EXERCISES

1. In 1979, his rookie year, Jeff Reardon pitched 21 innings for the New York Mets and gave up four earned runs. Calculate Reardon's ERA for 1979.
2. Roger Clemens's first year with the Boston Red Sox was 1984. During that season, he pitched 133.1 innings and gave up 64 earned runs. Calculate Clemens's ERA for 1984.
3. In 1987, Nolan Ryan had the lowest ERA of any pitcher in the major leagues. He gave up 65 earned runs and pitched 211.2 innings for the Houston Astros. Calculate Ryan's ERA for 1987.
4. During the 2015 season, Jake Arrieta of the Baltimore Orioles pitched 229 innings and had an ERA of 1.77. How many earned runs did he give up during the season?
5. Find the necessary statistics for a pitcher on your "home team," and calculate that pitcher's ERA.

EXERCISE SET 2.2

1. Provide two examples of situations in which unit rates are used.
2. Provide two examples of situations in which ratios are used.

■ In Exercises 3 to 8, write the expression as a unit rate.

3. 582 mi in 12 h
4. 138 mi on 6 gal of gasoline
5. 544 words typed in 8 min
6. 100 m in 8 s
7. $9100 for 350 shares of stock
8. 1000 ft^2 of wall covered with 2.5 gal of paint
9. **Wages** A machinist earns $682.50 for working a 35-hour week. What is the machinist's hourly rate of pay?

10. Space Vehicles The Space Shuttle's solid rocket boosters are a pair of rockets used during the first 2 min of powered flight. Each booster burns 680,400 kg of propellant in 2.5 min. How much propellant does each booster burn in 1 min?

11. Photography During filming, an IMAX camera uses 65-mm film at a rate of 5.6 ft/s.

a. At what rate per minute does the camera go through film?

b. How quickly does the camera use a 500-foot roll of 65-mm film? Round to the nearest second.

12. Consumerism Which is the more economical purchase, a 30-ounce jar of mayonnaise for $4.29 or a 48-ounce jar of mayonnaise for $6.29?

13. Consumerism Which is the more economical purchase, an 18-ounce box of corn flakes for $3.49 or a 24-ounce box of corn flakes for $3.89?

14. Wages You have a choice of receiving a wage of $34,000/year, $2840/month, $650 per week, or $16.50/h. Which pay choice would you take? Assume a 40-hour work week and 52 weeks of work per year.

Blank Archives/Getty Images

Babe Ruth

15. Baseball Baseball statisticians calculate a hitter's at-bats per home run by dividing the number of times the player has been at bat by the number of home runs the player has hit.

a. Calculate the at-bats per home run for each player in the table below. Round to the nearest tenth.

b. Which player has the lowest rate of at-bats per home run? Which player has the second lowest rate?

c. Why is this rate used for comparison rather than the number of home runs a player has hit?

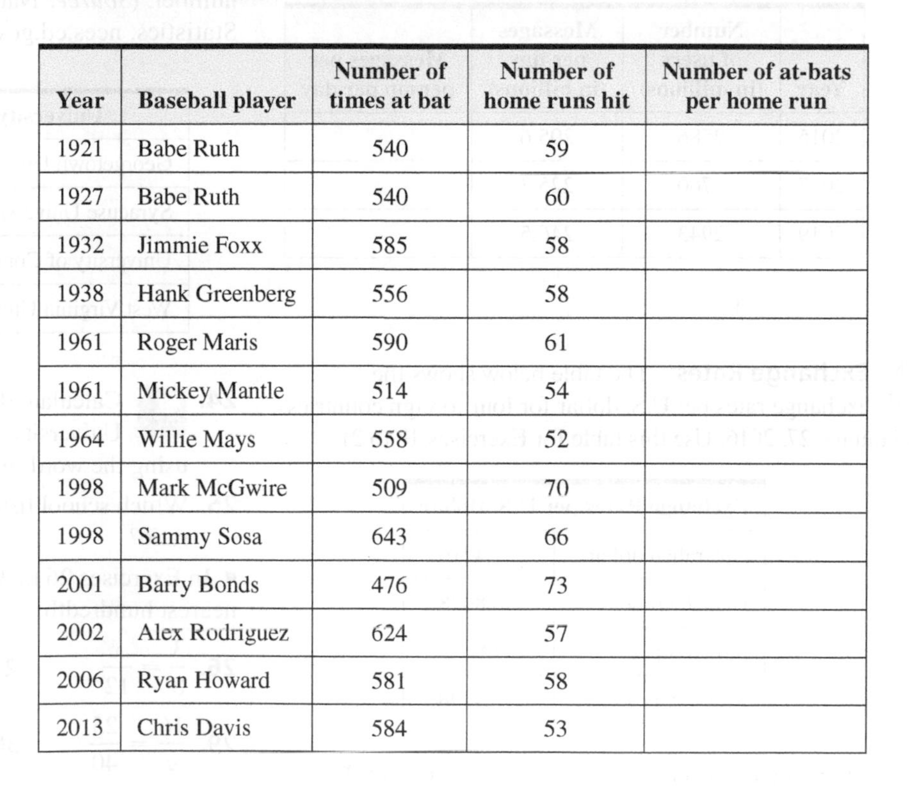

Year	Baseball player	Number of times at bat	Number of home runs hit	Number of at-bats per home run
1921	Babe Ruth	540	59	
1927	Babe Ruth	540	60	
1932	Jimmie Foxx	585	58	
1938	Hank Greenberg	556	58	
1961	Roger Maris	590	61	
1961	Mickey Mantle	514	54	
1964	Willie Mays	558	52	
1998	Mark McGwire	509	70	
1998	Sammy Sosa	643	66	
2001	Barry Bonds	476	73	
2002	Alex Rodriguez	624	57	
2006	Ryan Howard	581	58	
2013	Chris Davis	584	53	

16. **Population Density** The table below shows the population and area of three countries. The population density of a country is the number of people per square mile.

a. Which country has the lowest population density?

b. How many more people per square mile are there in India than in the United States? Round to the nearest whole number.

Country	Population	Area (in square miles)
Australia	22,751,000	2,938,000
India	1,251,696,000	1,146,000
United States	321,369,000	3,535,000

17. **E-mail** The Radicati Group compiled the following estimates on consumer use of e-mail worldwide.

a. Complete the last column of the table below by calculating the estimated number of messages per day that each user receives. Round to the nearest tenth.

b. The predicted number of messages per person per day in 2019 is how many times the estimated number in 2015? Round to the nearest hundredth.

Year	Number of users (in millions)	Messages per day (in billions)	Messages per person per day
2015	2586	205.6	
2017	2760	225.3	
2019	2943	246.5	

Exchange Rates The table below shows the exchange rates per U.S. dollar for four foreign countries on January 27, 2016. Use this table for Exercises 18 to 21.

Exchange Rates per U.S. Dollar	
Australian dollar	1.4216
Danish krone	6.8628
Indian rupee	67.8697
Mexican peso	18.4398

18. How many Danish kroner are equivalent to $5000?

19. Find the number of Indian rupees that would be exchanged for $45,000.

20. Find the cost, in Mexican pesos, of an order of American computer hardware costing $35,000.

21. Calculate the cost, in Australian dollars, of an American car costing $29,000.

Real Estate Dean Baker, co-director at the Center for Economic and Policy Research in Washington, D.C., suggests that the buy-versus-rent question can be answered using the price-to-rent ratio. Find two houses of similar size and quality in comparable neighborhoods, one for sale and the other for rent. Divide the price of the house for sale by the total cost of the rental for 1 year. If the quotient is higher than 20, renting might be the better option. If the quotient is below 15, buying might be the better option.

22. A house in San Diego, California, is priced at $530,000. The rent on a comparable house is $1800 per month. Find the price-to-rent ratio. Round to the nearest tenth. Does the ratio suggest that you buy or rent a home in San Diego?

23. A house in Orlando, Florida, is priced at $155,000. The rent on a comparable house is $1150 per month. Find the price-to-rent ratio. Round to the nearest tenth. Does the ratio suggest that you buy or rent a home in Orlando?

Student–Faculty Ratios The table below shows the number of full-time men and women undergraduates and the number of full-time faculty at several universities in the Big East. Use this table for Exercises 24 and 25. Round ratios to the nearest whole number. (*Source:* National Center for Education Statistics, nces.ed.gov)

University	Men	Women	Faculty
Georgetown University	3244	3982	1350
Syracuse University	6487	8045	1078
University of Connecticut	8851	8826	2007
West Virginia University	11,434	9429	2044

24. Calculate the student–faculty ratio at Syracuse University. Write the ratio using a colon and using the word *to*. What does this ratio mean?

25. Which school listed has the lowest student–faculty ratio?

■ In Exercises 26 to 37, solve the proportion. Round to the nearest hundredth.

26. $\frac{3}{8} = \frac{x}{12}$ **27.** $\frac{3}{y} = \frac{7}{40}$ **28.** $\frac{7}{12} = \frac{25}{d}$

29. $\frac{16}{d} = \frac{25}{40}$ **30.** $\frac{15}{45} = \frac{72}{c}$ **31.** $\frac{120}{c} = \frac{144}{25}$

32. $\frac{65}{20} = \frac{14}{a}$ **33.** $\frac{4}{a} = \frac{9}{5}$ **34.** $\frac{0.5}{2.3} = \frac{b}{20}$

35. $\frac{1.2}{2.8} = \frac{b}{32}$ **36.** $\frac{0.7}{1.2} = \frac{6.4}{x}$ **37.** $\frac{2.5}{0.6} = \frac{165}{x}$

38. Gravity The ratio of weight on the moon to weight on Earth is 1 : 6. How much would a 174-pound person weigh on the moon?

39. Management A management consulting firm recommends that the ratio of middle-management salaries to management trainee salaries be 5 : 4. Using this recommendation, what is the annual middle-management salary if the annual management trainee salary is $52,000?

40. Medication The dosage of a cold medication is 2 mg for every 80 lb of body weight. How many milligrams of this medication are required for a person who weighs 220 lb?

41. Fuel Consumption If your car can travel 70.5 mi on 3 gal of gasoline, how far can the car travel on 14 gal of gasoline under similar driving conditions?

42. Scale Drawings The scale on the architectural plans for a new house is 1 in. equals 3 ft. Find the length and width of a room that measures 5 in. by 8 in. on the drawing.

43. Scale Drawings The scale on a map is 1.25 in. equals 10 mi. Find the distance between two cities that are 2 in. apart on the map.

44. Art Leonardo da Vinci measured various distances on the human body in order to make accurate drawings. He determined that generally the ratio of the kneeling height of a person to the standing height of that person was $\frac{3}{4}$. Using this ratio, determine the standing height of a person who has a kneeling height of 48 in.

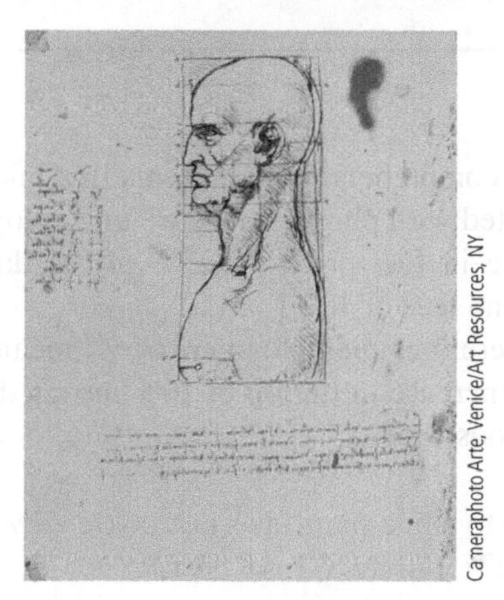

Cameraphoto Arte, Venice/Art Resources, NY

45. Art In one of Leonardo da Vinci's notebooks, he wrote that ". . . from the top to the bottom of the chin is the sixth part of a face, and it is the fifty-fourth part of the man." Suppose the distance from the top to the bottom of the chin of a person is 1.25 in. Using da Vinci's measurements, find the height of the person.

46. Elections A pre-election survey showed that two out of every three eligible voters would cast ballots in the county election. There are 240,000 eligible voters in the county. How many people are expected to vote in the election?

47. Food Waste One study estimated that in the U.S., the average family of four wastes $590 worth of food each year. Estimate the cost of food wasted by **a.** the average family of three and **b.** the average family of five.

48. Lotteries Three people put their money together to buy lottery tickets. The first person put in $25, the second person put in $30, and the third person put in $35. One of their tickets was a winning ticket. If they won $4.5 million, what was the first person's share of the winnings?

49. Nutrition A pancake 4 in. in diameter contains 5 g of fat. How many grams of fat are in a pancake 6 in. in diameter? Explain how you arrived at your answer.

Michael C. Gray/Shutterstock.com

EXTENSIONS

■ In Exercises 50 and 51, assume each denominator is a non-zero real number.

50. Determine whether the statement is true or false.

a. The quotient $a \div b$ is a ratio.

b. If $\frac{a}{b} = \frac{c}{d}$, then $\frac{b}{a} = \frac{d}{c}$.

c. If $\frac{a}{b} = \frac{c}{d}$, then $\frac{a}{c} = \frac{b}{d}$.

d. If $\frac{a}{b} = \frac{c}{d}$, then $\frac{a}{d} = \frac{c}{b}$.

51. If $\frac{a}{b} = \frac{c}{d}$, show that $\frac{a+b}{b} = \frac{c+d}{d}$.

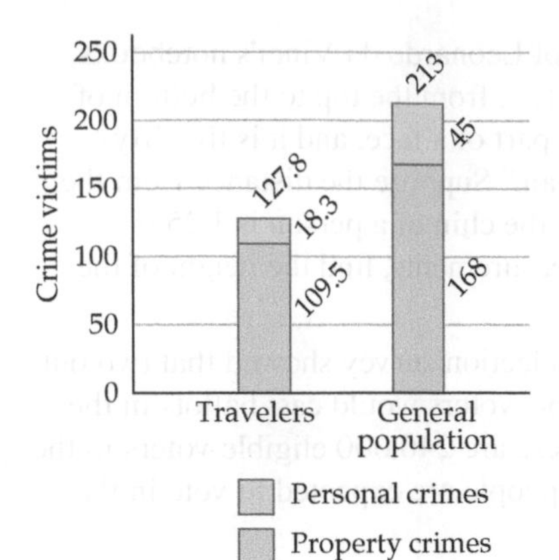

Crime Victims per 1000 Adults per Year

SOURCE: Travel Industry Association of America

52. **Crime Rates** According to a recent study, the crime rate against travelers in the United States is lower than that against the general population. The article reporting this study included a bar graph similar to the one at the left.

a. Why are the figures reported based on crime victims per 1000 adults per year?

b. Use the given figures to write the proportion

$$\frac{\text{personal crimes against travelers}}{\text{property crimes against travelers}} = \frac{\text{personal crimes against general population}}{\text{property crimes against general population}}$$

Is the proportion true?

c. Why might the crime rate against travelers be lower than that against the general population?

53. The House of Representatives The U.S. House of Representatives has a total of 435 members. These members represent the 50 states in proportion to each state's population. As stated in Article XIV, Section 2, of the Constitution of the United States, "Representatives shall be apportioned among the several states according to their respective numbers, counting the whole number of persons in each state."

Official White House Photo by Lawrence Jackson

U.S. House of Representatives

a. Find the population of each state according to the 2010 U.S. Census. Based on the state populations, determine how many representatives each state should elect to Congress.

b. Compare your list against the actual number of representatives that each state has.

SECTION 2.3 Percent

Percents

An understanding of percent is vital to comprehending the events that take place in our world today. We are constantly confronted with phrases such as "unemployment of 7%," "annual inflation of 4%," "6% increase in fuel prices," "25% of the daily minimum requirement," and "increase in tuition and fees of 10%."

Percent means "for every 100." Therefore, unemployment of 5% means that 5 out of every 100 people are unemployed. An increase in tuition of 10% means that tuition has gone up \$10 for every \$100 it cost previously.

POINT OF INTEREST

Of all the errors made on federal income tax returns, the four most common errors account for 76% of the mistakes. These errors include an omitted entry (30.7%), an incorrect entry (19.1%), an error in mathematics (17.4%), and an entry on the wrong line (8.8%).

QUESTION When adults were asked to name their favorite cookie, 52% said chocolate chip. What does this statistic mean? (*Source:* WEAREVER)

A percent is a ratio of a number to 100. Thus $\frac{1}{100} = 1\%$, $\frac{50}{100} = 50\%$, and $\frac{99}{100} = 99\%$. Because $1\% = \frac{1}{100}$ and $\frac{1}{100} = 0.01$, we can also write 1% as 0.01.

$$\mathbf{1\% = \frac{1}{100} = 0.01}$$

The equivalence $1\% = 0.01$ is used to write a percent as a decimal or to write a decimal as a percent.

ANSWER 52 out of every 100 people surveyed responded that their favorite cookie was chocolate chip. (In the same survey, the following responses were also given: oatmeal raisin, 10%; peanut butter, 9%; oatmeal, 7%; sugar, 4%; molasses, 4%; chocolate chip oatmeal, 3%.)

To write 17% as a decimal:

$$17\% = 17(1\%) = 17(0.01) = 0.17$$

Note that this is the same as removing the percent sign and moving the decimal point two places to the left.

To write 0.17 as a percent:

$$0.17 = 17(0.01) = 17(1\%) = 17\%$$

Note that this is the same as moving the decimal point two places to the right and writing a percent sign at the right of the number.

EXAMPLE 1 Write a Percent as a Decimal

Write the percent as a decimal.

a. 24% **b.** 183% **c.** 6.5% **d.** 0.9%

Solution

To write a percent as a decimal, remove the percent sign and move the decimal point two places to the left.

a. 24% = 0.24
b. 183% = 1.83
c. 6.5% = 0.065
d. 0.9% = 0.009

CHECK YOUR PROGRESS 1 Write the percent as a decimal.

a. 74% **b.** 152% **c.** 8.3% **d.** 0.6%

Solution See page S7.

EXAMPLE 2 Write a Decimal as a Percent

Write the decimal as a percent.

a. 0.62 **b.** 1.5 **c.** 0.059 **d.** 0.008

Solution

To write a decimal as a percent, move the decimal point two places to the right and write a percent sign.

a. 0.62 = 62%
b. 1.5 = 150%
c. 0.059 = 5.9%
d. 0.008 = 0.8%

POINT OF INTEREST

The National Safety Council estimates that 27% of car crashes in a recent year were attributable to cell phone use and texting.

CHECK YOUR PROGRESS 2 Write the decimal as a percent.

a. 0.3 **b.** 1.65 **c.** 0.072 **d.** 0.004

Solution See page S7.

The equivalence $1\% = \frac{1}{100}$ is used to write a percent as a fraction.

To write 16% as a fraction:

$$16\% = 16(1\%) = 16\left(\frac{1}{100}\right) = \frac{16}{100} = \frac{4}{25}$$

Note that this is the same as removing the percent sign and multiplying by $\frac{1}{100}$. The fraction is written in simplest form.

EXAMPLE 3 Write a Percent as a Fraction

Write the percent as a fraction.

a. 25% **b.** 120% **c.** 7.5% **d.** $33\frac{1}{3}\%$

Solution

To write a percent as a fraction, remove the percent sign and multiply by $\frac{1}{100}$. Then write the fraction in simplest form.

a. $25\% = 25\left(\frac{1}{100}\right) = \frac{25}{100} = \frac{1}{4}$

b. $120\% = 120\left(\frac{1}{100}\right) = \frac{120}{100} = 1\frac{20}{100} = 1\frac{1}{5}$

c. $7.5\% = 7.5\left(\frac{1}{100}\right) = \frac{7.5}{100} = \frac{75}{1000} = \frac{3}{40}$

d. $33\frac{1}{3}\% = \frac{100}{3}\% = \frac{100}{3}\left(\frac{1}{100}\right) = \frac{1}{3}$

CHECK YOUR PROGRESS 3 Write the percent as a fraction.

a. 8% **b.** 180% **c.** 2.5% **d.** $66\frac{2}{3}\%$

Solution See page S7.

TAKE NOTE

To write a fraction as a decimal, divide the number in the numerator by the number in the denominator. For example,

$\frac{4}{5} = 4 \div 5 = 0.8.$

To write a fraction as a percent, first write the fraction as a decimal. Then write the decimal as a percent.

EXAMPLE 4 Write a Fraction as a Percent

Write the fraction as a percent.

a. $\frac{3}{4}$ **b.** $\frac{5}{8}$ **c.** $\frac{1}{6}$ **d.** $1\frac{1}{2}$

Solution

To write a fraction as a percent, write the fraction as a decimal. Then write the decimal as a percent.

a. $\frac{3}{4} = 0.75 = 75\%$

b. $\frac{5}{8} = 0.625 = 62.5\%$

c. $\frac{1}{6} = 0.1\overline{66} = 16.\overline{6}\%$

d. $1\frac{1}{2} = 1.5 = 150\%$

CHECK YOUR PROGRESS 4 Write the fraction as a percent.

a. $\frac{1}{4}$ **b.** $\frac{3}{8}$ **c.** $\frac{5}{6}$ **d.** $1\frac{2}{3}$

Solution See page S7.

College Graduates' Job Expectations

The table below compares the expectations of 2015 college graduates with the realities of those who graduated in 2013 or 2014. (*Source:* Accenture)

Expectations of 2015 graduates	Realities of 2013–2014 graduates
80% believed their education prepared them well	64% felt their education prepared them well
72% completed an internship, apprenticeship, or co-op	47% found a job as a result of an internship, apprenticeship, or co-op
82% considered job availability before selecting a major	64% are working in their chosen field
85% expect to earn more than $25,000 per year	59% earn more than $25,000 per year

Percent Problems: The Proportion Method

Finding the solution of an application problem involving percent generally requires writing and solving an equation. Two methods of writing the equation will be developed in this section—the *proportion method* and the *basic percent equation.* We will present the proportion method first.

The proportion method of solving a percent problem is based on writing two ratios. One ratio is the percent ratio, written $\frac{\text{percent}}{100}$. The second ratio is the amount-to-base ratio, written $\frac{\text{amount}}{\text{base}}$, where the *base* is the number that the percentage will be taken of, and the *amount* is the result after the percentage is taken. These two ratios form the proportion used to solve percent problems.

The Proportion Used to Solve Percent Problems

$$\frac{\text{percent}}{100} = \frac{\text{amount}}{\text{base}}$$

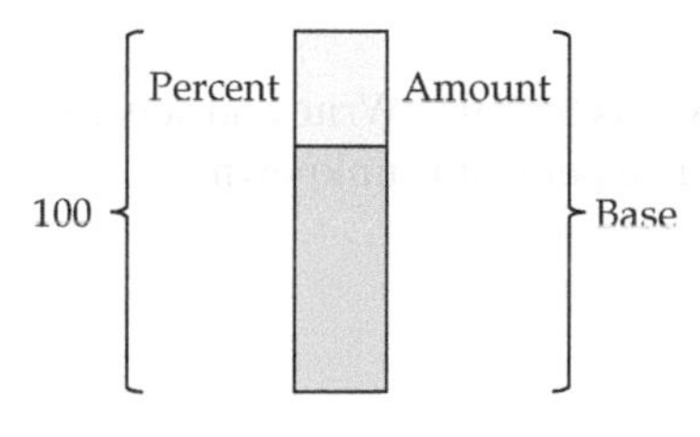

Diagram of the Proportion Method of Solving Percent Problems

The proportion method can be illustrated by a diagram. The rectangle at the left is divided into two parts. On the left, the whole rectangle is represented by 100 and the part by percent. On the right, the whole rectangle is represented by the base and the part by the amount. The ratio of percent to 100 is equal to the ratio of the amount to the base.

When solving a percent problem, first identify the percent, the base, and the amount. It is helpful to know that the base usually follows the phrase "percent of."

QUESTION In the statement "15% of 40 is 6," which number is the percent? Which number is the base? Which number is the amount?

ANSWER The percent is 15. The base is 40. (It follows the phrase "percent of.") The amount is 6.

EXAMPLE 5 Solve a Percent Problem for the Base Using the Proportion Method

The average size of a new single-family house in 2014 was 2690 ft². This is 158% of the average size of a new house in 1980. What was the average size of a new house in 1980? Round to the nearest whole number.

Solution

We want to answer the question "158% of what number is 2690?" Write and solve a proportion. The percent is 158%. The amount is 2690. The base is the average size of a new house in 1980.

$$\frac{\text{percent}}{100} = \frac{\text{amount}}{\text{base}}$$

$$\frac{158}{100} = \frac{2690}{B}$$

$$158 \cdot B = 100(2690)$$

$$158B = 269{,}000$$

$$\frac{158B}{158} = \frac{269{,}000}{158}$$

$$B \approx 1703$$

The average size of a new house in 1980 was 1703 ft².

CHECK YOUR PROGRESS 5 A used Toyota Corolla was purchased for $12,950. This is 70% of the cost when new. What was the cost of the Toyota Corolla when it was new?

Solution See page S7.

EXAMPLE 6 Solve a Percent Problem for the Percent Using the Proportion Method

According to the Bureau of Labor Statistics, in a recent year the average American family had an income of $66,877 and spent $6759 on food. What percent of the family income was spent on food? Round to the nearest percent.

Solution

We want to answer the question "What percent of $66,877 is $6759?" Write and solve a proportion. The base is $66,877. The amount is $6759. The percent is unknown.

$$\frac{\text{percent}}{100} = \frac{\text{amount}}{\text{base}}$$

$$\frac{p}{100} = \frac{6759}{66{,}877}$$

$$p \cdot 66{,}877 = 100(6759)$$

$$66{,}877p = 675{,}900$$

$$\frac{66{,}877p}{66{,}877} = \frac{675{,}900}{66{,}877}$$

$$p \approx 10$$

Ten percent of the family income was spent on food.

POINT OF INTEREST

According to the U.S. Department of Agriculture, of the 430 billion pounds of food produced annually in the United States, about 133 billion pounds are wasted. This is approximately 31% of all the food produced in the United States.

CHECK YOUR PROGRESS 6

An estimated 43.5 million adults in the United States are caretakers for an older friend or relative. Of these adults, 18.705 million said they feel they did not have a choice in this role. What percent of the adult caretakers in the United States feel they did not have a choice in this role? (*Source:* TIME, February 1, 2010)

Solution See page S7.

EXAMPLE 7 Solve a Percent Problem for the Amount Using the Proportion Method

Thirty-two percent of the world population of 7.3 billion people do not have access to improved sanitation facilities. How many people worldwide do not have access to improved sanitation facilities? (*Source:* World Health Organization, Fact Sheet No. 392, June 2015)

Solution

We want to answer the question, "32% of 7.3 billion is what number?" Write and solve a proportion. The percent is 32%. The base is 7.3 billion. The amount is the number of people who do not have access to improved sanitation facilities.

$$\frac{\text{percent}}{100} = \frac{\text{amount}}{\text{base}}$$

$$\frac{32}{100} = \frac{A}{7.3}$$

$$32(7.3) = 100(A)$$

$$233.6 = 100A$$

$$\frac{233.6}{100} = \frac{100A}{100}$$

$$2.336 = A$$

About 2.34 billion people worldwide do not have access to improved sanitation facilities.

CHECK YOUR PROGRESS 7 A General Motors buyer incentive program offered a 3.5% rebate on the selling price of a new car. What rebate would a customer receive who purchased a $32,500 car under this program?

Solution See page S7.

Percent Problems: The Basic Percent Equation

A second method of solving a percent problem is to use the basic percent equation.

The Basic Percent Equation

$PB = A$, where P is the percent, B is the base, and A is the amount.

When solving a percent problem using the proportion method, we have to first identify the percent, the base, and the amount. The same is true when solving percent problems using the basic percent equation. Remember that the base usually follows the phrase "percent of."

When using the basic percent equation, the percent must be written as a decimal or a fraction. This is illustrated in Example 8.

EXAMPLE 8 Solve a Percent Problem for the Amount Using the Basic Percent Equation

A real estate broker receives a commission of 3% of the selling price of a house. Find the amount the broker receives on the sale of a $275,000 home.

Solution

We want to answer the question "3% of $275,000 is what number?" Use the basic percent equation. The percent is $3\% = 0.03$. The base is 275,000. The amount is the amount the broker receives on the sale of the home.

$$PB = A$$
$$0.03(275{,}000) = A$$
$$8250 = A$$

The real estate broker receives a commission of $8250 on the sale.

CHECK YOUR PROGRESS 8 New Hampshire public school teachers contribute 5% of their wages to the New Hampshire Retirement System. What amount is contributed during one year by a teacher whose annual salary is $46,875?

Solution See page S7.

EXAMPLE 9 Solve a Percent Problem for the Base Using the Basic Percent Equation

An investor received a payment of $480, which was 12% of the value of the investment. Find the value of the investment.

Solution

We want to answer the question "12% of what number is 480?" Use the basic percent equation. The percent is $12\% = 0.12$. The amount is 480. The base is the value of the investment.

$$PB = A$$
$$0.12B = 480$$
$$\frac{0.12B}{0.12} = \frac{480}{0.12}$$
$$B = 4000$$

The value of the investment is $4000.

CHECK YOUR PROGRESS 9 A real estate broker receives a commission of 3% of the selling price of a house. If the broker receives a commission of $14,370 on the sale of a home, what was the selling price of the home?

Solution See page S7.

EXAMPLE 10 Solve a Percent Problem for the Percent Using the Basic Percent Equation

If you answer 96 questions correctly on a 120-question exam, what percent of the questions did you answer correctly?

Solution

We want to answer the question "What percent of 120 questions is 96 questions?" Use the basic percent equation. The base is 120. The amount is 96. The percent is unknown.

$$PB = A$$
$$P \cdot 120 = 96$$
$$\frac{P \cdot 120}{120} = \frac{96}{120}$$
$$P = 0.8$$
$$P = 80\%$$

You answered 80% of the questions correctly.

CHECK YOUR PROGRESS 10 If you answer 63 questions correctly on a 90-question exam, what percent of the questions did you answer correctly?

Solution See page S7.

cappi thompson/Shutterstock.com

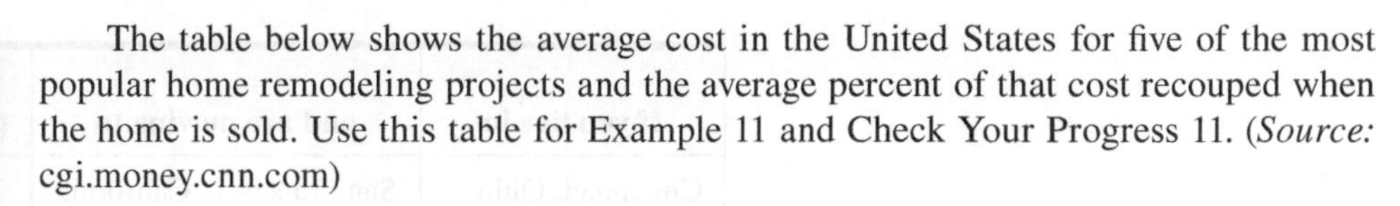

The table below shows the average cost in the United States for five of the most popular home remodeling projects and the average percent of that cost recouped when the home is sold. Use this table for Example 11 and Check Your Progress 11. (*Source:* cgi.money.cnn.com)

Home remodeling project	Average cost	Percent recouped
Addition to the master suite	$94,331	72%
Major kitchen remodeling	$54,241	80%
Home office remodeling	$20,057	63%
Bathroom remodeling	$12,918	85%
Basement remodeling	$56,724	79%

EXAMPLE 11 Solve an Application Using the Basic Percent Equation

Find the difference between the cost of remodeling the basement of your home and the amount by which the remodeling increases the sale price of your home.

Solution

The cost of remodeling the basement is $56,724, and the sale price increases by 79% of that amount. We need to find the difference between $56,724 and 79% of $56,724.

Use the basic percent equation to find 79% of $56,724. The percent is $79\% = 0.79$. The base is 56,724. The amount is unknown.

$$PB = A$$
$$0.79(56{,}724) = A$$
$$44{,}811.96 = A$$

Subtract 44,811.96 (the amount of the cost that is recouped when the home is sold) from 56,724 (the cost of remodeling the basement).

$$56{,}724 - 44{,}811.96 = 11{,}912.04$$

The difference between the cost of remodeling the basement and the increase in the value of your home is $11,912.04.

POINT OF INTEREST

According to Sallie Mae's *How America Pays for College* report, 54% of college students lived at home in 2014. That's up from 43% in 2010.

CHECK YOUR PROGRESS 11

Find the difference between the cost of a major kitchen remodeling in your home and the amount by which the remodeling increases the sale price of your home.

Solution See page S7.

Percent Increase

When a family moves from one part of the country to another, they are concerned about the difference in the cost of living. Will food, housing, and gasoline cost more in that part of the country? Will they need a larger salary in order to make ends meet?

We can use one number to represent the increased cost of living from one city to another so that no matter what salary you make, you can determine how much you will need to earn in order to maintain the same standard of living. That one number is a percent.

For example, look at the information in the table below. (*Source:* http://cgi.money.cnn.com/tools/costofliving/)

If you live in	and are moving to	you will need to make this percent of your current salary
Cincinnati, Ohio	San Francisco, California	191
St. Louis, Missouri	Boston, Massachusetts	153
Denver, Colorado	New York, New York	207

A family in Cincinnati living on \$60,000 per year would need 191% of their current income to maintain the same standard of living in San Francisco. Likewise, a family living on \$150,000 per year would need 191% of their current income.

$60{,}000(1.91) = 114{,}600 \qquad 150{,}000(1.91) = 286{,}500$

The family from Cincinnati living on \$60,000 would need an annual income of \$114,600 in San Francisco to maintain their standard of living. The family living on \$150,000 would need an annual income of \$286,500 in San Francisco to maintain their standard of living. No matter what a family's present income, they can use 191% to determine their necessary comparable income.

QUESTION How much would a family in Denver, Colorado, living on \$55,000 per year need in New York City to maintain a comparable lifestyle? Use the table above.

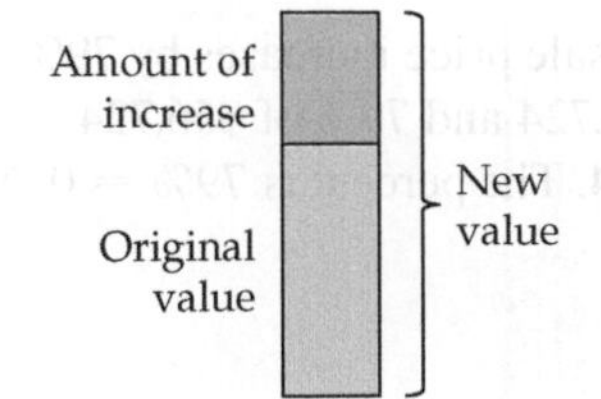

The cost of living in San Francisco is 191% of the cost of living in Cincinnati; this means that a family moving from Cincinnati to San Francisco will see a 91% *increase* in their cost of living. **Percent increase** is used to show how much a quantity has increased over its original value. Statements that illustrate the use of percent increase include "sales volume increased by 11% over last year's sales volume" and "employees received an 8% pay increase."

The **federal debt** is the amount the government owes after borrowing the money it needs to pay for its expenses. It is considered a good measure of how much of the

ANSWER In New York City, the family would need \$55,000(2.07) = \$113,850 per year to maintain a comparable lifestyle.

government's spending is financed by debt as opposed to taxation. The graph below shows the federal debt at the end of the fiscal years 1995, 2000, 2005, 2010, and 2015. A fiscal year is the 12-month period that the annual budget spans, from October 1 to September 30. Use the graph for Example 12 and Check Your Progress 12.

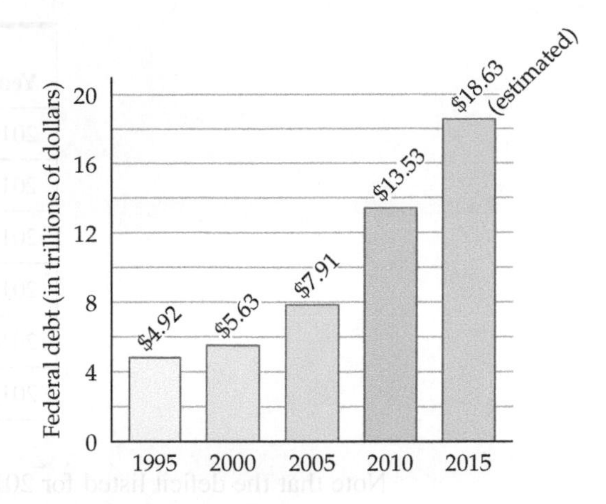

SOURCE: www.whitehouse.gov

EXAMPLE 12 Solve an Application Involving Percent Increase

The largest percent increase, for a single day, in the Dow Jones Industrial Average occurred on March 15, 1933. The Dow gained approximately 15% of its value.

Find the percent increase in the federal debt from 2005 to 2010. Round to the nearest tenth of a percent.

Solution

Calculate the amount of increase in the federal debt from 2005 to 2010.

$$13.53 - 7.91 = 5.62$$

We will use the basic percent equation. (The proportion method could also be used.) The base is the debt in 2005. The amount is the amount of increase in the debt. The percent is unknown.

$$PB = A$$
$$P \cdot 7.91 = 5.62$$
$$\frac{P \cdot 7.91}{7.91} = \frac{5.62}{7.91}$$
$$P \approx 0.710$$

The percent increase in the federal debt from 2005 to 2010 was 71.0%.

CHECK YOUR PROGRESS 12

Find the percent increase in the federal debt from 1995 to 2015. Round to the nearest tenth of a percent.

Solution See page S7.

Notice in Example 12 that the percent increase is a measure of the *amount of increase* over an *original value.* Therefore, in the basic percent equation, the amount A is the *amount of increase* and the base B is the *original value,* in this case the debt in 2005.

Percent Decrease

The federal debt is not the same as the federal deficit. The **federal deficit** is the amount by which government spending exceeds the federal budget. The table below shows projected federal deficits. (*Source:* www.usgovernmentspending.com)

Year	Federal deficit (in billions of dollars)
2010	\$1294
2011	\$1300
2012	\$1087
2013	\$680
2014	\$485
2015	\$439

Note that the deficit listed for 2013 is less than the deficit listed for 2012. This decrease can be expressed as a percent. First find the amount of decrease in the deficit from 2012 to 2013.

$$1087 - 680 = 407$$

We will use the basic percent equation to find the percent. The base is the deficit in 2012. The amount is the amount of decrease.

$$PB = A$$
$$P \cdot 1087 = 407$$
$$\frac{P \cdot 1087}{1087} = \frac{407}{1087}$$
$$P \approx 0.374$$

The federal deficit decreased by 37.4% from 2012 to 2013.

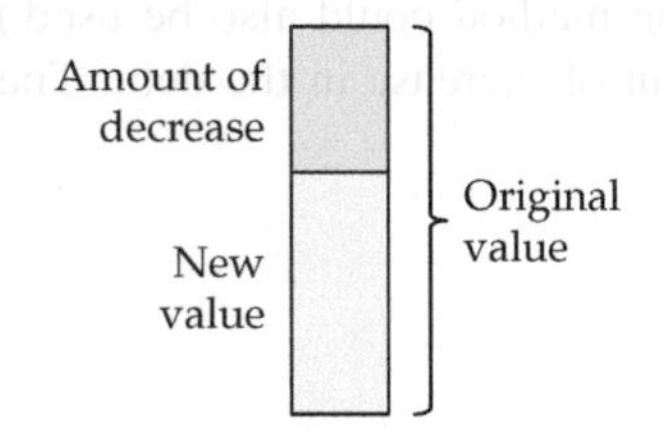

The percent used to measure the decrease in the federal deficit is a *percent decrease.* **Percent decrease** is used to show how much a quantity has decreased from its original value. Statements that illustrate the use of percent decrease include "the president's approval rating has decreased 9% over last month" and "there has been a 15% decrease in the number of industrial accidents."

Note in the deficit example above that the percent decrease is a measure of the *amount of decrease* over an *original value.* Therefore, in the basic percent equation, the amount A is the *amount of decrease* and the base B is the *original value,* in this case the deficit in 2012.

EXAMPLE 13 Solve an Application Involving Percent Decrease

According to the National Highway Traffic Safety Administration, there were 4668 deaths from motorcycle accidents in 2013 while there were 4986 deaths in 2012. This decrease reverses a rising trend from previous years. Find the percent decrease in deaths due to motorcycle accidents from 2012 to 2013. Round to the nearest tenth of a percent.

Solution

First find the amount of decrease.

$$4986 - 4668 = 318$$

We will use the basic percent equation to find the percent decrease. The base is the number of deaths in 2012 (4986). The amount is the decrease in the number of deaths (318).

$$PB = A$$
$$P \cdot 4986 = 318$$
$$\frac{P \cdot 4986}{4986} = \frac{318}{4986}$$
$$P \approx 0.064$$

The percent decrease in the number of deaths from motorcycle accidents is 6.4%.

CHECK YOUR PROGRESS 13

Find the percent decrease in the federal deficit from 2013 to 2014. Use the table on page 140. Round to the nearest tenth of a percent.

Solution See page S8.

EXCURSION

Federal Income Tax

Income taxes are the chief source of revenue for the federal government. If you are employed, your employer probably withholds some money from each of your paychecks for federal income tax. At the end of each year, your employer sends you a **Wage and Tax Statement Form (W-2 form)**, which states the amount of money you earned that year and how much was withheld for taxes.

Every employee is required by law to prepare an income tax return by April 15 of each year and send it to the Internal Revenue Service (IRS). On the income tax return, you must report your total income, or **gross income**. Then you subtract from the gross income any adjustments (such as deductions for charitable contributions or exemptions for people who are dependent on your income) to determine your **adjusted gross income**. You use your adjusted gross income and either a tax table or a tax rate schedule to determine your **tax liability**, or the amount of income you owe to the federal government.

After calculating your tax liability, compare it with the amount withheld for federal income tax, as shown on your W-2 form. If the tax liability is less than the amount withheld, you are entitled to a tax refund. If the tax liability is greater than the amount withheld, you owe the IRS money; you have a **balance due**.

The 2015 Tax Rate Schedules table is shown on page 142. To use this table for the exercises that follow, first classify the taxpayer as single, married filing jointly, or married filing separately. Then determine into which range the adjusted gross income falls. Then perform the calculations shown to the right of that range to determine the tax liability.

For example, consider a taxpayer who is single and has an adjusted gross income of \$48,720. To find this taxpayer's tax liability, use the portion of the table headed "Section A" for taxpayers whose filing status is single.

An income of \$48,720 falls in the range \$37,450 to \$90,750. The tax is \$5,156.25 + 25% of the amount over \$37,450. Find the amount over \$37,450.

$$\$48,720 - 37,450 = \$11,270$$

Calculate the tax liability:

$$\begin{aligned}\$5,156.25 + 25\%(\$11,270) &= \$5,156.25 + 0.25(\$11,270)\\ &= \$5,156.25 + \$2817.50\\ &= \$7973.75\end{aligned}$$

The taxpayer's liability is $7973.75.

2015 Tax Rate Schedules

Section A—If your filing status is Single

If your taxable income is: Over—	But not over—	The tax is:		of the amount over—
$0	$9,225	...	10%	$0
9,225	37,450	$922.50 + 15%		9,225
37,450	90,750	5,156.25 + 25%		37,450
90,750	189,300	18,481.25 + 28%		90,750
189,300	411,500	46,075.25 + 33%		189,300
411,500	413,200	119,401.25 + 35%		411,500
413,200	...	119,996.25 + 39.6%		413,200

Section B—If your filing status is Married filing jointly or Qualifying widow(er)

If your taxable income is: Over—	But not over—	The tax is:		of the amount over—
$0	$18,450	...	10%	$0
18,450	74,900	$1,845.00 + 15%		18,450
74,900	151,200	10,312.50 + 25%		74,900
151,200	230,450	29,387.50 + 28%		151,200
230,450	411,500	51,577.50 + 33%		230,450
411,500	464,850	111,324.00 + 35%		411,500
464,850	...	129,996.50 + 39.6%		464,850

Section C—If your filing status is Married filing separately

If your taxable income is: Over—	But not over—	The tax is:		of the amount over—
$0	$9,225	...	10%	$0
9,225	37,450	$922.50 + 15%		9,225
37,450	75,600	5,156.25 + 25%		37,450
75,600	115,225	14,693.75 + 28%		75,600
115,225	205,750	25,788.75 + 33%		115,225
205,750	232,425	55,662.00 + 35%		205,750
232,425	...	64,998.25 + 39.6%		232,425

EXCURSION EXERCISES

Use the 2015 Tax Rate Schedules to solve Exercises 1 to 6.

1. Joseph Abruzzio is married and filing separately. He has an adjusted gross income of $63,850. Find Joseph's tax liability.
2. Angela Lopez is single and has an adjusted gross income of $31,680. Find Angela's tax liability.

3. Dee Pinckney is married and filing jointly. She has an adjusted gross income of $58,120. The W-2 form shows the amount withheld as $7124. Find Dee's tax liability and determine her tax refund or balance due.
4. Jeremy Littlefield is single and has an adjusted gross income of $152,600. His W-2 form lists the amount withheld as $36,500. Find Jeremy's tax liability and determine his tax refund or balance due.
5. Does a taxpayer in the 33% tax bracket pay 33% of his or her earnings in income tax? Explain your answer.
6. In the table for single taxpayers, how were the figures $922.50 and $5156.25 arrived at?

EXERCISE SET 2.3

1. Name three situations in which percent is used.
2. Multiplying a number by 300% is the same as multiplying it by what whole number?

Complete the table of equivalent fractions, decimals, and percents.

	Fraction	Decimal	Percent
3.	$\frac{1}{2}$		
4.		0.75	
5.			40%
6.	$\frac{3}{8}$		
7.		0.7	
8.			56.25%
9.	$\frac{11}{20}$		
10.		0.52	
11.			15.625%
12.	$\frac{9}{50}$		

13. **e-Filed Tax Returns** The IRS reported that as of April 17, 2015, it had received 132 million tax returns for 2014. Of these, 90% were filed electronically. How many of the returns were filed electronically? Round to the nearest million.

14. **Credit Cards** A credit card company offers an annual 2% cash-back rebate on all gasoline purchases. If a family spent $6200 on gasoline purchases over the course of a year, what was the family's rebate at the end of the year?

15. **Charitable Contributions** During a recent year, charitable contributions in the United States totaled $358 billion. The graph at the right shows to whom this money was donated. Determine how much money was donated to educational organizations. (*Source:* Giving USA Foundation)

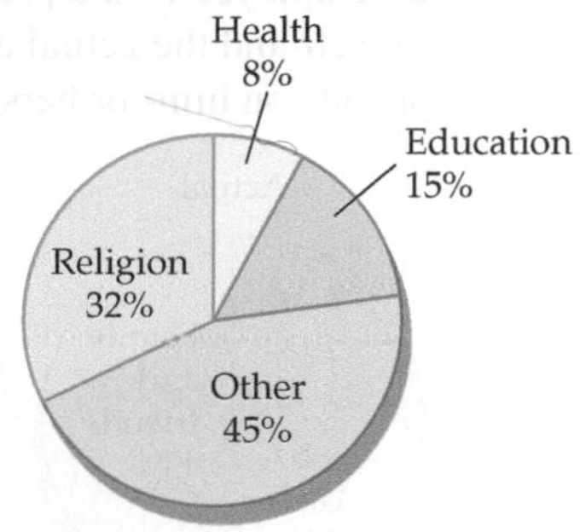

Recipients of Charitable Contributions in the United States

16. **Television** A survey by the *Boston Globe* questioned elementary and middle-school students about television. Sixty-eight students, or 42.5% of those surveyed, said that they had a television in their bedroom at home. How many students were included in the survey?

17. **Motorists** A survey of 1236 adults nationwide asked, "What irks you most about the actions of other motorists?" The response "tailgaters" was given by 293 people. What percent of those surveyed were most irked by tailgaters? Round to the nearest tenth of a percent. (*Source:* Reuters/Zogby)

18. **Wind Energy** In a recent year, wind machines in the United States generated 181.7 billion kWh of electricity, enough to serve over 16 million households. The nation's total electricity production that year was 4094 billion kWh. (*Source:* Energy Information Administration) What percent of the total energy production was generated by wind machines? Round to the nearest tenth of a percent.

TranceDrumer/Shutterstock.com

19. **Mining** During 1 year, approximately 2,240,000 oz of gold went into the manufacturing of electronic equipment in the United States. This is 16% of all the gold mined in the United States that year. How many ounces of gold were mined in the United States that year?

20. **Time Management** The two circle graphs show how surveyed employees actually spend their time and how they would prefer to spend their time. Assume that employees have 112 hours a week that are not spent sleeping. Round answers to the nearest tenth of an hour. (*Source: Wall Street Journal* Supplement from *Families and Work Institute*)

 a. What is the actual number of hours per week that employees spend with family and friends?
 b. What is the number of hours that employees would prefer to spend on their jobs or careers?
 c. What is the difference between the number of hours an employee would prefer to spend on him- or herself and the actual amount of time the employee spends on him- or herself?

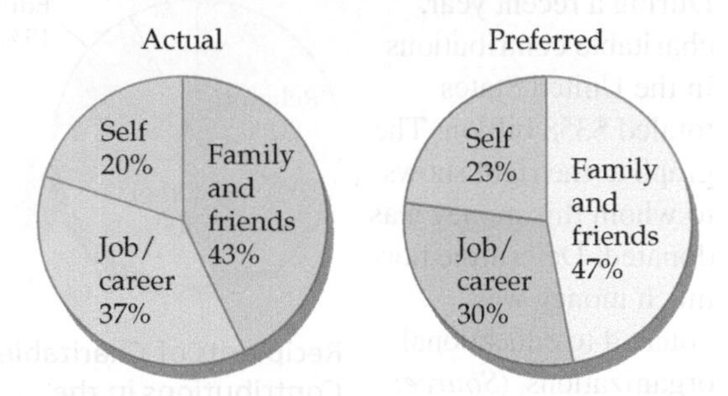

21. **Taxes** A TurboTax online survey asked people how they planned to use their tax refunds. Seven hundred forty people, or 22% of the respondents, said they would save the money. How many people responded to the survey?

22. **Diabetes** Approximately 9.3% of the American population has diabetes. Within this group, 21.0 million are diagnosed, while 8.1 million are undiagnosed. (*Source:* Centers for Disease Control and Prevention) What percent of Americans with diabetes have not been diagnosed with the disease? Round to the nearest tenth of a percent.

23. **Education** Of the 78 million baby boomers living in the United States, 45 million have some college experience but no college degree. (*Sources:* The National Center for Education Statistics; U.S. Census Bureau; *McCook Daily Gazette*) What percent of the baby boomers living in the United States have some college experience but have not earned a college degree? Round to the nearest tenth of a percent.

24. **Telecommunications** The number of Internet users worldwide went from 0.4 billion in 2000 to 3.2 billion in 2015. (*Source:* International Telecommunication Union) Find the percent increase in the number of Internet users from 2000 to 2015.

25. **Demographics** The graph below shows the projected growth of the number of Americans aged 85 and older.

 a. What is the percent increase in the population of this age group from 1995 to 2030?
 b. What is the percent increase in the population of this age group from 2030 to 2050?
 c. What is the percent increase in the population of this age group from 1995 to 2050?
 d. How many times larger is the population in 2050 than in 1995? How could you determine this number from the answer to part c?

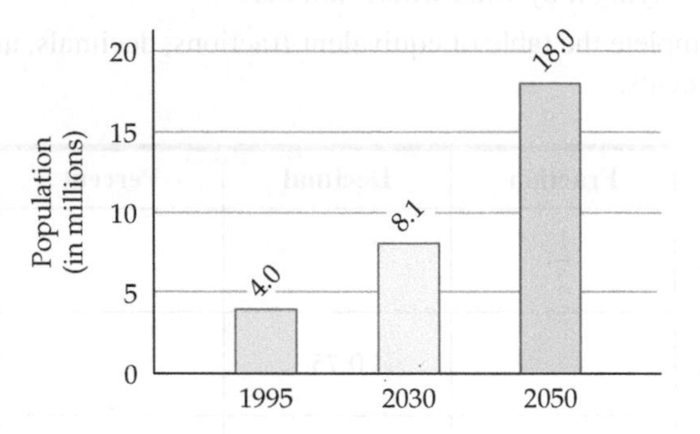

Projected Growth (in millions) of the Population of Americans Aged 85 and Older
SOURCE: U.S. Census Bureau

26. **Auto Sales** U.S. auto sales increased from 16.5 million in 2014 to 17.5 million in 2015. (*Source: Los Angeles Times*) Find the percent increase in auto sales from 2014 to 2015. Round to the nearest tenth of a percent.

27. **Cable TV** In 2006, 65.4 million people subscribed to cable television. In 2013, that number had decreased to 54.4 million. (*Source:* Federal Communications Commission) Find the percent decrease in the number of cable TV subscribers from 2006 to 2013. Round to the nearest tenth of a percent.

28. **Consumption of Eggs** During the last 50 years, the consumption of eggs in the United States has decreased by 17%. Fifty years ago, the average consumption was 307 eggs per person per year. What is the average consumption of eggs today?

29. **Millionaire Households** The following table shows the estimated number of millionaire households (households with a net worth of at least $1 million, not including primary residence) in the United States for selected years. (*Source:* Spectrem Group)

a. What is the percent increase in the estimated number of millionaire households from 2000 to 2007? Round to the nearest tenth of a percent.

b. Find the percent decrease in the estimated number of millionaire households from 2007 to 2008. Round to the nearest tenth of a percent.

Year	Millionaire households
2000	6,300,000
2007	9,200,000
2008	6,700,000
2013	9,600,000

30. **The Military** The graph below shows the number of active-duty U.S. military personnel, in thousands, in 1990 and 2014. Which branch of the military had the greatest percent decrease in personnel from 1990 to 2014? What was the percent decrease for this branch of the service? Round to the nearest tenth of a percent.

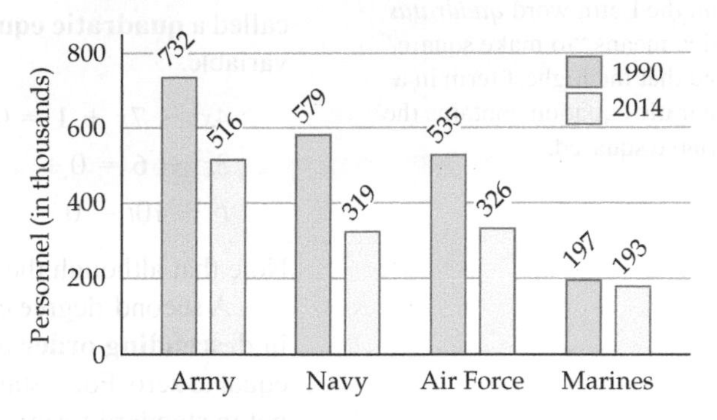

Number of Active-Duty U.S. Military Personnel

SOURCE: Department of Defense

EXTENSIONS

31. Salaries Your employer agrees to give you a 5% raise after 1 year on the job, a 6% raise the next year, and a 7% raise the following year. Is your salary after the third year greater than, less than, or the same as it would be if you had received a 6% raise each year?

32. **Work Habits** Approximately 73% of Americans who work in large offices work on weekends, either at home or in the office. The table below shows the average number of hours these workers report they work on a weekend. Approximately what percent of Americans who work in large offices work 11 or more hours on weekends?

Number of hours worked on weekends	Percent
0–1	3%
2–5	32%
6–10	42%
11 or more	23%

33. Nielsen Ratings Nielsen Media Research surveys television viewers to determine the numbers of people watching particular shows. They estimated that for the 2015–2016 television season, there were an estimated 113.3 million U.S. households with televisions. Each **rating point** represents 1% of that number, or 1,133,000. Therefore, for instance, if *60 Minutes* received a rating of 5.8, then 5.8% of all U.S. households with televisions, or (0.058)(113,300,000) = 6,571,400 households, were tuned to that program.

A rating point does not mean that 1,133,000 people are watching a program. A rating point refers to the number of households with television sets tuned to that program; there may be more than one person watching a television set in the household.

Nielsen Media Research also describes a program's share of the market. **Share** is the percent of households with television sets in use that are tuned to a program. Suppose that the same week that *60 Minutes* received 5.8 rating points, the show received a share of 11%. This would mean that 11% of all households with a television *turned on* were tuned to *60 Minutes*, whereas 5.8% of all households with a television were tuned to the program.

a. If *NCIS* received a Nielsen rating of 10.1 and a share of 17, how many TV households watched the program that week? How many TV households were watching television during that hour? Round to the nearest hundred thousand.

b. Suppose that *The Big Bang Theory* received a rating of 5.6 and a share of 11. How many TV households watched the program that week? How many TV households were watching television during that hour? Round to the nearest hundred thousand.

c. Suppose that *Modern Family* received a rating of 7.5 during a week in which 19,781,000 people were watching the show. Find the average number of people per TV household who watched the program. Round to the nearest tenth.

SECTION 2.4 Second-Degree Equations

Second-Degree Equations in Standard Form

POINT OF INTEREST

The word *quadratic* comes from the Latin word *quadratus*, which means "to make square." Note that the highest term in a quadratic equation contains the variable squared.

In Section 2.1, we introduced first-degree equations in one variable. A **second-degree equation in one variable** is an equation that can be written in the form $ax^2 + bx + c = 0$, where a and b are coefficients, c is a constant, and $a \neq 0$. An equation of this form is also called a **quadratic equation**. Here are three examples of second-degree equations in one variable.

$4x^2 - 7x + 1 = 0$ $\quad a = 4, b = -7, c = 1$

$3z^2 - 6 = 0$ $\quad a = 3, b = 0, c = -6$

$t^2 + 10t = 0$ $\quad a = 1, b = 10, c = 0$

Note that although the value of a cannot be 0, the value of b or c can be 0.

A second-degree equation is in **standard form** when the expression $ax^2 + bx + c$ is in **descending order** (the exponents on the variables decrease from left to right) and set equal to zero. For instance, $2x^2 + 8x - 3 = 0$ is written in standard form; $x^2 = 4x - 8$ is not in standard form.

QUESTION Which of the following are second-degree equations written in standard form?

a. $3y^2 + 5y - 2 = 0$ **b.** $8p - 4p^2 + 7 = 0$ **c.** $z^3 - 6z + 9 = 0$

d. $4r^2 + r - 1 = 6$ **e.** $v^2 - 16 = 0$

EXAMPLE 1 Write a Quadratic Equation in Standard Form

Write the equation $x^2 = 3x - 8$ in standard form.

Solution

Subtract $3x$ from each side of the equation.

$$x^2 = 3x - 8$$
$$x^2 - 3x = 3x - 3x - 8$$
$$x^2 - 3x = -8$$

Then add 8 to each side of the equation.

$$x^2 - 3x + 8 = -8 + 8$$
$$x^2 - 3x + 8 = 0$$

CHECK YOUR PROGRESS 1 Write $2s^2 = 6 - 4s$ in standard form.

Solution See page S8.

Solving Second-Degree Equations by Factoring

Recall that the multiplication property of zero states that the product of a number and zero is zero.

If a is a real number, then $a \cdot 0 = 0$.

ANSWER The equations in **a** and **e** are second-degree equations in standard form. The equation in **b** is not in standard form because $8p - 4p^2 + 7$ is not written in descending order. The equation in **c** is not a second-degree equation because there is an exponent of 3 on the variable. The equation in **d** is not in standard form because the expression on the left side is not set equal to 0.

Consider the equation $a \cdot b = 0$. If this is a true equation, then either $a = 0$ or $b = 0$. This is summarized in the principle of zero products.

Principle of Zero Products

If the product of two factors is zero, then at least one of the factors must be zero.

If $ab = 0$, then $a = 0$ or $b = 0$.

The principle of zero products is often used to solve equations. This is illustrated in Example 2.

EXAMPLE 2 **Solve an Equation Using the Principle of Zero Products**

Solve: $(x - 4)(x + 6) = 0$

Solution

In the expression $(x - 4)(x + 6)$, we are multiplying two numbers. Because their product is 0, one of the numbers must be equal to zero. The number $x - 4 = 0$ or the number $x + 6 = 0$. Solve each of these equations for x.

$$(x - 4)(x + 6) = 0$$

$$x - 4 = 0 \qquad x + 6 = 0$$
$$x = 4 \qquad x = -6$$

Check:

$(x - 4)(x + 6) = 0$		$(x - 4)(x + 6) = 0$	
$(4 - 4)(4 + 6)$	0	$(-6 - 4)(-6 + 6)$	0
$(0)(10)$	0	$(-10)(0)$	0
$0 = 0$		$0 = 0$	

TAKE NOTE

Note that both 4 and -6 check as solutions. The equation $(x - 4)(x + 6) = 0$ has two solutions.

The solutions are 4 and -6.

CHECK YOUR PROGRESS 2 Solve: $(n + 5)(2n - 3) = 0$

Solution See page S8.

HISTORICAL NOTE

Chu Shih-chieh, a Chinese mathematician who lived around 1300, wrote the book *Ssu-yuan yu-chien,* which dealt with equations of degree as high as 14.

A second-degree equation can be solved by using the principle of zero products when the expression $ax^2 + bx + c$ is factorable. This is illustrated in Example 3.

EXAMPLE 3 **Solve a Quadratic Equation by Factoring**

Solve: $2x^2 + x = 6$

Solution

In order to use the principle of zero products to solve a second-degree equation, the equation must be in standard form. Subtract 6 from each side of the given equation.

$$2x^2 + x = 6$$
$$2x^2 + x - 6 = 6 - 6$$
$$2x^2 + x - 6 = 0$$

Factor $2x^2 + x - 6$.

$$(2x - 3)(x + 2) = 0$$

CALCULATOR NOTE

These solutions can be checked on a scientific calculator. Many calculators require the following keystrokes.

2 [×] [(] 1.5 [INV] [x^2] [)] [+] 1.5 [=]

and

2 [×] [(] 2 [+/-] [INV] [x^2] [)] [+] 2 [+/-] [=]

On a graphing calculator, enter

2 [×] 1.5 [x^2] [+] 1.5 [ENTER]

and

2 [×] [(] [(-)] 2 [)] [x^2] [+] [(-)] 2 [ENTER]

In each case, the display is 6.

Use the principle of zero products. Set each factor equal to zero. Then solve each equation for x.

$$2x - 3 = 0 \qquad x + 2 = 0$$
$$2x = 3 \qquad x = -2$$
$$x = \frac{3}{2}$$

Check:

$2x^2 + x = 6$		$2x^2 + x = 6$	
$2\left(\frac{3}{2}\right)^2 + \frac{3}{2}$	6	$2(-2)^2 + (-2)$	6
$2\left(\frac{9}{4}\right) + \frac{3}{2}$	6	$2(4) + (-2)$	6
$\frac{9}{2} + \frac{3}{2}$	6	$8 + (-2)$	6
$6 = 6$		$6 = 6$	

The solutions are $\frac{3}{2}$ and -2.

CHECK YOUR PROGRESS 3 Solve: $2x^2 = x + 1$

Solution See page S8.

Note from Example 3 the steps involved in solving a second-degree equation by factoring. These are outlined below.

Steps in Solving a Second-Degree Equation by Factoring

1. Write the equation in standard form.
2. Factor the expression $ax^2 + bx + c$.
3. Use the principle of zero products to set each factor of the polynomial equal to zero.
4. Solve each of the resulting equations for the variable.

Solving Second-Degree Equations by Using the Quadratic Formula

When using only integers, not all second-degree equations can be solved by factoring. Any equation that cannot be solved easily by factoring can be solved by using the *quadratic formula,* which is given below.

HISTORICAL NOTE

The quadratic formula is one of the oldest formulas in mathematics. It is not known where it was first derived or by whom. However, there is evidence of its use as early as 2000 BC in ancient Babylonia (the area of the Middle East now known as Iraq). Hindu mathematicians were using it over a thousand years ago.

The Quadratic Formula

The solutions of the equation $ax^2 + bx + c = 0$, $a \neq 0$, are

$$x = \frac{-b + \sqrt{b^2 - 4ac}}{2a} \quad \text{and} \quad x = \frac{-b - \sqrt{b^2 - 4ac}}{2a}$$

The quadratic formula is frequently written in the form

$$x = \frac{-b \pm \sqrt{b^2 - 4ac}}{2a}$$

To use the quadratic formula, first write the second-degree equation in standard form. Determine the values of a, b, and c. Substitute the values of a, b, and c into the quadratic formula. Then evaluate the resulting expression.

EXAMPLE 4 Solve a Quadratic Equation by Using the Quadratic Formula

Solve the equation $2x^2 = 4x - 1$ by using the quadratic formula. Give exact solutions and approximate solutions to the nearest thousandth.

Solution

Write the equation in standard form by subtracting $4x$ from each side of the equation and adding 1 to each side of the equation. Then determine the values of a, b, and c.

$$2x^2 = 4x - 1$$
$$2x^2 - 4x + 1 = 0$$
$$a = 2, b = -4, c = 1$$

Substitute the values of a, b, and c into the quadratic formula. Then evaluate the resulting expression.

$$x = \frac{-b \pm \sqrt{b^2 - 4ac}}{2a}$$

$$x = \frac{-(-4) \pm \sqrt{(-4)^2 - 4(2)(1)}}{2(2)} = \frac{4 \pm \sqrt{16 - 8}}{4}$$

$$= \frac{4 \pm \sqrt{8}}{4} = \frac{4 \pm 2\sqrt{2}}{4} = \frac{2(2 \pm \sqrt{2})}{2(2)} = \frac{2 \pm \sqrt{2}}{2}$$

The exact solutions are $\frac{2 + \sqrt{2}}{2}$ and $\frac{2 - \sqrt{2}}{2}$.

$$\frac{2 + \sqrt{2}}{2} \approx 1.707 \qquad \frac{2 - \sqrt{2}}{2} \approx 0.293$$

To the nearest thousandth, the solutions are 1.707 and 0.293.

CALCULATOR NOTE

To find the decimal approximation of $\frac{2 + \sqrt{2}}{2}$ on a scientific calculator, use the following keystrokes.

(2 + 2 √) ÷ 2 =

Note that parentheses are used to ensure that the entire numerator is divided by the denominator.

On a graphing calculator, enter

(2 + 2nd √ 2)) ÷ 2 ENTER

CHECK YOUR PROGRESS 4 Solve the equation $2x^2 = 8x - 5$ by using the quadratic formula. Give exact solutions and approximate solutions to the nearest thousandth.

Solution See page S8.

The exact solutions to Example 4 are irrational numbers. It is also possible for a quadratic equation to have no real number solutions. This is illustrated in Example 5.

EXAMPLE 5 Solve a Quadratic Equation by Using the Quadratic Formula

Solve by using the quadratic formula: $t^2 + 7 = 3t$

Solution

Write the equation in standard form by subtracting $3t$ from each side of the equation. Then determine the values of a, b, and c.

$$t^2 + 7 = 3t$$
$$t^2 - 3t + 7 = 0$$
$$a = 1, b = -3, c = 7$$

Substitute the values of a, b, and c into the quadratic formula. Then evaluate the resulting expression.

$$t = \frac{-b \pm \sqrt{b^2 - 4ac}}{2a}$$

$$t = \frac{-(-3) \pm \sqrt{(-3)^2 - 4(1)(7)}}{2(1)}$$

$$= \frac{3 \pm \sqrt{9 - 28}}{2} = \frac{3 \pm \sqrt{-19}}{2}$$

$\sqrt{-19}$ is not a real number.

The equation has no real number solutions.

TAKE NOTE

The square root of a negative number is not a real number because there is no real number that, when squared, equals a negative number. Therefore, $\sqrt{-19}$ is not a real number.

CHECK YOUR PROGRESS 5 Solve by using the quadratic formula: $z^2 = -6 - 2z$

Solution See page S8.

MATH MATTERS The Discriminant

In Example 5, the second-degree equation has no real number solutions. In the quadratic formula, the quantity $b^2 - 4ac$ under the radical sign is called the **discriminant**. When a, b, and c are real numbers, the discriminant determines whether or not a quadratic equation has real number solutions.

The Effect of the Discriminant on the Solutions of a Second-Degree Equation

1. If $b^2 - 4ac \geq 0$, the equation has real number solutions.
2. If $b^2 - 4ac < 0$, the equation has no real number solutions.

For example, for the equation $x^2 - 4x - 5 = 0$, $a = 1$, $b = -4$, and $c = -5$.

$$b^2 - 4ac = (-4)^2 - 4(1)(-5) = 16 + 20 = 36$$
$$36 > 0$$

The discriminant is greater than 0. The equation has real number solutions.

Applications of Second-Degree Equations

Second-degree equations have many applications to the real world. Examples 6 and 7 illustrate two such applications.

AP Images/ROB GRIFFITHER

EXAMPLE 6 **Solve an Application of Quadratic Equations by Factoring**

An arrow is projected straight up into the air with an initial velocity of 48 ft/s. At what times will the arrow be 32 ft above the ground? Use the equation $h = 48t - 16t^2$, where h is the height, in feet, above the ground after t seconds.

Solution

We are asked to find the times when the arrow will be 32 ft above the ground, so we are given a value for h. Substitute 32 for h in the given equation and solve for t.

$$h = 48t - 16t^2$$
$$32 = 48t - 16t^2$$

> **TAKE NOTE**
>
> It would also be correct to subtract 32 from each side of the equation. However, many people prefer to have the coefficient of the squared term positive.

This is a second-degree equation. Write the equation in standard form by adding $16t^2$ to each side of the equation and subtracting $48t$ from each side of the equation.

$$16t^2 - 48t + 32 = 0$$
$$16(t^2 - 3t + 2) = 0$$
$$t^2 - 3t + 2 = 0 \quad \text{• Divide each side of the equation by 16.}$$
$$(t - 1)(t - 2) = 0$$
$$t - 1 = 0 \qquad t - 2 = 0$$
$$t = 1 \qquad t = 2$$

The arrow will be 32 ft above the ground 1 s after its release and 2 s after its release.

CHECK YOUR PROGRESS 6 An object is projected straight up into the air with an initial velocity of 64 ft/s. At what times will the object be on the ground? Use the equation $h = 64t - 16t^2$, where h is the height, in feet, above the ground after t seconds.

Solution See page S8.

EXAMPLE 7 **Solve an Application of Quadratic Equations by Using the Quadratic Formula**

A baseball player hits a ball. The height of the ball above the ground after t seconds can be approximated by the equation $h = -16t^2 + 75t + 5$. When will the ball hit the ground? Round to the nearest hundredth of a second.

Solution

We are asked to determine the number of seconds from the time the ball is hit until it is on the ground. When the ball is on the ground, its height above the ground is 0 ft. Substitute 0 for h and solve for t.

$$h = -16t^2 + 75t + 5$$
$$0 = -16t^2 + 75t + 5$$
$$16t^2 - 75t - 5 = 0$$

> **TAKE NOTE**
>
> The time until the ball hits the ground cannot be a negative number. Therefore, −0.07 s is not a solution of this application.

This is a second-degree equation. It is not easily factored. Use the quadratic formula to solve for t.

$$a = 16, b = -75, c = -5$$
$$t = \frac{-b \pm \sqrt{b^2 - 4ac}}{2a}$$
$$t = \frac{-(-75) \pm \sqrt{(-75)^2 - 4(16)(-5)}}{2(16)} = \frac{75 \pm \sqrt{5945}}{32}$$
$$t = \frac{75 + \sqrt{5945}}{32} \approx 4.75 \qquad t = \frac{75 - \sqrt{5945}}{32} \approx -0.07$$

The ball strikes the ground 4.75 s after the baseball player hits it.

CHECK YOUR PROGRESS 7 A basketball player shoots at a basket that is 25 ft away. The height h, in feet, of the ball above the ground after t seconds is given by $h = -16t^2 + 19t + 3.5$. How many seconds after the ball is released does it hit the basket? *Note:* The basket is 10 ft off the ground. Round to the nearest hundredth.

Solution See page S8.

EXCURSION

The Sum and Product of the Solutions of a Quadratic Equation

The solutions of the equation $x^2 + 3x - 10 = 0$ are -5 and 2.

$$x^2 + 3x - 10 = 0$$
$$(x + 5)(x - 2) = 0$$
$$x + 5 = 0 \qquad x - 2 = 0$$
$$x = -5 \qquad x = 2$$

Note that the sum of the solutions is equal to $-b$, the opposite of the coefficient of x.

$$-5 + 2 = -3$$

The product of the solutions is equal to c, the constant term.

$$-5(2) = -10$$

This illustrates the following theorem regarding the solutions of a quadratic equation.

TAKE NOTE

Look closely at the example at the right, in which -5 and 2 are solutions of the quadratic equation $(x + 5)(x - 2) = 0$. Using variables, we can state that if s_1 and s_2 are solutions of a quadratic equation, then the quadratic equation can be written in the form $(x - s_1)(x - s_2) = 0$.

The Sum and Product of the Solutions of a Quadratic Equation

If s_1 and s_2 are the solutions of a quadratic equation of the form $ax^2 + bx + c = 0$, $a \neq 0$, then

the sum of the solutions $s_1 + s_2 = -\frac{b}{a}$, and

the product of the solutions $s_1 s_2 = \frac{c}{a}$.

In this section, the method we used to check the solutions of a quadratic equation was to substitute the solutions back into the original equation. An alternative method is to use the sum and product of the solutions.

For example, let's check that -2 and 6 are the solutions of the equation $x^2 - 4x - 12 = 0$. For this equation, $a = 1$, $b = -4$, and $c = -12$. Let $s_1 = -2$ and $s_2 = 6$.

$s_1 + s_2 = -\frac{b}{a}$		$s_1 s_2 = \frac{c}{a}$	
$-2 + 6$	$-\frac{-4}{1}$	$-2(6)$	$\frac{-12}{1}$
$4 = 4$		$-12 = -12$	

TAKE NOTE

The result is the same if we let $s_1 = 6$ and $s_2 = -2$.

The solutions check.

In Example 4, we found that the exact solutions of the equation $2x^2 = 4x - 1$ are $\frac{2 + \sqrt{2}}{2}$ and $\frac{2 - \sqrt{2}}{2}$. Use the sum and product of the solutions to check these solutions.

Write the equation in standard form. Then determine the values of a, b, and c.

$$2x^2 = 4x - 1$$
$$2x^2 - 4x + 1 = 0$$
$$a = 2, b = -4, c = 1$$

Let $s_1 = \dfrac{2+\sqrt{2}}{2}$ and $s_2 = \dfrac{2-\sqrt{2}}{2}$.

$$
\begin{array}{c|c}
s_1 + s_2 & -\dfrac{b}{a} \\
\hline
\dfrac{2+\sqrt{2}}{2} + \dfrac{2-\sqrt{2}}{2} & -\dfrac{-4}{2} \\
\dfrac{2+\sqrt{2}+2-\sqrt{2}}{2} & 2 \\
\dfrac{4}{2} & 2 \\
\multicolumn{2}{c}{2 = 2}
\end{array}
\qquad
\begin{array}{c|c}
s_1 s_2 & \dfrac{c}{a} \\
\hline
\left(\dfrac{2+\sqrt{2}}{2}\right)\left(\dfrac{2-\sqrt{2}}{2}\right) & \dfrac{1}{2} \\
\dfrac{4-2}{4} & \dfrac{1}{2} \\
\dfrac{2}{4} & \dfrac{1}{2} \\
\multicolumn{2}{c}{\dfrac{1}{2} = \dfrac{1}{2}}
\end{array}
$$

The solutions check.

If we divide both sides of the equation $ax^2 + bx + c = 0$, $a \neq 0$, by a, the result is the equation

$$x^2 + \frac{b}{a}x + \frac{c}{a} = 0$$

Using this model and the sum and products of the solutions of a quadratic equation, we can find a quadratic equation given its solutions. The method is given below.

A Quadratic Equation with Solutions s_1 and s_2

A quadratic equation with solutions s_1 and s_2 is

$$x^2 - (s_1 + s_2)x + s_1 s_2 = 0$$

To write a quadratic equation that has solutions $\frac{2}{3}$ and 1, let $s_1 = \frac{2}{3}$ and $s_2 = 1$. Substitute these values into the equation $x^2 - (s_1 + s_2)x + s_1 s_2 = 0$ and simplify.

$$
\begin{aligned}
x^2 - (s_1 + s_2)x + s_1 s_2 &= 0 \\
x^2 - \left(\frac{2}{3} + 1\right)x + \left(\frac{2}{3} \cdot 1\right) &= 0 \\
x^2 - \frac{5}{3}x + \frac{2}{3} &= 0
\end{aligned}
$$

Assuming we want a, b, and c to be integers, then we can multiply each side of the equation by 3 to clear fractions.

$$
\begin{aligned}
3\left(x^2 - \frac{5}{3}x + \frac{2}{3}\right) &= 3(0) \\
3x^2 - 5x + 2 &= 0
\end{aligned}
$$

A quadratic equation with solutions $\frac{2}{3}$ and 1 is $3x^2 - 5x + 2 = 0$.

EXCURSION EXERCISES

In Exercises 1 to 8, solve the equation and then check the solutions using the sum and product of the solutions.

1. $x^2 - 10 = 3x$

2. $x^2 + 16 = 8x$

3. $3x^2 + 5x = 12$

4. $3x^2 + 8x = 3$

5. $x^2 = 6x + 3$
6. $x^2 = 2x + 5$
7. $4x + 1 = 4x^2$
8. $x + 1 = x^2$

In Exercises 9 to 16, write a quadratic equation that has integer coefficients and has the given pair of solutions.

9. -1 and 6
10. -5 and -4
11. 3 and $\frac{1}{2}$
12. $-\frac{3}{4}$ and 2
13. $\frac{1}{4}$ and $-\frac{3}{2}$
14. $\frac{2}{3}$ and $-\frac{2}{3}$
15. $2 + \sqrt{2}$ and $2 - \sqrt{2}$
16. $1 + \sqrt{3}$ and $1 - \sqrt{3}$

EXERCISE SET 2.4

■ In Exercises 1 to 24, first try to solve the equation by factoring. If you are unable to solve the equation by factoring, solve the equation by using the quadratic formula. For equations with solutions that are irrational numbers, give exact solutions and approximate solutions to the nearest thousandth.

1. $r^2 - 3r = 10$
2. $p^2 + 5p = 6$
3. $t^2 = t + 1$
4. $u^2 = u + 3$
5. $y^2 - 6y = 4$
6. $w^2 + 4w = 2$
7. $9z^2 - 18z = 0$
8. $4y^2 + 20y = 0$
9. $z^2 = z + 4$
10. $r^2 = r - 1$
11. $2s^2 = 4s + 5$
12. $3u^2 = 6u + 1$
13. $r^2 = 4r + 7$
14. $s^2 + 6s = 1$
15. $2x^2 = 9x + 18$
16. $3y^2 = 4y + 4$
17. $6x - 11 = x^2$
18. $-8y - 17 = y^2$
19. $4 - 15u = 4u^2$
20. $3 - 2y = 8y^2$
21. $6y^2 - 4 = 5y$
22. $6v^2 - 3 = 7v$
23. $y - 2 = y^2 - y - 6$
24. $8s - 11 = s^2 - 6s + 8$

25. Write a second-degree equation that you can solve by factoring.

26. Write a second-degree equation that you can solve by using the quadratic formula but not by factoring.

■ In Exercises 27 to 42, round answers to nearest hundredth where appropriate.

Paul Yates/Shutterstock.com

27. Golf The height h, in feet, of a golf ball t seconds after it has been hit is given by the equation $h = -16t^2 + 60t$. How many seconds after the ball is hit will the height of the ball be 36 ft?

28. Geometry The area A, in square meters, of a rectangle with a perimeter of 100 meters is given by the equation $A = 50w - w^2$, where w is the width of the rectangle in meters. What is the width of a rectangle if its area is 400 m^2?

29. Mathematics In the diagram below, the total number of circles T when there are n rows is given by $T = 0.5n^2 + 0.5n$. Verify the formula for the four figures shown. Determine the number of rows when the total number of circles is 55.

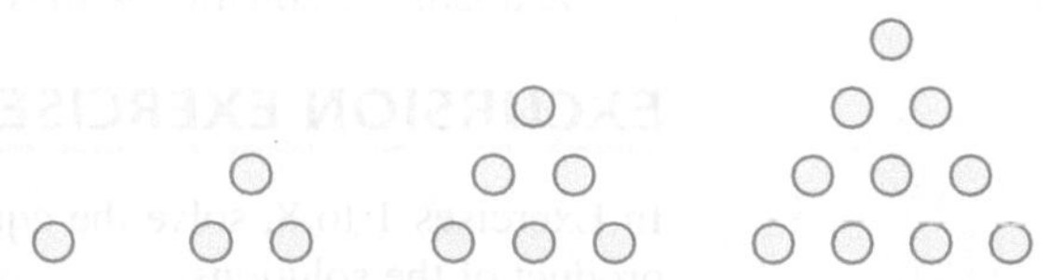

30. Astronautics If an astronaut on the moon throws a ball upward with an initial velocity of 6 m per second, its approximate height h, in meters, after t seconds is given by the equation $h = -0.8t^2 + 6t$. How long after it is released will the ball be 8 m above the surface of the moon?

31. Demography The equation $y = 0.03x^2 + 0.36x + 34.6$ describes the number of people y, in millions, aged 65 and older in the United States in year x, where $x = 0$ corresponds to the year 2000. Approximate the year in which there will be 50 million people aged 65 and older in the United States.

32. Alzheimer's The equation $y = 0.002x^2 + 0.05x + 2$ describes the number of Americans y, in millions, with Alzheimer's in year x, where $x = 0$ corresponds to the year 1980. Find the year in which 15 million Americans are expected to have Alzheimer's.

33. Stopping Distance When a driver decides to stop a car, it takes time first for the driver to react and put a foot on the brake, and then it takes additional time for the car to slow down. The total distance traveled during this period of time is called the *stopping distance* of the car. For some cars, the stopping distance d, in feet, is given by the equation $d = 0.05r^2 + r$, where r is the speed of the car in miles per hour.

a. Find the distance needed to stop a car traveling at 60 mph.

b. If skid marks at an accident site are 75 ft long, how fast was the car traveling?

Steve Allen/Stockbyte/Getty Images

34. Cliff Divers At La Quebrada in Acapulco, Mexico, cliff divers dive from a rock cliff that is 27 m above the water. The equation $h = -x^2 + 2x + 27$ describes the height h, in meters, of the diver above the water when the diver is x feet away from the cliff. Note that x is the horizontal distance between the diver's present position and the diver's "take off" point.

a. When the diver enters the water, how far is the diver from the cliff?

b. Does the diver ever reach a height of 28 m above the water? If so, how far is the diver from the cliff at that time?

c. Does the diver ever reach a height of 30 m above the water? If so, how far is the diver from the cliff at that time?

35. Football The hang time of a football that is kicked on the opening kickoff is given by $s = -16t^2 + 88t + 1$, where s is the height in feet of the football t seconds after leaving the kicker's foot. What is the hang time of a kickoff that hits the ground without being caught?

36. Softball In a slow pitch softball game, the height of a ball thrown by a pitcher can be approximated by the equation $h = -16t^2 + 24t + 4$, where h is the height, in feet, of the ball and t is the time, in seconds, since it was released by the pitcher. If a batter hits the ball when it is 2 ft off the ground, for how many seconds has the ball been in the air?

37. Fire Science The path of water from a hose on a fire tugboat can be approximated by the equation $y = -0.005x^2 + 1.2x + 10$, where y is the height, in feet, of the water above the ocean when the water is x feet from the tugboat. When the water from the hose is 5 ft above the ocean, at what distance from the tugboat is it?

38. Stopping Distance In Germany there are no speed limits on some portions of the autobahn (the highway). Other portions have a speed limit of 180 kph (approximately 112 mph). The distance d, in meters, required to stop a car traveling v kilometers per hour is $d = 0.0056v^2 + 0.14v$. Approximate the maximum speed a driver can be going and still be able to stop within 150 m.

German Autobahn System

39. Soccer A penalty kick in soccer is made from a penalty mark that is 36 ft from a goal that is 8 ft high. A possible equation for the flight of a penalty kick is $h = -0.002x^2 + 0.36x$, where h is the height, in feet, of the ball x feet from the goal. Assuming that the flight of the kick is toward the goal and that it is not touched by the goalie, will the ball land in the net?

40. Springboard Diving An event in the Summer Olympics is 10-meter springboard diving. In this event, the height h, in meters, of a diver above the water t seconds after jumping is given by the equation $h = -4.9t^2 + 7.8t + 10$. What is the height above the water of a diver after 2 s?

Hisham F. Ibrahim/Photodisc Blue/Getty Images

41. Fountains The Water Arc is a fountain that shoots water across the Chicago River from a water cannon. The path of the water can be approximated by the equation $h = -0.006x^2 + 1.2x + 10$, where x is the horizontal distance, in feet, from the cannon and h is the height, in feet, of the water above the river. On one particular day, some people were walking along the opposite side of the river from the Water Arc when a pulse of water was shot in their direction. If the distance from the Water Arc to the people was 220 ft, did they get wet from the cannon's water?

42. Model Rockets A model rocket is launched with an initial velocity of 200 ft per second. The height h, in feet, of the rocket t seconds after the launch is given by $h = -16t^2 + 200t$. How many seconds after the launch will the rocket be 300 ft above the ground?

43. First-Class Postage The graph below shows the cost for a first-class postage stamp from the 1950s to 2015. A second-degree equation that approximately models these data is $y = 0.00657x^2 - 0.330x - 0.0633$, $x \geq 50$, where $x = 50$ corresponds to the year 1950 and y is the cost in cents of a first-class stamp. Using the model equation, determine what the model predicts the cost of a first-class stamp will be in the year 2030. Round to the nearest cent.

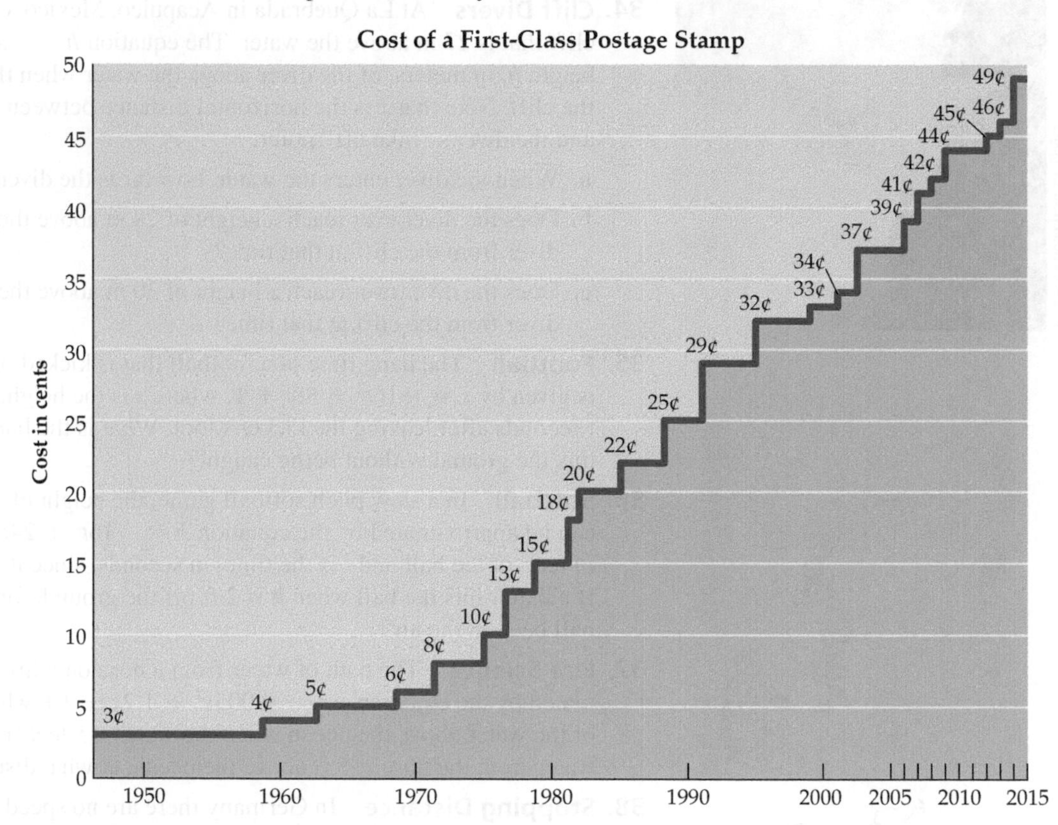

EXTENSIONS

44. Show that the solutions of the equation $ax^2 + bx = 0$, $a \neq 0$, are 0 and $-\frac{b}{a}$.

45. In a second-degree equation in standard form, why is the expression $ax^2 + bx + c$ factorable over the integers only when the discriminant is a perfect square? (See Math Matters, page 150.)

■ In Exercises 46 to 49, solve the equation for x.

46. $x^2 + 16ax + 48a^2 = 0$

47. $x^2 - 8bx + 15b^2 = 0$

48. $3x^2 - 4cx + c^2 = 0$

49. $2x^2 - xy - 3y^2 = 0$

50. Show that the equation $x^2 + bx - 1 = 0$ always has real number solutions, regardless of the value of b.

CHAPTER 2 SUMMARY

The following table summarizes essential concepts in this chapter. The references given in the right-hand column list Examples and Exercises that can be used to test your understanding of a concept.

Concept	References
2.1 First-Degree Equations and Formulas	
Steps for Solving a First-Degree Equation in One Variable **1.** If the equation contains fractions, multiply each side of the equation by the least common multiple (LCM) of the denominators to clear the equation of fractions. **2.** Use the distributive property to remove parentheses. **3.** Combine any like terms on the left side of the equation and any like terms on the right side of the equation. **4.** Use the addition or subtraction property to rewrite the equation with only one variable term and only one constant term. **5.** Use the multiplication or division property to rewrite the equation with the variable alone on one side of the equation and a constant term on the other side of the equation.	See **Example 2** on page 107, and then try Exercise 3 on page 158.
Applications of Solving First-Degree Equations The solution to an application problem may require solving a first-degree equation.	See **Examples 3, 4, and 5** on pages 109 and 110, and then try Exercises 11, 13, and 14 on page 158.
Solve a Literal Equation for One of the Variables The goal is to rewrite the equation so that the letter being solved for is alone on one side of the equation, and all numbers and other variables are on the other side.	See **Example 6** on page 111, and then try Exercises 9 and 10 on page 158.
2.2 Rate, Ratio, and Proportion	
Calculate a Unit Rate Divide the number in the numerator of the rate by the number in the denominator of the rate.	See **Example 1** on page 118, and then try Exercise 15 on page 158.
Write a Ratio A ratio can be written in three different ways: as a fraction, as two numbers separated by a colon (:), or as two numbers separated by the word *to*. Although units, such as hours, miles, or dollars, are written as part of a rate, units are not written as part of a ratio.	See **Example 5** on page 121, and then try Exercise 16 on page 158.
Cross-Products Method of Solving a Proportion If $\frac{a}{b} = \frac{c}{d}$, then $ad = bc$.	See **Examples 7 and 8** on pages 123 and 124, and then try Exercises 4 and 21 on pages 158 and 159.
2.3 Percent	
The Proportion Used to Solve Percent Problems $\frac{\text{percent}}{100} = \frac{\text{amount}}{\text{base}}$	See **Examples 5, 6, and 7** on pages 134 and 135, and then try Exercises 24 and 25 on page 160.
The Basic Percent Equation $PB = A$, where P is the percent, B is the base, and A is the amount.	See **Examples 8, 9, and 10** on pages 136 and 137, and then try Exercises 28 and 29 on page 160.

continued

Percent Increase and Percent Decrease The percent increase is the amount of increase divided by the original value, expressed as a percent. The percent decrease is the amount of decrease divided by the original value, expressed as a percent.	See **Examples 12 and 13** on pages 139 and 140, and then try Exercises 17, 26, and 27 on pages 159 and 160.
2.4 Second-Degree Equations	
Steps in Solving a Second-Degree Equation by Factoring **1.** Write the equation in standard form. **2.** Factor the polynomial $ax^2 + bx + c$. **3.** Use the principle of zero products to set each factor of the polynomial equal to zero. **4.** Solve each of the resulting equations for the variable.	See **Example 3** on page 147, and then try Exercise 6 on page 158.
The Quadratic Formula The solutions of the equation $ax^2 + bx + c = 0, a \neq 0$, are $x = \frac{-b \pm \sqrt{b^2 - 4ac}}{2a}$.	See **Examples 4 and 5** on page 149, and then try Exercises 7 and 8 on page 158.
Applications of Solving Second-Degree Equations The solution to an application problem may require solving a second-degree equation.	See **Examples 6 and 7** on pages 150 and 151, and then try Exercises 31 and 32 on page 160.

CHAPTER 2 REVIEW EXERCISES

■ In Exercises 1 to 8, solve the equation.

1. $5x + 3 = 10x - 17$

2. $3x + \frac{1}{8} = \frac{1}{2}$

3. $6x + 3(2x - 1) = -27$

4. $\frac{5}{12} = \frac{n}{8}$

5. $4y^2 + 9 = 0$

6. $x^2 - x = 30$

7. $x^2 = 4x - 1$

8. $x + 3 = x^2$

■ In Exercises 9 and 10, solve the formula for the given variable.

9. $4x + 3y = 12; y$

10. $f = v + at; t$

11. Meteorology In June, the temperature at various elevations of the Grand Canyon can be approximated by the equation $T = -0.005x + 113.25$, where T is the temperature in degrees Fahrenheit and x is the elevation (distance above sea level) in feet. Use this equation to find the elevation at Inner Gorge, the bottom of the canyon, where the temperature is 101°F.

Bryant Jayme/Shutterstock.com

The Grand Canyon

12. Falling Objects Find the time that it takes for the velocity of a falling object to increase from 4 ft/s to 100 ft/s. Use the equation $v = v_0 + 32t$, where v is the final velocity of the falling object, v_0 is the initial velocity, and t is the time it takes for the object to fall.

13. Chemistry A chemist mixes 100 g of water at 80°C with 50 g of water at 20°C. Use the formula $m_1(T_1 - T) = m_2(T - T_2)$ to find the final temperature of the water after mixing. In this equation, m_1 is the quantity of water at the hotter temperature, T_1 is the temperature of the hotter water, m_2 is the quantity of water at the cooler temperature, T_2 is the temperature of the cooler water, and T is the final temperature of water after mixing.

14. Telemarketing At a telemarketing firm, an employee is paid $12 an hour plus $0.75 for each call completed. During an 8-hour day, the employee's compensation was $159.75. How many calls did the employee complete?

15. Fuel Consumption An automobile was driven 326.6 mi on 11.5 gal of gasoline. Find the number of miles driven per gallon of gas.

16. Real Estate A house with an original value of $280,000 increased in value to $350,000 in 5 years. Write, as a fraction in simplest form, the ratio of the increase in value to the original value of the house.

17. **Social Media** In July 2012, Instagram announced 80 million users of its photo sharing app. In September 2015, they announced that the number of users had reached 400 million. Find the percent increase in the number of Instagram users during that time period. Round to the nearest percent.

18. **City Populations** The table below shows the population and area of the five most populous cities in the United States.

a. The cities are listed in the table according to population, from largest to smallest. Rank the cities according to population density, from largest to smallest.

b. How many more people per square mile are there in New York than in Houston? Round to the nearest whole number.

City	Population	Area (in square miles)
New York	8,400,000	321.8
Los Angeles	3,900,000	467.4
Chicago	2,900,000	228.469
Houston	2,300,000	594.03
Phoenix	1,600,000	136

19. **Student–Faculty Ratios** The table below shows the number of full-time men and women undergraduates, as well as the number of full-time faculty, at five colleges in Arizona. In parts a, b, and c, round ratios to the nearest whole number. (*Source:* National Center for Education Statistics, nces.ed.gov)

University	Men	Women	Faculty
Arizona State University	20,309	15,955	2018
Embry-Riddle Aeronautical University	1441	428	93
Northern Arizona University	8215	10,958	1055
Prescott College	156	215	56
University of Arizona	14,054	15,475	2343

a. Calculate the student–faculty ratio at Prescott College. Write the ratio using a colon and using the word *to*. What does this ratio mean?

b. Which school listed has the lowest student–faculty ratio? The highest?

c. Which schools listed have the same student–faculty ratio?

20. **Advertising** The Randolph Company spent $350,000 for advertising last year. Department A and Department B share the cost of advertising in the ratio 3:7. Find the amount allocated to each department.

21. **Gardening** Three tablespoons of a liquid plant fertilizer are to be added to every 4 gal of water. How many tablespoons of fertilizer are required for 10 gal of water?

22. **Federal Expenditures** The table below shows how each dollar of projected spending by the federal government for a recent year was distributed. (*Source:* Congressional Budget Office) Of the items listed, defense is the only discretionary spending by the federal government; all other items are fixed expenditures. The government predicted total expenses of $3.6 trillion for the year.

a. Is more or less than one-fifth of federal spending spent on health care?

b. Find the ratio of the fixed expenditures to the discretionary spending.

c. Find the amount of the budget to be spent on fixed expenditures.

d. Find the amount of the budget to be spent on Social Security.

How Your Federal Tax Dollar Is Spent	
Health care	21 cents
Social Security	20 cents
Defense	20 cents
Other social aid	14 cents
Remaining government agencies and programs	19 cents
Interest on national debt	6 cents

23. **Demographics** According to the U.S. Bureau of the Census, the population of males and females in the United States in 2025 and 2050 is projected to be as shown in the table below.

Year	Males	Females
2025	164,119,000	170,931,000
2050	193,234,000	200,696,000

a. What percent of the projected population in 2025 is female? Round to the nearest tenth of a percent.

b. Does the percent of the projected population that is female in 2050 differ by more or less than 1% from the percent that is female in 2025?

24. Diet Americans consume 7 billion hot dogs from Memorial Day through Labor Day. This is 35% of the hot dogs consumed annually in the United States. (*Source:* National Hot Dog & Sausage Council: American Meat Institute) How many hot dogs do Americans consume annually?

25. Boston Marathon In the 2015 Boston Marathon, 27,167 runners started the race and 26,598 finished. What percent of the runners who started the course finished the race? Round to the nearest tenth of a percent.

26. Nutrition The table below shows the fat, saturated fat, cholesterol, and calorie content of a 90-gram ground-beef burger and a 90-gram soy burger.

a. Compared to the beef burger, by what percent is the fat content decreased in the soy burger?

b. What is the percent decrease in cholesterol in the soy burger compared to the beef burger?

c. Calculate the percent decrease in calories in the soy burger compared to the beef burger.

	Beef burger	Soy burger
Fat	24 g	4 g
Saturated fat	10 g	1.5 g
Cholesterol	75 mg	0 mg
Calories	280	140

27. The Military On Veterans Day in 2000, there were 26.6 million U.S. veterans. By Veterans Day in 2010, the number of U.S. veterans had dropped to 23.1 million. (*Source:* Department of Veterans Affairs) Find the percent decrease in the number of veterans from 2000 to 2010. Round to the nearest tenth of a percent.

28. Police Officers The graph below shows the causes of death for all police officers killed in the line of duty during a recent year. What percent of the deaths were due to auto accidents? Round to the nearest percent.

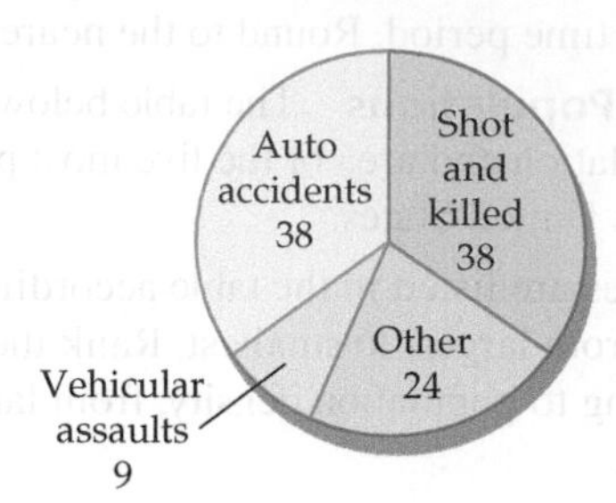

Causes of Death for Police Officers Killed in the Line of Duty
SOURCE: www.policespecial.com

29. Retirement Programs Massachusetts teachers enrolled in the Retirement-Plus savings program contribute 11% of their salaries to the program. What amount is contributed during 1 year by a member of this program who earns an annual salary of $64,000?

30. Vacation Days In Italy, workers take an average of 42 vacation days per year. This number is 3 more than three times the average number of vacation days that workers take each year in the United States. (*Source:* World Tourism Organization) On average, how many vacation days do U.S. workers take per year?

31. Model Rockets A small rocket is shot from the edge of a cliff. The height h, in meters, of the rocket above the cliff is given by $h = 30t - 5t^2$, where t is the time in seconds after the rocket is shot. Find the times at which the rocket is 25 m above the cliff.

32. Sports The height h, in feet, of a ball t seconds after being thrown from a height of 6 ft is given by the equation $h = -16t^2 + 32t + 6$. After how many seconds is the ball 18 ft above the ground? Round to the nearest tenth.

CHAPTER 2 TEST

■ In Exercises 1 to 5, solve the equation.

1. $\frac{x}{4} - 3 = \frac{1}{2}$

2. $x + 5(3x - 20) = 10(x - 4)$

3. $\frac{7}{16} = \frac{x}{12}$

4. $x^2 = 12x - 27$

5. $3x^2 - 4x = 1$

■ In Exercises 6 and 7, solve the formula for the given variable.

6. $x - 2y = 15; y$

7. $C = \frac{5}{9}(F - 32); F$

Old Faithful

8. Geysers Old Faithful is a geyser in Yellowstone National Park. It is so named because of its regular eruptions for the past 100 years. An equation that can predict the approximate time until the next eruption is $T = 12.4L + 32$, where T is the time, in minutes, until the next eruption and L is the duration, in minutes, of the last eruption. Use this equation to determine the duration of the last eruption when the time between two eruptions is 63 min.

9. Energy The cost of electricity in a certain city is $0.16 for each of the first 300 kWh and $0.20 for each kilowatt-hour over 300 kWh. Find the number of kilowatt-hours used by a family with a $74.25 electric bill.

10. Rate of Speed You drive 246.6 mi in 4.5 h. Find your average rate in miles per hour.

11. Parks The table below lists the largest city parks in the United States. The land acreage of Griffith Park in Los Angeles is 3 acres more than five times the acreage of New York's Central Park. What is the acreage of Central Park?

City park	Land acreage
Cullen Park (Houston)	10,534
Fairmount Park (Philadelphia)	8,700
Griffith Park (Los Angeles)	4,218
Eagle Creek Park (Indianapolis)	3,800
Pelham Bay Park (Bronx, NY)	2,764
Mission Bay Park (San Diego)	2,300

12. Baseball The table below shows six Major League lifetime record holders for batting. (*Source: Information Please Almanac*)

Baseball player	Number of times at bat	Number of home runs hit	Number of at-bats per home run
Ty Cobb	11,429	4,191	
Billy Hamilton	6,284	2,163	
Rogers Hornsby	8,137	2,930	
Joe Jackson	4,981	1,774	
Tris Speaker	10,195	3,514	
Ted Williams	7,706	2,654	

a. Calculate the number of at-bats per home run for each player in the table. Round to the nearest thousandth.

b. The players are listed in the table alphabetically. Rank the players according to the number of at-bats per home run, starting with the best rate.

13. Social Media In 2015, Twitter announced that they had 320 million monthly active users, and 80% of users were active on mobile devices. How many monthly active users were active on mobile devices in 2015?

14. Partnerships The two partners in a partnership share the profits of their business in the ratio 5:3. Last year the profits were $360,000. Find the amount received by each partner.

15. Gardening The directions on a bag of plant food recommend 0.5 lb for every 50 ft^2 of lawn. How many pounds of plant food should be used on a lawn that measures 275 ft^2?

16. Crime Rates The table below lists U.S. cities with populations over 100,000 that had a high number of violent crimes per 1000 residents per year. Violent crimes include murder, rape, aggravated assault, and robbery. (*Source:* FBI Uniform Crime Reports)

City	Violent crimes per 1000 people
Baltimore, Maryland	13.39
St. Louis, Missouri	16.79
Detroit, Michigan	19.89
Memphis, Tennessee	17.41
Oakland, California	16.85

a. Which city has the highest rate of violent crimes?

b. The population of Baltimore is approximately 624,000. Estimate the number of violent crimes committed in that city. Round to the nearest whole number.

17. Pets During a recent year, nearly 1.2 million dogs or litters were registered with the American Kennel Club. The most popular breed was the Labrador retriever, with 172,841 registered. What percent of the registrations were Labrador retrievers? Round to the nearest tenth of a percent. (*Source:* American Kennel Club)

18. Smartphone Sales Apple Inc. reported that it sold 74,779,000 iPhones during its first quarter of 2016. This is up from sales of 48,046,000 the previous quarter. Find the percent increase in iPhones sold in the first quarter of 2016 as compared to the previous quarter. Round to the nearest tenth of a percent.

19. Compact Disc Sales In 2005, the total number of music CDs sold was 598.9 million, while in 2015, it was 125.6 million. (*Source:* Soundscan)

a. Find the percent decrease in the number of CDs sold from 2005 to 2015. Round to the nearest tenth of a percent.

b. If the percent decrease in the number of CDs sold from 2015 to 2025 is the same as it was from 2005 to 2015, how many CDs will be sold in 2025?

20. Shot Put The equation $h = -16t^2 + 28t + 6$, where $0 \le t \le 1.943$, can be used to find the height h, in feet, of a shot t seconds after a shot putter has released it. After how many seconds is the shot 10 ft above the ground? Round to the nearest tenth of a second.

3

The Mathematics of Finance

We interact, on a daily basis, with people who want to separate us from our money. Advertisers tempt us to spend our hard-earned cash with images of cars, furniture, cruises, fast food, technology, and a million other products and services. At the same time, we are encouraged by banks and investment companies to save money for retirement or educational expenses by investing in retirement plans or college savings plans.

There are a multitude of ways to pay for both our purchases and our investments. We can pay for purchases by using credit in the form of bank loans, credit card loans, and mortgages. We can invest money through employer-sponsored 401(k) plans, state-sponsored college savings plans, IRAs (individual retirement accounts), mutual funds, and other investment vehicles. To assess these offers of financial assistance, we use a branch of mathematics called finance. The mathematics of finance is used by bankers, financial planners, hedge fund managers, stockbrokers, and hopefully you, after you finish this chapter.

Many of us are wary of investing our money in the stock market because of the risk involved and because the stock market seems very complicated. To give you a quick preview of how mathematics can help you make informed decisions, imagine that you have decided to hire a financial planner to assist you with your investment planning. Some good information about certified financial planners—individuals who have passed a series of tests on financial planning—can be found on the website www.cfp.net.

Financial planners charge fees for their services. It is very important to understand how these fees are structured because this will impact how the value of your investment grows. Let's assume that you begin with \$1000 and are committed to adding \$1000 each year to your investment. You want to know how much money you will have earned by the end of 25 years. This amount will depend on both the interest rate you expect to earn and the fee (normally a percentage of the value of your investment portfolio) charged by your financial advisor. For our example, we will assume that your investment earns 5% interest per year, on average. If your financial advisor charges an annual fee of 1% of your investment portfolio, then at the end of 25 years, your investment will be worth about \$44,000. If your advisor charges a fee of 0.25% per year, then after 25 years your investment will be worth about \$49,000, which is \$5000 more! Learning about the mathematics of finance is well worth the effort.

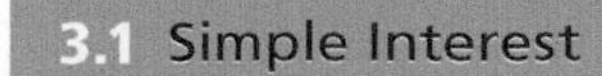

SECTION 3.1 Simple Interest

Simple Interest

HISTORICAL NOTE

The earliest loans date back to 3000 B.C., and interest on those loans may have extended over generations, not 4 or 5 years, as is the case for today's typical car loan. One of the first written records of an interest rate occurs in the Code of Hammurabi. Hammurabi ruled Babylon from 1795 to 1750 B.C. He is known for being the first ruler to write a set of laws that defined people's rights. In this Code, he allowed annual interest rates to be as high as 30%.

When you deposit money in a bank—for example, in a savings account—you are permitting the bank to use your money. The bank may lend the deposited money to customers to buy cars or make renovations on their homes. The bank pays you for the privilege of using your money. The amount paid to you is called **interest**. If you are the one borrowing money from a bank, the amount you pay for the privilege of using that money is also called interest.

The amount deposited in a bank or borrowed from a bank is called the **principal**. The amount of interest paid is usually given as a percent of the principal. The percent used to determine the amount of interest is called the **interest rate**. If you deposit $1000 in a savings account paying 5% interest per year, $1000 is the principal and the annual interest rate is 5%.

Interest paid on the original principal is called **simple interest**. The formula used to calculate simple interest is given below.

Simple Interest Formula

The simple interest formula is

$$I = Prt$$

where I is the interest, P is the principal, r is the interest rate, and t is the time period.

In the simple interest formula, the time t is expressed in the same units as the rate. For example, if the rate is given as an annual interest rate, then the time is measured in years; if the rate is given as a monthly interest rate, then the time must be expressed in months.

Interest rates are most commonly expressed as annual interest rates. Therefore, unless stated otherwise, we will assume the interest rate is an annual interest rate.

Interest rates are generally given as percents. Before performing calculations involving an interest rate, write the interest rate as a decimal.

EXAMPLE 1 Calculate Simple Interest

Calculate the simple interest earned in 1 year on a deposit of $1000 if the interest rate is 5%.

Solution

Use the simple interest formula. Substitute the following values into the formula: $P = 1000$, $r = 5\% = 0.05$, and $t = 1$.

$$I = Prt$$
$$I = 1000(0.05)(1)$$
$$I = 50$$

The simple interest earned is $50.

CHECK YOUR PROGRESS 1 Calculate the simple interest earned in 1 year on a deposit of $500 if the interest rate is 4%.

Solution See page S9.

EXAMPLE 2 **Calculate Simple Interest**

Calculate the simple interest due on a 3-month loan of \$2000 if the interest rate is 6.5%.

Solution

Use the simple interest formula. Substitute the values $P = 2000$ and $r = 6.5\% = 0.065$ into the formula. Because the interest rate is an annual rate, the time must be measured in years: $t = \frac{3 \text{ months}}{1 \text{ year}} = \frac{3 \text{ months}}{12 \text{ months}} = \frac{3}{12}$.

$$I = Prt$$
$$I = 2000(0.065)\left(\frac{3}{12}\right)$$
$$I = 32.5$$

The simple interest due is \$32.50.

CHECK YOUR PROGRESS 2 Calculate the simple interest due on a 4-month loan of \$1500 if the interest rate is 5.25%.

Solution See page S9.

EXAMPLE 3 **Calculate Simple Interest**

Calculate the simple interest due on a 2-month loan of \$500 if the interest rate is 1.5% per month.

Solution

Use the simple interest formula. Substitute the values $P = 500$ and $r = 1.5\% = 0.015$ into the formula. Because the interest rate is *per month,* the time period of the loan is expressed as the number of months: $t = 2$.

$$I = Prt$$
$$I = 500(0.015)(2)$$
$$I = 15$$

The simple interest due is \$15.

CHECK YOUR PROGRESS 3 Calculate the simple interest due on a 5-month loan of \$700 if the interest rate is 1.25% per month.

Solution See page S9.

POINT OF INTEREST

A PIRG (Public Interest Research Group) survey found that 29% of credit reports contained errors that could result in the denial of a loan. This is why financial advisors recommend that consumers check their credit ratings.

Remember that in the simple interest formula, time t is measured in the same period as the interest rate. Therefore, if the time period of a loan with an annual interest rate is given in days, it is necessary to convert the time period of the loan to a fractional part of a year. There are two methods for converting time from days to years: the exact method and the ordinary method. Using the exact method, the number of days of the loan is divided by 365, the number of days in a year.

$$\textbf{Exact method: } t = \frac{\text{number of days}}{365}$$

The ordinary method is based on there being an average of 30 days in a month and 12 months in a year ($30 \cdot 12 = 360$). Using this method, the number of days of the loan is divided by 360.

$$\textbf{Ordinary method: } t = \frac{\text{number of days}}{360}$$

The ordinary method is used by most businesses. Therefore, unless otherwise stated, the ordinary method will be used in this text.

EXAMPLE 4 Calculate Simple Interest

Calculate the simple interest due on a 45-day loan of $3500 if the annual interest rate is 8%.

Solution

Use the simple interest formula. Substitute the following values into the formula: $P = 3500$, $r = 8\% = 0.08$, and $t = \frac{\text{number of days}}{360} = \frac{45}{360}$.

$$I = Prt$$

$$I = 3500(0.08)\left(\frac{45}{360}\right)$$

$$I = 35$$

The simple interest due is $35.

CHECK YOUR PROGRESS 4 Calculate the simple interest due on a 120-day loan of $7000 if the annual interest rate is 5.25%.

Solution See page S9.

HISTORICAL NOTE

Some historians think that the dollar sign evolved from the Mexican or Spanish letters P and S, for pesos or piastres or pieces of eight. The S gradually came to be written over the P. The $ symbol was widely used before the adoption of the U.S. dollar in 1785.

The simple interest formula can be used to find the interest rate on a loan when the interest, principal, and time period of the loan are known. An example is given below.

EXAMPLE 5 Calculate the Simple Interest Rate

The simple interest charged on a 6-month loan of $3000 is $150. Find the simple interest rate.

Solution

Use the simple interest formula. Solve the equation for r.

$$I = Prt$$

$$150 = 3000(r)\left(\frac{6}{12}\right)$$

$$150 = 1500r \qquad \bullet\ 3000\left(\frac{6}{12}\right) = 1500$$

$$0.10 = r \qquad \bullet\ \text{Divide each side of the equation by 1500.}$$

$$r = 10\% \qquad \bullet\ \text{Write the decimal as a percent.}$$

The simple interest rate on the loan is 10%.

CHECK YOUR PROGRESS 5 The simple interest charged on a 6-month loan of $12,000 is $462. Find the simple interest rate.

Solution See page S9.

MATH MATTERS Is the American Dream Dead?

This chapter is about money, a topic of great importance to all of us. The possibility of going "from rags to riches" is a dream that has long attracted people from all over the world to the United States. Because the United States has such a large middle class, the leap from poverty to wealth, or even from the middle class to the upper class, is much easier to make than in almost any other country in the world. But many feel that the "American Dream" of starting out with nothing and working one's way to the top has become unattainable. Do you think this is true? Has the gap between the rich and the poor in the United States become insurmountable? Furthermore, do you think it is the government's responsibility to restore the middle class and decrease the income gap between the rich and the poor? Sixty-six percent of all Americans believe the government should be doing more in this regard. The breakdown by political affiliation is shown in the figure below. (*Source:* www.pbs.org (http://www.pbs.org/newshour/making-sense/why-half-of-u-s-adults-no-longer-believe-in-the-american-dream/)

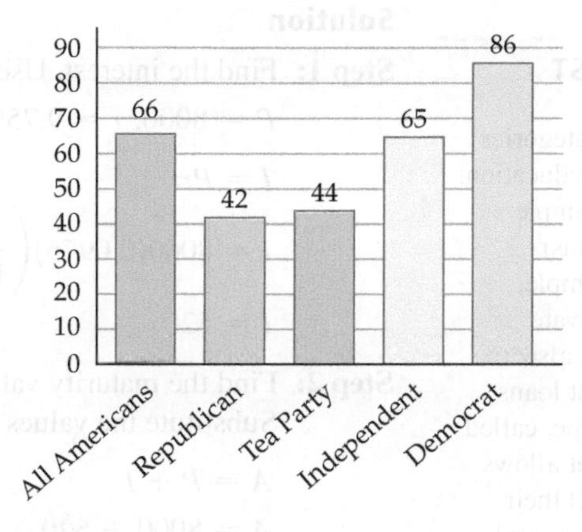

FIGURE 3.1 The percent of Americans who agree that the government should do more to reduce the gap between the rich and the poor, by political affiliation.

Future Value and Maturity Value

When you borrow money, the total amount to be repaid to the lender is the sum of the principal and interest. This sum is calculated using the following future value or maturity value formula for simple interest.

POINT OF INTEREST

You may have heard the term *legal tender.* Section 102 of the Coinage Act of 1965 states, in part, that

> All coins and currencies of the United States, regardless of when coins are issued, shall be legal tender for all debts, public and private, public charges, taxes, duties, and dues.

This means that when you offer U.S. currency to a creditor, you have made a valid and legal offer of payment of your debt.

Future Value or Maturity Value Formula for Simple Interest

The future or maturity value formula for simple interest is

$$A = P + I$$

where A is the amount after the interest, I, has been added to the principal, P.

This formula can be used for loans or investments. When used for a loan, A is the total amount to be repaid to the lender; this sum is called the **maturity value** of the loan. In Example 5, the simple interest charged on the loan of \$3000 was \$150. The maturity value of the loan is therefore \$3000 + \$150 = \$3150.

For an investment, such as a deposit in a bank savings account, A is the total amount on deposit after the interest earned has been added to the principal. This sum is called the **future value** of the investment.

QUESTION Is the stated sum a maturity value or a future value?

a. The sum of the principal and the interest on an investment

b. The sum of the principal and the interest on a loan

EXAMPLE 6 Calculate a Maturity Value

Calculate the maturity value of a simple interest, 8-month loan of \$8000 if the interest rate is 9.75%.

Solution

Step 1: Find the interest. Use the simple interest formula. Substitute the values $P = 8000$, $r = 9.75\% = 0.0975$, and $t = \frac{8}{12}$ into the formula.

$$I = Prt$$
$$I = 8000(0.0975)\left(\frac{8}{12}\right)$$
$$I = 520$$

Step 2: Find the maturity value. Use the maturity value formula for simple interest. Substitute the values $P = 8000$ and $I = 520$ into the formula.

$$A = P + I$$
$$A = 8000 + 520$$
$$A = 8520$$

The maturity value of the loan is \$8520.

POINT OF INTEREST

There are three major categories of loans used to pay for education: (1) student loans (for example, Stafford and Perkins loans), (2) parent loans (for example, PLUS loans), and (3) private student loans, which are also called alternative student loans. There is also a fourth type, called a consolidation loan, that allows borrowers to combine all their loans into one loan with a single payment.

CHECK YOUR PROGRESS 6 Calculate the maturity value of a simple interest, 9-month loan of \$4000 if the interest rate is 8.75%.

Solution See page S9.

Recall that the simple interest formula states that $I = Prt$. We can substitute Prt for I in the future or maturity value formula, as follows.

$$A = P + I$$
$$A = P + Prt$$
$$\mathbf{A = P(1 + rt)} \quad \text{• Factor } P \text{ from each term.}$$

In the final equation, A is the future value of an investment or the maturity value of a loan, P is the principal, r is the interest rate, and t is the time period.

We used the formula $A = P + I$ in Example 6. The formula $A = P(1 + rt)$ is used in Examples 7 and 8. Note that two steps were required to find the solution in Example 6, but only one step is required in Examples 7 and 8.

ANSWER **a.** Future value **b.** Maturity value

EXAMPLE 7 **Calculate the Maturity Value Using $A = P(1 + rt)$**

Calculate the maturity value of a simple interest, 3-month loan of $3800. The interest rate is 6%.

Solution

Substitute the following values into the formula $A = P(1 + rt)$: $P = 3800$, $r = 6\% = 0.06$, and $t = \frac{3}{12}$.

$$A = P(1 + rt)$$
$$A = 3800\left[1 + 0.06\left(\frac{3}{12}\right)\right]$$
$$A = 3800(1 + 0.015)$$
$$A = 3800(1.015)$$
$$A = 3857$$

The maturity value of the loan is $3857.

CHECK YOUR PROGRESS 7 Calculate the maturity value of a simple interest, 1-year loan of $6700. The interest rate is 8.9%.

Solution See page S9.

EXAMPLE 8 **Calculate the Future Value Using $A = P(1 + rt)$**

Find the future value after 1 year of $850 in an account earning 8.2% simple interest.

Solution

Because $t = 1$, $rt = r(1) = r$. Therefore, $1 + rt = 1 + r = 1 + 0.082 = 1.082$.

$$A = P(1 + rt)$$
$$A = 850(1.082)$$
$$A = 919.7$$

The future value of the account after 1 year is $919.70.

POINT OF INTEREST

The bill of largest value ever printed in the United States was a $100,000 bill. The statesman featured on the bill was Woodrow Wilson, the 28th president of the United States. The bill was used for transactions between Federal Reserve Banks only.

B Christopher/Alamy Stock Photo

CHECK YOUR PROGRESS 8 Find the future value after 1 year of $680 in an account earning 6.4% simple interest.

Solution See page S9.

Recall that the formula $A = P + I$ states that A is the amount after the interest has been added to the principal. Subtracting P from each side of this equation yields the following formula.

$$I = A - P$$

This formula states that the amount of interest paid is equal to the total amount minus the principal. This formula is used in Example 9.

EXAMPLE 9 **Calculate the Simple Interest Rate**

The maturity value of a 3-month loan of $4000 is $4085. What is the simple interest rate?

Solution

First find the amount of interest paid. Subtract the principal from the maturity value.

$$I = A - P$$
$$I = 4085 - 4000$$
$$I = 85$$

Find the simple interest rate by solving the simple interest formula for r.

$$I = Prt$$

$$85 = 4000(r)\left(\frac{3}{12}\right)$$

$$85 = 1000r \qquad \bullet\ 4000\left(\frac{3}{12}\right) = 1000$$

$$0.085 = r \qquad \bullet \text{ Divide each side of the equation by 1000.}$$

$$r = 8.5\% \qquad \bullet \text{ Write the decimal as a percent.}$$

The simple interest rate on the loan is 8.5%.

CHECK YOUR PROGRESS 9 The maturity value of a 4-month loan of $9000 is $9240. What is the simple interest rate?

Solution See page S9.

EXCURSION

Interest on a Car Loan

If you have a car loan, there is a good chance that each loan payment includes principal (the amount that goes toward paying off the original loan) and interest (the amount you are charged for borrowing), which is based on the outstanding balance. The *outstanding balance* refers to the portion of the original debt that has not yet been repaid. Because you pay some part of the principal each month, the outstanding balance decreases each month.

Here is an example. Suppose you obtain a 4-year car loan of $10,000 at an annual interest rate of 5%. The monthly payment on the loan is $230.29. Later in the chapter, we will show how that monthly payment is calculated.

One month after you obtain the loan, when your first payment is due, you still owe a total of $10,000 *plus interest.* The amount of interest owed can be calculated using the formula $I = Prt$. The principal is $10,000, the interest rate is $\frac{0.05}{12}$ (the annual interest rate, expressed as a decimal, divided by the number of months in a year), and the time is 1 month.

$$\begin{aligned} I &= Prt \\ &= 10{,}000\left(\frac{0.05}{12}\right)(1) \\ &\approx 41.67 \end{aligned}$$

The interest you owe for the first month is $41.67. By subtracting this amount from the monthly payment of $230.29, you can calculate the amount of the first payment that goes toward repaying the principal:

$$\$230.29 - \$41.67 = \$188.62$$

So, with the first payment, you have repaid $188.62 of the original $10,000 loan. You now owe $10,000 − $188.62 = $9811.38.

After two months, you owe $9811.38 plus the interest due on that amount. Performing a similar calculation, we have

$$I = Prt = 9811.38\left(\frac{0.05}{12}\right)(1) \approx 40.88$$

Note that the interest you owe for the second month is less than the interest you owed for the first month. This is because you have already paid back some of the loan. This time, the amount that goes toward reducing the principal is:

$$\$230.29 - \$40.88 = \$189.41$$

After the second payment is made, you have repaid $189.41 of the $9811.38 outstanding loan balance. You now owe $9811.38 − $189.41 = $9621.97.

Notice that the amount you paid toward reducing the principal is greater than the amount you paid toward the principal in the first month. Every month, more and more of your payment will go toward reducing the principal, and less and less will go toward interest charges.

EXCURSION EXERCISES

1. Find the amount of interest you owe for the third month.
2. How much of your payment goes toward reducing the principal in the third month?
3. How much do you owe after making the payment for the third month?
4. Find the amount of interest you owe for the fourth month.
5. How much of your payment goes toward reducing the principal in the fourth month?
6. How much do you owe after making the payment for the fourth month?
7. Your last payment of $230.29 includes the remaining balance of the loan plus the interest due on that remaining balance. Find the remaining balance of the loan for the last payment.

EXERCISE SET 3.1

1. Explain how to convert a number of months to a fractional part of a year.
2. Explain how to convert a number of days to a fractional part of a year.
3. Explain what each variable in the simple interest formula represents.

■ In Exercises 4 to 17, calculate the simple interest earned. Round to the nearest cent.

4. $P = \$2000$, $r = 6\%$, $t = 1$ year
5. $P = \$8000$, $r = 7\%$, $t = 1$ year
6. $P = \$3000$, $r = 5.5\%$, $t = 6$ months
7. $P = \$7000$, $r = 6.5\%$, $t = 6$ months
8. $P = \$4200$, $r = 8.5\%$, $t = 3$ months
9. $P = \$9000$, $r = 6.75\%$, $t = 4$ months
10. $P = \$12{,}000$, $r = 7.8\%$, $t = 45$ days
11. $P = \$3000$, $r = 9.6\%$, $t = 21$ days
12. $P = \$4000$, $r = 8.4\%$, $t = 33$ days
13. $P = \$7000$, $r = 7.2\%$, $t = 114$ days
14. $P = \$800$, $r = 1.5\%$ monthly, $t = 3$ months
15. $P = \$2000$, $r = 1.25\%$ monthly, $t = 5$ months
16. $P = \$3500$, $r = 1.8\%$ monthly, $t = 4$ months
17. $P = \$1600$, $r = 1.75\%$ monthly, $t = 6$ months

■ In Exercises 18 to 23, use the formula $A = P(1 + rt)$ to calculate the maturity value of the simple interest loan.

18. $P = \$8500$, $r = 6.8\%$, $t = 6$ months
19. $P = \$15{,}000$, $r = 8.9\%$, $t = 6$ months
20. $P = \$4600$, $r = 9.75\%$, $t = 4$ months
21. $P = \$7200$, $r = 7.95\%$, $t = 4$ months
22. $P = \$13{,}000$, $r = 1.4\%$ monthly, $t = 3$ months
23. $P = \$2800$, $r = 9.2\%$, $t = 3$ months

■ In Exercises 24 to 29, calculate the simple interest rate.

24. $P = \$8000$, $I = \$500$, $t = 1$ year
25. $P = \$1600$, $I = \$120$, $t = 1$ year
26. $P = \$4000$, $I = \$190$, $t = 6$ months
27. $P = \$2000$, $I = \$80$, $t = 6$ months
28. $P = \$500$, $I = \$10.25$, $t = 3$ months
29. $P = \$1200$, $I = \$37.20$, $t = 4$ months

30. Simple Interest Calculate the simple interest earned in 1 year on a deposit of $1900 if the interest rate is 8%.

31. Simple Interest You deposit $1500 in an account earning 5.2% interest. Calculate the simple interest earned in 6 months.

32. Simple Interest Calculate the simple interest due on a 2-month loan of $800 if the interest rate is 1.5% per month.

33. Simple Interest Calculate the simple interest due on a 45-day loan of $1600 if the interest rate is 9%.

34. Simple Interest Calculate the simple interest due on a 150-day loan of $4800 if the interest rate is 7.25%.

35. Maturity Value Calculate the maturity value of a simple interest, 8-month loan of $7000 if the interest rate is 8.7%.

36. Maturity Value Calculate the maturity value of a simple interest, 10-month loan of $6600 if the interest rate is 9.75%.

37. Maturity Value Calculate the maturity value of a simple interest, 1-year loan of $5200. The interest rate is 5.1%.

38. Future Value You deposit $880 in an account paying 9.2% simple interest. Find the future value of the investment after 1 year.

39. Future Value You deposit $750 in an account paying 7.3% simple interest. Find the future value of the investment after 1 year.

40. Simple Interest Rate The simple interest charged on a 6-month loan of $6000 is $270. Find the simple interest rate.

41. Simple Interest Rate The simple interest charged on a 6-month loan of $18,000 is $918. Find the simple interest rate.

42. Simple Interest Rate The maturity value of a 4-month loan of $3000 is $3097. Find the simple interest rate.

43. Simple Interest Rate Find the simple interest rate on a 3-month loan of $5000 if the maturity value of the loan is $5125.

44. Late Payments Your property tax bill is $1200. The county charges a penalty of 11% simple interest for late payments. How much do you owe if you pay the bill 2 months past the due date?

45. Late Payments Your electric bill is $132. You are charged 9% simple interest for late payments. How much do you owe if you pay the bill 1 month past the due date?

46. Certificate of Deposit If you withdraw part of your money from a certificate of deposit before the date of maturity, you must pay an interest penalty. Suppose you invested $5000 in a 1-year certificate of deposit paying 8.5% interest. After 6 months, you decide to withdraw $2000. Your interest penalty is 3 months simple interest on the $2000. What interest penalty do you pay?

47. Maturity Value $10,000 is borrowed for 140 days at an 8% interest rate. Calculate the maturity value by the exact method and by the ordinary method. Which method yields the greater maturity value? Who benefits from using the ordinary method rather than the exact method, the borrower or the lender?

EXTENSIONS

48.  Interest has been described as a rental fee for money. Explain why this is an apt description of interest.

49. On July 31, at 4 P.M., you open a money market account that pays 5% interest, compounded daily, and you deposit $500 in the account. Your deposit is credited as of August 1. At the beginning of September, you receive a statement from the bank that shows that during the month of August, you received $2.15 in interest. The interest has been added to your account, bringing the total deposit to $502.15. At the beginning of October, you receive a statement from the bank that shows that during the month of September, you received $2.09 in interest on the $502.15 on deposit. Why did you receive less interest during the second month, when there was more money on deposit?

SECTION 3.2 Compound Interest

Compound Interest

Simple interest is generally used for loans of 1 year or less. For loans of more than 1 year, the interest paid on the money borrowed is called *compound interest.* **Compound interest** is interest calculated not only on the original principal, but also on any interest that has already been earned.

POINT OF INTEREST

Warren Buffet, one of the richest men in the world, is sometimes referred to as "the Oracle of Omaha," a nod to his hometown of Omaha, Nebraska. When asked about the secret to his success, Buffet replied, "My wealth has come from a combination of living in America, some lucky genes, and compound interest." Compound interest is the topic of this section.

Lacy O'Toole/CNBC/NBCU/Getty Images

To illustrate compound interest, suppose you deposit \$1000 in a savings account earning 5% interest, compounded annually (once a year).

During the first year, the interest earned is calculated as follows.

$$I = Prt$$
$$I = \$1000(0.05)(1) = \$50$$

At the end of the first year, the total amount in the account is

$$A = P + I$$
$$A = \$1000 + \$50 = \$1050$$

During the second year, the interest earned is calculated using the amount in the account at the end of the first year.

$$I = Prt$$
$$I = \$1050(0.05)(1) = \$52.50$$

Note that the interest earned during the second year (\$52.50) is greater than the interest earned during the first year (\$50). This is because the interest earned during the first year was added to the original principal, and the interest for the second year was calculated using this sum. If the account earned simple interest rather than compound interest, the interest earned each year would be the same (\$50).

At the end of the second year, the total amount in the account is the sum of the amount in the account at the end of the first year and the interest earned during the second year.

$$A = P + I$$
$$A = \$1050 + 52.50 = \$1102.50$$

The interest earned during the third year is calculated using the amount in the account at the end of the second year (\$1102.50).

$$I = Prt$$
$$I = \$1102.50(0.05)(1) = \$55.125 \approx \$55.13$$

The interest earned each year keeps increasing. This is the effect of compound interest.

In this example, the interest is compounded annually. However, compound interest can be compounded semiannually (twice a year), quarterly (four times a year), monthly, or daily. The frequency with which the interest is compounded is called the **compounding period**.

If, in the preceding example, interest is compounded quarterly rather than annually, then the first interest payment on the \$1000 in the account occurs after 3 months $\left(t = \frac{3}{12} = \frac{1}{4};\ \text{3 months is one-quarter of a year}\right)$. That interest is then added to the account, and the interest earned for the second quarter is calculated using that sum.

End of 1st quarter: $I = Prt = \$1000(0.05)\left(\frac{3}{12}\right) = \$12.50$

$A = P + I = \$1000 + \$12.50 = \$1012.50$

End of 2nd quarter: $I = Prt = \$1012.50(0.05)\left(\frac{3}{12}\right) = \$12.65625 \approx \$12.66$

$A = P + I = \$1012.50 + \$12.66 = \$1025.16$

End of 3rd quarter: $I = Prt = \$1025.16(0.05)\left(\frac{3}{12}\right) = \$12.8145 \approx \$12.81$

$A = P + I = \$1025.16 + \$12.81 = \$1037.97$

End of 4th quarter: $I = Prt = \$1037.97(0.05)\left(\frac{3}{12}\right) = \$12.974625 \approx \$12.97$

$A = P + I = \$1037.97 + \$12.97 = \$1050.94$

The total amount in the account at the end of the first year is \$1050.94.

POINT OF INTEREST

The U.S. Bureau of Engraving and Printing is responsible for printing our currency. In addition to printing \$1, \$2, \$5, \$10, \$20, \$50, and \$100 bills, the Bureau also used to print \$500, \$1000, \$5000, and \$10,000 bills. Production of these large-denomination bills was stopped during World War II. In 1969, the Federal Reserve Board stopped distribution of these large-denomination bills. Below is an image of a \$5000 note.

PAUL J. RICHARDS/AAFP/Getty Images

When the interest is compounded quarterly, the account earns more interest ($50.94) than when the interest is compounded annually ($50). In general, an increase in the number of compounding periods results in an increase in the interest earned by an account.

In the example above, the formulas $I = Prt$ and $A = P + I$ were used to show the amount of interest added to the account each quarter. The formula $A = P(1 + rt)$ can be used to calculate A at the end of each quarter. For example, the amount in the account at the end of the first quarter is

$$A = P(1 + rt)$$
$$A = 1000\left[1 + 0.05\left(\frac{3}{12}\right)\right]$$
$$A = 1000(1.0125)$$
$$A = 1012.50$$

This amount, $1012.50, is the same as the amount calculated on the preceding page using the formula $A = P + I$ to find the amount at the end of the first quarter.

The formula $A = P(1 + rt)$ is used in Example 1.

EXAMPLE 1 Calculate Future Value

You deposit $500 in an account earning 6% interest, compounded semiannually. How much is in the account at the end of 1 year?

Solution

The interest is compounded every 6 months. Calculate the amount in the account after the first 6 months. $t = \frac{6}{12}$.

$$A = P(1 + rt)$$
$$A = 500\left[1 + 0.06\left(\frac{6}{12}\right)\right]$$
$$A = 515$$

Calculate the amount in the account after the second 6 months.

$$A = P(1 + rt)$$
$$A = 515\left[1 + 0.06\left(\frac{6}{12}\right)\right]$$
$$A = 530.45$$

The total amount in the account at the end of 1 year is $530.45.

CHECK YOUR PROGRESS 1 You deposit $2000 in an account earning 4% interest, compounded monthly. How much is in the account at the end of 6 months?

Solution See page S10.

POINT OF INTEREST

The top seven sources of financial news for professionals in the field of finance are listed below.

- MarketWatch News Viewer
- Boomerang Portal
- Reuters
- Forbes
- *The Wall Street Journal*
- *The Financial Times*
- CNBC

(*Source:* www.investopedia.com)

In calculations that involve compound interest, the sum of the principal and the interest that has been added to it is called the **compound amount**. In Example 1, the compound amount is $530.45.

The calculations necessary to determine compound interest and compound amounts can be simplified by using a formula. Consider an amount P deposited into an account paying an annual interest rate r, compounded annually.

The interest earned during the first year is

$$I = Prt$$
$$I = Pr(1) \quad \bullet\ t = 1.$$
$$I = Pr$$

The compound amount A in the account after 1 year is the sum of the original principal and the interest earned during the first year:

$$A = P + I$$
$$A = P + Pr$$
$$A = P(1 + r) \quad \text{• Factor } P \text{ from each term.}$$

During the second year, the interest is calculated on the compound amount at the end of the first year, $P(1 + r)$.

$$I = Prt$$
$$I = P(1 + r)r(1) \quad \text{• Replace } P \text{ with } P(1 + r);\ t = 1.$$
$$I = P(1 + r)r$$

The compound amount A in the account after 2 years is the sum of the compound amount at the end of the first year and the interest earned during the second year:

$$A = P + I$$
$$A = P(1 + r) + P(1 + r)r \quad \text{• Replace } P \text{ with } P(1 + r) \text{ and } I \text{ with } P(1 + r)r.$$
$$A = 1[P(1 + r)] + [P(1 + r)]r$$
$$A = P(1 + r)(1 + r) \quad \text{• Factor } P(1 + r) \text{ from each term.}$$
$$A = P(1 + r)^2 \quad \text{• Write } (1 + r)(1 + r) \text{ as } (1 + r)^2.$$

During the third year, the interest is calculated on the compound amount at the end of the second year, $P(1 + r)^2$.

$$I = Prt$$
$$I = P(1 + r)^2r(1) \quad \text{• Replace } P \text{ with } P(1 + r)^2;\ t = 1.$$
$$I = P(1 + r)^2r$$

The compound amount A in the account after 3 years is the sum of the compound amount at the end of the second year and the interest earned during the third year:

$$A = P + I$$
$$A = P(1 + r)^2 + P(1 + r)^2r \quad \text{• Replace } P \text{ with } P(1 + r)^2 \text{ and } I \text{ with } P(1 + r)^2r.$$
$$A = 1[P(1 + r)^2] + [P(1 + r)^2]r$$
$$A = P(1 + r)^2(1 + r) \quad \text{• Factor } P(1 + r)^2 \text{ from each term.}$$
$$A = P(1 + r)^3 \quad \text{• Write } (1 + r)^2(1 + r) \text{ as } (1 + r)^3.$$

Note that the compound amount at the end of each year is the previous year's compound amount multiplied by $(1 + r)$. The exponent on $(1 + r)$ is equal to the number of compounding periods. Generalizing from this, we can state that the compound amount after n years is $A = P(1 + r)^n$.

In deriving this equation, interest was compounded annually; therefore, $t = 1$. Applying a similar argument for more frequent compounding periods, we derive the following compound amount formula. This formula enables us to calculate the compound amount for any number of compounding periods per year.

Compound Amount Formula

The compound amount formula is

$$A = P\left(1 + \frac{r}{n}\right)^{nt}$$

where A is the compound amount, P is the amount of money deposited, r is the annual interest rate, n is the number of compounding periods per year, and t is the number of years.

POINT OF INTEREST

It is believed that U.S. currency is green because at the time of the introduction of the smaller-size bills in 1929, green pigment was readily available in large quantities. The color was resistant to chemical and physical changes, and green was psychologically associated with strong, stable government credit. (*Source*: www.moneyfactory.gov)

Alex Wong/Getty Images

Values of n (Number of Compounding Periods per Year)

If interest is compounded	then n =
annually	1
semiannually	2
quarterly	4
monthly	12
daily	360

To illustrate how to determine the values of the variables in this formula, consider depositing \$5000 in an account earning 6% interest, compounded quarterly, for a period of 3 years.

The amount deposited is P:	$P = 5000$
The annual interest rate is 6%:	$r = 6\% = 0.06$
When interest is compounded quarterly, there are four compounding periods per year:	$n = 4$
The time is 3 years:	$t = 3$

Recall that compound interest can be compounded annually (once a year), semiannually (twice a year), quarterly (four times a year), monthly, or daily. The possible values of n (the number of compounding periods per year) are recorded in the table at the left.

QUESTION What is the value of n when interest is compounded monthly?

Recall that the future value of an investment is the value of the investment after the original principal has been invested for a period of time. In other words, it is the principal plus the interest earned. Therefore, it is the compound amount A in the compound amount formula.

EXAMPLE 2 Calculate the Compound Amount

Calculate the compound amount when \$10,000 is deposited in an account earning 8% interest, compounded semiannually, for 4 years.

Solution

Use the compound amount formula.

$P = 10{,}000,\ r = 8\% = 0.08,\ n = 2,\ t = 4$

$$A = P\left(1 + \frac{r}{n}\right)^{nt}$$

$$A = 10{,}000\left(1 + \frac{0.08}{2}\right)^{2\cdot 4}$$

$$A = 10{,}000(1 + 0.04)^{8}$$

$$A = 10{,}000(1.04)^{8}$$

$$A \approx 10{,}000(1.368569)$$

$$A \approx 13{,}685.69$$

The compound amount after 4 years is approximately \$13,685.69.

CHECK YOUR PROGRESS 2 Calculate the compound amount when \$4000 is deposited in an account earning 6% interest, compounded monthly, for 2 years.

Solution See page S10.

TAKE NOTE

When using the compound amount formula, write the interest rate r as a decimal.

CALCULATOR NOTE

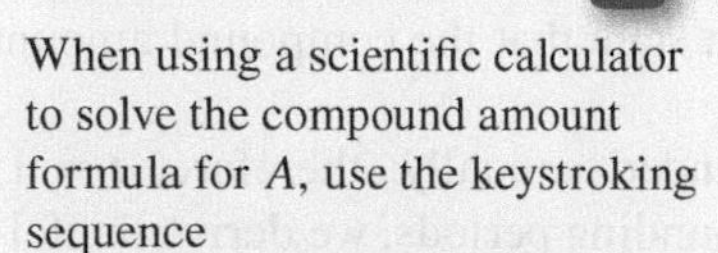

When using a scientific calculator to solve the compound amount formula for A, use the keystroking sequence

1 [+] r [÷] n [=] [y^x] [(] n [x] t [)] [x] P [=]

When using a graphing calculator, use the sequence

P [(] 1 [+] r [÷] n [)] [^] [(] n [x] t [)] [ENTER]

ANSWER $n = 12$.

EXAMPLE 3 Calculate Future Value

Calculate the future value of \$5000 earning 9% interest, compounded daily, for 3 years.

Solution

Use the compound amount formula.
$P = 5000, r = 9\% = 0.09, n = 360, t = 3$

$$A = P\left(1 + \frac{r}{n}\right)^{nt}$$

$$A = 5000\left(1 + \frac{0.09}{360}\right)^{360\cdot 3}$$

$$A = 5000(1 + 0.00025)^{1080}$$

$$A = 5000(1.00025)^{1080}$$

$$A \approx 5000(1.3099202)$$

$$A \approx 6549.60$$

The future value after 3 years is approximately \$6549.60.

CHECK YOUR PROGRESS 3 Calculate the future value of \$2500 earning 9% interest, compounded daily, for 4 years.

Solution See page S10.

POINT OF INTEREST

The majority of Americans say their children should start saving for retirement earlier than they did. The figure below shows the ages at which members of each generation started saving for retirement, and the amounts they are saving. (*Source:* money.cnn.com)

Age they started saving...

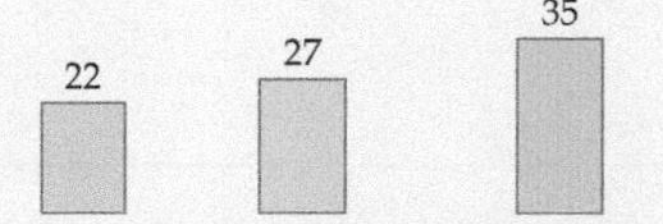

Millenials Generation X Baby Boomers

Amount of pay they are saving...

8% 7% 10%

Millenials Generation X Baby Boomers

The formula $I = A - P$ was used in Section 3.1 to find the interest earned on an investment or the interest paid on a loan. This same formula is used for compound interest. It is used in Example 4 to find the interest earned on an investment.

EXAMPLE 4 Calculate Compound Interest

How much interest is earned in 2 years on \$4000 deposited in an account paying 6% interest, compounded quarterly?

Solution

Calculate the compound amount. Use the compound amount formula.
$P = 4000, r = 6\% = 0.06, n = 4, t = 2$

$$A = P\left(1 + \frac{r}{n}\right)^{nt}$$

$$A = 4000\left(1 + \frac{0.06}{4}\right)^{4\cdot 2}$$

$$A = 4000(1 + 0.015)^{8}$$

$$A = 4000(1.015)^{8}$$

$$A \approx 4000(1.1264926)$$

$$A \approx 4505.97$$

Calculate the interest earned. Use the formula $I = A - P$.

$$I = A - P$$

$$I = 4505.97 - 4000$$

$$I = 505.97$$

The amount of interest earned is approximately \$505.97.

CHECK YOUR PROGRESS 4 How much interest is earned in 6 years on \$8000 deposited in an account paying 9% interest, compounded monthly?

Solution See page S10.

An alternative to using the compound amount formula is to use a calculator that has finance functions built into it. The TI-83/84 graphing calculator is used in Example 5.

EXAMPLE 5 Calculate Compound Interest

Use the finance feature of a calculator to determine the compound amount when $2000 is deposited in an account earning an interest rate of 12%, compounded quarterly, for 10 years.

Solution

On a TI-83/84 calculator, press APPS ENTER. The APPS key has red lettering on a black key.

Press ENTER to select 1: TVM Solver. TVM stands for time value of money.

N is the number of compounding periods, or $n \cdot t$ in the compound amount formula.

After N = , enter 4 × 10.

After I% = , enter 12.

After PV = , enter −2000. (See the note below.)

After PMT = , enter 0. Press ENTER twice.

After P/Y = , enter 4.

After C/Y = , enter 4.

Use the up arrow key to place the cursor at FV = .

Press ALPHA [Solve]. The ALPHA key has white lettering on a green key.

The solution is displayed to the right of FV = .

The compound amount is $6524.08.

Note: For most financial calculators and financial computer programs such as Excel, money that is paid out (such as the $2000 that is being deposited in this example) is entered as a negative number.

CALCULATOR NOTE

On the TI-83/84 calculator screen below, the variable N is the number of compounding periods, I% is the interest rate, PV is the present value of the money, PMT is the payment, P/Y is the number of payments per year, C/Y is the number of compounding periods per year, and FV is the future value of the money. TVM represents the time value of money.

Present value is discussed a little later in this section. Enter the principal for the present value amount.

"Solve" is located above the ENTER key on the calculator.

N=40
I%=12
PV=-2000
PMT=0
■FV=6524.075584
P/Y=4
C/Y=4
PMT: END BEGIN

TI-83/84 calculator screen display

CHECK YOUR PROGRESS 5 Use the finance feature of a calculator to determine the compound amount when $3500 is deposited in an account earning an interest rate of 6%, compounded semiannually, for 5 years.

Solution See page S10.

MATH MATTERS The Origins of the Federal Reserve

Joey Kotfica/Getty Images

The Federal Reserve Bank of San Francisco

In the late 1700s, before the Civil War began, there were two opposing views about banks in the United States. **Federalists** were in favor of a strong central bank, and **anti-Federalists** preferred to leave banks in the hands of the individual states. In 1791, the First Bank of the United States was created with a 20-year charter. Its main backer, Alexander Hamilton, was killed in a famous duel with Aaron Burr (who at the time was Thomas Jefferson's vice-president). When the charter expired, so did the first central bank. In 1816, the Second Bank of the United States was created, also with a 20-year charter, but President Andrew Jackson vetoed its renewal in 1832. The United States then entered the free banking era, which lasted until 1913, at which time the Third Bank of the United States was established. This bank was called the Federal Reserve System, and it is still the central bank of the United States today.

Present Value

The **present value** of an investment is the original principal invested, or the value of the investment before it earns any interest. Therefore, it is the principal, P, in the compound amount formula. Present value is used to determine how much money must be invested today in order for an investment to have a specific value at a future date.

The formula for the present value of an investment is found by solving the compound amount formula for P.

$$A = P\left(1 + \frac{r}{n}\right)^{nt}$$

$$\frac{A}{\left(1 + \frac{r}{n}\right)^{nt}} = \frac{P\left(1 + \frac{r}{n}\right)^{nt}}{\left(1 + \frac{r}{n}\right)^{nt}}$$ • Divide each side of the equation by $\left(1 + \frac{r}{n}\right)^{nt}$.

$$\frac{A}{\left(1 + \frac{r}{n}\right)^{nt}} = P$$

Present Value Formula

The present value formula is

$$P = \frac{A}{\left(1 + \frac{r}{n}\right)^{nt}}$$

where P is the original principal invested, A is the compound amount, r is the annual interest rate, n is the number of compounding periods per year, and t is the number of years.

The present value formula is used in Example 6.

EXAMPLE 6 Calculate Present Value

How much money should be invested in an account that earns 8% interest, compounded quarterly, in order to have $30,000 in 5 years?

Solution

Use the present value formula.

$A = 30{,}000$, $r = 8\% = 0.08$, $n = 4$, $t = 5$

$$P = \frac{A}{\left(1 + \frac{r}{n}\right)^{nt}}$$

$$P = \frac{30{,}000}{\left(1 + \frac{0.08}{4}\right)^{4 \cdot 5}} = \frac{30{,}000}{1.02^{20}} \approx \frac{30{,}000}{1.485947396}$$

$$P \approx 20{,}189.14$$

$20,189.14 should be invested in the account in order to have $30,000 in 5 years.

CALCULATOR NOTE 

To calculate P in the present value formula using a calculator, you can first calculate $\left(1 + \frac{r}{n}\right)^{nt}$. Next use the 1/x key or the x⁻¹ key. This will place the value of $\left(1 + \frac{r}{n}\right)^{nt}$ in the denominator. Then multiply by the value of A.

CHECK YOUR PROGRESS 6 How much money should be invested in an account that earns 9% interest, compounded semiannually, in order to have $20,000 in 5 years?

Solution See page S10.

EXAMPLE 7 Calculate Present Value

Use the finance feature of a calculator to determine how much money should be invested in an account that earns 7% interest, compounded monthly, in order to have $50,000 in 10 years.

Solution

On a TI-83/84 calculator, press APPS ENTER.

Press ENTER to select 1 TVM Solver.

After N = , enter 12 × 10.

After I% = , enter 7. Press ENTER twice.

After PMT = , enter 0.

After FV = , enter 50000.

After P/Y = , enter 12. • Number of payments per year

After C/Y = , enter 12. • Number of compounding periods per year

Use the up arrow key to place the cursor at PV = .

Press ALPHA [Solve].

The solution is displayed to the right of PV = .

$24,879.81 should be invested in the account in order to have $50,000 in 10 years.

```
N=120
I%=7
PV=
PMT=0
FV=50000
P/Y=12
C/Y=12
PMT: END BEGIN
```

```
N=120
I%=7
PV=-24879.81338
PMT=0
FV=50000
P/Y=12
C/Y=12
PMT: END BEGIN
```

TI-83/84 calculator screen displays

CHECK YOUR PROGRESS 7 Use the finance feature of a calculator to determine how much money should be invested in an account that earns 6% interest, compounded daily, in order to have $25,000 in 15 years.

Solution See page S11.

Inflation

POINT OF INTEREST

The average life of a dollar bill differs from the average lives of other denominations of U.S. currency. See the list below. (*Source:* www.federalreserve.gov)

$1	70 months
$5	66 months
$10	54 months
$20	95 months
$50	102 months
$100	180 months

We have discussed compound interest and its effect on the growth of an investment. After your money has been invested for a period of time in an account that pays interest, you will have more money than you originally deposited. But does that mean you will be able to buy more with the compound amount than you were able to buy with the original investment at the time you deposited the money? The answer is not necessarily, and the reason is the effect of inflation.

Suppose the price of a large-screen Smart LED TV is $1500. You have enough money to purchase the TV, but decide instead to invest the $1500 in an account paying 6% interest, compounded monthly. After 1 year, the compound amount is $1592.52. But during that same year, the rate of inflation was 7%. The TV now costs

$$\begin{aligned} \$1500 \text{ plus } 7\% \text{ of } \$1500 &= \$1500 + 0.07(\$1500) \\ &= \$1500 + \$105 \\ &= \$1605 \end{aligned}$$

Because $\$1592.52 < \$1605$, you have actually lost purchasing power. At the beginning of the year, you had enough money to buy the large-screen LED TV; at the end of the year, the compound amount is not enough to pay for that same TV. Your money has actually lost value because it can buy less now than it could 1 year ago.

Inflation is an economic condition during which there are increases in the costs of goods and services. Inflation is expressed as a percent; for example, we speak of an annual inflation rate of 7%.

To calculate the effects of inflation, we use the same procedure we used to calculate compound amount. This process is illustrated in Example 8. Although inflation rates vary dramatically, in this section we will assume constant annual inflation rates, and we will use annual compounding in solving inflation problems. In other words, $n = 1$ for these exercises.

EXAMPLE 8 **Calculate the Effect of Inflation on Salary**

Suppose your annual salary today is $35,000. You want to know what an equivalent salary will be in 20 years—that is, a salary that will have the same purchasing power. Assume a 6% inflation rate.

POINT OF INTEREST

Inflation rates can change dramatically over time. The table below shows the five lowest and the five highest inflation rates for the past 30 years. (*Source:* inflationdata.com)

The Five Lowest Inflation Rates

Inflation rate	Year
−0.34%	2009
0.12%	2015
1.47%	2013
1.55%	1998
1.59%	2002

The Five Highest Inflation Rates

Inflation rate	Year
13.58%	1980
10.35%	1981
6.16%	1982
5.39%	1990
4.83%	1989

Solution

Use the compound amount formula given on page 175, with $P = 35{,}000$, $r = 6\% = 0.06$, and $t = 20$. The inflation rate is an annual rate, so $n = 1$.

$$A = P\left(1 + \frac{r}{n}\right)^{nt}$$

$$A = 35{,}000\left(1 + \frac{0.06}{1}\right)^{1\cdot 20}$$

$$A = 35{,}000(1.06)^{20}$$

$$A \approx 35{,}000(3.20713547)$$

$$A \approx 112{,}249.74$$

Twenty years from now, you need to earn an annual salary of approximately $112,249.74 in order to have the same purchasing power.

CHECK YOUR PROGRESS 8 Assume that the average new car sticker price in 2013 was $28,000. Use an annual inflation rate of 5% to estimate the average new car sticker price in 2030.

Solution See page S11.

The present value formula can be used to determine the effect of inflation on the future purchasing power of a given amount of money. Substitute the inflation rate for the interest rate in the present value formula. The compounding period is 1 year. Again we will assume a constant rate of inflation.

EXAMPLE 9 **Calculate the Effect of Inflation on Future Purchasing Power**

Suppose you purchase an insurance policy in 2015 that will provide you with $250,000 when you retire in 2050. Assuming an annual inflation rate of 8%, what will be the purchasing power of the $250,000 in 2050?

Solution

Use the present value formula. $A = 250{,}000$, $r = 8\% = 0.08$, $t = 35$. The inflation rate is an annual rate, so $n = 1$.

$$P = \frac{A}{\left(1 + \frac{r}{n}\right)^{nt}}$$

$$P = \frac{250{,}000}{\left(1 + \frac{0.08}{1}\right)^{1\cdot 35}}$$

$$P = \frac{250{,}000}{(1 + 0.08)^{35}}$$

$$P \approx \frac{250{,}000}{14.785344}$$

$$P \approx 16{,}908.64$$

Assuming an annual inflation rate of 8%, the purchasing power of $250,000 will be about $16,908.64 in 2050.

CHECK YOUR PROGRESS 9 Suppose you purchase an insurance policy in 2015 that will provide you with $500,000 when you retire in 40 years. Assuming an annual inflation rate of 7%, what will be the purchasing power of half a million dollars in 2055?

Solution See page S11.

MATH MATTERS The Rule of 72

The **Rule of 72** states that the number of years necessary for prices to double is approximately equal to 72 divided by the annual inflation rate.

$$\text{Years to double} = \frac{72}{\text{annual inflation rate}}$$

For example, at an annual inflation rate of 6%, prices will double in approximately 12 years.

$$\text{Years to double} = \frac{72}{\text{annual inflation rate}} = \frac{72}{6} = 12$$

Effective Interest Rate

When interest is compounded, the annual rate of interest is called the **nominal rate**. The **effective rate** is the simple interest rate that would yield the same amount of interest after 1 year. When a bank advertises a "7% annual interest rate compounded daily and yielding 7.25%," the nominal interest rate is 7% and the effective rate is 7.25%.

QUESTION A bank offers a savings account that pays 2.75% annual interest, compounded daily and yielding 2.79%. What is the effective rate on this account? What is the nominal rate?

POINT OF INTEREST

According to the Federal Reserve Board, the value of U.S. currency in circulation increased 1013% from 1980 to 2015, to $1.39 trillion. (*Source:* www.federalreserve.gov)

Consider $100 deposited at 6%, compounded monthly, for 1 year.

The future value after 1 year is $106.17.

$$A = P\left(1 + \frac{r}{n}\right)^{nt}$$

$$A = 100\left(1 + \frac{0.06}{12}\right)^{12 \cdot 1}$$

$$A = 100(1 + 0.005)^{12}$$

$$A \approx 106.17$$

The interest earned in 1 year is $6.17.

$$I = A - P$$

$$I = 106.17 - 100$$

$$I = 6.17$$

ANSWER The effective rate is 2.79%. The nominal rate is 2.75%.

Now consider \$100 deposited at an annual simple interest rate of 6.17%.

The interest earned in 1 year is \$6.17.

$$I = Prt$$
$$I = 100(0.0617)(1)$$
$$I = 6.17$$

The interest earned on \$100 is the same when it is deposited at 6% compounded monthly as when it is deposited at an annual simple interest rate of 6.17%. 6.17% is the effective annual rate of a deposit that earns 6% compounded monthly.

In this example \$100 was used as the principal. When we use \$100 for P, we multiply the interest rate by 100. Remember that the interest rate is written as a decimal in the equation $I = Prt$, and a decimal is written as a percent by multiplying by 100. Therefore, when $P = 100$, the digits in the interest earned on the investment (\$6.17) are the same as the digits in the effective annual rate (6.17%).

EXAMPLE 10 Calculate the Effective Interest Rate

A credit union offers a certificate of deposit at an annual interest rate of 3%, compounded monthly. Find the effective rate. Round to the nearest hundredth of a percent.

Solution

Use the compound amount formula to find the future value of \$100 after 1 year.

$P = 100$, $r = 3\% = 0.03$, $n = 12$, $t = 1$

$$A = P\left(1 + \frac{r}{n}\right)^{nt}$$
$$A = 100\left(1 + \frac{0.03}{12}\right)^{12\cdot 1}$$
$$A = 100(1 + 0.0025)^{12}$$
$$A = 100(1.0025)^{12}$$
$$A \approx 100(1.030415957)$$
$$A \approx 103.04$$

Find the interest earned on the \$100.

$$I = A - P$$
$$I = 103.04 - 100$$
$$I = 3.04$$

The effective interest rate is 3.04%.

TAKE NOTE

To compare two investments or loan agreements, calculate the effective interest rate of each. When you are investing your money, you want the highest effective rate so that your money will earn more interest. If you are borrowing money, you want the lowest effective rate so that you will pay less interest on the loan.

CHECK YOUR PROGRESS 10 A bank offers a certificate of deposit at an annual interest rate of 4%, compounded quarterly. Find the effective rate. Round to the nearest hundredth of a percent.

Solution See page S11.

To compare two investments or loan agreements, we could calculate the effective annual rate of each. However, a shorter method involves comparing the compound amounts of each. Because the value of

$$\left(1 + \frac{r}{n}\right)^{nt}$$

is the compound amount of $1, we can compare the value of

$$\left(1 + \frac{r}{n}\right)^{nt}$$

for each alternative.

EXAMPLE 11 Compare Annual Yields

One bank advertises an interest rate of 5.5%, compounded quarterly, on a certificate of deposit. Another bank advertises an interest rate of 5.25%, compounded monthly. Which investment has the higher annual yield?

Solution

Calculate $\left(1 + \frac{r}{n}\right)^{nt}$ for each investment.

$$\left(1 + \frac{r}{n}\right)^{nt} = \left(1 + \frac{0.055}{4}\right)^{4\cdot 1} \approx 1.0561448 \qquad \left(1 + \frac{r}{n}\right)^{nt} = \left(1 + \frac{0.0525}{12}\right)^{12\cdot 1} \approx 1.0537819$$

Compare the two compound amounts.

$$1.0561448 > 1.0537819$$

An investment that earns 5.5% compounded quarterly has a higher annual yield than an investment that earns 5.25% compounded monthly.

CHECK YOUR PROGRESS 11 Which investment has the higher annual yield, one that earns 5% compounded quarterly or one that earns 5.25% compounded semiannually?

Solution See page S11.

MATH MATTERS Saving for Retirement

The graph below shows the results of a survey in which workers were asked to estimate the amount of money they would need to retire comfortably.

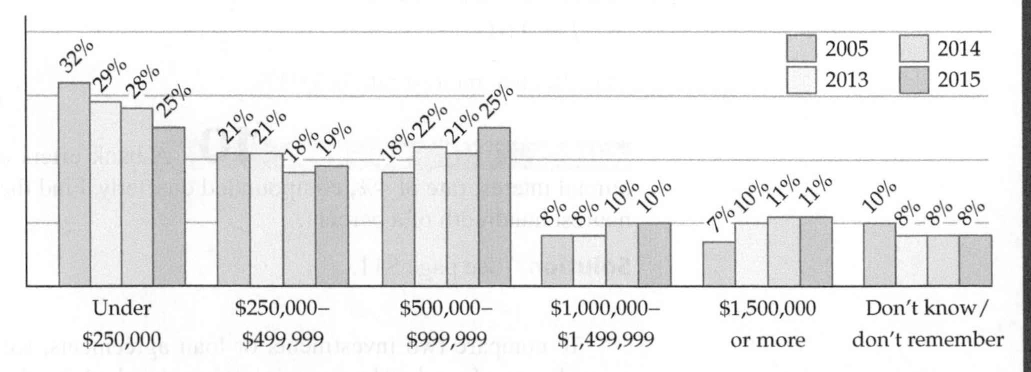

Source: Employee Benefit Research Institute and Greenwald & Associates, 2005–2015 Retirement Confidence Surveys

EXCURSION

Consumer Price Index

An **index number** measures the change in a quantity, such as cost, over a period of time. One of the most widely used indexes is the Consumer Price Index (CPI). The CPI, which includes the selling prices of key consumer goods and services, indicates the relative change in the price of these items over time. It measures the effect of inflation on the cost of goods and services.

The main components of the Consumer Price Index, shown below, are the costs of housing, food, transportation, medical care, clothing, recreation, and education.

TAKE NOTE

The category "Recreation" includes television sets, cable TV, pets and pet products, sports equipment, and admission tickets.

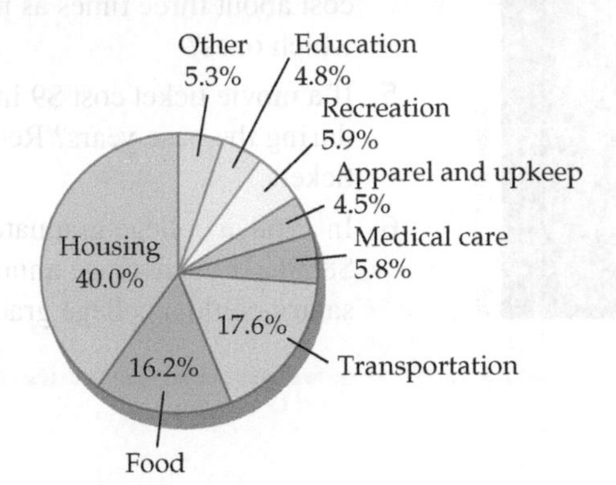

Components of the Consumer Price Index
SOURCE: U.S. Bureau of Labor Statistics

The CPI is a measure of the cost of living for consumers. The government publishes monthly and annual figures on the Consumer Price Index.

TAKE NOTE

You can obtain current and historical data on the Consumer Price Index by visiting the website of the Bureau of Labor Statistics at www.bls.gov.

The Consumer Price Index has a base period, 1982–1984, from which to make comparisons. The CPI for the base period is 100. The CPI for October 2010 was 218.9. This means that $100 in the period 1982–1984 had the same purchasing power as $218.90 in October of 2010.

An index number is actually a percent written without a percent sign. The CPI of 218.9 for October 2010 means that the average cost of consumer goods at that time was 218.9% of their cost in the 1982–1984 period.

The table below gives the CPI for various products in December 2015.

Product	CPI
All items	236.525
Food	247.903
Housing	282.394
Apparel	122.792
Transportation	294.081
Medical care	481.983
Recreation	115.626
Education	244.777

The Consumer Price Index, December 2015
SOURCE: U.S. Bureau of Labor Statistics

EXCURSION EXERCISES

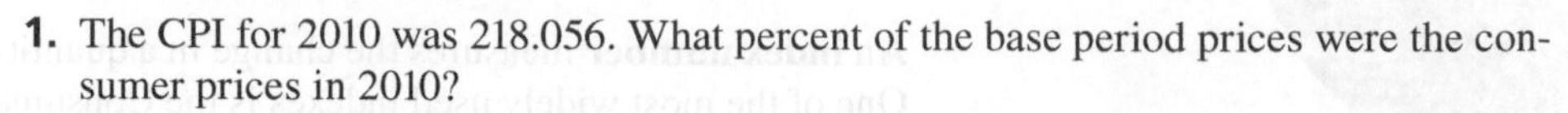

Solve the following.

Andersen Ross/Getty Images

1. The CPI for 2010 was 218.056. What percent of the base period prices were the consumer prices in 2010?
2. The CPI for 2014 was 236.736. The percent increase in consumer prices from 2014 to 2015 was 0.8%. Find the CPI for 2015. Round to the nearest hundredth.
3. The CPI for 2012 was 229.939. The CPI for 2015 was 237.017. Find the percent increase in consumer prices for this time period. Round to the nearest hundredth of a percent.
4. Of the items listed in the table on the preceding page, are there any items that cost about three times as much in 2015 as they cost during the base period? If so, which ones?
5. If a movie ticket cost $9 in 2015, what would a comparable movie ticket have cost during the base years? Recall that the category "Recreation" includes admission tickets.
6. In 1968, a college graduate could expect to earn an average annual starting salary of $8500. If the average annual inflation rate from 1968 to 2016 was 4.1%, what starting salary could a college graduate expect to earn in 2016?

EXERCISE SET 3.2

■ In Exercises 1 to 8, calculate the compound amount. Use the compound amount formula.

1. $P = \$1200$, $r = 7\%$ compounded semiannually, $t = 12$ years
2. $P = \$3500$, $r = 8\%$ compounded semiannually, $t = 14$ years
3. $P = \$500$, $r = 9\%$ compounded quarterly, $t = 6$ years
4. $P = \$7000$, $r = 4\%$ compounded quarterly, $t = 9$ years
5. $P = \$8500$, $r = 9\%$ compounded monthly, $t = 10$ years
6. $P = \$6400$, $r = 6\%$ compounded monthly, $t = 3$ years
7. $P = \$9600$, $r = 9\%$ compounded daily, $t = 3$ years
8. $P = \$1700$, $r = 9\%$ compounded daily, $t = 5$ years

■ In Exercises 9 to 14, calculate the compound amount. Use a calculator with a financial mode.

9. $P = \$1600$, $r = 8\%$ compounded quarterly, $t = 10$ years
10. $P = \$4200$, $r = 6\%$ compounded semiannually, $t = 8$ years
11. $P = \$3000$, $r = 5\%$ compounded monthly, $t = 5$ years
12. $P = \$9800$, $r = 10\%$ compounded quarterly, $t = 4$ years
13. $P = \$1700$, $r = 9\%$ compounded semiannually, $t = 3$ years
14. $P = \$8600$, $r = 3\%$ compounded semiannually, $t = 5$ years

■ In Exercises 15 to 20, calculate the future value.

15. $P = \$7500$, $r = 6\%$ compounded monthly, $t = 5$ years
16. $P = \$1800$, $r = 9.5\%$ compounded annually, $t = 10$ years
17. $P = \$4600$, $r = 5\%$ compounded semiannually, $t = 12$ years
18. $P = \$9000$, $r = 5.5\%$ compounded quarterly, $t = 3$ years
19. $P = \$22{,}000$, $r = 9\%$ compounded monthly, $t = 7$ years
20. $P = \$5200$, $r = 8.1\%$ compounded daily, $t = 9$ years

■ In Exercises 21 to 26, calculate the present value.

21. $A = \$25{,}000$, $r = 10\%$ compounded quarterly, $t = 12$ years
22. $A = \$20{,}000$, $r = 6\%$ compounded monthly, $t = 5$ years
23. $A = \$40{,}000$, $r = 7.5\%$ compounded annually, $t = 35$ years
24. $A = \$10{,}000$, $r = 4\%$ compounded semiannually, $t = 30$ years
25. $A = \$15{,}000$, $r = 8\%$ compounded quarterly, $t = 5$ years
26. $A = \$50{,}000$, $r = 3\%$ compounded monthly, $t = 5$ years

27. Compound Amount Calculate the compound amount when $8000 is deposited in an account earning 8% interest, compounded quarterly, for 5 years.

28. Compound Amount Calculate the compound amount when $3000 is deposited in an account earning 10% interest, compounded semiannually, for 3 years.

29. Compound Amount If you leave $2500 in an account earning 9% interest, compounded daily, how much money will be in the account after 4 years?

30. Compound Amount What is the compound amount when $1500 is deposited in an account earning an interest rate of 6%, compounded monthly, for 2 years?

31. Future Value What is the future value of $4000 earning 6% interest, compounded monthly, for 6 years?

32. Future Value Calculate the future value of $8000 earning 8% interest, compounded quarterly, for 10 years.

33. Compound Interest How much interest is earned in 3 years on $2000 deposited in an account paying 6% interest, compounded quarterly?

34. Compound Interest How much interest is earned in 5 years on $8500 deposited in an account paying 9% interest, compounded semiannually?

35. Compound Interest Calculate the amount of interest earned in 8 years on $15,000 deposited in an account paying 10% interest, compounded quarterly.

36. Compound Interest Calculate the amount of interest earned in 6 years on $20,000 deposited in an account paying 4% interest, compounded monthly.

37. Compound Interest How much money should be invested in an account that earns 6% interest, compounded monthly, in order to have $15,000 in 5 years?

38. Compound Interest How much money should be invested in an account that earns 7% interest, compounded quarterly, in order to have $10,000 in 5 years?

39. Compound Interest $1000 is deposited for 5 years in an account that earns 9% interest.

a. Calculate the simple interest earned.

b. Calculate the interest earned if interest is compounded daily.

c. How much more interest is earned on the account when the interest is compounded daily?

40. Compound Interest $10,000 is deposited for 2 years in an account that earns 5% interest.

a. Calculate the simple interest earned.

b. Calculate the interest earned if interest is compounded daily.

c. How much more interest is earned on the account when the interest is compounded daily?

41. Future Value $15,000 is deposited for 4 years in an account earning 8% interest.

a. Calculate the future value of the investment if interest is compounded semiannually.

b. Calculate the future value if interest is compounded quarterly.

c. How much greater is the future value of the investment when the interest is compounded quarterly?

42. Future Value $25,000 is deposited for 3 years in an account earning 6% interest.

a. Calculate the future value of the investment if interest is compounded annually.

b. Calculate the future value if interest is compounded semiannually.

c. How much greater is the future value of the investment when the interest is compounded semiannually?

43. Compound Interest $10,000 is deposited for 2 years in an account earning 8% interest.

a. Calculate the interest earned if interest is compounded semiannually.

b. Calculate the interest earned if interest is compounded quarterly.

c. How much more interest is earned on the account when the interest is compounded quarterly?

44. Compound Interest $20,000 is deposited for 5 years in an account earning 6% interest.

a. Calculate the interest earned if interest is compounded annually.

b. Calculate the interest earned if interest is compounded semiannually.

c. How much more interest is earned on the account when the interest is compounded semiannually?

45. Loans To help pay your college expenses, you borrow $7000 and agree to repay the loan at the end of 5 years at 8% interest, compounded quarterly.

a. What is the maturity value of the loan?

b. How much interest are you paying on the loan?

46. Loans You borrow $6000 to help pay your college expenses. You agree to repay the loan at the end of 5 years at 10% interest, compounded quarterly.

a. What is the maturity value of the loan?

b. How much interest are you paying on the loan?

47. Present Value A couple plans to save for their child's college education. What principal must be deposited by the parents when their child is born in order to have $40,000 when the child reaches the age of 18? Assume the money earns 8% interest, compounded quarterly.

Andresr/Shutterstock.com

48. Present Value A couple plans to invest money for their child's college education. What principal must be deposited by the parents when their child turns 10 in order to have $30,000 when the child reaches the age of 18? Assume that the money earns 8% interest, compounded quarterly.

49. Present Value You want to retire in 30 years with $1,000,000 in investments.

a. How much money would you have to invest today at 9% interest, compounded daily, in order to have $1,000,000 in 30 years?

b. How much will the $1,000,000 generate in interest each year if it is invested at 9% interest, compounded daily?

50. Present Value You want to retire in 40 years with $1,000,000 in investments.

a. How much money must you invest today at 8.1% interest, compounded daily, in order to have $1,000,000 in 40 years?

b. How much will the $1,000,000 generate in interest each year if it is invested at 8.1% interest, compounded daily?

51. Compound Amount You deposit $5000 in a two-year certificate of deposit (CD) earning 3.1% interest, compounded daily. At the end of the 2 years, you reinvest the compound amount in another 2-year CD. The interest rate on the second CD is 2.2%, compounded daily. What is the compound amount when the second CD matures?

52. Compound Amount You deposit $7500 in a 2-year certificate of deposit (CD) earning 2.4% interest, compounded daily. At the end of the 2 years, you reinvest the compound amount plus an additional $7500 in another 2-year CD. The interest rate on the second CD is 2.9%, compounded daily. What is the compound amount when the second CD matures?

53. Inflation The average monthly rent for a three-bedroom apartment in Denver, Colorado, is $1249. Using an annual inflation rate of 7%, find the average monthly rent in 15 years.

54. Inflation The average cost of housing in Greenville, North Carolina, is $140,300. Using an annual inflation rate of 7%, find the average cost of housing in 10 years.

55. Inflation Suppose your salary in 2015 is $40,000. Assuming an annual inflation rate of 7%, what salary do you need to earn in 2020 in order to have the same purchasing power?

56. Inflation Suppose your salary in 2015 is $50,000. Assuming an annual inflation rate of 6%, what salary do you need to earn in 2025 in order to have the same purchasing power?

57. Inflation In 2014, you purchase an insurance policy that will provide you with $125,000 when you retire in 2054. Assuming an annual inflation rate of 6%, what will be the purchasing power of the $125,000 in 2054?

58. Inflation You purchase an insurance policy in the year 2015 that will provide you with $250,000 when you retire in 25 years. Assuming an annual inflation rate of 8%, what will be the purchasing power of the quarter-of-a-million dollars in 2040?

59. Inflation A retired couple have a fixed income of $3500 per month. Assuming an annual inflation rate of 7%, what is the purchasing power of their monthly income in 5 years?

60. Inflation A retired couple have a fixed income of $46,000 per year. Assuming an annual inflation rate of 6%, what is the purchasing power of their annual income in 10 years?

■ In Exercises 61 to 68, calculate the effective annual rate for an investment that earns the given rate of return. Round to the nearest hundredth of a percent.

61. 7.2% interest compounded quarterly

62. 8.4% interest compounded quarterly

63. 7.5% interest compounded monthly

64. 6.9% interest compounded monthly

65. 8.1% interest compounded daily

66. 6.3% interest compounded daily

67. 5.94% interest compounded monthly

68. 6.27% interest compounded monthly

■ **Inflation** In Exercises 69 to 76, you are given the 2009 price of an item. Use an inflation rate of 6% to calculate its price in 2014, 2019, and 2029. Round to the nearest cent.

69. Gasoline: $3.00 per gallon

70. Milk: $3.35 per gallon

71. Loaf of bread: $2.69

72. Sunday newspaper: $2.25

73. Ticket to a movie: $9

74. Paperback novel: $12.00

75. House: $275,000

76. Car: $24,000

■ In Exercises 77 to 82, calculate the purchasing power using an annual inflation rate of 7%. Round to the nearest cent.

77. $50,000 in 10 years

78. $25,000 in 8 years

79. $100,000 in 20 years

80. $30,000 in 15 years

81. $75,000 in 5 years

82. $20,000 in 25 years

83. a. Complete the table.

Nominal rate	Effective rate
4% annual compounding	
4% semiannual compounding	
4% quarterly compounding	
4% monthly compounding	
4% daily compounding	

b. As the number of compounding periods increases, does the effective rate increase or decrease?

84. Effective Interest Rate Beth Chipman has money in a savings account that earns an annual interest rate of 3%, compounded quarterly. What is the effective rate of interest on Beth's account? Round to the nearest hundredth of a percent.

85. Effective Interest Rate Blake Hamilton has money in a savings account that earns an annual interest rate of 3%, compounded monthly. What is the effective rate of interest on Blake's savings? Round to the nearest hundredth of a percent.

86. Annual Yield One bank advertises an interest rate of 6.6%, compounded quarterly, on a certificate of deposit. Another bank advertises an interest rate of 6.25%, compounded monthly. Which investment has the higher annual yield?

87. Annual Yield Which has the higher annual yield, 6% compounded quarterly or 6.25% compounded semiannually?

88. Annual Yield Which investment has the higher annual yield, one earning 7.8% compounded monthly or one earning 7.5% compounded daily?

89. Annual Yield One bank advertises an interest rate of 5.8%, compounded quarterly, on a certificate of deposit. Another bank advertises an interest rate of 5.6%, compounded monthly. Which investment has a higher annual yield?

EXTENSIONS

90. Continuous Compounding In our discussion of compound interest, we used annual, semiannual, monthly, quarterly, and daily compounding periods. When interest is compounded daily, it is compounded 360 times a year. If interest were compounded twice daily, it would be compounded $360(2) = 720$ times a year. If interest were compounded four times a day, it would be compounded $360(4) = 1440$ times a year. Remember that the more frequent the compounding period, the more interest earned on the account. Therefore, if interest is compounded more frequently than daily, an investment will earn even more interest than it would if interest were compounded daily.

Some banking institutions advertise **continuous compounding**, which means that the number of compounding periods per year gets very, very large. When compounding continuously, instead of using the compound amount formula $A = P\left(1 + \frac{r}{n}\right)^{nt}$, we use the following formula.

$$A = Pe^{rt}$$

In this formula, A is the compound amount when P dollars are deposited at an annual interest rate of r percent compounded continuously for t years. The number e is approximately equal to 2.7182818.

The number e is found in many real-world applications. It is an irrational number, so its decimal representation never terminates or repeats. Calculators have an $\boxed{e^x}$ key for evaluating exponential expressions in which e is the base.

To calculate the compound amount when $10,000 is invested for 5 years at an interest rate of 10%, compounded continuously, use the formula for continuous compounding. Substitute the following values into the formula: $P = 10{,}000$, $r = 10\% = 0.10$, and $t = 5$.

$$A = Pe^{rt}$$
$$A \approx 10{,}000(2.7182818)^{0.10(5)}$$
$$A \approx 16{,}487.21$$

The compound amount is $16,487.21.

In the following exercises, calculate the compound interest when interest is compounded continuously.

a. $P = \$5000$, $r = 8\%$, $t = 6$ years
b. $P = \$8000$, $r = 7\%$, $t = 15$ years
c. $P = \$12{,}000$, $r = 9\%$, $t = 10$ years
d. $P = \$7000$, $r = 6\%$, $t = 8$ years
e. $P = \$3000$, $r = 7.5\%$, $t = 4$ years
f. $P = \$9000$, $r = 8.6\%$, $t = 5$ years

Solve the following exercises.

g. Calculate the compound amount when $2500 is deposited in an account earning 11% interest, compounded continuously, for 12 years.
h. What is the future value of $15,000 earning 9.5% interest, compounded continuously, for 7 years?
i. How much interest is earned in 9 years on $6000 deposited in an account paying 10% interest, compounded continuously?
j. $25,000 is deposited for 10 years in an account that earns 8% interest. Calculate the future value of the investment if interest is compounded quarterly and if interest is compounded continuously. How much greater is the future value of the investment when interest is compounded continuously?

SECTION 3.3 Credit Cards and Consumer Loans

Credit Cards

When a customer uses a credit card to make a purchase, the customer is actually receiving a loan. Therefore, there is frequently an added cost to the consumer who purchases on credit. This added cost may be in the form of an annual fee or interest charges on purchases. A **finance charge** is an amount paid in excess of the cash price; it is the cost to the customer for the use of credit.

Most credit card companies issue monthly bills. The due date on the bill is usually 1 month after the billing date (the date the bill is prepared and sent to the customer). If the bill is paid in full by the due date, the customer pays no finance charge. If the bill is not paid in full by the due date, a finance charge is added to the next bill.

Suppose a credit card billing date is the 10th day of each month. If a credit card purchase is made on April 15, then May 10 is the billing date (the 10th day of the month following April). The due date is June 10 (one month from the billing date). If the bill is paid in full before June 10, no finance charge is added. However, if the bill is not paid in full, interest charges on the outstanding balance will start to accrue (be added) on June 10, and any purchase made after June 10 will immediately start accruing interest.

The most common method of determining finance charges is the **average daily balance method**. Interest charges are based on the credit card's average daily balance, which is calculated by dividing the sum of the total amounts owed each day of the month by the number of days in the billing period.

Nerthuz/Shutterstock.com

Average Daily Balance

$$\text{Average daily balance} = \frac{\text{sum of the total amounts owed each day of the month}}{\text{number of days in the billing period}}$$

POINT OF INTEREST

The average American has 2.24 credit cards. There are about 180 million credit card holders in the United States. Of these, 58% pay the full balance on the card each month. For the remaining card holders, the average credit card balance is $6600.

An example of calculating the average daily balance follows.

Suppose an unpaid bill for $315 had a due date of April 10. A purchase of $28 was made on April 12, and $123 was charged on April 24. A payment of $50 was made on April 15. The next billing date is May 10. The interest on the average daily balance is 1.5% per month. Find the finance charge on the May 10 bill.

Solution

To find the finance charge, first prepare a table showing the unpaid balance for each purchase, the number of days the balance is owed, and the product of these numbers. A negative sign in the Payments or Purchases column of the table indicates that a payment was made on that date.

Date	Payments or purchases	Balance each day	Number of days until balance changes	Unpaid balance times number of days
April 10–11		$315	2	$630
April 12–14	$28	$343	3	$1029
April 15–23	−$50	$293	9	$2637
April 24–May 9	$123	$416	16	$6656
Total				$10,952

The sum of the total amounts owed each day of the month is $10,952.

Find the average daily balance.

$$\text{Average daily balance} = \frac{\text{sum of the total amounts owed each day of the month}}{\text{number of days in the billing period}}$$

$$= \frac{10{,}952}{30} \approx 365.07$$

Find the finance charge.

$$I = Prt$$
$$I = 365.07(0.015)(1)$$
$$I \approx 5.48$$

The finance charge on the May 10 bill is $5.48.

EXAMPLE 1 **Calculate Interest on a Credit Card Bill**

An unpaid bill for $620 had a due date of March 10. A purchase of $214 was made on March 15, and $67 was charged on March 30. A payment of $200 was made on March 22. The interest on the average daily balance is 1.5% per month. Find the finance charge on the April 10 bill.

Solution

First calculate the sum of the total amounts owed each day of the month.

Date	Payments or purchases	Balance each day	Number of days until balance changes	Unpaid balance times number of days
March 10–11		$620	5	$3100
March 15–21	$214	$834	7	$5838
March 22–29	−$200	$634	8	$5072
March 30–April 9	$67	$701	11	$7711
Total				$21,721

The sum of the total amounts owed each day of the month is $21,721.

POINT OF INTEREST

In 1950, Frank McNamara issued to 200 friends a card that could be used to pay for food at various restaurants in New York. The card, called a Diner's Card, spawned the credit card industry.

B Christopher/Alamy Stock Photo

Find the average daily balance.

$$\text{Average daily balance} = \frac{\text{sum of the total amounts owed each day of the month}}{\text{number of days in the billing period}}$$

$$= \frac{21{,}721}{31} \approx \$700.68$$

Find the finance charge.

$I = Prt$

$I = 700.68(0.015)(1)$

$I \approx 10.51$

The finance charge on the April 10 bill is $10.51.

CHECK YOUR PROGRESS 1 A bill for $1024 was due on July 1. Purchases of $315 were made on July 7, and $410 was charged on July 22. A payment of $400 was made on July 15. The interest on the average daily balance is 1.2% per month. Find the finance charge on the August 1 bill.

Solution See page S11.

MATH MATTERS Credit Card Debt

The graph below shows how long it would take you to pay off a credit card debt of $5000 if you paid the minimum monthly payment* plus an additional amount each month. For instance, the bar above 50 shows that it would take approximately 57 months to repay the credit card balance if you paid the minimum monthly payment plus $50. The number inside the bar shows approximately how much interest you would pay over the repayment period.

If you have credit card debt and want to determine how long it will take you to pay off the debt, enter "debt payoff calculator" in a search engine on the Internet. Find a calculator that will calculate how long it will take to pay off the debt and the total amount of interest you will pay.

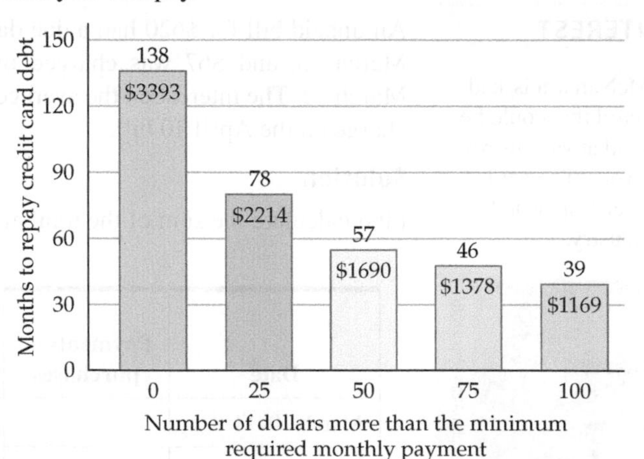

SOURCE: CardWeb.com

Note from the graph that if you paid $100 more than the minimum due each month, the debt would be repaid approximately 99 months sooner and you would save approximately $2224 in interest charges.

*For this illustration, we are assuming that the minimum monthly payment is 2% of the credit card balance plus the interest accrued for one month. The monthly interest rate on the credit card balance is 1.5%.

Annual Percentage Rate

TAKE NOTE

Note that both the effective interest rate discussed in Section 3.2 and the annual percentage rate discussed here reflect the cost of a loan on a yearly basis. Both are useful to the consumer interested in comparing loan offers.

Federal law, in the form of the Truth in Lending Act, requires that credit customers be made aware of the cost of credit. This law, passed by Congress in 1969, requires that a business issuing credit inform the consumer of all details of a credit transaction, including the true annual interest rate. The **true annual interest rate**, also called the **annual percentage rate (APR)** or **annual percentage yield (APY)**, is the effective annual interest rate on which credit payments are based.

The idea behind the APR is that interest is owed only on the *unpaid balance* of the loan. For instance, suppose you decide to borrow \$2400 from a bank that advertises a 10% *simple* interest rate. You want a 6-month loan and agree to repay the loan in six equal monthly payments. The simple interest due on the loan is

$$I = Prt$$
$$I = \$2400(0.10)\left(\frac{6}{12}\right)$$
$$I = \$120$$

The total amount to be repaid to the bank is

$$A = P + I$$
$$A = \$2400 + \$120$$
$$A = \$2520$$

The amount of each monthly payment is

$$\text{Monthly payment} = \frac{2520}{6} = \$420$$

During the first month, you still owe a total of \$2400. The interest on that amount is

$$I = Prt$$
$$I = \$2400(0.10)\left(\frac{1}{12}\right)$$
$$I = \$20$$

At the end of the first month, of the \$420 payment you make, \$20 is the interest payment and \$400 is applied to reducing the loan. Therefore, during the second month, you owe \$2400 − \$400 = \$2000. The interest on that amount is

$$I = Prt$$
$$I = \$2000(0.10)\left(\frac{1}{12}\right) \approx 16.667$$
$$I = \$16.67$$

At the end of the second month, of the \$420 payment you make, \$16.67 is the interest payment and \$403.33 is applied to reducing the loan. Therefore, during the third month, you owe \$2000 − \$403.33 = \$1596.67.

The point of these calculations is to demonstrate that each month, the amount you owe is decreasing, and not by a constant amount. From our calculations, the loan decreased by \$400 the first month and by \$403.33 the second month. Similar calculations were made in the car loan example presented in the Excursion at the end of Section 3.1.

The Truth in Lending Act stipulates that the interest rate for a loan be calculated only on the amount owed at a particular time, not on the original amount borrowed. All loans must be stated according to this standard, thereby making it possible for a consumer to compare different loans.

CALCULATOR NOTE 

You can calculate APR using the Finance option on a TI-83/84 by pressing [APPS] and then selecting Finance. Press [ENTER]. Input the values. Note on the screen below that the payment is entered as a negative number. Amounts paid out are normally entered as negative numbers.

```
N=6
I%=0
PV=2400
PMT=-420
FV=0
P/Y=12
C/Y=12
PMT: END BEGIN
```

Move the cursor to I% and then press [ALPHA] [SOLVE]. The actual APR is then displayed next to I%.

```
N=6
I%=16.94488071
PV=2400
PMT=-420
FV=0
P/Y=12
C/Y=12
PMT: END BEGIN
```

The APR is approximately 16.9%.

We can use the following formula to estimate the annual percentage rate (APR) on a simple interest rate installment loan.

Approximate Annual Percentage Rate (APR) Formula for a Simple Interest Rate Loan

The annual percentage rate (APR) of a simple interest rate loan can be approximated by

$$\text{APR} \approx \frac{2nr}{n+1}$$

where n is the number of payments and r is the simple interest rate.

For the loan described on the preceding page, $n = 6$ and $r = 10\% = 0.10$.

$$\text{APR} \approx \frac{2nr}{n+1}$$

$$\approx \frac{2(6)(0.10)}{6+1} = \frac{1.2}{7} \approx 0.171$$

The annual percentage rate on the loan is approximately 17.1%. Recall that the simple interest rate was 10%, much less than the actual rate. The Truth in Lending Act provides the consumer with a standard interest rate, APR, so that it is possible to compare loans. The 10% simple interest loan described above is equivalent to an APR loan of about 17%.

EXAMPLE 2 Calculate a Finance Charge and an APR

You purchase a refrigerator for $675. You pay 20% down and agree to repay the balance in 12 equal monthly payments. The finance charge on the balance is 9% simple interest.

a. Find the finance charge.

b. Estimate the annual percentage rate. Round to the nearest tenth of a percent.

Solution

a. To find the finance charge, first calculate the down payment.

$$\text{Down payment} = \text{percent down} \times \text{purchase price}$$
$$= 0.20 \times 675 = 135$$

$$\text{Amount financed} = \text{purchase price} - \text{down payment}$$
$$= 675 - 135 = 540$$

Calculate the interest owed on the loan.

$$\text{Interest owed} = \text{finance rate} \times \text{amount financed}$$
$$= 0.09 \times 540 = 48.60$$

The finance charge is $48.60.

b. Use the APR formula to estimate the annual percentage rate.

$$\text{APR} \approx \frac{2nr}{n+1}$$

$$\approx \frac{2(12)(0.09)}{12+1} = \frac{2.16}{13} \approx 0.166$$

The annual percentage rate is approximately 16.6%.

CHECK YOUR PROGRESS 2 You purchase a washing machine and dryer for $750. You pay 20% down and agree to repay the balance in 12 equal monthly payments. The finance charge on the balance is 8% simple interest.

a. Find the finance charge.

b. Estimate the annual percentage rate. Round to the nearest tenth of a percent.

Solution See page S12.

Consumer Loans: Calculating Monthly Payments

The stated interest rate for most consumer loans, such as a car loan, is normally the annual percentage rate, APR, as required by the Truth in Lending Act. The payment amount for these loans is given by the following formula.

Payment Formula for an APR Loan

The payment for a loan based on APR is given by

$$PMT = A\left(\frac{\frac{r}{n}}{1-\left(1+\frac{r}{n}\right)^{-nt}}\right)$$

where PMT is the payment, A is the loan amount, r is the annual interest rate, n is the number of payments per year, and t is the number of years.

CALCULATOR NOTE

You can calculate the monthly payment using the Finance option on a TI-83/84 calculator. Press APPS ENTER ENTER. Input the known values. Typically, financial calculations use PV (present value) for the loan amount and FV (future value) for the amount owed at the end of the loan period, usually 0. P/Y = 12 and C/Y = 12 mean that payments and interest are calculated monthly (12 times a year). Now place the cursor at PMT= and press ALPHA [SOLVE].

```
N=48
I%=9.5
PV=5995
PMT=-150.6132
FV=0
P/Y=12
C/Y=12
PMT: END BEGIN
```

The monthly payment is $150.61.

QUESTION For a 4-year loan repaid on a monthly basis, what is the value of nt in the formula above?

The payment formula given above is used to calculate monthly payments on most consumer loans. In Example 3 we calculate the monthly payment for a new refrigerator, and in Example 4 we calculate the monthly payment for a car loan.

EXAMPLE 3 **Calculate a Monthly Payment**

Integrated Technologies is offering anyone who purchases a refrigerator an annual interest rate of 9.5% for 4 years. If Andrea Smyer purchases a luxury model refrigerator for $5995 from Integrated Technologies, find her monthly payment.

Solution

To calculate the monthly payment, you will need a calculator. The following keystrokes will work on most scientific calculators. You could also use a calculator with a finance app, as shown in the Calculator Note at the left.

First calculate $\frac{r}{n}$ and store the result.

$$\frac{r}{n} = \frac{0.095}{12} \approx 0.00791667$$

Keystrokes: 0.095 ÷ 12 ≈ 0.00791667 STO

ANSWER nt = (number of payments per year)(number of years) = (12)(4) = 48.

Calculate the monthly payment. For a 4-year loan, $nt = 12(4) = 48$.

$$PMT = A\left(\frac{\frac{r}{n}}{1 - \left(1 + \frac{r}{n}\right)^{-nt}}\right)$$

$$= 5995\left(\frac{0.095/12}{1 - (1 + 0.095/12)^{-48}}\right) \approx 150.61$$

Keystrokes: 5995 [x] [RCL] [=] [÷] [(] 1 [−] [(] 1 [+] [RCL] [)] [y^x] 48 [+/−] [)] [=]

The monthly payment is $150.61.

CHECK YOUR PROGRESS 3 Carlos Menton purchases a new laptop computer from Knox Computer Solutions for $1499. If the sales tax is 4.25% of the purchase price and Carlos finances the total cost, including sales tax, for 3 years at an annual interest rate of 8.4%, find the monthly payment.

Solution See page S12.

EXAMPLE 4 Calculate a Car Payment

A web page designer purchases a car for $18,395.

a. If the sales tax is 6.5% of the purchase price, find the amount of the sales tax.

b. If the car license fee is 1.2% of the purchase price, find the amount of the license fee.

c. If the designer makes a $2500 down payment, find the amount of the loan the designer needs.

d. Assuming the designer gets the loan in part c at an annual interest rate of 7.5% for 4 years, determine the monthly car payment.

Solution

a. Sales tax $= 0.065(18{,}395) = 1195.675$

The sales tax is $1195.68.

b. License fee $= 0.012(18{,}395) = 220.74$

The license fee is $220.74.

c. Loan amount = purchase price + sales tax + license fee − down payment

$= 18{,}395 + 1195.68 + 220.74 - 2500$

$= 17{,}311.42$

The loan amount is $17,311.42.

d. To calculate the monthly payment, you will need a calculator. The following keystrokes will work on most scientific calculators.

First calculate $\frac{r}{n}$ and store the result.

$$\frac{r}{n} = \frac{0.075}{12} = 0.00625$$

Keystrokes: 0.075 [÷] 12 = 0.00625 [STO]

CALCULATOR NOTE

A typical TI-83/84 screen for the calculation in Example 4 is shown below.

```
N=48
I%=7.5
PV=17311.42
PMT=-418.5711
FV=0
P/Y=12
C/Y=12
PMT: END BEGIN
```

The monthly payment is $418.57.

Calculate the monthly payment. For a 4-year loan, $nt = 12(4) = 48$.

$$PMT = A\left(\frac{\frac{r}{n}}{1-\left(1+\frac{r}{n}\right)^{-nt}}\right)$$

$$= 17{,}311.42\left(\frac{0.00625}{1-(1+0.00625)^{-48}}\right) \approx 418.57$$

Keystrokes:

17311.42 [x] [RCL] [=] [÷] [(] 1 [−] [(] 1 [+] [RCL] [)] [y^x] 48 [+/−] [)] [=]

The monthly payment is $418.57.

CHECK YOUR PROGRESS 4 A school superintendent purchases a new sedan for $26,788.

a. If the sales tax is 5.25% of the purchase price, find the amount of the sales tax.

b. The superintendent makes a $2500 down payment and the license fee is $145. Find the amount the superintendent must finance.

c. Assuming the superintendent gets the loan in part b at an annual interest rate of 8.1% for 5 years, determine the superintendent's monthly car payment.

Solution See page S12.

MATH MATTERS Payday Loans

mikeledray/Shutterstock.com

An ad reads,

Get cash until payday! Loans of $100 or more available.

These ads refer to *payday loans*, which go by a variety of names, such as cash advance loans, check advance loans, post-dated check loans, or deferred deposit check loans. These types of loans are offered by finance companies and check-cashing companies.

Typically a borrower writes a personal check payable to the lender for the amount borrowed plus a *service fee*. The company gives the borrower the amount of the check minus the fee, which is normally a percent of the amount borrowed. The amount borrowed is usually repaid after payday, normally within a few weeks.

Under the Truth in Lending Act, the cost of a payday loan must be disclosed. Along with other information, the borrower must receive, in writing, a statement of the APR for such a loan. To understand just how expensive these loans can be, suppose a borrower receives a loan for $100 for 2 weeks and pays a fee of $10. The APR for this loan can be calculated using the formula in this section or a graphing calculator. Screens for a TI-83/84 calculator are shown below.

TAKE NOTE

Some states have enacted laws that regulate the amount a person can borrow on a payday loan and the maximum fee that can be charged. In California, for instance, the maximum amount that can be borrowed at one time is $300, and the maximum fee is $45. The borrower receives $265. The APR on the loan is 460% for a two-week loan!

```
N=1
I%=0
PV=100
PMT=-110
FV=0
P/Y=26
C/Y=26
PMT: END BEGIN
```

$N = 1$ (number of payments)
I% is unknown.
$PV = 100$ (amount borrowed)
$PMT = -110$ (the payment)
$FV = 0$ (no money is owed after all the payments)
$P/Y = 26$ (There are 26 2-week periods in 1 year.)
$C/Y = 26$

continued

```
N=1
I%=260
PV=100
PMT=-110
FV=0
P/Y=26
C/Y=26
PMT: END BEGIN
```

Place the cursor at I%=. Press ALPHA [SOLVE].

The annual interest rate is 260%.

To give you an idea of the enormity of a 260% APR, if the loan on the refrigerator in Example 3, page 195, were based on a 260% interest rate, the monthly payment on the refrigerator would be $1299.02!

Consumer Loans: Calculating Loan Payoffs

Sometimes a consumer wants to pay off a loan before the end of the loan term. For instance, suppose you have a five-year car loan but would like to purchase a new car after owning your car for 4 years. Because there is still 1 year remaining on the loan, you must pay off the remaining loan amount before purchasing another car.

This is not as simple as just multiplying the monthly car payment by 12 to arrive at the payoff amount. The reason, as we mentioned earlier, is that each payment includes both interest and principal. By solving the payment formula for an APR loan (see page 195) for A, the amount of the loan, we can calculate the payoff amount, which is just the remaining principal.

TAKE NOTE

The APR loan payoff formula applies only to those situations in which all regular payments that have come due have been paid on time and no extra money has been paid toward the principal.

APR Loan Payoff Formula

The payoff amount for a loan based on APR is given by

$$A = PMT\left(\frac{1-\left(1+\frac{r}{n}\right)^{-U}}{\frac{r}{n}}\right)$$

where A is the loan payoff, PMT is the payment, r is the annual interest rate, n is the number of payments per year, and U is the number of *remaining* (or *unpaid*) payments.

EXAMPLE 5 Calculate a Payoff Amount

Allison Werke wants to pay off the loan on her jet ski that she has owned for 18 months. Allison's monthly payment is $284.67 on a 2-year loan at an annual percentage rate of 8.7%. Find the payoff amount.

Solution

Because Allison has owned the jet ski for 18 months of a 24-month (two-year) loan, she has six payments remaining. Thus $U = 6$, the number of unpaid or remaining payments. Here are the keystrokes to find the loan payoff.

Calculate $\frac{r}{n}$ and store the result.

$$\frac{r}{n} = \frac{0.087}{12} = 0.00725$$

Keystrokes: 0.087 [÷] 12 [=] 0.00725 [STO]

Use the APR loan payoff formula.

$$A = PMT\left(\frac{1-\left(1+\frac{r}{n}\right)^{-U}}{\frac{r}{n}}\right)$$

$$= 284.67\left(\frac{1-(1+0.00725)^{-6}}{0.00725}\right) \approx 1665.50$$

Keystrokes: 284.67 [×] [(] 1 [−] [(] 1 [+] [RCL] [)] [y^x] 6 [+/−] [)] [÷] [RCL] [=]

The loan payoff is $1665.50.

CHECK YOUR PROGRESS 5 Aaron Jefferson has a 5-year car loan based on an annual percentage rate of 8.4%. The monthly payment is $592.57. After 3 years, Aaron decides to purchase a new car and must pay off his car loan. Find the payoff amount.

Solution See page S12.

Student Loans

The student loan program that benefits many students today was part Title IV of the Higher Education Act of 1965. In 1988, Congress renamed the student loan program after Senator Robert T. Stafford, who authored a number of bills in support of students seeking post-secondary education. Stafford loans, as they are now called, are available to students through the Department of Education. Because the U.S. government guarantees the repayment of these loans to lenders, the interest rate on Stafford loans is usually lower than the rate on private student loans.

There are basically two types of Stafford loans: subsidized and unsubsidized. For a subsidized loan, the interest on the loan is paid by the government while the student is in school. For unsubsidized loans, the student is responsible for all the interest on the loan while in school. In 2011, Congress eliminated subsidized loans for students in any graduate school program.

There are many different repayment plans for student loans. We will look at payment plans that are fixed for the entire term of the loan. For a summary of all payment plans, see https://studentloans.gov.

EXAMPLE 6 Calculate the Monthly Payment of a Subsidized Student Loan

Lois Wellington received a 9-year subsidized student loan of $32,000 at an annual interest rate of 4.5%. Determine her monthly payment on the loan after she graduates in 3 years.

Solution

Because Lois has a subsidized loan, she does not have to pay the interest that would normally accrue on a loan during the time she does not make payments. Therefore, her payment can be calculated using the payment formula for an APR loan. The payment can be calculated using the keystrokes shown in Example 4. For this example, we will use Excel's PMT function.

	A	B
1	Present value	32000
2	Annual interest rate as a decimal	0.045
3	Number of years to repay loan	9
4	Monthly payment	−$360.88

Each cell in a spreadsheet is defined by its column and row. Present value is in cell A1; 32000 is in cell B1. Calculation of the monthly payment is based on the PMT function. Here is the format.

= PMT(rate, nper, pv, [fv], [type])

The equals sign is used to tell Excel that a formula follows: *PMT* is the name of the function, *rate* is the interest rate per period, *nper* is the total number of payments, *pv* is the present value (amount of the loan), [*fv*] is the future value of the loan, and [*type*] indicates whether the payment is due at the end of a period (type = 0) or the beginning of a period (type = 1). The brackets around *fv* and *type* indicate that these values are optional. If values are not given, Excel assumes they are 0.

For this example, the PMT function is

= PMT(B2/12,B3*12,B1,0,0)

TAKE NOTE

The negative sign in front of the monthly payment is used to show that Lois must make a payment—money is subtracted from her account.

Note that the *cell locations* are placed in the formula, not the actual values. Also note that because B2 is the annual interest rate, we must divide by 12 to get the monthly interest rate; because B3 is the number of years of the loan, we must multiply by 12 to get the number of monthly payments.

The monthly payment is calculated in B4. Lois's monthly payment is $360.88.

CHECK YOUR PROGRESS 6 Hudson Zavello received a 10-year subsidized student loan of $25,000 at an annual interest rate of 4.9%. Determine his monthly payment after he graduates in 2 years.

Solution See page S12.

For a non-subsidized loan, interest on the loan accrues from the beginning of the loan. This interest is added to the loan amount and then the monthly payment is calculated. To emphasize the difference, we are going to rework Example 6 assuming a non-subsidized loan.

EXAMPLE 7 Calculate the Monthly Payment of a Non-subsidized Student Loan

Lois Wellington received a 9-year non-subsidized student loan of $32,000 at an annual interest rate of 4.5%. Determine her monthly payment on the loan after she graduates in 3 years.

Solution

Because this is a non-subsidized loan, Lois owes interest on the loan for the 3 years she is not making payments. This is a simple interest loan, so we use the simple interest rate formula.

$I = Prt$ • Simple interest rate formula

$= 32{,}000(0.045)(3)$ • $P = 32{,}000, r = 0.045, t = 3$

$= 4320$

When Lois begins making monthly payments, she owes $4320 in interest plus the $32,000 she borrowed, for a total of $36,320. To calculate her monthly payment, we will use the spreadsheet in Example 6. Lois's monthly payment is $409.60.

	A	B
1	Present value	36320
2	Annual interest rate as a decimal	0.045
3	Number of years to repay loan	9
4	Monthly payment	−$409.60

Note that this payment is almost $50 more per month than that of the subsidized loan.

CHECK YOUR PROGRESS 7 Hudson Zavello received a 10-year non-subsidized student loan of $25,000 at an annual interest rate of 4.9%. Determine his monthly payment after he graduates in 2 years.

Solution See page S12.

Examples 6 and 7 illustrate some of the power of using a spreadsheet. Because the calculation is based on the number in the cell, changing that number automatically recalculates any value that depends on that number.

EXCURSION

Car Leases

Leasing a car may result in lower monthly car payments. However, at the end of the lease term, you do not own the car. Ownership of the car reverts to the dealer, who can then sell it as a used car and realize the profit from the sale.

The value of the car at the end of the lease term is called the **residual value** of the car. The residual value of a car is frequently based on a percent of the manufacturer's suggested retail price (MSRP) and normally varies between 40% and 60% of the MSRP, depending on the type of lease.

For instance, suppose the MSRP of a car is $18,500, and the residual value is 45% of the MSRP. Then

$$\text{Residual value} = 0.45 \cdot 18{,}500$$
$$= 8325$$

The residual value is $8325. This is the amount the dealer thinks the car will be worth at the end of the lease period. The person leasing the car, the lessee, usually has the option of purchasing the car at that price at the end of the lease.

In addition to the residual value of the car, the monthly lease payment for a car takes into consideration *net capitalized cost, the money factor, average monthly finance charge,* and *average monthly depreciation.* Each of these terms is defined below.

$$\textbf{Net capitalized cost} = \text{negotiated price} - \text{down payment} - \text{trade-in value}$$

$$\textbf{Money factor} = \frac{\text{annual interest rate}}{24}$$

$$\textbf{Average monthly finance charge}$$
$$= (\text{net capitalized cost} + \text{residual value}) \times \text{money factor}$$

$$\textbf{Average monthly depreciation} = \frac{\text{net capitalized cost} - \text{residual value}}{\text{term of the lease in months}}$$

Using these definitions, we have the following formula for a monthly lease payment.

Monthly Lease Payment Formula

The monthly lease payment formula is given by $P = F + D$, where P is the monthly lease payment, F is the average monthly finance charge, and D is the average monthly depreciation of the car.

Here is an example of calculating a monthly lease payment for a car.

The director of human resources for a company decides to lease a car for 30 months. Suppose the annual interest rate is 8.4%, the negotiated price is $29,500, there is no trade-in, and the down payment is $5000. Find the monthly lease payment. Assume that the residual value is 55% of the MSRP of $33,400.

Solution

$$\text{Net capitalized cost} = \text{negotiated price} - \text{down payment} - \text{trade-in value}$$
$$= 29{,}500 - 5000 - 0 = 24{,}500$$

$$\text{Residual value} = 0.55(33{,}400) = 18{,}370$$

$$\text{Money factor} = \frac{\text{Annual interest rate}}{24} = \frac{0.084}{24} = 0.0035$$

Average monthly finance charge

$$= (\text{net capitalized cost} + \text{residual value}) \times \text{money factor}$$
$$= (24{,}500 + 18{,}370) \times 0.0035$$
$$\approx 150.05$$

$$\text{Average monthly depreciation} = \frac{\text{net capitalized cost} - \text{residual value}}{\text{term of the lease in months}}$$
$$= \frac{24{,}500 - 18{,}370}{30}$$
$$\approx 204.33$$

Monthly lease payment

$$= \text{average monthly finance charge} + \text{average monthly depreciation}$$
$$= 150.05 + 204.33$$
$$= 354.38$$

The monthly lease payment is \$354.38.

TAKE NOTE

When a person purchases a car, any state sales tax must be paid at the time of the purchase. However, with a lease, you make a state sales tax payment each month.

Suppose, for instance, that in this example the state sales tax is 6% of the monthly lease payment. Then,

Total monthly lease payment

$$= 354.38 + 0.06(354.38)$$
$$\approx 375.64$$

EXCURSION EXERCISES

1. Suppose you decide to obtain a 4-year lease for a car and negotiate a selling price of \$28,990, including license fees. The trade-in value of your old car is \$3850. If you make a down payment of \$2400, the money factor is 0.0027, and the residual value is \$15,000, find each of the following.

a. The net capitalized cost

b. The average monthly finance charge

c. The average monthly depreciation

d. The monthly lease payment

2. Marcia Scripps obtains a 5-year lease for a Ford pickup and negotiates a selling price of \$37,115, including license fees. The trade-in value of her old car is \$2950. Assuming that she makes a down payment of \$3000, the money factor is 0.0035, and the residual value is \$16,500, find each of the following.

a. The net capitalized cost

b. The average monthly finance charge

c. The average monthly depreciation

d. The monthly lease payment

3. Jorge Cruz obtains a 3-year lease for an economy sedan and negotiates a selling price of \$22,100. The annual interest rate is 8.1%, the residual value is \$15,000, and Jorge makes a down payment of \$1000. Find each of the following.

a. The net capitalized cost

b. The money factor

c. The average monthly finance charge

d. The average monthly depreciation

e. The monthly lease payment

4. Suppose you obtain a 5-year lease for a Porsche and negotiate a selling price of \$165,000. The annual interest rate is 8.4%, the residual value is \$85,000, and you make a down payment of \$5000. Find each of the following.

a. The net capitalized cost

b. The money factor

c. The average monthly finance charge

d. The average monthly depreciation

e. The monthly lease payment

5. Find the monthly lease payment for a car for which the negotiated price is $31,900, the annual interest rate is 8%, the length of the lease is 5 years, and the residual value is 40% of the MSRP of $33,395. There is no down payment or trade-in.

6. Find the monthly lease payment for a car for which the negotiated price is $32,450, the annual interest rate is 3%, the length of the lease is 3 years, and the residual value is 35% of the MSRP of $34,990. There is no down payment or trade-in.

EXERCISE SET 3.3

■ In Exercises 1 to 4, calculate the finance charge for a credit card that has the given average daily balance and interest rate.

1. Average daily balance: $118.72; monthly interest rate: 1.25%
2. Average daily balance: $391.64; monthly interest rate: 1.75%
3. Average daily balance: $10,154.87; monthly interest rate: 1.5%
4. Average daily balance: $20,346.91; monthly interest rate: 1.25%
5. **Average Daily Balance** A credit card account had a $244 balance on March 5. A purchase of $152 was made on March 12, and a payment of $100 was made on March 28. Find the average daily balance if the billing date is April 5.
6. **Average Daily Balance** A credit card account has a $768 balance on April 1. A purchase of $316 was made on April 5, and a payment of $200 was made on April 18. Find the average daily balance if the new billing date is May 1.
7. **Finance Charges** A charge account had a balance of $944 on May 5. A purchase of $255 was made on May 17, and a payment of $150 was made on May 20. The interest on the average daily balance is 1.5% per month. Find the finance charge on the June 5 bill.
8. **Finance Charges** A charge account had a balance of $655 on June 1. A purchase of $98 was made on June 17, and a payment of $250 was made on June 15. The interest on the average daily balance is 1.2% per month. Find the finance charge on the July 1 bill.
9. **Finance Charges** On August 10, a credit card account had a balance of $345. A purchase of $56 was made on August 15, and $157 was charged on August 27. A payment of $75 was made on August 15. The interest on the average daily balance is 1.25% per month. Find the finance charge on the September 10 bill.
10. **Finance Charges** On May 1, a credit card account had a balance of $189. Purchases of $213 were made on May 5, and $102 was charged on May 21. A payment of $150 was made on May 25. The interest on the average daily balance is 1.5% per month. Find the finance charge on the June 1 bill.

In Exercises 11 and 12, you may want to use the spreadsheet program available on our companion site at CengageBrain.com. This spreadsheet automates the finance charge procedure shown in this section.

11. **Finance Charges** The activity date, company, and amount for a credit card bill are shown below. The due date of the bill is September 15. On August 15, there was an unpaid balance of $1236.43. Find the finance charge if the interest rate is 1.5% per month.

Activity date	Company	Amount
August 15	Unpaid balance	1236.43
August 16	Veterinary clinic	125.00
August 17	Gasoline	23.56
August 18	Olive's restaurant	53.45
August 20	Seaside market	41.36
August 22	Monterey Hotel	223.65
August 25	Airline tickets	310.00
August 30	Bike 101	23.26
September 1	Trattoria Maria	36.45
September 12	Seaside Market	41.25
September 13	Credit card payment	−1345.00

12. Finance Charges The activity date, company, and amount for a credit card bill are shown below. The due date of the bill is July 10. On June 10, there was an unpaid balance of $987.81. Find the finance charge if the interest rate is 1.8% per month.

Activity date	Company	Amount
June 10	Unpaid balance	987.81
June 11	Jan's Surf Shop	156.33
June 12	Albertson's	45.61
June 15	The Down Shoppe	59.84
June 16	News Mart	18.54
June 20	Cardiff Delicatessen	23.09
June 22	The Olde Golf Mart	126.92
June 28	Lee's Hawaiian Restaurant	41.78
June 30	City Food Drive	100.00
July 2	Credit card payment	−1000.00
July 8	Safeway Stores	161.38

Use a calculator for Exercises 13 to 39.

■ In Exercises 13 to 16, use the approximate annual percentage rate formula.

13. APR Chuong Ngo borrows $2500 from a bank that advertises a 9% simple interest rate and repays the loan in three equal monthly payments. Estimate the APR. Round to the nearest tenth of a percent.

14. APR Charles Ferrara borrows $4000 from a bank that advertises an 8% simple interest rate. If he repays the loan in six equal monthly payments, estimate the APR. Round to the nearest tenth of a percent.

15. APR Kelly Ang buys a computer system for $2400 and makes a 15% down payment. If Kelly agrees to repay the balance in 24 equal monthly payments at an annual simple interest rate of 10%, estimate the APR for Kelly's loan.

16. APR Jill Richards purchases a stereo system for $1500. She makes a 20% down payment and agrees to repay the balance in 12 equal payments. If the finance charge on the balance is 7% simple interest, estimate the APR. Round to the nearest tenth of a percent.

17. Monthly Payments Arrowood's Camera Store advertises a Canon Power Shot S95 camera for $400, including taxes. If you finance the purchase of this camera for 1 year at an annual percentage rate of 6.9%, find the monthly payment.

18. Monthly Payments Optics Mart offers a Meade ETX-LS 6 telescope for $1249, including taxes. If you finance the purchase of this telescope for 2 years at an annual percentage rate of 7.2%, what is the monthly payment?

19. Buying on Credit A surf shop offers a Channel Islands 6′10 MBM surfboard for $649. The sales tax is 7.25% of the purchase price.

a. What is the total cost, including sales tax?

b. If you make a down payment of 25% of the total cost, find the down payment.

c. Assuming you finance the remaining cost at an annual interest rate of 5.7% for 6 months, find the monthly payment.

20. Buying on Credit Waterworld marina offers a motorboat with a mercury engine for $38,250. The sales tax is 6.5% of the purchase price.

a. What is the total cost, including sales tax?

b. If you make a down payment of 20% of the total cost, find the down payment.

c. Assuming you finance the remaining cost at an annual interest rate of 5.7% for 3 years, find the monthly payment.

21. Buying on Credit After becoming a commercial pilot, Lorna Kao decides to purchase a 1978 Cessna 182 for $64,995. Assuming the sales tax is 5.5% of the purchase price, find each of the following.

a. What is the total cost, including sales tax?

b. If Lorna makes a down payment of 20% of the total cost, find the down payment.

c. Assuming Lorna finances the remaining cost at an annual interest rate of 7.15% for 10 years, find the monthly payment.

Paul Bowen/Science Faction/ Getty Images

22. Buying on Credit Donald Savchenko purchased new living room furniture for $2488. Assuming the sales tax is 7.75% of the purchase price, find each of the following.

a. What is the total cost, including sales tax?

b. If Donald makes a down payment of 15% of the total cost, find the down payment.

c. Assuming that Donald finances the remaining cost at an annual interest rate of 8.16% for 2 years, find the monthly payment.

23. **Car Payments** Luis Mahla purchases a used Porsche Boxster for $42,600 and finances the entire amount at an annual interest rate of 5.7% for 5 years. Find the monthly payment. Assume the sales tax is 6% of the purchase price and the license fee is 1% of the purchase price.

24. **Car Payments** Suppose you negotiate a selling price of $26,995 for a Ford Explorer. You make a down payment of 10% of the selling price and finance the remaining balance for 3 years at an annual interest rate of 7.5%. The sales tax is 7.5% of the selling price, and the license fee is 0.9% of the selling price. Find the monthly payment.

25. **Car Payments** Margaret Hsi purchases a classic car for $24,500. She makes a down payment of $3000 and finances the remaining amount for 4 years at an annual interest rate of 8.5%. The sales tax is 5.5% of the selling price and the license fee is $331. Find the monthly payment.

26. **Car Payments** Chris Schmaltz purchases a Toyota Avalon for $34,119. Chris makes a down payment of $5000 and finances the remaining amount for 5 years at an annual interest rate of 7.6%. The sales tax is 6.25% of the selling price, and the license fee is $429. Find the monthly payment.

27. **Car Payments** Suppose you purchase a car for a total price of $25,445, including taxes and license fee, and finance that amount for 4 years at an annual interest rate of 8%.
    a. Find the monthly payment.
    b. What is the total amount of interest paid over the term of the loan?

28. **Car Payments** Adele Paolo purchased an SUV for a total price of $21,425, including taxes and license fee, and financed that amount for 5 years at an annual interest rate of 7.8%.
    a. Find the monthly payment.
    b. What is the total amount of interest paid over the term of the loan?

29. **Loan Payoffs** Angela Montery has a 5-year car loan for a Jeep Wrangler at an annual interest rate of 6.3% and a monthly payment of $603.50. After 3 years, Angela decides to purchase a new car. What is the payoff on Angela's loan?

30. **Loan Payoffs** Suppose you have a 4-year car loan at an annual interest rate of 7.2% and a monthly payment of $587.21. After $2\frac{1}{2}$ years, you decide to purchase a new car. What is the payoff on your loan?

31. **Loan Payoffs** Suppose you have a 4-year car loan at an annual interest rate of 8.9% and a monthly payment of $303.52. After 3 years, you decide to purchase a new car. What is the payoff on your loan?

32. **Loan Payoffs** Ming Li has a 3-year car loan at an annual interest rate of 9.3% and a monthly payment of $453.68. After 1 year, Ming decides to purchase a new car. What is the payoff on his loan?

33. **Student Loans** Samuel Ng received a 5-year subsidized student loan of $12,000 at an annual interest rate of 5%. What are Samuel's monthly loan payments for this loan when he graduates from college in 2 years?

34. **Student Loans** Melissa Hernandez received an 8-year subsidized student loan of $21,000 at an annual interest rate of 4.1%. What are Melissa's monthly loan payments for this loan when she graduates in 1 year?

35. **Student Loans** Angelica Reardon received a 5-year non-subsidized student loan of $17,000 at an annual interest rate of 6.2%. What are Angelica's monthly loan payments for this loan after she graduates in 4 years?

36. **Student Loans** Jeffery Wei received a 6-year non-subsidized student loan of $30,000 at an annual interest rate of 5.2%. What are Jeffery's monthly loan payments for this loan after he graduates in 4 years?

EXTENSIONS

37. **Car Trade-Ins** You may have heard advertisements from car dealerships that say something like "Bring in your car, paid for or not, and we'll take it as a trade-in for a new car." The advertisement does not go on to say that you have to pay off the remaining loan balance or that balance gets added to the price of the new car.
    a. Suppose you are making payments of $235.73 per month on a 4-year car loan that has an annual interest rate of 8.4%. After making payments for 3 years, you decide to purchase a new car. What is the loan payoff?
    b. You negotiate a price, including taxes, of $18,234 for the new car. What is the actual amount you owe for the new car when the loan payoff is included?
    c. If you finance the amount in part b for 4 years at an annual interest rate of 8.4%, what is the new monthly payment?

38. Credit Card Debt The APR loan payoff formula can be used to determine how many months it will take to pay off a credit card debt if the minimum monthly payment is made each month. For instance, suppose that you have a credit card bill of $620.50, the minimum payment is $13, and the interest rate is 18% per year. Using a graphing calculator, we can determine the number of months, n, it will take to pay off the debt. Enter the values shown on the TI-83/84 calculator screen below. Move the cursor to N= and press ALPHA [SOLVE]. It will take over 84 months (or approximately 7 years) to pay off the credit card debt, assuming you do not make additional purchases.

```
N=84.53746933
I%=18
PV=620.5
PMT=-13
FV=0
P/Y=12
C/Y=12
PMT: END BEGIN
```

a. Find the number of months it will take to pay off a credit card debt of $1283.34 if the minimum payment is $27 and the annual interest rate is 19.6%. Round to the nearest month.

b. How much interest will be paid on the credit card debt in part a?

c. If you have credit card debt, determine how many months it would take to pay off your debt by making the minimum monthly payments. How much interest would you pay? You may want to use a debt payoff calculator, as mentioned in the Math Matters on page 192, to determine the answers.

39. Student Loans Suppose a graduate student receives a non-subsidized student loan of $12,000 for each of the 4 years the student pursues a PhD. If the annual interest rate is 5% and the student has a 10-year repayment program, what are the student's monthly payments on the loans after graduation?

SECTION 3.4 Stocks, Bonds, and Mutual Funds

Stocks

Stocks, bonds, and mutual funds are investment vehicles, but they differ in nature.

When owners of a company want to raise money, generally to expand their business, they may decide to sell part of the company to investors. An investor who purchases a part of the company is said to own *stock* in the company. Stock is measured in shares; a **share of stock** in a company is a certificate that indicates partial ownership in the company. The owners of the certificates are called **stockholders** or **shareholders**. As owners, the stockholders share in the profits or losses of the corporation.

A company may distribute profits to its shareholders in the form of **dividends**. A dividend is usually expressed as a per-share amount—for example, $0.07 per share.

HISTORICAL NOTE

Topham/The Image Works

Have you heard the tongue-in-cheek advice for making a fortune in the stock market that goes something like "Buy low, sell high"? The phrase is adapted from a comment made by Hetty Green (1834–1916), who was also known as the Witch of Wall Street. She turned a $1 million inheritance into $100 million and became the richest woman in the world at that time. In today's terms, that $100 million would be worth over $2 billion. When asked how she became so successful, she replied, "There is no secret in fortune making. All you have to do is buy cheap and sell dear, act with thrift and shrewdness, and be persistent."

EXAMPLE 1 Calculate Dividends Paid to a Stockholder

A stock pays an annual dividend of $0.84 per share. Calculate the dividends paid to a shareholder who has 200 shares of the company's stock.

Solution

($0.84 per share) × (200 shares) = $168

The shareholder receives $168 in dividends.

CHECK YOUR PROGRESS 1 A stock pays an annual dividend of $0.72 per share. Calculate the dividends paid to a shareholder who has 550 shares of the company's stock.

Solution See page S12.

The **dividend yield**, which is used to compare companies' dividends, is the amount of the dividend divided by the stock price and is expressed as a percent. Determining a dividend yield is similar to calculating the simple interest rate earned on an investment. You can think of the dividend as the interest earned, the stock price as the principal, and the yield as the interest rate.

EXAMPLE 2 Calculate a Dividend Yield

POINT OF INTEREST

Usually the dividends earned on shares of stock are sent to shareholders. However, in a **dividend reinvestment plan**, or DRIP, the dividends earned are applied toward the purchase of more shares.

A stock pays an annual dividend of \$1.75 per share. The stock is trading at \$70. Find the dividend yield.

Solution

$I = Prt$

$1.75 = 70r(1)$ • Let $I =$ annual dividend and $P =$ the stock price. The time is 1 year.

$1.75 = 70r$

$0.025 = r$ • Divide each side of the equation by 70.

The dividend yield is 2.5%.

CHECK YOUR PROGRESS 2 A stock pays an annual dividend of \$0.82 per share. The stock is trading at \$51.25. Find the dividend yield.

Solution See page S13.

The **market value** of a share of stock is the price for which a stockholder is willing to sell a share of the stock and a buyer is willing to purchase it. Shares are always sold to the highest bidder. A **brokerage firm** is a dealer of stocks that acts as your agent when you want to buy or sell shares of stock. The **brokers** in the firm charge commissions for their service. Most trading of stocks happens on a stock exchange. **Stock exchanges** are businesses whose purpose it is to bring together buyers and sellers of stock. The largest stock exchange in the United States is the New York Stock Exchange. Shares of stock are also bought and sold through the National Association of Securities Dealers Automated Quotation System, which is commonly referred to as the NASDAQ. Every working day, each stock exchange provides financial institutions, Internet website hosts, newspapers, and other publications with data on the trading activity of all the stocks traded on that exchange. Table 3.1 shows a portion of a stock table.

TABLE 3.1
Selected Stocks from the Dow Jones Industrial Average for a Day in 2015

Name	Symbol	Open	High	Low	Close	Net chg	% Chg	Volume	52-week high	52-week low	Div	Yield	PE	YTD %chg
Apple	APPL	113.84	115.01	113.61	115.01	1.73	1.51	41654100	134.54	92.	2.08	2.14	10.05	8.48
Boeing	BA	141.13	146.45	141.05	145.41	5.09	3.5	6976300	158.83	115.02	4.36	3.63	15.8	0.56
International Business Machines	IBM	140.42	143.72	140.30	142.75	3.14	2.2	5583200	176.3	118.	5.20	4.17	9.16	3.59
Johnson & Johnson	JNJ	97.134	99.08	96.42	98.802	1.89	1.91	9887900	105.49	81.79	3.00	2.87	18.88	−3.97
General Electric	GE	28.74	29.52	28.70	29.36	0.72	2.47	81476400	31.49	19.37	0.92	3.16	16.97	−6.1
Procter & Gamble	PG	73.22	74.96	72.97	74.20	1.25	1.68	14080900	86.78	65.02	2.65	3.25	27.17	−6.09

The meaning of each column head is given below. The information refers to the first company in the table, Apple.

Open The number 113.84 in the "Open" column indicates that the opening price of the stock was \$113.84. This means that in the first trade of the day, the price of a share of Apple stock was \$113.84.

High/low On the day in question, the highest price paid for a share of Apple stock was \$115.01, and the lowest price paid was \$113.61.

Close The next number, 115.01, indicates that the closing price of the stock was \$115.01. This means that in the final trade of the day, before the market closed, the price of a share of Apple stock was \$115.01.

Net chg The number 1.73 indicates that the stock's closing price was \$1.73 higher than it was on the previous trading day.

%Chg 1.51 represents the percent change in the price from the previous day's closing price to today's closing price. A positive number indicates a percent increase in price. A negative number indicates a percent decrease in price.

Vol Vol refers to the volume of shares sold. 41,654,100 shares of Apple stock were sold on the day in question.

52-week high/low The next two numbers show that, in the last 52 weeks, the highest price a share of Apple stock sold for was \$134.54, and the lowest price was \$92.00.

Div The number 2.08 means that the company is currently paying an annual dividend of \$2.08 per share of stock.

Yield The current yield on the company's stock is 2.14%. The dividend of \$2.08 is 2.14% of the current purchase price of a share of the stock.

PE The heading PE refers to the price-to-earnings ratio, the purchase price per share divided by the earnings per share.

YTD %chg The number 8.48 in the last column indicates that the price of a share of Apple stock has increased 8.48% thus far in the given calendar year.

POINT OF INTEREST

According to the Board of Governors of the Federal Reserve System, the percent of Americans who own stock decreased from 2007 to 2015. The table below gives the percents of stock owned, by annual income and by age group, for both years.

	% in 2007	% in 2015
All adults	65	55
\$75K and up	90	88
\$30K–\$75K	72	56
Less than \$30K	28	21
18–34 years	52	49
35–54 years	73	58
55 and older	65	57

EXAMPLE 3 Calculate Profits or Losses and Expenses in Selling Stock

Suppose you owned 500 shares of stock in General Electric. You purchased the shares at a price of \$22.08 per share and sold them at the closing price of the stock given in Table 3.1.

a. Ignoring dividends, what was your profit or loss on the sale of the stock?

b. If your broker charges 2.4% of the total sale price, what was the broker's commission?

Solution

a. From Table 3.1, the selling price per share was \$29.36.

The selling price per share is greater than the purchase price per share.

You made a profit on the sale of the stock.

$$\begin{aligned} \text{Profit} &= \text{selling price} - \text{purchase price} \\ &= 500(\$29.36) - 500(\$22.08) \\ &= \$14{,}680 - \$11{,}040 \\ &= \$3640 \end{aligned}$$

The profit on the sale of the stock was \$3640.

b.
$$\begin{aligned} \text{Commission} &= 2.4\%(\text{selling price}) \\ &= 0.024(\$14{,}680) \\ &= \$352.32 \end{aligned}$$

The broker's commission was \$352.32.

CHECK YOUR PROGRESS 3 Use Table 3.1. Suppose you bought 300 shares of General Electric at the 52-week low and sold the shares at the 52-week high.

a. Ignoring dividends, what was your profit or loss on the sale of the stock?

b. If your broker charges 2.1% of the total sale price, what was the broker's commission? Round to the nearest cent.

Solution See page S13.

Bonds

When a corporation issues stock, it is *selling* part of the company to the stockholders. When it issues a **bond**, the corporation is *borrowing* money from the bondholders; a **bondholder** lends money to a corporation. Corporations, the federal government, government agencies, states, and cities all issue bonds. These entities need money to operate—for example, to fund the federal deficit, repair roads, or build a new factory—so they borrow money from the public by issuing bonds.

Bonds are usually issued in units of $1000. The price paid for the bond is the **face value**. The issuer promises to repay the bondholder on a particular day, called the **maturity date**, at a given rate of interest, called the **coupon**.

Assume that a bond with a $1000 face value has a 5% coupon and a 10-year maturity date. The bondholder collects interest payments of $50 in each of those 10 years. The payments are calculated using the simple interest formula, as shown below.

$$I = Prt$$
$$I = 1000(0.05)(1)$$
$$I = 50$$

At the end of the 10-year period, the bondholder receives from the issuer the $1000 face value of the bond.

POINT OF INTEREST

Municipal bonds are issued by states, cities, counties, and other governments to raise money to build schools, highways, sewer systems, hospitals, and other projects for the public good. The income from many municipal bonds is exempt from federal and/or state taxes.

EXAMPLE 4 Calculate Interest Payments on a Bond

A bond with a $10,000 face value has a 3% coupon and a 5-year maturity date. Calculate the total of the interest payments paid to the bondholder.

Solution

Use the simple interest formula to find the annual interest payments. Substitute the following values into the formula: $P = 10{,}000$, $r = 3\% = 0.03$, and $t = 1$.

$$I = Prt$$
$$I = 10{,}000(0.03)(1)$$
$$I = 300$$

Multiply the annual interest payment by the term of the bond (5 years).

$$300(5) = 1500$$

The total of the interest payments paid to the bondholder is $1500.

CHECK YOUR PROGRESS 4 A bond has a $15,000 face value, a 4-year maturity, and a 3.5% coupon. What is the total of the interest payments paid to the bondholder?

Solution See page S13.

A key difference between stocks and bonds is that stocks make no promises about dividends or returns, whereas the issuer of a bond guarantees that, provided the issuer remains solvent, it will pay back the face value of the bond plus interest.

Mutual Funds

An **investment trust** is a company whose assets are stocks and bonds. These companies do not manufacture a product but instead purchase stocks and bonds with the hope that their value will increase. A **mutual fund** is an example of an investment trust.

When investors purchase shares in a mutual fund, they are adding their money to a pool along with many other investors. The investments within a mutual fund are called the fund's **portfolio**. The investors in a mutual fund share the fund's profits or losses from the investments in the portfolio.

An advantage of owning shares in a mutual fund is that your money is managed by full-time professionals whose job it is to research and evaluate stocks; you own stocks without having to choose which individual stocks to buy or decide when to sell them. Another advantage is that by owning shares in the fund, you have purchased shares of stock in many different companies. This diversification helps to reduce some of the risks of investing.

Because a mutual fund owns many different stocks, each share of the fund represents a fractional interest in each stock. Each day, the value of a share in the fund, called the **net asset value of the fund**, or **NAV**, depends on the performance of the stocks in the fund. It is calculated by the following formula.

Net Asset Value of a Mutual Fund

The net asset value (NAV) of a mutual fund is given by

$$NAV = \frac{A - L}{N}$$

where A is the total fund assets, L is the total fund liabilities, and N is the number of shares outstanding.

EXAMPLE 5 Calculate the Net Asset Value of, and the Number of Shares Purchased in, a Mutual Fund

A mutual fund has $600 million worth of stock, $5 million worth of bonds, and $1 million in cash. The fund's total liabilities amount to $2 million. There are 25 million shares outstanding. You invest $15,000 in this fund.

a. Calculate the NAV.

b. How many shares are you purchasing?

Solution

a. $NAV = \frac{A - L}{N}$

$= \frac{606 \text{ million} - 2 \text{ million}}{25 \text{ million}}$

• $A = 600$ million $+ 5$ million $+ 1$ million $= 606$ million, $L = 2$ million, $N = 25$ million

$= 24.16$

The NAV of the fund is $24.16.

b. $\frac{15{,}000}{24.16} \approx 620$

• Divide the amount invested by the cost per share of the fund. Round down to the nearest whole number.

You are purchasing 620 shares of the mutual fund.

CHECK YOUR PROGRESS 5 A mutual fund has $750 million worth of stock, $750,000 in cash, and $1,500,000 in other assets. The fund's total liabilities amount to $1,500,000. There are 20 million shares outstanding. You invest $10,000 in this fund.

a. Calculate the NAV.

b. How many shares are you purchasing?

Solution See page S13.

MATH MATTERS Growth of Mutual Funds

Where do Americans invest their money? You might correctly assume that the largest number of Americans invest in real estate, as every homeowner is considered to have an investment in real estate. But more and more Americans are investing their money in the stock market, and many of them are doing so by purchasing shares in mutual funds. The table below shows data on mutual funds for selected years from 1980 to 2015. (*Source:* Investment Company Institute)

Year	Total number of U.S. households (millions)	Total value of mutual funds owned by U.S. households (millions of $)	Percent of U.S. households owning mutual funds
1980	80.8	4.6	5.7
1990	93.3	23.4	25.1
2000	106.4	48.6	45.7
2010	117.5	53.2	45.3
2015	124.6	53.6	43.0

EXCURSION

Treasury Bills

The bonds issued by the United States government are called Treasuries. Some investors prefer to invest in Treasuries, rather than the stock market, because their investment is backed by the federal government. For this reason, Treasuries are considered the safest of all investments. They are grouped into three categories.

U.S. Treasury bills have maturities of under 1 year.

U.S. Treasury notes have maturities ranging from 2 to 10 years.

U.S. Treasury bonds have maturities ranging from 10 to 30 years.

This Excursion will focus on Treasury bills.

The **face value** of a Treasury bill is the amount of money received by the investor on the maturity date of the bill. Treasury bills are sold on a **discount basis**; that is, the interest on the bill is computed and subtracted from the face value to determine the bill's cost.

TAKE NOTE

You can obtain more information about the various Treasury securities at http://www.publicdebt.treas.gov. Using this site, investors can buy securities directly from the government, thereby avoiding the service fee charged by banks and brokerage firms. This website also provides information about Treasury bills. In the past, paper bills were issued, but now all Treasury bills are issued and held electronically.

Suppose a company invests in a $50,000 United States Treasury bill at 3.35% interest for 28 days. The bank through which the bill is purchased charges a service fee of $15. What is the cost of the Treasury bill?

To find the cost, first find the interest. Use the simple interest formula.

$$I = Prt$$
$$= 50{,}000(0.0335)\left(\frac{28}{360}\right)$$
$$\approx 130.28$$

The interest earned is $130.28.

Find the cost of the Treasury bill.

$$\text{Cost} = (\text{face value} - \text{interest}) + \text{service fee}$$
$$= (50{,}000 - 130.28) + 15$$
$$= 49{,}869.72 + 15$$
$$= 49{,}884.72$$

The cost of the Treasury bill is $49,884.72.

EXCURSION EXERCISES

1. The face value of a Treasury bill is $30,000. The interest rate is 2.32% and the bill matures in 182 days. The bank through which the bill is purchased charges a service fee of $15. What is the cost of the Treasury bill?
2. The face value of a 91-day Treasury bill is $20,000. The interest rate is 2.96%. The purchaser buys the bill through Treasury Direct and pays no service fee. Calculate the cost of the Treasury bill.
3. A company invests in a 29-day, $60,000 United States Treasury bill at 2.28% interest. The bank through which the bill is purchased charges a service fee of $35. Calculate the cost of the Treasury bill.
4. A $40,000 United States Treasury bill, purchased at 1.96% interest, matures in 92 days. The purchaser is charged a service fee of $20. What is the cost of the Treasury bill?

EXERCISE SET 3.4

1. **Annual Dividends** A stock pays an annual dividend of $1.02 per share. Calculate the dividends paid to a shareholder who has 375 shares of the company's stock.
2. **Annual Dividends** A stock pays an annual dividend of $0.58 per share. Calculate the dividends paid to a shareholder who has 1500 shares of the company's stock.
3. **Annual Dividends** Calculate the dividends paid to a shareholder who has 850 shares of a stock that is paying an annual dividend of $0.63 per share.
4. **Annual Dividends** Calculate the dividends paid to a shareholder who has 400 shares of a stock that is paying an annual dividend of $0.91 per share.
5. **Dividend Yield** Find the dividend yield for a stock that pays an annual dividend of $1.24 per share and has a current price of $49.375. Round to the nearest hundredth of a percent.
6. **Dividend Yield** The Blackburn Computer Company has declared an annual dividend of $0.50 per share. The stock is trading at $40 per share. Find the dividend yield.
7. **Dividend Yield** A stock that pays an annual dividend of $0.58 per share has a current price of $31.75. Find the dividend yield. Round to the nearest hundredth of a percent.
8. **Dividend Yield** The Moreau Corporation is paying an annual dividend of $0.65 per share. If the price of a share of the stock is $81.25, what is the dividend yield on the stock?

Use the partial stock table shown below for Exercises 9 to 16. Round dollar amounts to the nearest cent when necessary.

TABLE 3.1
Selected Stocks from the Dow Jones Industrial Average for a Day in 2015

Name	Symbol	Open	High	Low	Close	Net chg	% Chg	Volume	52-week high	52-week low	Div	Yield	PE	YTD %chg
Apple	APPL	113.84	115.01	113.61	115.01	1.73	1.51	41654100	134.54	92.	2.08	2.14	10.05	8.48
Boeing	BA	141.13	146.45	141.05	145.41	5.09	3.5	6976300	158.83	115.02	4.36	3.63	15.8	0.56
International Business Machines	IBM	140.42	143.72	140.30	142.75	3.14	2.2	5583200	176.3	118.	5.20	4.17	9.16	3.59
Johnson & Johnson	JNJ	97.134	99.08	96.42	98.802	1.89	1.91	9887900	105.49	81.79	3.00	2.87	18.88	−3.97
General Electric	GE	28.74	29.52	28.70	29.36	0.72	2.47	81476400	31.49	19.37	0.92	3.16	16.97	−6.1
Procter & Gamble	PG	73.22	74.96	72.97	74.20	1.25	1.68	14080900	86.78	65.02	2.65	3.25	27.17	−6.09

9. Stock Tables For Boeing (BA):

a. What is the difference between the highest and lowest prices paid for this stock during the last 52 weeks?

b. Suppose that you own 750 shares of this stock. What dividend do you receive this year?

c. How many shares of this stock were sold during the trading day?

d. Did the price of a share of this stock increase or decrease during the day shown in the table?

e. What was the price of a share of this stock at the start of the trading day?

10. Stock Tables For International Business Machines (IBM):

a. What is the difference between the highest and lowest prices paid for this stock during the last 52 weeks?

b. Suppose that you own 750 shares of this stock. What dividend do you receive this year?

c. How many shares of this stock were sold during the trading day?

d. Did the price of a share of this stock increase or decrease during the day shown in the table?

e. What was the price of a share of this stock at the start of the trading day?

11. Stock Purchases At the closing price per share of Johnson & Johnson (JNJ), how many shares of the stock can you purchase for $5000?

12. Stock Purchases At the closing price per share of General Electric (GE), how many shares of the stock can you purchase for $2500?

13. Stock Sale Suppose that you owned 1000 shares of stock in Procter & Gamble (PG). You purchased the shares at a price of $48.96 per share and sold them at the closing price of the stock given in the table.

a. Ignoring dividends, what was your profit or loss on the sale of the stock?

b. If your broker charges 1.9% of the total sale price, what was the broker's commission?

14. Stock Sale Gary Walters owned 400 shares of stock in General Electric (GE). He purchased the shares at a price of $38.06 per share and sold them at the closing price of the stock given in the table.

a. Ignoring dividends, what was Gary's profit or loss on the sale of the stock?

b. If his broker charges 2.5% of the total sale price, what was the broker's commission?

15. Stock Sale Michele Desjardins bought 800 shares of Apple (APPL) at the 52-week low and sold the shares at the 52-week high shown in the table.

a. Ignoring dividends, what was Michele's profit or loss on the sale of the stock?

b. If her broker charges 2.3% of the total sale price, what was the broker's commission?

16. Stock Sale Suppose that you bought 1200 shares of IBM at the 52-week low and sold the shares at the 52-week high shown in the table.

a. Ignoring dividends, what was your profit or loss on the sale of the stock?

b. If your broker charges 2.25% of the total sale price, what was the broker's commission?

17. **Bonds** A bond with a face value of $6000 and a 4.2% coupon has a 5-year maturity. Find the annual interest paid to the bondholder.
18. **Bonds** The face value on a bond is $15,000. It has a 10-year maturity and a 3.75% coupon. What is the annual interest paid to the bondholder?
19. **Bonds** A bond with an $8000 face value has a 3.5% coupon and a 3-year maturity. What is the total of the interest payments paid to the bondholder?
20. **Bonds** A bond has a $12,000 face value, an 8-year maturity, and a 2.95% coupon. Find the total of the interest payments paid to the bondholder.
21. **Mutual Funds** A mutual fund has total assets of $50,000,000 and total liabilities of $5,000,000. There are 2,000,000 shares outstanding. Find the net asset value of the mutual fund.
22. **Mutual Funds** A mutual fund has total assets of $25,000,000 and total liabilities of $250,000. There are 1,500,000 shares outstanding. Find the net asset value of the mutual fund.
23. **Mutual Funds** A mutual fund has total assets of $15 million and total liabilities of $1 million. There are 2 million shares outstanding. You invest $5000 in this fund. How many shares are you purchasing?
24. **Mutual Funds** A mutual fund has total assets of $12 million and total liabilities of $2 million. There are 1 million shares outstanding. You invest $2500 in this fund. How many shares are you purchasing?
25. **Mutual Funds** A mutual fund has $500 million worth of stock, $500,000 in cash, and $1 million in other assets. The fund's total liabilities amount to $2 million. There are 10 million shares outstanding. You invest $12,000 in this fund. How many shares are you purchasing?
26. **Mutual Funds** A mutual fund has $250 million worth of stock, $10 million worth of bonds, and $1 million in cash. The fund's total liabilities amount to $1 million. There are 13 million shares outstanding. You invest $10,000 in this fund. How many shares are you purchasing?

EXTENSIONS

27. **Load and No-Load Funds** All mutual funds carry fees. One type of fee is called a "load." This is an additional fee that generally is paid at the time you invest your money in the mutual fund. A no-load mutual fund does not charge this up-front fee.

    Suppose you invested $2500 in a 4% load mutual fund 2 years ago. The 4% fee was paid out of the $2500 invested. The fund has earned 8% during each of the past 2 years. There was a management fee of 0.015% charged at the end of each year. A friend of yours invested $2500 2 years ago in a no-load fund that has earned 6% during each of the past 2 years. This fund charged a management fee of 0.15% at the end of each year. Find the difference between the values of the two investments now.
28. **Investing in the Stock Market** (This activity assumes that the class has been divided into groups of three or four students.) Imagine that your group has $10,000 to invest in each of 10 stocks. Use the stock table in today's paper or the Internet to determine the price you would pay per share. Determine the number of shares of each stock you will purchase. Check the value of each stock every business day for the next four weeks. Assume that you sell your shares at the end of the fourth week. Calculate the group's profit or loss over the 4-week period. Compare your profits or losses with those of the other groups in your class.
29. Find a mutual fund table in a daily newspaper. You can find one in the same section where the stock tables are printed. Explain the meaning of the heading of each column in the table.

SECTION 3.5 Home Ownership

POINT OF INTEREST

The U.S. Census Bureau keeps a vast selection of statistics. Two categories for which data are collected are the prices of existing homes and the prices of new homes. Recent statistics showed that the median price of an existing home was $210,000, while the median price of a new home was $283,000.

Initial Expenses

When you purchase a home, you generally make a down payment and finance the remainder of the purchase price with a loan obtained through a bank or savings and loan association. The amount of the down payment can vary, but it is normally between 10% and 30% of the selling price. The **mortgage** is the amount that is borrowed to buy the real estate. The amount of the mortgage is the difference between the selling price and the down payment.

Mortgage = selling price − down payment

This formula is used to find the amount of the mortgage. For example, suppose you buy a $240,000 home with a down payment of 25%. First find the down payment by computing 25% of the purchase price.

$$\text{Down payment} = 25\% \text{ of } 240{,}000 = 0.25(240{,}000)$$
$$= 60{,}000$$

Then find the mortgage by subtracting the down payment from the selling price.

$$\begin{aligned}\text{Mortgage} &= \text{selling price} - \text{down payment}\\ &= 240{,}000 - 60{,}000\\ &= 180{,}000\end{aligned}$$

The mortgage is $180,000.

The down payment is generally the largest initial expense in purchasing a home, but there are other expenses associated with the purchase. These payments are due at the closing, when the sale of the house is finalized, and are called **closing costs**. The bank may charge fees for attorneys, credit reports, loan processing, and title searches. There may also be a **loan origination fee**. This fee is usually expressed in **points**. One point is equal to 1% of the mortgage.

Suppose you purchase a home and obtain a loan for $180,000. The bank charges a fee of 1.5 points. To find the charge for points, multiply the loan amount by 1.5%.

TAKE NOTE

1.5 points means 1.5%.
1.5% = 0.015

$$\begin{aligned}\text{Points} &= 1.5\% \text{ of } 180{,}000 = 0.015(180{,}000)\\ &= 2700\end{aligned}$$

The charge for points is $2700.

EXAMPLE 1 Calculate a Down Payment and the Closing Costs

The purchase price of a home is $392,000. A down payment of 20% is made. The bank charges $450 in fees plus $2\frac{1}{2}$ points. Find the total of the down payment and the closing costs.

Andy Dean Photography/Shutterstock.com

Solution

First find the down payment.

$$\begin{aligned}\text{Down payment} &= 20\% \text{ of } 392{,}000 = 0.20(392{,}000)\\ &= 78{,}400\end{aligned}$$

The down payment is $78,400.

Next find the mortgage.

$$\begin{aligned}\text{Mortgage} &= \text{selling price} - \text{down payment}\\ &= 392{,}000 - 78{,}400\\ &= 313{,}600\end{aligned}$$

The mortgage is $313,600.

Then, calculate the charge for points.

$$\begin{aligned}\text{Points} &= 2\tfrac{1}{2}\% \text{ of } 313{,}600 = 0.025(313{,}600)\\ &= 7840\end{aligned}$$

• $2\frac{1}{2}\% = 2.5\% = 0.025$

The charge for points is $7840.

Finally, find the sum of the down payment and the closing costs.

$$78{,}400 + 450 + 7840 = 86{,}690$$

The total of the down payment and the closing costs is $86,690.

CHECK YOUR PROGRESS 1 The purchase price of a home is $410,000. A down payment of 25% is made. The bank charges $375 in fees plus 1.75 points. Find the total of the down payment and the closing costs.

Solution See page S13.

Mortgages

When a bank agrees to provide you with a mortgage, you agree to pay off that loan in monthly payments. If you fail to make the payments, the bank has the right to **foreclose**, which means that the bank takes possession of the property and has the right to sell it.

There are many types of mortgages available to home buyers today, so the terms of mortgages differ considerably. Some mortgages are **adjustable rate mortgages (ARMs)**. The interest rate charged on an ARM is adjusted periodically to more closely reflect current interest rates. The mortgage agreement specifies exactly how often and by how much the interest rate can change.

A **fixed-rate mortgage**, or **conventional mortgage**, is one in which the interest rate charged on the loan remains the same throughout the life of the mortgage. For a fixed-rate mortgage, the amount of the monthly payment also remains unchanged throughout the term of the loan.

The term of a mortgage can vary. Terms of 15, 20, 25, and 30 years are most common.

The monthly payment on a mortgage is the **mortgage payment**. The amount of the mortgage payment depends on the amount of the mortgage, the interest rate on the loan, and the term of the loan. This payment is calculated by using the payment formula for an APR loan given in Section 3.3. We will restate the formula here.

Mortgage Payment Formula

The mortgage payment for a mortgage is given by

$$PMT = A\left(\frac{\frac{r}{n}}{1-\left(1+\frac{r}{n}\right)^{-nt}}\right)$$

where PMT is the monthly mortgage payment, A is the amount of the mortgage, r is the annual interest rate, n is the number of payments per year, and t is the number of years.

EXAMPLE 2 Calculate a Mortgage Payment

Suppose Allison Sommerset purchases a condominium and secures a loan of \$134,000 for 30 years at an annual interest rate of 6.5%.

a. Find the monthly mortgage payment.

b. What is the total of the payments over the life of the loan?

c. Find the amount of interest paid on the loan over the 30 years.

Solution

a. First calculate $\frac{r}{n}$ and store the result.

$$\frac{r}{n} = \frac{0.065}{12} \approx 0.00541667$$

Keystrokes: 0.065 [÷] 12 ≈ 0.00541667 [STO]

Calculate the monthly payment. For a 30-year loan, $nt = 12(30) = 360$.

$$PMT = A\left(\frac{\frac{r}{n}}{1-\left(1+\frac{r}{n}\right)^{-nt}}\right)$$

$$= 134{,}000\left(\frac{0.065/12}{1-(1+0.065/12)^{-360}}\right) \approx 846.97$$

Keystrokes:

134000 [x] [RCL] [=] [÷] [(] 1 [-] [(] 1 [+] [RCL] [)] [y^x] 360 [+/-] [)] [=]

The monthly mortgage payment is \$846.97.

POINT OF INTEREST

The national home ownership rate in the United States in 2016 was approximately 63%, a rate comparable to the rate in 1990. The highest rate on record was about 69%, which occurred during the housing boom of 2006.

b. To determine the total of the payments, multiply the number of payments (360) by the monthly payment ($846.97).

$$846.97(360) = 304{,}909.20$$

The total of the payments over the life of the loan is $304,909.20.

c. To determine the amount of interest paid, subtract the mortgage from the total of the payments.

$$304{,}909.20 - 134{,}000 = 170{,}909.20$$

The amount of interest paid over the life of the loan is $170,909.20.

CHECK YOUR PROGRESS 2 Suppose Antonio Scarletti purchases a home and secures a loan of $223,000 for 25 years at an annual interest rate of 7%.

a. Find the monthly mortgage payment.

b. What is the total of the payments over the life of the loan?

c. Find the amount of interest paid on the loan over the 25 years.

Solution See page S13.

A portion of a mortgage payment pays the current interest owed on the loan, and the remaining portion of the mortgage payment is used to reduce the principal owed on the loan. This process of paying off the principal and the interest, which is similar to paying a car loan, is called **amortizing the loan**.

In Example 2, the mortgage payment on a $134,000 mortgage at 6.5% for 30 years was $846.97. The amount of the first payment that is interest and the amount that is applied to the principal can be calculated using the simple interest formula.

$$I = Prt$$

$$= 134{,}000(0.065)\left(\frac{1}{12}\right)$$ • $P = 134{,}000$, the current loan amount; $r = 0.065$; $t = \frac{1}{12}$

$$\approx 725.83$$ • Round to the nearest cent.

Of the $846.97 mortgage payment, $725.83 is an interest payment. The remainder is applied toward reducing the principal.

Principal reduction = $846.97 − $725.83 = $121.14

After the first month's mortgage payment, the balance on the loan (the amount that remains to be paid) is calculated by subtracting the principal paid on the mortgage from the mortgage.

Loan balance after first month = $134,000 − $121.14 = $133,878.86

The portion of the second mortgage payment that is applied to interest and the portion that is applied to the principal can be calculated in the same manner. In the calculation, the figure used for the principal, P, is the current balance on the loan, $133,878.86.

$$I = Prt$$

$$= 133{,}878.86(0.065)\left(\frac{1}{12}\right)$$ • $P = 133{,}878.86$, the current loan amount; $r = 0.065$; $t = \frac{1}{12}$

$$\approx 725.18$$ • Round to the nearest cent.

Principal reduction = $846.97 − $725.18 = $121.79

Of the second mortgage payment, $725.18 is an interest payment and $121.79 is a payment toward the principal.

Loan balance after second month = $133,878.86 − $121.79 = $133,757.07

The interest payment, principal payment, and balance on the loan can be calculated in this manner for all of the mortgage payments throughout the life of the loan—all 360 of them! Alternatively, a computer can be programmed to make these calculations and print out the information. The printout is called an **amortization schedule**. It lists, for each mortgage payment, the payment number, the interest payment, the amount applied toward the principal, and the resulting balance to be paid.

Each month, the amount of the mortgage payment that is an interest payment decreases and the amount applied toward the principal increases. This is because you are paying interest on a decreasing balance each month. Mortgage payments early in the life of a mortgage are largely interest payments; mortgage payments late in the life of a mortgage are largely payments toward the principal.

The partial amortization schedule below shows the breakdown of the monthly payments for the first 12 months of the loan discussed in Example 2.

TAKE NOTE

You can find a spreadsheet on our companion site at CengageBrain.com, that will enable you to obtain a complete amortization schedule for any fixed-rate loan. Because car loans and home loans are calculated using the same formula, the spreadsheet can also be used to show the principal and interest payments on a car loan.

Amortization Schedule

Loan Amount	$134,000.00	
Interest Rate	6.50%	
Term of Loan	30	
Monthly Payment	$846.97	

Month	Amount of interest	Amount of principal	New loan amount
1	$725.83	$121.14	$133,878.86
2	$725.18	$121.79	$133,757.07
3	$724.52	$122.45	$133,634.61
4	$723.85	$123.12	$133,511.50
5	$723.19	$123.78	$133,387.71
6	$722.52	$124.45	$133,263.26
7	$721.84	$125.13	$133,138.13
8	$721.16	$125.81	$133,012.32
9	$720.48	$126.49	$132,885.84
10	$719.80	$127.17	$132,758.66
11	$719.11	$127.86	$132,630.80
12	$718.42	$128.55	$132,502.25

QUESTION Using the amortization schedule above, how much of the loan has been paid off after 1 year?

ANSWER After 1 year (12 months), the loan amount is $132,502.25. The original loan was $134,000. The amount that has been paid off is

$134,000 − $132,502.25 = $1497.75.

POINT OF INTEREST

According to the Joint Center for Housing Studies at Harvard University, consumers in the United States spend an average of 49% of their income on housing costs, which include costs associated with their residence, utilities, household supplies, and home furnishings.

EXAMPLE 3 Calculate Principal and Interest for a Mortgage Payment

You purchase a condominium for $98,750 and obtain a 30-year, fixed-rate mortgage at 7.25%. After paying a down payment of 20%, how much of the second payment is interest and how much is applied toward the principal?

Solution

First find the down payment by multiplying the percent of the purchase price that is the down payment by the purchase price.

$0.20(98{,}750) = 19{,}750$

The down payment is $19,750.

Find the mortgage by subtracting the down payment from the purchase price.

$98{,}750 - 19{,}750 = 79{,}000$

The mortgage is $79,000.

Calculate $\frac{r}{n}$ and store the result.

$$\frac{r}{n} = \frac{\text{annual interest rate}}{\text{number of payments per year}} = \frac{0.0725}{12} \approx 0.00604167$$

Keystrokes: 0.0725 [÷] 12 ≈ 0.00604167 [STO]

Calculate the monthly payment. For a 30-year loan, $nt = 12(30) = 360$.

$$PMT = A\left(\frac{\frac{r}{n}}{1 - \left(1 + \frac{r}{n}\right)^{-nt}}\right)$$

$$= 79{,}000\left(\frac{0.0725/12}{1 - (1 + 0.0725/12)^{-360}}\right) \approx 538.92$$

Keystrokes:

79000 [×] [RCL] [=] [÷] [(] 1 [−] [(] 1 [+] [RCL] [)] [yˣ] 360 [+/−] [)] [=]

The monthly payment is $538.92.

Find the amount of interest paid on the first mortgage payment by using the simple interest formula.

$I = Prt$

$= 79{,}000(0.0725)\left(\frac{1}{12}\right)$ • $P = 79{,}000$, the current loan amount; $r = 0.0725$; $t = \frac{1}{12}$

≈ 477.29 • Round to the nearest cent.

Find the principal paid on the first mortgage payment by subtracting the interest paid from the monthly mortgage payment.

$538.92 - 477.29 = 61.63$

Calculate the balance on the loan after the first mortgage payment by subtracting the principal paid from the mortgage.

$79{,}000 - 61.63 = 78{,}938.37$

Find the amount of interest paid on the second mortgage payment.

$I = Prt$

$= 78{,}938.37(0.0725)\left(\frac{1}{12}\right)$ • $P = 78{,}938.37$, the current loan amount; $r = 0.0725$; $t = \frac{1}{12}$

≈ 476.92 • Round to the nearest cent.

The interest paid on the second payment was $476.92.

Find the principal paid on the second mortgage payment.

$538.92 - 476.92 = 62.00$

The principal paid on the second payment was $62.

CHECK YOUR PROGRESS 3 You purchase a home for $295,000. You obtain a 30-year conventional mortgage at 6.75% after paying a down payment of 25% of the purchase price. Of the first month's payment, how much is interest and how much is applied toward the principal?

Solution See page S13.

When a home is sold before the term of the loan has expired, the homeowner must pay the lender the remaining balance on the loan. To calculate that balance, we can use the APR loan payoff formula from Section 3.3.

APR Loan Payoff Formula

The payoff amount for a mortgage is given by

$$A = PMT\left(\frac{1-\left(1+\frac{r}{n}\right)^{-U}}{\frac{r}{n}}\right)$$

where A is the loan payoff, PMT is the mortgage payment, r is the annual interest rate, n is the number of payments per year, and U is the number of *remaining* (or *unpaid*) payments.

EXAMPLE 4 Calculate a Mortgage Payoff

A homeowner has a monthly mortgage payment of $645.32 on a 30-year loan at an annual interest rate of 7.2%. After making payments for 5 years, the homeowner decides to sell the house. What is the payoff for the mortgage?

Solution

Use the APR loan payoff formula. The homeowner has been making payments for 5 years, or 60 months. There are 360 months in a 30-year loan, so there are $360 - 60 = 300$ unpaid or remaining payments; $U = 300$.

$$A = PMT\left(\frac{1-\left(1+\frac{r}{n}\right)^{-U}}{\frac{r}{n}}\right)$$

$$= 645.32\left(\frac{1-(1+0.006)^{-300}}{0.006}\right) \qquad \bullet\ PMT = 645.32;\ \frac{r}{n} = \frac{0.072}{12} = 0.006;$$

$U = 300$, the number of remaining payments

$$\approx 89{,}679.01$$

N=300
I%=7.2
PV=89679.0079
PMT=-645.32
FV=0
P/Y=12
C/Y=12
PMT: END BEGIN

Here are the keystrokes to compute the payoff on a scientific calculator. The same calculation using a graphing calculator is shown at the left.

Calculate i: 0.072 [÷] 12 [=] 0.006 [STO]

Calculate the payoff: 645.32 [×] [(] 1 [−] [(] 1 [+] [RCL] [)] [yˣ] 300 [+/−] [)] [÷] [RCL] [=]

The loan payoff is $89,679.01.

CHECK YOUR PROGRESS 4 Ava Rivera has a monthly mortgage payment of $846.82 on her condo. After making payments for 4 years, she decides to sell the condo. If she has a 25-year loan at an annual interest rate of 6.9%, what is the payoff for the mortgage?

Solution See page S13.

MATH MATTERS Biweekly and Two-Step Mortgages

A variation of the fixed-rate mortgage is the *biweekly mortgage.* Borrowers make payments on a 30-year loan, but they pay half of a monthly payment every 2 weeks, which adds up to 26 half-payments a year, or 13 monthly payments. By making one extra monthly payment each year, the homeowner can pay off the mortgage in about $17\frac{1}{2}$ years.

Another type of mortgage is the *two-step mortgage.* Its name is derived from the fact that the life of the loan has two stages. The first step is a low fixed rate for the first 7 years of the loan, and the second step is a different, and probably higher, fixed rate for the remaining 23 years of the loan. This loan is appealing to those homeowners who do not anticipate owning the home beyond the initial low-interest-rate period; they do not need to worry about the increased interest rate during the second step.

Ongoing Expenses

In addition to a monthly mortgage payment, there are other ongoing expenses associated with home ownership. Among these expenses are the costs of insurance, property tax, and utilities such as heat, electricity, and water.

Services such as schools, police and fire protection, road maintenance, and recreational services, which are provided by cities and counties, are financed by the revenue received from taxes levied on real property, or property taxes. Property tax is normally an annual expense that can be paid on a monthly, quarterly, semiannual, or annual basis.

Homeowners who obtain a mortgage must carry fire insurance. This insurance guarantees that the lender will be repaid in the event of a fire.

POINT OF INTEREST

The home ownership rate in the United States for the fourth quarter of 2015 was 63.8%. The following list gives home ownership rates by region during the same quarter.

Northeast: 61.6%

Midwest: 68.1%

South: 65.3%

West: 59.0%

It is interesting to note that the home ownership rate in the United States in 1950 was 55.0%, significantly lower than it is today. (*Source:* U.S. Bureau of the Census)

EXAMPLE 5 Calculate a Total Monthly Payment

A homeowner has a monthly mortgage payment of $1145.60 and an annual property tax bill of $1074. The annual fire insurance premium is $600. Find the total monthly payment for the mortgage, property tax, and fire insurance.

Solution

Find the monthly property tax bill by dividing the annual property tax bill by 12.

$$1074 \div 12 = 89.50$$

The monthly property tax bill is $89.50.

Find the monthly fire insurance bill by dividing the annual fire insurance bill by 12.

$$600 \div 12 = 50$$

The monthly fire insurance bill is $50.

Find the sum of the mortgage payment, the monthly property tax bill, and the monthly fire insurance bill.

$$1145.60 + 89.50 + 50.00 = 1285.10$$

The monthly payment for the mortgage, property tax, and fire insurance is $1285.10.

CHECK YOUR PROGRESS 5 A homeowner has a monthly mortgage payment of $1492.89, an annual property tax bill of $2332.80, and an annual fire insurance premium of $450. Find the total monthly payment for the mortgage, property tax bill, and fire insurance.

Solution See page S14.

EXCURSION

Home Ownership Issues

There are a number of issues that a person must think about when purchasing a home. One such issue is the difference between the interest rate on which the loan payment is based and the APR. For instance, a bank may offer a loan at an annual interest rate of 6.5%, but then go on to say that the APR is 7.1%.

The discrepancy is a result of the Truth in Lending Act. This act requires that the APR be based on all loan fees. This includes points and other fees associated with the purchase. To calculate the APR, a computer or financial calculator is necessary.

Suppose that you decide to purchase a home and you secure a 30-year, $285,000 loan at an annual interest rate of 6.5%.

EXCURSION EXERCISES

1. Calculate the monthly payment for the loan.
2. If points are 1.5% of the loan amount, find the fee for points.
3. Add the fee for points to the loan amount. This is the modified mortgage on which the APR is calculated.
4. Using the result from Excursion Exercise 3 as the mortgage and the monthly payment from Excursion Exercise 1, determine the interest rate. (This is where the financial or graphing calculator is necessary. See page 194 for details.) The result is the APR required by the Truth in Lending Act. For this example we have included only points. In most situations, other fees would be included as well.

Another issue to research when purchasing a home is that of points and mortgage interest rates. Usually, higher points are associated with a lower mortgage interest rate. The question for the homebuyer is: Should I pay higher points for a lower mortgage interest rate, or pay lower points for a higher mortgage interest rate? The answer to that question depends on many factors, one of which is the amount of time the homeowner plans on staying in the home.

Consider two typical situations for a 30-year, $100,000 mortgage. Option 1 offers an annual mortgage interest rate of 7.25% and a loan origination fee of 1.5 points. Option 2 offers an annual interest rate of 7% and a loan origination fee of 2 points.

5. Calculate the monthly payments for Option 1 and Option 2.
6. Calculate the loan origination fees for Option 1 and Option 2.
7. What is the total amount paid, including points, after 2 years for each option?
8. What is the total amount paid, including points, after 3 years for each option?
9. Which option is more cost effective if you stay in the home for 2 years or less? Which option is more cost effective if you stay in the home for 3 years or more? Explain your answer.

EXERCISE SET 3.5

1. **Mortgages** You buy a $258,000 home with a down payment of 25%. Find the amount of the down payment and the mortgage amount.
2. **Mortgages** Greg Walz purchases a home for $325,000 with a down payment of 10%. Find the amount of the down payment and the mortgage amount.
3. **Points** Clarrisa Madison purchases a home and secures a loan of $250,000. The bank charges a fee of 2.25 points. Find the charge for points.
4. **Points** Jerome Thurber purchases a home and secures a loan of $170,000. The bank charges a fee of $2\frac{3}{4}$ points. Find the charge for points.
5. **Closing Costs** The purchase price of a home is $309,000. A down payment of 30% is made. The bank charges $350 in fees plus 3 points. Find the total of the down payment and the closing costs.
6. **Closing Costs** The purchase price of a home is $243,000. A down payment of 20% is made. The bank charges $425 in fees plus 4 points. Find the total of the down payment and the closing costs.
7. **Closing Costs** The purchase price of a condominium is $121,500. A down payment of 25% is made. The bank charges $725 in fees plus $3\frac{1}{2}$ points. Find the total of the down payment and the closing costs.
8. **Closing Costs** The purchase price of a manufactured home is $159,000. A down payment of 20% is made. The bank charges $815 in fees plus 1.75 points. Find the total of the down payment and the closing costs.
9. **Mortgage Payments** Find the mortgage payment for a 25-year loan of $129,000 at an annual interest rate of 7.75%.
10. **Mortgage Payments** Find the mortgage payment for a 30-year loan of $245,000 at an annual interest rate of 6.5%.
11. **Mortgage Payments** Find the mortgage payment for a 15-year loan of $223,500 at an annual interest rate of 8.15%.
12. **Mortgage Payments** Find the mortgage payment for a 20-year loan of $149,900 at an annual interest rate of 8.5%.
13. **Mortgage Payments** Leigh King purchased a townhouse and obtained a 30-year loan of $152,000 at an annual interest rate of 7.75%.
    a. What is the mortgage payment?
    b. What is the total of the payments over the life of the loan?
    c. Find the amount of interest paid on the mortgage loan over the 30 years.
14. **Mortgage Payments** Richard Miyashiro purchased a condominium and obtained a 25-year loan of $199,000 at an annual interest rate of 8.25%.
    a. What is the mortgage payment?
    b. What is the total of the payments over the life of the loan?
    c. Find the amount of interest paid on the mortgage loan over the 25 years.
15. **Interest Paid** Ira Patton purchased a home and obtained a 15-year loan of $219,990 at an annual interest rate of 8.7%. Find the amount of interest paid on the loan over the 15 years.
16. **Interest Paid** Leona Jefferson purchased a home and obtained a 30-year loan of $437,750 at an annual interest rate of 7.5%. Find the amount of interest paid on the loan over the 30 years.
17. **Principal and Interest** Marcel Thiessen purchased a home for $208,500 and obtained a 15-year, fixed-rate mortgage at 9% after paying a down payment of 10%. Of the first month's mortgage payment, how much is interest and how much is applied to the principal?
18. **Principal and Interest** You purchase a condominium for $173,000. You obtain a 30-year, fixed-rate mortgage loan at 12% after paying a down payment of 25%. Of the second month's mortgage payment, how much is interest and how much is applied to the principal?
19. **Principal and Interest** You purchase a cottage for $185,000. You obtain a 20-year, fixed-rate mortgage loan at 12.5% after paying a down payment of 30%. Of the second month's mortgage payment, how much is interest and how much is applied to the principal?

Rafal Mielczarek/Shutterstock.com

20. **Principal and Interest** Fay Nguyen purchased a second home for $183,000 and obtained a 25-year, fixed-rate mortgage loan at 9.25% after paying a down payment of 30%. Of the second month's mortgage payment, how much is interest and how much is applied to the principal?
21. **Loan Payoffs** After making payments of $913.10 for 6 years on your 30-year loan at 8.5%, you decide to sell your home. What is the loan payoff?

22. **Loan Payoffs** Christopher Chamberlain has a 25-year mortgage loan at an annual interest rate of 7.75%. After making payments of $1011.56 for $3\frac{1}{2}$ years, Christopher decides to sell his home. What is the loan payoff?

23. **Loan Payoffs** Iris Chung has a 15-year mortgage loan at an annual interest rate of 7.25%. After making payments of $672.39 for 4 years, Iris decides to sell her home. What is the loan payoff?

24. **Loan Payoffs** After making payments of $736.98 for 10 years on your 30-year loan at 6.75%, you decide to sell your home. What is the loan payoff?

25. **Total Monthly Payment** A homeowner has a mortgage payment of $996.60, an annual property tax bill of $594, and an annual fire insurance premium of $300. Find the total monthly payment for the mortgage, property tax, and fire insurance.

26. **Total Monthly Payment** Malcolm Rothschild has a mortgage payment of $1753.46, an annual property tax bill of $1023, and an annual fire insurance premium of $780. Find the total monthly payment for the mortgage, property tax, and fire insurance.

27. **Total Monthly Payment** Baka Onegin obtains a 25-year mortgage loan of $259,500 at an annual interest rate of 7.15%. Her annual property tax bill is $1320 and her annual fire insurance premium is $642. Find the total monthly payment for the mortgage, property tax, and fire insurance.

28. **Total Monthly Payment** Suppose you obtain a 20-year mortgage loan of $198,000 at an annual interest rate of 8.4%. The annual property tax bill is $972 and the annual fire insurance premium is $486. Find the total monthly payment for the mortgage, property tax, and fire insurance.

29. **Mortgage Loans** Consider a mortgage loan of $150,000 at an annual interest rate of 8.125%.
    a. How much greater is the mortgage payment if the term is 15 years rather than 30 years?
    b. How much less is the amount of interest paid over the life of the 15-year loan than over the life of the 30-year loan?

30. **Mortgage Loans** Consider a mortgage loan of $359,960 at an annual interest rate of 7.875%.
    a. How much greater is the mortgage payment if the term is 15 years rather than 30 years?
    b. How much less is the amount of interest paid over the life of the 15-year loan than over the life of the 30-year loan?

31. **Mortgage Loans** The Mendez family is considering a mortgage loan of $349,500 at an annual interest rate of 6.75%.
    a. How much greater is their mortgage payment if the term is 20 years rather than 30 years?
    b. How much less is the amount of interest paid over the life of the 20-year loan than over the life of the 30-year loan?

32. **Mortgage Loans** Herbert Bloom is considering a mortgage loan of $322,495 at an annual interest rate of 7.5%.
    a. How much greater is his mortgage payment if the term is 20 years rather than 30 years?
    b. How much less is the amount of interest paid over the life of the 20-year loan than over the life of the 30-year loan?

33. **Affordability** A couple has saved $25,000 for a down payment on a home. Their bank requires a minimum down payment of 20%. What is the maximum price they can offer for a house in order to have enough money for the down payment?

34. **Affordability** You have saved $18,000 for a down payment on a house. Your bank requires a minimum down payment of 15%. What is the maximum price you can offer for a home in order to have enough money for the down payment?

35. **Affordability** You have saved $39,400 to make a down payment and pay the closing costs on your future home. Your bank informs you that a 15% down payment is required and that the closing costs should be $380 plus 4 points. What is the maximum price you can offer for a home in order to have enough money for the down payment and the closing costs?

EXTENSIONS

36. **Amortization Schedules** Suppose you have a 30-year mortgage loan for $119,500 at an annual interest rate of 8.25%. For which monthly payment does the amount of principal paid first exceed the amount of interest paid? For this exercise, you will need a spreadsheet program for producing amortization schedules. You can find one on our companion site at CengageBrain.com.

37. **Amortization Schedules** Does changing the amount of the loan in Exercise 36 change the number of the monthly payment for which the amount of principal paid first exceeds the amount of interest paid? For this exercise, you will need a spreadsheet program for producing amortization schedules. You can find one on our companion site at CengageBrain.com.

38. WWW **Amortization Schedules** Does changing the interest rate of the loan in Exercise 36 change the number of the monthly payment for which the amount of principal paid first exceeds the amount of interest paid? For this exercise, you will need a spreadsheet program for producing amortization schedules. You can find one on our companion site at CengageBrain.com.

39. Buying and Selling a Home Suppose you buy a house for $208,750, make a down payment that is 30% of the purchase price, and secure a 30-year loan for the balance at an annual interest rate of 7.75%. The points on the loan are 1.5% and there are additional lender fees of $825.

a. How much is due at closing? Note that the down payment is due at closing.

b. After 5 years, you decide to sell your house. What is the loan payoff?

c. Because of inflation, you are able to sell your house for $248,000. Assuming that the selling fees are 6% of the selling price, what are the proceeds of the sale after deducting selling fees? Do not include the interest paid on the mortgage. Remember to consider the loan payoff.

d. The percent return on an investment equals $\frac{\text{proceeds from sale}}{\text{total closing costs}} \times 100$. Find the percent return on your investment. Round to the nearest percent.

CHAPTER 3 SUMMARY

The following table summarizes essential concepts in this chapter. The references given in the right-hand column list Examples and Exercises that can be used to test your understanding of a concept.

3.1 Simple Interest	
Simple Interest Formula The simple interest formula is $I = Prt$, where I is the interest, P is the principal, r is the interest rate, and t is the time period.	See **Examples 2, 4, and 5** on pages 165 and 166, and then try Exercises 1, 2, and 3 on page 227.
Future Value or Maturity Value Formula for Simple Interest The future or maturity value formula for simple interest is $$A = P + I$$ where A is the amount after the interest, I, has been added to the principal, P. The future value or maturity value formula can also be written $A = P(1 + rt)$, where A is the future or maturity value, P is the principal, r is the interest rate, and t is the time period.	See **Examples 6 and 7** on pages 168 and 169, and then try Exercise 4 on page 227.
3.2 Compound Interest	
Compound Amount Formula The compound amount formula is $$A = P\left(1 + \frac{r}{n}\right)^{nt}$$ where A is the compound amount, P is the amount of money deposited, r is the annual interest rate, n is the number of compounding periods per year, and t is the number of years.	See **Examples 2, 3, and 4** on pages 176 and 177, and then try Exercises 7, 8, and 9 on page 227.
Present Value Formula The present value formula is $$P = \frac{A}{\left(1 + \frac{r}{n}\right)^{nt}}$$ where P is the original principal invested, A is the compound amount, r is the annual interest rate, n is the number of compounding periods per year, and t is the number of years.	See **Example 6** on page 179, and then try Exercises 10 and 12 on pages 227 and 228.

continued

Inflation To calculate the effects of inflation, use the same procedure used to calculate compound amount. Assume a constant annual inflation rate, and use $n = 1$ in the calculation.	See **Examples 8 and 9** on page 181, and then try Exercises 15 and 16 on page 228.
Effective Interest Rate When interest is compounded, the annual rate of interest is the nominal rate. The effective rate is the simple interest rate that would yield the same amount of interest after 1 year.	See **Examples 10 and 11** on pages 183 and 184, and then try Exercises 17 and 18 on page 228.
3.3 Credit Cards and Consumer Loans	
Average Daily Balance Average daily balance = $\dfrac{\text{sum of the total amounts owed each day of the month}}{\text{number of days in the billing cycle}}$	See **Example 1** on page 191, and then try Exercises 19 and 20 on page 228.
Approximate Annual Percentage Rate (APR) Formula for a Simple Interest Loan The annual percentage rate (APR) of a simple interest rate loan can be approximated by $\text{APR} \approx \dfrac{2nr}{n+1}$ where n is the number of payments and r is the simple interest rate.	See **Example 2** on page 194, and then try Exercises 21 and 22 on page 228.
Payment Formula for an APR Loan The payment for a loan based on APR is given by $PMT = A\left(\dfrac{\frac{r}{n}}{1-\left(1+\frac{r}{n}\right)^{-nt}}\right)$ where PMT is the payment, A is the loan amount, r is the annual interest rate, n is the number of payments per year, and t is the number of years.	See **Examples 3 and 4** on pages 195 and 196, and then try Exercises 23, 24, and 25 on page 228.
APR Loan Payoff Formula The payoff amount for a loan based on APR is given by $A = PMT\left(\dfrac{1-\left(1+\frac{r}{n}\right)^{-U}}{\frac{r}{n}}\right)$ where A is the loan payoff, PMT is the payment, r is the annual interest rate, n is the number of payments per year, and U is the number of *remaining* (or *unpaid*) payments.	See **Example 5** on page 198, and then try Exercise 26 on page 228.
3.4 Stocks, Bonds, and Mutual Funds	
Stocks A company may distribute profits to its shareholders in the form of dividends. A dividend is usually expressed as a per-share amount. The dividend yield is the amount of the dividend divided by the stock price and is expressed as a percent.	See **Examples 1 and 2** on pages 206 and 207, and then try Exercise 13 on page 228.

Bonds The price paid for a bond is the face value. The issuer promises to repay the bondholder on a particular day, called the maturity date, at a given interest rate, called the coupon.	See **Example 4** on page 209, and then try Exercise 14 on page 228.
Net Asset Value of a Mutual Fund The net asset value of a mutual fund is given by $$NAV = \frac{A - L}{N}$$ where A is the total fund assets, L is the total fund liabilities, and N is the number of shares outstanding.	See **Example 5** on page 210, and then try Exercise 28 on page 228.
3.5 Home Ownership	
Mortgage Payment Formula The mortgage payment for a mortgage is given by $$PMT = A\left(\frac{\frac{r}{n}}{1-\left(1+\frac{r}{n}\right)^{-nt}}\right)$$ where PMT is the monthly mortgage payment, A is the amount of the mortgage, r is the annual interest rate, n is the number of payments per year, and t is the number of years.	See **Examples 2 and 3** on pages 216–217 and 218–219, and then try Exercise 30 on page 229.
APR Loan Payoff Formula The payoff amount for a mortgage is given by $$A = PMT\left(\frac{1-\left(1+\frac{r}{n}\right)^{-U}}{\frac{r}{n}}\right)$$ where A is the loan payoff, PMT is the mortgage payment, r is the annual interest rate, n is the number of payments per year, and U is the number of *remaining* (or *unpaid*) payments.	See **Example 4** on page 220, and then try Exercise 26 on page 228.

CHAPTER 3 REVIEW EXERCISES

1. **Simple Interest** Calculate the simple interest due on a 4-month loan of $2750 if the interest rate is 6.75%.
2. **Simple Interest** Find the simple interest due on an 8-month loan of $8500 if the interest rate is 1.15% per month.
3. **Simple Interest** What is the simple interest earned in 120 days on a deposit of $4000 if the interest rate is 6.75%?
4. **Maturity Value** Calculate the maturity value of a simple interest, 108-day loan of $7000 if the interest rate is 10.4%.
5. **Simple Interest Rate** The simple interest charged on a 3-month loan of $6800 is $127.50. Find the simple interest rate.
6. **Compound Amount** Calculate the compound amount when $3000 is deposited in an account earning 6.6% interest, compounded monthly, for 3 years.
7. **Compound Amount** What is the compound amount when $6400 is deposited in an account earning an interest rate of 6%, compounded quarterly, for 10 years?
8. **Future Value** Find the future value of $6000 earning 9% interest, compounded daily, for 3 years.
9. **Compound Interest** Calculate the amount of interest earned in 4 years on $600 deposited in an account paying 7.2% interest, compounded daily.
10. **Present Value** How much money should be invested in an account that earns 8% interest, compounded semiannually, in order to have $18,500 in 7 years?

11. Loans To help pay your college expenses, you borrow $8000 and agree to repay the loan at the end of 5 years at 7% interest, compounded quarterly.

a. What is the maturity value of the loan?

b. How much interest are you paying on the loan?

12. Present Value A couple plans to save for their child's college education. What principal must be deposited by the parents when their child is born in order to have $80,000 when the child reaches the age of 18? Assume the money earns 8% interest, compounded quarterly.

13. Dividend Yield A stock pays an annual dividend of $0.66 per share. The stock is trading at $60. Find the dividend yield.

14. Bonds A bond with a $20,000 face value has a 4.5% coupon and a 10-year maturity. Calculate the total of the interest payments paid to the bondholder.

15. Inflation In 2011, the price of 1 lb of baking potatoes was $0.89. Use an annual inflation rate of 6% to calculate the price of 1 lb of baking potatoes in 2021. Round to the nearest cent.

16. Inflation You purchase a bond that will provide you with $75,000 in 8 years. Assuming an annual inflation rate of 7%, what will be the purchasing power of the $75,000 in 8 years?

17. Effective Interest Rate Calculate the effective interest rate of 5.90% compounded monthly. Round to the nearest hundredth of a percent.

18. Annual Yield Which has the higher annual yield, 5.2% compounded quarterly or 5.4% compounded semiannually?

19. Average Daily Balance A credit card account had a $423.35 balance on March 11. A purchase of $145.50 was made on March 18, and a payment of $250 was made on March 29. Find the average daily balance if the billing date is April 11.

20. Finance Charges On September 10, a credit card account had a balance of $450. A purchase of $47 was made on September 20, and $157 was charged on September 25. A payment of $175 was made on September 28. The interest on the average daily balance is 1.25% per month. Find the finance charge on the October 10 bill.

21. APR Arlene McDonald borrows $1500 from a bank that advertises a 7.5% simple interest rate and repays the loan in six equal monthly payments.

a. Find the monthly payment.

b. Estimate the APR. Round to the nearest tenth of a percent.

22. APR Suppose you purchase a laptop computer for $449, make a 10% down payment, and agree to repay the balance in 12 equal monthly payments. The finance charge on the balance is 7% simple interest.

a. Find the monthly payment.

b. Estimate the APR. Round to the nearest tenth.

23. Monthly Payments Photo Experts offers a Nikon camera for $999, including taxes. If you finance the purchase of this camera for 2 years at an annual interest rate of 8.5%, find the monthly payment.

24. Monthly Payments Abeni Silver purchases a Samsung 4K Ultra HD TV for $9499. The sales tax is 6.25% of the purchase price.

a. What is the total cost, including sales tax?

b. If Abeni makes a down payment of 20% of the total cost, find the down payment.

c. Assuming that Abeni finances the remaining cost at an annual interest rate of 8% for 3 years, find the monthly payment.

25. Car Payments Suppose that you decide to purchase a new car. You go to a credit union to get preapproval for your loan. The credit union offers you an annual interest rate of 3.25% for 3 years. The purchase price of the car you select is $28,450, including taxes, and you make a 20% down payment. What is your monthly payment?

26. Loan Payoffs Dasan Houston obtains a $28,000, 5-year loan for a hybrid car at an annual interest rate of 5.9%.

a. Find the monthly payment.

b. After 3 years, Dasan decides to purchase a new car. What is the payoff on his loan?

27. Stock Sale Suppose that you purchased 500 shares of stock at a price of $28.75 per share and sold them for $39.40 per share.

a. Ignoring dividends, what was your profit or loss on the sale of the stock?

b. If your broker charges 1.3% of the total sale price, what was the broker's commission?

28. Mutual Funds A mutual fund has total assets of $34 million and total liabilities of $4 million. There are 2 million shares outstanding. You invest $3000 in this fund. How many shares are you purchasing?

29. Closing Costs The purchase price of a seaside cottage is $459,000. A down payment of 20% is made. The bank charges $815 in fees plus 1.75 points. Find the total of the down payment and the closing costs.

30. **Mortgage Payments** Suppose you purchase a condominium and obtain a 30-year loan of $255,800 at an annual interest rate of 6.75%.
   a. What is the mortgage payment?
   b. What is the total of the payments over the life of the loan?
   c. Find the amount of interest paid on the mortgage loan over the 30 years.

31. **Mortgage Payments and Loan Payoffs** Garth Santacruz purchased a condominium and obtained a 25-year loan of $189,000 at an annual interest rate of 7.5%.
   a. What is the mortgage payment?
   b. After making payments for 10 years, Garth decides to sell his home. What is the loan payoff?

32. **Total Monthly Payments** Geneva Goldberg obtains a 15-year loan of $278,950 at an annual interest rate of 7%. Her annual property tax bill is $1134 and her annual fire insurance premium is $681. Find the total monthly payment for the mortgage, property tax, and fire insurance.

33. **Student Loans** A student receives a non-subsidized Stafford loan of $17,000 at an annual interest rate of 4.1% for 6 years. What are the monthly payments on the loan when the student graduates 2 years later?

CHAPTER 3 TEST

1. **Simple Interest** Calculate the simple interest due on a 3-month loan of $5250 if the interest rate is 8.25%.
2. **Simple Interest** Find the simple interest earned in 180 days on a deposit of $6000 if the interest rate is 6.75%.
3. **Maturity Value** Calculate the maturity value of a simple interest, 200-day loan of $8000 if the interest rate is 9.2%.
4. **Simple Interest Rate** The simple interest charged on a 2-month loan of $7600 is $114. Find the simple interest rate.
5. **Compound Amount** What is the compound amount when $4200 is deposited in an account earning an interest rate of 7%, compounded monthly, for 8 years?
6. **Compound Interest** Calculate the amount of interest earned in 3 years on $1500 deposited in an account paying 6.3% interest, compounded daily.
7. **Maturity Value** To help pay for a new truck, you borrow $10,500 and agree to repay the loan in 4 years at 9.5% interest, compounded monthly.
   a. What is the maturity value of the loan?
   b. How much interest are you paying on the loan?
8. **Present Value** A young couple wants to save money to buy a house. What principal must be deposited by the couple in order to have $30,000 in 5 years? Assume the money earns 6.25% interest, compounded daily.
9. **Dividend Yield** A stock that has a market value of $40 pays an annual dividend of $0.48 per share. Find the dividend yield.
10. **Bonds** Suppose you purchase a $5000 bond that has a 3.8% coupon and a 10-year maturity. Calculate the total of the interest payments that you will receive.
11. **Inflation** In 2016, the median value of a single-family house was $224,000. Use an annual inflation rate of 4.3% to calculate the median value of a single family house in 2029. (*Source:* money.cnn.com)
12. **Effective Interest Rate** Calculate the effective interest rate of 6.25% compounded quarterly. Round to the nearest hundredth of a percent.
13. **Annual Yield** Which has the higher annual yield, 4.4% compounded monthly or 4.6% compounded semiannually?
14. **Finance Charges** On October 15, a credit card account had a balance of $515. A purchase of $75 was made on October 20, and a payment of $250 was made on October 28. The interest on the average daily balance is 1.8% per month. Find the finance charge on the November 15 bill.
15. **APR** Suppose that you purchase a 2-in-1 laptop computer for $629, make a 15% down payment, and agree to repay the balance in 12 equal monthly payments. The finance charge on the balance is 9% simple interest.
   a. Find the monthly payment.
   b. Estimate the APR. Round to the nearest tenth of a percent.
16. **Monthly Payments** Technology Pro offers a new computer for $1899, including taxes. If you finance the purchase of this computer for 3 years at an annual percentage rate of 4.5%, find your monthly payment.

17. Stock Sale Suppose you purchased 800 shares of stock at a price of $31.82 per share and sold them for $25.70 per share.

a. Ignoring dividends, what was your profit or loss on the sale of the stock?

b. If your broker charges 1.1% of the total sale price, what was the broker's commission?

18. Mutual Funds A mutual fund has total assets of $42 million and total liabilities of $6 million. There are 3 million shares outstanding. You invest $2500 in this fund. How many shares are you purchasing?

19. Monthly Payments Kalani Canfield purchases a deluxe hot tub for $6575. The sales tax is 6.25% of the purchase price.

a. What is the total cost, including sales tax?

b. If Kalani makes a down payment of 20% of the total cost, find the down payment.

c. Assuming Kalani finances the remaining cost at an annual interest rate of 7.8% for 3 years, find the monthly payment.

20. Closing Costs The purchase price of a house is $262,250. A down payment of 20% is made. The bank charges $815 in fees plus 3.25 points. Find the total of the down payment and the closing costs.

21. Mortgage Payments and Loan Payoffs Bernard Mason purchased a house and obtained a 30-year loan of $236,000 at an annual interest rate of 6.75%.

a. What is the mortgage payment?

b. After making payments for 5 years, Bernard decides to sell his home. What is the loan payoff?

22. Total Monthly Payment Zelda MacPherson obtains a 20-year loan of $312,000 at an annual interest rate of 7.25%. Her annual property tax bill is $1044 and her annual fire insurance premium is $516. Find the total monthly payment for the mortgage, property tax, and fire insurance.

4

Statistics

The U.S. government collects data on the population of the United States. It then issues *statistical* reports that indicate changes and trends in the U.S. population. For instance, according to *The World Factbook*, published by the Central Intelligence Agency (CIA), in 2015 there were approximately 105 males for every 100 females between the ages of 15 and 24. However, in the category of people 65 years old and older, there were approximately 79 men for every 100 women. See the graph below.

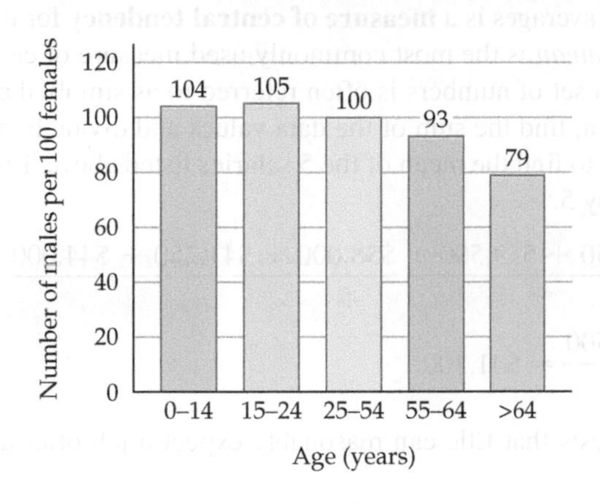

SOURCE: CIA, *The World Factbook*

Here are some other statistics from *The World Factbook*:

- There are 2.45 physicians per 1000 people in the United States.
- In 1910, the mean annual family income in the United States was $687. In 2015, the mean annual family income was approximately $68,500.

However, the *median* annual family income was approximately $51,900. The difference between the mean and the median is one of the topics of this chapter.

SECTION 4.1 Measures of Central Tendency

The Arithmetic Mean

Statistics involves the collection, organization, summarization, presentation, and interpretation of data. The branch of statistics that involves the collection, organization, summarization, and presentation of data is called **descriptive statistics**. The branch that interprets and draws conclusions from the data is called **inferential statistics**.

One of the most basic statistical concepts involves finding *measures of central tendency* of a set of numerical data. It is often helpful to find numerical values that locate, in some sense, the *center* of a set of data. Suppose Elle is a senior at a university. In a few months she plans to graduate and start a career as a landscape architect. A survey of five landscape architects from last year's senior class shows that they received job offers with the following yearly salaries.

$43,750 $39,500 $38,000 $41,250 $44,000

Before Elle interviews for a job, she wishes to determine an *average* of these 5 salaries. This average should be a "central" number around which the salaries cluster. We will consider three types of averages, known as the *arithmetic mean*, the *median*, and the *mode*. Each of these averages is a **measure of central tendency** for the numerical data.

The *arithmetic mean* is the most commonly used measure of central tendency. The arithmetic mean of a set of numbers is often referred to as simply the *mean*. To find the mean for a set of data, find the sum of the data values and divide by the number of data values. For instance, to find the mean of the 5 salaries listed above, Elle would divide the sum of the salaries by 5.

$$\text{Mean} = \frac{\$43{,}750 + \$39{,}500 + \$38{,}000 + \$41{,}250 + \$44{,}000}{5}$$

$$= \frac{\$206{,}500}{5} = \$41{,}300$$

The mean suggests that Elle can reasonably expect a job offer at a salary of about $41,300.

In statistics it is often necessary to find the sum of a set of numbers. The traditional symbol used to indicate a summation is the Greek letter *sigma*, Σ. Thus the notation Σx, called **summation notation**, denotes the sum of all the numbers in a given set. We can define the mean using summation notation.

Mean

The **mean** of n numbers is the sum of the numbers divided by n.

$$\text{Mean} = \frac{\Sigma x}{n}$$

Statisticians often collect data from small portions of a large group in order to determine information about the group. In such situations the entire group under consideration is known as the **population**, and any subset of the population is called a **sample**. It is traditional to denote the mean of a *sample* by $\bar{x}$ (which is read as "x bar") and to denote the mean of a *population* by the Greek letter μ (lowercase mu).

EXAMPLE 1 Find a Mean

Six friends in a biology class of 20 students received test grades of

92, 84, 65, 76, 88, and 90

Find the mean of these test scores.

Solution

The 6 friends are a sample of the population of 20 students. Use $\bar{x}$ to represent the mean.

$$\bar{x} = \frac{\Sigma x}{n} = \frac{92 + 84 + 65 + 76 + 88 + 90}{6} = \frac{495}{6} = 82.5$$

The mean of these test scores is 82.5.

CHECK YOUR PROGRESS 1 A doctor ordered 4 separate blood tests to measure a patient's total blood cholesterol levels. The test results were

245, 235, 220, and 210

Find the mean of the blood cholesterol levels.

Solution See page S14.

The Median

Another type of average is the *median*. Essentially, the median is the *middle number* or the *mean of the two middle numbers* in a list of numbers that have been arranged in numerical order from smallest to largest or largest to smallest. Any list of numbers that is arranged in numerical order from smallest to largest or largest to smallest is a **ranked list.**

POINT OF INTEREST

Peter French/Pacific Stock/Design Pics/Superstock

The average price of the homes in a neighborhood is often stated in terms of the median price of the homes that have been sold over a given time period. The median price, rather than the mean, is used because it is easy to calculate and less sensitive to extreme prices.

Median

The median of a ranked list of n numbers is:

- the middle number if n is odd.
- the mean of the two middle numbers if n is even.

EXAMPLE 2 Find a Median

Find the median of the data in the following lists.

a. 4, 8, 1, 14, 9, 21, 12 **b.** 46, 23, 92, 89, 77, 108

Solution

a. The list 4, 8, 1, 14, 9, 21, 12 contains 7 numbers. The median of a list with an odd number of entries is found by ranking the numbers and finding the middle number. Ranking the numbers from smallest to largest gives

1, 4, 8, 9, 12, 14, 21

The middle number is 9. Thus 9 is the median.

b. The list 46, 23, 92, 89, 77, 108 contains 6 numbers. The median of a list of data with an even number of entries is found by ranking the numbers and computing the mean of the two middle numbers. Ranking the numbers from smallest to largest gives

23, 46, 77, 89, 92, 108

The two middle numbers are 77 and 89. The mean of 77 and 89 is 83. Thus 83 is the median of the data.

CHECK YOUR PROGRESS 2 Find the median of the data in the following lists.

a. 14, 27, 3, 82, 64, 34, 8, 51

b. 21.3, 37.4, 11.6, 82.5, 17.2

Solution See page S14.

QUESTION The median of the ranked list 3, 4, 7, 11, 17, 29, 37 is 11. If the maximum value 37 is increased to 55, what effect will this have on the median?

The Mode

A third type of average is the *mode*.

Mode

The **mode** of a list of numbers is the number that occurs most frequently.

Some lists of numbers do not have a mode. For instance, in the list 1, 6, 8, 10, 32, 15, 49, each number occurs exactly once. Because no number occurs more often than the other numbers, there is no mode.

A list of numerical data can have more than one mode. For instance, in the list 4, 2, 6, 2, 7, 9, 2, 4, 9, 8, 9, 7, the number 2 occurs three times and the number 9 occurs three times. Each of the other numbers occurs less than three times. Thus 2 and 9 are both modes for the data.

EXAMPLE 3 Find a Mode

Find the mode of the data in the following lists.

a. 18, 15, 21, 16, 15, 14, 15, 21 **b.** 2, 5, 8, 9, 11, 4, 7, 23

Solution

a. In the list 18, 15, 21, 16, 15, 14, 15, 21, the number 15 occurs more often than the other numbers. Thus 15 is the mode.

b. Each number in the list 2, 5, 8, 9, 11, 4, 7, 23 occurs only once. Because no number occurs more often than the others, there is no mode.

CHECK YOUR PROGRESS 3 Find the mode of the data in the following lists.

a. 3, 3, 3, 3, 3, 4, 4, 5, 5, 5, 8 **b.** 12, 34, 12, 71, 48, 93, 71

Solution See page S14.

POINT OF INTEREST

Daniel Acker/Bloomberg/Getty Images

For professional sports teams, the salaries of a few very highly paid players can lead to large differences between the mean and the median salary. In 2015, the median Major League Baseball (MLB) salary was about $1.65 million. The mean salary was $4.2 million, about 2.5 times the median. (*Source:* sports.yahoo.com)

The mean, the median, and the mode are all averages; however, they are generally not equal. The mean of a set of data is the most sensitive of the averages. A change in any of the numbers changes the mean, and the mean can be changed drastically by changing an extreme value.

In contrast, the median and the mode of a set of data are usually not changed by changing an extreme value.

When a data set has one or more extreme values that are very different from the majority of data values, the mean will not necessarily be a good indicator of an average value. In the following example, we compare the mean, median, and mode for the salaries of 5 employees of a small company.

Salaries: $370,000 $60,000 $36,000 $20,000 $20,000

The sum of the 5 salaries is $506,000. Hence the mean is

$$\frac{506{,}000}{5} = 101{,}200$$

ANSWER The median will remain the same because 11 will still be the middle number in the ranked list.

The median is the middle number, \$36,000. Because the \$20,000 salary occurs the most, the mode is \$20,000. The data contain one extreme value that is much larger than the other values. This extreme value makes the mean considerably larger than the median. Most of the employees of this company would probably agree that the median of \$36,000 better represents the average of the salaries than does either the mean or the mode.

MATH MATTERS Average Rate for a Round Trip

Suppose you average 60 mph on a one-way trip of 60 mi. On the return trip you average 30 mph. You might be tempted to think that the average of 60 mph and 30 mph, which is 45 mph, is the average rate for the entire trip. However, this is not the case. Because you were traveling more slowly on the return trip, the return trip took longer than the original trip to your destination. More time was spent traveling at the slower speed. Thus the average rate for the round trip is less than the average (mean) of 60 mph and 30 mph.

To find the actual average rate for the round trip, use the formula

$$\text{Average rate} = \frac{\text{total distance}}{\text{total time}}$$

The total round-trip distance is 120 mi. The time spent traveling to your destination was 1 h, and the time spent on the return trip was 2 h. The total time for the round trip was 3 h. Thus,

$$\text{Average rate} = \frac{\text{total distance}}{\text{total time}} = \frac{120}{3} = 40 \text{ mph}$$

The Weighted Mean

A value called the *weighted mean* is often used when some data values are more important than others. For instance, many professors determine a student's course grade from the student's tests and the final examination. Consider the situation in which a professor counts the final examination score as 2 test scores. To find the weighted mean of the student's scores, the professor first assigns a weight to each score. In this case the professor could assign each of the test scores a weight of 1 and the final exam score a weight of 2. A student with test scores of 65, 70, and 75 and a final examination score of 90 has a weighted mean of

$$\frac{(65 \times 1) + (70 \times 1) + (75 \times 1) + (90 \times 2)}{5} = \frac{390}{5} = 78$$

Note that the numerator of the weighted mean above is the sum of the products of each test score and its corresponding weight. The number 5 in the denominator is the sum of all the weights $(1 + 1 + 1 + 2 = 5)$. The procedure for finding the weighted mean can be generalized as follows.

The Weighted Mean

The **weighted mean** of the n numbers $x_1, x_2, x_3, \ldots, x_n$ with the respective assigned weights $w_1, w_2, w_3, \ldots, w_n$ is

$$\text{Weighted mean} = \frac{\Sigma(x \cdot w)}{\Sigma w}$$

where $\Sigma(x \cdot w)$ is the sum of the products formed by multiplying each number by its assigned weight, and Σw is the sum of all the weights.

Many colleges use the 4-point grading system:

A = 4, B = 3, C = 2, D = 1, F = 0

A student's grade point average (GPA) is calculated as a weighted mean, where the student's grade in each course is given a weight equal to the number of units (or credits) that course is worth. Use this 4-point grading system for Example 4 and Check Your Progress 4.

EXAMPLE 4 **Find a Weighted Mean**

TABLE 4.1
Dillon's Grades, Fall Semester

Course	Course grade	Course units
English	B	4
History	A	3
Chemistry	D	3
Algebra	C	4

Table 4.1 shows Dillon's fall semester course grades. Use the weighted mean formula to find Dillon's GPA for the fall semester.

Solution

The B is worth 3 points, with a weight of 4; the A is worth 4 points with a weight of 3; the D is worth 1 point, with a weight of 3; and the C is worth 2 points, with a weight of 4. The sum of all the weights is 4 + 3 + 3 + 4, or 14.

$$\text{Weighted mean} = \frac{(3 \times 4) + (4 \times 3) + (1 \times 3) + (2 \times 4)}{14}$$

$$= \frac{35}{14} = 2.5$$

Dillon's GPA for the fall semester is 2.5.

TABLE 4.2
Janet's Grades, Spring Semester

Course	Course grade	Course units
Biology	A	4
Statistics	B	3
Business	C	3
Psychology	F	2
CAD	B	2

CHECK YOUR PROGRESS 4 Table 4.2 shows Janet's spring semester course grades. Use the weighted mean formula to find Janet's GPA for the spring semester. Round to the nearest hundredth.

Solution See page S14.

Data that have not been organized or manipulated in any manner are called **raw data**. A large collection of raw data may not provide much readily observable information. A **frequency distribution**, which is a table that lists observed events and the frequency of occurrence of each observed event, is often used to organize raw data. For instance, consider the following table, which lists the number of laptop computers owned by families in each of 40 homes in a subdivision.

TABLE 4.3
Number of Laptop Computers per Household

2	0	3	1	2	1	0	4
2	1	1	7	2	0	1	1
0	2	2	1	3	2	2	1
1	4	2	5	2	3	1	2
2	1	2	1	5	0	2	5

The frequency distribution in Table 4.4 on the next page was constructed using the data from Table 4.3. The first column of the frequency distribution consists of the numbers 0, 1, 2, 3, 4, 5, 6, and 7. The corresponding frequency of occurrence, *f*, of each of the numbers in the first column is listed in the second column.

TABLE 4.4

A Frequency Distribution for Table 4.3

Observed event Number of laptop computers, x	*Frequency* Number of households, f, with x laptop computers
0	5
1	12
2	14
3	3
4	2
5	3
6	0
7	1
	40 total

This row indicates that there are 14 households with 2 laptop computers.

The formula for a weighted mean can be used to find the mean of the data in a frequency distribution. The only change is that the weights $w_1, w_2, w_3, \ldots, w_n$ are replaced with the frequencies $f_1, f_2, f_3, \ldots, f_n$. This procedure is illustrated in the next example.

EXAMPLE 5 Find the Mean of Data Displayed in a Frequency Distribution

Find the mean of the data in Table 4.4.

Solution

The numbers in the right-hand column of Table 4.4 are the frequencies f for the numbers in the first column. The sum of all the frequencies is 40.

$$\text{Mean} = \frac{\Sigma(x \cdot f)}{\Sigma f}$$

$$= \frac{(0 \cdot 5) + (1 \cdot 12) + (2 \cdot 14) + (3 \cdot 3) + (4 \cdot 2) + (5 \cdot 3) + (6 \cdot 0) + (7 \cdot 1)}{40}$$

$$= \frac{79}{40}$$

$$= 1.975$$

The mean number of laptop computers per household for the homes in the subdivision is 1.975.

CHECK YOUR PROGRESS 5 A housing division consists of 45 homes. The following frequency distribution shows the number of homes in the subdivision that are two-bedroom homes, the number that are three-bedroom homes, the number that are four-bedroom homes, and the number that are five-bedroom homes. Find the mean number of bedrooms for the 45 homes.

Observed event Number of bedrooms, x	*Frequency* Number of homes with x bedrooms
2	5
3	25
4	10
5	5
	45 total

Solution See page S14.

EXCURSION

Linear Interpolation and Animation

Linear interpolation is a method used to find a particular number between two given numbers. For instance, if a table lists the two entries 0.3156 and 0.8248, then the value exactly halfway between the numbers is the mean of the numbers, which is 0.5702. To find the number that is 0.2 of the way from 0.3156 to 0.8248, compute 0.2 times the difference between the numbers and, because the first number is smaller than the second number, add this result to the smaller number.

$$0.8248 - 0.3156 = 0.5092 \longleftarrow \text{Difference between the table entries}$$

$$0.2 \cdot (0.5902) = 0.10184 \longleftarrow \text{0.2 of the above difference}$$

$$0.3156 + 0.10184 = 0.41744 \longleftarrow \text{Interpolated result, which is 0.2 of the way between the two table entries}$$

The above linear interpolation process can be used to find an intermediate number that is any specified fraction of the difference between two given numbers.

EXCURSION EXERCISES

1. Use linear interpolation to find the number that is 0.7 of the way from 1.856 to 1.972.

2. Use linear interpolation to find the number that is 0.3 of the way from 0.8765 to 0.8652. Note that because 0.8765 is larger than 0.8652, three-tenths of the difference between 0.8765 and 0.8652 must be subtracted from 0.8765 to find the desired number.

3. A calculator shows that $\sqrt{2} \approx 1.414$ and $\sqrt{3} \approx 1.732$. Use linear interpolation to estimate $\sqrt{2.4}$. *Hint:* Find the number that is 0.4 of the difference between 1.414 and 1.732 and add this number to the smaller number, 1.414. Round your estimate to the nearest thousandth.

4. We know that $2^1 = 2$ and $2^2 = 4$. Use linear interpolation to estimate $2^{1.2}$.

5. At the present time, a football player weighs 325 lb. There are 90 days until the player needs to report to spring training at a weight of 290 lb. The player wants to lose weight at a constant rate. That is, the player wants to lose the same amount of weight each day of the 90 days. What weight, to the nearest tenth of a pound, should the player attain in 25 days?

Graphic artists use computer drawing programs, such as Adobe Illustrator, to draw the intermediate frames of an animation. For instance, in the following figure, the artist drew the small green apple on the left and the large ripe apple on the right. The drawing program used interpolation procedures to draw the five apples between the two apples drawn by the artist.

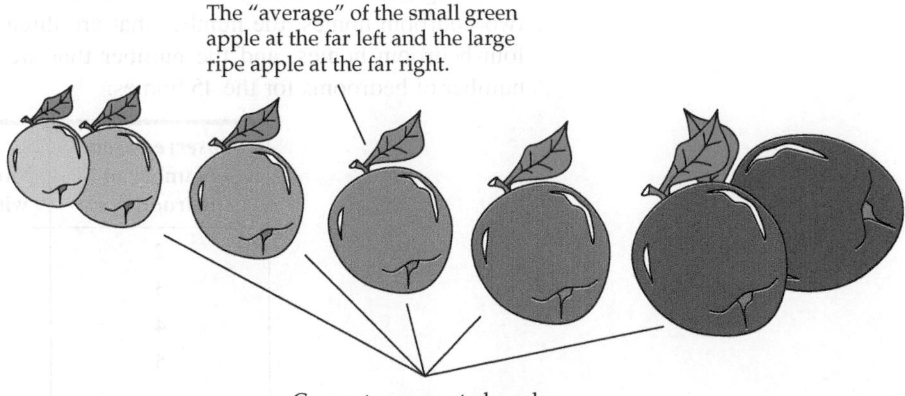

EXERCISE SET 4.1

■ In Exercises 1 to 10, find the mean, median, and mode(s), if any, for the given data. Round noninteger means to the nearest tenth.

1. 2, 7, 5, 7, 14
2. 8, 3, 3, 17, 9, 22, 19
3. 11, 8, 2, 5, 17, 39, 52, 42
4. 101, 88, 74, 60, 12, 94, 74, 85
5. 2.1, 4.6, 8.2, 3.4, 5.6, 8.0, 9.4, 12.2, 56.1, 78.2
6. 5, 5, 5, 5, 5, 5, 5, 5, 5, 5, 5, 5
7. 255, 178, 192, 145, 202, 188, 178, 201
8. 118, 105, 110, 118, 134, 155, 166, 166, 118
9. −12, −8, −5, −5, −3, 0, 4, 9, 21
10. −8.5, −2.2, 4.1, 4.1, 6.4, 8.3, 9.7

11. a. If exactly one number in a set of data is changed, will this necessarily change the mean of the set? Explain.

b. If exactly one number in a set of data is changed, will this necessarily change the median of the set? Explain.

12. If a set of data has a mode, then *must* the mode be one of the numbers in the set? Explain.

13. **Academy Awards** The following table displays the ages of female actors when they starred in their Oscar-winning Best Actor performances.

Ages of Best Female Actor Award Recipients, Academy Awards, 1980–2015

41	33	31	74	33	49	38	61	21	41	26	80
42	29	33	36	45	49	39	34	26	25	33	35
35	28	30	29	61	32	33	45	66	25	46	55

Find the mean and the median for the data in the table. Round to the nearest tenth.

14. **Academy Awards** The following table displays the ages of male actors when they starred in their Oscar-winning Best Actor performances.

Ages of Best Male Actor Award Recipients, Academy Awards, 1980–2015

40	42	37	76	39	53	45	36	62	43	51	32
42	54	52	37	38	32	45	60	46	40	36	47
29	43	37	38	45	50	48	60	43	58	46	33

Find the mean and the median for the data in the table. Round to the nearest tenth.

15. **Dental Schools** Dental schools provide urban statistics to their students.

a. Use the following data to decide which of the two cities you would pick to set up your practice in.

Cloverdale: Population, 18,250
Median price of a home, $167,000
Dentists, 12; median age, 49
Mean number of patients, 1294.5

Barnbridge: Population, 27,840
Median price of a home, $204,400
Dentists, 17.5; median age, 53
Mean number of patients, 1148.7

b. Explain how you made your decision.

16. **Expense Reports** A salesperson records the following daily expenditures during a 10-day trip.

$185.34 $234.55 $211.86 $147.65 $205.60
$216.74 $1345.75 $184.16 $320.45 $88.12

In your opinion, does the mean or the median of the expenditures best represent the salesperson's average daily expenditure? Explain your reasoning.

Grade Point Average In some 4.0 grading systems, a student's grade point average (GPA) is calculated by assigning letter grades the following numerical values.

A = 4.00	B− = 2.67	D+ = 1.33
A− = 3.67	C+ = 2.33	D = 1.00
B+ = 3.33	C = 2.00	D− = 0.67
B = 3.00	C− = 1.67	F = 0.00

■ In Exercises 17 to 20, use the above grading system to find each student's GPA. Round to the nearest hundredth.

17. Jerry's Grades, Fall Semester

Course	Course grade	Course units
English	A	3
Anthropology	A	3
Chemistry	B	4
French	C+	3
Theatre	B−	2

18. Rhonda's Grades, Spring Semester

Course	Course grade	Course units
English	C	3
History	D+	3
Computer science	B+	2
Calculus	B−	3
Photography	A−	1

19. Tessa's cumulative GPA for 3 semesters was 3.24 for 46 course units. Her fourth semester GPA was 3.86 for 12 course units. What is Tessa's cumulative GPA for all 4 semesters?

20. Richard's cumulative GPA for 3 semesters was 2.0 for 42 credits. His fourth semester GPA was 4.0 for 14 course units. What is Richard's cumulative GPA for all 4 semesters?

21. Calculate a Course Grade A professor grades students on 5 tests, a project, and a final examination. Each test counts as 10% of the course grade. The project counts as 20% of the course grade. The final examination counts as 30% of the course grade. Samantha has test scores of 70, 65, 82, 94, and 85. Samantha's project score is 92. Her final examination score is 80. Use the weighted mean formula to find Samantha's average for the course. *Hint:* The sum of all the weights is 100% = 1.

22. Calculate a Course Grade A professor grades students on 4 tests, a term paper, and a final examination. Each test counts as 15% of the course grade. The term paper counts as 20% of the course grade. The final examination counts as 20% of the course grade. Alan has test scores of 80, 78, 92, and 84. Alan received an 84 on his term paper. His final examination score was 88. Use the weighted mean formula to find Alan's average for the course. *Hint:* The sum of all the weights is 100% = 1.

Baseball In baseball, a batter's *slugging average*, which measures the batter's power as a hitter, is a type of weighted mean. If s, d, t, and h represent the numbers of singles, doubles, triples, and home runs, respectively, that a player achieves in n times at bat, then the player's slugging average is $\frac{s + 2d + 3t + 4h}{n}$.

Transcendental Graphics/Getty Images

■ In Exercises 23 to 26, find the player's slugging average for the season or seasons described. Slugging averages are given to the nearest thousandth.

23. Babe Ruth, in his first season with the New York Yankees (1920), was at bat 458 times and achieved 73 singles, 36 doubles, 9 triples, and 54 home runs. In this season, Babe Ruth achieved his highest slugging average, which stood as a major league record until 2001.

24. Babe Ruth, over his 22-year career, was at bat 8399 times and hit 1517 singles, 506 doubles, 136 triples, and 714 home runs.

25. Albert Pujols, in his 2006 season with the St. Louis Cardinals, was at bat 535 times and achieved 94 singles, 33 doubles, 1 triple, and 49 home runs.

26. Albert Pujols, during 10 years with the St. Louis Cardinals (2001–2010), was at bat 5733 times and hit 1051 singles, 426 doubles, 15 triples, and 408 home runs.

■ In Exercises 27 to 30, find the mean, the median, and all modes for the data in the given frequency distribution.

27. Points Scored by Lynn

Points scored in a basketball game	Frequency
2	6
4	5
5	6
9	3
10	1
14	2
19	1

28. Mystic Pizza Company

Hourly pay rates for employees	Frequency
$8.00	14
$11.50	9
$14.00	8
$16.00	5
$19.00	2
$22.50	1
$35.00	1

29. Quiz Scores

Scores on a biology quiz	Frequency
2	1
4	2
6	7
7	12
8	10
9	4
10	3

30. Ages of Science Fair Contestants

Age	Frequency
7	3
8	4
9	6
10	15
11	11
12	7
13	1

Meteorology In Exercises 31 to 34, use the following information about another measure of central tendency for a set of data, called the *midrange*. The **midrange** is defined as the value that is halfway between the minimum data value and the maximum data value. That is,

$$\text{Midrange} = \frac{\text{minimum value} + \text{maximum value}}{2}$$

The midrange is often stated as the *average* of a set of data in situations in which there are a large amount of data and the data are constantly changing. Many weather reports state the average daily temperature of a city as the midrange of the temperatures achieved during that day. For instance, if the minimum daily temperature of a city was 60° and the maximum daily temperature was 90°, then the midrange of the temperatures is $\frac{60° + 90°}{2} = 75°$.

31. Find the midrange of the following daily temperatures, which were recorded at 3-hour intervals.

52°, 65°, 71°, 74°, 76°, 75°, 68°, 57°, 54°

32. Find the midrange of the following daily temperatures, which were recorded at three-hour intervals.

−6°, 4°, 14°, 21°, 25°, 26°, 18°, 12°, 2°

33. During a 24-hour period on January 23–24, 1916, the temperature in Browning, Montana, decreased from a high of 44°F to a low of −56°F. Find the midrange of the temperatures during this 24-hour period. (*Source:* National Oceanic and Atmospheric Administration)

34. During a 2-minute period on January 22, 1943, the temperature in Spearfish, South Dakota, increased from a low of −4°F to a high of 45°F. Find the midrange of the temperatures during this 2-minute period. (*Source:* National Oceanic and Atmospheric Administration)

35. Test Scores After 6 biology tests, Ruben has a mean score of 78. What score does Ruben need on the next test to raise his average (mean) to 80?

36. Test Scores After 4 algebra tests, Alisa has a mean score of 82. One more 100-point test is to be given in this class. All of the test scores are of equal importance. Is it possible for Alisa to raise her average (mean) to 90? Explain.

37. Baseball For the first half of a baseball season, a player had 92 hits out of 274 times at bat. The player's batting average was $\frac{92}{274} \approx 0.336$. During the second half of the season, the player had 60 hits out of 282 times at bat. The player's batting average was $\frac{60}{282} \approx 0.213$.

a. What is the average (mean) of 0.336 and 0.213?

b. What is the player's batting average for the complete season?

c. Does the answer in part a equal the average in part b?

38. Commuting Times Mark averaged 60 mph during the 30-mile trip to college. Because of heavy traffic he was able to average only 40 mph during the return trip. What was Mark's average speed for the round trip?

EXTENSIONS

Consider the data in the following table.

Summary of Yards Gained in Two Football Games

	Game 1	Game 2	Combined statistics for both games
Warren	12 yds on 4 carries Average: 3 yds/carry	78 yds on 16 carries Average: 4.875 yds/carry	90 yds on 20 carries Average: 4.5 yds/carry
Barry	120 yds on 30 carries Average: 4 yds/carry	100 yds on 20 carries Average: 5 yds/carry	220 yds on 50 carries Average: 4.4 yds/carry

- In the first game, Barry has the better average.
- In the second game, Barry has the better average.
- If the statistics for the games are combined, Warren has the better average.

You may be surprised by the above results. After all, how can it be that Barry has the better average in game 1 and game 2, but he does not have the better average for both games? In statistics, an example such as this is known as a **Simpson's paradox**.

■ Form groups of three or four students to work Exercises 39 and 40.

39. Consider the following data.

Batting Statistics for Two Baseball Players

	First month	Second month	Both months
Dawn	2 hits; 5 at-bats Average: ?	19 hits; 49 at-bats Average: ?	? hits; ? at-bats Average: ?
Joanne	29 hits; 73 at-bats Average: ?	31 hits; 80 at-bats Average: ?	? hits; ? at-bats Average: ?

Is this an example of a Simpson's paradox? Explain.

40. Consider the following data.

Test Scores for Two Students

	English	History	English and history combined
Wendy	84, 65, 72, 91, 99, 84 Average: ?	66, 84, 75, 77, 94, 96, 81 Average: ?	Average: ?
Sarah	90, 74 Average: ?	68, 78, 98, 76, 68, 92, 88, 86 Average: ?	Average: ?

Is this an example of a Simpson's paradox? Explain.

SECTION 4.2 Measures of Dispersion

The Range

TABLE 4.5
Soda Dispensed (ounces)

Machine 1	Machine 2
9.52	8.01
6.41	7.99
10.07	7.95
5.85	8.03
8.15	8.02
$\bar{x} = 8.0$	$\bar{x} = 8.0$

In the preceding section we introduced three types of average values for a data set—the mean, the median, and the mode. Some characteristics of a set of data may not be evident from an examination of averages. For instance, consider a soft-drink dispensing machine that should dispense 8 oz of your selection into a cup. Table 4.5 shows data for two of these machines.

The mean data value for each machine is 8 oz. However, look at the variation in data values for Machine 1. The quantity of soda dispensed is very inconsistent—in some cases the soda overflows the cup, and in other cases too little soda is dispensed. The machine obviously needs adjustment. Machine 2, on the other hand, is working just fine. The quantity dispensed is very consistent, with little variation

This example shows that average values do not reflect the *spread* or *dispersion* of data. To measure the spread or dispersion of data, we must introduce statistical values known as the *range* and the *standard deviation.*

Range

The **range** of a set of data values is the difference between the greatest data value and the least data value.

EXAMPLE 1 Find a Range

Find the range of the numbers of ounces dispensed by Machine 1 in Table 4.5.

Solution

The greatest number of ounces dispensed is 10.07 and the least is 5.85. The range of the numbers of ounces dispensed is $10.07 - 5.85 = 4.22$ oz.

CHECK YOUR PROGRESS 1 Find the range of the numbers of ounces dispensed by Machine 2 in Table 4.5.

Solution See page S14.

MATH MATTERS A World Record Range

Robert Wadlow

Bettmann/Getty Images

The tallest man for whom there is irrefutable evidence was Robert Pershing Wadlow. On June 27, 1940, Wadlow was 8 ft 11.1 in. tall. The shortest man for whom there is reliable evidence is Chandra Bahadur Dangi. On February 26, 2012, he was 21.5 in. tall. (*Source:* Guinness World Records) The range of the heights of these men is $107.1 - 21.5 = 85.6$ in.

The Standard Deviation

The range of a set of data is easy to compute, but it can be deceiving. The range is a measure that depends only on the two most extreme values, and as such it is very sensitive. A measure of dispersion that is less sensitive to extreme values is the *standard deviation*. The standard deviation of a set of numerical data makes use of the amount by which each individual data value deviates from the mean. These deviations, represented by $(x - \bar{x})$, are positive when the data value x is greater than the mean $\bar{x}$ and are negative when x is less than the mean $\bar{x}$. The sum of all the deviations $(x - \bar{x})$ is 0 for all sets of data. This is shown in Table 4.6 for the Machine 2 data of Table 4.5.

TABLE 4.6
Machine 2: Deviations from the Mean

x	$x - \bar{x}$
8.01	$8.01 - 8 = 0.01$
7.99	$7.99 - 8 = -0.01$
7.95	$7.95 - 8 = -0.05$
8.03	$8.03 - 8 = 0.03$
8.02	$8.02 - 8 = 0.02$
Sum of deviations $= 0$	

Because the sum of all the deviations of the data values from the mean is *always* 0, we cannot use the sum of the deviations as a measure of dispersion for a set of data. Instead, the standard deviation uses the sum of the *squares* of the deviations.

TAKE NOTE

You may question why a denominator of $n - 1$ is used instead of n when we compute a sample standard deviation. The reason is that a sample standard deviation is often used to estimate the population standard deviation, and it can be shown mathematically that the use of $n - 1$ tends to yield better estimates.

Standard Deviations for Populations and Samples

If $x_1, x_2, x_3, \dots, x_n$ is a *population* of n numbers with a mean of μ, then the **standard deviation** of the population is $\sigma = \sqrt{\frac{\Sigma(x - \mu)^2}{n}}$ (1).

If $x_1, x_2, x_3, \dots, x_n$ is a *sample* of n numbers with a mean of $\bar{x}$, then the **standard deviation** of the sample is $s = \sqrt{\frac{\Sigma(x - \bar{x})^2}{n - 1}}$ (2).

Most statistical applications involve a sample rather than a population, which is the complete set of data values. Sample standard deviations are designated by the lowercase letter s. In those cases in which we *do* work with a population, we designate the standard deviation of the population by σ, which is the lowercase Greek letter sigma. We can use the following procedure to calculate the standard deviation of n numbers.

Procedure for Computing a Standard Deviation

1. Determine the mean of the n numbers.
2. For each number, calculate the deviation (difference) between the number and the mean of the numbers.
3. Calculate the square of each deviation and find the sum of these squared deviations.
4. If the data is a *population*, then divide the sum by n. If the data is a *sample*, then divide the sum by $n - 1$.
5. Find the square root of the quotient in Step 4.

EXAMPLE 2 Find the Standard Deviation

The following numbers were obtained by sampling a population.

2, 4, 7, 12, 15

Find the standard deviation of the sample.

Solution

Step 1: The mean of the numbers is

$$\bar{x} = \frac{2 + 4 + 7 + 12 + 15}{5} = \frac{40}{5} = 8$$

Step 2: For each number, calculate the deviation between the number and the mean.

x	$x - \bar{x}$
2	$2 - 8 = -6$
4	$4 - 8 = -4$
7	$7 - 8 = -1$
12	$12 - 8 = 4$
15	$15 - 8 = 7$

TAKE NOTE

Because the sum of the deviations is always 0, you can use this as a means to check your arithmetic. That is, if your deviations from the mean do not add to 0, then you know you have made an error.

Step 3: Calculate the square of each deviation in Step 2, and find the sum of these squared deviations.

x	$x - \bar{x}$	$(x - \bar{x})^2$
2	$2 - 8 = -6$	$(-6)^2 = 36$
4	$4 - 8 = -4$	$(-4)^2 = 16$
7	$7 - 8 = -1$	$(-1)^2 = 1$
12	$12 - 8 = 4$	$4^2 = 16$
15	$15 - 8 = 7$	$7^2 = 49$
		118 ← Sum of the squared deviations

Step 4: Because we have a sample of $n = 5$ values, divide the sum 118 by $n - 1$, which is 4.

$$\frac{118}{4} = 29.5$$

Step 5: The standard deviation of the sample is $s = \sqrt{29.5}$. To the nearest hundredth, the standard deviation is $s = 5.43$.

CHECK YOUR PROGRESS 2 A student has the following quiz scores: 5, 8, 16, 17, 18, 20. Find the standard deviation for this population of quiz scores.

Solution See page S14.

In the next example we use standard deviations to determine which company produces batteries that are most consistent with regard to their life expectancy.

EXAMPLE 3 Use Standard Deviations

A consumer group has tested a sample of 8 size-D batteries from each of 3 companies. The results of the tests are shown in the following table. According to these tests, which company produces batteries for which the values representing hours of constant use have the smallest standard deviation?

Company	Hours of constant use per battery
EverSoBright	6.2, 6.4, 7.1, 5.9, 8.3, 5.3, 7.5, 9.3
Dependable	6.8, 6.2, 7.2, 5.9, 7.0, 7.4, 7.3, 8.2
Beacon	6.1, 6.6, 7.3, 5.7, 7.1, 7.6, 7.1, 8.5

Solution

The mean for each sample of batteries is 7 h.
The batteries from EverSoBright have a standard deviation of

$$s_1 = \sqrt{\frac{(6.2-7)^2 + (6.4-7)^2 + \cdots + (9.3-7)^2}{7}}$$

$$= \sqrt{\frac{12.34}{7}} \approx 1.328 \text{ h}$$

The batteries from Dependable have a standard deviation of

$$s_2 = \sqrt{\frac{(6.8-7)^2 + (6.2-7)^2 + \cdots + (8.2-7)^2}{7}}$$

$$= \sqrt{\frac{3.62}{7}} \approx 0.719 \text{ h}$$

The batteries from Beacon have a standard deviation of

$$s_3 = \sqrt{\frac{(6.1-7)^2 + (6.6-7)^2 + \cdots + (8.5-7)^2}{7}}$$

$$= \sqrt{\frac{5.38}{7}} \approx 0.877 \text{ h}$$

The batteries from Dependable have the smallest standard deviation. According to these results, the Dependable company produces the most consistent batteries with regard to life expectancy under constant use.

CHECK YOUR PROGRESS 3 A consumer testing agency has tested the strengths of 3 brands of $\frac{1}{8}$-inch rope. The results of the tests are shown in the following table. According to the sample test results, which company produces $\frac{1}{8}$-inch rope for which the breaking point has the smallest standard deviation?

Company	Breaking point of $\frac{1}{8}$-inch rope in pounds
Trustworthy	122, 141, 151, 114, 108, 149, 125
Brand X	128, 127, 148, 164, 97, 109, 137
NeverSnap	112, 121, 138, 131, 134, 139, 135

Solution See page S14.

Many calculators have built-in statistics features for calculating the mean and standard deviation of a set of numbers. The next example illustrates these features on a TI-83/84 graphing calculator.

EXAMPLE 4 Use a Calculator to Find the Mean and Standard Deviation

Use a graphing calculator to find the mean and standard deviation of the times in the following table. Because the table contains all the winning times for this race (up to the year 2012), the data set is a population.

Olympic Women's 400-Meter Dash Results, in Seconds, 1969–2012

52.0	51.08	49.29	48.88	48.83	48.65	48.83	48.25	49.11	49.41	49.62	49.55

Solution

On a TI-83/84 calculator, press STAT ENTER and then enter the above times into list L1. Press STAT ▷ ENTER ENTER. The calculator displays the mean and standard deviations shown below. Because we are working with a population, we are interested in the population standard deviation. From the calculator screen, $\bar{x} \approx 49.458$ s and $\sigma x \approx 1.021$ s.

TAKE NOTE

Because the calculations of the population mean and the sample mean are the same, a graphing calculator uses the same symbol $\bar{x}$ for both. The symbols for the population standard deviation, σx, and the sample standard deviation, sx, are different.

TI-83/84 **Display of List 1**

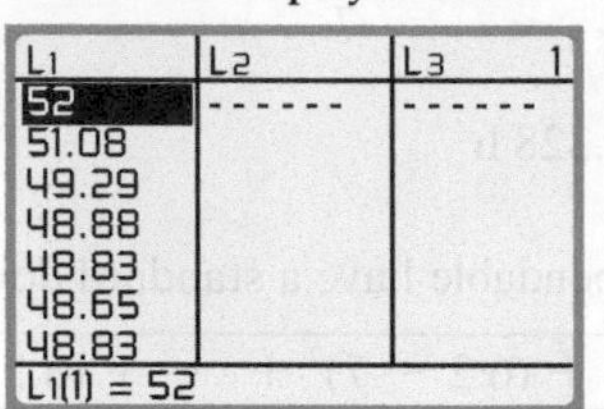

TI-83/84 **Display of $\bar{x}$, s, and σ**

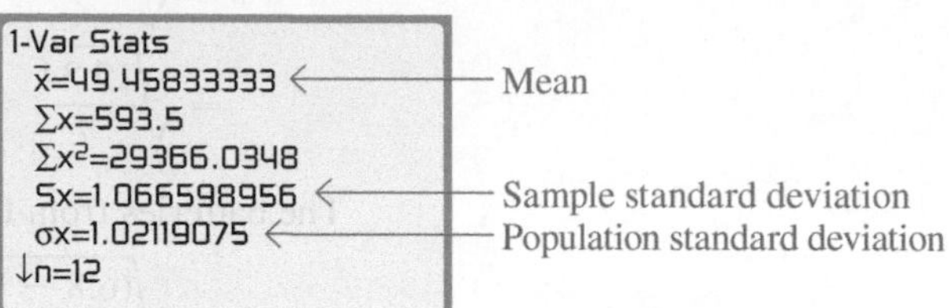

CHECK YOUR PROGRESS 4 Use a graphing calculator to find the mean and the population standard deviation of the race times in the following table.

Olympic Men's 400-Meter Dash Results, in Seconds, 1900–2012

49.4	49.2	53.2	50.0	48.2	49.6	47.6	47.8	46.2
46.5	46.2	45.9	46.7	44.9	45.1	43.8	44.66	44.26
44.60	44.27	43.87	43.50	43.49	43.84	44.00	43.75	43.94

Solution See page S14.

The Variance

A statistic known as the *variance* is also used as a measure of dispersion. The **variance** for a given set of data is the square of the standard deviation of the data. The following chart shows the mathematical notations that are used to denote standard deviations and variances.

Notations for Standard Deviation and Variance

σ is the standard deviation of a population.

σ^2 is the variance of a population.

s is the standard deviation of a sample.

s^2 is the variance of a sample.

EXAMPLE 5 **Find the Variance**

Find the variance for the sample given in Example 2.

Solution

In Example 2, we found $s = \sqrt{29.5}$. The variance is the square of the standard deviation. Thus the variance is $s^2 = (\sqrt{29.5})^2 = 29.5$.

CHECK YOUR PROGRESS 5 Find the variance for the population given in Check Your Progress 2.

Solution See page S14.

QUESTION Can the variance of a data set be less than the standard deviation of the data set?

Although the variance of a set of data is an important measure of dispersion, it has a disadvantage that is not shared by the standard deviation: the variance does not have the same unit of measure as the original data. For instance, if a set of data consists of times measured in hours, then the variance of the data will be measured in *square* hours. The standard deviation of this data set is the square root of the variance, and as such it is measured in hours, which is a more intuitive unit of measure.

ANSWER Yes. The variance is less than the standard deviation whenever the standard deviation is less than 1.

EXCURSION

A Geometric View of Variance and Standard Deviation[1]

The following geometric explanation of the variance and standard deviation of a set of data is designed to provide you with a deeper understanding of these important concepts.

Consider the data $x_1, x_2, \ldots, x_n$, which are arranged in ascending order. The average, or mean, of these data is

$$\mu = \frac{\Sigma x_i}{n}$$

and the variance is

$$\sigma^2 = \frac{\Sigma(x_i - \mu)^2}{n}$$

In the last formula, each term $(x_i - \mu)^2$ can be pictured as the area of a square whose sides are of length $|x_i - \mu|$, the distance between the ith data value and the mean. We will refer to these squares as *tiles*, denoting by T_i the area of the tile associated with the data value x_i. Thus $\sigma^2 = \frac{\Sigma T_i}{n}$, which means that the variance may be thought of as the *area of the average-sized tile* and the standard deviation as the length of a side of this average-sized tile. By drawing the tiles associated with a data set, as shown on the next page, you can

TAKE NOTE

Up to this point we have used $\mu = \frac{\Sigma x}{n}$ as the formula for the mean. However, many statistics texts use the formula $\mu = \frac{\Sigma x_i}{n}$ for the mean. Letting the subscript i vary from 1 to n helps us to remember that we are finding the sum of all the numbers $x_1, x_2, x_3, \ldots, x_n$.

[1] Adapted with permission from "Chebyshev's Theorem: A Geometric Approach," *The College Mathematics Journal*, Vol. 26, No. 2, March 1995. Article by Pat Touhey, College Misericordia, Dallas, PA 18612.

visually estimate an average-sized tile, and thus you can roughly approximate the variance and standard deviation.

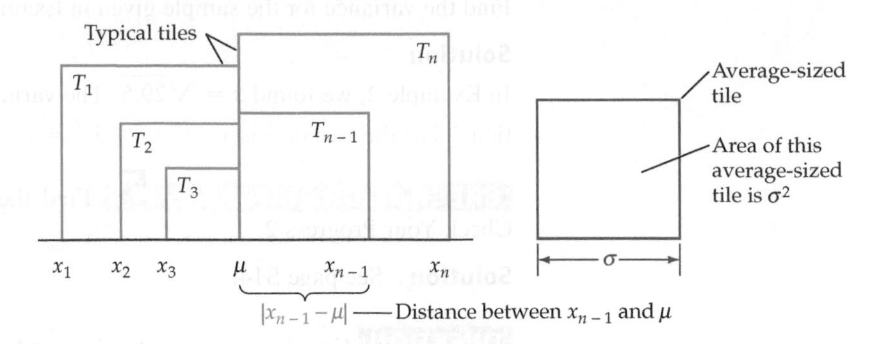

A typical data set, with its associated tiles and average-sized tile

These geometric representations of variance and standard deviation enable us to visualize how these values are used as measures of the dispersion of a set of data. If all of the data are bunched up near the mean, it is clear that the average-sized tile will be small and, consequently, so will its side length, which represents the standard deviation. But if even a small portion of the data lies far from the mean, the average-sized tile may be rather large, and thus its side length will also be large.

EXCURSION EXERCISES

1. This exercise makes use of the geometric procedure just explained to calculate the variance and standard deviation of the population 2, 5, 7, 11, 15. The following figure shows the given set of data labeled on a number line, along with its mean, which is 8.

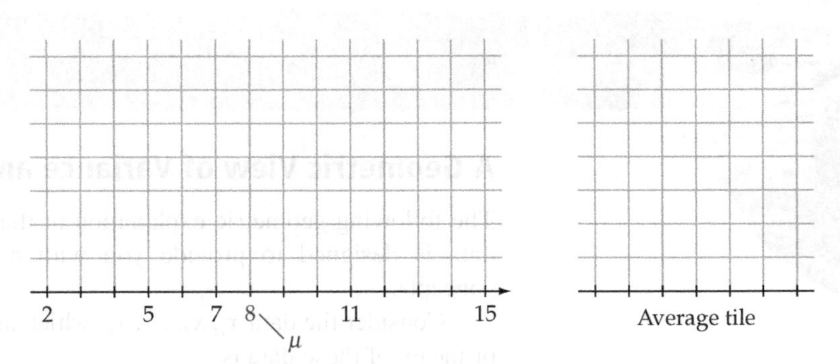

a. Draw the tile associated with each of the five data values 2, 5, 7, 11, and 15.

b. Label each tile with its area.

c. Find the sum of the areas of all the tiles.

d. Find the average (mean) of the areas of all 5 tiles.

e. To the right of the above number line, draw a tile whose area is the average found in part d.

f. What is the variance of the data? What geometric figure represents the variance?

g. What is the standard deviation of the data? What geometric figure represents the standard deviation?

2. a. to **g.** Repeat all of the steps described in Excursion Exercise 1 for the data set

6, 8, 9, 11, 16

h. Which of the data sets in these two Excursion exercises has the larger mean? Which data set has the larger standard deviation?

EXERCISE SET 4.2

1. **Meteorology** During a 12-hour period on December 24, 1924, the temperature in Fairfield, Montana, dropped from a high of 63°F to a low of −21°F. What was the range of the temperatures during this period? (*Source:* National Oceanic and Atmospheric Administration)

2. **Meteorology** During a 2-hour period on January 12, 1911, the temperature in Rapid City, South Dakota, dropped from a high of 49°F to a low of −13°F. What was the range of the temperatures during this period? (*Source:* National Oceanic and Atmospheric Administration)

■ In Exercises 3 to 12, find the range, the standard deviation, and the variance for the given *samples*. Round noninteger results to the nearest tenth.

3. 1, 2, 5, 7, 8, 19, 22
4. 3, 4, 7, 11, 12, 12, 15, 16
5. 2.1, 3.0, 1.9, 1.5, 4.8
6. 5.2, 11.7, 19.1, 3.7, 8.2, 16.3
7. 48, 91, 87, 93, 59, 68, 92, 100, 81
8. 93, 67, 49, 55, 92, 87, 77, 66, 73, 96, 54
9. 4, 4, 4, 4, 4, 4, 4, 4, 4, 4, 4, 4, 4, 4, 4, 4
10. 8, 6, 8, 6, 8, 6, 8, 6, 8, 6, 8, 6, 8
11. −8, −5, −12, −1, 4, 7, 11
12. −23, −17, −19, −5, −4, −11, −31

13. **Mountain Climbing** A mountain climber plans to buy some rope to use as a lifeline. Which of the following would be the better choice? Explain your choice.

    Rope A: Mean breaking strength: 500 lb; standard deviation of 100 lb

    Rope B: Mean breaking strength: 500 lb; standard deviation of 10 lb

14. **Lotteries** Which would you expect to be larger: the standard deviation of 5 random numbers picked from 1 to 47 in the California Super Lotto, or the standard deviation of 5 random numbers picked from 1 to 69 in the multistate PowerBall lottery?

15. **Weights of Students** Which would you expect to be the larger standard deviation: the standard deviation of the weights of 25 students in a first-grade class, or the standard deviation of the weights of 25 students in a college statistics course?

16. Evaluate the accuracy of the following statement: When the mean of a data set is large, the standard deviation will be large.

17. **Fuel Efficiency** The fuel efficiency, in miles per gallon, of 10 small utility trucks was measured. The results are recorded in the table below.

Fuel Efficiency (mpg)

22	25	23	27	15	24	24	32	23	22	25	22

Find the mean and sample standard deviation of these data. Round to the nearest hundredth.

18. **Waiting Times** A customer at a specialty coffee shop observed the amount of time, in minutes, that each of 20 customers spent waiting to receive an order. The results are recorded in the table below.

Time (min) to receive order

3.2	4.0	3.8	2.4	4.7	5.1	4.6	3.5	3.5	6.2
3.5	4.9	4.5	5.0	2.8	3.5	2.2	3.9	5.3	2.9

Find the mean and sample standard deviation of these data. Round to the nearest hundredth.

19. **Fast-food Calories** A survey of 10 fast-food restaurants noted the number of calories in a mid-sized hamburger. The results are given in the table below.

Calories in a mid-sized hamburger

514	507	502	498	496	506	458	478	463	514

Find the mean and sample standard deviation of these data. Round to the nearest hundredth.

20. **Energy Drinks** A survey of 16 energy drinks noted the caffeine concentration of each drink in milligrams per ounce. The results are given in the table below.

Concentration of caffeine (mg/oz)

9.1	7.5	7.8	8.9	9.0	8.2	9.1	8.7
9.0	7.7	8.8	8.9	9.0	9.1	8.2	8.9

Find the mean and sample standard deviation of these data. Round to the nearest hundredth.

21. **Weekly Commute Times** A survey of 15 large cities noted the average weekly commute times, in hours, of the residents of each city. The results are recorded in the table below.

Weekly commute time (h)

4.5	4.0	5.8	5.4	4.7
4.0	3.6	3.9	4.7	3.7
4.6	3.4	3.5	3.9	4.4

Find the mean and sample standard deviation of these data. Round to the nearest hundredth.

22. Biology Some studies show that the mean normal human body temperature is actually somewhat lower than the commonly given value of 98.6°F. This is reflected in the following data set of body temperatures.

Body Temperatures (°F) of 30 Healthy Adults

97.1	97.8	98.0	98.7	99.5	96.3
98.4	98.5	98.0	100.8	98.6	98.2
99.0	99.3	98.8	97.6	97.4	99.0
97.4	96.4	98.0	98.1	97.8	98.5
98.7	98.8	98.2	97.6	98.2	98.8

a. Find the mean and *sample* standard deviation of the body temperatures. Round each result to the nearest hundredth.

b. Are there any temperatures in the data set that do not lie within 2 standard deviations of the mean? If so, list them.

23. Recording Industry The table below shows a random sample of the lengths of songs in a playlist.

Lengths of Songs (minutes:seconds)

3:42	3:40	3:50	3:17	3:15	3:37
2:27	3:01	3:47	3:49	4:02	3:30

a. Find the mean and *sample* standard deviation of the song lengths, in seconds. Round each result to the nearest second.

b. Are there any song lengths in the data set that do not lie within 1 standard deviation of the mean? If so, list them.

EXTENSIONS

24. Pick 5 numbers and compute the *population* standard deviation of the numbers.

a. Add a nonzero constant c to each of your original numbers, and compute the standard deviation of this new population.

b. Use the results of part a and inductive reasoning to state what happens to the standard deviation of a population when a nonzero constant c is added to each data item.

25. Pick 6 numbers and compute the *population* standard deviation of the numbers.

a. Double each of your original numbers and compute the standard deviation of this new population.

b. Use the results of part a and inductive reasoning to state what happens to the standard deviation of a population when each data item is multiplied by a positive constant k.

26. a. All of the numbers in a sample are the same number. What is the standard deviation of the sample?

b. If the standard deviation of a sample is 0, must all of the numbers in the sample be the same number?

c. If two samples both have the same standard deviation, are the samples necessarily identical?

27. Under what condition would the variance of a sample be equal to the standard deviation of the sample?

SECTION 4.3 Measures of Relative Position

z-Scores

Consider an Internet site that offers movie downloads. Based on data kept by the site, an estimate of the mean time to download a certain movie is 12 min, with a standard deviation of 4 min. When you download this movie, the download takes 20 min, which you think is an unusually long time for the download. On the other hand, when your friend downloads the movie, the download takes only 6 min, and your friend is pleasantly surprised at how quickly she receives the movie. In each case, a data value far from the mean is unexpected.

The graph below shows the download times for this movie using two different measures: the number of *minutes* a download time is from the mean and the number of *standard deviations* the download time is from the mean.

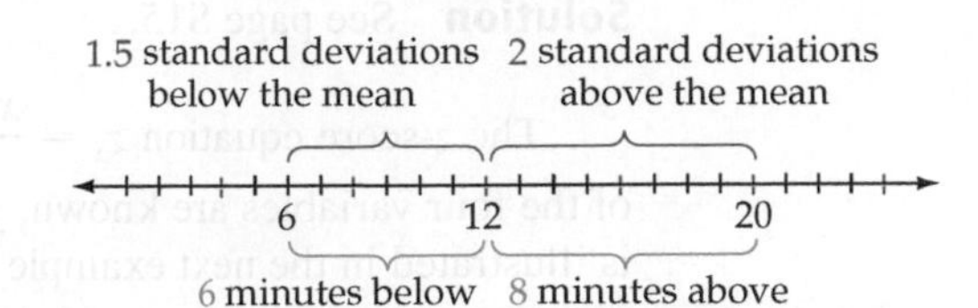

The number of standard deviations between a data value and the mean is known as the data value's *z-score* or *standard score.*

z-Score

The **z-score** for a given data value x is the number of standard deviations that x is above or below the mean of the data. The following formulas show how to calculate the z-score for a data value x in a population and in a sample.

$$\text{Population: } z_x = \frac{x - \mu}{\sigma} \qquad \text{Sample: } z_x = \frac{x - \bar{x}}{s}$$

QUESTION What does a z-score of 3 for a data value x represent? What does a z-score of -1 for a data value x represent?

In the next example, we use a student's z-scores for two tests to determine how well the student did on each test in comparison to the other students.

EXAMPLE 1 Compare z-Scores

Raul has taken two tests in his chemistry class. He scored 72 on the first test, for which the mean of all scores was 65 and the standard deviation was 8. He received a 60 on a second test, for which the mean of all scores was 45 and the standard deviation was 12. In comparison to the other students, did Raul do better on the first test or the second test?

Solution

Find the z-score for each test.

$$z_{72} = \frac{72 - 65}{8} = 0.875 \qquad z_{60} = \frac{60 - 45}{12} = 1.25$$

Raul scored 0.875 standard deviation above the mean on the first test and 1.25 standard deviations above the mean on the second test. These z-scores indicate that, in comparison to his classmates, Raul scored better on the second test than he did on the first test.

ANSWER A z-score of 3 for a data value x means that x is 3 standard deviations above the mean. A z-score of -1 for a data value x means that x is 1 standard deviation below the mean.

CHECK YOUR PROGRESS 1 Cheryl has taken two quizzes in her history class. She scored 15 on the first quiz, for which the mean of all scores was 12 and the standard deviation was 2.4. Her score on the second quiz, for which the mean of all scores was 11 and the standard deviation was 2.0, was 14. In comparison to her classmates, did Cheryl do better on the first quiz or the second quiz?

Solution See page S15.

The z-score equation $z_x = \dfrac{x - \bar{x}}{s}$ involves four variables. If the values of any three of the four variables are known, you can solve for the unknown variable. This procedure is illustrated in the next example.

EXAMPLE 2 **Use z-Scores**

A consumer group tested a sample of 100 light bulbs. It found that the mean life expectancy of the bulbs was 842 h, with a standard deviation of 90. One particular light bulb from the DuraBright Company had a z-score of 1.2. What was the life span of this light bulb?

Solution

Substitute the given values into the z-score equation and solve for x.

$$z_x = \frac{x - \bar{x}}{s}$$

$$1.2 = \frac{x - 842}{90} \qquad \bullet\ z_x = 1.2,\ \bar{x} = 842,\ s = 90$$

$$108 = x - 842 \qquad \bullet\ \text{Solve for } x.$$

$$950 = x$$

The light bulb had a life span of 950 h.

CHECK YOUR PROGRESS 2 Roland received a score of 70 on a test for which the mean score was 65.5. Roland has learned that the z-score for his test is 0.6. What is the standard deviation for this set of test scores?

Solution See page S15.

Percentiles

Most standardized examinations provide scores in terms of *percentiles*, which are defined as follows:

> **pth Percentile**
>
> A value x is called the ***p*th percentile** of a data set provided $p\%$ of the data values are less than x.

EXAMPLE 3 **Using Percentiles**

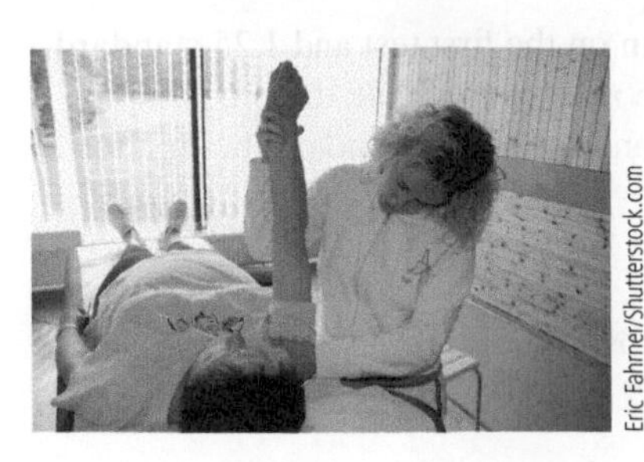
Eric Fahrner/Shutterstock.com

In a recent year, the median annual salary for a physical therapist was $74,480. If the 90th percentile for the annual salary of a physical therapist was $105,900, find the percent of physical therapists whose annual salary was

a. more than $74,480.

b. less than $105,900.

c. between $74,480 and $105,900.

Solution

a. By definition, the median is the 50th percentile. Therefore, 50% of the physical therapists earned more than $74,480 per year.

b. Because $105,900 is the 90th percentile, 90% of all physical therapists made less than $105,900.

c. From parts a and b, 90% − 50% = 40% of the physical therapists earned between $74,480 and $105,900.

CHECK YOUR PROGRESS 3 The median annual salary for a police dispatcher in a large city was $44,528. If the 25th percentile for the annual salary of a police dispatcher was $32,761, find the percent of police dispatchers whose annual salaries were

a. less than $44,528.

b. more than $32,761.

c. between $32,761 and $44,528.

Solution See page S15.

The following formula can be used to find the percentile that corresponds to a particular data value in a set of data.

Percentile for a Given Data Value

Given a set of data and a data value x,

$$\text{Percentile of score } x = \frac{\text{number of data values less than } x}{\text{total number of data values}} \cdot 100$$

EXAMPLE 4 **Find a Percentile**

On a reading examination given to 900 students, Elaine's score of 602 was higher than the scores of 576 of the students who took the examination. What is the percentile for Elaine's score?

Solution

$$\text{Percentile} = \frac{\text{number of data values less than 602}}{\text{total number of data values}} \cdot 100$$

$$= \frac{576}{900} \cdot 100$$

$$= 64$$

Elaine's score of 602 places her at the 64th percentile.

CHECK YOUR PROGRESS 4 On an examination given to 8600 students, Hal's score of 405 was higher than the scores of 3952 of the students who took the examination. What is the percentile for Hal's score?

Solution See page S15.

MATH MATTERS Standardized Tests and Percentiles

Standardized tests, such as the Scholastic Assessment Test (SAT), are designed to measure all students by a *single* standard. The SAT is used by many colleges as part of their admissions criteria. The SAT I is a 3-hour examination that measures verbal and mathematical reasoning skills. Scores on each portion of the test range from 200 to 800 points. SAT scores are generally reported in points and percentiles. Sometimes students are confused by the percentile score. For instance, if a student scores 650 points on the mathematics portion of the SAT and is told that this score is in the 85th percentile, this *does not* indicate that the student answered 85% of the questions correctly. An 85th percentile score means that the student scored higher than 85% of the students who took the test. Consequently, the student scored lower than 15% (100% − 85%) of the students who took the test.

Quartiles

The three numbers Q_1, Q_2, and Q_3 that partition a ranked data set into four (approximately) equal groups are called the **quartiles** of the data. For instance, for the data set below, the values $Q_1 = 11$, $Q_2 = 29$, and $Q_3 = 104$ are the quartiles of the data.

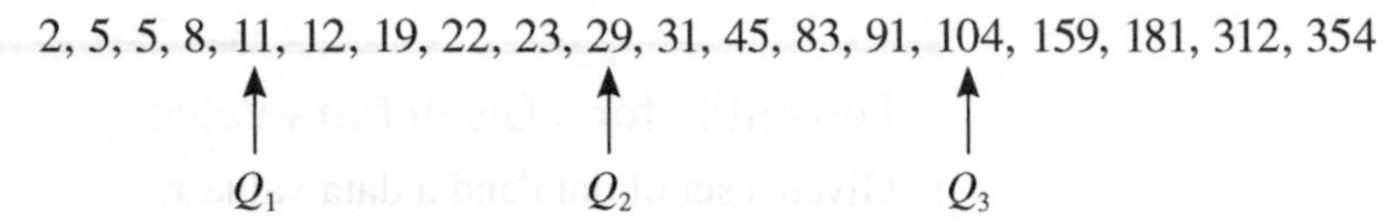

The quartile Q_1 is called the *first quartile*. The quartile Q_2 is called the *second quartile*. It is the median of the data. The quartile Q_3 is called the *third quartile*. The following method of finding quartiles makes use of medians.

The Median Procedure for Finding Quartiles

1. Rank the data.
2. Find the median of the data. This is the second quartile, Q_2.
3. The first quartile, Q_1, is the median of the data values less than Q_2. The third quartile, Q_3, is the median of the data values greater than Q_2.

EXAMPLE 5 Use Medians to Find the Quartiles of a Data Set

The following table lists the calories per 100 milliliters of 25 popular sodas. Find the quartiles for the data.

Calories, per 100 milliliters, of Selected Sodas

43	37	42	40	53	62	36	32	50	49
26	53	73	48	45	39	45	48	40	56
41	36	58	42	39					

Solution

Step 1: Rank the data as shown in the following table.

1) 26	2) 32	3) 36	4) 36	5) 37	6) 39	7) 39	8) 40	9) 40
10) 41	11) 42	12) 42	13) 43	14) 45	15) 45	16) 48	17) 48	18) 49
19) 50	20) 53	21) 53	22) 56	23) 58	24) 62	25) 73		

Step 2: The median of these 25 data values has a rank of 13. Thus the median is 43. The second quartile Q_2 is the median of the data, so $Q_2 = 43$.

Step 3: There are 12 data values less than the median and 12 data values greater than the median. The first quartile is the median of the data values less than the median. Thus Q_1 is the mean of the data values with ranks of 6 and 7.

$$Q_1 = \frac{39 + 39}{2} = 39$$

The third quartile is the median of the data values greater than the median. Thus Q_3 is the mean of the data values with ranks of 19 and 20.

$$Q_3 = \frac{50 + 53}{2} = 51.5$$

CHECK YOUR PROGRESS 5 The following table lists the weights, in ounces, of 15 avocados in a random sample. Find the quartiles for the data.

Weights, in ounces, of Avocados

12.4	10.8	14.2	7.5	10.2	11.4	12.6	12.8	13.1	15.6
9.8	11.4	12.2	16.4	14.5					

Solution See page S15.

Box-and-Whisker Plots

A **box-and-whisker plot** (sometimes called a **box plot**) is often used to provide a visual summary of a set of data. A box-and-whisker plot shows the median, the first and third quartiles, and the minimum and maximum values of a data set. See the figure below.

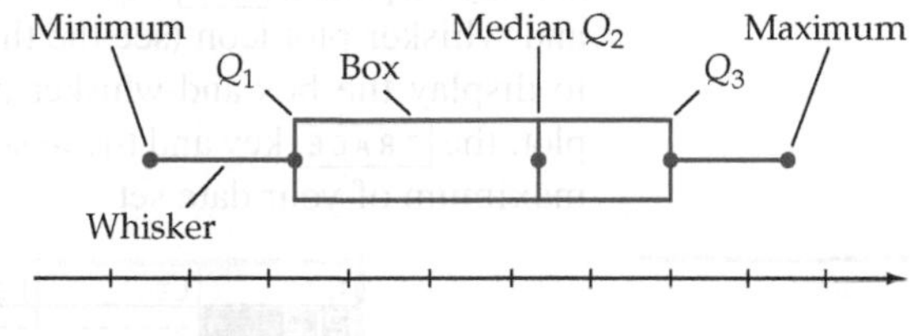

A box-and-whisker plot

TAKE NOTE

If a set of data is not ranked, then you need to rank the data so that you can easily determine the median, the first and third quartiles, and the minimum and maximum.

Construction of a Box-and-Whisker Plot

1. Draw a horizontal scale that extends from the minimum data value to the maximum data value.
2. Above the scale, draw a rectangle (box) with its left side at Q_1 and its right side at Q_3.
3. Draw a vertical line segment across the rectangle at the median, Q_2.
4. Draw a horizontal line segment, called a whisker, that extends from Q_1 to the minimum and another whisker that extends from Q_3 to the maximum.

HISTORICAL NOTE

John W. Tukey (1915–2000) made many important contributions to the field of statistics during his career at Princeton University and Bell Labs. He invented box plots when he was working on exploratory data analysis.

EXAMPLE 6 Construct a Box-and-Whisker Plot

Construct a box-and-whisker plot for the data set in Example 5.

Solution

For the data set in Example 5, we determined that $Q_1 = 39$, $Q_2 = 43$, and $Q_3 = 51.5$. The minimum data value for the data set is 26, and the maximum data value is 73. Thus the box-and-whisker plot is as shown below.

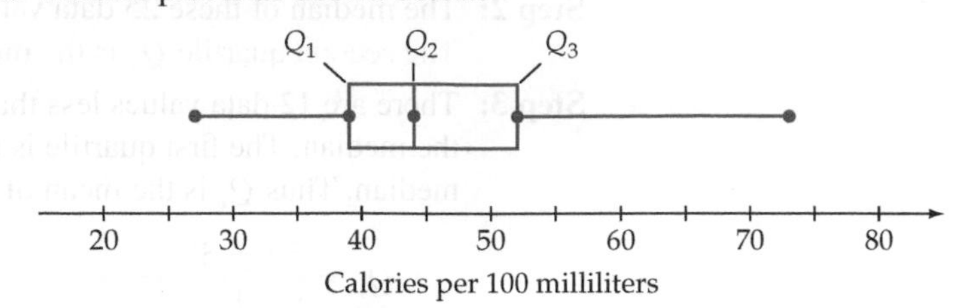

CHECK YOUR PROGRESS 6 Construct a box-and-whisker plot for the following data.

Number of Rooms Occupied in a Resort during an 18-Day Period

86	77	58	45	94	96	83	76	75
65	68	72	78	85	87	92	55	61

Solution See page S15.

Box plots are popular because they are easy to construct and they illustrate several important features of a data set in a simple diagram. Note from the box plot in Example 6 that we can easily estimate

- the quartiles of the data.
- the range of the data.
- the position of the middle half of the data as shown by the length of the box.

Some graphing calculators can be used to produce box-and-whisker plots. For instance, on a TI-83/84, you enter the data into a list, as shown on the first screen in Figure 4.1. The `WINDOW` menu is used to enter appropriate boundaries that contain all the data. Use the key sequence `2nd` `[STAT PLOT]` `ENTER` and choose from the `Type` menu the box-and-whisker plot icon (see the third screen in Figure 4.1). The `GRAPH` key is then used to display the box-and-whisker plot. After the calculator displays the box-and-whisker plot, the `TRACE` key and the ▷ key enable you to view Q_1, Q_2, Q_3, and the minimum and maximum of your data set.

TAKE NOTE

The following data were used to produce the box plot shown in Figure 4.1.

21.2, 20.5, 17.0, 16.8, 16.8, 16.5, 16.2, 14.0, 13.7, 13.3, 13.1, 13.0, 12.4, 12.1, 12.0

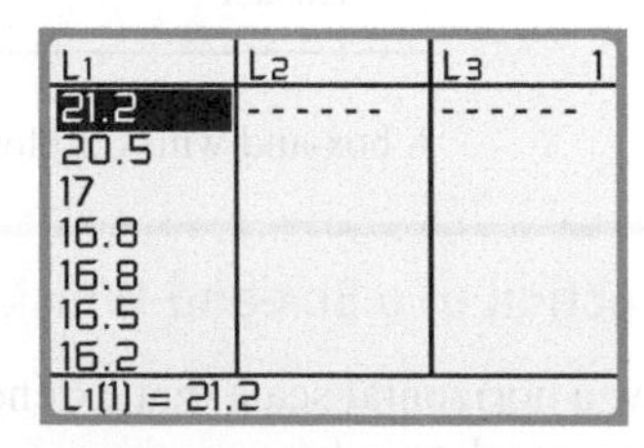

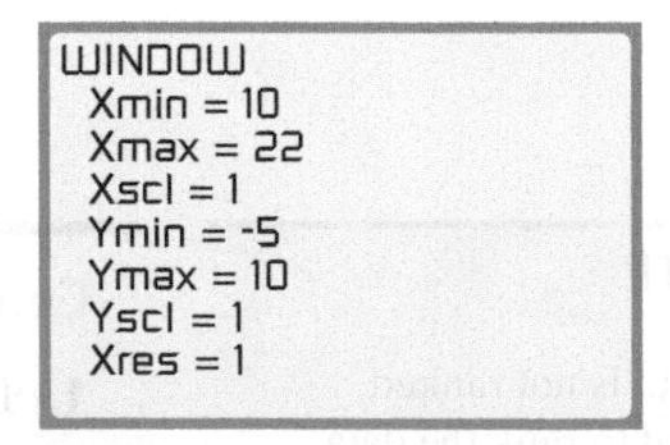

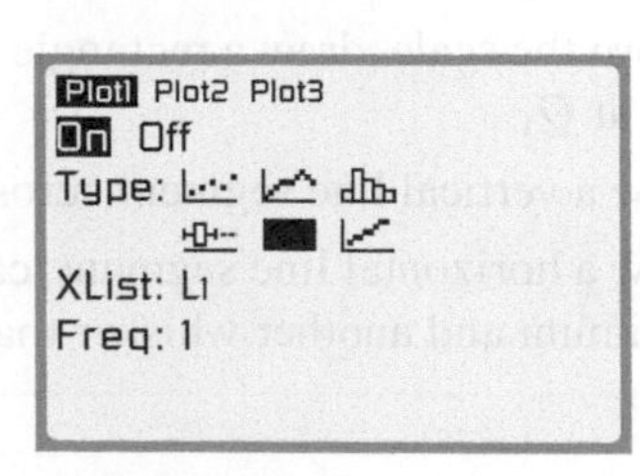

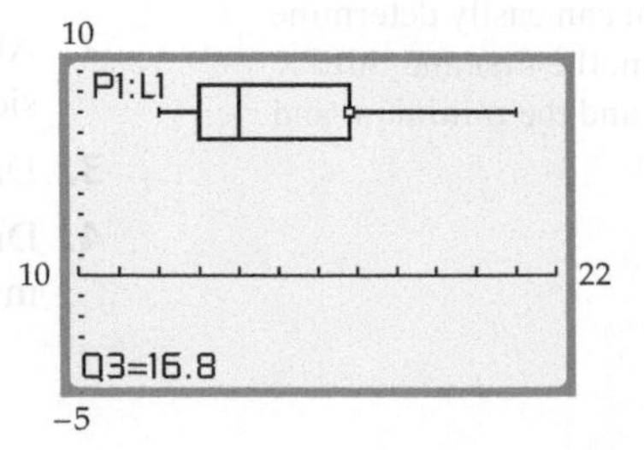

FIGURE 4.1 TI-83/84 screen displays

EXCURSION

Stem-and-Leaf Diagrams

The relative position of each data value in a small set of data can be graphically displayed by using a *stem-and-leaf diagram*. For instance, consider the following history test scores:

65, 72, 96, 86, 43, 61, 75, 86, 49, 68, 98, 74, 84, 78, 85, 75, 86, 73

A Stem-and-Leaf Diagram of a Set of History Test Scores

Stems	Leaves
4	3 9
5	
6	1 5 8
7	2 3 4 5 5 8
8	4 5 6 6 6
9	6 8

Legend: 8|6 represents 86

In the stem-and-leaf diagram at the left, we have organized the history test scores by placing all of the scores that are in the 40s in the top row, the scores that are in the 50s in the second row, the scores that are in the 60s in the third row, and so on. The tens digits of the scores have been placed to the left of the vertical line. In this diagram, they are referred to as *stems*. The ones digits of the test scores have been placed in the proper row to the right of the vertical line. In this diagram, they are the *leaves*. It is now easy to make observations about the distribution of the scores. Only two of the scores are in the 90s. Six of the scores are in the 70s, and none of the scores are in the 50s. The lowest score is 43, and the highest is 98.

Steps in Construction of a Stem-and-Leaf Diagram

1. Determine the stems and list them in a column from smallest to largest or largest to smallest.
2. List the remaining digit of each stem as a leaf to the right of the stem.
3. Include a *legend* that explains the meaning of the stems and the leaves. Include a title for the diagram.

The choice of how many leading digits to use as the stem will depend on the particular data set. For instance, consider the following data set, in which a travel agent has recorded the amount spent by customers for a cruise.

Amount Spent for a Cruise

$3600	$4700	$7200	$2100	$5700	$4400	$9400
$6200	$5900	$2100	$4100	$5200	$7300	$6200
$3800	$4900	$5400	$5400	$3100	$3100	$4500
$4500	$2900	$3700	$3700	$4800	$4800	$2400

One method of choosing the stems is to let each thousands digit be a stem and each hundreds digit be a leaf. If the stems and leaves are assigned in this manner, then the notation 2|1, with a stem of 2 and a leaf of 1, represents a cost of $2100, and 5|4 represents a cost of $5400. A stem-and-leaf diagram can now be constructed by writing all of the stems in a column from smallest to largest to the left of a vertical line and writing the corresponding leaves to the right of the line. See the diagram below.

Amount Spent for a Cruise

Stems	Leaves
2	1 1 4 9
3	1 1 6 7 7 8
4	1 4 5 5 7 8 8 9
5	2 4 4 7 9
6	2 2
7	2 3
8	
9	4

Legend: 7|3 represents $7300

Sometimes two sets of data can be compared by using a *back-to-back stem-and-leaf diagram*, in which common stems are listed in the middle column of the diagram. Leaves from one data set are displayed to the right of the stems, and leaves from the other data set are displayed to the left. For instance, the back-to-back stem-and-leaf diagram below shows the test scores for two classes that took the same test. It is easy to see that the 8 A.M. class did better on the test because it had more scores in the 80s and 90s and fewer scores in the 40s, 50s, and 60s. The number of scores in the 70s was the same for both classes.

Biology Test Scores

8 A.M. class		10 A.M. class
2	4	5 8
7	5	6 7 9 9
5 8	6	2 3 4 8
1 2 3 3 3 7 8	7	1 3 3 5 5 6 8
4 4 5 5 6 8 8 9	8	2 3 6 6 6
2 4 5 5 8	9	4 5

Legend: 3|7 represents 73 Legend: 8|2 represents 82

EXCURSION EXERCISES

1. The following table lists the ages of customers who purchased a cruise. Construct a stem-and-leaf diagram for the data.

Ages of Customers Who Purchased a Cruise

32	45	66	21	62	68	72
61	55	23	38	44	77	64
46	50	33	35	42	45	51
51	28	40	41	52	52	33

2. Two groups of people were part of a test to determine how long, in seconds, it took to solve a logic problem when exposed to different ambient noise levels. Group 1 was given the problem in a room where a constant decibel (dB) level of 65 dB was maintained. For Group 2, the decibel level was maintained at 30 dB. The results are shown in the stem-and-leaf diagram below.

Group 1	Stem	Group 2
	3	3
4	4	2 2 6 8
8 3 1	5	0 4 4 4 5 8
6 2 2 2 1	6	2 3 5
5 3 2 1	7	4
6 1	8	

Legend: 8|5 represents 58 seconds Legend: 5|8 represents 58 seconds

a. How many people in Group 1 required more than 60 s to solve the problem?

b. How many people in Group 2 required more than 60 s to solve the problem?

c. By just looking at the stem-and-leaf diagram, which group appears to have the larger mean time to solve the problem?

3. The exercise heart rate, in beats per minute (bpm), of 20 people was tested before and after a 10-week training program. The results are recorded in the table below.

Before	128	128	131	151	141	139	128	139	161	156
	136	134	134	136	116	174	158	148	156	144
After	125	107	121	140	150	149	126	119	134	138
	164	140	134	129	123	133	139	117	128	139

Draw a back-to-back stem-and-leaf diagram for these data.

EXERCISE SET 4.3

■ In Exercises 1 to 4, round each z-score to the nearest hundredth.

1. A data set has a mean of $\bar{x} = 75$ and a standard deviation of 11.5. Find the z-score for each of the following.

a. $x = 85$ **b.** $x = 95$

c. $x = 50$ **d.** $x = 75$

2. A data set has a mean of $\bar{x} = 212$ and a standard deviation of 40. Find the z-score for each of the following.

a. $x = 200$ **b.** $x = 224$

c. $x = 300$ **d.** $x = 100$

3. A data set has a mean of $\bar{x} = 6.8$ and a standard deviation of 1.9. Find the z-score for each of the following.

a. $x = 6.2$ **b.** $x = 7.2$

c. $x = 9.0$ **d.** $x = 5.0$

4. A data set has a mean of $\bar{x} = 4010$ and a standard deviation of 115. Find the z-score for each of the following.

a. $x = 3840$ **b.** $x = 4200$

c. $x = 4300$ **d.** $x = 4030$

5. Blood Pressure A blood pressure test was given to 450 women ages 20 to 36. It showed that their mean systolic blood pressure was 119.4 mm Hg, with a standard deviation of 13.2 mm Hg.

a. Determine the z-score, to the nearest hundredth, for a woman who had a systolic blood pressure reading of 110.5 mm Hg.

b. The z-score for one woman was 2.15. What was her systolic blood pressure reading?

6. Fruit Juice A random sample of 1000 oranges showed that the mean amount of juice per orange was 7.4 fluid ounces, with a standard deviation of 1.1 fluid ounces.

a. Determine the z-score, to the nearest hundredth, of an orange that produced 6.6 fluid ounces of juice.

b. The z-score for one orange was 3.15. How much juice was produced by this orange? Round to the nearest tenth of a fluid ounce.

7. Cholesterol A test involving 380 men ages 20 to 24 found that their blood cholesterol levels had a mean of 182 mg/dl and a standard deviation of 44.2 mg/dl.

a. Determine the z-score, to the nearest hundredth, for one of the men who had a blood cholesterol level of 214 mg/dl.

b. The z-score for one man was -1.58. What was his blood cholesterol level? Round to the nearest hundredth.

8. Tire Wear A random sample of 80 tires showed that the mean mileage per tire was 41,700 mi, with a standard deviation of 4300 mi.

a. Determine the z-score, to the nearest hundredth, for a tire that provided 46,300 mi of wear.

b. The z-score for one tire was -2.44. What mileage did this tire provide? Round your result to the nearest hundred miles.

9. Test Scores Which of the following three test scores is the highest relative score?

a. A score of 65 on a test with a mean of 72 and a standard deviation of 8.2

b. A score of 102 on a test with a mean of 130 and a standard deviation of 18.5

c. A score of 605 on a test with a mean of 720 and a standard deviation of 116.4

10. Physical Fitness Which of the following fitness scores is the highest relative score?

a. A score of 42 on a test with a mean of 31 and a standard deviation of 6.5

b. A score of 1140 on a test with a mean of 1080 and a standard deviation of 68.2

c. A score of 4710 on a test with a mean of 3960 and a standard deviation of 560.4

11. Reading Test On a reading test, Shaylen's score of 455 was higher than the scores of 4256 of the 7210 students who took the test. Find the percentile, rounded to the nearest percent, for Shaylen's score.

12. Placement Exams On a placement examination, Rick scored lower than 1210 of the 12,860 students who took the exam. Find the percentile, rounded to the nearest percent, for Rick's score.

13. Test Scores Kevin scored at the 65th percentile on a test given to 9840 students. How many students scored lower than Kevin?

14. Test Scores Rene scored at the 84th percentile on a test given to 12,600 students. How many students scored higher than Rene?

15. Median Income In 2015, the median family income in the United States was $66,650. (*Source:* U.S. Census Bureau) If the 90th percentile for the 2015 median four-person family income was $178,500, find the percentage of families whose 2015 income was

a. more than $66,650. **b.** more than $178,500.
c. between $66,650 and $178,500.

16. Monthly Rents A recent survey by the U.S. Census Bureau determined that the median monthly housing rent was $708. If the first quartile for monthly housing rent was $570, find the percent of monthly housing rents that were

a. more than $570. **b.** less than $708.
c. between $570 and $708.

17. Commute to School A survey was given to 18 students. One question asked about the one-way distance the student had to travel to attend college. The results, in miles, are shown in the following table. Use the median procedure for finding quartiles to find the first, second, and third quartiles for the data.

Miles Traveled to Attend College								
12	18	4	5	26	41	1	8	10
10	3	28	32	10	85	7	5	15

18. Prescriptions The following table shows the number of prescriptions a doctor wrote each day for a 36-day period. Use the median procedure for finding quartiles to find the first, second, and third quartiles for the data.

Number of Prescriptions Written per Day					
8	12	14	10	9	16
7	14	10	7	11	16
11	12	8	14	13	10
9	14	15	12	10	8
10	14	8	7	12	15
14	10	9	15	10	12

19. Home Sales The accompanying table shows the median selling prices of existing single-family homes in the United States in the four regions of the country for an 11-year period. Prices have been rounded to the nearest hundred. Draw a box-and-whisker plot of the data for each of the four regions. Write a few sentences that explain any differences you found.

Median Prices of Homes Sold in the United States over an 11-year Period

Year	Northwest	Midwest	South	West
1	227,400	169,700	148,000	196,400
2	246,400	172,600	155,400	213,600
3	264,300	178,000	163,400	238,500
4	264,500	184,300	168,100	260,900
5	315,800	205,000	181,100	283,100
6	343,800	216,900	197,300	332,600
7	346,000	213,500	208,200	337,700
8	320,200	208,600	217,700	330,900
9	343,600	198,900	203,700	294,800
10	302,500	189,200	194,800	263,700
11	335,500	197,600	196,000	259,700

SOURCE: U.S. Census Bureau

20. The table below shows the heights, in inches, of 15 randomly selected National Basketball Association (NBA) players and 15 randomly selected Division I National Collegiate Athletic Association (NCAA) players.

NBA	84	76	79	75	81	81	76	85
	78	79	78	78	84	75	76	
NCAA	78	73	73	78	77	76	75	74
	74	81	75	78	78	79	73	

Using the same scale, draw a box-and-whisker plot for each of the two data sets, placing the second plot below the first. Write a valid conclusion based on the data.

21. The table below shows the numbers of bushels of barley cultivated per acre for 12 one-acre plots of land for two different strains of barley, PHT-34 and CBX-21.

PHT-34	CBX-21
43	56
49	47
47	44
38	45
47	46
45	50
50	48
46	60
46	53
46	50
45	49
43	52

Using the same scale, draw a box-and-whisker plot for each of the two data sets, placing the PHT-34 plot below the CBX-21 plot. Write a valid conclusion based on the data.

22. The blood lead concentrations, in micrograms per deciliter (μg/dL), of 20 children from two different neighborhoods were measured. The results are recorded in the table.

Neighborhood 1	3.97	3.91	3.98	3.70	4.13	3.97	4.01	3.88	4.11	3.70
	3.96	3.77	4.30	4.08	4.12	4.93	3.93	3.94	3.85	3.83
Neighborhood 2	4.31	4.22	3.78	4.10	4.34	4.20	4.35	4.20	4.01	4.04
	4.28	4.12	4.59	4.12	4.01	3.85	3.96	4.28	4.39	4.13

Using the same scale, draw a box-and-whisker plot for each of the two data sets, placing the second plot below the first. Considering that high blood lead concentrations are harmful to humans, in which of the two neighborhoods would you prefer to live?

EXTENSIONS

23. a. The population 3, 4, 9, 14, and 20 has a mean of 10 and a standard deviation of 6.356. The z-scores for each of the five data values are $z_3 \approx -1.101$, $z_4 \approx -0.944$, $z_9 \approx -0.157$, $z_{14} \approx 0.629$, and $z_{20} \approx 1.573$. Find the mean and the standard deviation of these z-scores.

b. The population 2, 6, 12, 17, 22, and 25 has a mean of 14 and a standard deviation of 8.226. The z-scores for each of the six data values are $z_2 \approx -1.459$, $z_6 \approx -0.973$, $z_{12} \approx -0.243$, $z_{17} \approx 0.365$, $z_{22} \approx 0.973$, and $z_{25} \approx 1.337$. Find the mean and the standard deviation of these z-scores.

c. Use the results of part a and part b to make a conjecture about the mean and standard deviation of the z-scores for any set of population data.

24. For each of the following, determine whether the statement is true or false.

a. For any given set of data, the median of the data equals the mean of Q_1 and Q_3.

b. For any given set of data, $Q_3 - Q_2 = Q_2 - Q_1$.

c. A z-score for a given data value x in a set of data can be a negative number.

d. If a student answers 75% of the questions on a test correctly, then the student's score on the test will place the student at the 75th percentile.

SECTION 4.4 Normal Distributions

Frequency Distributions and Histograms

Large sets of data are often displayed using a *grouped frequency distribution* or a *histogram.* For instance, consider the following situation. An Internet service provider (ISP) has installed new computers. To estimate the new download times its subscribers will experience, the ISP surveyed 1000 of its subscribers to determine the time required for each subscriber to download a particular file from an Internet site. The results of that survey are summarized in Table 4.7 on the next page.

TABLE 4.7
A Grouped Frequency Distribution with 12 Classes

Download time (in seconds)	Number of subscribers
0–5	6
5–10	17
10–15	43
15–20	92
20–25	151
25–30	192
30–35	190
35–40	149
40–45	90
45–50	45
50–55	15
55–60	10

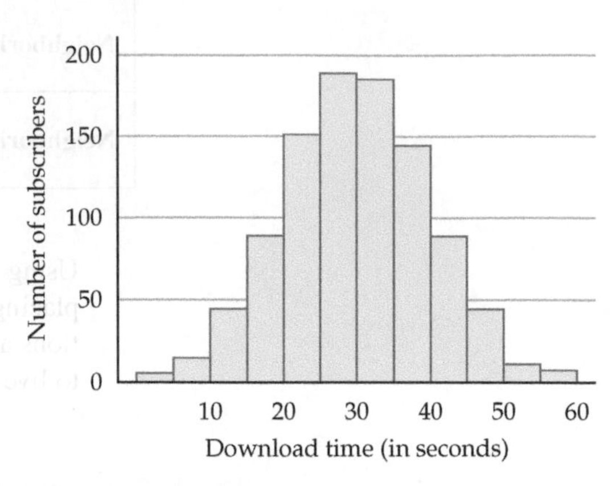

FIGURE 4.2 A histogram for the frequency distribution in Table 4.7

Table 4.7 is called a **grouped frequency distribution**. It shows how often (frequently) certain events occurred. Each interval, 0–5, 5–10, and so on, is called a **class**. This distribution has 12 classes. For the 10–15 class, 10 is the **lower class boundary** and 15 is the **upper class boundary**. Any data value that lies on a common boundary is assigned to the higher class. The *graph* of a frequency distribution is called a **histogram**. A histogram provides a pictorial view of how the data are distributed. In Figure 4.2, the height of each bar of the histogram indicates how many subscribers experienced the download times shown by the class on the base of the bar.

Examine the distribution in Table 4.8 below. It shows the *percent* of subscribers that are in each class, as opposed to the frequency distribution in Table 4.7, which shows the *number* of customers in each class. The type of frequency distribution that lists the *percent* of data in each class is called a **relative frequency distribution**. The **relative frequency histogram** in Figure 4.3 was drawn by using the data in the relative frequency distribution. It shows the *percent* of subscribers along its vertical axis.

TABLE 4.8
A Relative Frequency Distribution

Download time (in seconds)	Percent of subscribers
0–5	0.6
5–10	1.7
10–15	4.3
15–20	9.2
20–25	15.1
25–30	19.2
30–35	19.0
35–40	14.9
40–45	9.0
45–50	4.5
50–55	1.5
55–60	1.0

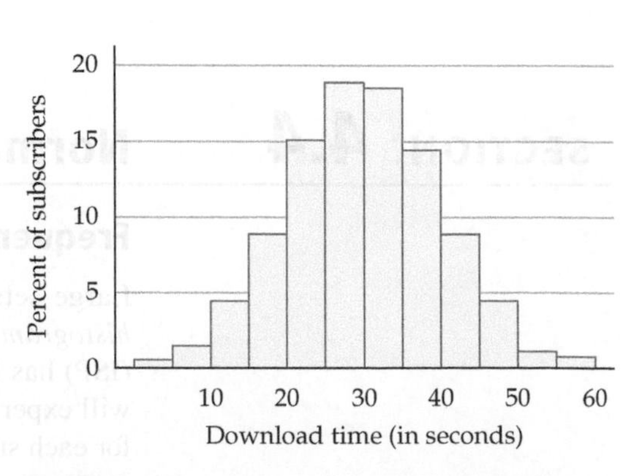

FIGURE 4.3 A relative frequency histogram

One advantage of using a relative frequency distribution instead of a grouped frequency distribution is that there is a direct correspondence between the percent values of the relative frequency distribution and probabilities. For instance, in the relative frequency distribution in Table 4.8, the percent of the data that lies between 35 s and 40 s is 14.9%. Thus, if a subscriber is chosen at random, the probability that the subscriber will require at least 35 s but less than 40 s to download the file is 0.149.

EXAMPLE 1 Use a Relative Frequency Distribution

Use the relative frequency distribution in Table 4.8 to determine the

a. *percent* of subscribers who required at least 25 s to download the file.

b. *probability* that a subscriber chosen at random will require at least 5 s but less than 20 s to download the file.

Solution

a. The percent of data in all the classes with a lower boundary of 25 s or more is the sum of the percents printed in red in Table 4.9 below. Thus the percent of subscribers who required at least 25 s to download the file is 69.1%.

TABLE 4.9

Download time (in seconds)	Percent of subscribers	
0–5	0.6	
5–10	1.7	Sum is 15.2%
10–15	4.3	
15–20	9.2	
20–25	15.1	
25–30	19.2	Sum is 69.1%
30–35	19.0	
35–40	14.9	
40–45	9.0	
45–50	4.5	
50–55	1.5	
55–60	1.0	

b. The percent of data in all the classes with a lower boundary of 5 s and an upper boundary of 20 s is the sum of the percents printed in blue in Table 4.9 above. Thus the percent of subscribers who required at least 5 s but less than 20 s to download the file is 15.2%. The probability that a subscriber chosen at random will require at least 5 s but less than 20 s to download the file is 0.152.

CHECK YOUR PROGRESS 1 Use the relative frequency distribution in Table 4.8 to determine the

a. *percent* of subscribers who required less than 25 s to download the file.

b. *probability* that a subscriber chosen at random will require at least 10 s but less than 30 s to download the file.

Solution See page S15.

Normal Distributions and the Empirical Rule

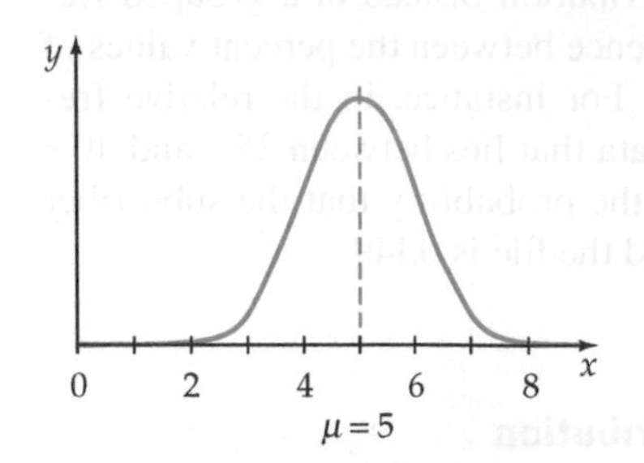

One of the most important statistical distributions of data is known as a *normal distribution*. This distribution occurs in a variety of applications. Types of data that may demonstrate a normal distribution include the lengths of leaves on a tree, the weights of newborns in a hospital, the lengths of time of a student's trip from home to school over a period of months, the SAT scores of a large group of students, and the life spans of light bulbs.

A **normal distribution** forms a bell-shaped curve that is symmetric about a vertical line through the mean of the data. A graph of a normal distribution with a mean of 5 is shown at the left.

Properties of a Normal Distribution

Every normal distribution has the following properties.

- The graph is symmetric about a vertical line through the mean of the distribution.
- The mean, median, and mode are equal.
- The y-value of each point on the curve is the *percent* (expressed as a decimal) of the data at the corresponding x-value.
- Areas under the curve that are symmetric about the mean are equal.
- The total area under the curve is 1.

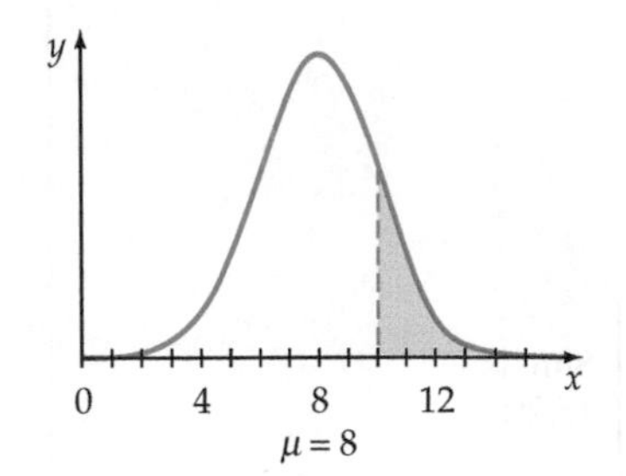

QUESTION What is the area under the curve to the right of the mean for a normal distribution?

In the normal distribution shown at the left, the area of the shaded region is 0.159 units. This region represents the fact that 15.9% of the data values are greater than or equal to 10. Because the area under the curve is 1, the unshaded region under the curve has area 1 − 0.159, or 0.841, representing the fact that 84.1% of the data are less than 10.

The following rule, called the Empirical Rule, describes the percents of data that lie within 1, 2, and 3 standard deviations of the mean in a normal distribution.

Empirical Rule for a Normal Distribution

In a normal distribution, approximately

- 68% of the data lie within 1 standard deviation of the mean.
- 95% of the data lie within 2 standard deviations of the mean.
- 99.7% of the data lie within 3 standard deviations of the mean.

A normal distribution

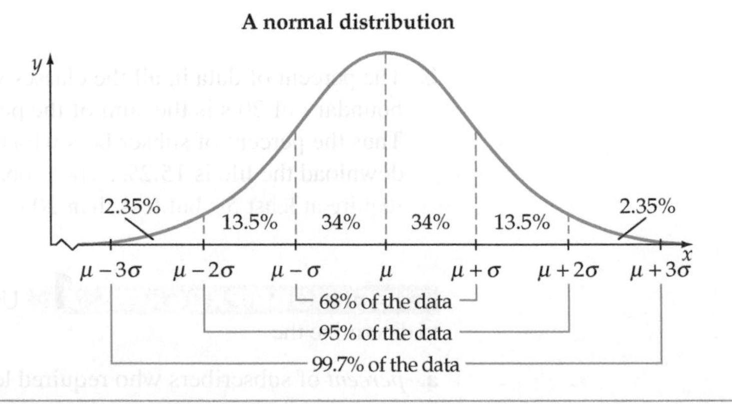

ANSWER Because a normal distribution is symmetric about the mean, the area under the curve to the right of the mean is one-half the total area. The total area under a normal distribution is 1, so the area under the curve to the right of the mean is 0.5.

EXAMPLE 2 Use the Empirical Rule to Solve an Application

A survey of 1000 U.S. gas stations found that the price charged for a gallon of regular gas could be closely approximated by a normal distribution with a mean of \$3.10 and a standard deviation of \$0.18. How many of the stations charge

a. between \$2.74 and \$3.46 for a gallon of regular gas?

b. less than \$3.28 for a gallon of regular gas?

c. more than \$3.46 for a gallon of regular gas?

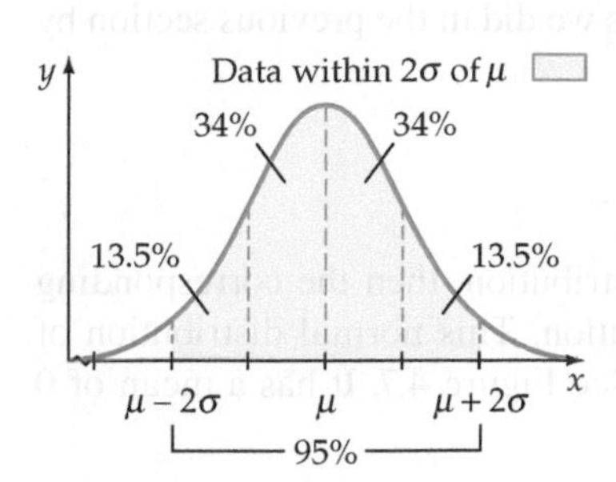

FIGURE 4.4

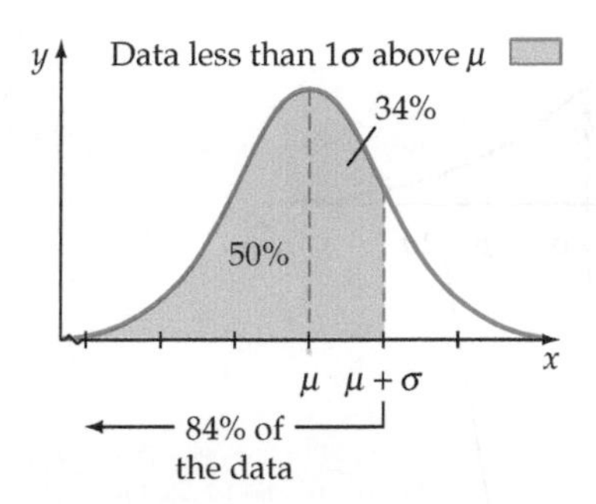

FIGURE 4.5

Solution

a. The \$2.74 per gallon price is 2 standard deviations below the mean. The \$3.46 price is 2 standard deviations above the mean. In a normal distribution, 95% of all data lie within 2 standard deviations of the mean. See Figure 4.4. Therefore approximately

$$(95\%)(1000) = (0.95)(1000) = 950$$

of the stations charge between \$2.74 and \$3.46 for a gallon of regular gas.

b. The \$3.28 price is 1 standard deviation above the mean. See Figure 4.5. In a normal distribution, 34% of all data lie between the mean and 1 standard deviation above the mean. Thus, approximately

$$(34\%)(1000) = (0.34)(1000) = 340$$

of the stations charge between \$3.10 and \$3.28 for a gallon of regular gasoline. Half of the 1000 stations, or 500 stations, charge less than the mean. Therefore about 340 + 500 = 840 of the stations charge less than \$3.28 for a gallon of regular gas.

c. The \$3.46 price is 2 standard deviations above the mean. In a normal distribution, 95% of all data are within 2 standard deviations of the mean. This means that the other 5% of the data will lie either more than 2 standard deviations above the mean or more than 2 standard deviations below the mean. We are interested only in the data that are more than 2 standard deviations above the mean, which is $\frac{1}{2}$ of 5%, or 2.5%, of the data. See Figure 4.6. Thus about 2.5%)(1000) = (0.025)(1000) = 25 of the stations charge more than \$3.46 for a gallon of regular gas.

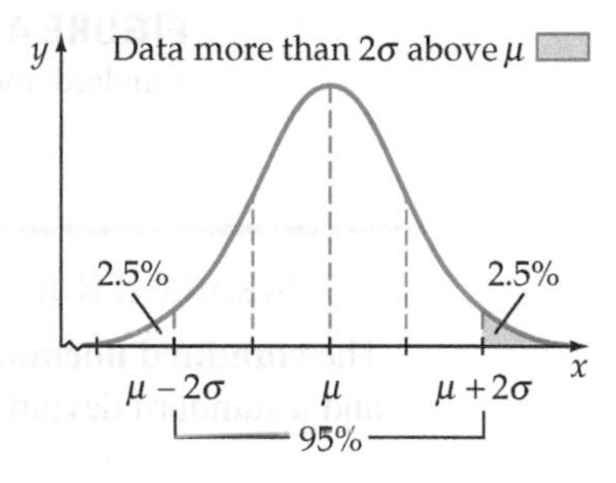

FIGURE 4.6

CHECK YOUR PROGRESS 2 A vegetable distributor knows that during the month of August, the weights of its tomatoes are normally distributed with a mean of 0.61 lb and a standard deviation of 0.15 lb.

a. What percent of the tomatoes weigh less than 0.76 lb?

b. In a shipment of 6000 tomatoes, how many tomatoes can be expected to weigh more than 0.31 lb?

c. In a shipment of 4500 tomatoes, how many tomatoes can be expected to weigh from 0.31 lb to 0.91 lb?

Solution See pages S15.

QUESTION Can the Empirical Rule be applied to all data sets?

The Standard Normal Distribution

It is often helpful to convert data values x to z-scores, as we did in the previous section by using the z-score formulas:

$$z_x = \frac{x - \mu}{\sigma} \quad \text{or} \quad z_x = \frac{x - \overline{x}}{s}$$

If the original distribution of x values is a normal distribution, then the corresponding distribution of z-scores will also be a normal distribution. This normal distribution of z-scores is called the *standard normal distribution*. See Figure 4.7. It has a mean of 0 and a standard deviation of 1.

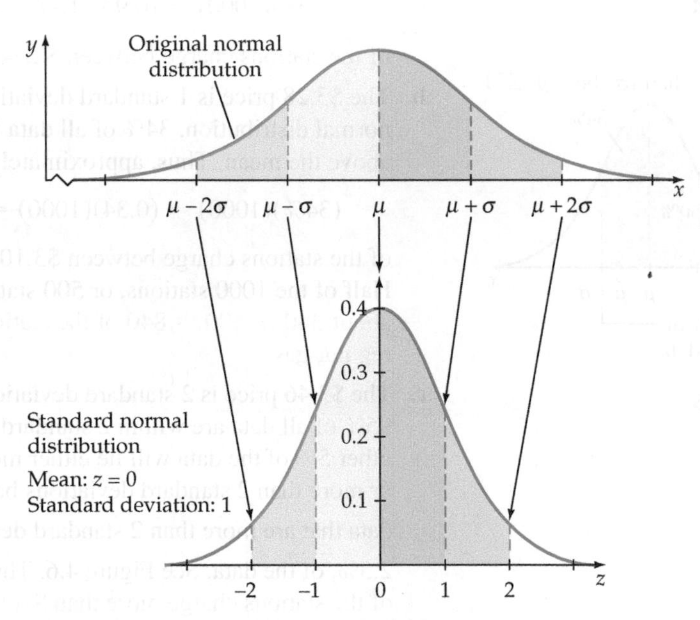

FIGURE 4.7 Conversion of a normal distribution to the standard normal distribution

> **The Standard Normal Distribution**
>
> The **standard normal distribution** is the normal distribution that has a mean of 0 and a standard deviation of 1.

Tables and calculators are often used to determine the area under a portion of the standard normal curve. We will refer to this type of area as an *area of the standard normal distribution*. Table 4.10 gives the approximate areas of the standard normal distribution between the mean 0 and z standard deviations from the mean. See Figure 4.8. Table 4.10 indicates that the area A of the standard normal distribution from the mean 0 up to $z = 1.34$ is 0.410 square unit.

ANSWER No. The Empirical Rule can only be applied to normal distributions.

TAKE NOTE

In Table 4.10, the entries below A give the area under the standard normal curve from 0 to the z-value listed to the left of the A value. The A values have been rounded to the nearest thousandth.

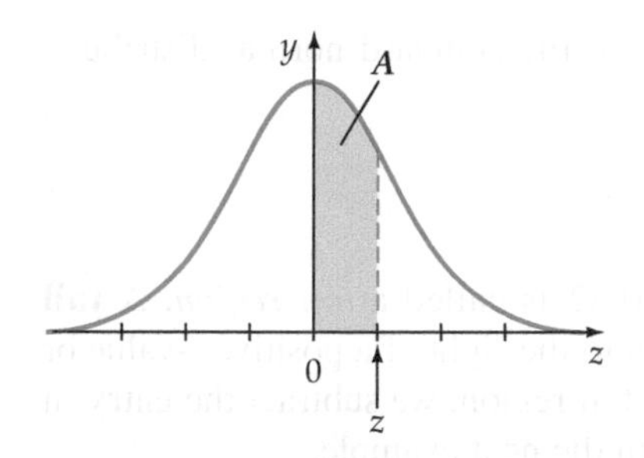

FIGURE 4.8 A is the area of the shaded region.

TAKE NOTE

To find the A value for the z-score 0.382, round 0.382 to the nearest hundredth to produce 0.38. Then use Table 4.10 to find that $A \approx 0.148$.

TABLE 4.10
Area Under the Standard Normal Curve

z	A	z	A	z	A	z	A	z	A	z	A
0.00	0.000	0.56	0.212	1.12	0.369	1.68	0.454	2.24	0.487	2.80	0.497
0.01	0.004	0.57	0.216	1.13	0.371	1.69	0.454	2.25	0.488	2.81	0.498
0.02	0.008	0.58	0.219	1.14	0.373	1.70	0.455	2.26	0.488	2.82	0.498
0.03	0.012	0.59	0.222	1.15	0.375	1.71	0.456	2.27	0.488	2.83	0.498
0.04	0.016	0.60	0.226	1.16	0.377	1.72	0.457	2.28	0.489	2.84	0.498
0.05	0.020	0.61	0.229	1.17	0.379	1.73	0.458	2.29	0.489	2.85	0.498
0.06	0.024	0.62	0.232	1.18	0.381	1.74	0.459	2.30	0.489	2.86	0.498
0.07	0.028	0.63	0.236	1.19	0.383	1.75	0.460	2.31	0.490	2.87	0.498
0.08	0.032	0.64	0.239	1.20	0.385	1.76	0.461	2.32	0.490	2.88	0.498
0.09	0.036	0.65	0.242	1.21	0.387	1.77	0.462	2.33	0.490	2.89	0.498
0.10	0.040	0.66	0.245	1.22	0.389	1.78	0.462	2.34	0.490	2.90	0.498
0.11	0.044	0.67	0.249	1.23	0.391	1.79	0.463	2.35	0.491	2.91	0.498
0.12	0.048	0.68	0.252	1.24	0.393	1.80	0.464	2.36	0.491	2.92	0.498
0.13	0.052	0.69	0.255	1.25	0.394	1.81	0.465	2.37	0.491	2.93	0.498
0.14	0.056	0.70	0.258	1.26	0.396	1.82	0.466	2.38	0.491	2.94	0.498
0.15	0.060	0.71	0.261	1.27	0.398	1.83	0.466	2.39	0.492	2.95	0.498
0.16	0.064	0.72	0.264	1.28	0.400	1.84	0.467	2.40	0.492	2.96	0.498
0.17	0.067	0.73	0.267	1.29	0.401	1.85	0.468	2.41	0.492	2.97	0.499
0.18	0.071	0.74	0.270	1.30	0.403	1.86	0.469	2.42	0.492	2.98	0.499
0.19	0.075	0.75	0.273	1.31	0.405	1.87	0.469	2.43	0.492	2.99	0.499
0.20	0.079	0.76	0.276	1.32	0.407	1.88	0.470	2.44	0.493	3.00	0.499
0.21	0.083	0.77	0.279	1.33	0.408	1.89	0.471	2.45	0.493	3.01	0.499
0.22	0.087	0.78	0.282	1.34	0.410	1.90	0.471	2.46	0.493	3.02	0.499
0.23	0.091	0.79	0.285	1.35	0.411	1.91	0.472	2.47	0.493	3.03	0.499
0.24	0.095	0.80	0.288	1.36	0.413	1.92	0.473	2.48	0.493	3.04	0.499
0.25	0.099	0.81	0.291	1.37	0.415	1.93	0.473	2.49	0.494	3.05	0.499
0.26	0.103	0.82	0.294	1.38	0.416	1.94	0.474	2.50	0.494	3.06	0.499
0.27	0.106	0.83	0.297	1.39	0.418	1.95	0.474	2.51	0.494	3.07	0.499
0.28	0.110	0.84	0.300	1.40	0.419	1.96	0.475	2.52	0.494	3.08	0.499
0.29	0.114	0.85	0.302	1.41	0.421	1.97	0.476	2.53	0.494	3.09	0.499
0.30	0.118	0.86	0.305	1.42	0.422	1.98	0.476	2.54	0.494	3.10	0.499
0.31	0.122	0.87	0.308	1.43	0.424	1.99	0.477	2.55	0.495	3.11	0.499
0.32	0.126	0.88	0.311	1.44	0.425	2.00	0.477	2.56	0.495	3.12	0.499
0.33	0.129	0.89	0.313	1.45	0.426	2.01	0.478	2.57	0.495	3.13	0.499
0.34	0.133	0.90	0.316	1.46	0.428	2.02	0.478	2.58	0.495	3.14	0.499
0.35	0.137	0.91	0.319	1.47	0.429	2.03	0.479	2.59	0.495	3.15	0.499
0.36	0.141	0.92	0.321	1.48	0.431	2.04	0.479	2.60	0.495	3.16	0.499
0.37	0.144	0.93	0.324	1.49	0.432	2.05	0.480	2.61	0.495	3.17	0.499
0.38	0.148	0.94	0.326	1.50	0.433	2.06	0.480	2.62	0.496	3.18	0.499
0.39	0.152	0.95	0.329	1.51	0.434	2.07	0.481	2.63	0.496	3.19	0.499
0.40	0.155	0.96	0.331	1.52	0.436	2.08	0.481	2.64	0.496	3.20	0.499
0.41	0.159	0.97	0.334	1.53	0.437	2.09	0.482	2.65	0.496	3.21	0.499
0.42	0.163	0.98	0.336	1.54	0.438	2.10	0.482	2.66	0.496	3.22	0.499
0.43	0.166	0.99	0.339	1.55	0.439	2.11	0.483	2.67	0.496	3.23	0.499
0.44	0.170	1.00	0.341	1.56	0.441	2.12	0.483	2.68	0.496	3.24	0.499
0.45	0.174	1.01	0.344	1.57	0.442	2.13	0.483	2.69	0.496	3.25	0.499
0.46	0.177	1.02	0.346	1.58	0.443	2.14	0.484	2.70	0.497	3.26	0.499
0.47	0.181	1.03	0.348	1.59	0.444	2.15	0.484	2.71	0.497	3.27	0.499
0.48	0.184	1.04	0.351	1.60	0.445	2.16	0.485	2.72	0.497	3.28	0.499
0.49	0.188	1.05	0.353	1.61	0.446	2.17	0.485	2.73	0.497	3.29	0.499
0.50	0.191	1.06	0.355	1.62	0.447	2.18	0.485	2.74	0.497	3.30	0.500
0.51	0.195	1.07	0.358	1.63	0.448	2.19	0.486	2.75	0.497	3.31	0.500
0.52	0.198	1.08	0.360	1.64	0.449	2.20	0.486	2.76	0.497	3.32	0.500
0.53	0.202	1.09	0.362	1.65	0.451	2.21	0.486	2.77	0.497	3.33	0.500
0.54	0.205	1.10	0.364	1.66	0.452	2.22	0.487	2.78	0.497		
0.55	0.209	1.11	0.367	1.67	0.453	2.23	0.487	2.79	0.497		

Because the standard normal distribution is symmetrical about the mean of 0, we can also use Table 4.10 to find the area of a region that is located to the left of the mean. This process is explained in Example 3.

EXAMPLE 3 Use Symmetry to Determine an Area

Find the area of the standard normal distribution between $z = -1.44$ and $z = 0$.

Solution

Because the standard normal distribution is symmetrical about the center line $z = 0$, the area of the standard normal distribution between $z = -1.44$ and $z = 0$ is equal to the area between $z = 0$ and $z = 1.44$. See Figure 4.9. The entry in Table 4.10 associated with $z = 1.44$ is 0.425. Thus the area of the standard normal distribution between $z = -1.44$ and $z = 0$ is 0.425 square unit.

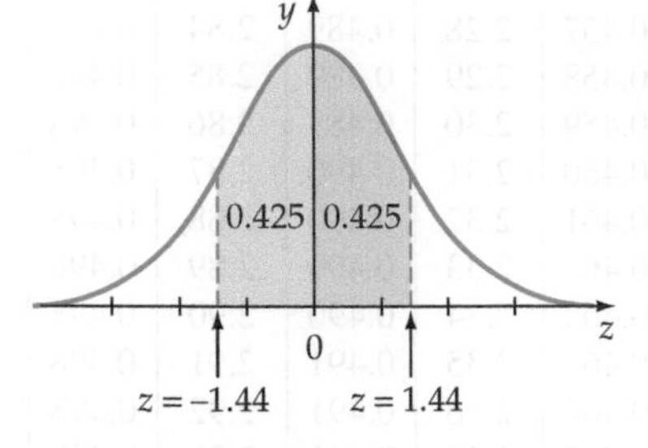

FIGURE 4.9 Symmetrical region

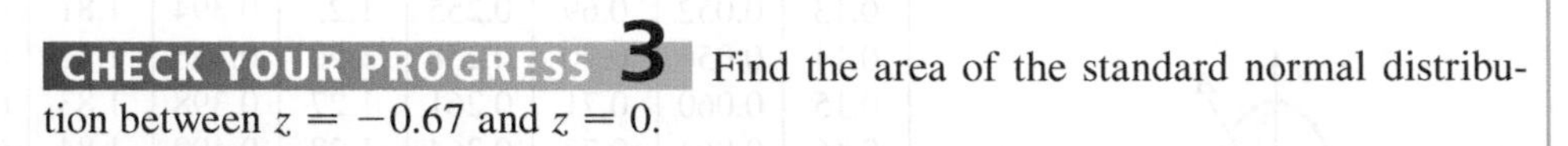

CHECK YOUR PROGRESS 3 Find the area of the standard normal distribution between $z = -0.67$ and $z = 0$.

Solution See page S15.

In Figure 4.10, the region to the right of $z = 0.82$ is called a *tail region*. A **tail region** is a region of the standard normal distribution to the right of a positive z-value or to the left of a negative z-value. To find the area of a tail region, we subtract the entry in Table 4.10 from 0.500. This procedure is illustrated in the next example.

EXAMPLE 4 Find the Area of a Tail Region

Find the area of the standard normal distribution to the right of $z = 0.82$.

Solution

Table 4.10 indicates that the area from $z = 0$ to $z = 0.82$ is 0.294 square unit. The area to the right of $z = 0$ is 0.500 square unit. Thus the area to the right of $z = 0.82$ is $0.500 - 0.294 = 0.206$ square unit. See Figure 4.10.

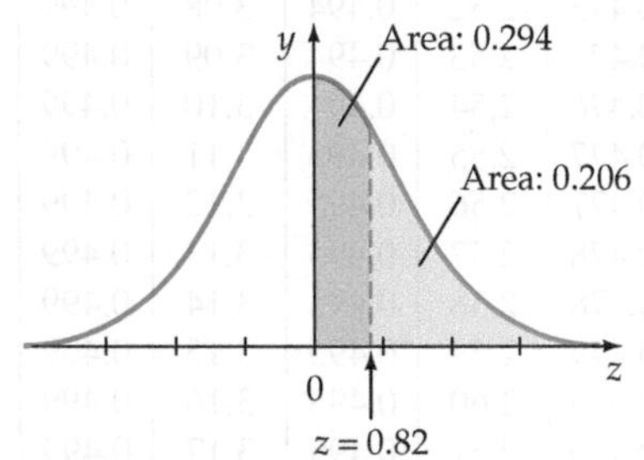

FIGURE 4.10 Area of a tail region

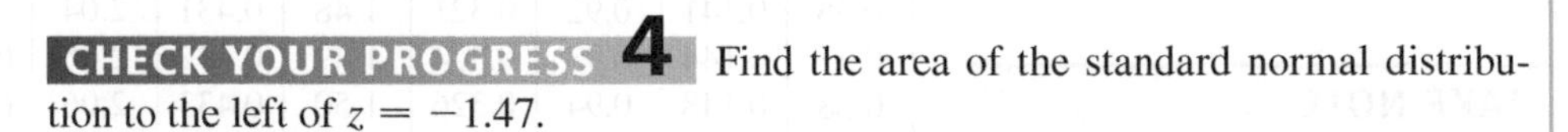

CHECK YOUR PROGRESS 4 Find the area of the standard normal distribution to the left of $z = -1.47$.

Solution See page S15.

The Standard Normal Distribution, Areas, Percentages, and Probabilities

In the standard normal distribution, the area of the distribution from $z = a$ to $z = b$ represents

- the *percentage* of z-values that lie in the interval from a to b.
- the *probability* that z lies in the interval from a to b.

Because the area of a portion of the standard normal distribution can be interpreted as a percentage of the data or as a probability that the variable lies in a particular interval, we can use the standard normal distribution to solve many application problems.

EXAMPLE 5 Solve an Application

A soda machine dispenses soda into 12-ounce cups. Tests show that the actual amount of soda dispensed is normally distributed, with a mean of 11.5 oz and a standard deviation of 0.2 oz.

a. What percent of cups will receive less than 11.25 oz of soda?

b. What percent of cups will receive between 11.2 oz and 11.55 oz of soda?

c. If a cup is filled at random, what is the probability that the machine will overflow the cup?

Solution

a. Recall that the formula for the z-score for a data value x is

$$z_x = \frac{x - \bar{x}}{s}$$

The z-score for 11.25 oz is

$$z_{11.25} = \frac{11.25 - 11.5}{0.2} = -1.25$$

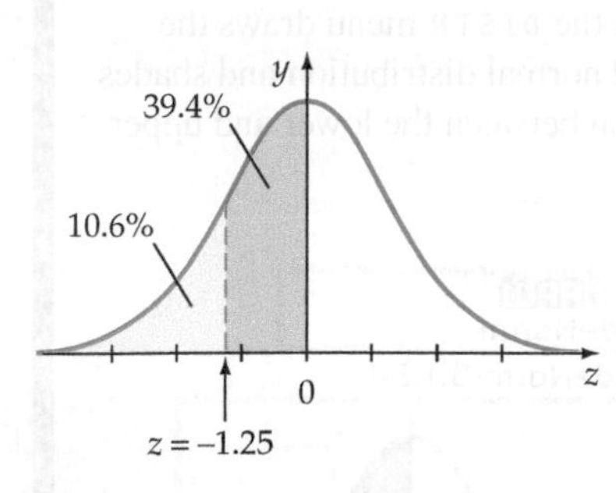

FIGURE 4.11 Portion of data to the left of $z = -1.25$

Table 4.10 indicates that 0.394 (39.4%) of the data in a normal distribution are between $z = 0$ and $z = 1.25$. Because the data are normally distributed, 39.4% of the data is also between $z = 0$ and $z = -1.25$. The percent of data to the left of $z = -1.25$ is 50% − 39.4% = 10.6%. See Figure 4.11. Thus 10.6% of the cups filled by the soda machine will receive less than 11.25 oz of soda.

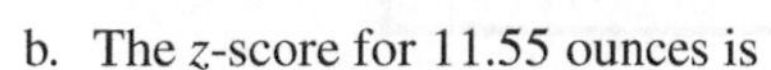

b. The z-score for 11.55 ounces is

$$z_{11.55} = \frac{11.55 - 11.5}{0.2} = 0.25$$

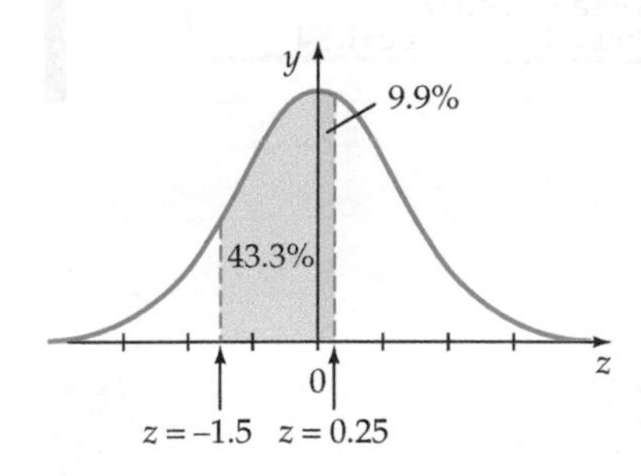

FIGURE 4.12 Portion of data between two z-scores

Table 4.10 indicates that 0.099 (9.9%) of the data in a normal distribution is between $z = 0$ and $z = 0.25$.

The z-score for 11.2 oz is

$$z_{11.2} = \frac{11.2 - 11.5}{0.2} = -1.5$$

Table 4.10 indicates that 0.433 (43.3%) of the data in a normal distribution are between $z = 0$ and $z = 1.5$. Because the data are normally distributed, 43.3% of the data are also between $z = 0$ and $z = -1.5$. See Figure 4.12. Thus the percent of the cups that the vending machine will fill with between 11.2 oz and 11.55 oz of soda is 43.3% + 9.9% = 53.2%.

c. A cup will overflow if it receives more than 12 oz of soda. The z-score for 12 oz is

$$z_{12} = \frac{12 - 11.5}{0.2} = 2.5$$

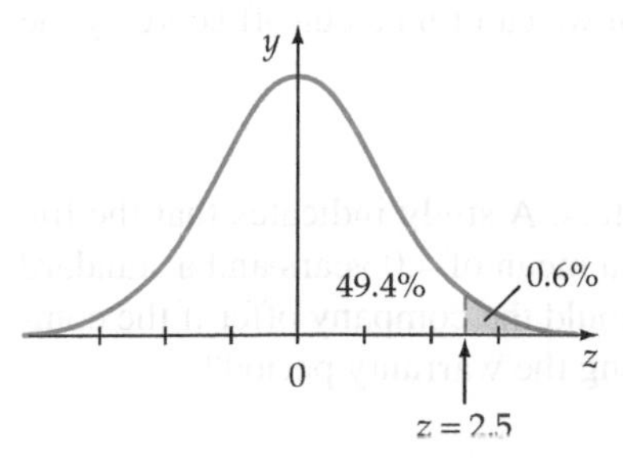

FIGURE 4.13 Portion of data to the right of $z = 2.5$

Table 4.10 indicates that 0.494 (49.4%) of the data in the standard normal distribution are between $z = 0$ and $z = 2.5$. The percent of data to the right of $z = 2.5$ is determined by subtracting 49.4% from 50%. See Figure 4.13. Thus 0.6% of the time the machine produces an overflow, and the probability that a cup filled at random will overflow is 0.006.

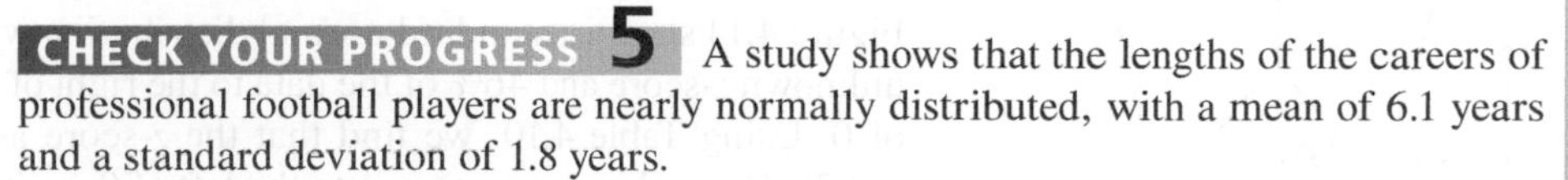

CHECK YOUR PROGRESS 5 A study shows that the lengths of the careers of professional football players are nearly normally distributed, with a mean of 6.1 years and a standard deviation of 1.8 years.

a. What percent of professional football players have a career of more than 9 years?

b. If a professional football player is chosen at random, what is the probability that the player will have a career of between 3 and 4 years?

Solution See page S15–S16.

MATH MATTERS Find the Area of a Portion of the Standard Normal Distribution by Using a Calculator

Some calculators can be used to find the area of a portion of the standard normal distribution. For instance, the TI-83/84 screen displays below indicate that the area of the standard normal distribution from a lower bound of $z = 0$ to an upper bound of $z = 1.34$ is about 0.409877 square unit. This is a more accurate value than the entry given in Table 4.10, which is 0.410.

Select the `normalcdf(` function from the `DISTR` menu. Enter your lower bound, followed by a comma and your upper bound. Press `ENTER`.

The `ShadeNorm` instruction under `DRAW` in the `DISTR` menu draws the standard normal distribution and shades the region between the lower and upper bounds.

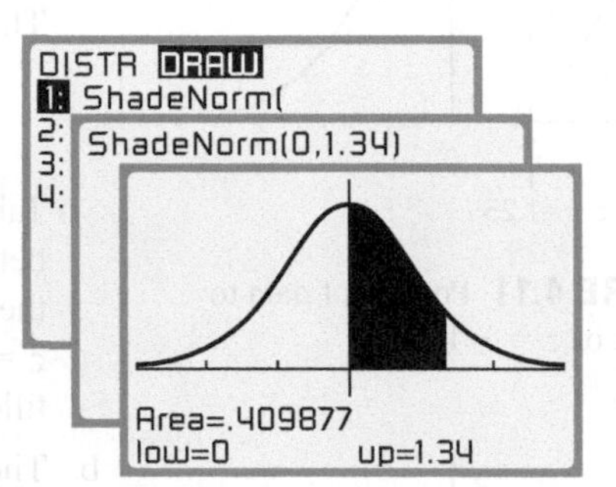

EXCURSION

Cut-Off Scores

A *cut-off score* is a score that separates data into two groups such that the data in one group satisfy a certain requirement and the data in the other group do not satisfy the requirement. If the data are normally distributed, then we can find a cut-off score by the method shown in the following example.

EXAMPLE

The OnTheGo company manufactures laptop computers. A study indicates that the life spans of its computers are normally distributed, with a mean of 4.0 years and a standard deviation of 1.2 years. How long a warranty period should the company offer if the company wishes less than 4% of its computers to fail during the warranty period?

Solution

Figure 4.14 shows a standard normal distribution with 4% of the data to the left of some unknown z-score and 46% of the data to the right of the z-score but to the left of the mean of 0. Using Table 4.10, we find that the z-score associated with an area of $A = 0.46$ is 1.75. Our unknown z-score is to the left of 0, so it must be negative. Thus $z_x = -1.75$. If we let x represent the time in years that a computer is in use, then x is related to the z-scores by the formula

$$z_x = \frac{x - \bar{x}}{s}$$

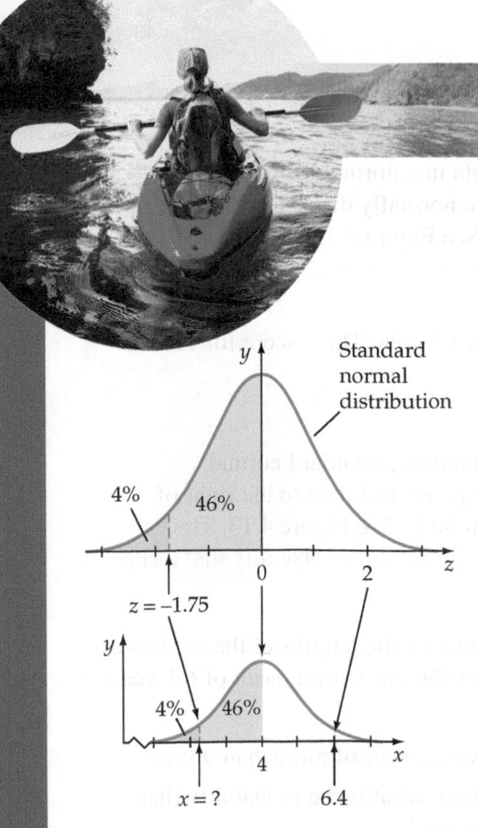

FIGURE 4.14 Finding a cut-off score

Solving for x with $\bar{x} = 4.0$, $s = 1.2$, and $z = -1.75$ gives us

$$
\begin{aligned}
-1.75 &= \frac{x - 4.0}{1.2} \\
(-1.75)(1.2) &= x - 4.0 \\
x &= 4.0 - 2.1 \\
x &= 1.9 \quad \text{The cut-off score}
\end{aligned}
$$

Hence the company can provide a 1.9-year warranty and expect less than 4% of its computers to fail during the warranty period.

EXCURSION EXERCISES

1. A professor finds that the grades in a large class are normally distributed. The mean of the grades is 64, and the standard deviation is 10. If the professor decides to give an A grade to the students in the top 9% of the class, what is the cut-off score for an A?

2. The results of a statewide examination of the reading skills of sixth-grade students are normally distributed, with a mean score of 104 and a standard deviation of 16. The students in the top 10% are to receive an award, and those in the bottom 14% will be required to take a special reading class.

a. What score does a student need in order to receive an award?

b. What is the cut-off score that will be used to determine whether a student will be required to take the special reading class?

3. A secondary school system finds that the 440-yard-dash times of its female students are normally distributed, with an average time of 72 s and a standard deviation of 5.5 s. What time does a runner need in order to be in the 9% of runners with the best times? Round to the nearest hundredth of a second.

EXERCISE SET 4.4

1. **Boys' Heights** Humans are, on average, taller today than they were 200 years ago. Today, the mean height of 14-year-old boys is about 65 in. Use the following relative frequency distribution of heights of a group of 14-year-old boys from the 19th century to answer the following questions.

Heights of a Group of 19th-Century Boys, Age 14

Height (in inches)	Percent of boys
Under 50	0.2
50–54	7.0
55–59	46.0
60–64	41.0
65–69	5.8

SOURCE: *Journal of the Anthropological Institute of Great Britain and Ireland*

a. What percent of the group of 19th-century boys was at least 65 in. tall?

b. What is the probability that one of the 19th-century boys selected at random was at least 55 in. tall but less than 65 in. tall?

2. **Biology** A biologist measured the lengths of hundreds of cuckoo bird eggs. Use the relative frequency distribution below to answer the questions that follow.

Lengths of Cuckoo Bird Eggs

Length (in millimeters)	Percent of eggs
18.75–19.75	0.8
19.75–20.75	4.0
20.75–21.75	17.3
21.75–22.75	37.9
22.75–23.75	28.5
23.75–24.75	10.7
24.75–25.75	0.8

SOURCE: Biometrika

a. What percent of the group of eggs was less than 21.75 mm long?

b. What is the probability that one of the eggs selected at random was at least 20.75 mm long but less than 24.75 mm long?

■ In Exercises 3 to 8, use the Empirical Rule to answer each question.

3. In a normal distribution, what percent of the data lie

a. within 2 standard deviations of the mean?

b. more than 1 standard deviation above the mean?

c. between 1 standard deviation below the mean and 2 standard deviations above the mean?

4. In a normal distribution, what percent of the data lie

a. within 3 standard deviations of the mean?

b. more than 2 standard deviations below the mean?

c. between 2 standard deviations below the mean and 3 standard deviations above the mean?

5. Shipping During 1 week, an overnight delivery company found that the weights of its parcels were normally distributed, with a mean of 24 oz and a standard deviation of 6 oz.

a. What percent of the parcels weighed between 12 oz and 30 oz?

b. What percent of the parcels weighed more than 42 oz?

6. Baseball A baseball franchise finds that the attendance at its home games is normally distributed, with a mean of 16,000 and a standard deviation of 4000.

a. What percent of the home games have an attendance between 12,000 and 20,000 people?

b. What percent of the home games have an attendance of fewer than 8000 people?

7. Traffic A highway study of 8000 vehicles that passed by a checkpoint found that their speeds were normally distributed, with a mean of 61 mph and a standard deviation of 7 mph.

a. How many of the vehicles had a speed of more than 68 mph?

b. How many of the vehicles had a speed of less than 40 mph?

8. Women's Heights A survey of 1000 women ages 20 to 30 found that their heights were normally distributed, with a mean of 65 in. and a standard deviation of 2.5 in.

a. How many of the women have a height that is within 1 standard deviation of the mean?

b. How many of the women have a height that is between 60 in. and 70 in.?

■ In Exercises 9 to 16, find the area, to the nearest thousandth, of the standard normal distribution between the given z-scores.

9. $z = 0$ and $z = 1.5$

10. $z = 0$ and $z = 1.9$

11. $z = 0$ and $z = -1.85$

12. $z = 0$ and $z = -2.3$

13. $z = 1$ and $z = 1.9$

14. $z = 0.7$ and $z = 1.92$

15. $z = -1.47$ and $z = 1.64$

16. $z = -0.44$ and $z = 1.82$

■ In Exercises 17 to 24, find the area, to the nearest thousandth, of the indicated region of the standard normal distribution.

17. The region where $z > 1.3$

18. The region where $z > 1.92$

19. The region where $z < -2.22$

20. The region where $z < -0.38$

21. The region where $z > -1.45$

22. The region where $z < 1.82$

23. The region where $z < 2.71$

24. The region where $z < 1.92$

■ In Exercises 25 to 30, find the z-score, to the nearest hundredth, that satisfies the given condition.

25. 0.200 square unit of the area of the standard normal distribution is to the right of z.

26. 0.227 square unit of the area of the standard normal distribution is to the right of z.

27. 0.184 square unit of the area of the standard normal distribution is to the left of z.

28. 0.330 square unit of the area of the standard normal distribution is to the left of z.

29. 0.363 square unit of the area of the standard normal distribution is to the right of z.

30. 0.440 square unit of the area of the standard normal distribution is to the left of z.

■ In Exercises 31 to 40, answer each question. Round z-scores to the nearest hundredth and then find the required A values using Table 4.10 on page 267.

31. Cholesterol Levels The cholesterol levels of a group of young women at a university are normally distributed, with a mean of 185 and a standard deviation of 39. What percent of the young women have a cholesterol level

a. greater than 219?

b. between 190 and 225?

32. Biology A biologist found the wingspans of a group of monarch butterflies to be normally distributed, with a mean of 52.2 mm and a standard deviation of 2.3 mm. What percent of the butterflies had a wingspan

a. less than 48.5 mm?

b. between 50 and 55 mm?

33. Light Bulbs A manufacturer of light bulbs finds that one light bulb model has a mean life span of 1025 h with a standard deviation of 87 h. What percent of these light bulbs will last

a. at least 950 h?

b. between 800 and 900 h?

34. Heart Rates The resting heart rates of a group of healthy adult men were found to have a mean of 73.4 beats per minute, with a standard deviation of 5.9 beats per minute. What percent of these men had a resting heart rate of

a. greater than 80 beats per minute?

b. between 70 and 85 beats per minute?

35. Cereal Weight The weights of all the boxes of corn flakes filled by a machine are normally distributed, with a mean weight of 14.5 oz and a standard deviation of 0.4 oz. What percent of the boxes will

a. weigh less than 14 oz?

b. weigh between 13.5 oz and 15.5 oz?

36. Telephone Calls A telephone company has found that the lengths of its long distance telephone calls are normally distributed, with a mean of 225 s and a standard deviation of 55 s. What percent of its long distance calls are

a. longer than 340 s?

b. between 200 and 300 s?

37. Rope Strength The breaking point of a particular type of rope is normally distributed, with a mean of 350 lb and a standard deviation of 24 lb. What is the probability that a piece of this rope chosen at random will have a breaking point of

a. less than 320 lb?

b. between 340 and 370 lb?

38. Tire Mileage The mileage for WearEver tires is normally distributed, with a mean of 48,000 mi and a standard deviation of 7400 mi. What is the probability that the WearEver tires you purchase will provide a mileage of

a. more than 60,000 mi?

b. between 40,000 and 50,000 mi?

39. Grocery Store Lines The amount of time customers spend waiting in line at a grocery store is normally distributed, with a mean of 2.5 min and a standard deviation of 0.75 min. Find the probability that the time a customer spends waiting is

a. less than 3 min.

b. less than 1 min.

40. IQ Tests A psychologist finds that the intelligence quotients of a group of patients are normally distributed, with a mean of 102 and a standard deviation of 16. Find the percent of the patients with IQs

a. above 114.

b. between 90 and 118.

41. Heights Consider the data set of the heights of all babies born in the United States during a particular year. Do you think this data set is nearly normally distributed? Explain.

42. Weights Consider the data set of the weights of all Valencia oranges grown in California during a particular year. Do you think this data set is nearly normally distributed? Explain.

EXTENSIONS

■ In Exercises 43 to 49, determine whether the given statement is true or false.

43. The standard normal distribution has a mean of 0.

44. Every normal distribution is a bell-shaped distribution.

45. In a normal distribution, the mean, the median, and the mode of the distribution are all located at the center of the distribution.

46. The mean of a normal distribution is always larger than the standard deviation of the distribution.

47. The standard deviation of the standard normal distribution is 1.

48. If a data value x from a normal distribution is positive, then its z-score also must be positive.

49. All normal distributions have a mean of 0.

50. a. Make a sketch of two normal distributions that have the same standard deviation but different means.

b. Make a sketch of two normal distributions that have the same mean but different standard deviations.

51. Determine the approximate z-scores for the first quartile and the third quartile of the standard normal distribution.

SECTION 4.5 Linear Regression and Correlation

Linear Regression

When performing research studies, scientists often wish to know whether two variables are related. If the variables are determined to be related, a scientist may then wish to find an equation that can be used to model the relationship. For instance, a geologist might want to know whether there is a relationship between the duration of an eruption of a geyser and the time between eruptions. A first step in this determination is to collect some data. Data involving two variables are called **bivariate data**. Table 4.11 gives bivariate data showing the time between two eruptions and the duration of the second eruption for 10 eruptions of the geyser Old Faithful.

TABLE 4.11

Time between eruptions (in seconds), x	272	227	237	238	203	270	218	226	250	245
Duration of eruption (in seconds), y	89	79	83	82	81	85	78	81	85	79

Once the data are collected, a **scatter diagram** or **scatter plot** can be drawn, as shown in Figure 4.15.

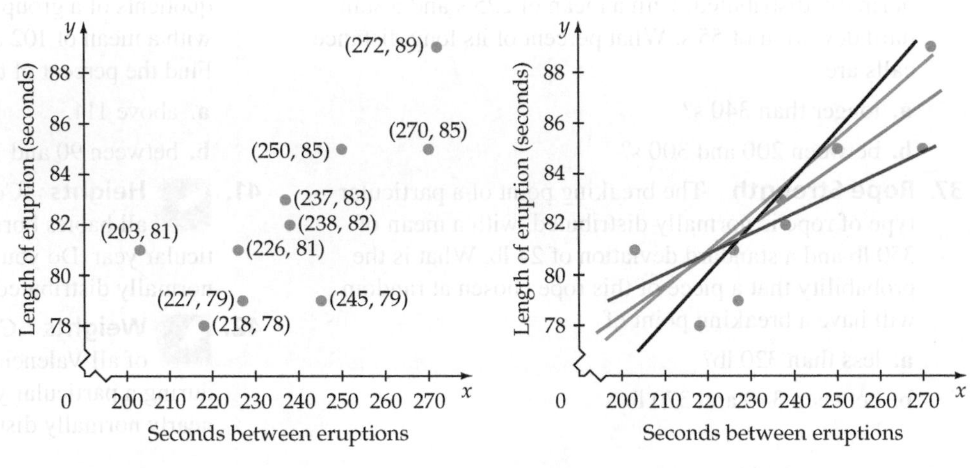

FIGURE 4.15

FIGURE 4.16

One way for the geologist to create a model of the relationship between the time between two eruptions and the duration of the second eruption is to find a line that *approximates* the data points plotted in the scatter plot. There are many such lines that can be drawn, as shown in Figure 4.16.

Of all the possible lines that can be drawn, the one that is usually of most interest is called the *line of best fit* or the *least-squares regression line*. The least-squares regression line is the line that fits the data better than any other line that might be drawn. The least-squares regression line is defined as follows.

The Least-Squares Regression Line

The **least-squares regression line** for a set of bivariate data is the line that minimizes the sum of the squares of the vertical deviations from each data point to the line.

In this definition, the phrase "minimizes the sum of the squares of the vertical deviations" is somewhat daunting. Referring to Figure 4.17, it means that of all the lines possible, the linear equation that minimizes the sum

$$d_1^2 + d_2^2 + d_3^2 + d_4^2 + d_5^2 + d_6^2 + d_7^2 + d_8^2 + d_9^2 + d_{10}^2$$

is the equation of the line of best fit. In this expression, each d_n represents the distance from data point n to the line.

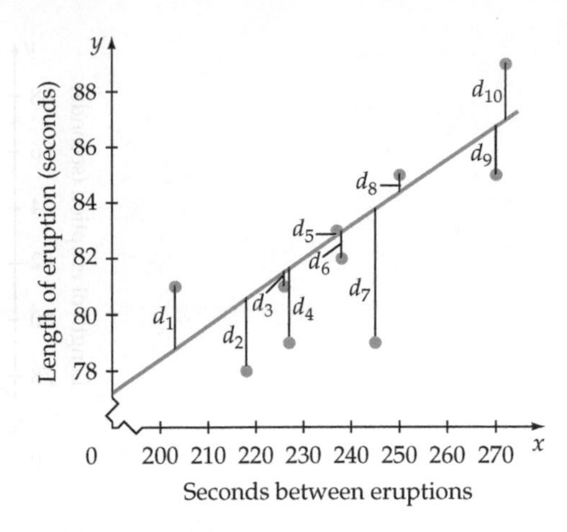

FIGURE 4.17

Applying some techniques from calculus, it is possible to find a formula for the least-squares line.

> **TAKE NOTE**
>
> It is traditional to use the symbol $\hat{y}$ (pronounced "y-hat") in place of y in the equation of the least-squares line. This helps distinguish between the line's y-values (the values calculated from the equation) and the data's y-values (the values given in the table).

The Formula for the Least-Squares Line

The equation of the least-squares line for the n ordered pairs

$$(x_1, y_1), (x_2, y_2), (x_3, y_3), \ldots, (x_n, y_n)$$

is $\hat{y} = ax + b$, where

$$a = \frac{n\Sigma xy - (\Sigma x)(\Sigma y)}{n\Sigma x^2 - (\Sigma x)^2} \quad \text{and} \quad b = \overline{y} - a\overline{x}$$

To apply this formula to the data for Old Faithful, we first find the value of each summation.

$$\Sigma x = 2386 \qquad \Sigma y = 822 \qquad \Sigma x^2 = 573{,}560 \qquad \Sigma xy = 196{,}636$$

> **TAKE NOTE**
>
> There are other lines, such as the median–median line, that can be used to approximate a set of data.

Next, we use these values to find the value of a.

$$a = \frac{n\Sigma xy - (\Sigma x)(\Sigma y)}{n\Sigma x^2 - (\Sigma x)^2}$$

$$a = \frac{(10)(196{,}636) - (2386)(822)}{(10)(573{,}560) - (2386)^2} \approx 0.1189559666$$

We then find the values of $\overline{x}$ and $\overline{y}$,

$$\overline{x} = \frac{\Sigma x}{n} = \frac{2386}{10} = 238.6 \quad \text{and} \quad \overline{y} = \frac{\Sigma y}{n} = \frac{822}{10} = 82.2$$

and use them to find the y-intercept, b.

$$\begin{aligned} b &= \overline{y} - a\overline{x} \\ &\approx 82.2 - 0.1189559666(238.6) \\ &= 53.81710637 \end{aligned}$$

The regression equation is $\hat{y} = 0.1189559666x + 53.81710637$. The graph of the regression equation and a scatter plot of the data are shown below.

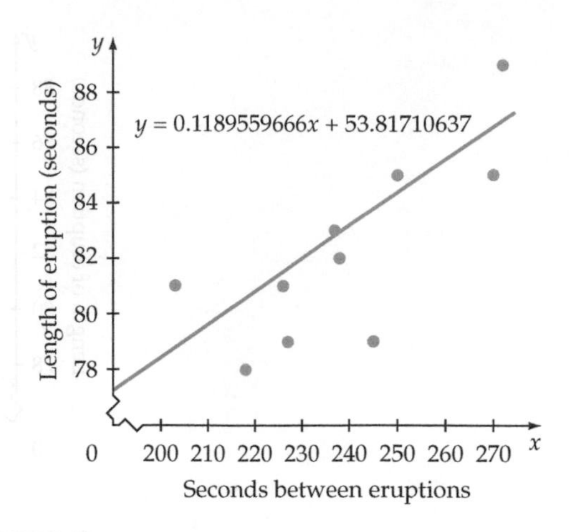

We can now use the regression equation to estimate the duration of an eruption given the time between eruptions. For instance, if the time between two eruptions is 200 seconds, then the estimated duration of the second eruption is

$$\begin{aligned}\hat{y} &= 0.1189559666x + 53.81710637\\ &= 0.1189559666(200) + 53.81710637\\ &\approx 78\end{aligned}$$

The approximate duration of the eruption is 78 seconds.

As our example demonstrates, it can be challenging to calculate all of the values needed to find a regression line. Fortunately, many computer programs and calculators can perform these calculations. The following example shows the use of a TI-84 to find the regression line for the Old Faithful data.

Enter the data from Table 4.11 into L1 and L2, as shown at the right.

L1	L2	L3 1
272	89	------
227	79	
237	83	
238	82	
203	81	
270	85	
218	78	

L1(1) = 272

Press the STAT key, tab to CALC, and scroll to 4:. Then press ENTER.

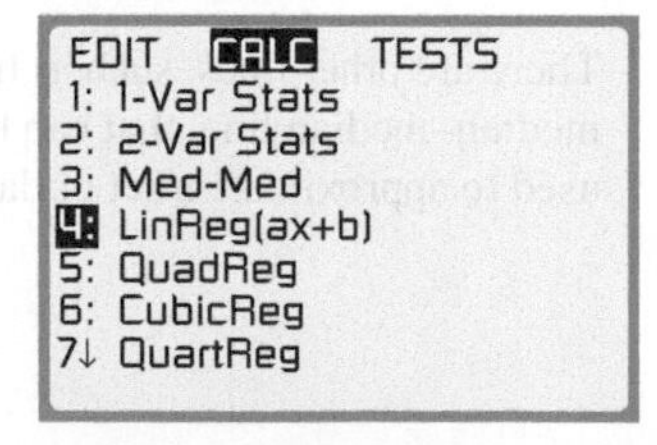

Scroll to the Store RegEQ line. Press the VARS key and scroll to Y-VARS. Press ENTER twice.

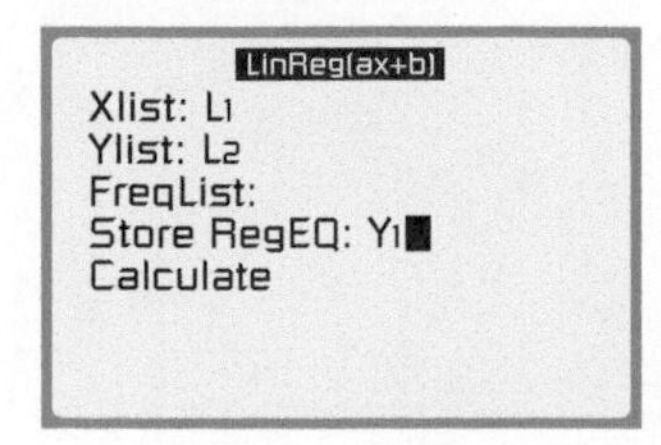

Press ENTER twice. The slope a and y-intercept b of the least-squares line are shown. You will see two additional values, r^2 and r, displayed on the screen. We will discuss the meanings of these values later.

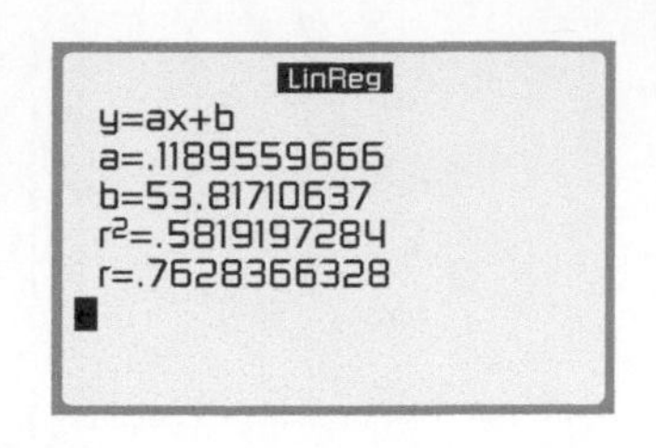

The equation for the regression line is stored in Y1. Using 200 seconds as the time between eruptions, as we did above, we can calculate the expected duration of the eruption as follows.

Press the VARS key and scroll to Y-VARS. Press ENTER twice. Now enter "(200)" and press ENTER. The predicted duration of the eruption is approximately 78 seconds.

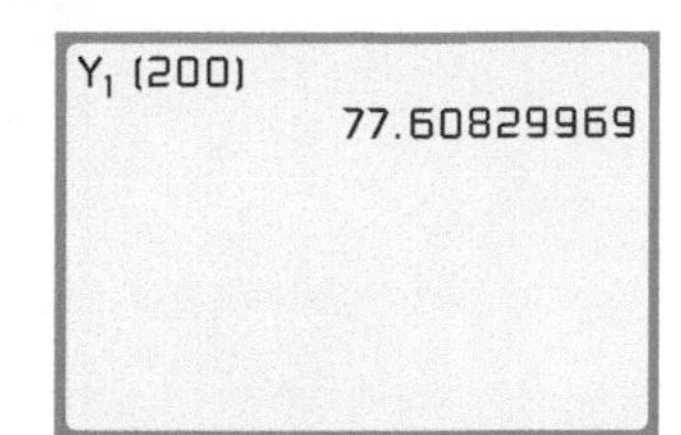

Here is an additional example of calculating regression lines. Professor R. McNeill Alexander wanted to determine whether the *stride length* of a dinosaur, as shown by its fossilized footprints, could be used to estimate the speed of the dinosaur. Stride length for an animal is defined as the distance x from a particular point on a footprint to that same point on the next footprint of the same foot. (See the figure at the left.) Because dinosaurs are extinct, Alexander and fellow scientist A. S. Jayes carried out experiments with many types of animals, including adult men, dogs, camels, ostriches, and elephants. Some of the results from these experiments are recorded in Table 4.12. These data will be used in the examples that follow.

TABLE 4.12

Speeds for Selected Stride Lengths

a. Adult men

Stride length (m)	2.5	3.0	3.3	3.5	3.8	4.0	4.2	4.5
Speed (m/s)	3.4	4.9	5.5	6.6	7.0	7.7	8.3	8.7

b. Dogs

Stride length (m)	1.5	1.7	2.0	2.4	2.7	3.0	3.2	3.5
Speed (m/s)	3.7	4.4	4.8	7.1	7.7	9.1	8.8	9.9

c. Camels

Stride length (m)	2.5	3.0	3.2	3.4	3.5	3.8	4.0	4.2
Speed (m/s)	2.3	3.9	4.4	5.0	5.5	6.2	7.1	7.6

EXAMPLE 1 Find the Equation of a Least-Squares Line

Find the equation of the least-squares line for the ordered pairs in Table 4.12a.

Solution

Enter the data into a calculator or software program that supports regresson equations. Here are the results using a TI-84 calculator.

L1	L2	L3
2.5	3.4	
3	4.9	
3.3	5.5	
3.5	6.6	
3.8	7	
4	7.7	
4.2	8.3	

L1(1) = 2.5

LinReg(ax+b)
Xlist: L1
Ylist: L2
FreqList:
Store RegEQ: Y1
Calculate

LinReg
y=ax+b
a=2.730263158
b=-3.316447368
r^2=.9874692177
r=.9937148574

The regression equation is $\hat{y} = 2.730263158x - 3.316447368$.

CHECK YOUR PROGRESS 1 Find the equation of the least-squares line for the stride length and speed of camels given in Table 4.12c.

Solution See page S16.

It can be proved that for any set of ordered pairs, the graph of the ordered pair $(\bar{x}, \bar{y})$ is a point on the least-squares line that models the set. This fact can serve as a check. If you have calculated the least-squares line for a set of ordered pairs and you find that the point $(\bar{x}, \bar{y})$ does not lie on your line, then you know that you have made an error.

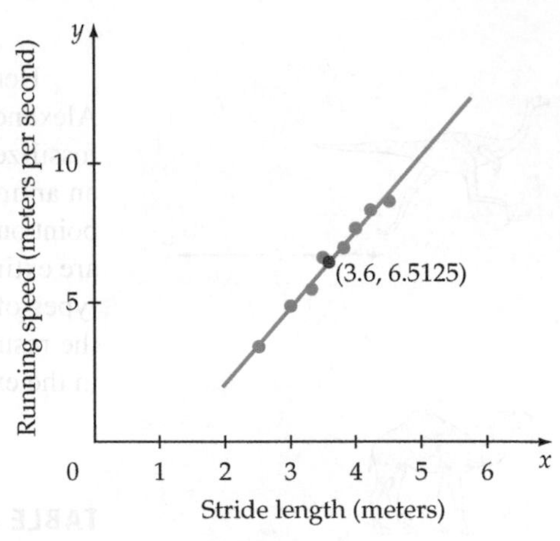

Once the equation of the least-squares line is found, it can be used to make predictions. This procedure is illustrated in the next example.

EXAMPLE 2 Use a Least-Squares Line to Make a Prediction

Use the equation of the least-squares line from Example 1 to predict the average speed of an adult man for each of the following stride lengths. Round your results to the nearest tenth of a meter per second.

a. 2.8 m **b.** 4.8 m

Solution

a. From Example 1, the regression equation is $\hat{y} = 2.730263158x - 3.316447368$. Substitute 2.8 for x and evaluate the resulting expression.

$$\begin{aligned}\hat{y} &= 2.730263158x - 3.316447368\\ &= 2.730263158(2.8) - 3.316447368 \approx 4.328\end{aligned}$$

The predicted average speed of an adult man with a stride length of 2.8 m is 4.3 m/s.

b. From Example 1, the regression equation is $\hat{y} = 2.730263158x - 3.316447368$. Substitute 4.8 for x and evaluate the resulting expression.

$$\begin{aligned}\hat{y} &= 2.730263158x - 3.316447368\\ &= 2.730263158(4.8) - 3.316447368 \approx 9.789\end{aligned}$$

The predicted average speed of an adult man with a stride length of 4.8 m is 9.8 m/s.

CHECK YOUR PROGRESS 2 Use the equation of the least-squares line from Check Your Progress 1 to predict the average speed of a camel for each of the following stride lengths. Round your results to the nearest tenth of a meter per second.

a. 2.7 m

b. 4.5 m

Solution See page S16.

> **TAKE NOTE**
>
> Sometimes values predicted by extrapolation are not reasonable. For instance, if we wish to predict the speed of a man with a stride length of $x = 20$ m, the least-squares equation $\hat{y} = 2.730263158x - 3.316447368$ gives us a speed of about 51.3 m/s. Because the maximum stride length of adult men is considerably less than 20 m, we should not trust this prediction.

The procedure in Example 2a made use of an equation to determine a point between given data points. This procedure is referred to as **interpolation**. In Example 2b, an equation was used to determine a point to the right of the given data points. The process of using an equation to determine a point to the right or left of given data points is referred to as **extrapolation**. See Figure 4.18.

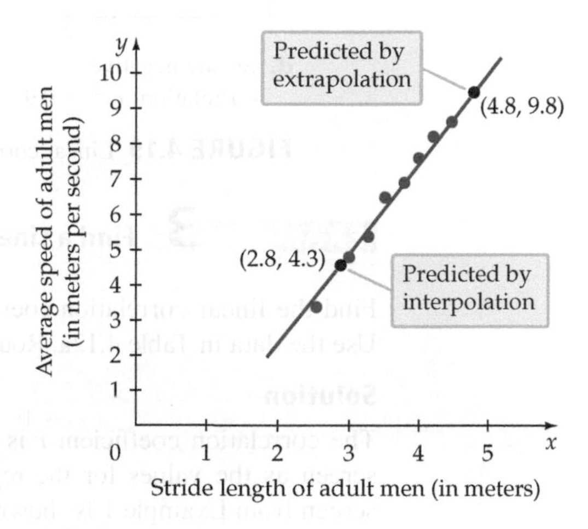

FIGURE 4.18 Interpolation and extrapolation

Linear Correlation Coefficient

To determine the strength of a linear relationship between two variables, statisticians use a statistic called the *linear correlation coefficient*, which is denoted by the variable r and is defined as follows.

> **HISTORICAL NOTE**
>
> **Karl Pearson** (pîr'sən) spent most of his career as a mathematics professor at University College, London. Some of his major contributions concerned the development of statistical procedures such as regression analysis and correlation. He was particularly interested in applying these statistical concepts to the study of heredity. The term *standard deviation* was invented by Pearson, and because of his work in the area of correlation, the formal name given to the linear correlation coefficient is the *Pearson product moment coefficient of correlation.* Pearson was a co-founder of the statistical journal *Biometrika.*

Linear Correlation Coefficient

For the n ordered pairs $(x_1, y_1), (x_2, y_2), (x_3, y_3), \ldots, (x_n, y_n)$, the **linear correlation coefficient** r is given by

$$r = \frac{n(\Sigma xy) - (\Sigma x)(\Sigma y)}{\sqrt{n(\Sigma x^2) - (\Sigma x)^2} \cdot \sqrt{n(\Sigma y^2) - (\Sigma y)^2}}$$

If the linear correlation coefficient r is positive, the relationship between the variables has a **positive correlation**. In this case, if one variable increases, the other variable also tends to increase. If r is negative, the linear relationship between the variables has a **negative correlation**. In this case, if one variable increases, the other variable tends to decrease.

Figure 4.19 on the next page shows some scatter diagrams along with the type of linear correlation that exists between the x and y variables. The closer $|r|$ is to 1, the stronger the linear relationship is between the variables.

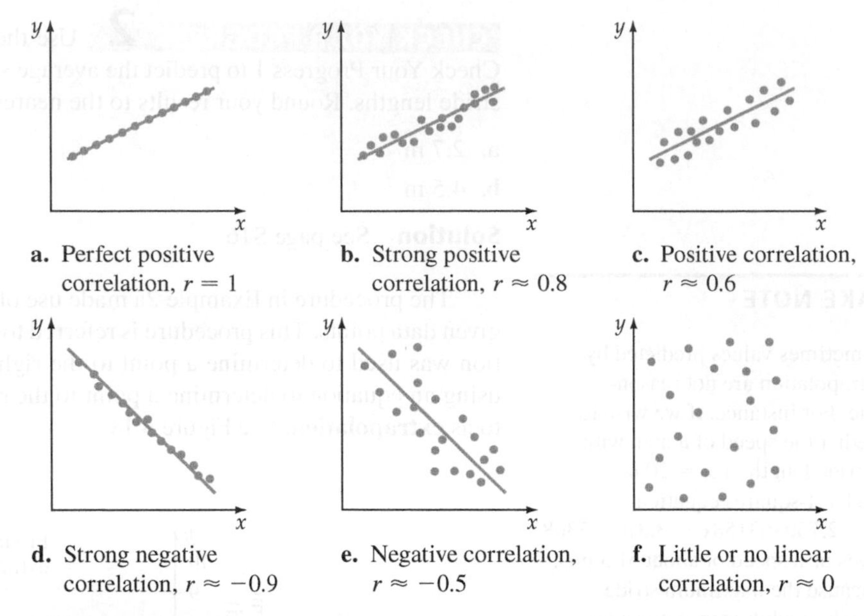

a. Perfect positive correlation, $r = 1$

b. Strong positive correlation, $r \approx 0.8$

c. Positive correlation, $r \approx 0.6$

d. Strong negative correlation, $r \approx -0.9$

e. Negative correlation, $r \approx -0.5$

f. Little or no linear correlation, $r \approx 0$

FIGURE 4.19 Linear correlation

EXAMPLE 3 Find a Linear Correlation Coefficient

Find the linear correlation coefficient for stride length versus speed of an adult man. Use the data in Table 4.12a. Round your result to the nearest hundredth.

Solution

```
LinReg
y=ax+b
a=2.730263158
b= -3.316447368
r²=.9874692177
r=.9937148574
```

The correlation coefficient r is displayed on the same screen as the values for the regression equation. The screen from Example 1 is shown again at the right.

The linear correlation coefficient, rounded to the nearest hundredth, is 0.99.

CHECK YOUR PROGRESS 3 Find the linear correlation coefficient for stride length versus speed of a camel as given in Table 4.12c. Round your result to the nearest hundredth.

Solution See page S16.

QUESTION What is the significance of the fact that the linear correlation coefficient is positive in Example 3?

The linear correlation coefficient indicates the strength of a linear relationship between two variables; however, it does not indicate the presence of a *cause-and-effect relationship.* For instance, the data in Table 4.13 show the hours per week that a student spent playing pool and the student's weekly algebra test scores for those same weeks.

TABLE 4.13

Algebra Test Scores vs. Hours Spent Playing Pool

Hours per week spent playing pool	4	5	7	8	10
Weekly algebra test score	52	60	72	79	83

ANSWER It indicates a positive correlation between a man's stride length and his speed. That is, as a man's stride length increases, his speed also increases.

The linear correlation coefficient for the ordered pairs in the table is $r \approx 0.98$. Thus there is a strong positive linear relationship between the student's algebra test scores and the time the student spent playing pool. This does not mean that the higher algebra test scores were caused by the increased time spent playing pool. The fact that the student's test scores increased with the increase in the time spent playing pool could be due to many other factors, or it could just be a coincidence.

In your work with applications that involve the linear correlation coefficient r, it is important to remember the following properties of r.

Properties of the Linear Correlation Coefficient

1. The linear correlation coefficient r is always a real number between -1 and 1, inclusive. In the case in which
   - all of the ordered pairs lie on a line with positive slope, r is 1.
   - all of the ordered pairs lie on a line with negative slope, r is -1.
2. For any set of ordered pairs, the linear correlation coefficient r and the slope of the least-squares line both have the same sign.
3. Interchanging the variables in the ordered pairs does not change the value of r. Thus the value of r for the ordered pairs $(x_1, y_1), (x_2, y_2), \ldots, (x_n, y_n)$ is the same as the value of r for the ordered pairs $(y_1, x_1), (y_2, x_2), \ldots, (y_n, x_n)$.
4. The value of r does not depend on the units used. You can change the units of a variable from, for example, feet to inches, and the value of r will remain the same.

EXCURSION

Exponential Regression

Earlier in this chapter we examined linear regression models. In some cases, an exponential function may more closely model a set of data. For example, suppose a diamond merchant has determined the values of several white diamonds that have different weights, measured in carats, but are similar in quality. See the table below.

4.00 ct	3.00 ct	2.00 ct	1.75 ct	1.50 ct	1.25 ct	1.00 ct	0.75 ct	0.50 ct
\$14,500	\$10,700	\$7900	\$7300	\$6700	\$6200	\$5800	\$5000	\$4600

TAKE NOTE

The value of a diamond is generally determined by its color, cut, clarity, and carat weight. These characteristics of a diamond are known as the four c's. In the example at the right we have assumed that the color, cut, and clarity of all of the diamonds are similar. This assumption enables us to model the value of each diamond as a function of just its carat weight.

We can use the data in the table to determine an exponential growth function that models the values of the diamonds as a function of their weights, and then use the model to predict the value of a 3.5-carat diamond of similar quality. Using a graphing calculator, the exponential regression equation is $y \approx 4067.6(1.3816)^x$, where x is the carat weight of the diamond and y is the value of the diamond.

```
ExpReg
 y = a*b^x
 a = 4067.641145
 b = 1.381644186
 r² = .994881215
 r = .9974373238
```

POINT OF INTEREST

The Hope Diamond, shown below, is the world's largest deep-blue diamond. It weighs 45.52 carats. We should not expect the function $y \approx 4067.6(1.3816)^x$ to yield an accurate value of the Hope Diamond because the Hope Diamond is not the same type of diamond as the diamonds in the example, and its weight is much larger.

The Hope Diamond is on display at the Smithsonian Museum of Natural History in Washington, D.C.

To use the regression equation to predict the value of a 3.5-carat diamond of similar quality, substitute 3.5 for x and evaluate.

$$y \approx 4067.6(1.3816)^x$$
$$y \approx 4067.6(1.3816)^{3.5}$$
$$y \approx 12{,}609$$

According to the modeling function, the value of a 3.5-carat diamond of similar quality is \$12,609.

Note on the calculator screen on the preceding page that r^2, the coefficient of determination, is about 0.9949, which is very close to 1. This indicates that the equation $y \approx 4067.6(1.3816)^x$ provides a good fit for the data.

EXCURSION EXERCISE

1. The following table shows Earth's atmospheric pressure P at an altitude of a kilometers. Find an exponential function that models the atmospheric pressure as a function of altitude. Use the function to estimate, to the nearest tenth, the atmospheric pressure at an altitude of 11 km.

Altitude, a, in kilometers above sea level	Atmospheric pressure, P, in newtons per square centimeter
0	10.3
2	8.0
4	6.4
6	5.1
8	4.0
10	3.2
12	2.5
14	2.0
16	1.6
18	1.3

EXERCISE SET 4.5

1. Which of the scatter diagrams below suggests the
   a. strongest positive linear correlation between the x and y variables?
   b. strongest negative linear correlation between the x and y variables?

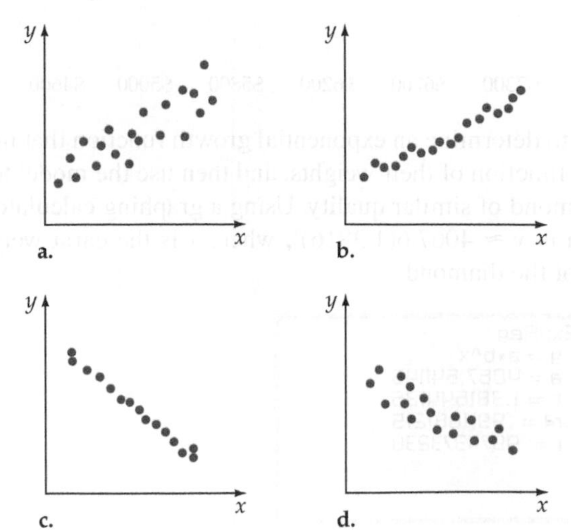

2. Which of the scatter diagrams below suggests
   a. a nearly perfect positive linear correlation between the x and y variables?
   b. little or no linear correlation between the x and y variables?

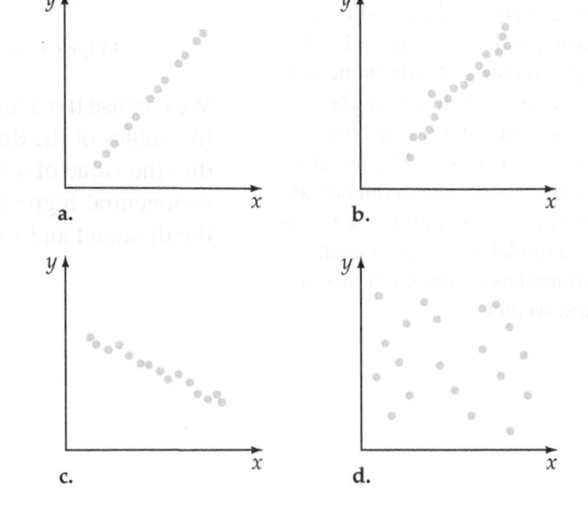

3. Given the bivariate data:

x	1	2	3	5	6
y	7	5	3	2	1

a. Draw a scatter diagram for the data.

b. Find n, Σx, Σy, Σx^2, $(\Sigma x)^2$, and Σxy.

c. Find a, the slope of the least-squares line, and b, the y-intercept of the least-squares line.

d. Draw the least-squares line on the scatter diagram from part a.

e. Is the point $(\overline{x}, \overline{y})$ on the least-squares line?

f. Use the equation of the least-squares line to predict the value of y when $x = 3.4$.

g. Find, to the nearest hundredth, the linear correlation coefficient.

4. Given the bivariate data:

x	3	4	5	6	7
y	2	3	3	5	5

a. Draw a scatter diagram for the data.

b. Find n, Σx, Σy, Σx^2, $(\Sigma x)^2$, and Σxy.

c. Find a, the slope of the least-squares line, and b, the y-intercept of the least-squares line.

d. Draw the least-squares line on the scatter diagram from part a.

e. Is the point $(\overline{x}, \overline{y})$ on the least-squares line?

f. Use the equation of the least-squares line to predict the value of y when $x = 7.3$.

g. Find, to the nearest hundredth, the linear correlation coefficient.

■ In Exercises 5 to 10, find the equation of the least-squares line and the linear correlation coefficient for the given data. Round the constants, a, b, and r to the nearest hundredth.

5. $\{(2, 6), (3, 6), (4, 8), (6, 11), (8, 18)\}$

6. $\{(2, -3), (3, -4), (4, -9), (5, -10), (7, -12)\}$

7. $\{(-3, 11.8), (-1, 9.5), (0, 8.6), (2, 8.7), (5, 5.4)\}$

8. $\{(-7, -11.7), (-5, -9.8), (-3, -8.1), (1, -5.9), (2, -5.7)\}$

9. $\{(1, 4.1), (2, 6.0), (4, 8.2), (6, 11.5), (8, 16.2)\}$

10. $\{(2, 5), (3, 7), (4, 8), (6, 11), (8, 18), (9, 21)\}$

In Exercises 11 to 18, use the statistics features of a graphing calculator.

11. Value of a Corvette The following table gives retail values of a 2010 Corvette for various odometer readings. (*Source:* Kelley Blue Book website)

Odometer reading	Retail value
13,000	\$52,275
18,000	\$51,525
20,000	\$51,200
25,000	\$50,275
29,000	\$49,625
32,000	\$49,075

a. Find the equation of the least-squares line for the data. Round constants to the nearest thousandth.

b. Use the equation from part a to predict the retail price of a 2010 Corvette with an odometer reading of 30,000.

c. Find the linear correlation coefficient for these data.

d. What is the significance of the fact that the linear correlation coefficient is negative for these data?

12. Paleontology The following table shows the length, in centimeters, of the humerus and the total wingspan, in centimeters, of several pterosaurs, which are extinct flying reptiles. (*Source:* Southwest Educational Development Laboratory)

Pterosaur Data

Humerus	Wingspan	Humerus	Wingspan
24	600	20	500
32	750	27	570
22	430	15	300
17	370	15	310
13	270	9	240
4.4	68	4.4	55
3.2	53	2.9	50
1.5	24		

a. Find the equation of the least-squares line for the data. Round constants to the nearest hundredth.

b. Use the equation from part a to determine, to the nearest centimeter, the projected wingspan of a pterosaur if its humerus is 54 cm.

13. **Health** The U.S. Centers for Disease Control and Prevention (CDC) use a measure called body mass index (BMI) to determine whether a person is overweight. A BMI between 25.0 and 29.9 is considered overweight, and a BMI of 30.0 or more is considered obese. The following table shows the percents of U.S. males 18 years old or older who were obese in the years indicated, judging on the basis of BMI. (*Source:* Centers for Disease Control and Prevention)

Year	Percent obese
2003	22.7
2004	23.9
2005	24.9
2006	25.3
2007	26.5
2008	26.6
2009	27.6

a. Using 3 for 2003, 4 for 2004, and so on, find the equation of the least-squares line for the data.

b. Use the equation from part a to predict the percent of overweight males in 2015.

14. **Health** The U.S. Centers for Disease Control and Prevention (CDC) use a measure called body mass index (BMI) to determine whether a person is overweight. A BMI between 25.0 and 29.9 is considered overweight, and a BMI of 30.0 or more is considered obese. The following table shows the percents of U.S. females 18 years old or older who were overweight in the years indicated, judging on the basis of BMI. (*Source:* Centers for Disease Control and Prevention)

Year	Percent obese
2003	23.3
2004	23.7
2005	24.3
2006	25.6
2007	25.2
2008	27.6
2009	26.8

a. Using 3 for 2003, 4 for 2004, and so on, find the equation of the least-squares line for the data.

b. Use the equation from part a to predict the percent of overweight females in 2015.

15. **Wireless Phone** The following table shows the approximate numbers of wireless telephone subscriptions in the United States for recent years.

U.S. Wireless Telephone Subscriptions

Year	2005	2006	2007	2008	2009	2010
Subscriptions, in millions	194	220	243	263	277	293

SOURCE: CTIA Semi-Annual Wireless Survey, Midyear 2010

a. Find the linear correlation coefficient for the data.

b. On the basis of the value of the linear correlation coefficient, would you conclude, at the $|r| > 0.9$ level, that the data can be reasonably modeled by a linear equation? Explain.

16. **Life Expectancy** The average remaining lifetimes for men of various ages in the United States are given in the following table. (*Source:* National Institutes of Health)

Average Remaining Lifetimes for Men

Age	Years	Age	Years
0	74.9	65	16.8
15	60.6	75	10.2
35	42.0		

Use the linear correlation coefficient to determine whether there is a strong correlation, at the level $|r| > 0.9$, between a man's age and the average remaining lifetime of that man.

17. **Life Expectancy** The average remaining lifetimes for women of various ages in the United States are given in the following table. (*Source:* National Institutes of Health)

Average Remaining Lifetimes for Women

Age	Years	Age	Years
0	79.9	65	19.5
15	65.6	75	12.1
35	46.2		

a. Find the equation of the least-squares line for the data.

b. Use the equation from part a to estimate the remaining lifetime of a woman of age 25.

c. Is the procedure in part b an example of interpolation or extrapolation?

18. **Fitness** An aerobic exercise instructor remembers the data given in the following table, which shows the recommended maximum exercise heart rates for individuals of the given ages.

Age (x years)	20	40	60
Maximum heart rate (y beats per minute)	170	153	136

a. Find the linear correlation coefficient for the data.

b. What is the significance of the value found in part a?

c. Find the equation of the least-squares line.

d. Use the equation from part c to predict the maximum exercise heart rate for a person who is 72.

e. Is the procedure in part d an example of interpolation or extrapolation?

EXTENSIONS

19. Tuition The following table shows the average annual tuition and fees at private and public 4-year colleges and universities for the school years 2009–2010 through 2014–2015. (*Source:* National Center for Education Statistics)

Four-year Colleges and Universities Tuition and Fees

Year	Private	Public
2009–2010	31,448	15,014
2010–2011	32,617	15,918
2011–2012	33,674	16,805
2012–2013	35,074	17,474
2013–2014	36,193	18,372
2014–2015	37,385	19,203

a. Using 1 for 2009–2010, 2 for 2010–2011, and so on, find the linear correlation coefficient and the equation of the least-squares line for the tuition and fees at private 4-year colleges and universities, based on the year.

b. Using 1 for 2009–2010, 2 for 2010–2011, and so on, find the linear correlation coefficient and the equation of the least-squares line for the tuition and fees at public 4-year colleges and universities, based on the year.

c. Based on the linear correlation coefficients you found in parts a and b, are the equations you wrote in parts a and b good models of the growth in tuition and fees at 4-year colleges and universities?

d. The equation of a least-squares line is written in the form $\hat{y} = ax + b$. Explain the meaning of the value of a for each equation you wrote in parts a and b.

20. Search for bivariate data (in a magazine, in a newspaper, in an almanac, or on the Internet) that can be closely modeled by a linear equation.

a. Draw a scatter diagram of the data.

b. Find the equation of the least-squares line and the linear correlation coefficient for the data.

c. Graph the least-squares line on the scatter diagram in part a.

d. Use the equation of the least-squares line to predict a range value for a specific domain value.

CHAPTER 4 SUMMARY

The following table summarizes essential concepts in this chapter. The references given in the right-hand column list Examples and Exercises that can be used to test your understanding of a concept.

4.1 Measures of Central Tendency	
Mean, Median, and Mode The *mean* of n numbers is the sum of the numbers divided by n. The *median* of a ranked list of n numbers is the middle number if n is odd, or the mean of the two middle numbers if n is even. The *mode* of a list of numbers is the number that occurs most frequently.	See **Examples 1, 2, and 3** on pages 232 to 234, and then try Exercise 1 on page 288.

continued

Weighted Mean The formula for the weighted mean of the n numbers $x_1, x_2, x_3, \ldots, x_n$ is $$\text{Weighted mean} = \frac{\Sigma(x \cdot w)}{\Sigma w}$$ where $\Sigma(x \cdot w)$ is the sum of the products formed by multiplying each number by its assigned weight, and Σw is the sum of all the weights.	See **Example 4** on page 236, and then try Exercise 7 on page 288.
4.2 Measures of Dispersion	
Range The range of a set of data values is the difference between the greatest data value and the least data value.	See **Example 1** on page 242, and then try Exercise 5 on page 288.
Standard Deviation and Variance If $x_1, x_2, x_3, \ldots, x_n$ is a *population* of n numbers with mean μ, then the standard deviation of the population is $\sigma = \sqrt{\frac{\Sigma(x-\mu)^2}{n}}$, and the variance is $\frac{\Sigma(x-\mu)^2}{n}$. If $x_1, x_2, x_3, \ldots, x_n$ is a *sample* of n numbers with mean $\bar{x}$, then the standard deviation of the population is $s = \sqrt{\frac{\Sigma(x-\bar{x})^2}{n-1}}$, and the variance is $\frac{\Sigma(x-\bar{x})^2}{n-1}$.	See **Examples 2 and 5** on pages 244 and 247, and then try Exercise 9 on page 288.
4.3 Measures of Relative Position	
***z*-score** The z-score for a given data value x is the number of standard deviations that x is above or below the mean. z-score for a population data value: $z_x = \frac{x-\mu}{\sigma}$ z-score for a sample data value: $z_x = \frac{x-\bar{x}}{s}$	See **Example 1** on page 251, and then try Exercises 8a and 12 on page 288.
Percentiles A value x is called the pth percentile of a data set provided $p\%$ of the data values are less than x. Given a set of data and a data value x, $$\text{Percentile score of } x = \frac{\text{number of data values less than } x}{\text{total number of data values}} \cdot 100$$	See **Example 4** on page 253, and then try Exercise 8b on page 288.
Quartiles and Box-and-Whisker Plots The quartiles of a data set are the three numbers Q_1, Q_2, and Q_3 that partition the ranked data into four (approximately) equal groups. Q_2 is the median of the data, Q_1 is the median of the data values less than Q_2, and Q_3 is the median of the data values greater than Q_2. A box-and-whisker plot is a display used to show the quartiles and the maximum and minimum values of a data set.	See **Examples 5 and 6** on pages 254 to 256, and then try Exercise 13 on page 288.

4.4 Normal Distributions

Frequency Distributions A frequency distribution displays a data set by dividing the data into intervals, or classes, and listing the number of data values that fall into each interval. A relative freqency distribution lists the percent of data in each interval.	See **Example 1** on page 263, and then try Exercise 15 on page 289.
Normal Distributions and the Empirical Rule A normal distribution of data is a bell-shaped curve that is symmetric about a vertical line through the mean. The y-value of each point on the curve is the *percent* (expressed as a decimal) of the data at the corresponding x-value. The total area under the curve is 1. The Empirical Rule for a normal distribution states that approximately 68% of the data lie within 1 standard deviation of the mean, 95% of the data lie within 2 standard deviations of the mean, and 99.7% of the data lie within 3 standard deviations of the mean.	See **Example 2** on page 265, and then try Exercise 20 on page 289.
Using the Standard Normal Distribution The standard normal distribution is the normal distribution that has a mean of 0 and a standard deviation of 1. Any normal distribution can be converted into the standard normal distribution by converting data values to their z-scores. Then the percent of data values that lie in a given interval can be found as the area under the standard normal curve between the z-scores of the endpoints of the given interval. Table 4.10 on page 267 gives the areas under the standard normal curve for z-scores between 0 and 3.33.	See **Example 5** on page 269, and then try Exercise 21 on page 289.

4.5 Linear Regression and Correlation

Least-Squares Line Bivariate data are data given as ordered pairs. The least-squares regression line, or least-squares line, for a set of bivariate data is the line that minimizes the sum of the squares of the vertical deviations from each data point to the line. The equation of the least-squares line for the n ordered pairs $(x_1, y_1), (x_2, y_2), (x_3, y_3), \ldots, (x_n, y_n)$ is $\hat{y} = ax + b$, where $a = \dfrac{n\Sigma xy - (\Sigma x)(\Sigma y)}{n(\Sigma x^2) - (\Sigma x)^2}$ and $b = \bar{y} - a\bar{x}$. The equation of the least-squares line can be used to predict the value of one variable when the value of the other variable is known.	See **Examples 1 and 2** on page 278, and then try Exercises 24b and 24c on page 290.
Linear Correlation Coefficient The linear correlation coefficient r measures the strength of a linear relationship between two variables. The closer $\lvert r \rvert$ is to 1, the stronger the linear relationship is between the variables. For the n ordered pairs $(x_1, y_1), (x_2, y_2), (x_3, y_3), \ldots, (x_n, y_n)$, the linear correlation coefficient is $r = \dfrac{n\Sigma xy - (\Sigma x)(\Sigma y)}{\sqrt{n\Sigma x^2 - (\Sigma x)^2} \cdot \sqrt{n\Sigma y^2 - (\Sigma y)^2}}$	See **Example 3** on page 280, and then try Exercise 24a on page 290.

CHAPTER 4 REVIEW EXERCISES

1. Find the mean, median, mode, range, population variance, and population standard deviation for the following data. Round noninteger values to the nearest tenth.

   12, 17, 14, 12, 8, 19, 21

2. A set of data has a mean of 16, a median of 15, and a mode of 14. Which of these numbers must be a value in the data set?

3. Write a set of data with five data values for which the mean, median, and mode are all 55.

4. State whether the mean, median, or mode is being used.
   a. In 2002, there were as many people aged 25 and younger in the world as there were people aged 25 and older.
   b. The majority of full-time students carry a load of 15 credit hours per semester.
   c. The average annual return on an investment is 6.5%.

5. **Bridges** The lengths of cantilever bridges in the United States are shown below. Find the mean, median, mode, and range of the data.

   Bridge Length (in feet)

   Baton Rouge (Louisiana), 1235
   Commodore John Barry (Pennsylvania), 1644
   Greater New Orleans (Louisiana), 1576
   Longview (Washington), 1200
   Patapsco River (Maryland), 1200
   Queensboro (New York), 1182
   Tappan Zee (New York), 1212
   Transbay Bridge (California), 1400

6. **Average Speed** Cleone traveled 45 mi to her sister's house in 1 h. The return trip took 1.5 h. What was Cleone's average rate for the entire trip?

7. **Grade Point Average** In a 4.0 grading system, each letter grade has the following numerical value.

A = 4.00	B− = 2.67	D+ = 1.33
A− = 3.67	C+ = 2.33	D = 1.00
B+ = 3.33	C = 2.00	D− = 0.67
B = 3.00	C− = 1.67	F = 0.00

   Use the weighted mean formula to find the grade point average for a student with the following grades. Round to the nearest hundredth.

Course	Credits	Grade
Mathematics	3	A
English	3	C+
Computers	2	B−
Biology	4	B
Art	1	A

8. **Test Scores** A teacher finds that the test scores of a group of 40 students have a mean of 72 and a standard deviation of 8.
   a. If Ann has a test score of 82, what is Ann's z-score?
   b. Ann's score is higher than that of 35 of the 40 students who took the test. Find the percentile, rounded to the nearest percent, for Ann's score.

9. **Airline Industry** An airline recorded the times it took for a ground crew to unload the baggage from an airplane. The recorded times, in minutes, were 12, 18, 20, 14, and 16. Find the *sample* standard deviation and the variance of these times. Round your results to the nearest hundredth of a minute.

10. **Ticket Prices** The following table gives the average annual admission prices to U.S. movie theaters for the years 2006 to 2015.

   Average Annual Admission Price, 2006–2015

\$6.55	\$6.88	\$7.18	\$7.50	\$7.89
\$7.93	\$7.96	\$8.15	\$8.17	\$8.12

   SOURCE: Theatrical Market Statistics, 2015, Motion Picture Association of America

   Find the mean, median, and standard deviation for this *sample* of admission prices. Round to the nearest cent.

11. **Test Scores** One student received test scores of 85, 92, 86, and 89. A second student received scores of 90, 97, 91, and 94 (exactly 5 points more on each test).
   a. What is the relationship between the means of the 2 students' test scores?
   b. What is the relationship between the standard deviations of the 2 students' test scores?

12. A *population* data set has a mean of 81 and a standard deviation of 5.2. Find the z-scores for each of the following. Round to the nearest hundredth.
   a. $x = 72$ b. $x = 84$

13. **Cholesterol Levels** The cholesterol levels for 10 adults are shown below. Draw a box-and-whisker plot of the data.

   Cholesterol Levels

310	185	254	221	170
214	172	208	164	182

14. Test Scores The following histogram shows the distribution of the test scores for a history test.

a. How many students scored at least 84 on the test?

b. How many students took the test?

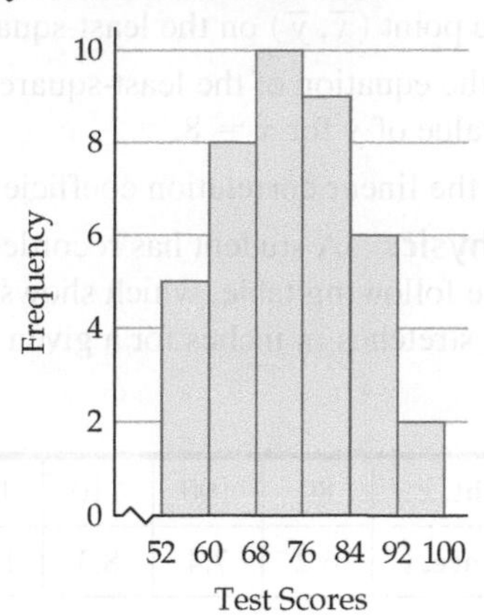

15. Teacher Salaries Use the following relative frequency distribution to determine the

a. *percent* of the states that paid an average teacher salary of at least $48,000.

b. *probability, as a decimal,* that a state selected at random paid an average teacher salary of at least $56,000 but less than $72,000.

Average Salaries of Public School Teachers, 2014–2015

Average salary, s	Number of states	Relative frequency
$40,000 ≤ s < $44,000	2	4%
$44,000 ≤ s < $48,000	9	18%
$48,000 ≤ s < $52,000	14	28%
$52,000 ≤ s < $56,000	4	8%
$56,000 ≤ s < $60,000	9	18%
$60,000 ≤ s < $64,000	2	4%
$64,000 ≤ s < $68,000	4	8%
$68,000 ≤ s < $72,000	2	4%
$72,000 ≤ s < $76,000	3	6%
$76,000 ≤ s < $80,000	1	2%

SOURCE: National Education Association

16. Greenhouse Gas Emissions The table below shows annual greenhouse gas emissions, in tons of carbon dioxide (CO_2), by vehicle fuel efficiency rating in miles per gallon (mpg).

MPG rating	15	20	25	30	35	40	45	50
Tons of CO_2	12	9	7.2	6	5.1	4.5	4	4.8

SOURCE: fueleconomy.gov

Is there a linear relation, at the $|r| > 0.9$ level, between vehicle fuel efficiency and greenhouse gas emissions?

17. Alternative Fuels Alternative fuel vehicles that run on nonpetroleum-based fuels cannot refuel at traditional gas stations. Use the table of the numbers of alternative fuel stations in the United States to answer the questions below.

Alternative Fuel Stations in the U.S.

Year	Number
2011	10,071
2012	20,498
2013	27,159
2014	36,805
2015	39,963

SOURCE: U.S. Department of Energy

a. Using 11 for 2011, 12 for 2012, and so on, find the equation of the least-squares line for the data.

b. Use your equation from part a to predict the number of alternative fuel stations in the United States in 2015.

18. Test Scores A professor gave a final examination to 110 students. Eighteen students had scores that were more than standard deviation above the mean. With this information, can you conclude that 18 of the students had scores that were more than 1 standard deviation below the mean? Explain.

19. Waiting Time The amount of time customers spend waiting in line at the ticket counter of an amusement park is normally distributed, with a mean of 6.5 min and a standard deviation of 1 min. Find the probability that the time a customer will spend waiting is:

a. less than 8 min. **b.** less than 6 min.

20. Pet Food The weights of all the sacks of dog food filled by a machine are normally distributed, with an average weight of 50 lb and a standard deviation of 0.5 lb. What percent of the sacks will

a. weigh less than 49.5 lb?

b. weigh between 49 and 51 lb?

21. Telecommunication A telephone manufacturer finds that the life spans of its telephones are normally distributed, with a mean of 6.5 years and a standard deviation of 0.5 year.

a. What percent of its telephones will last at least 7.25 years?

b. What percent of its telephones will last between 5.8 years and 6.8 years?

c. What percent of its telephones will last less than 6.9 years?

22. Astronomy The following table gives the distances, in millions of miles, of Earth from the sun at selected times during the year.

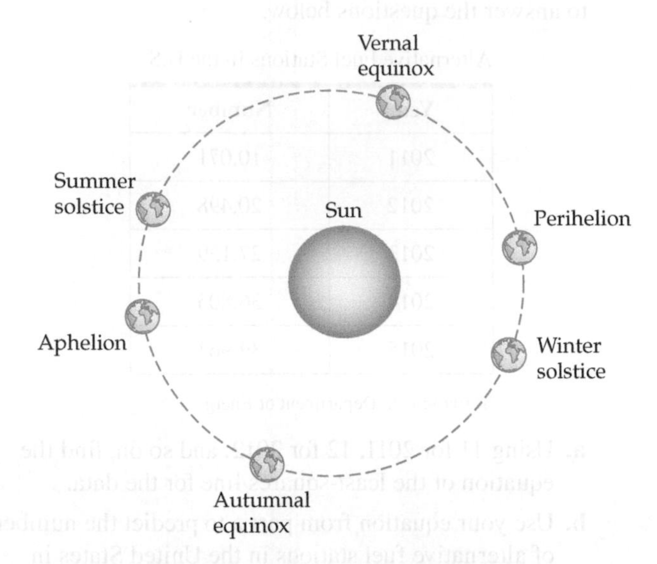

Position	Distance (millions of miles)
Perihelion	91.4
Vernal equinox	92.6
Summer solstice	94.5
Aphelion	94.6
Autumnal equinox	94.3
Winter solstice	91.5

On the basis of these data, what is the mean distance of Earth from the sun?

23. Given the bivariate data

x	10	12	14	15	16
y	8	7	5	4	1

a. Draw a scatter diagram for the data.

b. Find n, Σx, Σy, Σx^2, $(\Sigma x)^2$, and Σxy.

c. Find a, the slope of the least-squares regression line, and b, the y-intercept of the least-squares line.

d. Draw the least-squares line on the scatter diagram from part a.

e. Is the point $(\overline{x}, \overline{y})$ on the least-squares line?

f. Use the equation of the least-squares line to predict the value of y for $x = 8$.

g. Find the linear correlation coefficient.

24. Physics A student has recorded the data in the following table, which shows the distance a spring stretches in inches for a given weight in pounds.

Weight, x	80	100	110	150	170
Distance, y	6.2	7.4	8.3	11.1	12.7

a. Find the linear correlation coefficient.

b. Find the equation of the least-squares line.

c. Use the equation of the least-squares line from part b to predict the distance a weight of 195 lb will stretch the spring.

25. Internet A test of an Internet service provider showed the following download times (in seconds) for files of various sizes (in megabytes).

Download Times

Size	Time	Size	Time
10.5	0.20	110	2.01
12.9	0.24	156	2.68
15	0.27	163	2.87
20	0.36	175	3.10
60	1.09	200	3.64
75	1.42	250	4.61

a. Find the equation of the least-squares line for these data.

b. On the basis of the value of the linear correlation coefficient, is a linear model of these data a reasonable model?

c. Use the equation of the least-squares line from part a to predict the expected download time of a file that is 100 megabytes in size.

26. Blood alcohol content (BAC) is measured in grams of alcohol per deciliter of blood. For instance, a BAC reading of 0.08% (a level that is considered legally intoxicated in most states) means that one deciliter of the person's blood contains 0.08 gram of alcohol. A toxicologist recorded the times elapsed, in hours, until the blood alcohol levels of eight adults who had consumed various amounts of alcohol were less than 0.005%. The results are given in the table.

BAC (%)	0.01	0.05	0.08	0.02	0.03	0.16	0.1	0.04
Time (h) for BAC level to reach 0.005%	0.8	3.5	5.4	0.9	2.1	9.2	6.4	2.1

a. Find the regression equation and linear correlation coefficient for these data.

b. Use the equation to predict the time it would take for a person with a BAC of 0.06% to reach a BAC level of less than 0.005%. Round to the nearest tenth.

CHAPTER 4 TEST

1. Find the mean, median, and mode for the following data. Round noninteger values to the nearest tenth.

3, 7, 11, 12, 7, 9, 15

2. Grade Point Average Use the 4.0 grading system:

A = 4, B = 3, C = 2, D = 1, F = 0

A student's grade point average (GPA) is calculated as a weighted mean, where the student's grade in each course is given a weight equal to the number of units that course is worth. Find Justin's GPA for the fall semester. Round to the nearest hundredth.

Justin's Grades, Fall Semester

Course	Course grade	Course units
Algebra	A	3
English	B	3
Biology	C	4
History	C	3
Psychology	A	2

3. Find the range, standard deviation, and variance for the following sample data.

7, 11, 12, 15, 31, 22

4. A *sample* data set has a mean of $\bar{x} = 65$ and a standard deviation of 10.2. Find the *z*-scores for each of the following. Round to the nearest hundredth.

a. $x = 77$ **b.** $x = 60$

5. Basketball Draw a box-and-whisker plot for the following data.

Points Scored by Top 20 Women's National Basketball Association Players in a Recent Year

729	716	702	656	618	606	575
555	548	535	528	522	521	509
484	479	470	465	453	422	

SOURCE: Women's National Basketball Association

6. Movie Attendance Use the following relative frequency distribution to estimate the *percent* of the movie attendees who were

a. at least 40 years of age.

b. at least 18 but less than 40 years of age.

Movie Attendance by Age Group

Age group	Percent of total yearly admissions
2–11	15%
12–17	12%
18–24	12%
25–39	23%
40–49	15%
50–59	11%
≥60	11%

7. During 1 month, an overnight delivery company found that the weights of its parcels were normally distributed, with a mean of 34 oz and a standard deviation of 10 oz. Use the Empirical Rule to determine

a. the percent of the parcels that weighed between 34 oz and 54 oz.
b. the percent of the parcels that weighed less than 24 oz.

8. Box Weights The weights of all the boxes of cake mix filled by a machine are normally distributed, with a mean weight of 18.0 oz and a standard deviation of 0.8 oz. What percent of the boxes will

a. weigh less than 17 oz?
b. weigh between 18.4 and 19.0 oz?

9. A psychologist wants to determine whether there is a relationship between how long it takes a subject to complete a manual task and the number of hours of sleep the subject had the night before. The results from a study of 10 people are given in the following table.

Hours of sleep	6.2	8.1	7.5	8.4	5.0	6.2	4.8	8.0	3.8	5.9
Minutes to complete task	9.0	8.6	8.4	8.6	10.0	9.3	9.9	8.9	10.4	9.1

a. Find the linear correlation coefficient for the data.
b. On the basis of your answer to part a, is there a strong linear relationship, at the $|r| > 0.9$ level, between hours of sleep and minutes to complete a task?

10. Nutrition The following table shows the percent of water and the number of calories in various canned soups to which 100 g of water are added.

Percent Water In Soups

% Water	Calories
93.2	28
92.3	26
91.9	39
89.5	56
89.6	56
90.5	36
91.9	32
91.7	32

a. Find the equation of the least-squares line for the data. Round constants to the nearest hundredth.
b. Use the equation in part a to find the expected number of calories in a soup that is 89% water. Round to the nearest whole number.

Answers to Selected Exercises

CHAPTER 1

EXERCISE SET 1.1 page 9

1. 72 in. **3.** 180 in. **5.** 4 lb **7.** 24 oz **9.** 20 fl oz **11.** 56 pt **13.** 620 mm **15.** 321 cm **17.** 7.421 kg **19.** 4.5 dg **21.** 0.0075 L **23.** 435 cm^3 **25.** 65.91 kg **27.** 48.3 km/h **29.** \$8.70/L **31.** 1.38 in. **33.** \$4.55/lb **35.** 2.3×10^{-12} Y **37.** 6.5×10^{11} G **39.** 4.01×10^{-9} E **41.** 3×10^{-13} Zm/s **43.** 0.000000000001 s

EXERCISE SET 1.2 page 19

1. $\angle O$, $\angle AOB$, and $\angle BOA$ **3.** A 28° angle **5.** An 18° angle **7.** An acute angle **9.** An obtuse angle **11.** 14 cm **13.** 28 ft **15.** 86° **17.** 71° **19.** 30° **21.** 127° **23.** 116° **25.** 20° **27.** 20° **29.** 141° **31.** 106° **33.** 11° **35.** $m\angle a = 38°$, $m\angle b = 142°$ **37.** $m\angle a = 47°$, $m\angle b = 133°$ **39.** 20° **41.** 47° **43.** $m\angle x = 155°$, $m\angle y = 70°$ **45.** $m\angle a = 45°$, $m\angle b = 135°$ **47.** 60° **49.** 35° **51.** False **53.** True **55.** 360° **57.** $\angle AOC$ and $\angle BOC$ are supplementary angles; therefore, $m\angle AOC + m\angle BOC = 180°$. Because $m\angle AOC = m\angle BOC$, by substitution, $m\angle AOC + m\angle AOC = 180°$. Therefore, $2(m\angle AOC) = 180°$, and $m\angle AOC = 90°$. Hence $\overline{AB} \perp \overline{CD}$.

EXERCISE SET 1.3 page 35

1. a. Perimeter is not measured in square units. **b.** Area is measured in square units. **3. a.** 30 m **b.** 50 m^2 **5. a.** 40 km **b.** 100 km^2 **7. a.** 40 ft **b.** 72 ft^2 **9. a.** 8π cm; 25.13 cm **b.** 16π cm^2; 50.27 cm^2 **11. a.** 11π mi; 34.56 mi **b.** 30.25π mi^2; 95.03 mi^2 **13. a.** 17π ft; 53.41 ft **b.** 72.25π ft^2; 226.98 ft^2 **15.** 20 in. **17.** 10 mi **19.** 2 packages **21.** Perimeter of the square **23.** 144 m^2 **25.** 9 in. **27.** 39 ft **29.** 10×20 unit **31.** 136.5 ft^2 **33.** 160 km^2 **35.** 2 qt **37.** \$480 **39.** \$912 **41.** 176 m^2 **43.** 13.19 ft **45.** 12,064 in. **47.** 62.83 ft **49.** 2500π ft^2 **51.** 339.29 in^2 larger; more than twice the size **53.** 222.2 mi^2 **55.** $8r^2 - 2\pi r^2$ **57.** 4 times as large **59.** 12.1 in^2 **b.** 29.8 cm^2 **c.** 3 in., 4 in., 5 in.

EXERCISE SET 1.4 page 48

1. $\frac{1}{2}$ **3.** $\frac{3}{4}$ **5.** 7.2 cm **7.** 3.3 m **9.** 12 m **11.** 12 in. **13.** 56.3 cm^2 **15.** 18 ft **17.** 16 m **19.** $14\frac{3}{8}$ ft **21.** 15 m **23.** 8 ft **25.** 13 cm **27.** 35 m **29.** Yes, SAS theorem **31.** Yes, SSS theorem **33.** Yes, ASA theorem **35.** No **37.** Yes, SAS theorem **39.** No **41.** No **43.** 5 in. **45.** 8.6 cm **47.** 11.2 ft **49.** 4.5 cm **51.** 12.7 yd **53.** 8.5 cm **55.** 24.3 cm **57. a.** Always true **b.** Sometimes true **c.** Always true **d.** Always true

EXERCISE SET 1.5 page 60

1. 840 in^3 **3.** 15 ft^3 **5.** 4.5π cm^3; 14.14 cm^3 **7.** 94 m^2 **9.** 56 m^2 **11.** 96π in^2; 301.59 in^2 **13.** 34 m^3 **15.** 15.625 in^3 **17.** 36π ft^3 **19.** 8143.01 cm^3 **21.** 75π in^3 **23.** 120 in^3 **25.** Sphere **27.** 7.80 ft^3 **29.** 35,380,400 gal **31.** 69.36 m^2 **33.** 225π cm^2 **35.** 402.12 in^2 **37.** 6π ft^2 **39.** 297 in^2 **41.** 2.5 ft **43.** 11 cans **45.** 22.53 cm^2 **47.** 5 m^3 **49.** 69.12 in^3 **51.** 192 in^3 **53.** 208 in^2 **55.** 204.57 cm^2 **57.** 95,000 L **59.** \$4860

61. a. Drawings will vary. For example:

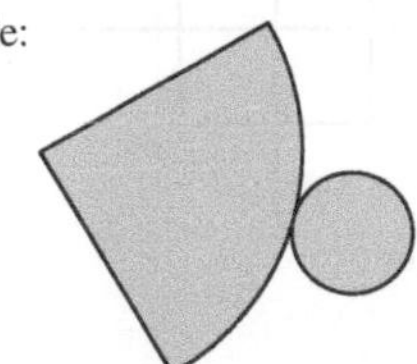

b. Drawings will vary. For example:

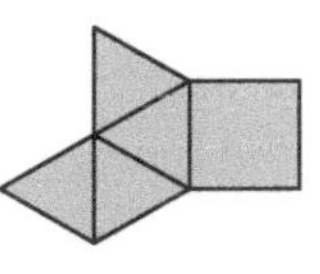

63. a. Always true **b.** Never true **c.** Sometimes true **65. a.** For example, make a cut perpendicular to the top and bottom faces and parallel to two of the sides. **b.** For example, beginning at an edge that is perpendicular to the bottom face, cut at an angle through to the bottom face. **c.** For example, beginning at the top face at a distance *d* from the vertex, cut at an angle to the bottom face, ending at a distance greater than *d* from the opposite vertex. **d.** For example, beginning on the top face at a distance *d* from a vertex, cut across the cube to a point just above the opposite vertex.

EXERCISE SET 1.6 *page 70*

1. a. $\frac{a}{c}$ **b.** $\frac{b}{c}$ **c.** $\frac{b}{c}$ **d.** $\frac{a}{c}$ **e.** $\frac{a}{b}$ **f.** $\frac{b}{a}$ **3.** $\sin\theta = \frac{5}{13}, \cos\theta = \frac{12}{13}, \tan\theta = \frac{5}{12}$
5. $\sin\theta = \frac{24}{25}, \cos\theta = \frac{7}{25}, \tan\theta = \frac{24}{7}$ **7.** $\sin\theta = \frac{8}{\sqrt{113}}, \cos\theta = \frac{7}{\sqrt{113}}, \tan\theta = \frac{8}{7}$ **9.** $\sin\theta = \frac{1}{2}, \cos\theta = \frac{\sqrt{3}}{2}, \tan\theta = \frac{1}{\sqrt{3}}$
11. 0.6820 **13.** 1.4281 **15.** 0.9971 **17.** 1.9970 **19.** 0.8878 **21.** 0.8453 **23.** 0.8508 **25.** 0.6833
27. 38.6° **29.** 41.1° **31.** 21.3° **33.** 38.0° **35.** 72.5° **37.** 0.6° **39.** 66.1° **41.** 29.5°
43. 841.8 ft **45.** 13.6° **47.** 29.1 ft **49.** 52.9 ft **51.** 13.6 ft **53.** 1056.6 ft **55.** 29.6 yd
57. 4 radians **59.** $\frac{2}{3}$ radian **61.** $\left(\frac{180}{\pi}\right)^\circ$ **63.** $\frac{\pi}{4}$ radian; 0.7854 radian **65.** $\frac{7\pi}{4}$ radians; 5.4978 radians
67. $\frac{7\pi}{6}$ radians; 3.6652 radians **69.** 60° **71.** 240° **73.** $\left(\frac{540}{\pi}\right)^\circ$; 171.8873°

EXERCISE SET 1.7 *page 82*

1. a. Through a given point not on a given line, exactly one line can be drawn parallel to the given line. **b.** Through a given point not on a given line, there are at least two lines parallel to the given line. **c.** Through a given point not on a given line, there exist no lines parallel to the given line. **3.** Carl Friedrich Gauss **5.** Imaginary geometry **7.** A geodesic is a curve on a surface such that for any two points of the curve, the portion of the curve between the points is the shortest path on the surface that joins these points. **9.** An infinite saddle surface
11. π square units **13.** $d_E(P, Q) = \sqrt{49} = 7$ blocks, $d_C(P, Q) = 7$ blocks **15.** $d_E(P, Q) = \sqrt{89} \approx 9.4$ blocks, $d_C(P, Q) = 13$ blocks
17. $d_E(P, Q) = \sqrt{72} \approx 8.5$ blocks, $d_C(P, Q) = 12$ blocks **19.** $d_E(P, Q) = \sqrt{37} \approx 6.1$ blocks, $d_C(P, Q) = 7$ blocks
21. $d_C(P, Q) = 7$ blocks **23.** $d_C(P, Q) = 5$ blocks **25.** $d_C(P, Q) = 5$ blocks **27.** A city distance may be associated with more than one Euclidean distance. For example, if $P = (0, 0)$ and $Q = (2, 0)$, then the city distance between the points is 2 blocks and the Euclidean distance is also 2 blocks. However, if $P = (0, 0)$ and $Q = (1, 1)$, then the city distance between the points is still 2 blocks, but the Euclidean distance is $\sqrt{2}$ blocks.

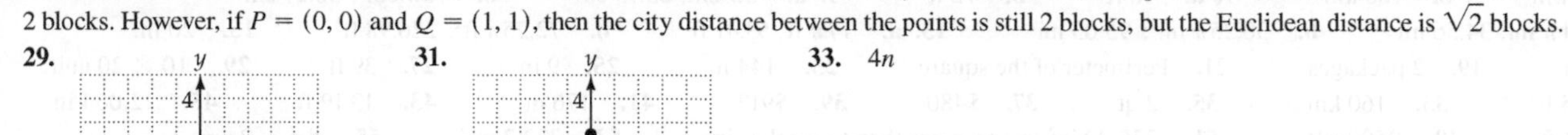

29. **31.** **33.** $4n$

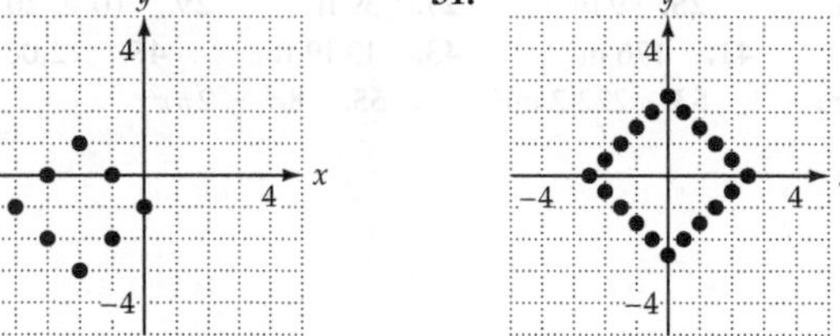

35. a. **b.** **37. a.** 10 **b.** 3

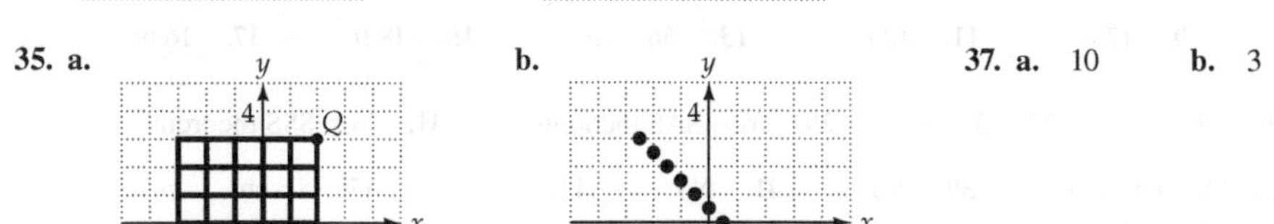

EXERCISE SET 1.8 *page 93*

1. **3.** **5.**

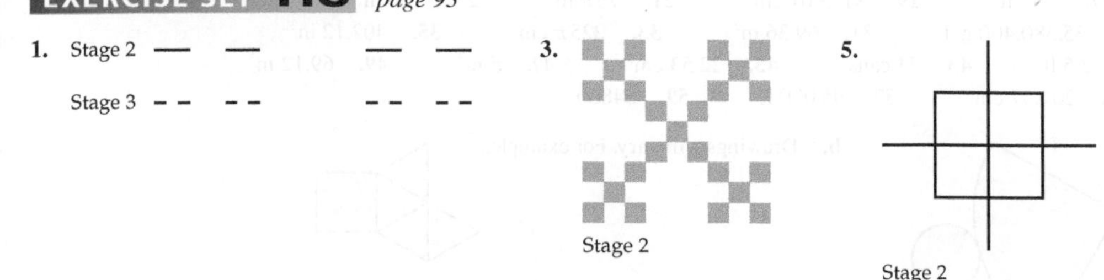

7.
9.

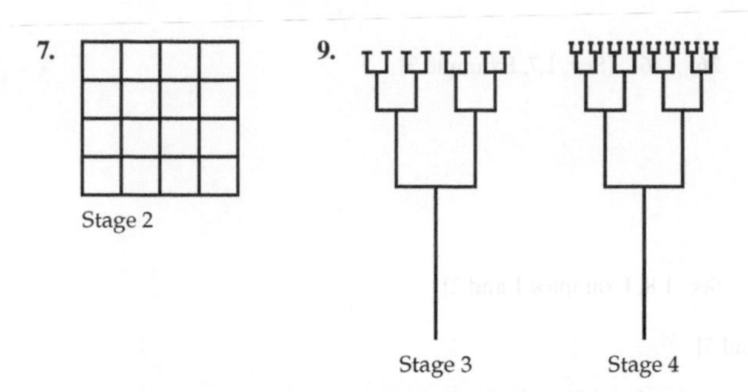

11. 0.631 **13.** 1.465 **15.** 2.000 **17.** 2.000 **19.** 1.613
21. a. Sierpinski carpet, 1.893; variation 2, 1.771; variation 1, 1.465 **b.** The Sierpinski carpet
23. The binary tree fractal is not a strictly self-similar fractal.

CHAPTER 1 REVIEW EXERCISES *page 99*

1. $2\frac{1}{4}$ [Sec. 1.1] **2.** $7\frac{1}{2}$ [Sec. 1.1] **3.** 3.7 [Sec. 1.1] **4.** 678 [Sec. 1.1] **5.** 1.273 [Sec. 1.1]
6. \$3.36 per qt [Sec. 1.1] **7.** $m\angle x = 22°$; $m\angle y = 158°$ [Sec. 1.2] **8.** 24 in. [Sec. 1.4] **9.** 240 in^3 [Sec. 1.5]
10. 68° [Sec. 1.2] **11.** 220 ft^2 [Sec. 1.5] **12.** 40π m^2 [Sec. 1.5] **13.** 44 cm [Sec. 1.2]
14. $m\angle w = 30°$; $m\angle y = 30°$ [Sec. 1.2] **15.** 27 in^2 [Sec. 1.3] **16.** 96 cm^3 [Sec. 1.5] **17.** 14.1 m [Sec. 1.3]
18. $m\angle a = 138°$; $m\angle b = 42°$ [Sec. 1.2] **19.** A 148° angle [Sec. 1.2] **20.** 39 ft^3 [Sec. 1.5] **21.** 95° [Sec. 1.2]
22. 8 cm [Sec. 1.3] **23.** 288π mm^3 [Sec. 1.5] **24.** 21.5 cm [Sec. 1.3] **25.** 4 cans [Sec. 1.5] **26.** 208 yd [Sec. 1.3]
27. 90.25 m^2 [Sec. 1.3] **28.** 276 m^2 [Sec. 1.3] **29.** The triangles are congruent by the SAS theorem. [Sec. 1.4]
30. 9.7 ft [Sec. 1.4] **31.** $\sin\theta = \frac{5\sqrt{89}}{89}$, $\cos\theta = \frac{8\sqrt{89}}{89}$, $\tan\theta = \frac{5}{8}$ [Sec. 1.6] **32.** $\sin\theta = \frac{\sqrt{3}}{2}$, $\cos\theta = \frac{1}{2}$, $\tan\theta = \sqrt{3}$ [Sec. 1.6]
33. 25.7° [Sec. 1.6] **34.** 29.2° [Sec. 1.6] **35.** 53.8° [Sec. 1.6] **36.** 1.9° [Sec. 1.6] **37.** 100.1 ft [Sec. 1.6]
38. 153.2 mi [Sec. 1.6] **39.** 56.0 ft [Sec. 1.6] **40.** Spherical geometry or elliptical geometry [Sec. 1.7]
41. Hyperbolic geometry [Sec. 1.7] **42.** Lobachevskian or hyperbolic geometry [Sec. 1.7] **43.** Riemannian or spherical geometry [Sec. 1.7]
44. 120π in^2 [Sec. 1.7] **45.** $\frac{25\pi}{3}$ ft^2 [Sec. 1.7] **46.** $d_E(P, Q) = 5$ blocks, $d_C(P, Q) = 7$ blocks [Sec. 1.7]
47. $d_E(P, Q) = \sqrt{113} \approx 10.6$ blocks, $d_C(P, Q) = 15$ blocks [Sec. 1.7] **48.** $d_E(P, Q) = \sqrt{37} \approx 6.1$ blocks, $d_C(P, Q) = 7$ blocks [Sec. 1.7]
49. $d_E(P, Q) = \sqrt{89} \approx 9.4$ blocks, $d_C(P, Q) = 13$ blocks [Sec. 1.7] **50. a.** P and Q **b.** P and R [Sec. 1.7]
51. Stage 0 Yes. The Koch curve is a strictly self-similar fractal. [Sec. 1.8] **52.**

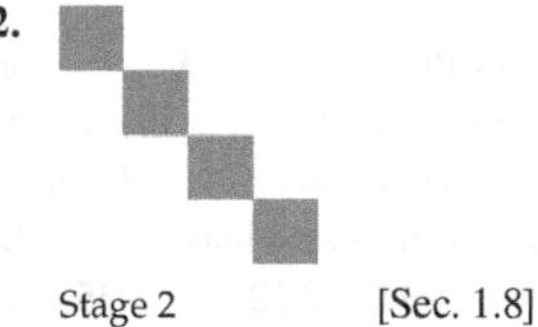

53. a. 2 **b.** 2 **c.** $D = \frac{\log 2}{\log 2} = 1$ [Sec. 1.8] **54.** $\frac{\log 5}{\log 4} \approx 1.161$ [Sec. 1.8]

CHAPTER 1 TEST *page 101*

1. 169.6 m^3 [Sec. 1.5, Example 3] **2.** 6.8 m [Sec. 1.3, Example 1] **3.** A 58° angle [Sec. 1.2, Example 2]
4. 3.1 m^2 [Sec. 1.3, Example 10] **5.** 150° [Sec. 1.2, Example 5] **6.** $m\angle a = 45°$; $m\angle b = 135°$ [Sec. 1.2, Example 5]
7. 1200 cm [Sec. 1.1, Example 4] **8.** 448π cm^3 [Sec. 1.5, Example 3] **9.** $1\frac{1}{5}$ ft [Sec. 1.4, Example 2]
10. 90° and 50° [Sec. 1.2, Example 8] **11.** 125° [Sec. 1.2, Example 7] **12.** 32 m^2 [Sec. 1.3, Example 7]
13. 25 ft [Sec. 1.4, Example 2] **14.** 113.1 in^2 [Sec. 1.3, Example 11] **15.** The triangles are congruent by the SAS theorem. [Sec. 1.4, Example 3] **16.** 7.5 cm [Sec. 1.4, Example 4] **17.** $\sin\theta = \frac{4}{5}$, $\cos\theta = \frac{3}{5}$, $\tan\theta = \frac{4}{3}$ [Sec. 1.6, Example 1]
18. 127 ft [Sec. 1.6, Example 6] **19.** 103.9 ft^2 [Sec. 1.3, Example 11] **20.** 780 in^3 [Sec. 1.5, Check Your Progress 1]
21. 26.82 m/s [Sec. 1.1, Example 9] **22.** Through a given point not on a given line, exactly one line can be drawn parallel to the given line. [Sec. 1.7, Example 2] **23.** A great circle of a sphere is a circle on the surface of the sphere whose center is at the center of the sphere.
$S = (m\angle A + m\angle B + m\angle C - 180°)\left(\frac{\pi}{180°}\right)r^2$ [Sec. 1.7, Example 1] **24.** 80π ft$^2 \approx 251.3$ ft^2 [Sec. 1.7, Example 1]

25. $d_E(P, Q) = \sqrt{82} \approx 9.1$ blocks, $d_C(P, Q) = 10$ blocks [Sec. 1.7, Example 3] **26.** 16 [Sec. 1.7, Example 3]

27. Stage 2 [Sec. 1.8, Examples 1 and 2]

28.

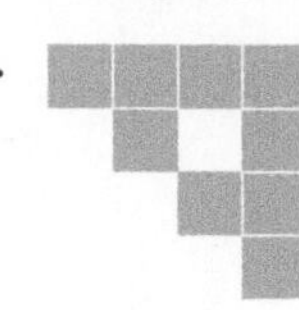

Stage 2 [Sec. 1.8, Examples 1 and 2]

29. Replacement ratio: 2; scale ratio: 2; similarity dimension: 1 [Sec. 1.8, Examples 4 and 5]

30. Replacement ratio: 3; scale ratio: 2; similarity dimension: $\frac{\log 3}{\log 2} \approx 1.585$ [Sec. 1.8, Examples 4 and 5]

CHAPTER 2

EXERCISE SET 2.1 *page 114*

1. An equation expresses the equality of two mathematical expressions. An equation contains an equals sign. An expression does not.
3. Substitute the solution back into the original equation and confirm the equality. **5.** 12 **7.** 22 **9.** −8 **11.** −20 **13.** 8
15. −1 **17.** 1 **19.** $-\frac{1}{3}$ **21.** $\frac{2}{3}$ **23.** −2 **25.** 4 **27.** 2 **29.** 2 **31.** $\frac{1}{4}$ **33.** −2
35. 4 **37.** 8 **39.** 1 **41.** −32 **43.** $19,004.18 **45.** 80 ft **47.** 1998 **49.** 136 ft **51.** 24.3°C
53. 168.75 **55. a.** 1725 children **b.** 465 children **57.** 3 h **59.** 150 research assistants **61.** $2000 and $3000
63. 13 GB **65.** $b = P - a - c$ **67.** $R = \frac{E}{I}$ **69.** $r = \frac{I}{Pt}$ **71.** $C = \frac{5}{9}(F - 32)$ **73.** $t = \frac{A - P}{Pr}$
75. $f = \frac{T + gm}{m}$ **77.** $S = C - Rt$ **79.** $b_2 = \frac{2A}{h} - b_1$ **81.** $h = \frac{S}{2\pi r} - r$ **83.** $y = 2 - \frac{4}{3}x$ **85.** $x = \frac{y - y_1}{m} + x_1$
87. Every real number is a solution. **89.** $x = \frac{d - b}{a - c}$. $a \neq c$ or the denominator equals zero and the expression is undefined.
91. $T = 750m + 30{,}000$, where T is the total number of miles driven and m is the number of months you have owned the car.
93. $C = 29.95d + 0.50(m - 100)$, where C is the total cost, d is the number of days, and m is the number of miles driven.

EXERCISE SET 2.2 *page 126*

1. Examples will vary. **3.** 48.5 mph **5.** 68 words/min **7.** $26 per share **9.** $19.50/hr **11. a.** 336 ft/min **b.** 89 s
13. 24 ounces for $3.89 **15. a.** 9.2, 9, 10.1, 9.6, 9.7, 9.5, 10.7, 7.3, 9.7, 6.5, 10.9, 10.0, 11.0 **b.** Barry Bonds; Mark McGwire
c. Explanations may vary. **17. a.** 79.5, 81.6, 83.8 **b.** 1.05 times greater **19.** 3,054,136.5 Indian rupees
21. 41,226.4 Australian dollars **23.** 11.2; buy **25.** Georgetown University **27.** 17.14 **29.** 25.6
31. 20.83 **33.** 2.22 **35.** 13.71 **37.** 39.6 **39.** $65,000 **41.** 329 mi **43.** 16 mi
45. 67.5 in. **47. a.** $442.50 **b.** $737.50 **49.** 11.25 g. Explanations will vary.

51.
$$\frac{a}{b} = \frac{c}{d}$$
$$\frac{a}{b} + 1 = \frac{c}{d} + 1$$
$$\frac{a}{b} + \frac{b}{b} = \frac{c}{d} + \frac{d}{d}$$
$$\frac{a + b}{b} = \frac{c + d}{d}$$

53. a. and b. The number of seats per state is AL 7, AK 1, AZ 8, AR 4, CA 53, CO 7, CT 5, DE 1, DC 3, FL 25, GA 13, HI 2, ID 2, IL 19, IN 9, IA 5, KS 4, KY 6, LA 7, ME 2, MD 8, MA 10, MI 15, MN 8, MS 4, MO 9, MT 1, NE 3, NV 3, NH 2, NJ 13, NM 3, NY 29, NC 13, ND 1, OH 18, OK 5, OR 5, PA 19, RI 2, SC 6, SD 1, TN 9, UT 3, VT 1, VA 11, WA 9, WV 3, WI 8, WY 1. Students will find that the calculated number of representatives per state does not match the actual number of representatives in the following states: AZ, FL, GA, IL, IA, LA, MA, MI, MN, MO, NV, NJ, NY, OH, PA, SC, TX, UT, WA.

EXERCISE SET 2.3 *page 143*

1. Answers will vary. **3.** 0.5; 50% **5.** $\frac{2}{5}$; 0.4 **7.** $\frac{7}{10}$; 70% **9.** 0.55; 55% **11.** $\frac{5}{32}$; 0.15625
13. 119 million returns **15.** $53.7 billion **17.** 23.7% **19.** 14 million oz **21.** 3364 people **23.** 57.7%
25. a. 102.5% **b.** 122.2% **c.** 350% **d.** It is 4.5 times larger. Convert the percent to a decimal and add 1.
27. 16.8% **29. a.** 46.0% **b.** 27.2% **31.** Less than **33. a.** 11,400,000 TV households; 67,100,000 TV households
b. 6,300,000 TV households; 57,300,000 TV households **c.** 2.3 people

EXERCISE SET 2.4 *page 154*

1. −2 and 5 **3.** $\frac{1+\sqrt{5}}{2}$ and $\frac{1-\sqrt{5}}{2}$; −0.618 and 1.618 **5.** $3+\sqrt{13}$ and $3-\sqrt{13}$; −0.606 and 6.606
7. 0 and 2 **9.** $\frac{1+\sqrt{17}}{2}$ and $\frac{1-\sqrt{17}}{2}$; −1.562 and 2.562 **11.** $\frac{2+\sqrt{14}}{2}$ and $\frac{2-\sqrt{14}}{2}$; −0.871 and 2.871
13. $2+\sqrt{11}$ and $2-\sqrt{11}$; −1.317 and 5.317 **15.** $-\frac{3}{2}$ and 6 **17.** No real number solutions **19.** −4 and $\frac{1}{4}$
21. $-\frac{1}{2}$ and $\frac{4}{3}$ **23.** $1+\sqrt{5}$ and $1-\sqrt{5}$; −1.236 and 3.236 **25.** Answers will vary. **27.** 0.75 s and 3 s
29. $T = 0.5(1)^2 + 0.5(1) = 1$; $T = 0.5(2)^2 + 0.5(2) = 3$; $T = 0.5(3)^2 + 0.5(3) = 6$; $T = 0.5(4)^2 + 0.5(4) = 10$; 10 rows
31. 2017 **33. a.** 240 ft **b.** 30 mph **35.** 5.51 s **37.** 244.10 ft **39.** No **41.** No **43.** 68 cents
45. If the discriminant is not a perfect square, the radical expression in the quadratic formula will not simplify to a whole number.
47. $3b$ and $5b$ **49.** $-y$ and $\frac{3}{2}y$

CHAPTER 2 REVIEW EXERCISES *page 158*

1. 4 [Sec. 2.1] **2.** $\frac{1}{8}$ [Sec. 2.1] **3.** −2 [Sec. 2.1] **4.** $\frac{10}{3}$ [Sec. 2.2] **5.** No real number solutions [Sec. 2.4]
6. −5 and 6 [Sec. 2.4] **7.** $2+\sqrt{3}$ and $2-\sqrt{3}$ [Sec. 2.4] **8.** $\frac{1+\sqrt{13}}{2}$ and $\frac{1-\sqrt{13}}{2}$ [Sec. 2.4] **9.** $y = -\frac{4}{3}x + 4$ [Sec. 2.1]
10. $t = \frac{f-v}{a}$ [Sec. 2.1] **11.** 2450 ft [Sec. 2.1] **12.** 3 s [Sec. 2.1] **13.** 60°C [Sec. 2.1] **14.** 85 calls [Sec. 2.1]
15. 28.4 mi/gal [Sec. 2.2] **16.** $\frac{1}{4}$ [Sec. 2.2] **17.** 400% [Sec. 2.3] **18. a.** New York, Chicago, Phoenix, Los Angeles, Houston
b. 22,231 more people per square mile [Sec. 2.2] **19. a.** 7 : 1, 7 to 1. There are 7 students for each faculty member at the university.
b. Prescott College, Embry-Riddle Aeronautical University **c.** Arizona State University and Northern Arizona University [Sec. 2.2]
20. Department A: $105,000; Department B: $245,000 [Sec. 2.2] **21.** 7.5 tablespoons [Sec. 2.2] **22. a.** More than one-fifth
b. 4:1 **c.** $2.88 trillion **d.** $0.72 trillion or $720 billion [Sec. 2.2] **23. a.** 51.0% **b.** Less than [Sec. 2.3]
24. 20 billion hot dogs [Sec. 2.3] **25.** 97.9% [Sec. 2.3] **26. a.** $83.\overline{3}\%$ **b.** 100% **c.** 50% [Sec. 2.3]
27. 13.2% [Sec. 2.3] **28.** 35% [Sec. 2.3] **29.** $7040 [Sec. 2.3] **30.** 13 days [Sec. 2.1] **31.** 1 s and 5 s [Sec. 2.4]
32. 0.5 s and 1.5 s [Sec. 2.4]

CHAPTER 2 TEST *page 160*

1. 14 [Sec. 2.1, Example 2c] **2.** 10 [Sec. 2.1, Example 2b] **3.** $\frac{21}{4}$ [Sec. 2.2, Example 7] **4.** 3 and 9 [Sec. 2.4, Example 3]
5. $\frac{2+\sqrt{7}}{3}$ and $\frac{2-\sqrt{7}}{3}$ [Sec. 2.4, Example 4] **6.** $y = \frac{1}{2}x - \frac{15}{2}$ [Sec. 2.1, Example 6a] **7.** $F = \frac{9}{5}C + 32$ [Sec. 2.1, Example 6a]
8. 2.5 min [Sec. 2.1, Example 3] **9.** 431.25 kWh [Sec. 2.1, Example 4] **10.** 54.8 mph [Sec. 2.2, Example 1]
11. 843 acres [Sec. 2.1, Check Your Progress 4] **12. a.** 2.727, 2.905, 2.777, 2.808, 2.901, 2.904
b. Ty Cobb, Rogers Hornsby, Joe Jackson, Tris Speaker, Ted Williams, Billy Hamilton [Sec. 2.2, Example 1]
13. 256 million [Sec. 2.3, Example 7] **14.** $225,000 and $135,000 [Sec. 2.2, Check Your Progress 9]
15. 2.75 lb [Sec. 2.2, Example 10] **16. a.** Detroit, Michigan **b.** 8355 violent crimes [Sec. 2.2, Example 4]
17. 14.4% [Sec. 2.3, Check Your Progress 6] **18.** 55.6% [Sec. 2.3, Example 12] **19. a.** 79.0% **b.** 26.4 million [Sec. 2.3, Example 13]
20. 0.2 s and 1.6 s [Sec. 2.4, Example 7]

CHAPTER 3

EXERCISE SET 3.1 *page 171*

1. Divide the number of months by 12. **3.** I is the interest, P is the principal, r is the interest rate, and t is the time period.
5. $560 **7.** $227.50 **9.** $202.50 **11.** $16.80 **13.** $159.60 **15.** $125 **17.** $168
19. $15,667.50 **21.** $7390.80 **23.** $2864.40 **25.** 7.5% **27.** 8% **29.** 9.3% **31.** $39
33. $18 **35.** $7406 **37.** $5465.20 **39.** $804.75 **41.** 10.2% **43.** 10% **45.** $132.99
47. The ordinary method. The lender benefits. **49.** There are fewer days in September than there are in August.

EXERCISE SET 3.2 page 186

1. $2739.99 3. $852.88 5. $20,836.54 7. $12,575.23 9. $3532.86 11. $3850.08 13. $2213.84
15. $10,116.38 17. $8320.14 19. $41,210.44 21. $7641.78 23. $3182.47 25. $10,094.57
27. $11,887.58 29. $3583.16 31. $5728.18 33. $391.24 35. $18,056.35 37. $11,120.58
39. a. $450 b. $568.22 c. $118.22 41. a. $20,528.54 b. $20,591.79 c. $63.25
43. a. $1698.59 b. $1716.59 c. $18.00 45. a. $10,401.63 b. $3401.63 47. $9612.75
49. a. $67,228.19 b. $94,161.98 51. $5559.09 53. $3446.03 55. $56,102.07 57. $12,152.77
59. $2495.45 61. 7.40% 63. 7.76% 65. 8.44% 67. 6.10% 69. $4.01, $5.37, $9.62
71. $3.60, $4.82, $8.63 73. $12.04, $16.12, $28.86 75. $368,012.03, $492,483.12, $881,962.25 77. $25,417.46
79. $25,841.90 81. $53,473.96 83. a. 4.0%, 4.04%, 4.06%, 4.07%, 4.08% b. increase 85. 3.04%
87. 6.25% compounded semiannually 89. 5.8% compounded quarterly

EXERCISE SET 3.3 page 203

1. $1.48 3. $152.32 5. $335.87 7. $15.34 9. $5.00 11. $26.87 13. 13.5% 15. 19.2%
17. $34.59 19. a. $696.05 b. $174.01 c. $88.46 21. a. $68,569.73 b. $13,713.95 c. $641.17
23. $874.88 25. $571.31 27. a. $621.19 b. $4372.12 29. $13,575.25 31. $3472.57
33. $226.45 35. $412.14 37. a. $2704.15 b. $20,938.15 c. $515.10 39. $572.75

EXERCISE SET 3.4 page 212

1. $382.50 3. $535.50 5. 2.51% 7. 1.83% 9. a. $43.81 b. $3270.00 c. 6,976,300 shares
d. increase e. $141.13 11. 50 shares 13. a. Profit of $25,240.00 b. $1409.80 15. a. Profit of $34,032
b. $2475.54 17. $252 19. $840 21. $22.50 23. 714 shares 25. 240 shares
27. The no-load fund's value ($2800.58) is $2.06 greater than the load fund's value ($2798.52). 29. Answers will vary.

EXERCISE SET 3.5 page 223

1. $64,500; $193,500 3. $5625 5. $99,539 7. $34,289.38 9. $974.37 11. $2155.28
13. a. $1088.95 b. $392,022 c. $240,022 15. $174,606 17. Interest: $1407.38; principal: $495.89
19. Interest: $1347.68; principal: $123.62 21. $112,025.49 23. $61,039.75 25. $1071.10 27. $2022.50
29. a. $330.57 b. $140,972.40 31. a. $390.62 b. $178,273.20 33. $125,000 35. $212,065 37. No
39. a. $65,641.88 b. $138,596.60 c. $28,881.52 d. 44%

CHAPTER 3 REVIEW EXERCISES page 227

1. $61.88 [Sec. 3.1] 2. $782 [Sec. 3.1] 3. $90 [Sec. 3.1] 4. $7218.40 [Sec. 3.1] 5. 7.5% [Sec. 3.1]
6. $3654.90 [Sec. 3.2] 7. $11,609.72 [Sec. 3.2] 8. $7859.52 [Sec. 3.2] 9. $200.23 [Sec. 3.2]
10. $10,683.29 [Sec. 3.2] 11. a. $11,318.23 b. $3318.23 [Sec. 3.2] 12. $19,225.50 [Sec. 3.2]
13. 1.1% [Sec. 3.4] 14. $9000 [Sec. 3.4] 15. $1.59 [Sec. 3.2] 16. $43,650.68 [Sec. 3.2]
17. 6.06% [Sec. 3.2] 18. 5.4% compounded semiannually [Sec. 3.2] 19. $431.16 [Sec. 3.3]
20. $6.12 [Sec. 3.3] 21. a. $259.38 b. 12.75% [Sec. 3.3] 22. a. $36.03 b. 12.9% [Sec. 3.3]
23. $45.41 [Sec. 3.3] 24. a. $10,092.69 b. $2018.54 c. $253.01 [Sec. 3.3] 25. $664.40 [Sec. 3.3]
26. a. $540.02 b. $12,196.80 [Sec. 3.3] 27. a. Profit of $5325 b. $256.10 [Sec. 3.4]
28. 200 shares [Sec. 3.4] 29. $99,041 [Sec. 3.5] 30. a. $1659.11 b. $597,279.60 c. $341,479.60 [Sec. 3.5]
31. a. $1396.69 b. $150,665.74 [Sec. 3.5] 32. $2658.53 [Sec. 3.5] 33. $288.62 [Sec. 3.3]

CHAPTER 3 TEST page 229

1. $108.28 [Sec. 3.1, Example 2] 2. $202.50 [Sec. 3.1, Example 1] 3. $8408.89 [Sec. 3.1, Example 6]
4. 9% [Sec. 3.1, Example 5] 5. $7340.87 [Sec. 3.2, Check Your Progress 2] 6. $312.03 [Sec. 3.2, Example 4]
7. a. $15,331.03 b. $4831.03 [Sec. 3.1, Example 6] 8. $21,949.06 [Sec. 3.2, Example 6] 9. 1.2% [Sec. 3.4, Example 2]
10. $1900 [Sec. 3.4, Example 4] 11. $387,207.74 [Sec. 3.2, Check Your Progress 8] 12. 6.40% [Sec. 3.2, Check Your Progress 10]
13. 4.6% compounded semiannually [Sec. 3.2, Example 11] 14. $7.79 [Sec. 3.3, Example 1] 15. a. $48.56
b. 16.6% [Sec. 3.3, Example 2] 16. $56.49 [Sec. 3.3, Example 3] 17. a. Loss of $4896 b. $226.16 [Sec. 3.4, Example 3]
18. 208 shares [Sec. 3.4, Example 5] 19. a. $6985.94 b. $1397.19 c. $174.62 [Sec. 3.3, Example 4]
20. $60,083.50 [Sec. 3.5, Example 1] 21. a. $1530.69 [Sec. 3.5, Example 2a] b. $221,546.46 [Sec. 3.5, Example 4]
22. $2595.97 [Sec. 3.5, Example 2a, Example 5]

CHAPTER 4

EXERCISE SET 4.1 page 239

1. 7; 7; 7 **3.** 22; 14; no mode **5.** 18.8; 8.1; no mode **7.** 192.4; 190; 178 **9.** 0.1; −3; −5
11. a. Yes. The mean is computed by using the sum of all the data. **b.** No. The median is not affected unless the middle value, or one of the two middle values, in a data set is changed. **13.** ≈40.0 years; 35 years **15. a.** Answers will vary. **b.** Answers will vary.
17. 3.22 **19.** 3.37 **21.** 82 **23.** 0.847 **25.** 0.671 **27.** ≈6.1 points; 5 points; 2 points and 5 points
29. ≈7.2; 7; 7 **31.** 64° **33.** −6°F **35.** 92 **37. a.** ≈0.275 **b.** ≈0.273 **c.** No
39. Yes. Joanne has a smaller average for the first month and the second month, but she has a larger average for both months.

EXERCISE SET 4.2 page 249

1. 84°F **3.** 21; 8.2; 67.1 **5.** 3.3; 1.3; 1.7 **7.** 52; 17.7; 311.6 **9.** 0; 0; 0 **11.** 23; 8.3; 69.6
13. Opinions will vary. However, many climbers would consider rope B to be safer because of its smaller standard deviation in breaking strength.
15. The students in the college statistics course because the range of weights is greater. **17.** 23.67 mpg; 3.92 mpg **19.** 493.6 cal; 20.30 cal
21. 4.27 h; 0.69 h **23. a.** 210 s, or 3 min 30 s; 26 s **b.** Yes; 2:27, 3:01, 4:02 **25. a.** Answers will vary.
b. The standard deviation of the new data is *k* times the standard deviation of the original data. **27.** If the variance is 0 or 1

EXERCISE SET 4.3 page 259

1. a. ≈0.87 **b.** ≈1.74 **c.** ≈−2.17 **d.** 0.0 **3. a.** ≈−0.32 **b.** ≈0.21 **c.** ≈1.16 **d.** ≈−0.95
5. a. ≈−0.67 **b.** 147.78 mm Hg **7. a.** ≈0.72 **b.** ≈112.16 mg/dl **9.** The score in part a. **11.** ≈59th percentile
13. 6396 students **15. a.** 50% **b.** 10% **c.** 40% **17.** $Q_1 = 5$, $Q_2 = 10$, $Q_3 = 26$

19. Northeast
Midwest
South
West

150,000 200,000 250,000 300,000 350,000

Answers will vary. Here are some possibilities. The region with the lowest median was the South; the region with the highest median was the Northeast. The range of prices was greatest for the West.

21.
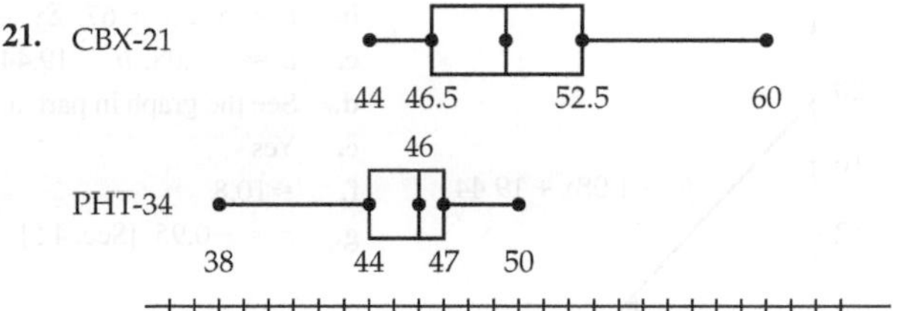

Answers will vary. Here is one possibility: The maximum number of bushels cultivated per acre for PHT-34 is approximately equal to the median number of bushels cultivated per acre for CBX-21.

23. a. $\mu = 0, \sigma = 1$ **b.** $\mu = 0, \sigma = 1$ **c.** $\mu = 0, \sigma = 1$

EXERCISE SET 4.4 page 271

1. a. 5.8% **b.** 0.87 **3. a.** 95% **b.** 16% **c.** 81.5% **5. a.** 81.5% **b.** 0.15%
7. a. 1280 vehicles **b.** 12 vehicles **9.** 0.433 square unit **11.** 0.468 square unit **13.** 0.130 square unit
15. 0.878 square unit **17.** 0.097 square unit **19.** 0.013 square unit **21.** 0.926 square unit **23.** 0.997 square unit
25. $z = 0.84$ **27.** $z = -0.90$ **29.** $z = 0.35$ **31. a.** 19.2% **b.** 29.6% **33. a.** 80.5% **b.** 7%
35. a. 10.6% **b.** 98.8% **37. a.** 0.106 **b.** 0.460 **39. a.** 0.749 **b.** 0.023 **41.** Answers will vary.
43. True **45.** True **47.** True **49.** False **51.** ≈−0.67 and 0.67

EXERCISE SET 4.5 page 282

1. a. b **b.** c **3. a.**

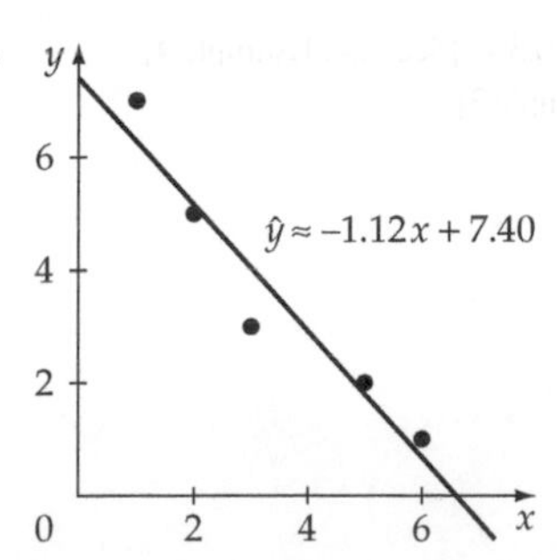

b. $n = 5$, $\Sigma x = 17$, $\Sigma y = 18$, $\Sigma x^2 = 75$, $(\Sigma x)^2 = 289$, $\Sigma xy = 42$
c. $a = -\frac{48}{43} \approx -1.12$, $b = \frac{318}{43} \approx 7.40$
d. See the graph in part a.
e. Yes
f. $y \approx 3.6$
g. $r \approx -0.96$

5. $\hat{y} \approx 2.01x + 0.56$; $r \approx 0.96$ **7.** $\hat{y} \approx -0.72x + 9.23$; $r \approx -0.96$ **9.** $\hat{y} \approx 1.66x + 2.25$; $r \approx 0.99$
11. a. $\hat{y} \approx -0.170x + 54{,}545.585$ **b.** $49,444 **c.** $r \approx -0.999$ **d.** As the number of miles the car is driven increases, the value of the car decreases. **13. a.** $\hat{y} \approx 0.775x + 20.707$ **b.** $\approx$32.3%
15. a. $r \approx 0.99$ **b.** Yes, at least for the years 2005 to 2010. The correlation coefficient is very close to 1, which indicates a strong correlation.
17. a. $\hat{y} \approx -0.91x + 79.21$ **b.** $\approx$56 years **c.** Interpolation **19. a.** $r = 0.999525765$; $y = 1194.657x + 30{,}217.2$
b. $r = 0.9993403551$; $y = 827.8857x + 14{,}233.4$ **c.** Yes **d.** The value of a indicates the approximate yearly increase in tuition and fees. For instance, the number 827.8857 in part b means that tuition and fees at public universities increased by about $828 each year.

CHAPTER 4 REVIEW EXERCISES *page 288*

1. 14.7; 14; 12; 9; 17.6; 4.2 [Sec. 4.1/4.2] **2.** The mode [Sec. 4.1] **3.** Answers will vary. [Sec. 4.1]
4. a. Median **b.** Mode **c.** Mean [Sec. 4.1] **5.** 1331.125 ft; 1223.5 ft; 1200 ft; 462 ft [Sec. 4.1/4.2]
6. 36 mph [Sec. 4.1] **7.** $\approx$3.20 [Sec. 4.1] **8. a.** 1.25 **b.** The 88th percentile [Sec. 4.3] **9.** $\approx$3.16; $\approx$10.00 [Sec. 4.2]
10. $7.63; $7.91; $0.58 [Sec. 4.1/4.2] **11. a.** The second student's mean is 5 points higher than the first student's mean.
b. They are the same. [Sec. 4.1/4.2] **12. a.** ≈ -1.73 **b.** $\approx$0.58 [Sec. 4.3]
13.

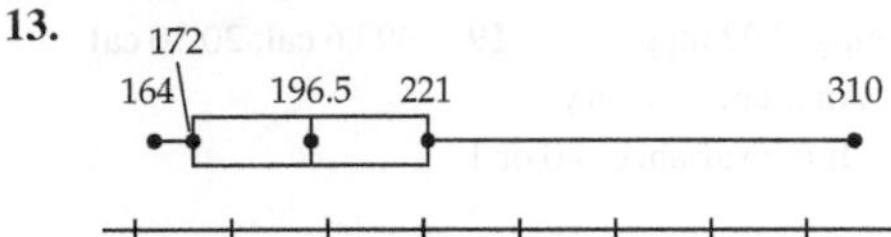

[Sec. 4.3]

14. a. 8 **b.** 40 [Sec. 4.4]
15. a. 78% **b.** 0.34 [Sec. 4.4] **16.** Yes. $r \approx -0.9004$, which indicates a strong linear correlation. [Sec. 4.5]
17. a. $\hat{y} \approx 7609.1x - 72{,}019.1$ **b.** 42,117 stations [Sec. 4.5]
18. No. No information is given about how the scores are distributed below the mean. [Sec. 4.4]
19. a. 0.933 **b.** 0.309 [Sec. 4.4] **20. a.** 16% **b.** 95% [Sec. 4.4]
21. a. 6.7% **b.** 64.5% **c.** 78.8% [Sec. 4.4] **22.** 93.15 million mi [Sec. 4.1]
23. a.

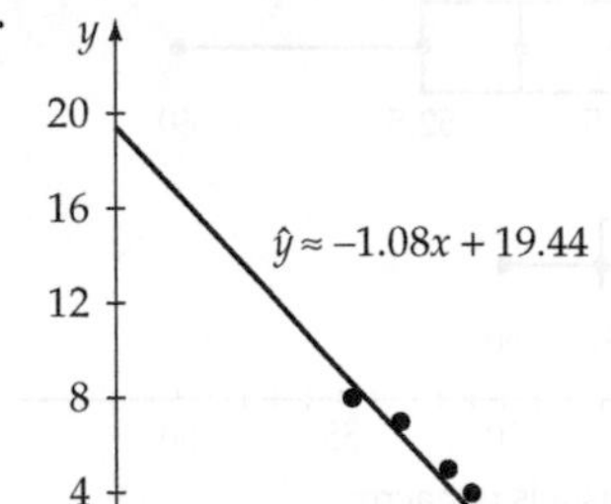

b. $n = 5$, $\Sigma x = 67$, $\Sigma y = 25$, $\Sigma x^2 = 921$, $(\Sigma x)^2 = 4489$, $\Sigma xy = 310$
c. $a \approx -1.08$, $b \approx 19.44$
d. See the graph in part a.
e. Yes
f. $\approx$10.8
g. $r \approx -0.95$ [Sec. 4.5]

24. a. $r \approx 0.999$ **b.** $\hat{y} \approx 0.07x + 0.29$ **c.** 13.94 in. [Sec. 4.5]
25. a. $\hat{y} \approx 0.018x + 0.0005$ **b.** Yes. $r \approx 0.999$, which is very close to 1. **c.** 1.80 s [Sec. 4.5]
26. a. $\hat{y} = 58.89921372x + 0.1924231594$; $r \approx 0.9911051145$ **b.** 3.7 h [Sec. 4.5]

CHAPTER 4 TEST *page 291*

1. 9.1; 9; 7 [Sec. 4.1, Examples 1, 2, and 3] **2.** 2.87 [Sec. 4.1, Example 4]
3. 24; $\approx$8.76; $\approx$76.7 [Sec. 4.2, Examples 1, 2, and 3] **4. a.** $\approx$1.18 **b.** ≈ -0.49 [Sec. 4.3, Example 1]
5.

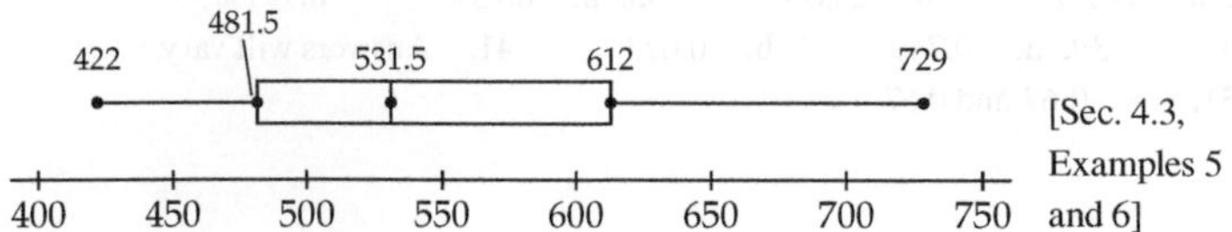

[Sec. 4.3, Examples 5 and 6]

6. a. 37% **b.** 35% [Sec. 4.4, Example 1]
7. a. 47.5% **b.** 16% [Sec. 4.4, Example 2] **8. a.** 10.6% **b.** 20.3% [Sec. 4.4, Example 4]
9. a. $r = -0.9308039961$ **b.** Yes. $|-0.9308039961| > 0.9$ [Sec. 4.5, Example 3]
10. a. $\hat{y} \approx -7.98x + 767.12$ **b.** 57 calories [Sec. 4.5, Examples 1 and 2]

Solutions to Check Your Progress Problems

CHAPTER 1

SECTION 1.1

Check your progress 1, *page 3*

$$14 \text{ ft} = 14 \cancel{\text{ft}} \times \frac{1 \text{ yd}}{3 \cancel{\text{ft}}} = \frac{14 \text{ yd}}{3} = 4\frac{2}{3} \text{ yd}$$

Check your progress 2, *page 3*

$$3 \text{ lb} = 3 \cancel{\text{lb}} \times \frac{16 \text{ oz}}{1 \cancel{\text{lb}}} = 48 \text{ oz}$$

Check your progress 3, *page 3*

First convert pints to quarts, and then convert quarts to gallons.

$$18 \text{ pt} = 18 \cancel{\text{pt}} \times \frac{1 \cancel{\text{qt}}}{2 \cancel{\text{pt}}} \times \frac{1 \text{ gal}}{4 \cancel{\text{qt}}}$$

$$= \frac{18 \text{ gal}}{8} = 2\frac{1}{4} \text{ gal}$$

Check your progress 4, *page 4*

3.07 m = 307 cm

Check your progress 5, *page 5*

42.3 mg = 0.0423 g

Check your progress 6, *page 6*

2 kl = 2000 L

2 kl 167 L = 2000 L + 167 L

= 2167 L

Check your progress 7, *page 7*

$$\frac{\$3.69}{\text{gal}} \approx \frac{\$3.69}{\cancel{\text{gal}}} \times \frac{1 \cancel{\text{gal}}}{3.79 \text{ L}}$$

$$= \frac{\$3.69}{3.79 \text{ L}} \approx \frac{\$.97}{\text{L}}$$

\$3.69/gal ≈ \$.97/L

Check your progress 8, *page 7*

$$45 \text{ cm} = \frac{45 \cancel{\text{cm}}}{1} \times \frac{1 \text{ in.}}{2.54 \cancel{\text{cm}}}$$

$$= \frac{45 \text{ in.}}{2.54} \approx 17.72 \text{ in.}$$

45 cm ≈ 17.72 in.

Check your progress 9, *page 7*

$$\frac{75 \text{ km}}{\text{h}} \approx \frac{75 \cancel{\text{km}}}{\text{h}} \times \frac{1 \text{ mi}}{1.61 \cancel{\text{km}}}$$

$$= \frac{75 \text{ mi}}{1.61 \text{ h}} \approx 46.58 \text{ mi/h}$$

75 km/h ≈ 46.58 mi/h

SECTION 1.2

Check your progress 1, *page 11*

$AB + BC = AC$

$\frac{1}{4}(BC) + BC = AC$

$\frac{1}{4}(16) + 16 = AC$

$4 + 16 = AC$

$20 = AC$

$AC = 20$ ft

Check your progress 2, *page 13*

Supplementary angles are two angles the sum of whose measures is 180°. To find the supplement, let x represent the supplement of a 129° angle.

$x + 129 = 180$

$x = 51$

The supplement of a 129° angle is a 51° angle.

Check your progress 3, *page 14*

$m\angle a + 68° = 118°$

$m\angle a = 50°$

Check your progress 4, *page 15*

$m\angle b + m\angle a = 180°$

$m\angle b + 35° = 180°$

$m\angle b = 145°$

$m\angle c = m\angle a = 35°$

$m\angle d = m\angle b = 145°$

$m\angle b = 145°$, $m\angle c = 35°$, and $m\angle d = 145°$.

Check your progress 5, *page 16*

$m\angle b = m\angle g = 124°$

$m\angle d = m\angle g = 124°$

$m\angle c + m\angle b = 180°$

$m\angle c + 124° = 180°$

$m\angle c = 56°$

$m\angle b = 124°$, $m\angle c = 56°$, and $m\angle d = 124°$.

Check your progress 6, *page 17*

Let x represent the measure of the third angle.

$x + 90° + 27° = 180°$

$x + 117° = 180°$

$x = 63°$

The measure of the third angle is 63°.

Check your progress 7, *page 18*

$m\angle b + m\angle d = 180°$
$m\angle b + 105° = 180°$
$m\angle b = 75°$

$m\angle a + m\angle b + m\angle c = 180°$
$m\angle a + 75° + 35° = 180°$
$m\angle a + 110° = 180°$
$m\angle a = 70°$

$m\angle e = m\angle a = 70°$

SECTION 1.3

Check your progress 1, *page 26*

$P = 2L + 2W$
$P = 2(12) + 2(8)$
$P = 24 + 16$
$P = 40$

You will need 40 ft of molding to edge the top of the walls.

Check your progress 2, *page 26*

$P = 4s$
$P = 4(24)$
$P = 96$

The homeowner should purchase 96 ft of fencing.

Check your progress 3, *page 27*

$C = \pi d$
$C = 9\pi$

The circumference of the circle is 9π km.

Check your progress 4, *page 27*

12 in. = 1 ft

$C = \pi d$
$C = \pi(1)$
$C = \pi$

$12C = 12\pi \approx 37.70$

The tricycle travels approximately 37.70 ft when the wheel makes 12 revolutions.

Check your progress 5, *page 28*

$A = LW$
$A = 308(192)$
$A = 59{,}136$

59,136 cm^2 of fabric is needed.

Check your progress 6, *page 29*

$A = s^2$
$A = 24^2$
$A = 576$

The area of the floor is 576 ft^2.

Check your progress 7, *page 30*

$A = bh$
$A = 14(8)$
$A = 112$

The area of the patio is 112 m^2.

Check your progress 8, *page 31*

$A = \frac{1}{2}bh$

$A = \frac{1}{2}(18)(9)$

$A = 9(9)$
$A = 81$

81 in^2 of felt is needed.

Check your progress 9, *page 32*

$A = \frac{1}{2}h(b_1 + b_2)$

$A = \frac{1}{2} \cdot 9(12 + 20)$

$A = \frac{1}{2} \cdot 9(32)$

$A = \frac{9}{2} \cdot (32)$

$A = 144$

The area of the patio is 144 ft^2.

Check your progress 10, *page 32*

$r = \frac{1}{2}d = \frac{1}{2}(12) = 6$

$A = \pi r^2$
$A = \pi(6)^2$
$A = 36\pi$

The area of the circle is 36π km^2.

Check your progress 11, *page 33*

$r = \frac{1}{2}d = \frac{1}{2}(4) = 2$

$A = \pi r^2$
$A = \pi(2)^2$
$A = \pi(4)$
$A \approx 12.57$

Approximately 12.57 ft^2 of material is needed.

SECTION 1.4

Check your progress 1, *page 41*

$\frac{AC}{DF} = \frac{CH}{FG}$

$\frac{10}{15} = \frac{7}{FG}$

$10(FG) = (15)7$
$10(FG) = 105$
$FG = 10.5$

The height FG of triangle DEF is 10.5 m.

Check your progress 2, *page 43*

$\angle A$ and $\angle D$ are right angles. Therefore, $\angle A = \angle D$. $\angle AOB$ and $\angle COD$ are vertical angles. Therefore, $\angle AOB = \angle COD$. Because two angles of triangle AOB are equal in measure to two angles of triangle DOC, triangles AOB and DOC are similar triangles.

$$\frac{AO}{DO} = \frac{AB}{DC}$$
$$\frac{AO}{3} = \frac{10}{4}$$
$$4(AO) = 3(10)$$
$$4(AO) = 30$$
$$AO = 7.5$$
$$A = \frac{1}{2}bh$$
$$A = \frac{1}{2}(10)(7.5)$$
$$A = 5(7.5)$$
$$A = 37.5$$

The area of triangle AOB is 37.5 cm^2.

Check your progress 3, *page 45*

Because two sides and the included angle of one triangle are equal in measure to two sides and the included angle of the second triangle, the triangles are congruent by the SAS theorem.

Check your progress 4, *page 46*

$a^2 + b^2 = c^2$ • Use the Pythagorean theorem.

$2^2 + b^2 = 6^2$ • $a = 2, c = 6$

$4 + b^2 = 36$

$b^2 = 32$ • Solve for b^2. Subtract 4 from each side.

$\sqrt{b^2} = \sqrt{32}$ • Take the square root of each side of the equation.

$b \approx 5.66$ • Use a calculator to approximate $\sqrt{32}$.

The length of the other leg is approximately 5.66 m.

SECTION 1.5

Check your progress 1, *page 55*

$$V = LWH$$
$$V = 5(3.2)(4)$$
$$V = 64$$

The volume of the solid is 64 m^3.

Check your progress 2, *page 55*

$$V = \frac{1}{3}s^2h$$
$$V = \frac{1}{3}(15)^2(25)$$
$$V = \frac{1}{3}(225)(25)$$
$$V = 1875$$

The volume of the pyramid is 1875 m^3.

Check your progress 3, *page 56*

$$r = \frac{1}{2}d = \frac{1}{2}(16) = 8$$
$$V = \pi r^2 h$$
$$V = \pi(8)^2(30)$$
$$V = \pi(64)(30)$$
$$V = 1920\pi$$

$$\frac{1}{4}(1920\pi) = 480\pi$$
$$\approx 1507.96$$

Approximately 1507.96 ft^3 are not being used for storage.

Check your progress 4, *page 58*

$$r = \frac{1}{2}d = \frac{1}{2}(6) = 3$$

$$S = 2\pi r^2 + 2\pi rh$$
$$S = 2\pi(3)^2 + 2\pi(3)(8)$$
$$S = 2\pi(9) + 2\pi(3)(8)$$
$$S = 18\pi + 48\pi$$
$$S = 66\pi$$
$$S \approx 207.35$$

The surface area of the cylinder is approximately 207.35 ft^2.

SECTION 1.6

Check your progress 1, *page 65*

Use the Pythagorean theorem to find the length of the hypotenuse.

$$a^2 + b^2 = c^2$$
$$3^2 + 4^2 = c^2$$
$$9 + 16 = c^2$$
$$25 = c^2$$
$$\sqrt{25} = \sqrt{c^2}$$
$$5 = c$$

$$\sin\theta = \frac{\text{opp}}{\text{hyp}} = \frac{3}{5},$$
$$\cos\theta = \frac{\text{adj}}{\text{hyp}} = \frac{4}{5},$$
$$\tan\theta = \frac{\text{opp}}{\text{adj}} = \frac{3}{4}$$

Check your progress 2, *page 67*

We are given the measure of $\angle B$ and the hypotenuse. We want to find the length of side a. The cosine function involves the side adjacent and the hypotenuse.

$$\cos B = \frac{\text{adj}}{\text{hyp}}$$
$$\cos 48° = \frac{a}{12}$$
$$12(\cos 48°) = a$$
$$8.0 \approx a$$

The length of side a is approximately 8.0 ft.

Check your progress 3, *page 67*

$\tan^{-1}(0.3165) \approx 17.6°$

Check your progress 4, *page 68*

$$\theta \approx \tan^{-1}(0.5681)$$
$$\theta \approx 29.6°$$

Check your progress 5, *page 68*

We want to find the measure of $\angle A$, and we are given the length of the side opposite $\angle A$ and the hypotenuse. The sine function involves the side opposite an angle and the hypotenuse.

$$\sin A = \frac{\text{opp}}{\text{hyp}}$$

$$\sin A = \frac{7}{11}$$

$$A = \sin^{-1}\frac{7}{11}$$

$$A \approx 39.5°$$

The measure of $\angle A$ is approximately 39.5°.

Check your progress 6, *page 69*

Let d be the distance from the base of the lighthouse to the boat.

$$\tan 25° = \frac{20}{d}$$

$$d(\tan 25°) = 20$$

$$d = \frac{20}{\tan 25°}$$

$$d \approx 42.9$$

The boat is approximately 42.9 m from the base of the lighthouse.

SECTION 1.7

Check your progress 1, *page 76*

$$S = (m\angle A + m\angle B + m\angle C - 180°)\left(\frac{\pi}{180°}\right)r^2$$

$$= (200° + 90° + 90° - 180°)\left(\frac{\pi}{180°}\right)(6)^2$$

$$= (200°)\left(\frac{\pi}{180°}\right)(36)$$

$= 40\pi$ in^2 • Exact area

≈ 125.66 in^2 • Approximate area

Check your progress 2, *page 77*

In Example 2, we observed that only Riemannian geometry has the property that there exist no lines parallel to a given line. Thus, in this Check Your Progress, the type of geometry must be Riemannian.

Check your progress 3, *page 80*

a. $d_E(P, Q) = \sqrt{(x_2 - x_1)^2 + (y_2 - y_1)^2}$

$= \sqrt{[3 - (-1)]^2 + [2 - 4]^2}$

$= \sqrt{4^2 + (-2)^2}$

$= \sqrt{20} \approx 4.5$ blocks

$d_C(P, Q) = |x_2 - x_1| + |y_2 - y_1|$

$= |3 - (-1)| + |2 - 4|$

$= |4| + |-2|$

$= 4 + 2$

$= 6$ blocks

b. $d_E(P, Q) = \sqrt{(x_2 - x_1)^2 + (y_2 - y_1)^2}$

$= \sqrt{[(-1) - 3]^2 + [5 - (-4)]^2}$

$= \sqrt{(-4)^2 + 9^2}$

$= \sqrt{97} \approx 9.8$ blocks

$d_C(P, Q) = |x_2 - x_1| + |y_2 - y_1|$

$= |(-1) - 3| + |5 - (-4)|$

$= |-4| + 9$

$= 4 + 9$

$= 13$ blocks

SECTION 1.8

Check your progress 1, *page 87*

Replace each line segment with a scaled version of the generator. As you move from left to right, your first zig should be to the left.

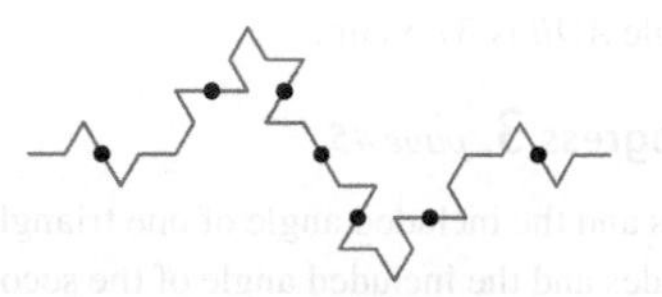

Stage 2 of the zig-zag curve

Check your progress 2, *page 87*

Replace each square with a scaled version of the generator.

Stage 2 of the Sierpinski carpet

Check your progress 3, *page 89*

a. Any portion of the box curve replicates the entire fractal, so the box curve is a strictly self-similar fractal.

b. Any portion of the Sierpinski gasket replicates the entire fractal, so the Sierpinski gasket is a strictly self-similar fractal.

Check your progress 4, *page 90*

a. The generator of the Koch curve consists of four line segments, and the initiator consists of only one line segment. Thus the replacement ratio of the Koch curve is 4:1, or 4. The initiator of the Koch curve is a line segment that is 3 times as long as the replica line segments in the generator. Thus the scaling ratio of the Koch curve is 3:1, or 3.

b. The generator of the zig-zag curve consists of six line segments, and the initiator consists of only one line segment. Thus the replacement ratio of the zig-zag curve is 6:1, or 6. The initiator of the zig-zag curve is a line segment that is 4 times as long as the replica line segments in the generator. Thus the scaling ratio of the zig-zag curve is 4:1, or 4.

Check your progress 5, *page 90*

a. In Example 4, we determined that the replacement ratio of the box curve is 5 and the scaling ratio of the box curve is 3. Thus the similarity dimension of the box curve is $D = \frac{\log 5}{\log 3} \approx 1.465$.

b. The replacement ratio of the Sierpinski carpet is 8, and the scaling ratio of the Sierpinski carpet is 3. Thus the similarity dimension of the Sierpinski carpet is $D = \frac{\log 8}{\log 3} \approx 1.893$.

CHAPTER 2

SECTION 2.1

Check your progress 1, *page 106*

a.
$$\begin{aligned} c - 6 &= -13 \\ c - 6 + 6 &= -13 + 6 \\ c &= -7 \end{aligned}$$

The solution is -7.

b.
$$\begin{aligned} 4 &= -8z \\ \frac{4}{-8} &= \frac{-8z}{-8} \\ -\frac{1}{2} &= z \end{aligned}$$

The solution is $-\frac{1}{2}$.

c.
$$\begin{aligned} 22 + m &= -9 \\ 22 - 22 + m &= -9 - 22 \\ m &= -31 \end{aligned}$$

The solution is -31.

d.
$$\begin{aligned} 5x &= 0 \\ \frac{5x}{5} &= \frac{0}{5} \\ x &= 0 \end{aligned}$$

The solution is 0.

Check your progress 2, *page 108*

a.
$$\begin{aligned} 4x + 3 &= 7x + 9 \\ 4x - 7x + 3 &= 7x - 7x + 9 \\ -3x + 3 &= 9 \\ -3x + 3 - 3 &= 9 - 3 \\ -3x &= 6 \\ \frac{-3x}{-3} &= \frac{6}{-3} \\ x &= -2 \end{aligned}$$

The solution is -2.

b.
$$\begin{aligned} 7 - (5x - 8) &= 4x + 3 \\ 7 - 5x + 8 &= 4x + 3 \\ 15 - 5x &= 4x + 3 \\ 15 - 5x - 4x &= 4x - 4x + 3 \\ 15 - 9x &= 3 \\ 15 - 15 - 9x &= 3 - 15 \\ -9x &= -12 \\ \frac{-9x}{-9} &= \frac{-12}{-9} \\ x &= \frac{4}{3} \end{aligned}$$

The solution is $\frac{4}{3}$.

c.
$$\begin{aligned} \frac{3x - 1}{4} + \frac{1}{3} &= \frac{7}{3} \\ 12\left(\frac{3x - 1}{4} + \frac{1}{3}\right) &= 12\left(\frac{7}{3}\right) \\ 12 \cdot \frac{3x - 1}{4} + 12 \cdot \frac{1}{3} &= 12 \cdot \frac{7}{3} \\ 9x - 3 + 4 &= 28 \\ 9x + 1 &= 28 \\ 9x + 1 - 1 &= 28 - 1 \\ 9x &= 27 \\ \frac{9x}{9} &= \frac{27}{9} \\ x &= 3 \end{aligned}$$

The solution is 3.

Check your progress 3, *page 109*

a.
$$\begin{aligned} P &= 0.05Y - 96 \\ P &= 0.05(2015) - 96 \\ P &= 100.75 - 96 \\ P &= 4.75 \end{aligned}$$

The amount of garbage was about 4.75 lb/day.

b.
$$\begin{aligned} P &= 0.05Y - 96 \\ 5.5 &= 0.05Y - 96 \\ 5.5 + 96 &= 0.05Y - 96 + 96 \\ 101.5 &= 0.05Y \\ \frac{101.5}{0.05} &= \frac{0.05Y}{0.05} \\ 2030 &= Y \end{aligned}$$

The year will be 2030.

Check your progress 4, *page 110*

\$340 for the first four lines + \$76 for each additional line	=	**\$948**

Let L = the number of lines in the ad.

$$\begin{aligned} 340 + 76(L - 4) &= 948 \\ 340 + 76L - 304 &= 948 \\ 36 + 76L &= 948 \\ 36 - 36 + 76L &= 948 - 36 \\ 76L &= 912 \\ \frac{76L}{76} &= \frac{912}{76} \\ L &= 12 \end{aligned}$$

The ad can contain 12 lines.

Check your progress 5, *page 111*

Let n = the number of years after 2014.

The 2014 population of Cleveland minus an annual decrease times *n*	=	**The 2014 population of Tampa plus the annual increase times *n***

$$\begin{aligned} 389{,}500 - 1600n &= 358{,}700 + 5700n \\ 389{,}500 - 1600n + 1600n &= 358{,}700 + 5700n + 1600n \\ 389{,}500 &= 358{,}700 + 7300n \\ 389{,}500 - 358{,}700 &= 358{,}700 - 358{,}700 + 7300n \\ 30{,}800 &= 7300n \\ \frac{30{,}800}{7300} &= \frac{7300n}{7300} \\ 4 &\approx n \end{aligned}$$

$2014 + 4 = 2018$

The populations would be the same in 2018.

Check your progress 6, *page 112*

a.

$$s = \frac{A + L}{2}$$
$$2 \cdot s = 2 \cdot \frac{A + L}{2}$$
$$2s = A + L$$
$$2s - A = A - A + L$$
$$2s - A = L$$

b.

$$L = a(1 + ct)$$
$$\frac{L}{a} = \frac{a(1 + ct)}{a}$$
$$\frac{L}{a} = 1 + ct$$
$$\frac{L}{a} - 1 = 1 - 1 + ct$$
$$\frac{L}{a} - 1 = ct$$
$$\frac{\frac{L}{a} - 1}{t} = \frac{ct}{t}$$
$$\frac{\frac{L}{a} - 1}{t} = c$$
$$\left(\frac{L}{a} - 1\right)\left(\frac{1}{t}\right) = c$$
$$\frac{L}{at} - \frac{1}{t} = c$$

SECTION 2.2

Check your progress 1, *page 118*

$6.75 \div 1.5 = 4.5$

$\frac{\$6.75}{1.5 \text{ lb}} = \frac{\$4.50}{1 \text{ lb}} = \$4.50/\text{pound}$

The hamburger costs $4.50/lb.

Check your progress 2, *page 118*

Find the difference in the hourly wage.

$\$10.00 - \$7.25 = \$2.75$

Multiply the difference in the hourly wage by 35.

$\$2.75(35) = \$96.25$

An employee's pay for working 35 h and earning the California minimum wage is $96.25 greater.

Check your progress 3, *page 119*

$\frac{\$6.29}{32 \text{ oz}} \approx \frac{\$0.197}{1 \text{ oz}}$ $\frac{\$8.29}{48 \text{ oz}} \approx \frac{\$0.173}{1 \text{ oz}}$

$\$0.197 > \$0.173$

The more economical purchase is 48 oz of detergent for $8.29.

Check your progress 4, *page 120*

a. $20{,}000(1.4574) = 29{,}148$

29,148 Canadian dollars would be needed to pay for an order costing $20,000.

b. $25{,}000(0.9156) = 22{,}890$

22,890 euros would be exchanged for $25,000.

Check your progress 5, *page 121*

$\frac{24 \text{ h}}{1 \text{ day}} \cdot 7 \text{ days} = (24 \text{ h})(7) = 168 \text{ h}$

$\frac{72 \text{ h}}{1 \text{ wk}} = \frac{72 \text{ h}}{168 \text{ h}} = \frac{72}{168} \approx \frac{3}{7}$

The ratio is $\frac{3}{7}$.

Check your progress 6, *page 122*

$8849 + 9824 = 18{,}673$

$\frac{18{,}673}{1364} \approx \frac{13.69}{1} \approx \frac{14}{1}$

The ratio is 14 to 1.

Check your progress 7, *page 123*

$$\frac{42}{x} = \frac{5}{8}$$
$$42 \cdot 8 = x \cdot 5$$
$$336 = 5x$$
$$\frac{336}{5} = \frac{5x}{5}$$
$$67.2 = x$$

The solution is 67.2.

Check your progress 8, *page 124*

$$\frac{15 \text{ km}}{2 \text{ cm}} = \frac{x \text{ km}}{7 \text{ cm}}$$
$$\frac{15}{2} = \frac{x}{7}$$
$$15 \cdot 7 = 2 \cdot x$$
$$105 = 2x$$
$$\frac{105}{2} = \frac{2x}{2}$$
$$52.5 = x$$

The distance between the two cities is 52.5 km.

Check your progress 9, *page 125*

$$\frac{7}{5} = \frac{\$84{,}000}{x \text{ dollars}}$$
$$\frac{7}{5} = \frac{84{,}000}{x}$$
$$7 \cdot x = 5 \cdot 84{,}000$$
$$7x = 420{,}000$$
$$\frac{7x}{7} = \frac{420{,}000}{7}$$
$$x = 60{,}000$$

The other partner receives $60,000.

Check your progress 10, *page 125*

$$\frac{11.0 \text{ deaths}}{1{,}000{,}000 \text{ people}} = \frac{d \text{ deaths}}{318{,}000{,}000 \text{ people}}$$
$$11.0(318{,}000{,}000) = 1{,}000{,}000 \cdot d$$
$$3{,}498{,}000{,}000 = 1{,}000{,}000d$$
$$\frac{3{,}498{,}000{,}000}{1{,}000{,}000} = \frac{1{,}000{,}000d}{1{,}000{,}000}$$
$$3498 = d$$

Approximately 3500 people died from fire in the United States in 2013.

SECTION 2.3

Check your progress 1, *page 131*

a. $74\% = 0.74$

b. $152\% = 1.52$

c. $8.3\% = 0.083$

d. $0.6\% = 0.006$

Check your progress 2, *page 131*

a. $0.3 = 30\%$

b. $1.65 = 165\%$

c. $0.072 = 7.2\%$

d. $0.004 = 0.4\%$

Check your progress 3, *page 132*

a. $8\% = 8\left(\frac{1}{100}\right) = \frac{8}{100} = \frac{2}{25}$

b. $180\% = 180\left(\frac{1}{100}\right) = \frac{180}{100} = 1\frac{80}{100} = 1\frac{4}{5}$

c. $2.5\% = 2.5\left(\frac{1}{100}\right) = \frac{2.5}{100} = \frac{25}{1000} = \frac{1}{40}$

d. $66\frac{2}{3}\% = \frac{200}{3}\% = \frac{200}{3}\left(\frac{1}{100}\right) = \frac{2}{3}$

Check your progress 4, *page 132*

a. $\frac{1}{4} = 0.25 = 25\%$

b. $\frac{3}{8} = 0.375 = 37.5\%$

c. $\frac{5}{6} = 0.83\overline{3} = 83.\overline{3}\%$

d. $1\frac{2}{3} = 1.66\overline{6} = 166.\overline{6}\%$

Check your progress 5, *page 134*

$$\frac{\text{percent}}{100} = \frac{\text{amount}}{\text{base}}$$
$$\frac{70}{100} = \frac{12{,}950}{B}$$
$$70 \cdot B = 100(12{,}950)$$
$$70B = 1{,}295{,}000$$
$$\frac{70B}{70} = \frac{1{,}295{,}000}{70}$$
$$B = 18{,}500$$

The Corolla cost $18,500 when it was new.

Check your progress 6, *page 135*

$$\frac{\text{percent}}{100} = \frac{\text{amount}}{\text{base}}$$
$$\frac{p}{100} = \frac{18{,}705{,}000}{43{,}500{,}000}$$
$$p \cdot 43{,}500{,}000 = 100(18{,}705{,}000)$$
$$43{,}500{,}000p = 1{,}870{,}500{,}000$$
$$\frac{43{,}500{,}000p}{43{,}500{,}000} = \frac{1{,}870{,}500{,}000}{43{,}500{,}000}$$
$$p = 43$$

43% of the adult caretakers felt that they did not have a choice in this role.

Check your progress 7, *page 135*

$$\frac{\text{percent}}{100} = \frac{\text{amount}}{\text{base}}$$
$$\frac{3.5}{100} = \frac{A}{32{,}500}$$
$$3.5(32{,}500) = 100(A)$$
$$113{,}750 = 100A$$
$$\frac{113{,}750}{100} = \frac{100A}{100}$$
$$1137.5 = A$$

The customer would receive a rebate of $1137.50.

Check your progress 8, *page 136*

$$PB = A$$
$$0.05(46{,}875) = A$$
$$2343.75 = A$$

The teacher contributes $2343.75.

Check your progress 9, *page 136*

$$PB = A$$
$$0.03B = 14{,}370$$
$$\frac{0.03B}{0.03} = \frac{14{,}370}{0.03}$$
$$B = 479{,}000$$

The selling price of the home was $479,000.

Check your progress 10, *page 137*

$$PB = A$$
$$P \cdot 90 = 63$$
$$\frac{P \cdot 90}{90} = \frac{63}{90}$$
$$P = 0.7$$
$$P = 70\%$$

You answered 70% of the questions correctly.

Check your progress 11, *page 138*

$$PB = A$$
$$0.80(54{,}241) = A$$
$$43{,}392.80 = A$$
$$54{,}241 - 43{,}392.80 = 10{,}848.20$$

The difference between the cost of the remodeling and the increase in value of your home is $10,848.20.

Check your progress 12, *page 139*

$$18.63 - 4.92 = 13.71$$
$$PB = A$$
$$P \cdot 4.92 = 13.71$$
$$\frac{P \cdot 4.92}{4.92} = \frac{13.71}{4.92}$$
$$P \approx 2.787$$

The percent increase in the federal debt from 1995 to 2015 was 278.7%.

Check your progress 13, *page 141*

$680 - 485 = 195$

$$PB = A$$
$$P \cdot 680 = 195$$
$$\frac{P \cdot 680}{680} = \frac{195}{680}$$
$$P \approx 0.287$$

The federal deficit decreased by 28.7% from 2013 to 2014.

SECTION 2.4

Check your progress 1, *page 146*

$$2s^2 = 6 - 4s$$
$$2s^2 + 4s = 6 - 4s + 4s$$
$$2s^2 + 4s = 6$$
$$2s^2 + 4s - 6 = 6 - 6$$
$$2s^2 + 4s - 6 = 0$$

Check your progress 2, *page 147*

$(n + 5)(2n - 3) = 0$

$n + 5 = 0 \qquad 2n - 3 = 0$

$n = -5 \qquad 2n = 3$

$n = \frac{3}{2}$

Check:

$(n + 5)(2n - 3) = 0$	
$(-5 + 5)[2(-5) - 3]$	0
$0(-13)$	0
$0 = 0$	

$(n + 5)(2n - 3) = 0$	
$\left(\frac{3}{2} + 5\right)\left(2 \cdot \frac{3}{2} - 3\right)$	0
$\frac{13}{2}(3 - 3)$	0
$0 = 0$	

The solutions are -5 and $\frac{3}{2}$.

Check your progress 3, *page 148*

$$2x^2 = x + 1$$
$$2x^2 - x = x - x + 1$$
$$2x^2 - x = 1$$
$$2x^2 - x - 1 = 1 - 1$$
$$2x^2 - x - 1 = 0$$
$$(2x + 1)(x - 1) = 0$$

$2x + 1 = 0 \qquad x - 1 = 0$

$2x = -1 \qquad x = 1$

$x = -\frac{1}{2}$

Check:

$2x^2 = x + 1$	
$2\left(-\frac{1}{2}\right)^2$	$-\frac{1}{2} + 1$
$2\left(\frac{1}{4}\right)$	$\frac{1}{2}$
$\frac{1}{2} = \frac{1}{2}$	

$2x^2 = x + 1$	
$2(1)^2$	$1 + 1$
$2(1)$	2
$2 = 2$	

The solutions are $-\frac{1}{2}$ and 1.

Check your progress 4, *page 149*

$$2x^2 = 8x - 5$$
$$2x^2 - 8x + 5 = 0$$

$a = 2, b = -8, c = 5$

$$x = \frac{-b \pm \sqrt{b^2 - 4ac}}{2a}$$
$$x = \frac{-(-8) \pm \sqrt{(-8)^2 - 4(2)(5)}}{2(2)} = \frac{8 \pm \sqrt{64 - 40}}{4}$$
$$= \frac{8 \pm \sqrt{24}}{4} = \frac{8 \pm 2\sqrt{6}}{4} = \frac{2(4 \pm \sqrt{6})}{2(2)} = \frac{4 \pm \sqrt{6}}{2}$$

The exact solutions are $\frac{4 + \sqrt{6}}{2}$ and $\frac{4 - \sqrt{6}}{2}$.

$$\frac{4 + \sqrt{6}}{2} \approx 3.225 \qquad \frac{4 - \sqrt{6}}{2} \approx 0.775$$

To the nearest thousandth, the solutions are 3.225 and 0.775.

Check your progress 5, *page 150*

$$z^2 = -6 - 2z$$
$$z^2 + 2z + 6 = 0$$

$a = 1, b = 2, c = 6$

$$z = \frac{-b \pm \sqrt{b^2 - 4ac}}{2a}$$
$$z = \frac{-(2) \pm \sqrt{(2)^2 - 4(1)(6)}}{2(1)}$$
$$= \frac{-2 \pm \sqrt{4 - 24}}{2} = \frac{-2 \pm \sqrt{-20}}{2}$$

$\sqrt{-20}$ is not a real number.

The equation has no real number solutions.

Check your progress 6, *page 151*

$$h = 64t - 16t^2$$
$$0 = 64t - 16t^2$$
$$16t^2 - 64t = 0$$
$$16t(t - 4) = 0$$

$16t = 0 \qquad t - 4 = 0$

$t = 0 \qquad t = 4$

The object will be on the ground at 0 s and after 4 s.

Check your progress 7, *page 151*

$$h = -16t^2 + 19t + 3.5$$
$$10 = -16t^2 + 19t + 3.5$$
$$16t^2 - 19t + 3.5 = 0$$

$a = 16, b = -19, c = 3.5$

$$t = \frac{-b \pm \sqrt{b^2 - 4ac}}{2a}$$
$$t = \frac{-(-19) \pm \sqrt{(-19)^2 - 4(16)(3.5)}}{2(16)} = \frac{19 \pm \sqrt{137}}{32}$$
$$t = \frac{19 + \sqrt{137}}{32} \approx 0.96 \qquad t = \frac{19 - \sqrt{137}}{32} \approx 0.23$$

The solution $t \approx 0.23$ s is not reasonable because we know from experience that the ball cannot reach the basket in 0.23 s. The ball hits the basket 0.96 s after the ball is released.

CHAPTER 3

SECTION 3.1

Check your progress 1, *page 164*

$P = 500,\ r = 4\% = 0.04,\ t = 1$

$I = Prt$
$I = 500(0.04)(1)$
$I = 20$

The simple interest earned is \$20.

Check your progress 2, *page 165*

$P = 1500,\ r = 5.25\% = 0.0525$

$t = \frac{4 \text{ months}}{1 \text{ year}} = \frac{4 \text{ months}}{12 \text{ months}} = \frac{4}{12}$

$I = Prt$

$I = 1500(0.0525)\left(\frac{4}{12}\right)$

$I = 26.25$

The simple interest due is \$26.25.

Check your progress 3, *page 165*

$P = 700,\ r = 1.25\% = 0.0125,\ t = 5$

$I = Prt$
$I = 700(0.0125)(5)$
$I = 43.75$

The simple interest due is \$43.75.

Check your progress 4, *page 166*

$P = 7000,\ r = 5.25\% = 0.0525$

$t = \frac{\text{number of days}}{360} = \frac{120}{360}$

$I = Prt$

$I = 7000(0.0525)\left(\frac{120}{360}\right)$

$I = 122.5$

The simple interest due is \$122.50.

Check your progress 5, *page 166*

$I = Prt$

$462 = 12{,}000(r)\left(\frac{6}{12}\right)$

$462 = 6000r$
$0.077 = r$
$r = 7.7\%$

The simple interest rate on the loan is 7.7%.

Check your progress 6, *page 168*

Find the interest.

$P = 4000,\ r = 8.75\% = 0.0875,\ t = \frac{9}{12}$

$I = Prt$

$I = 4000(0.0875)\left(\frac{9}{12}\right)$

$I = 262.50$

Find the maturity value.
$A = P + I$
$A = 4000 + 262.50$
$A = 4262.50$

The maturity value of the loan is \$4262.50.

Check your progress 7, *page 169*

$P = 6700,\ r = 8.9\% = 0.089,\ t = 1$

$A = P(1 + rt)$
$A = 6700[1 + 0.089(1)]$
$A = 6700(1 + 0.089)$
$A = 6700(1.089)$
$A = 7296.30$

The maturity value of the loan is \$7296.30.

Check your progress 8, *page 169*

$P = 680,\ r = 6.4\% = 0.064,\ t = 1$

$A = P(1 + rt)$
$A = 680[1 + 0.064(1)]$
$A = 680(1 + 0.064)$
$A = 680(1.064)$
$A = 723.52$

After 1 year, \$723.52 is in the account.

Check your progress 9, *page 170*

$I = A - P$
$I = 9240 - 9000$
$I = 240$

$I = Prt$

$240 = 9000(r)\left(\frac{4}{12}\right)$

$240 = 3000r$
$0.08 = r$
$r = 8\%$

The simple interest rate on the loan is 8%.

SECTION 3.2

Check your progress 1, *page 174*

$A = P(1 + rt)$

$A = 2000\left[1 + 0.04\left(\frac{1}{12}\right)\right]$

$A \approx 2006.67$

$A = P(1 + rt)$

$A \approx 2006.67\left[1 + 0.04\left(\frac{1}{12}\right)\right]$

$A \approx 2013.36$

$A = P(1 + rt)$

$A = 2013.36\left[1 + 0.04\left(\frac{1}{12}\right)\right]$

$A \approx 2020.07$

$A = P(1 + rt)$

$A = 2020.07\left[1 + 0.04\left(\frac{1}{12}\right)\right]$

$A \approx 2026.80$

$A = P(1 + rt)$

$A = 2026.80\left[1 + 0.04\left(\frac{1}{12}\right)\right]$

$A \approx 2033.56$

$A = P(1 + rt)$

$A = 2033.56\left[1 + 0.04\left(\frac{1}{12}\right)\right]$

$A \approx 2040.34$

The total amount in the account at the end of 6 months is \$2040.34.

Check your progress 2, *page 176*

Use the compound amount formula.

$P = 4000, r = 6\% = 0.06, n = 12, t = 2$

$A = P\left(1 + \frac{r}{n}\right)^{nt}$

$A = 4000\left(1 + \frac{0.06}{12}\right)^{12 \cdot 2}$

$A = 4000(1 + 0.005)^{24}$

$A = 4000(1.005)^{24}$

$A \approx 4000(1.127160)$

$A \approx 4508.64$

The compound amount after 2 years is approximately \$4508.64.

Check your progress 3, *page 177*

Use the compound amount formula.

$P = 2500, r = 9\% = 0.09, n = 360, t = 4$

$A = 2500\left(1 + \frac{0.09}{360}\right)^{360 \cdot 4}$

$A = 2500(1 + 0.00025)^{1440}$

$A = 2500(1.00025)^{1440}$

$A \approx 2500(1.4332649)$

$A \approx 3583.16$

The future value after 4 years is approximately \$3583.16.

Check your progress 4, *page 177*

Calculate the compound amount. Use the compound amount formula.

$P = 8000, r = 9\% = 0.09, n = 12, t = 6$

$A = P\left(1 + \frac{r}{n}\right)^{nt}$

$A = 8000\left(1 + \frac{0.09}{12}\right)^{12 \cdot 6}$

$A = 8000(1 + 0.0075)^{72}$

$A = 8000(1.0075)^{72}$

$A \approx 8000(1.7125527)$

$A \approx 13{,}700.42$

$I = A - P$

$I = 13{,}700.42 - 8000$

$I = 5700.42$

The amount of interest earned is approximately \$5700.42.

Check your progress 5, *page 178*

The following solution utilizes the finance feature of a TI-83/84 calculator.

Press APPS ENTER.

Press ENTER to select 1: TVM Solver.

N is the number of compounding periods, or $n \cdot t$ in the compound amount formula.

After N =, enter 2×5.
After I% =, enter 6.
After PV =, enter -3500.
After PMT =, enter 0. Press ENTER twice.
After P/Y =, enter 2.
After C/Y =, enter 2.
Use the up arrow key to place the cursor at FV =.

Press ALPHA [Solve].

The solution is displayed to the right of FV =.

The compound amount is \$4703.71.

Check your progress 6, *page 179*

Use the present value formula.

$A = 20{,}000, r = 9\% = 0.09, n = 2, t = 5$

$P = \frac{A}{\left(1 + \frac{r}{n}\right)^{nt}}$

$P = \frac{20{,}000}{\left(1 + \frac{0.09}{2}\right)^{2 \cdot 5}}$

$P = \frac{20{,}000}{(1 + 0.045)^{10}}$

$P \approx \frac{20{,}000}{1.552969}$

$P \approx 12{,}878.55$

\$12,878.55 should be invested in the account.

Check your progress 7, *page 180*

The following solution utilizes the finance feature of a TI-83/84 calculator.

Press APPS ENTER.

Press ENTER to select 1: TVM Solver.

After N =, enter 360 × 15.
After I% =, enter 6. Press ENTER twice.
After PMT =, enter 0.
After FV =, enter 25000.
After P/Y =, enter 360.
After C/Y =, enter 360.
Use the up arrow key to place the cursor at PV =.

Press ALPHA [Solve].

The solution is displayed to the right of PV =.

$10,165.00 should be invested in the account.

Check your progress 8, *page 181*

Use the compound amount formula.

$P = 28{,}000, r = 5\% = 0.05, t = 17$

The inflation rate is an annual rate, so $n = 1$.

$$A = P\left(1 + \frac{r}{n}\right)^{nt}$$
$$A = 28{,}000\left(1 + \frac{0.05}{1}\right)^{1 \cdot 17}$$
$$A = 28{,}000(1 + 0.05)^{17}$$
$$A = 28{,}000(1.05)^{17}$$
$$A \approx 28{,}000(2.2920183)$$
$$A \approx 64{,}176.51$$

The average new car sticker price in 2030 will be approximately $64,176.51.

Check your progress 9, *page 182*

Use the present value formula.

$A = 500{,}000, r = 7\% = 0.07, t = 40$

The inflation rate is an annual rate, so $n = 1$.

$$P = \frac{A}{\left(1 + \frac{r}{n}\right)^{nt}}$$
$$P = \frac{500{,}000}{\left(1 + \frac{0.07}{1}\right)^{1 \cdot 40}}$$
$$P = \frac{500{,}000}{(1 + 0.07)^{40}}$$
$$P \approx \frac{500{,}000}{14.9744578}$$
$$P \approx 33{,}390.19$$

In 2055, the purchasing power of $500,000 will be approximately $33,390.19.

Check your progress 10, *page 183*

$P = 100, r = 4\% = 0.04, n = 4, t = 1$

$$A = P\left(1 + \frac{r}{n}\right)^{nt}$$
$$A = 100\left(1 + \frac{0.04}{4}\right)^{4 \cdot 1}$$
$$A = 100(1 + 0.01)^4$$
$$A = 100(1.01)^4$$
$$A \approx 100(1.040604)$$
$$A \approx 104.06$$

$$I = A - P$$
$$I = 104.06 - 100$$
$$I = 4.06$$

The effective interest rate is 4.06%.

Check your progress 11, *page 184*

$$\left(1 + \frac{r}{n}\right)^{nt} = \left(1 + \frac{0.05}{4}\right)^{4 \cdot 1} \approx 1.050945 \qquad \left(1 + \frac{r}{n}\right)^{nt} = \left(1 + \frac{0.0525}{2}\right)^{2 \cdot 1} \approx 1.053189$$

An investment that earns 5.25% compounded semiannually has a higher annual yield than an investment that earns 5% compounded quarterly.

SECTION 3.3

Check your progress 1, *page 192*

Date	Payments or purchases	Balance each day	Number of days until balance changes	Unpaid balance times number of days
July 1–6		$1024	6	$6144
July 7–14	$315	$1339	8	$10,712
July 15–21	−$400	$939	7	$6573
July 22–31	$410	$1349	10	$13,490
Total				$36,919

$$\text{Average daily balance} = \frac{\text{sum of the total amounts owed each day of the month}}{\text{number of days in the billing period}}$$
$$= \frac{36{,}919}{31} \approx \$1190.94$$

$$I = Prt$$
$$I = 1190.94(0.012)(1)$$
$$I \approx 14.29$$

The finance charge on the August 1 bill is $14.29.

Check your progress 2, *page 195*

a. Down payment = Percent down × purchase price

$= 0.20 \times 750 = 150$

Amount financed = purchase price − down payment

$= 750 - 150 = 600$

Interest owed = finance rate × amount financed

$= 0.08 \times 600 = 48$

The finance charge is $48.

b. $\text{APR} \approx \dfrac{2nr}{n+1}$

$\approx \dfrac{2(12)(0.08)}{12+1} \approx \dfrac{1.92}{13} \approx 0.148$

The annual percentage rate is approximately 14.8%.

Check your progress 3, *page 196*

Sales tax amount = sales tax rate × purchase price

$= 0.0425 \times 1499 \approx 63.71$

Amount financed = purchase price + sales tax amount

$= 1499 + 63.71 = 1562.71$

$$\frac{r}{n} = \frac{0.084}{12} = 0.007$$

$$nt = 12(3) = 36$$

$$PMT = A\left(\frac{\frac{r}{n}}{1-\left(1+\frac{r}{n}\right)^{-nt}}\right)$$

$$PMT = 1562.71\left(\frac{0.007}{1-(1+0.007)^{-36}}\right)$$

$$PMT \approx 49.26$$

The monthly payment is $49.26.

Check your progress 4, *page 197*

a. Sales tax $= 0.0525(26{,}788) = 1406.37$

b. Loan amount

= purchase price + sales tax + license fee − down payment

$= 26{,}788 + 1406.37 + 145 - 2500$

$= 25{,}839.37$

c. $\dfrac{r}{n} = \dfrac{0.081}{12} = 0.00675$

$nt = 12(5) = 60$

$$PMT = A\left(\frac{\frac{r}{n}}{1-\left(1+\frac{r}{n}\right)^{-nt}}\right)$$

$$PMT = 25{,}839.37\left(\frac{0.00675}{1-(1+0.00675)^{-60}}\right)$$

$$PMT \approx 525.17$$

The monthly payment is $525.17.

Check your progress 5, *page 199*

Because Aaron has owned the car for 36 months of a 60-month (5-year) loan, he has 24 payments remaining. Thus $U = 24$, the number of unpaid or remaining payments.

$$\frac{r}{n} = \frac{0.084}{12} = 0.007$$

$$A = PMT\left(\frac{1-\left(1+\frac{r}{n}\right)^{-U}}{\frac{r}{n}}\right)$$

$$A = 592.57\left(\frac{1-(1+0.007)^{-24}}{0.007}\right)$$

$$A \approx 13{,}049.34$$

The loan payoff is $13,049.34.

Check your progress 6, *page 200*

Using the spreadsheet from Example 6, we have

	A	B
1	Present value	25000
2	Annual interest rate as a decimal	0.049
3	Number of years to repay loan	10
4	Monthly payment	-$263.94

His monthly payment is $263.94.

Check your progress 7, *page 200*

First, calculate the interest owed on the loan for the 2 years before payments begin.

$I = Prt$ • Simple interest rate formula

$= 25{,}000(0.049)(2)$ • $P = 25{,}000,\ r = 0.049,\ t = 2$

$= 2450$

Add this amount to the amount borrowed, $25,000, to determine the present value on which the loan payment will be calculated.

Present value $= 25{,}000 + 2450 = 27{,}450.$

Using the spreadsheet from Example 7, we have

	A	B
1	Present value	27450
2	Annual interest rate as a decimal	0.049
3	Number of years to repay loan	10
4	Monthly payment	-$289.81

Hudson's monthly payment is $289.81.

SECTION 3.4

Check your progress 1, *page 206*

($0.72 per share) × (550 shares) = $396

The shareholder receives $396 in dividends.

Check your progress 2, *page 207*

$I = Prt$

$0.82 = 51.25r(1)$ • Let I = annual dividend and P = the stock price. The time is 1 year.

$0.82 = 51.25r$

$0.016 = r$ • Divide each side of the equation by 51.25.

The dividend yield is 1.6%.

Check your progress 3, *page 209*

a. From Table 3.1, the selling price per share was \$31.49. The purchase price per share was \$19.37. The selling price per share is greater than the purchase price per share. You made a profit on the sale of the stock.

$$\begin{aligned}\text{Profit} &= \text{selling price} - \text{purchase price}\\ &= 300(\$31.49) - 300(\$19.37)\\ &= \$9447 - \$5811\\ &= \$3636\end{aligned}$$

The profit on the sale of the stock was \$3636.

b.
$$\begin{aligned}\text{Commission} &= 2.1\%(\text{selling price})\\ &= 0.021(\$9447)\\ &\approx \$198.387\end{aligned}$$

The broker's commission was \$198.39.

Check your progress 4, *page 209*

Use the simple interest formula to find the annual interest payments. Substitute the following values into the formula: $P = 15{,}000$, $r = 3.5\% = 0.035$, and $t = 1$.

$I = Prt$

$I = 15{,}000(0.035)(1)$

$I = 525$

Multiply the annual interest payment by the term of the bond.

$525(4) = 2100$

The total of the interest payments paid to the bondholder is \$2100.

Check your progress 5, *page 211*

a.
$$\begin{aligned}A - L &= (750 \text{ million} + 0.75 \text{ million} + 1.5 \text{ million}) - 1.5 \text{ million}\\ &= 750.75 \text{ million}\end{aligned}$$

$N = 20$ million

$$\text{NAV} = \frac{A - L}{N} = \frac{750.75 \text{ million}}{20 \text{ million}} = 37.5375$$

The NAV of the fund is \$37.5375.

b. $\dfrac{10{,}000}{37.5375} \approx 266$ • Divide the amount invested by the cost per share of the fund. Round down to the nearest whole number.

You are purchasing 266 shares of the mutual fund.

SECTION 3.5

Check your progress 1, *page 215*

$$\begin{aligned}\text{Down payment} &= 25\% \text{ of } 410{,}000 = 0.25(410{,}000)\\ &= 102{,}500\end{aligned}$$

$$\begin{aligned}\text{Mortgage} &= \text{selling price} - \text{down payment}\\ &= 410{,}000 - 102{,}500\\ &= 307{,}500\end{aligned}$$

$$\begin{aligned}\text{Points} &= 1.75\% \text{ of } 307{,}500 = 0.0175(307{,}500)\\ &= 5381.25\end{aligned}$$

$\text{Total} = 102{,}500 + 375 + 5381.25 = 108{,}256.25$

The total of the down payment and the closing costs is \$108,256.25.

Check your progress 2, *page 217*

a. $\dfrac{r}{n} = \dfrac{0.07}{12} \approx 0.00583333$

$nt = 12(25) = 300$

$$PMT = A\left(\frac{\frac{r}{n}}{1 - \left(1 + \frac{r}{n}\right)^{-nt}}\right)$$

$$PMT \approx 223{,}000\left(\frac{0.00583333}{1 - (1 + 0.00583333)^{-300}}\right)$$

$PMT \approx 1576.12$

The monthly payment is \$1576.12.

b. $\text{Total} = 1576.12(300) = 472{,}836$

The total of the payments over the life of the loan is \$472,836.

c. $\text{Interest} = 472{,}836 - 223{,}000 = 249{,}836$

The amount of interest paid over the life of the loan is \$249,836.

Check your progress 3, *page 220*

$\text{Down payment} = 0.25(295{,}000) = 73{,}750$

$\text{Mortgage} = 295{,}000 - 73{,}750 = 221{,}250$

$\dfrac{r}{n} = \dfrac{0.0675}{12} = 0.005625$

$nt = 12(30) = 360$

$$PMT = A\left(\frac{\frac{r}{n}}{1 - \left(1 + \frac{r}{n}\right)^{-nt}}\right)$$

$$PMT = 221{,}250\left(\frac{0.005625}{1 - (1 + 0.005625)^{-360}}\right)$$

$PMT \approx 1435.02$

The monthly payment is \$1435.02.

$$\begin{aligned}I &= Prt\\ &= 221{,}250(0.0675)\left(\frac{1}{12}\right)\\ &\approx 1244.53\end{aligned}$$

The interest paid on the first payment is \$1244.53.

$\text{Principal} = 1435.02 - 1244.53 = 190.49$

The principal paid on the first payment is \$190.49.

Check your progress 4, *page 221*

Use the APR loan payoff formula. The homeowner has been making payments for 4 years, or 48 months. There are 300 payments in a 25-year loan, so there are $300 - 48 = 252$ unpaid or remaining payments; $U = 252$.

$\dfrac{r}{n} = \dfrac{0.069}{12} = 0.00575$

$$A = PMT\left(\frac{1 - \left(1 + \frac{r}{n}\right)^{-U}}{\frac{r}{n}}\right)$$

$$A = 846.82\left(\frac{1 - (1 + 0.00575)^{-252}}{0.00575}\right)$$

$A \approx 112{,}548.79$

The mortgage payoff is \$112,548.79.

Check your progress 5, *page 222*

Monthly property tax = 2332.80 ÷ 12 = 194.40
Monthly fire insurance = 450 ÷ 12 = 37.50
Total monthly payment = 1492.89 + 194.40 + 37.50 = 1724.79

The total monthly payment for mortgage, property tax, and fire insurance is $1724.79.

CHAPTER 4

SECTION 4.1

Check your progress 1, *page 233*

The four tests are a complete population. Use μ to represent the mean.

$$\mu = \frac{\Sigma x}{n} = \frac{245 + 235 + 220 + 210}{4} = \frac{910}{4} = 227.5$$

The mean of the patient's blood cholesterol levels is 227.5.

Check your progress 2, *page 233*

a. The list 14, 27, 3, 82, 64, 34, 8, 51 contains 8 numbers. The median of a list of data with an even number of numbers is found by ranking the numbers and computing the mean of the two middle numbers. Ranking the numbers from smallest to largest gives 3, 8, 14, 27, 34, 51, 64, 82. The two middle numbers are 27 and 34. The mean of 27 and 34 is 30.5. Thus 30.5 is the median of the data.

b. The list 21.3, 37.4, 11.6, 82.5, 17.2 contains 5 numbers. The median of a list of data with an odd number of numbers is found by ranking the numbers and finding the middle number. Ranking the numbers from smallest to largest gives 11.6, 17.2, 21.3, 37.4, 82.5. The middle number is 21.3. Thus 21.3 is the median.

Check your progress 3, *page 234*

a. In the list 3, 3, 3, 3, 3, 4, 4, 5, 5, 5, 8, the number 3 occurs more often than the other numbers. Thus 3 is the mode.

b. In the list 12, 34, 12, 71, 48, 93, 71, the numbers 12 and 71 both occur twice and the other numbers occur only once. Thus 12 and 71 are both modes for the data.

Check your progress 4, *page 236*

The A is worth 4 points, with a weight of 4; the B in Statistics is worth 3 points, with a weight of 3; the C is worth 2 points, with a weight of 3; the F is worth 0 points, with a weight of 2; and the B in CAD is worth 3 points, with a weight of 2. The sum of all the weights is 4 + 3 + 3 + 2 + 2, or 14.

$$\text{Weighted mean} = \frac{(4 \times 4) + (3 \times 3) + (2 \times 3) + (0 \times 2) + (3 \times 2)}{14}$$
$$= \frac{37}{14} \approx 2.64$$

Janet's GPA for the spring semester is approximately 2.64.

Check your progress 5, *page 237*

$$\text{Mean} = \frac{\Sigma(x \cdot f)}{\Sigma f}$$
$$= \frac{(2 \cdot 5) + (3 \cdot 25) + (4 \cdot 10) + (5 \cdot 5)}{45}$$
$$= \frac{150}{45}$$
$$= 3\frac{1}{3}$$

The mean number of bedrooms per household for the homes in the subdivision is $3\frac{1}{3}$.

SECTION 4.2

Check your progress 1, *page 243*

The greatest number of ounces dispensed is 8.03, and the least is 7.95. The range of the number of ounces is 8.03 − 7.95 = 0.08 oz.

Check your progress 2, *page 244*

$$\mu = \frac{5 + 8 + 16 + 17 + 18 + 20}{6} = \frac{84}{6} = 14$$

x	$x - \mu$	$(x - \mu)^2$
5	5 − 14 = −9	$(-9)^2 = 81$
8	8 − 14 = −6	$(-6)^2 = 36$
16	16 − 14 = 2	$2^2 = 4$
17	17 − 14 = 3	$3^2 = 9$
18	18 − 14 = 4	$4^2 = 16$
20	20 − 14 = 6	$6^2 = 36$
		Sum: 182

$$\sigma = \sqrt{\frac{\Sigma(x - \mu)^2}{n}} = \sqrt{\frac{182}{6}} \approx \sqrt{30.33} \approx 5.51$$

The standard deviation for this population is approximately 5.51.

Check your progress 3, *page 245*

The mean for each sample of rope is 130 lb.

The rope from Trustworthy has a breaking point standard deviation of

$$s_1 = \sqrt{\frac{(122 - 130)^2 + (141 - 130)^2 + \cdots + (125 - 130)^2}{6}}$$
$$= \sqrt{\frac{1752}{6}} \approx 17.1 \text{ lb}$$

The rope from Brand X has a breaking point standard deviation of

$$s_2 = \sqrt{\frac{(128 - 130)^2 + (127 - 130)^2 + \cdots + (137 - 130)^2}{6}}$$
$$= \sqrt{\frac{3072}{6}} \approx 22.6 \text{ lb}$$

The rope from NeverSnap has a breaking point standard deviation of

$$s_3 = \sqrt{\frac{(112 - 130)^2 + (121 - 130)^2 + \cdots + (135 - 130)^2}{6}}$$
$$= \sqrt{\frac{592}{6}} \approx 9.9 \text{ lb}$$

The breaking point values of the rope from NeverSnap have the lowest standard deviation.

Check your progress 4, *page 246*

The mean is approximately 46.092.

The population standard deviation is approximately 2.476.

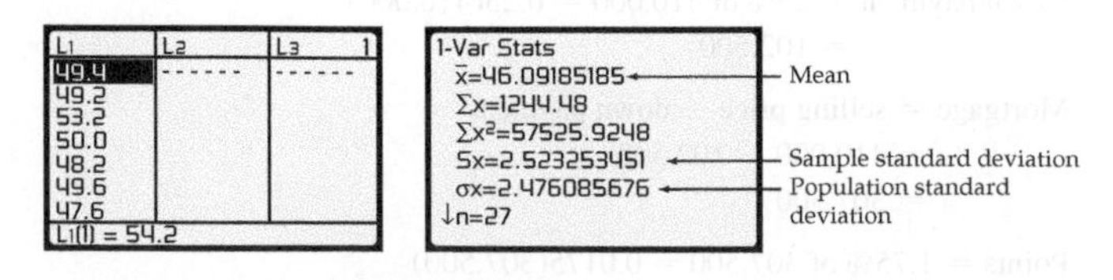

Check your progress 5, *page 247*

In Check Your Progress 2, we found $\sigma \approx \sqrt{30.33}$. Variance is the square of the standard deviation. Thus the variance is $\sigma^2 \approx \left(\sqrt{30.33}\right)^2 = 30.33$.

SECTION 4.3

Check your progress 1, *page 252*

$$z_{15} = \frac{15 - 12}{2.4} = 1.25 \qquad z_{14} = \frac{14 - 11}{2.0} = 1.5$$

These z-scores indicate that in comparison to her classmates, Cheryl did better on the second quiz than she did on the first quiz.

Check your progress 2, *page 252*

$$z_x = \frac{x - \mu}{\sigma}$$

$$0.6 = \frac{70 - 65.5}{\sigma}$$

$$\sigma = \frac{4.5}{0.6} = 7.5$$

The standard deviation for this set of test scores is 7.5.

Check your progress 3, *page 253*

a. By definition, the median is the 50th percentile. Therefore, 50% of the police dispatchers earned less than \$44,528 per year.

b. Because \$32,761 is in the 25th percentile, 100% − 25% = 75% of all police dispatchers made more than \$32,761.

c. From parts a and b, 50% − 25% = 25% of the police dispatchers earned between \$32,761 and \$44,528.

Check your progress 4, *page 253*

$$\text{Percentile} = \frac{\text{number of data values less than 405}}{\text{total number of data values}} \cdot 100$$

$$= \frac{3952}{8600} \cdot 100$$

$$\approx 46$$

Hal's score of 405 places him at the 46th percentile.

Check your progress 5, *page 255*

Rank the data.

7.5 9.8 10.2 10.8 11.4 11.4 12.2 12.4 12.6 12.8 13.1 14.2 14.5 15.6 16.4

The median of these 15 data values has a rank of 8. Thus the median is 12.4. The second quartile, Q_2, is the median of the data, so $Q_2 = 12.4$.

The first quartile is the median of the seven values less than Q_2. Thus Q_1 has a rank of 4, so $Q_1 = 10.8$.

The third quartile is the median of the values greater than Q_2. Thus Q_3 has a rank of 12, so $Q_3 = 14.2$.

Check your progress 6, *page 256*

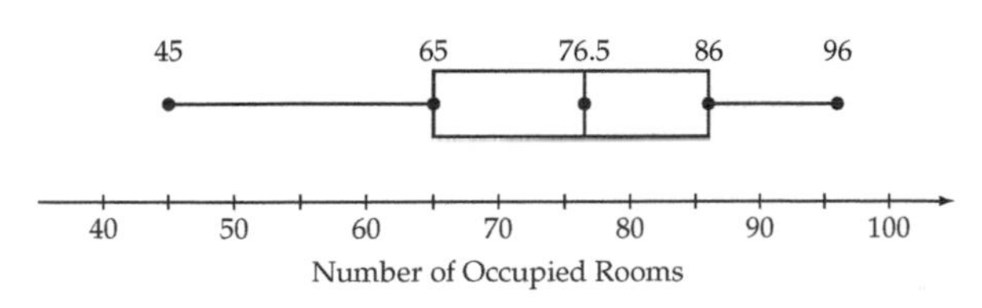

SECTION 4.4

Check your progress 1, *page 263*

a. The percent of data in all classes with an upper bound of 25 s or less is the sum of the percents for the first five classes in Table 4.8. Thus the percent of subscribers who required less than 25 s to download the file is 30.9%.

b. The percent of data in all the classes with a lower bound of at least 10 s and an upper bound of 30 s or less is the sum of the percents in the third through sixth classes in Table 4.8. Thus the percent of subscribers who required from 10 s to 30 s to download the file is 47.8%. The probability that a subscriber chosen at random will require from 10 s to 30 s to download the file is 0.478.

Check your progress 2, *page 265*

a. 0.76 lb is 1 standard deviation above the mean of 0.61 lb. In a normal distribution, 34% of all data lie between the mean and 1 standard deviation above the mean, and 50% of all data lie below the mean. Thus 34% + 50% = 84% of the tomatoes weigh less than 0.76 lb.

b. 0.31 lb is 2 standard deviations below the mean of 0.61 lb. In a normal distribution, 47.5% of all data lie between the mean and 2 standard deviations below the mean, and 50% of all data lie above the mean. This gives a total of 47.5% + 50% = 97.5% of the tomatoes that weigh more than 0.31 lb. Therefore

$$(97.5\%)(6000) = (0.975)(6000) = 5850$$

of the tomatoes can be expected to weigh more than 0.31 lb.

c. 0.31 lb is 2 standard deviations below the mean of 0.61 lb and 0.91 lb is 2 standard deviations above the mean of 0.61 lb. In a normal distribution, 95% of all data lie within 2 standard deviations of the mean. Therefore

$$(95\%)(4500) = (0.95)(4500) = 4275$$

of the tomatoes can be expected to weigh from 0.31 lb to 0.91 lb.

Check your progress 3, *page 268*

The area of the standard normal distribution between $z = -0.67$ and $z = 0$ is equal to the area between $z = 0$ and $z = 0.67$. The entry in Table 4.10 associated with $= 0.67$ is 0.249. Thus the area of the standard normal distribution between $z = -0.67$ and $z = 0$ is 0.249 square unit.

Check your progress 4, *page 268*

Table 4.10 indicates that the area from $= 0$ to $= -1.47$ is 0.429 square unit. The area to the left of $z = 0$ is 0.500 square unit. Thus the area to the left of $z = -1.47$ is $0.500 - 0.429 = 0.071$ square unit.

Check your progress 5, *page 269*

Round z-scores to the nearest hundredth so you can use Table 4.10.

a. $z_9 = \dfrac{9 - 6.1}{1.8} \approx 1.61$

Table 4.10 indicates that 0.446 (44.6%) of the data in the standard normal distribution are between $z = 0$ and $z = 1.61$. The percent of the data to the right of $z = 1.61$ is 50% − 44.6% = 5.4%.

Approximately 5.4% of professional football players have careers of more than 9 years.

b. $z_3 = \dfrac{3 - 6.1}{1.8} \approx -1.72 \qquad z_4 = \dfrac{4 - 6.1}{1.8} \approx -1.17$

From Table 4.10:

$A_{1.72} = 0.457 \qquad A_{1.17} = 0.379$

$0.457 - 0.379 = 0.078$

The probability that a professional football player chosen at random will have a career of between 3 and 4 years is about 0.078.

SECTION 4.5

Check your progress 1, *page 278*

Here are the results using a TI-84 calculator.

L1	L2	L3 1
2.5	2.3	------
3	3.9	
3.2	4.4	
3.4	5	
3.5	5.5	
3.8	6.2	
4	7.1	

L1(1) = 2.5

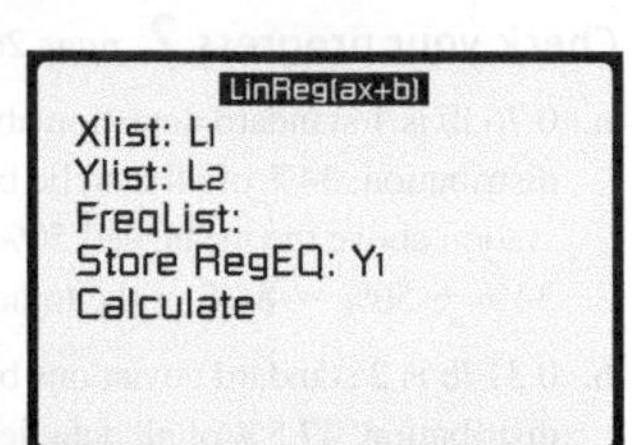

LinReg
y=ax+b
a=3.12962963
b= -5.547222222
r²=.9969979404
r=.998497842

The regression equation is $\hat{y} \approx 3.12962963x - 5.547222222$.

Check your progress 2, *page 279*

Use the regression equation from Check Your Progress 1.

a. Evaluate the equation when $x = 2.7$ m.

$\hat{y} \approx 3.12962963x - 5.547222222$

$\approx 3.12962963(2.7) - 5.547222222 \approx 2.903$

The average speed of a camel with a 2.7 m stride is 2.9 m/s.

b. Evaluate the equation when $x = 4.5$ m.

$\hat{y} \approx 3.12962963x - 5.547222222$

$\approx 3.12962963(4.5) - 5.547222222 \approx 8.536$

The average speed of a camel with a 4.5 m stride is 8.5 m/s.

Check your progress 3, *page 280*

The TI-84 screenshot from Check Your Progress 1 is repeated here.

LinReg
y=ax+b
a=3.12962963
b= -5.547222222
r²=.9969979404
r=.998497842

Rounded to the nearest hundredth, the linear correlation coefficient is 1.00.